A New Devil's Dictionary

Dictionary:
n. A malevolent literary device for cramping the growth
of a language and making it hard and inelastic.
This dictionary, however, is a most useful work.

Ambrose Bierce

Praise for *A New Devil's Dictionary*

"This latest addition to the literature put out by my father's least satisfactory tenant proves once again that it was quite right to have him evicted him from paradise. The text is poorly written, riddled with errors and awash with non sequiturs. I urge you instead to buy the Evangelists' bestselling and entirely objective account of my life and miracles."

J. Christ: *The Galilean Journal*

"Despite it having been pointed out by the CEO of Goldman Sachs that the financial sector is selflessly engaged in God's work, this book continues irresponsibly to peddle misinformation to the effect that bankers, financiers, fund managers etc. are principally engaged in transferring money from the pockets of clients, investors, savers and taxpayers into their own. Of course, nothing could be further from the truth."

Frederick G. Shred: *The Digital Banker* (incorporating *Bonus Monthly*)

"Although we have repeatedly explained that the British Civil Service is the Rolls Royce of world bureaucracy, this work repeats the old error of confusing Applebies (our magnificent achievements) with pears (things that go pear-shaped). Unhelpful phrases like "not fit for purpose" are bandied around, together with misinformation that challenges our own.

Sir Humphrey Appleby: *Proceedings of the Association of Civil Servants*

Thank you for sending me this text for peer review. The author has brilliantly worked over the very material upon which I am myself presently engaged, so it is of the utmost importance that this work should not be published by yourselves. I am retaining the manuscript you sent me for use in my own study.

Judas Iscariot Jobsworth: *University of The Wash*

This fascinating text constitutes a zone of decreation that deactivates its habitual signifying and informative functions in order to communicate communicability itself. The metalanguage of negative impulse unfolds an unindividuated aspect of being — the void, the impersonal, the neuter, the absolute, Genius etc., whereby the myth of authorship dissolves momentarily into a thingly, asignifying language that now speaks itself. The telling becomes the teller and the thing *in* itself becomes the thing *of* itself.

Hofrat Heuschrecke: *Journal of Derridian Studies*

"This is the sort of book that makes you wonder why it was ever written. Why should anyone want to read it? God knows, there are enough good books around (mine for instance.) "

Orlando Figleaf: *The Burkbeck Review of Books*

A New Devil's Dictionary

Lexicon for Contrarians

Nicholas T. Parsons

ISBN-13: 978-1535420440

ISBN-10: 1535420448

First published in Hungary by Magánkiadó,
Nicholas T. Parsons 2016

Cover design by Zee Wilson from an idea by Thalia Murray

Printed and bound in the European Union

Acknowledgements

The author would like to express his heartfelt thanks to Ilona Badics and Edit Horváth for their superb and patient work in preparing this book for publication. Thanks also to Ronny Karlsson for all his hard work on the initial phases of the book as well as much forbearance; and to Holly Karlsson for advice on design.

A number of friends have been supportive and helpful as the book was gestating, though they most certainly cannot be held accountable in any way for its errors or other shortcomings. In particular I would like to thank Andrew Schuller, Lonnie Johnson, Maggie Saunders, Brian Coats and Piers Burton Page.

The author / publisher gratefully acknowledges permission to reprint copyright material as follows:

"Their Sex Life", from **The Really Short Poems by A. R. Ammons** by A. R. Ammons. Copyright ©1990 by A. R. Ammons. Used by permission of W.W. Norton & Company, Inc.

"Much Madness is divinest Sense" and *"Tell all the Truth, but tell it slant"* from **The Poems of Emily Dickinson,** edited by Thomas H. Johnson, Cambridge, Mass.: The Belknap Press of Harvard University Press, Copyright © 1951, 1955 by the President and Fellows of Harvard College. Copyright © renewed 1979, 1983 by the President and Fellows of Harvard College. Copyright © 1914, 1918, 1919, 1924, 1929, 1930, 1932, 1935, 1937, 1942, by Martha Dickinson Bianchi. Copyright © 1952, 1957, 1958, 1963, 1965, by Mary L. Hampson.

An extract of 24 lines from *"Toads"* by **Philip Larkin from Philip Larkin: Collected Poems,** edited by Anthony Thwaite (Faber & Faber,

Contents

By Way of a Preface...

"Most people are other people... their thoughts are someone else's opinions, their lives a mimicry, their passions a quotation."

Oscar Wilde: *De Profundis*

"To a man with a hammer, everything looks like a nail..."

Mark Twain (attributed.)

"The supreme function of reason is to show that some things are beyond reason."

Blaise Pascal

"A serious and good philosophical work could be written entirely consisting of jokes."

Ludwig Wittgenstein

Introduction

A Lexicon for Contrarians

"A lie told often enough becomes the truth."
Vladimir Ilyich Lenin.

"Repetition does not transform a lie into a truth."
Franklin Delano Roosevelt.

Most people with a certain expertise in one field or another, indeed anyone who is simply a careful reader or listener, will be uneasily aware of the disingenuousness and unreliability of much public discourse All too often people with an axe to grind do not quite say what they mean or mean what they say: as the scientist Bob Carter put it, *"there is an insidious focus on 'correct' terminology from a range of interest groups. The lesson for all of us must be to look behind the words."*

In order to facilitate a better understanding of misleading language, this "dictionary" has been conceived as a disrespectful guide to the manipulative rhetoric of journalists, politicians, plausible PR men, bankers, businessmen and (last but not least) academics. Words like *"progressive," "nativist," "empowerment," "deregulation," "edgy," "resonant"* and even *"service"* are frequently degraded in the media to mere, and usually dishonest, slogans. Some formulations are deliberately deceitful (*"secular fundamentalist,"* for instance, *"advocacy science," "market adjustment"* and a host of terms used in the financial sector to make sharp practice seem anodyne or even respectable.) Insincerity is the hallmark of such discourse, like the cold caller who asks solicitously after your health and patronisingly addresses you with your Christian name. Often apparently innocuous words and phrases are combined in a meaningless and inappropriately applied mantra: a very funny Cuban film some years ago featured a decrepit bus that broke down and stranded the passengers for days as the drivers tried to get hold of unobtainable spares. Each loudspeaker announcement, which in fact had nothing to announce, ended with the words *"Thank you for choosing the Cuban Na-*

tional Bus Company" (there being no other bus company on the island.) Probably we shouldn't laugh too loudly at the Cubans…

This is of course not the first attempt to produce a contrarian dictionary. One such was compiled in the late 19th century by a marvellous American writer named Ambrose Bierce. It arose out of his newspaper column and was originally called *"The Cynic's Wordbook"* (1906). The American reading public being somewhat po-faced and prim, there were apparently objections made to a title that seemed to undermine the religiously based all-American ideals of progress, uplift and optimism. So Bierce changed the title of its second, enlarged edition to *"The Devil's Dictionary"* (1911), thus (to his evident satisfaction) causing even more offence.[1] But the Devil has the best tunes, as everyone admits, and his Dictionary established itself as a valuable guide to the prevailing hypocrisies and euphemisms of his day. Bierce said it was aimed at *"enlightened souls who prefer dry wines to sweet, sense to sentiment, wit to humour and clean English to slang."* Of course it needed continuous updating. The present work is not exactly like the output of a *"tribute band"* (the contemporary term for a pop band that makes good money out of imitating an original product) and it does not exactly follow Bierce's formula. Nevertheless it is inspired by Bierce's creative iconoclasm and I have shamelessly pinched his title.

The claims attached to a particular use of a word or phrase in a given political context usually incorporate abuse of those who would derive different claims from a different use of the same words or phrases. Pablo Iglesias, leader of the radical left Spanish party Podemos, recently said in an interview: *"Reality is defined by words. So whoever owns the words has the power to shape reality."* The most significant word in this observation is *"owns."* In a world full of tendentious media reporting, politicians' verbal evasions and academic obfuscation, the layman (perhaps without realising it) is often the cannon fodder in the ongoing struggle for "ownership" of words. By the same token, language originally designed to be consensually descriptive is taken hostage by vested interests. An ex-

---

1 In his preface to the 1911 edition of *The Devil's Dictionary* Bierce actually says that the "more reverent title" of *"The Cynic's Word Book"* "had previously been forced upon him by the religious scruples of the last newspaper in which a part of the work had appeared." The volume provoked a deluge of feeble copycat publications featuring "cynic" in their titles, with the result that the word was brought so deeply into disfavour "that any book bearing it was discredited in advance of publication."

ample is the word *"migrant,"* which seems to have become shorthand for *"economic migrant,"* a person who does not enjoy the automatic right of entry to EU countries that a *"refugee"* does. Evidently this was why the News Editor of *Al Jazeera* banned the word *"migrant"* from his TV channel altogether in 2015, ordering that the word *"refugee"* should be substituted in every case. This was an act of deliberate censorship, given that a fair proportion of those seeking to enter Europe in the vast flow of humans reaching its shores in 2015-16 were in fact "economic migrants" — or at any rate not "refugees" under the terms of the Geneva Convention, since they came from allegedly safe havens. The News Editor's ukase was an especially elegant example of *"virtue signalling,"* (*q.v.*) given that *Al Jazeera* is based in Doha, capital of Qatar, which (like the other Arab states of the Gulf) does not take any refugees at all.[2]

Analogous examples of word manipulation may be encountered well beyond the realm of politics and broadcasting, most obviously in academe, where a new form of scholasticism has taken hold; in economics where it has become polluted by financial interests; in journalism and in social life generally, where the turf wars over identity and victimhood are fought. For those of us the Germans describe as *Normalverbraucher* ("average consumer," a phrase on which Langenscheidt's dictionary hangs the cautionary tag of *"humor"*), unravelling what lies behind the use of a particular word in a particular context has become quite a time-consuming task. Dull or obscure prolixity is itself is a weapon of disingenuous power and bureaucratic tyranny. The self-congratulatory officialese of the EU bureaucracy, for example, reflects only palely any recognition of the latter's malfunctions, its directives being lumbering verbal monstrosities of red tape and legalese. As the historian John Julius Norwich drily points out: *"The Lord's Prayer contains 69 words. The Ten Commandments contain 297 words. The American Declaration of Independence contains 310 words. The European Union Directive on the Exportation of Duck Eggs contains 28,911 words."*[3]

A recurring feature, therefore, of *A New Devil's Dictionary* is the explo-

---

2 They do, however, help to finance refugee camps in the region, from which most of the inhabitants are desperate to escape for a better life in Europe.

3 This comparative statistic was a contribution sent to Lord Norwich by an EU official and reprinted in his 2012 *Christmas Cracker*, an annual collection of anecdote and oddity that he has been publishing for many years.

ration of the ways in which an increasingly oppressive *bureaucracy* (*q.v.*), whether operating for government or business, uses a type of language that is authoritarian, yet pretends to be citizen or consumer oriented. It will soon become apparent to those who study them that *"mission statements"* (*q.v.*) and other communications from business to consumers are often a cover for the opposite of their proclaimed intentions. "Customer service" turns out to be "customer control," usually in the interests of marketing ("data-mining"), but possibly on behalf of an inquisitive state. Any questioning of questionable behaviour is met with bland rebuttals full of assertions about things the firm "takes very seriously" and is "working hard," probably with "stakeholders," to improve or remedy. Such blandness falls like a continuous warm piss on the citizen, the consumer and the voter, its progenitors being concerned with creating a general impression of benevolence and integrity which seldom accords with reality.

Too often "corporate-speak" is designed to circumvent admission of guilt or acceptance of personal responsibility.[4] Executives *"step down"* (which gives the impression of self-sacrifice) rather than resign (which would remind people of the fact they were forced to).[5] Organisations issue statements saying that *"lessons have been learned"* — but why do you need to *"learn"* a lesson (e.g. that fraud is wrong) which you already know? The very job descriptions posted in advertisements for public sector workers reek of factitious dynamism and impressive-sounding but ill-defined activity. They tend to be packed with managerial buzz words like *"transformation"* — a favourite with New Labour — *"stakeholders," "catalyst," "excellence," "partners," "sustainable," "best practice," "diversity"* and so forth. *"You'll develop innovative, sustainable policies and programmes for consultation and engagement and provide expert advice to managers, councillors and partners in this specialised area,"* runs a not untypical advertisement in *The Guardian* for a "Consultation and Community Engagement Officer," whatever that might be. *"High on your list of priorities will be ensur-*

4 The scourge of corporate guff is the journalist Lucy Kellaway on the *Financial Times*, who not only regularly exposes cringe-making messages to staff from Chief Executives, but has initiated a *"Guffopedia"* to which employees who feel insulted and patronized by semi-literate executives can send in examples of inappropriate messages they have received from the same.

5 Sometimes they just *"step back,"* may be calculating that the furore will die down after a while and they can then step forward again…

ing that we [Merton] *meet the requirements of the Duty to Involve and capitalising on the opportunities presented by new neighbourhood governance arrangements."*[6] The only concrete information one can glean from such a job definition is that the lucky successful candidate will definitely have a telephone and a computer for producing spreadsheets. *"New neighbourhood governance arrangements"* even sounds faintly sinister: as the Viennese satirist Karl Kraus mordantly remarked: *"What I demand from a city I choose to live in is asphalt, street cleaning, a key to the door of the house, heating and a warm water supply. The conviviality is provided by myself..."*[7]

All in all the jargon of management consultancy that has infected both business and government seems to be addressed to a class of insiders who are adept at working the system, ticking boxes and making the right-sounding noises, but whose actual activities are hard to pin down. Such people are the modern equivalent of what Sir Thomas Elyot, in the Latin-English Dictionary he compiled in 1538, magnificently labelled as *logodaedalus*: *"he that speaketh craftily to deceiue; or in eloquente words induceth sentences vayne, or of lyttel purpose."*

In Defence of the Devil

One of the amusing conceits underlying Daniel Defoe's satire *The Political History of the Devil* (1726) is that the Devil is shocked by the deplorable behaviour of mankind and indignant at getting the blame for it. The idea is an inversion of the situation in Dostoevsky's great parable of *The Grand Inquisitor*,[8] in which Christ returns to earth and is haughtily put in his place by the Inquisitor for being far too radical. *Mutatis mu-*

6 Quoted in David Craig and Matthew Elliott: *Fleeced: How we've been betrayed by the politicians, bureaucrats and bankers and how much they've cost us* (Constable, London, 2009) P. 160.

7 *"Ich verlange von einer Stadt, in der ich leben soll: Asphalt, Strassenspülung, Haustorschlüssel, Luftheizung, Warmwasserleitung. Gemütlich bin ich selber."* *"Gemütlichkeit,"* an Austrian concept implying a sentimental feeling of cosiness and geniality, is almost impossible to render in English. Karl Kraus, the scourge of Viennese and Austrian complacency, was of course anything but either convivial or genial.

8 The encounter features in a chapter in *The Brothers Karamazov* where Christ is imagined as returning to Seville when the Inquisition is in full swing and the Grand Inquisitor explains to him that he must be sent to the stake because he is interfering with the church's mission on earth.

tandis, many of us may be inclined to feel sympathy for the Devil when we consider the extent to which his agenda has today been hijacked by the most celebrated and best remunerated members of society, although he would surely regard contemporary levels of would-be demonic hand-iwork as cheap and tasteless (in W.H.Auden's *The Song of the Devil* (1963) he gives vent to his frustration: "I'm so bored with the whole fucking crowd of you / I could *scream!*") As the Introduction to the Non-such reprint (2007) of the *Political History* puts it: "The prescience of [Defoe's] text is astonishing... as we grow ever more conscious of our powerlessness over megalomania, and as mass media puts names and faces to the perpetrators of evil and injustice on earth, there are many who, like Defoe have never felt more sympathy for the Devil."[9]

Although it is true that "Lucifer," one of the Devil's many names, actu-ally means "bringer of light," many refuse to see him as anything other than the "Prince of Darkness." A left-wing writer like Angus Calder likens the Devil's contemporary profile to the Leviathan of Hobbes's po-litical philosophy, an all-embracing tyranny dispensing sweeteners to the enslaved. "The System deals out Justice, based on carefully pondered ra-tional principles or it flourishes pseudo-rational business plans. Because it perceives that its own security depends on being respected and, if at all possible, loved, it is generous to those who play along with it and serve it unreservedly. It usually offers some variant of the Welfare State, in which no one is allowed to starve or die of hypothermia if this can be managed without undue inconvenience to the rich. All the price that it charges for its handouts and fringe benefits is docile conformity."[10]

Such sentiments mark out a territory where the libertarian left meets the libertarian right. *Pace* Calder, this is actually the Devil's terrain too, because he is a libertarian at heart. It is rather the Leviathan that claims a monopoly of virtue and employs an armoury of *bien pensant* verbal abuse against those who question its dogmas. And it is this abuse that makes the Devil a contrarian, inclined, I'm afraid, to play the *devil's advocate* and ask awkward questions — such as whether "poor people in rich coun-tries" should be giving money through their taxes to corrupt "rich people

9 Daniel Defoe: *The Political History of the Devil* (1726, reprinted 2007 by Non-such Publishing, Dublin). Introduction, P. 9.

10 Angus Calder: *Gods, Mongrels and Demons: 101 Brief but Essential Lives* (Bloomsbury, London, 2003), P. 99.

in poor countries;" or whether football should really be called the "beautiful game" when it could, with equal accuracy, be described as an orgy of bribery, cheating and ritualised violence;[11] or whether the gospels of the marketplace are actually adhered to by those who force them upon society; or whether *"eco-salvationism"* is not a new tyranny in the making, albeit plausibly dressed up as altruism; or whether shareholders, depositors and taxpayers should be expected not only to bail out those who have swindled them, but also subsidise the latter's rehabilitation through their taxes and nil interest deposit accounts; or whether the bland label of *"multiculturalism"* (which the French philosopher Pascal Bruckner calls the "racism of the anti-racists") is not providing cover for anxious appeasement of violent intolerance; or whether, if a lecturer can claim that *Gardeners' Question Time* is a racist radio programme in Britain because it refers to *"native species,"* we might possibly be better off with fewer "lecturers," indeed fewer "universities."[12]

As one might expect, the Devil takes a particular and regrettable interest in saints, both official ones like Mother Theresa or St Joseph of Copertino and unofficial ones like Sir Jimmy Savile[13] and Bono. Not to mention moralising self-publicists like the German writer Günter Grass, who

11 At a football game in Algeria in August 2014, Albert Ebosse, despite scoring his side's only goal was killed by a stone thrown by one of its supporters. While this is an extreme example of fan barbarism, violence on and off the pitch is routine everywhere, vicious strategic fouling during the game being particularly rife. There has also been unbelievable corruption at Fifa, football's international governing body and some match-fixing organised by Asian betting syndicates (also in cricket and tennis). The drugs scene in athletics and cycling is another indication of the way sport, even as it is milked for role models, often represents the most repellent aspects of our greedy, hypocritical and sophisticatedly barbarous culture. Virtually no male politician in Europe will let slip an opportunity to ingratiate himself with voters by professing undying allegiance to one or other of the football clubs, just as Roman emperors were careful to cheer up the proletariat with bread and circuses. David Cameron came a cropper in an interview during the 2015 UK general election by getting confused about which football club he so passionately supported...

12 In case some of the observations here and in the rest of the *Introduction* should strain the reader's credulity, I should point out that all the examples given relate actual events or persons and are explored in more detail in the *Dictionary* itself.

13 Sir James Wilson Vincent Savile, OBE, KCSG (1926–2011). When the revelations of his long career of sexual abuse of minors, which BBC colleagues claimed not to know about, was finally revealed, he was stripped of his titles and the aura of sanctity in which he had hitherto basked abruptly evaporated...

made a fortune out of German war guilt, but for sixty years forgot to mention that he had been drafted into the SS at the end of the war.[14] His [the Devil's] perception of such people enjoying antinomian privilege is, of course, liable to give offence in certain quarters; and further offence may be caused by his mischievous claim that many people probably agree with him, but would never say so, not at least in public. What is the use of hypocrisy if it cannot protect your career, enhance your status, and keep up the flow of awards, appointments and honours?

The key to avoiding unwelcome exposure is to master the appropriate language, and likewise the key to *our* understanding of what is going on is to do the same. So *A New Devil's Dictionary* offers an Ariadne's thread through the labyrinth of contemporary jargon, cliché, sloganeering and downright mendacity. For much of this there is actually a new language (mostly abusive) that has not yet made it into conventional dictionaries (for example, *apologism, churnalism, fraudit, frenemy, humblebrag, cyberchondria, selfare* and *virtue signalling*.) Some of the lexicon's entries are only a few words long, many are short essays, and a few are quite lengthy pieces of analysis. There are also sketches of heroes and villains (past and present) in the war against obfuscation, cliché and general disingenuousness. A few poems have crept in, because poems say things that other literary forms cannot and discover meanings in unsuspected places. Finally there are quite a lot of jokes which hopefully will save the reader from indignation fatigue and serve to remind those of us who are optimists that scepticism, or occasionally ridicule, is more effective against abuse of power, mendacity and rent-seeking in a free society than throwing bombs. Thankfully, there are still many who value linguistic integrity, and who are determined to resist the corruption of public discourse and the commodification of everything. It is to those kindred spirits that the author has addressed this cheerful little book.

---

14 Many youths were drafted, of course, who were not necessarily convinced Nazis. What outraged Grass's critics was that he had suppressed this hardly irrelevant detail of his life through a long career of preaching to his compatriots about moral responsibility. He finally revealed it on publication of a memoir, well timed therefore to create a scandal generating huge publicity — and of course huge sales. In addition, Günther's attention-seeking claim that the reunification of Germany could be likened to the Nazi *Anschlusss* with Austria in 1938 was not exactly received with enthusiasm…

xviii

A

Absurdity:

A statement or belief manifestly inconsistent with one's own opinion

Ambrose Bierce: *The Devil's Dictionary*

Abacus 2007–AC1: Type of deal devised by Goldman Sachs for its clients based on the old banking principle of "heads I win, tails you lose."

Goldman Sachs would probably have expected, or at least hoped, that this type of glittering subprime mortgage deal would remain under the radar after their clever Mr Fabrice Tourre came up with it. It certainly should have done, as the investors in it were quite unaware of its true nature. Mr Tourre somehow forgot to inform them that a hedge fund had *helped to select* the mortgages bundled into the deal, and that the said fund was planning *to bet against it* thereafter. The upshot was that the investors lost $1bn, Goldman collected $15m in fees and Mr Tourre earned $1.7m in pay and bonuses.[1] I'm sure all sensible people can agree that these rewards were amply justified. Unfortunately New York's Securities and Exchange Commission thought otherwise and seized e-mails relating to Abacus sent by Tourre to his mates. One to his girlfriend joked about selling Abacus to "widows and orphans" and advised her to click on a link with the name *www.mortgageimplode.com* for a good laugh. The SEC didn't find all this quite so hilarious, but that kind of killjoy attitude is typical of its officials and just shows they have no sense of humour.

Anyway it seems terribly unfair to pick on the unfortunate Mr Tourre, who has done rather well for the son of a pedicurist and an office furniture salesman. Indeed he complained after his (well paid) suspension that he was "hoping to come back to Goldman Sachs and in the mean-

---

1 Figures from the *Weekend FT,* 27th/28th July, 2013.

1

time make the SEC understand this transaction." Evidently he doesn't feel the need to make the investors "understand" the transaction; that of course may be because they now understand it all too well and have perhaps intimated as much to him.

Actuary: Person who finds accountancy too exciting:
In reality an actuary has the exciting job of predicting life expectancy in a given population. The more sophisticated **Sicilian actuary** can predict the names and addresses of the deceased, the year of their death and where they will be buried, if at all.

Addiction: Fashionable malady, useful as a way of medicalising lack of self-control (e.g. the "sex addiction" of priapic Hollywood stars.)
Some really uncool people persist in claiming that there are alternatives to addiction, like the journalist who wrote: "Avoid using cigarettes, alcohol, and drugs as alternatives to being an interesting person."[2]
A book entitled *Addiction by Design*[3] describes how the Las Vegas casinos build their interiors as confusing mazes leading eventually to the apotheosis of the *digitalised slot machine*. When dazed punters end up at these (after haemorrhaging cash along the way), they are equipped with "play money" and so become "umbilically attached" to the machines via a casino charge card. True, this ingenious casino layout means that paramedics take far longer to reach those that get cardiac arrests while playing (and irate slot-players also obstruct the medics from getting to the casualty if their game is interrupted thereby.) But the good news is that punters *don't notice how long they are spending on the machine.*
But you don't have to be a gambler to be routinely exploited in the wider economy — for example by the deliberate bamboozlement of multi-part (sometimes as many as 30) tariffs for mobile phones, cable TV or electricity. Journalist Tim Harford notes that his phone company regularly sends an e-mail assuring him he is on the cheapest possible plan, which prompts him to research the matter, which research invariably reveals the claim to be untrue. When he cancelled with one provider

---

2 Marilyn Vos Savant, an American columnist who was celebrated by the *Guinness Book of Records* for her high IQ.
3 Natasha Dow Schüll: *Addiction by Design: Machine Gambling in Las Vegas* (Princeton University Press, 2012).

because their gizmo broke down, the company swivelled in 48 hours from claiming he had broken it to offering him hundreds of pounds to stay with them. *"When your phone company starts using the playbook of an emotionally abusive spouse,"* comments Harford, *"this is not a market in good working order."*[4]

Advertising: Excellent training for writers of fiction:
The legendary American advertising executive Philip Dusenberry (advertising executives, for some reason, are always "legendary") had it about right when he said: *"I have always believed that writing advertisements is the second most profitable form of writing. The first, of course, is ransom notes...* (Dusenberry is also famous for presiding over the Pepsi commercial in which Michael Jackson's hair accidentally caught fire.)

George Orwell described advertising as *"the rattling of a stick inside a swill bucket."* This is a little too generous.

Advocacy Science: Euphemism for the substitution of propaganda, invariably alarmist, usually with a thinly concealed ideological agenda, for genuine science:

Advocacy science embraces *"confirmation bias"* (cherry-picking data to fit a pre-conceived conclusion) and false assertions of *"scientific consensus"* (with concomitant claims that *"the science is settled"* — the view, you will recall, of Galileo's persecutors.)

An offshoot of *"advocacy science"* is the notion of *"post-normal science"* associated with Jerome Ravetz and others, which hints at subordinating *"science"* (i.e. facts that have been subject to empirical testing) to *"social values"* (i.e. someone's ideological agenda). An article in *The Guardian* (14 March, 2007) by Mike Hulme states the following : *"In order to make progress about how we manage climate change , we have to take science off centre stage."* We already have an example of what can happen when you subordinate science to ideology, namely Lysenkoism in the former Soviet Union. Bogus, but Communist Party-approved, Lysenko's theory of how to achieve greater crop yields was rigorously enforced under Nikita Khrushchev and led to millions dying of starvation.

4 Tim Harford: "Casino's worrying knack for consumer manipulation" *Financial Times* Jan. 3, 2014.

Agitator: In the French and Russian revolutions, someone who helped to build the system that killed him. In modern Britain, a student politician preparing for a political career of dull conformity:

"*The secret of the agitator,*" wrote Karl Kraus, "*is to make himself as stupid as his audience, so that they think they are as clever as he is.*" [*See also* **Andropause** *below.*]

"Demagogues," wrote the Austrian Kabarettist Helmut Qualtinger, "*are people who speak into the wind they themselves have let off...*"

Aid to Third World Governments: A process by which poor people in rich countries give money to rich people in poor countries:[5]

Hayekian economist Peter Bauer observed that bilateral aid to Third World *governments* "increases the power of rulers [at the expense of the people], encourages corruption, misallocates resources and erodes civil society." Or, as Herbert Samuel once put it, "where there are two PhDs in a developing country, one is head of state and the other is in exile." Politicians mostly know this, but must seem to be in favour of aid, ever more of it, for fear of appearing uncaring. Of course it is taxpayers' money they are spending, and nothing is more seductive than the prospect of raising your moral profile on somebody else's money. "It cannot be stressed too much," Ex-Chancellor Nigel Lawson has said, "that government policies need to be justified not by their intentions, which in the case of aid are irreproachable, but by their results, which in the case of aid are on balance harmful."[6] A quarter of Britain's foreign aid goes as 'budget support' into the treasuries of some of the world's least competent, honest or responsible governments.[7] In 2014 that was a quarter of £12bn, the total being more than is disbursed by any other EU state and second only to what the USA spends.[8] All this at a time when the government was planning further austerity for its own constituency

5 This aphorism was originally coined by Hungarian born Péter Tamás Bauer (Lord Bauer), a developmental economist and adviser to the Thatcher government.

6 Letter to *The Spectator* 8/2/2014.

7 Jonathan Forman: "The great aid mystery" in *The Spectator*, 5 January, 2013.

8 See the *Weekend FT* leader, 6-7 December, 2014. It points out that the "*doctrinaire*" declaration of the World Council of Churches in the 1960s that developed countries should devote 0.7% of gross national income to international aid is based on "*outdated growth models*" and "*wrongly puts the priority on the quantity of money that Britain spends on aid rather than the quality of its projects.*"

4

in Britain, with a plan to reduce public expenditure to 35% of GDP when re-elected in 2015, which (by some measures) will be its lowest level since the 1930s. This may or may not be a sound policy, but it certainly makes spraying taxpayers' money on other governments look a touch overgenerous.

Ghanaian intellectual George Ayittey, Ugandan Andrew Mwenda or Zambian Dambisa Moyo will gladly point out to you that most of such "aid" has sustained African kleptocracies, subsidised warlords and sponsored genocidal civil wars. Doling out insufficiently monitored cash (that also remunerates, on a scale bordering on the grotesque, the vast aid industry with its fat tail of agencies)[9] simply traps nations in a vicious cycle of dependency and poor governance. Aid to Africa doubled in the 1980s as a percentage of the continent's GDP; *growth* simultaneously collapsed from 2 per cent to zero.[10] Moyo writes: "Aid doesn't work, hasn't worked, and won't work ... no longer part of the potential solution, it is part of the problem — in fact aid *is* the problem."

That is partly why India politely asked Britain *to stop* giving it money, the other reason being that it no longer wishes to be patronised in this neo-colonialist manner. Moyo quotes a body called the Asymmetric Threats Contingency Alliance (ATCA), a worldwide philanthropic net-

9 Figures cited in *a Financial Times* leading article in 2013 showed that 30 staff at 14 leading UK foreign aid charities were paid £100,000 or more in the previous year. In some cases salaries rose although income had fallen. The FT also drew attention to the fact that governments increasingly use charities to carry out public policy. This casts doubt on whether such "charities" (taxpayers already contribute 38% to their income) can correctly be described as such. It also leads to charity bosses assuming they can claim private, or even public, sector pay scales. According to the Institute of Economic Affairs, some 27,000 charities depend on the state for more than three-quarters of their income and there are top name ones that receive more from government than from private donors (figures quoted in *The Spectator*, 8th Feb. 2014).

A letter to the *Sunday Telegraph* (5/01/14) has a sensible suggestion to deal with the problem of "health tourism," which means unentitled foreigners arriving in UK to have babies or operations on the NHS without paying. *Simply deduct the cost from the overseas aid budget*: it's fair, easy to administer and above all effective. It would also ensure that "aid" actually goes to some who clearly need it...

10 Matt Ridley: *The Rational Optimist* (Fourth Estate, London, 2011). P. 317. Quoting Dambisa Moyo: *Dead Aid* (Allen Lane, London, 2009) Ridley adds that the aid given to Zambia since 1960, had it been invested in assets with a reasonable rate of return, would by now have raised the Zambian per capita income to the same level of the Portuguese — $20,000 instead $500.

work of politicians, businessmen, academics, editors and others, which calculates that Indians have some **US$1.5tn** residing in Swiss banks — *"more unaccounted for monies than the rest of the world put together"* and ten times the country's foreign debt.[11] Until the Indian government locates the owners of this money and taxes it, it is hard to see why British (or any other) taxpayers should support India's vast web of official corruption. The Indians are, after all, disarmingly frank about it, admitting in a report released in May 2011 that 70 million of our 388 million pounds recently handed over to them by our generous rulers had been stolen or lost.[12] Still, that is probably only the tip of an iceberg — when the secret accounts at the Swiss branch of HSBC were revealed in 2015, there was found to be $700m from Eritrea sitting there and $560m from Kenya. Eritrea is one of the poorest countries in the world and both it and Kenya receive substantial aid from the developed world. As a percentage of their home countries' GDP these deposits are as large, or larger, than illicit deposits from the rich countries nestling at HSBC and doubtless elsewhere. Probably a lot of this money is only recycled aid anyway…

"Like other pseudo-religions," writes Jonathan Foreman, "aid has its own myths, iconography, priesthoods; its state and private elements; its conflicts between fundamentalists and moderates; its guardians of purity, its true believers and cynical hucksters, its genuine saints and its ruthless bureaucrats. And it offers believers an almost spiritual sense of their own goodness — which goes some way towards explaining their extreme reluctance to listen to the evidence against it."[13]

Of course only a quarter of Britain's "aid" money is spent or squandered bilaterally. Much of the rest is sieved through multilateral institutions like the EU, which the left-wing Labour Minister Clare Short, on closer acquaintance with it, described as "an outrage," "a disgrace" and "the worst development agency in the world." The British government spent £11.7 billion, or the full 0.7 per cent of national revenue on aid in

---

11 Dambisa Moyo: *How The West Was Lost* (Allen Lane, London, 2011) P. 20.

12 In 2015, Narendra Modi, the Indian Prime Minister threatened jail terms of 10 years for tax dodgers, when local newspapers reported that, in 2006-7, 1,200 wealthy Indians had $5.6bn stashed away in HSBC's Swiss private bank. Between 2002 and 2011 more than $300bn is estimated to have been sent abroad from India illicitly. See a report by Amy Kazmin in the *Financial Times*, 5th March 2015 "India's Modi threatens jail terms for holders of 'black money' "

13 Jonathan Foreman op cit.

2014. Commenting on this, the respected authors[14] of *"Why Nations Fail"* say they are certainly not against aid *per se*, but (with unwonted honesty among aid advocates) they point out that most of the diminution of poverty that has actually occurred had nothing to do with aid, but has been the result of economic growth in Asia; that is, in countries which received little aid.

Meanwhile more than a quarter of the countries in sub-Saharan Africa are poorer now than in 1960 — despite massive aid programmes. Poverty is created and sustained by "extractive" institutions, they say, that bar anyone outside a small elite from sharing in the national income. This is a widespread phenomenon. The cousin of the Syrian dictator Bashar al-Assad controls government monopolies and is the richest man in the country. The richest woman in Angola, concluded an investigation by *Forbes* magazine, takes a chunk of any company that wants to do business in the country or is cut in on any business deal by fiat of the President, who just happens to be her father. Africa's greatest kleptocrat, Mobutu Sese Seko, was largely sustained by western aid, but South Africa's apartheid regime was undermined by sanctions — which is the opposite of foreign aid! While government office remains the preferred route to individual wealth in these countries, most of the government supplied "aid" to them emanating from the EU is little better than Robin Hoodery in reverse.[15]

Even worse seems to have been the impact of Bob Geldof's Band Aid and its patronising song *"Don't they know it's Christmas."* Originally inspired by the famine in Northern Ethiopia, Band Aid's dreadful song generated huge amounts of cash and matching increases in bilateral aid, much of the latter ending up helping a vicious totalitarian regime in its

---

14 Daron Acemoglu and James A. Robinson: *Why Nations Fail* (Crown Publishers, 2012). An article by Acemoglu and Robinson summarising their research and criticising the idea that "large donations can remedy poverty" appeared in *The Spectator*, 25th January 2014. David Cameron claims that their work is one of his "five favourite books of all time"; but this doesn't seem to have affected his determination to sluice out aid at 0.7% of GDP to governments that are all too keen to have it so that their members can sustain their lifestyles.

15 However, before western democrats get too smug, one should point out that the median net wealth of an American family is $113,000, but for members of Congress it is over $1m apiece. "The truth is that both main American political parties are up for rent," as Edward Luce puts it (*Financial Times* March 31, 2014).

coercive policies. Although the Band Aid Trust successfully fought off claims that its money went directly to the agents of oppression, or to arm their opponents, it did take the pressure off the government to help its own people. This is why Pascal Bruckner calls Band Aid the "biggest moral swindle of the 1980s, that enabled the Mengistu regime to arm itself and to accelerate the herding of the rural populations into controlled zones."[16] In 2014, an article by Ian Birrell in the *Daily Mail* points out that this pattern of human rights abuse indirectly supported by aid has continued : "The most terrible atrocities are inflicted on those who resist, including mass killings, torture, rape and being burned from their villages by rampaging troops, as I have seen for myself when I interviewed scarred victims whose families had been slaughtered.

"This is carried out by a one-party state renowned for repression, with the fertile land — sometimes flecked with seams of gold beneath it — being snatched and handed to regime officials or sold to foreign investors. "Astonishingly, this project is backed by big chunks of British aid. Ethiopia has become the biggest recipient of our assistance, handed an incredible £328 million this year [2014] despite mounting condemnation over horrific human rights abuses." Indeed, Ethiopia is among the biggest beneficiaries of the global aid boom. It will rake in £1.3 billion from Britain over the course of the coalition, while another £2 billion pours in each year from other international donors. "Inevitably, Ethiopia exerts a special hold on the aid industry after Band Aid influenced an entire generation."[17] The success of all this giving may be measured by the continued flow of desperate asylum seekers from that part of the world, many of whom drown as they try and cross the Mediterranean to Europe in the hands of brutal people traffickers.

Ethiopia is not an isolated case. In his book *The Tyranny of Experts*, development expert William Easterly describes how farmers of the Mubende District in Uganda were driven from their homes, their crops and livestock burned, in order to establish forestry on the land in a scheme sponsored by the World Bank. No doubt the technocrats of the bank had the best intentions (namely to raise incomes and establish profits through the scheme), but unfortunately the farmers were in the way

16 Pascal Bruckner: *The Temptation of Innocence: Living in the Age of Entitlement* (Algora Publishing,New York, 2000 — No translator cited), P. 285.

17 Ian Birrell, *Mail Online*, 12 November, 2014.

8

and the experts failed to take into account that they would be vulnerable to companies ruthlessly taking advantage of World Bank largesse in a land where governance was weak, human rights mostly honoured in the breach thereof, and corruption ubiquitous.[18]

Meanwhile one billion Euros that the EU recently handed to a brand new and supposedly more user-friendly government in Egypt has simply disappeared — just like in the good old days under Hosni Mubarak. To avoid this sort of thing, Matt Ridley in his book *The Rational Optimist* advocates that aid be democratised via the Internet[19] so that individuals could contribute to specific projects. This would take aid "out of the hands of inefficient international bureaucrats and corrupt African officials, [and away from] idealistic free-market shock therapists, [and have it] separated from arms deals, removed from big industrial projects, distanced from patronising do-gooders and given person to person."[20] There are a lot of people on both sides of the aid racket who would die in the ditches (or perhaps drown in their champagne baths) rather than see that happen.

Altruism: Something to which successful businessmen are attracted once they have made their pile through skill, diligence, monopoly, luck or crookery:

Adam Smith wrote that "it is not from the benevolence of the butcher, the brewer, or the baker, that we expect our dinner, but from their regard to their own self-interest"[21] — which is part of the gospel of free market capitalism. He was also prescient about the inadvisability of taking businessmen at their own estimation of themselves: "People of the same trade seldom meet together, even for merriment and diversion, but the conversation ends in a conspiracy against the public, or in some contrivance to raise prices."[22]

The Russian-Jewish-American novelist and pseudo-philosopher Ayn Rand was of the opinion that *"if civilisation is to survive it is the moral-*

18 Reports of this appeared in *the New York Times* of September 21st, 2011 and in a report by Oxfam. The full story may be read in William Easterly: *The Tyranny of Experts* (Basic Books, New York, 2013), *Introduction* Pp.3-16.

19 e.g. through Globalgiving.com

20 Ridley op cit. P. 319.

21 Adam Smith: *An Inquiry into the Nature and Causes of the Wealth of Nations* (1776).

22 Adam Smith, op cit.Bk.1, ch.10, Pt.2.

*ity of **altruism** that men have to reject.*" This will of course be regarded as a grossly anti-social view by all right-thinking people.[23] But turn it round to William Blake's formulation "*the road to hell is paved with good intentions*" and it suddenly becomes an almost *salonfähiger* view, even among liberals. Nor should you forget the old maxim that if you help someone, you earn a friend; but if you help somebody too much, you make an enemy.

Gore Vidal was not impressed by Rand and wrote waspishly of "this odd little woman attempting to give a moral sanction to greed and self-interest." However the "odd little woman's" cult now looms large in America on the libertarian right, though it has divided the Tea Party crazies between those who love her promotion of egoism and those who are furious at her dismissal of religion. Sadly Rand's much praised hostility to the welfare state is a shade less convincing since she herself, suffering from lung cancer and having exhausted her considerable fortune on rapacious American capitalist medicine, applied for Social Security and Medicare — none of which would exist if society was totally lacking in altruism.

The Rand cult nevertheless continues to boom in the USA, where it is now called "*anarcho-capitalism*". Linda and Morris Tannehill have written a book[24] claiming that the state should be abolished on the grounds that it is a "coercive monopoly." (This kind of attitude is of course not new: a gritty Frenchman called Frédéric Bastiat [*q.v.*] claimed in the 19th century that "the State is that great fictitious entity by which everyone seeks to live at the expense of everyone else.") "Altruism is an 'inverted morality,' pursue Linda and Morris, "the 'morality of death.' It teaches man that his interests are opposed to the interests of everyone else and that the only 'moral' thing he can do is to sacrifice his interests. This means that whatever is practical for a man is 'immoral' and conversely whatever is 'moral' for him is impractical and destructive of his values."

Mother Teresa is a borderline case. Idolised by conservative Christians like Malcolm Muggeridge, the exposé written by taboo desecrator

---

23 c.f. John Maynard Keynes's remark that "capitalism is the extraordinary belief that the nastiest of men, for the nastiest of reasons, will somehow work for the benefit of us all." It is not entirely clear whether Keynes regarded this as an erroneous belief or "extraordinary" but true…

24 Linda and Morris Tannehill: *The Market for Liberty* (Ludwig von Mises Institute, Auburn, Alabama, 2007).

Christopher Hitchens[25] cast her in a very different light. After she wrote somewhat disingenuously to the judge presiding in the case of mega-fraudster Charles Keating, who had generously given money to her refuge (unfortunately other people's money), the District Attorney wrote her a masterpiece of restrained derision to explain why Keating was not deserving of the extenuation she had unctuously requested:

"Mr. Keating," he wrote, "was convicted of defrauding 17 individuals of more than $900.000. These 17 persons were representative of 17,000 individuals from whom Mr. Keating stole $252,000,000… Their money was being used to fund Mr. Keating's exorbitant and extravagant lifestyle."… "The biblical slogan of your [Mother Teresa's] organization is: 'As long as you did it to one of these My least brethren, You did it to me.'" [This admonition, with some chutzpah, had in fact been advanced in Mother Teresa's letter to the judge].

The D.A. went on to point out that Mr. Keating not only showed no remorse for his actions but persistently tried to shift the blame for them to other people. "What would Jesus do if he were in possession of money that had been stolen?" he concluded by asking. "I submit that Jesus would promptly and unhesitatingly return the stolen property to its rightful owners. You should do the same." The D.A.'s letter remained unanswered and no one can account for the missing money. "Saints, it seems," writes Hitchens, "are immune to audit."

Idi Amin (born Idi Awo-Ongo Angoo): Soldier who served with distinction in the British army and was regarded as an excellent rugby player:

The complete list of Amin's self-awarded titles combines the innocent charm of operetta with the less appealing megalomania of the Emperor Nero. As they exceeded the space normally allowed for such things on the *Court and Circular* pages of the press, the opportunity is taken here to record them in full: His Excellency President for Life, Field Marshal *Al Hadji*, Doctor Idi Amin Dada VC, DSO, MC, Lord of All the Beasts of the Earth and Fishes of the Sea and Conqueror of the British Empire in Africa in General and Uganda in Particular. He was also the self-

---

25 Christopher Hitchens: *The Missionary Position: Mother Teresa in Theory and Practice* (Atlantic Books, 2013). Mother Teresa's letter to the trial judge and Mr Turley's letter to Mother Teresa are quoted in full on Pp.71-75.

appointed King of Scotland, a land for which he felt some affection because of its long struggle against the dastardly English.

When Amin served in the King's African Rifles, his British commanding officer described him as „a splendid type and a good rugby player;" although, after he had terrorised the opposition on the rugby pitch, he was always excluded from the white officers' celebratory drinking in the bar, a racist slight that he did not forget. Fighting the Mau Mau insurgency in Kenya, Amin's methods (getting the men of a suspect village to lay their penises on a stone block and chopping off the said penises unless every hidden weapon was yielded up) were remarkably effective, though not an ideal advertisement for the superior civilisation the Brits claimed to be upholding.

For eight years the „splendid type" ruled Uganda in a manner reminiscent of a black comedy by Evelyn Waugh. He routinely fed his opponents to crocodiles and forced prisoners to beat each other's brains out with hammers. He collected so many severed human heads that he had to install an especially large deep freezer in his residence to store them all. He loved to play the accordion interminably at parties, maniacally beaming at the terrified dancers. After he fled Uganda in 1979, the evening of his days was passed comfortably on a Saudi pension in Riyadh, where he spent much of his time in shopping malls.

The Saudis obviously appreciated Amin as a good Muslim (with his four wives and fifty children), one who piously went to the mosque each day. True, he had killed at least 250,000 Ugandans during his dictatorship, may be even double that number. However this impressive record of slaughter did not prevent him from being elected Chairman of the Organisation of African Unity in 1975 (though Julius Nyerere and some others boycotted the vote.) Evidently the majority of the OAU's members agreed with Amin's modest description of himself as "the hero of Africa." The Russian Ambassador with difficulty dissuaded him from erecting a massive monument to Adolf Hitler on the shores of Lake Victoria.

Amin's foreign diplomacy was erratic, but sometimes touching (for example, he sent President Nixon a "Get Well Soon Card" at the height of the Watergate crisis, when Nixon was suffering from phlebitis.) Sadly his offer of sexual favours to Queen Elizabeth II was ignored, such is the ingratitude of Britain's ruling house.

Andropause: Male menopause characterised by a reversion to radical posturing by 68ers who have done well out of capitalism:

It was said that the great 19th century Liberal William Gladstone became more radical as he grew older, whereas usually the reverse tendency is to be expected. Now there is a new phenomenon of the newly retired "68ers," flush with final salary index-linked pensions, who are rediscovering what a terrible thing capitalism is. This is particularly marked among the chattering classes and in the arts. If Pascal Bruckner is to be believed, statist France has the most thriving European sector of the new "bourgeois bolshevism." "There is no journalist, no actor, who does not claim to be subversive, especially if he or she receives a government subsidy," he writes.[26]

Anti-Capitalist: A person who condemns unethical business behaviour: Vince Cable, the saintly Liberal Democrat Cabinet Minister, once rashly referred to the "spivs and gamblers" of the City of London in a speech to the Lib Dem conference. This was deemed an unacceptably candid description of the bankers who had nearly bankrupted the Britain, but personally and in most cases paid minor or no penalties for doing so. The remark recalled a similar, if more sophisticated, insight of John Maynard Keynes, namely that "the businessman, regarded as a means, is tolerable; as an end he is not so satisfactory." Moreover Keynes put his finger on the same neuralgic point of capitalism about which Cable was reminding his audience of city hucksters when he said that "capitalism is the astonishing belief that the nastiest motives of the nastiest men somehow or other work for the best results in the best of all possible worlds."

Cable compounded his offence with a statement of the obvious, namely that the interests of powerful "business people" do not *necessarily* coincide with those of the rest of us. This instantly provoked a tantrum in financial circles, which denounced him *inter alia* as an "anti-capitalist." (It was Tacitus who remarked: *"You always hate most the persons you have injured most."*)

No sooner are regulations introduced to limit the unscrupulous behaviour of business than business starts lobbying against them, usually with

26 Pascal Bruckner: *The Tyranny of Guilt: As Essay on Western Masochism* (Translated by Steven Rendall. Princeton University Press, Princeton and Oxford, 2010) Pp. 180-181.

some success. The arguments advanced always combine blackmail with disingenuousness (jobs will be lost or companies will move to a more lenient (i.e. more corrupt) jurisdiction.) In 2015, a key element in the Dodd-Frank reforms in the USA was rolled back by being slipped into a "must pass" funding bill not otherwise concerned with it. The former chair of the Federal Deposit Insurance Corporation commented that *"there was no way this would have passed muster if people had openly debated it."* The repeal of this clause left banks holding $10tn of risky derivatives which they would have otherwise been obliged to offload, but wanted to keep on their books because their margins were higher thereby. Why should they care if they are confident the state will bail them out in the event it all goes belly-up? There will be many more such manoeuvres as corrupt Congressmen and Senators hasten to do the bidding of their paymasters.[27]

The blanket accusation of being an *"anti-"* this or that will be familiar to those who've been smeared as *"anti-Semitic"* for criticising Israeli policy, or *"anti-American"* for opposing the Iraq war. The idea is to disbar your opponent from speaking rather than having to argue your case with him or her. A current favourite is to label anyone who questions the appropriateness of Britain's current relationship with the EU as *"anti-European."*

As the Inquisition knew, shouting down (or preferably burning) your critics saves you the trouble of engaging with their arguments. Similarly, being disrespectful of bankers who have appropriated billions from savers and investors is condemned as *"envy"* of high earners. And envy, you know, is a *sin*. Nevertheless one cannot but admire the *chutzpah* of this rhetorical tactic: it's as if you were to catch a burglar red-handed helping himself from the safe in your living room and furiously ordered him out of your house — whereat he responds by telling you to get counselling for anger management.

A similar ploy may be observed in the use of the suffix "— *bashing.*" As soon as the bankers thought it safe to return to business as usual, increasingly disapproving references to *"banker-bashing"* began to appear in banker-friendly sections of the press. The clear implication was that criticism of bankers was becoming ill-informed or vulgar — and worse,

---

27 See a report in the *Financial Times*, 11th November, 2015, "Warren attacks Dodd-Frank rollback" by Barney Jopson and Ben Mclannahan.

no longer fashionable. The millions who had been disadvantaged by the banking fraud, and then been forced as taxpayers to pick up the tab for it, should simply *"get over it"* and *"move on".*[28] Unfortunately, just as this casuistical propaganda was getting into its stride, yet another avalanche of banking criminality burst over the heads of a weary public and the egregious spin had to be hastily abandoned.

A particularly disingenuous use of the "— *bashing*" suffix is to be found amongst the politically correct when commenting on politics in the new democracies of Central and Eastern Europe. Even guidebook writers fall for the old Communist /new Liberal or Socialist line that it is indelicate to continue harping on the evils of the former Communist regimes, especially when ex-Communists are doing so remarkably well out of the new dispensation. To neutralise a well-founded suspicion in some countries that the Communists have lost the war but won the peace, the phrase *"Commie-bashing"* (with its whiff of McCarthyism) is wheeled into service. Former victims of Communist oppression, especially those who churlishly express their dismay when the new power holders turn out to be the old Communist establishment in drag, are stigmatised as intolerant boors who can't let bygones be bygones. The old perpetrators appear before our wondering eyes as the new victims.

A simple test will expose the dishonesty of using the phrase *"Commie-bashing"* to distract attention from Communist atrocities in the past: just write an article incorporating the phrase *"Nazi-bashing"* in the same disinfecting way that *"Commie-bashing"* is sometimes used by journalists and wait for the tsunami of furious denunciation to roll in….

[Q.V. *"rant,"* *"populist"* and other diversionary terms of abuse.]

Aphorism: A remark plucked from its context and placed in anthologies for future misuse by politicians, journalists, lexicon compilers etc.:

Dr Johnson thought most aphorisms were apocryphal. In his view, *"pointed axioms and acute replies fly loose about the world and are assigned successively to those whom it may be the fashion to celebrate."*

---

28 Or as Bob Diamond, the unrepentant rent-seeker-in-chief of Barclays Bank put it: *"the period of remorse and apology needed to be over."* Few had noticed that it had begun, apart from one humiliating grilling of temporarily embarrassed bankers before a House of Commons Committee.

André Gide was hardly more flattering about the genre, remarking in *Le Traité du Narcisse* that *"Everything has been said before; but because nobody pays any attention, we have to keep saying it again."*

On the other hand, Friedrich Schlegel defended the aphorism from such rude handling: *"it ought,"* he said, *"to be entirely isolated from the surrounding world and a work of art complete in itself, like a hedge-hog."* Alan E. Williams, quoting this in an article on the music of György Kurtág, adds the following: *"Kurtág's most closed fragments are also like hedgehogs, in that they are curled up in themselves, perfect in form, but point their spikes at the world, resisting and inviting exegesis at the same time."* (This observation neatly summarizes the rebarbative nature of atonal modern music. *"Bad music always sounds pleasant,"* says Pierre Boulez grimly, *"but good music makes you gnash your teeth."* Arnold Schoenberg, whose music caused a riot at an early performance in Vienna, made the same point differently when he talked of *"the emancipation of dissonance."* However it appeared that it was not so much dissonance that needed to be emancipated as the public, regrettably in thrall to Boulez's "pleasant" sounds even today. *"To listen is an effort,"* said Stravinsky (another provoker of riots), *"and just to hear is no merit. A duck also hears."*)

As to aphorisms, Karl Kraus said they *"need not be true, but should* **surpass** *truth. They must go beyond it with one leap."* So they should be used sparingly, like Angostura bitters. Moreover there is a danger of them becoming a substitute for thought rather than a stimulant to it. The Viennese writer Hermann Bahr, in a sly attack on his aphorist-coining rival, observed that *"many an aphorism is the gravestone of a great thought prematurely deceased."*

Apocaholic: A person whose mental health, but not his bank balance, is adversely affected by doom mongering:

Given the human race's evident preference for pessimism over optimism it is a wonder that so much of it has not only survived but modestly improved its living arrangements since the Stone Age. The story goes that Árpád, the leader of the 9th century Magyars who was hoping to lead his seven tribes across the Carpathians in 896 AD, was faced with truculent opposition from his famously obdurate and pessimistic people. So he consulted the shaman, who told him: "Just tell them that you've changed your mind and we should return to our lands by the Dniester and Dnieper rivers, as intelligence has reached you that there has been a bumper harvest and the outlook is good. That should move them in the opposite direction — they're Magyars after all." And indeed as dawn broke the following day, the air was rent with cries and the dust-clouds rose as the Magyars prepared to move on hastily to the new homeland that Árpád envisaged for them in the Carpathian Basin. (It is true that any Magyar worth his salt will hasten to inform you that, since that fateful evening at the Verecke mountain pass, Hungarian history has been an unmitigated disaster and he will (if you let him) relate his entire national narrative in a manner that may make it difficult to disbelieve him. But he is merely being true to his perception of the world, which has been summed up in the aphorism: "an optimist is merely a pessimist who is badly informed." Some good things have happened, but mostly they were bad things in disguise. That light at the end of the tunnel is unfortunately the headlights of an oncoming train.)

Modern apocaholics have far more means at their disposal than 9th century Magyars to spread alarm and despondency — as Matt Ridley points out: "For 200 years pessimists have had all the headlines, even though optimists have far more often been right. Arch-pessimists are fêted, showered with honours and rarely challenged, let alone confronted with their past mistakes."[29] To take a not untypical example of the latter, in 1984 the German "*Stern* magazine reported that a third of Germany's forests were already dead or dying, that experts believed all its conifers would be gone by 1990 and that the Federal Ministry of the Interior predicted all forests would be gone by 2002. All of them! Professor Bernd Ulrich said it was *already too late* for Germany's forests: 'They cannot be saved.'" This was at the height of the "acid rain" scare, with similarly apocalyptic warnings across the Atlantic. As it turned out, European and American forests were thriving — a ten year government sponsored study in the USA subsequently showed as much, although the US Environment Agency tried to prevent the findings being shown to Congress.

---

29 Matt Ridley: *The Rational Optimist* (Fourth Estate, London, 2011) P. 295. Also the following quotations and paraphrase of passages in his entertaining book may be found on Pp. 304-5 and generally in Chapter 9 (*Turning Points. Pessimism after 1900* and Chapter 10 (*The two great pessimisms of today: Africa and climate after 2010*), and the *Postscript* on the history of the concept of optimism.

Analogous examples of wildly wrong or exaggerated predictions can be endlessly replicated, but the tide of apocalyptic doom-mongering rolls on. Solvable problems are presented as ineluctable catastrophes, local ones are projected onto a worldwide canvas, successful solutions or the retreat of much reported threatening phenomena are scarcely reported or not at all. When the fossil fuel reserves did not run out in thirty years as predicted at the end of the sixties (on the contrary they have increased), when famines diminish, populations begin to stabilise, the green revolution makes more food available more efficiently, life expectancy steadily rises, deaths diminish through better medical outreach or drugs, and so on and so forth, the apocaholics are unimpressed. Next year's scare is already in the oven (an asteroid is on its way to us like the one that wiped out the dinosaurs — hadn't you heard?)

Oil is an interesting example. Part of the odium directed at it by environmentalists is because it stubbornly refuses to run out. Its certain disappearance within thirty years was predicted in the 1970s, when the eco-salvationists first worked up a head of steam about the iniquity of fossil fuels. But new oil was discovered in the North Sea and elsewhere, while the price per barrel proved to be cyclical. At the turn of the millennium the same prediction of oil's demise was again to be found everywhere in the media when the phrase "peak oil" was coined (for good measure, the alarmists threw in iron ore, copper, rare earths and cereals), meaning that the availability and price of these would soon make them unobtainable, thus causing a worldwide crisis of unprecedented dimensions. This was good news for unscrupulous investment bankers like Goldman Sachs, who speculate in commodities' prices and who predicted in March 2008 that oil would shortly reach $200 a barrel. What actually happened was that oil peaked at $150 a barrel, before the financial crisis sent it steadily lower to only $35 a barrel by February 2016. Meanwhile the Americans made themselves self-sufficient in oil through fracking (one of the reasons the environmentalists target that process, since it both ensures continuity of supply and refutes the doom mongering, although quite a high oil price is required to make its extraction through fracking economic.) In addition Saudi Arabia started pumping oil at a loss (the SA break-even price is $105 a barrel), in an effort to make the American extraction uneconomic; moreover the possible solution of the Iranian crisis could mean a veritable tsunami of oil coming on the market from that source. In short, in 2015 the world was

18

awash with oil and potentially could soon be even more so. So now Goldman Sachs was saying the price could be stuck at $50 for years — Sell those futures (through us, please)!

Optimism as a concept seems to have appeared around 1737, but did not then mean a sanguine view *of the future*; rather it suggested that the world was at its "optimum", a notion that Voltaire was later to ridicule as *"everything being for the best in the best of all possible worlds"* (the disrespectful aphorism deliberately echoed Gottfried Wilhelm Leibniz's solemn claim that *"we live in the best of all possible worlds."*) In 1755 Voltaire, who was a sceptical Deist, wrote a poem to undermine the Catholic Church's rather feeble attempt to deflect blame from the Almighty for the loss of 60,000 mostly innocent lives in the Lisbon earthquake of that year by implausibly claiming that these unfortunate persons had (justly) incurred God's wrath:

> And can you then impute a sinful deed
> To babes who on their mothers' bosoms bleed?
> Was then more vice in fallen Lisbon found,
> Than Paris, where voluptuous joys abound?
> Was less debauchery to London known,
> Where opulence luxurious holds the throne?[30]

Dr. Pangloss in Voltaire's witty **Candide, ou l'Optimisme** (1759) more or less did for optimism in the Leibniz sense, since anyone subsequently embracing it could be written off as a Panglossian, a complacent fool. But the actual origin of optimism in theodicy (the implausible notion that even the most terrible events can be reconciled with God's mercy) has long since vanished, leaving only its perverted legacy in a sort of hysterical and mendacious glee in doom-mongering taken by the boulevard press, academics on the make, dodgy politicians and grant-thirsty lobbies with their publicity agendas. Pseudo-scientists and sensation-seeking journalists rejoice in anything that can be presented as the first blast of the last trump[31] — the eschatological fate that mankind, for far too long, has tried to dodge. Any attempt to question doom-mongering

---

30 *Poème sur le désastre de Lisbonne*, published by Voltaire in 1756.

31 *"We shall not all sleep, but we shall all be changed, in a moment, in the twinkling of an eye, at the last trump."* I Corinthians 15:51-52.

The Lisbon earthquake, 1755, which provoked an ironic Voltaire to ponder God's mercy.

may lead to ostracism and abuse. When the Danish statistician Bjørn Lomborg ventured to question some articles of faith of the climate change apocaholics, the latter immediately went ballistic in a reaction reminiscent of the Salem witch trials. Lomborg was arraigned by a total-itarian-sounding body called the Danish Committee on Scientific Dishonesty (DCSD), which operated under the aegis of the Ministry of Science, and which "convicted" him of "scientific dishonesty." All this because, although Lomborg thought global warming was happening, he argued heretically that it would be better and cheaper for the world to adapt to it rather than cut carbon emissions. Unfortunately for apocaholics it proved irritatingly difficult to smear a "mild-mannered, bicycle-riding leftish vegetarian" as a "corporate apologist" and each attempt to do so resulted in a satisfactory rise in the sales of his excellent book *The Skeptical Environmentalist* (2001).

After a petition by a large number of Danish scientists and a formal complaint by Lomborg himself regarding his kangaroo trial at which he was not even allowed to defend himself (Galileo was accorded better treatment), the Ministry annulled the "conviction," stating not unreasonably that "the DCSD has not documented where [Dr. Lomborg] has allegedly been biased in his choice of data and in his argumentation,

20

and … [its] ruling is completely void of argumentation for why the DCSD find that the complainants are right in their criticisms of [his] working methods. It is not sufficient that the criticisms of a researcher's working methods exist; the DCSD must consider the criticisms and take a position on whether or not the criticisms are justified, and why." Naturally the Committee did not take up the Ministry's invitation to substantiate its criticisms, nor to re-investigate the claims of Lomborg's critics, arguing that renewed scrutiny would, in all likelihood, result in the same conclusion. In other words, even if we're wrong (but we won't let you find out whether we are or not), we're right. Lomborg was subsequently appointed head of the Environmental Assessment Institute for the Danish government.

Although the modern advances in media technology (itself presumably a remarkable indication of progress for all but the most determined pessimists) make it easier to indulge in what has been described as *catastrophilia* and propagate the comparatively new religion of *eco-salvationism*, these phenomena are as old as the hills that hopefully contain lots of minerals or fossil fuels awaiting exploitation. "I have observed," said John Stuart Mill in his speech on *Perfectibility*, "that not the man who hopes when others despair, but the man who despairs when others hope, is admired by a large class of persons as a sage." Adam Smith was articulating a similar view when he remarked (on the eve of the industrial revolution which laid the foundation for our modern prosperity) that "five years have seldom passed away in which some book or pamphlet has not been published pretending to demonstrate that the wealth of nations was fast declining, that the country was depopulated, agriculture neglected, manufactures decaying and trade undone." Five years! Nowadays it's more like five minutes. The decline of mainstream Christianity in the western democracies has led to a secular eschatology pouring into the psychological void left by organised religion like the fire and brimstone of the scriptures ("*Upon the wicked He shall rain snares, fire and brimstone, and an horrible tempest.*")[32] Like the Manichean doctrine of Babylon and early Christianity, apocaholism is energised by the identification of enemies, satanic figures like Lomborg who work ceaselessly for the forces of darkness against the revealed truths of the doomsters. As Tom Stacey has written: "That there is no evidence of the climate

32 Psalm 11:6

21

going awry in the long view of climate history… is a proposition offensive to many since it removes from them what has become the alleviation of a neurosis — that is, removes the justification to relieve their opaque sense of guilt by loading guilt on others."[33]

Of course there is always a good supply of promising news to fuel this process. The Arab spring and its consequent civil wars, the rise of ISIL and the migration flood from failed African states, provide the apocaholic of 2015 with plenty of red meat. All of these, he observes with satisfaction are anyway the fault of the West and colonialism (past and present). Any suggestion that African rulers might consider abandoning the wholesale plunder of the states they rule, or indeed that such states are themselves in any way at all responsible for their misery is of course to be deprecated. However much aid, technology transfer, and logistical support the West might offer them, it can never assuage the terrible guilt of past imperialism or reduce the necessity to dish out yet more cash and material aid — thus freeing local rulers of the obligation to serve their people rather than themselves.

In any case apocalyptic visions are sexy and have bred a number of *Führer*-style sects, some harmlessly eccentric, some, like Jim Jones or David Koresh, rather less so. The futurologist Matthias Horx reproduces in his book *"Risk the Future"* a splendidly opportunistic letter from an old sixty-eighter called Friedrich Theodor (originally "von Theodor," then not, then again "von," presumably in accordance with the changing fashions of the alternative society's self-image.)[34] Friedrich, or Freddie as he preferred to be called, lived much of his life as a trust fund hippie and was an expert on Gramsci, Marx (Karl, not Groucho), Hegel, Castaneda, Kant and long-legged blondes. At the height of the 2008 financial crisis he wrote to Horch from his latest perch on a South Seas island pointing out that the "greedy self-destructive monetary system is nearing its end," "financial and economic disasters are piling up," as also are "environmental catastrophes, floods, earthquakes, extreme weather events, terrorist attacks, social unrest and

33 Tom Stacey in the *Prefatory Essay* to Professor Robert M. Carter: *Climate: The Counter Consensus* (Stacey International, London, 2010) P. 18.

34 Matthias Horx: *Zukunft wagen: über den klugen Umgang mit dem Unvorhersehbaren* (DeutscheVerlags-Anstalt, München, 2013) Pp.143, 145, 146, 160,161. (Translations N. P.)

killers running amok; all of which recalls the seven plagues of the Bible and other prophecies... Many leaders now assume that the human species will not survive the 21st century..." In order to save humanity from itself, Freddie von Theodor was staging a congress on his agreeable volcanic South Seas island with the working title *"Dancing on the Volcano."* Matthias Horch, together with others drawn from the "most important visionaries and thinkers" of the day was cordially invited to participate in its urgent deliberations to avert the end of civilisation as we know it.

Horch replies that he has decided against attending Freddie's world rescue congress, not because he fears that the local volcano might suddenly erupt while he's there; not even because he objects to Freddie (now again "von") Theodor's newly formulated "peace treaty with capital" ("with your three tax efficient residences in three continents, I understand that this may be a necessity.") No, none of that, but on account of a far more worrying apostasy: "I have, in short, parted company with the basic idea that the world is on a knife-edge. And that it must unquestioningly and unswervingly be rescued. Instead I am going to state something outrageous; namely that, taking one thing with another, the world is doing OK." It may even be, hints Horch, that the world needs to be *rescued* from its *rescuers*... he recognises that this is an even more horrifying prospect for the doomsters than their end of the world scenarios:

"Let us imagine that the world simply does not need rescuing," he writes, "and that she is quite capable of rescuing herself. What a dreadful thought! Truly an apocalyptic notion! What point would there be to our existence, what would remain of our interpretative power, of our world mission?!"[35]

The good news, if one may use such a deplorable phrase, is that there are still plenty of health resorts around the world with benign climatic conditions where stressed out apocaholics can recover, perhaps in the embrace of self-help groups like Apocaholics Anonymous. Tuvalu or the Maldives, for instance, to name but two destinations that have not (yet) sunk beneath the waves despite thirty years of predictions that they would. [See also **Z: Climate Change Zealotry**]

---

35 Matthias Horx: *Op cit.* Pp. 162-3. (Translation N.P.)

Apologism: The doctrine, much favoured in identity politics, that the apology is merely an extension of the original offence:

Annie Teriba, a black lesbian activist at Wadham College, Oxford, had to resign her many important posts in 2015 since she discovered one morning (as one does) that she had indulged in non-consensual sex the night before. It appears that "the other party" informed her over the bacon and eggs that the sex was not consensual and she (Teriba) had failed to *"properly establish consent before the act."* In other words, both of them were pissed out of their minds. There followed a tsunami of remorse and cringing apology from Annie on Facebook, with an added confession that the previous year she had *"touched somebody in a sexual manner without their consent,"* again when pissed. Annie resigned as Editor of *No HeterOx*, which is "a magazine for Oxford's Queer and Trans Voices", and also as the Wadham Students Union's "people of colour and racial equality officer." She also left her post as the "lesbian, gay, bi and transsexual women's representative" for the black section of the NUS and sacked herself from the committee of the National Campaign Against Fees and Cuts. (Did she have any time left for studying, one wonders?)

Sadly this orgy of *mea culpa* left the women's campaign of the Oxford Students Union unimpressed. They condemned her statement as being *"rife with APOLOGISM"* and added for the uninitiated that *"Rape APOLOGISM manifests itself in infinite forms: we define it as any discourse that refers to sexual assault as anything other than what it is — inacceptable and appalling abuse."* This seems rather hard on Annie, who, after all, was at pains to say that: *"In failing to clarify that the person consented to our entire encounter, I caused serious, irreparable harm."* Nice try, mate, but it seems your career as a victimhood activist is over.[36]

This will surely be a grave disappointment to her — after all she was so good at it! For example she was leading demands to have a statue of Cecil Rhodes removed from its place in the city on the grounds that it was racist. Evidently it would "trigger" trauma in passers by — except of course in elderly white dons, who are closet racists anyway. *"There's violence,"* she has said, *"in having to walk past the statue every day on the way to your lecture."* Let us hope someone else will swiftly take up

36 The details of Annie Teriba's troubles were reported in *The Times* of October 14th, 2015.

the baton from her and complete the good work on Cecil Rhodes.[37] Meanwhile all concerned citizens must be sure to add APOLOGISM to the list of crimes that so many of us are committing every day, probably without even knowing it…

The fact is, however, that it is becoming difficult to keep up with verbal sexual etiquette,[38] at least if you're not in Annie Teriba's milieu, because sensitive people are now declaring themselves *"pansexual,"* *"genderfluid,"* and *"genderqueer"* — like pop singer Miley Cyrus, who has declared that she can be attracted to any of the above categories and also to *"transgender"* persons who are trapped in a biological sexuality which they reject (this is rather a growth market.) However there are apparently also persons who are *"non-binary and genderqueer"* who may identify with being a woman, say on Monday, and with being a man, say on Thursday. This is even more of a growth market and has afforded some promising new perspectives for identity politics by generating demands that those enjoying *"cis privilege"* (that is, the privilege of identifying with the sex you were born into) show proper respect for all these fluctuating identities.

However not all feminists, and especially not all who have been in the midst of the feminist struggle for years, seem to welcome these new competitors in the already crowded market for victimhood. For example, Germaine Greer was characteristically blunt at a Cambridge Union meeting in 2015, remarking *en passant* that trans women do not know what it is to have a *"big, fat, hairy, smelly vagina."* This provoked an adverse reaction from those who thought they might be the target of her allusion, and who condemned the decision to invite *"the unapologetic transmisogynist Germaine Greer."* Coming from a *"non-binary trans,"* that is pretty much as rude as you can get short of accusing someone of being a paedophile or a Tory. Meanwhile the rest of us must keep up with the alphabet soup (LGB is woefully insufficient, now it must be at least LGBTQ) and be careful not to trigger trauma by applying the wrong gender for the day of the week to our gender queer friends. Still,

37 In December 2015, Oriel College decided to keep the Rhodes statue and the Chancellor of the university said those who objected to the university's historical monuments should think about being educated elsewhere.

38 See, for example, an article on this topic in *The Spectator*, 17th October, 2015, by Jenny McCartney, and Sam Leith's comments on acronyms for gender identity in the *Evening Standard* of 19th October, 2015.

it might be a wise precautionary measure to form a proactive victim-hood group for those being discriminated against on account of their *"cis privilege"*…

Appeasement: The wisest course — or the most counterproductive, depending on circumstance:

Winston Churchill's fame as a statesman rests substantially on his rejection of the appeasement of Hitler at a time (the 1930s) when *bien pensant* opinion on the right and the left thought this was not only a good idea, but the *only* good idea in town. So it is all the more intriguing that he once said that *"appeasement has its place in all policy. Make sure you put it in the right place. Appease the weak; defy the strong."* One wonders if this is altogether a good idea, or whether Machiavelli would have agreed with it.

It has been said rather unkindly of the British Foreign Office that its *modus operandi* may be summed up as follows: "Find out what our opponents want and give it to them." As a strategy for withdrawal from empire that arguably has its merits. When Chris Patten became the last British Governor of Hong Kong before the handover to China and decided to give the local inhabitants some of the rights the British had managed to deny them for 150 years, he was furiously opposed by the FO mandarin and China expert Sir Percy Cradock, who was just as defiantly "on message" as Patten was off it. Although *The Economist* infamously compared Cradock and Mrs Thatcher(!) to Neville Chamberlain at Munich, Cradock represented a "realist" line of diplomacy and was the prime mover behind the Joint Declaration between China and the UK on Hong Kong's future status signed in 1984. In his view Patten (whom he dubbed "the incredible shrinking governor") put all that at risk, while Patten evidently regarded it as far too much of a compromise and denounced Cradock as a "dyspeptic retired ambassador" suffering from "Cradockitis." This episode was a classic stand-off between "realist" diplomacy by professional diplomats, which the ignorant call appeasement, and Churchill's recommended policy of "defying the strong." Ten years after the handover in 1997 it was hard to tell who was right, a US Congressional Report beginning its summary with the statement *"10 years after the handover, much has changed and little has changed."* Sir Humphrey could not have improved on that sentence.

The accusation of defeatism has dogged the FO in modern times, though it is easy for those who have no direct responsibility in the matter to urge irresponsibility and bravado when it might be more prudent to find a face-saving formula. Should one pick a fight with a Goliath like China (an "enemy") or the USA (a "friend," with its eye on one's assets)? At the post-war Bretton Woods negotiations, the brilliant John Maynard Keynes had to do battle with an aggressive American negotiator called Harry Dexter White. Keynes had already warned his defeatist sponsors in London that the Americans were intent on "picking the eyes out of the British Empire" (although he did not then know that Roosevelt's adviser Harry Hopkins regarded the British Empire as a greater threat to world peace than Soviet Russia.) The Liberal Keynes was no swivel-eyed nationalist, but even he lamented that "if there was no one left to appease, the FO would feel out of a job altogether."

Anyway White was secretly supplying confidential information to the Soviet Union and had been its agent for years. As in the cases of the dreadful Alger Hiss and the Rosenbergs, American leftists have successfully portrayed these unrepentant traitors to their country as highly principled persons maligned by McCarthyists etc. etc. If, as Dr Johnson maintained, patriotism is the last refuge of a scoundrel, what the Italians delightfully call "Cashmere Communism" is the first.

In a splendid letter to the *New Statesman*[39] after the Nazi-Soviet Pact wrong-footed Communist fellow-travellers in the UK before World War II, Keynes pinned down the sort of appeasement that exhibited neither the rationality of prudence nor the courage of principle: "The intelligentsia of the left were the loudest in demanding that Nazi aggression should be resisted at all costs," he wrote. "When it comes to a showdown, scarce four weeks have passed before they remember they are pacifists and write defeatist letters to your columns, leaving the defence of freedom and civilisation to Colonel Blimp and the Old School Tie, for whom Three Cheers." This must have cost him a large number of dinner invitations.

Archaeology: A challenging profession, for example involving the difficulty of looking for ancient Greek locks, where either the lock can be found, but not the key, or *vice versa*. A dead end where there is no end to the dead:

"Absence of evidence is not evidence of absence" (old adage of archaeologists c.f. Donald Rumsfeld's *"known unknowns"* etc.). This is a

39 *New Statesman*, October 14, 1939.

very handy notion that may be applied to global warming, adultery, the intelligence of one's children and, by hypochondriacs, to the insistence of their GPs that there is nothing wrong with them...

Astrologers: Persons who cannot predict the future:
The most redundant part of the daily newspaper after the Editorial leader is the astrology column. Like the ancient oracle at Delphi, the Mystic Megs who write these columns in the boulevard press employ handily vague formulas that would more or less do for any situation arising. Humour is to be rigorously avoided, particularly of the type that is regrettably evident in the countercultural astrology published as *"You Were Born On A Rotten Day."*

A Fleet Street anecdote records how a newspaper astrologer returned well refreshed from a lengthy journalists' lunch and found on his desk a *billet* less than *doux* from his Editor. It began: "As you would know if you were any good at your job, I've decided to fire you..."

Of course many people still consult astrologers, who are no less likely to be right in their predictions than the people in other professions who are paid vast sums to make them. As the economist Ezra Solomon mordantly remarked of his colleagues: "The only function of economic forecasting is to make astrology look respectable."[40] The business analyst Andrew Smithers, who was actually more accurate than most in his predictions, was similarly unimpressed by market practitioners who claim that stock markets are predictable. "If predictability were good," he observed with some asperity, "even investors would notice."[41]

[See also **B: *Queen Witch Brataria Buzea***]

Oxford auditions: Bizarre rituals affording Oxford dons opportunities to exhibit eccentricity; likewise the hapless candidates being interviewed:
Such auditions are famous (or notorious) for the dangerously bland questions of the interviewers, which are supposedly designed to elicit answers of startling originality from the interviewees. Take, for example, the student who was asked about the causes of the First World War

---

40 This remark is sometimes attributed to John Kenneth Galbraith, but may be he was quoting Solomon.

41 *Weeekend FT*, March1/2, 2014, "Lunch with the FT: Andrew Smithers – 'I don't have any faith in forecasts.'"

and firmly ascribed it to "Belgian aggression" — not a bad answer when you think of the Belgians, but still not quite right (although Konrad Adenauer did once describe his fellow-countrymen as "Belgians with megalomania.")

On another occasion, a sarcastic admissions tutor, idly perusing a newspaper on his desk, glanced with distaste at the candidate and barked: "Surprise me!" The interviewee whipped out his cigarette lighter and set fire to the newspaper, which in turn ignited the tutor's beard.

The public prints are full of college admissions tutors or prospective employers bewailing the innumeracy, illiteracy etc. of candidates for admission or employment. It is even implied in the right-wing press that the more radical teachers of today evidently feel that grammar, spelling, syntax and so forth are part of a conspiracy by the middle class elite to catch out honest, underprivileged youngsters and disbar them from achievement. After all, you don't need grammar for texting on mobile phones.

English spelling is particularly insidious, being arbitrary and often unrelated to pronunciation. The whole thing is clearly a typical trick by a privileged class to do down the rest, just as the priests of the ancient world administered opaque mysteries that ordinary mortals were not allowed to penetrate. As George Bernard Shaw remarked, given the eccentricities of English spelling, there is no reason not to spell the word "*fish*" as "*photi*" ("ph" as in "photo", "o" as in "women" and "ti" as in "nation.")

All the same, it is a little frustrating where the profession applied for might conceivably require basic grammatical and semantic skills. The journalist Michael Skapinker tells of an American professor teaching MBA students who tried to assign them the task of writing a single page memorandum each week, which he would mark for clarity of expression and correctness of English. The students instantly and violently rebelled (on the grounds that business is nowadays done through e-mails and tweets, so correct English was not required) and the Dean took their side (after all, these students are mostly paying big bucks for their courses …) Still, says Skapinker, "I can't be the only customer who assumes that a banker who doesn't know where an apostrophe goes is going to be equally careless with my money…"

The head of one of Britain's drama schools recently described how difficult it was to pick potential acting talent from candidates who could barely read. One was asked to read a Shakespeare sonnet, but the interviewer was unable to understand a word of it (neither, it seemed, could the candidate). Anxious to give the applicant a fair chance, the interviewer finally said: "*OK. Just pick out the nouns in the text and tell me what they mean.*" "*What's a noun?*" asked the candidate.

Austrian turns of phrase: Creative culture of everyday insults:
Backhendlfriedhof: "Cemetery of fried chickens" (Viennese term for a paunch, the last resting place of an untold number of Austrian chickens each year.)

Supposed bureaucratic, managerial or professorial indifference to the concerns of citizens, customers or voters in Austria is a leitmotif of the country's private and media discourse. It is given heartfelt expression in the complaint: „*Er hat mich nicht einmal ignoriert!*" („He didn't even bother to ignore me!").

The *Adabei* is a far from flattering characterisation of "*einer der überall 'auch dabei' sein will (Neugieriger; Wichtigmacher)* "[one who pokes his nose into everything, or always insists on being involved, whether it is appropriate or not — a nosy parker; a pompous ass.] Indeed *Wichtigtuerei* [self-importance] attracts considerable opprobrium in Austria where overbearing officials and the like are often dismissed with the phrase "*er will sich wichtig machen.*" At the opposite linguistic pole to these officiously industrious persons are to be found those given unappetising nomenclature such as *Schnorrer* and *Schmarotzer* (scroungers and freeloaders).

"*Totschweigen*" is another vivid Austrian phrase meaning "killing by silence" (for example, the artistic work ignored by a partisan establishment, or the source heavily used but unmentioned in the footnotes or bibliography.) On the other hand, if you are much in the public eye in a media-conscious environment, the (potentially) prominent people you ignore become negative contributors to your own profile.

There have been people in Austria who were vilified in one context and ignored in another. This is what happened to the entirely estimable Eugénie Schwarzwald, a feminist reformer and educationalist in turn of the century Vienna. Unfortunately she fell foul of the misogynistic Karl Kraus, who pilloried her in his journal *Die Fackel* and cut her socially.

Vienna being a small world, their paths constantly crossed, Kraus always affecting not to recognise his victim. Eventually Schwarzwald attempted to call his bluff when they met one day at a salon, remonstrating with the irascible polemicist that he never seemed to remember her and never greeted her. "You must excuse me, Madam," came the reply, "I thought you were that dreadful Schwarzwald woman."

Author Blurb: Book flap eulogies designed to impress potential readers, intimidate the opposition and flatter the egos of their neurotically insecure subjects:

In a survey of authors' potted biographies, Stephanie Merritt of *The Observer* shrewdly advises readers to „be wary of any author who tries to be ironic and /or uses exclamation marks !!! e.g. *'John Mate lives in London and likes windsurfing and playing the guitar — though not at the same time!'* Similarly, avoid the author who „*divides his time.*" Note that he always „*divides his time*" between New York and Provence, or West London and the British Virgin Islands. Never do you read of someone dividing their time between their flat in Camden and the Coach and Horses".

Pierre Bayle, the discursive lexicographer who compiled a *Historical and Critical Dictionary* (1697), gives a charming example of the completely useless "author biography," *viz:*

"*Caniceus, James: Author of some love letters. I relate this fact only on the testimony of Agrippa, and to excite the curious to discover who this writer was, whose name I have not found in any bibliography; no more than of James Calandrus, an author of the same type, according to the same Agrippa.*"

A "Christian skeptic" with a taste for lewd anecdotes, Bayle thought reason was as dangerous as it was useful. "*Philosophy at first refutes errors,*" he wrote, "*but if it is not stopped at this point, it goes on to attack truths.*" This is very close to the thinking of the Vatican.

Modesty in the author's description of himself is not considered desirable, and may even arouse suspicion: one hears of an author who supplied the following accurate one-line biography to his German publisher for use on a book cover: "[X] *is a freelance writer living in London*". An editor rang him up from Frankfurt: "You can't say that; people will think you're unemployed." "Well, at the moment I *am* unemployed". "Of course, of course! But you can't *say* so. Germans are not prepared to buy books by unemployed persons."

Authority: That which is invoked when respect for it is no longer deserved:

After the summer riots in Britain in 2011 conservative pundits lamented the loss of *respect for authority* in the UK.

What "authority" might that be, one wonders? MPs had been revealed as chisellers and the police exposed as being on the take. The then Archbishop of Canterbury was toying with the idea of allowing parts of *shari'a* to operate in Britain. The London School of Economics had eagerly accepted money stolen from the Libyan people by their oppressors; and a few years earlier a former Foreign Secretary, his bottom still warm from the F.C.O. ministerial chair, had rushed to do well-remunerated business deals with the Serbian mass-murderer, Slobodan Milosevich.

Then again, left-leaning judges had begun decreeing that the "right" to a [usually fictitious] "family life" for rapists and murderers, illegally resident in Britain, trumped the right of the state to have them deported (not to mention the rights of their victims). Bankers held the country to ransom. In a surreal insult to honest citizens, the banks had even been given the job of policing money laundering and tax avoidance, although many of them had themselves for years been involved in such. Much of the intellectual, and virtually all of the political and economic elite of Britain supported or pushed through what Martin Wolf calls "a huge and, for the financial sector, hugely profitable bet on the expansion of debt... lulled by fantasies of self-stabilising financial markets," following "headlong financial liberalisation" promoted by self-seeking ideologues and ineffably greedy bankers. When the crash came, its architects were not the ones to pay the bill. "The belief," adds Wolf laconically, "that the powerful sacrificed taxpayers to the interests of the guilty is correct."[42]

CEOs were paid up to one hundred times the average salaries of their employees. When, as not infrequently happened, they spectacularly failed to deliver the goods, further huge sums were paid to get rid of them. This represented decades of ratcheting and connivance by "remuneration boards" whose members were mostly drawn from the same narrow pool and themselves expect to be similarly rewarded by those they reward. Plato thought the wealthiest Athenians should not have incomes above five times those of the poorest citizens, though admittedly the

42 Martin Wolf: *Failing elites threaten our future* (Financial Times 15 January, 2014.)

slaves (of which he had five) were not reckoned in this figure. In the 1970s the management guru Peter Drucker shared the view expressed a century earlier by financier John Pierpoint Morgan that Chief Executives should not take home more than twenty times the median wage in the firm. Companies with large low paid workforces have even bigger gaps between boss and worker, the former routinely making off with over 400 times the median employee wage, but they are not necessarily the worst offenders when millions, sometimes billions, are being paid out to bankers and chiefs of international concerns. In 2014 Barclays bank *raised* its bonuses by ten per cent despite a *one third fall* in profits. Even the feeblest attempt to pretend that pay reflected performance seemed to have been abandoned.

Furthermore auditors, posing as the watchdogs of corporate integrity, had decided that it was more profitable to whitewash company accounts in order not to prejudice their sales of business services to the companies they audited (or "fraudited" q.v.). Ratings agencies took money from firms pushing worthless or risky bonds and delivered the requisite risk rating (notably giving glowing ratings for banks just before they collapsed.)

Meanwhile back in the Westminster loop, the Glaswegian Labour politician and Speaker, who spent taxpayers' money trying to conceal the abuse of expenses by MPs, and furthermore allowed police into Parliament to rifle the offices an opposition MP who had annoyed the Government, was rewarded for disgracing the office of Speaker of the House of Commons with "elevation" to the House of Lords. (*"In accordance with tradition, as soon as Martin's successor as Speaker was installed, the first motion passed by the House of Commons was a resolution directing that a humble Address be presented to The Queen, asking her „to confer some signal mark of Her Royal favour" upon Martin „for his **eminent services** during the important period in which he presided with such **distinguished ability and dignity** in the Chair of this House." The „signal mark of Her Royal favour" is traditionally the grant of a peerage.* — Wikipedia). The Lords of course contained other peers described as "colourful", including perjurers, paedophiles and dodgy businessmen who had given money to political parties and thus effectively purchased their peerages.

One could go on, but you've probably got the point…

Awards: The proceedings of the Mutual Admiration Society:
Apparently awards can be more easily obtained in the UK if you avail yourself of the advice provided by an outfit called Awards Intelligence. *The Spectator* has revealed that even taxpayers' money is shovelled to this company, in order that public sector drones can bone up on the boxes of political correctness that have to be ticked so as to get in line for an award.

Naturally GS4, the firm that screwed up so spectacularly on the security for the London Olympics, came to the job garlanded with industry "awards." And not so long ago the phone-hacking (and now defunct) *News of the World* won the "Newspaper of the Year" award *three years' running*, an eloquent demonstration of the fact that not only the cash, but also the honours, routinely go to the least-deserving members of our society (arise, Sir Jimmy Savile!)

But then again we all got an award in 2012 as citizens of the EU. No doubt this was as deserved as the award of the Nobel Peace prize to Barack Obama just nine months into his term of office, which many people assumed was his reward for "not being George W. Bush", a rather low set bar. As for the citizens of the EU, we (and Obama) thus joined an illustrious line of Nobel Peace Prize winners that includes Woodrow Wilson, whose Versailles Peace Treaty was such a spectacular success that it caused the Second World War, Henry Kissinger, whose trail of destruction ranges from Chile to Cambodia, not to mention cuddly Yasser Arafat. It's a shame that Osama bin Laden died before he could be awarded his Peace Prize.

B

Bore:
A person who talks when you wish him to listen.

Ambrose Bierce: *The Devil's Dictionary*

Bankster: Term that fuses "banker" and "gangster," now commonly used to describe the former.

Barclays Bank: Rent-seeking (*q.v.*) and mis-selling behemoth:
The following is a quick round-up on the excellent job Barclays plc has been doing for its customers and shareholders since 2009: (1): Fined *£2.45* million by the FSA for falsely reporting transactions (2009). (2): Fined *£7.7m*, plus *£59m* compensation paid to Barclays customers who were mis-sold high- risk Aviva funds (2010) (3): Fined *$298m* for violating US sanctions and embargoes (2010). (4): Forced by HMRC to pay *£500m* in back taxes following "highly abusive" tax avoidance scheme (2011). (5): Obliged to pay **£2 billion** compensation for mis-selling PPI, on which many of the "insured" could never have claimed (2011-12). (6): *Similar costs expected* for mis-selling credit swaps to small businesses, while concealing their massive downside.

(7): *£290m* fine for manipulating LIBOR (i.e. falsifying interest rates in order to generate illicit profits) (2012). (8) Achieved dubious distinction of incurring the biggest bank penalty in British history *($2.4bn)* when fined by US and UK regulators for manipulation of foreign exchange markets (FOREX) (2015).[1] One reason for the size of this partic-

---

1 Barclays was one of a group of six malefactors (the other five were Citigroup, J. P. Morgan Chase, Royal Bank of Scotland, Bank of America and UBS) collectively sanctioned to the tune of $5.6bn dollars (£3.84 bn) in May of 2015. Civil litigation is to follow and the lawyers are rubbing their hands...

ular penalty was that the FOREX swindling came after a settlement for the same sort of cheating on LIBOR, part of which settlement was an undertaking by the banks *not to undertake any further rigging of markets* (most magnanimous of them). But the culture was such that, as one Barclays barrow boy put it, *"If you ain't cheating, you ain't trying."* (9): Fined *$435m* by US regulators for Enron-style manipulation of US energy markets, plus repayment of *$35m* of illegal profits on same (2012). (10): Investigated for *massive kickbacks* allegedly paid by Barclays to secure bail-out from Qatar sovereign wealth fund (2012). (11): Investigation into *kickbacks* paid to secure Saudi Arabian banking licence (2012).

(12): Continued use of offshore tax avoidance vehicles despite having admitted that in 2009 it had paid only *£113m* in corporation tax and had promised to clean up its act (2012). (13): Settlement with a care home operator and a Portuguese property company, 16 unsuitable and costly derivative transactions allegedly having been pressed on the latter by the Barclays' Portuguese branch, all of them "contrary to the claimant's interests and objectives" (2014), but evidently related to manipulation of Libor and Euribor. (14): Obliged to pay a penalty in November 2015 of *$150m* for dishonestly withholding electronic trades for hundreds of milliseconds, only processing them if the markets had moved in favour of the bank.

(15): In late November 2015 the chickens were still coming home to roost for Barclays. The U.K. Financial Conduct Authority fined it **£72 million** ($109 million) for evading its own rules for background checks on clients to determine the origin of their cash and whether they featured on international sanctions lists. Regulators remarked on the elaborate manoeuvres the responsible Barclays employees had pursued in 2011-2012 in order to hide the £1.9 billion transaction ($2.8 billion) even from the bank's own staff, manoeuvres which it said (with nicely judged understatement) „*threatened confidence in the U.K. financial system.*" The bank had been unduly anxious to accommodate a number of „ultra high net worth clients" who might have been "politically exposed persons" (i.e. potentially crooks and money launderers). It was known as an "elephant deal," bringing with it a cool £52 million in "commission," so it's not hard to see why the bankers involved thought it worth risking the bank's reputation, what was left of it.

All of which entertainingly highlights the irony-free zone of the bank's "**mission statement**" (2011), in which it promises to be "*customer-focused,*" to deliver "*superb products and services*" [*sic*] and "*contribute positively*" to the community. That's the thing about mission statements: they're written by the dumbos in "Compliance"… [C. f. **R: Rent-seeking**]

"Sound banker": Person who makes money by squandering other people's:

In 2014, elegant, silver-haired and universally admired (by bankers) Jamie Dimon presided over J. P. Morgan, which by then had incurred fines of a mere $18bn for past malfeasance of one kind or another. In January of that year it made a further settlement of $2.6bn for civil claims linked to its behaviour in respect of Bernard Madoff's Ponzi scheme. No reason to sack Mr Dimon of course, since the bank was still making bumper profits, so the fines were just a business cost as far as Chairman Dimon and his admirers were concerned. "In no other business," wrote Philip Stephens in the *Financial Times* "would a chief executive survive such expensive ignominy. Bankers have made themselves the exception. The fines make only a small dent in the vast rents they extract from the productive sector. They may even be tax-deductible."[2] In any case, banks that are "too big to fail", of which J.P.Morgan was one, were still effectively subsidised by the taxpayer, so why should they care?[3]

Thomas Jefferson once said: "*Every bank in America is an enormous tax upon the people for the profit of individuals.*" This remark has been proved remarkably prescient: since the Lehman Brothers implosion in 2008, central banks have kept interest rates artificially low in order to subsidise the banking system as it rebuilds its balance sheets. This has devastated the return on savings for ordinary people, who were still in most cases receiving zero interest on their deposit accounts in 2015 (interest on their overdrafts, of course, stood at 19.90 per cent EAR vari-

2 Philip Stephens: "*Nothing can dent the Divine Right of Bankers*", *Financial Times*, January 17th 2014.

3 Mr Dimon's pay package was cut in half in 2012, to a mere $11.5 million, so we can see he was doing his bit. On the other hand his 2013 pay package soared by 74% to $20 million. The rank and file bankers were not so lucky, their pay being "down year on year" according to the FT (Jan 25/26 2014). Poor fellows.

able.)[4] To add insult to the injury of what is effectively a stealth tax on savers, the government decided in 2015 to cut the guarantee on savers' deposits from an already meagre £85,000 to £75,000, pleading an initiative of the European Union. As a letter to the *Financial Times* caustically pointed out *"Westminster is continuously at odds with Brussels opting out of this or that directive, but is suddenly toeing the line when dealing with the protection of our savings."*[5] To put it another way, not only have all those who manage their affairs prudently been made to pay for the recklessness of the banks, but the government has also now decided that their much diminished savings deposits should be even less protected than before. It is an interesting version of capitalism where prudent people are punished for doing the right thing in order to rescue crooks, who did the wrong thing.

Not so long ago, the retiring Chairman of J. P. Morgan's rival Merrill Lynch was widely described as a *sound banker* by his peers, despite presiding over $7.9bn mortgage-related losses. The blow of his eventual resignation was somewhat softened, one would hope, with a package of stock options, unvested shares, deferred compensation, pension payments and "other benefits" of circa $160m. The *Financial Times* helpfully explained that these were the rewards for "risk-taking" (shareholders took the risks and Mr O'Neal took the money.) Also, these sorts of incentives are needed to attract other "sound bankers" to replace those who have lost their shareholders their shirts. *"Confused?"* asks the FT. *"That shows you are not clever enough to be a banker."*

Frédéric Bastiat (1801–1850): Genial Frenchman who objected to the legalised theft of people's money by the state and quarrelled with Proudhon:

"Socialism," wrote Bastiat, "like the ancient ideas from which it springs, confuses the distinction between government and society. As a result of this, every time we object to a thing being done by the government, the socialists conclude that we object to its being done at all. We disapprove of state education. Then socialists say that we are opposed to

---

4 "Equivalent Annual Rate" if you were overdrawn for a year, higher than the advertised annual rate times 12 because of the effect of compound interest. Moreover the "fees" charged by the bank to a customer going overdrawn are not included.

5 Letter from A. Albert of London SW3 to the *Financial Times*, 11th–12th July, 2015.

any education. We object to a state religion. Then the socialists say we want no religion at all. We object to a state-enforced equality. Then they say we are against equality. And so on, and so on. It is as if the socialists were to accuse us of not wanting persons to eat because we do not want the state to raise grain."

Writing more than 150 years ago, Bastiat foresaw and caricatured arguments about the size and role of the state that exercise us today. He would have been scathing about the insidious but almost universal assumption that citizens are customarily *granted* by the government out of its generosity the money that is theirs in the first place (hence the references at budget time of Chancellors "giving away" money to taxpayers.) Mrs Thatcher, knowingly or not, was a true Bastiatian when she opined that *"the trouble with Socialism is that eventually you run out of other people's money."*

"Sometimes the law defends plunder and participates in it," pursues Bastiat in *The Law*: "Thus the beneficiaries are spared the shame and danger that their acts would otherwise involve... But how is this legal plunder to be identified? Quite simply. See if the law takes from some persons what belongs to them and gives it to the other persons to whom it doesn't belong. See if the law benefits one citizen at the expense of another by doing what the citizen himself cannot do without committing a crime. Then abolish that law without delay. No legal plunder: this is the principle of justice, peace, order, stability, harmony and logic."

It is no accident that Bastiat had a spectacular verbal punch-up with the anarchist Proudhon[6], whose views on property (*"Qu'est ce que la propriété? C'est le vol!"*) were, as Bastiat put it, "the exact antithesis to my serious approach." This splendidly condescending put-down caused Proudhon to lose his temper: "Your intelligence sleeps, or rather it has never been awake," he snapped. "You are a man for whom logic does not exist... You do not hear anything, you do not understand anything... You are without philosophy, without science, without humanity... Your ability to reason, like your ability to pay attention and make comparisons is zero... scientifically, M. Bastiat, you are a dead man." It is amusing (though not for their victims) that the putative enforcers of Proudhon's

6 Pierre-Joseph Proudhon (1809–1865), the inventor of Mutualist philosophy and (as he claimed, at least) the first political thinker to call himself an anarchist. His most famous observation (quoted above) translates as: *"What is property? Property is theft!"*

most socialistic views under Soviet Communism could be described in almost exactly the same terms.

Yet Proudhon shared Bastiat's distrust of government — they were, after all, both libertarians — and claimed that " *the government of men over others is slavery!*"; he just thought that if you abolished governments everything would go swimmingly when society was spontaneously guided by anarcho-syndicalist associations of workers. Bastiat, on the other hand, thought everything would be just fine if the government stopped confiscating people's money and limited itself to what company directors are pleased to call its "core functions." Property was the guarantee of liberty for Bastiat, the negation of it for Proudhon.

Bastiat was ahead of his time in being against monopolies and protectionism. In his *Economic Sophisms* he relates the parable of the French candle makers and tallow producers who lobby the Chamber of Deputies under the July Monarchy to block out the sun in order to prevent "unfair" competition with their products. (Of course one might consider the sun a bit of a monopoly, since our planet only has one of them.) This was his *reductio ad absurdum* of what he called the "legal plunder" of "tariffs, protection, benefits, subsidies, encouragements, progressive taxation, public schools, guaranteed jobs, guaranteed profits, minimum wages, a right to relief, a right to the tools of labour, free credit, and so on, and so on." He therefore concluded: "As long as it is admitted that the law may be diverted from its true purpose — that it may violate property instead of protecting it — then everyone will want to participate in making the law, either to protect himself against plunder or to use it to plunder." Bastiat's list of restrictive practices has the merit of highlighting not only the abuse by the state of public money for buying votes, but more especially the megahypocrisy of US big business, which preaches entrepreneurism (for oth-

Frédéric Bastiat (1801-1850): "Everyone tries to live at the expense of everyone else..."

ers), but itself tries to live off what J.K. Galbraith has dubbed "corporate welfare" (tax breaks, discriminatory tariffs and so forth).

If we look at the situation of mature democracies today, where the entire political debate revolves around how much money can be gouged from the government for this or that, Bastiat seems like a voice in the wilderness. Furthermore those who raise their heads above the consensual parapet are usually crooked bankers or corrupt economists who are unlikely to carry much weight with a public still picking up the enormous tab for these gentlemen's malfeasance. As Bastiat himself sadly remarked: *"The worst thing that can happen to a good cause is, not to be skilfully attacked, but to be ineptly defended."*

Jean Baudrillard: Whimsical French philosopher whose "simulacrum" disappeared in 2007 (it's called death if it happens to you and me):

Baudrillard is celebrated for announcing that the first Gulf War of 1991 would not take place. When it did, he said it was not really taking place. After its conclusion he announced that it had not taken place. His obituarist hastened to defend him from charges of delusion. Baudrillard was pointing out that the campaign was a "war-game enacted for the viewing public as a simulation."

All of which may remind us that Boswell once remarked to Dr Johnson that it was difficult to refute Bishop Berkeley's sophistries proving the non-existence of matter. "I shall never," writes Boswell, "forget the alacrity with which Johnson answered, striking his foot with mighty force against a large stone, till he rebounded from it, and roaring 'I refute it ***thus***.' "

According to Baudrillard, events were "on strike" in the 1990's and only went back to work when 9/11 occurred. The philosopher was also an expert on dustbins, pointing out that, while the Marxists had invented the "dustbin of history", they had themselves fallen into it. Now there are no more dustbins for *passé* ideologies, "because history itself has become its own dustbin, just as the planet itself is becoming its own dustbin."

Beatification: Propaganda device of the Roman Catholic Church:
A good example is that of the last Habsburg Emperor, Karl the First (or "Karl the Sudden" as the Vienna coffee-house wits called him, when he unexpectedly became heir to the throne in 1914): it is hard to see him in the same light as, for instance, King Saint Stephen of Hungary

or Saint Leopold of Babenberg, but it seems to have been decided at some Vatican PR meeting that he should be set on the path to sainthood. May be he was at least harmless, and the Habsburg name still has brand recognition.

An attested miracle is required for beatification, but happily it could be demonstrated that a Polish lady with varicose veins had prayed to the dead Emperor, who obligingly cured her of her affliction. Moreover, as the Pope himself has stressed, Karl was a man who "really abhorred war." Obviously that was why he authorised the use of mustard gas on the Italian front during World War One. Here he was following the precept of the German commander, General Von Moltke (the Younger and Nastier), who observed that using gas is a purely humanitarian measure, since it shortens the war for all concerned. Surely no one would want to disagree with that?

In his autobiography, Christopher Hitchens describes his unlikely (or unwitting) role as Devil's Advocate for the canonisation of Mother Teresa as follows: "When the late Pope John Paul II decided to place the woman so strangely known as "Mother" Teresa on the fast track for beatification, and thus to qualify her for eventual sainthood, the Vatican felt obliged to solicit my testimony and I thus spent several hours in a closed hearing room with a priest, a deacon, and a monsignor, no doubt making their day as I told off, as from a rosary, the frightful faults and crimes of the departed fanatic. In the course of this, I discovered that the pope during his tenure had surreptitiously abolished the famous office of "Devil's Advocate," in order to fast–track still more of his many candidates for canonization. I can thus claim to be the only living person to have represented the Devil *pro bono*."[7]

"Many people," wrote George Orwell, "genuinely do not wish to be saints, and it is probable that some who achieve or aspire to sainthood have never felt much temptation to be human beings. If one could follow it to its psychological roots, one would, I believe, find that the main motive for „non-attachment" is a desire to escape from the pain of living, and above all from love, which, sexual or non-sexual, is hard work."[8]

7 Christopher Hitchens: *Hitch-22: A Memoir*.
8 George Orwell: *The Collected Essays, Journalism and Letters of George Orwell 1903–1950*.

42

Saul Bellow (Solomon Bellows): Writer and serial monogamist (five wives):

"All a writer has to do to get a woman," Bellow once wrote, *"is to say he's a writer. It's an aphrodisiac."* Not such a good deal for the ladies, however. And evidently the writer ploy didn't *always* work, since Bellow used to describe a woman who is lusted after, but unobtainable, as a *"noli-me-tangerine."*

Sam Tanenhaus, writing in the *New York Times Book Review* in 2007, commented on the unhappy fate of Bellow's cast-offs, which, though better than being beaten up like a Norman Mailer wife, was more long-lasting. They joined a club of the *"punitively caricatured ex-wives drawn from the teeming annals of the novelist's own marital discord."*

A fine novelist, he moved his political allegiance from left-wing to right-wing over the years and fell out with almost everyone, except his readers, and intermittently his wives; but what else can you expect of someone who wrote: *"We mustn't forget how quickly the visions of genius become the canned goods of intellectuals"*?

Nor did he hold with multiculturalism and its intellectually flabby egalitarianism: „*Who is the Tolstoy of the Zulus?"* he asked, *"The Proust of the Papuans? I'd be glad to read him."*

Alan Bennett: Accident-prone British author and national treasure:
The bisexual Bennett has said that being asked about his sexuality (actor Ian McKellen aggressively demanded to know whether Bennett was gay) is like asking a man who has just crawled across the Sahara to choose between Perrier and Malvern water. Despite his acute powers of observation, his disarming persona is that of a bumbling provincial with a broad Yorkshire accent. Incurably accident-prone, he has been beaten over the head with a steel bar by hoodlums while on an Italian holiday and even mugged in his local Marks & Spencer. Upgrading to first class on a rail trip, he was told by the ticket collector: "You don't belong in here. These are proper first class people." Once he arrived at Claridges to meet the film maker John Huston and was redirected to the tradesman's entrance. In 1971 he got the *Evening Standard* award for the best comedy of the year for a play (*"Getting On"*) which he hadn't even intended to be funny (*"It's as if you entered a marrow for the show and were given the cucumber prize."*) Impressive success as a writer has neither increased his self-esteem nor re-

duced his accident rate. *"Life,"* he has observed ruefully, *"is generally something that happens elsewhere."*

Bennett's public, and in particular his political, pronouncements are invariably self-deprecating (subsequent to interviews, he always claims to feel he has made a fool of himself). Refusing an honorary history degree from Oxford, he pointed out that the university had accepted an endowment for a Chair of Language and Communication from the bullying media mogul, Rupert Murdoch. In Bennett's view, you might as well have a Saddam Hussein Chair of Peace Studies.

As a writer, Bennett's greatest skill is highly focused eavesdropping, which generally reveals more about the British character and attitudes than any number of carefully crafted plays and novels. For example, an entry in his 1997 *Diary* recalls the following remark made by a Morningside lady as she came away from an Edinburgh performance of Chekhov: „There was a lot of laughter at the end of the first act, but I soon put a stop to *that!*" In Perth the play concerned (*The Cherry Orchard*) was billed as *The Cheery Orchard*. In Luxor Bennett overheard one British tourist saying to another: "Palm trees are nothing to us — we're from Torquay." Sometimes he himself seems to be supplying good material for eavesdroppers, as in the charmingly Bennettian remark: "We started off trying to set up a small anarchist community, but people wouldn't obey the rules…"

Thomas Bernhard: Celebrated Austrian author and curmudgeon: Bodies that were rash enough to honour Bernhard with a literary prize were customarily told in his acceptance speech that he was only taking the award from such a contemptible source because he needed the money. He was himself a member of a prize-giving body, the *"Deutsche Akademie für Sprache und Dichtung"* [German Academy for Language and Literature], from which he resigned on hearing that a former *Bundespräsident* (and ex-Nazi) had been elected to it. As he explained in his resignation letter, this gentleman's election demonstrated beyond a peradventure that the *"Academy"* had nothing to do with *"Language,"* still less with *"Literature"*.

Moreover, he said, warming to his theme, the pages of its *Yearbook* were filled with contributions from *"linguistically challenged windbags,"* padded out with lists of obscure and often implausible *"honours"* accorded to the same, plus brown-nosing obituaries of stupendous hypocrisy. *"Sadly,"* he concludes, *"the Academy's Yearbook is printed on such fancy paper that it won't burn in my solid-fuel stove."*

The authentic flavour of Bernhard resides not so much in one-liners such as *"instead of committing suicide, people go to work"*, but rather in the crescendo-building effect of his deadpan prose, as for instance in *The Voice Imitator:* "There was a woman in Atzbach [Upper Austria] who was murdered by her husband because, in his opinion, she had rescued the wrong child when their house was on fire. That is, she had not rescued their eight-year-old son, for whom the husband had special plans, but instead had rescued the daughter, to whom he was largely indifferent. Asked in court what were the plans for his son that had so concerned him, he replied that he had intended he should become an anarchist and mass murderer of dictatorships — and so a destroyer of the state."

On the other hand there is an elegiac Bernhard mode based on his evident belief that *"everything is ridiculous, when one thinks of death."* For example, the following passage from a work entitled "Frost": *"Women were like rivers, their banks were unreachable, the night often rang with the cries of the drowned."*

Bruno Bettelheim: Fashionable, if cantankerous, child psychologist whose reputation began to unravel after his death:

"To be told that our child's behavior is 'normal,'" wrote Bettelheim, "offers little solace … when we worry that his actions are harmful at the moment or may be injurious to his future. It does not help me as a parent nor lessen my worries when my child drives carelessly, even dangerously, if I am told that this is „normal" behavior for children of his age. I'd much prefer him to deviate from the norm and be a cautious driver!"

Bettelheim talked a good game, but as soon a he was safely dead, details began to leak out of his alleged maltreatment of his young charges in the Orthogenic School of Chicago University; indeed, he eventually came to be known to his critics as *"Beno Brutalheim."* Besides being accused of having knocked about the children in his care and of sexually abusing a girl, it was further claimed that he had faked his credentials, done research of dubious integrity and plagiarised other people's work.

The interesting thing about Bettelheim is not so much the question of whether all this was true (most of those in the field of child psychiatry now seem to accept that some of it was and some of it wasn't), but the way he cruised to a position of authority without proper academic or official scrutiny by exuding charm and menace in equal proportions. It also helped that he seemed to be basing his ideas on Freud at a time when impressionable American academics were still deeply in love with the latter — and long before anyone dared to question some of Dr Freud's's own questionable methods and claims.

Having decided that autism was the result of maternal failure to show the child affection, Bettelheim constructed a dogma about *"refrigerator mothers"* and in due course advocated what he called *"parentodectomy,"* which turned out to mean bringing children into the care of his institute. In one case he described the mother of a child he claimed was autistic as "a devouring witch, an infanticidal king and an SS concentration camp guard." For some reason the lady concerned took this amiss.

The SS epithet reflected another side of Bettelheim, namely his propensity for crossing the road for an argument whenever the opportunity presented itself, or even if it didn't. A survivor of the concentration camps himself, he lectured to Jewish audiences on their "ghetto mentality" and even suggested that their fate was partly their own fault. Then again, he accused the student radicals of the sixties of being "like the Hitler youth" — hardly surprising that trainees on his staff referred to his educational technique as "the Nazi-Socratic method."

The British writer Michael Frayn has suggested an altogether more humane approach to parent-training than the Bettelheim battering ram. In his *Spock's Guide to Parent Care*, which every caring child should possess, and which pleasingly captures the tone the great doctor (Spock) had considered appropriate for addressing moronic parents, Frayn advises children on parent-handling skills. Headings include: PARENTS ARE JUST LARGE HUMAN BEINGS, EVERY PARENT IS DIFFERENT and BE FRIENDLY BUT FIRM. Under REMEMBER, YOU'RE HELPING THEM TO GROW UP we read: „It's your job to help your parents grow into mature, responsible old-age pensioners, self-confident, armed with a workable code of morals and manners, and too exhausted in mind and body to make trouble for anyone else."

Bias: Something that exists in the eye of the beholder, but unfortunately elsewhere too:

Claims that left-leaning bias is the default position of the mainstream media are usually dismissed (in the same media, of course) as "conspiracy theories;" so the following report about France in the impeccably liberal and *bien pensant* pages of *The Economist* (August 18th 2012) may provide some wry amusement for such theorists: "In 2010 the public targeting of Roma camps by [the Conservative] Nicolas Sarkozy… ran into virulent opposition from the left. However, as a Socialist government embarks on the same course, the reaction is more muted. Some are even arguing that it is all different now… but the policy is essentially the same." Then again, placing would-be immigrants to Australia in offshore holding camps, was angrily denounced by Australia's Labour Prime Minister (then in opposition) as "inhumane" when introduced by a conservative government. Of course she reinstated the policy — to hardly a squeak from the liberal press.

"Metropolitan liberals" (now a term of abuse on the right) do not accept that the BBC (for example) is biased towards their world view. Like BBC producers, they start from the premise that there is an ascertainably sensible ("moderate") line to take on any issue (i.e. theirs). Any views that depart from this template towards the left are probably "extremist", but no doubt well-intentioned; or if they depart towards the right, are "populist" and dangerous. To some extent this is a legacy of Lord Reith's paternalistic view of the BBC's educative role — very desirable, if the aim is to get people to think for themselves; less desirable if this laudable aim segues into a feeling that they ought to be persuaded to think like you — and broadcasting can bring that about. Christopher Booker, a stubborn campaigner for unfashionable causes (such as that of parents grievously wronged by the UK's incipiently totalitarian family courts, which are able to act in almost total secrecy through blanket restrictions on reporting) claims that the BBC has a "party line" on the main issues of the day "dictating what can and cannot be said, who it invites on and who it excludes: from the EU and global warming to gay marriage; from wind farms to government "cuts"; from Israel to fracking. This is to the point where too many of its programmes are little more than propaganda, put over by self-regarding presenters who frequently cannot hide their impatience with anyone who doesn't agree with the groupthink."[9]

This is the classic conservative view of the BBC and assumes a homogeneity of outlook among BBC staffers that is certainly exaggerated. By comparison with the left-liberal bias in some European flagship broad-

9 Christopher Booker: "The BBC's groupthink is an enemy to free speech," *The Sunday Telegraph*, April 20th, 2014.

casters on the one hand, or the violent and mendacious rightwing propaganda of Fox News in the USA on the other, the BBC is a model of fairness. It is however curious that almost no one ever seems to accuse the BBC of *right-wing* bias…

Part of the problem is purely semantic. As development economist William Easterly has pointed out, contributors to economic and political debate (in this case aid and development) risk being branded as ideologues through a simple process of counting the number of times certain "code" words occur in their discourse. "Mention markets and you are presumed to favour a world with zero government. Mention liberty too often and you are presumed to be in favour of some extreme right -wing ideology [quite ironic that for large swathes of academe, an emphasis on liberty can be considered dangerously right-wing]. Mention Friedrich Hayek's book *The Road to Serfdom* and you are presumed to be to the right of ranting talk-show hosts.

"Less commonly recognized is a perceptional slippery slope on the left. If you mention *colonialism*, *racism*, or *imperialism* too often, as concepts still relevant to understanding development past or present, you risk being seen as a leftist ideologue… If our exclusion of extremists is too broad, however, we will just wind up endlessly repeating a consensus whose origin is unclear… The history of ideas matters but does not automatically disqualify ideas that have some dubious progenitors."[10] However it is of course the media that decides what progenitors are "dubious." A character in Umberto Eco's novel *Numero Zero* makes the point in an elegant aphorism: "*It is not the news that makes the newspaper, but the newspaper that makes the news.*"

The bottom line is that it is difficult to be a good challenging journalist without basic values from which the challenges are issued. Being the devil's advocate as a day job requires a barrister's suppleness of mind and a suppression of personal feelings that few are capable of. "An attitude of permanent indignation signifies great mental poverty," wrote Paul Valéry in *Tel Quel*: "Politics compels its votaries to take that line and you can see their minds growing more impoverished every day, from one burst of righteous anger to the next."

See also ***Churnalism***

10 William Easterly: *The Tyranny of Experts: Economists, Dictators, and the Forgotten Rights of the Poor*, Basic Books, New York, 2013, Pp. 12-15.

48

"Birtspeak" and "Blue Skies Thinking": Managerial psychobabble: Lord Birt, mercurial Liverpudlian and protagonist of the bogus cult of „the manager" (i.e. a person who leaps from one highly paid job to another, leaving a trail of destruction behind him) was at one point pondering solutions for the railways; doubtless, wrote Chris Horrie, with a view to introducing his famous Birtian system of „business units" that nearly destroyed the BBC under his leadership.

Under the Birtian system, said Horrie, a train driver would be given not a train for his projected journey but „a huge budget, a flipchart and an eight-day 'empowerment' session with management consultants. Instead of simply driving the train between stations, preferably keeping it on the rails, under a Birt system the driver would commission amazingly expensive market research to find out where passengers want to go. This would discover what everybody already knows: they want to get to work."

Perhaps the most entertainingly risible example of "blue skies thinking" was the sudden decision of Britain's Royal Mail to rebrand itself (at huge cost) as "Consignia." This name had everything the modern yuppie manager could desire: it distanced itself from the snobby and obviously uncool association with royalty; its Latin base made it sound suitably pretentious; it might have suggested to the more literate members of the public what the mail actually did (it consigned things… more or less), and even suggested a little play on words (consigning Royal Mail to oblivion). It is pleasant to ponder the number of people that might have been involved in the brainstorming that produced such a turkey, and how much they were paid. Despite all the dramatic forehead clutching, shouts of "*Eureka!*" and high fives that attended its birth, Consignia failed to catch on either with the public or the press. To the consternation of the "blue skies" thinkers, the public simply continued to refer to the Royal Mail as if Consignia had never been invented. The press seemed to think the whole thing was a joke and kept suggesting alternatives like "*Sorry-You-Weren't-Inya.*"

David Blunkett: Blind ex-Cabinet Minister and would-be Lothario: On leaving office, Blunkett published some rather touching diaries. For example, he explained how he was always having to parry well-meaning attempts to render assistance on account of his blindness — once indeed from the Queen herself at an official dinner: "Her Majesty," writes Blunkett, "twice asked me if I would like my meat cutting up." The obvious kindness of this thought was only slightly undermined by her adding: "*You know, I often do it for the corgis.*"

***Bono, aka Bozo*[11]*:** Paul David Hewson, self-publicising egomaniac and member of the band U2:

Unfortunately some of the rock stars cashing in on the philanthropy for Africa campaign known as "Make Poverty History" were found to be keeping their own earnings in havens out of reach from the taxman ("*Steueroase: Cui Bono?*" as Austria's *Die Presse* disrespectfully inquired.) These arrangements naturally did not prevent them from lecturing Gordon Brown on how much the British taxpayer should be coughing up for Africa.

Bono epitomises what is most suspect about "celebrity philanthropy," by means of which self-aggrandising publicity binges finance counterproductive methods for putting the world to rights. Nowadays jigging around at a rock concert featuring your favourite stars counts as charitable "giving" (Frank Zappa called Live Aid "the biggest cocaine money-laundering scheme of all time.") *Self-absorption* being the highest good of contemporary society, the idea of *self-denial* does not fit with celebrity philanthropy.

It has been pointed out by those who have analysed the matter (Anthony Daniels, Dambisa Moyo and others) that Africa is the only continent to have got poorer over a period of 40 years, despite receiving some $500 billion in aid and soft loans. Eighty cents of every dollar lent or given is said to have ended up in the secret bank accounts of the rulers. But gesture politics is all the rage — in keeping with the spirit of our times, how you feel about yourself is more important than how others feel, or whether indeed they can afford the luxury of feeling anything other than suicidal.

His biographer does concede that the funniest story about Saint Bono is almost certainly apocryphal, namely that he once hushed an audience at a gig and began slowly clapping his hands, whispering as he did so: "Every time I clap my hands a child in Africa dies." *Voice from the audience*: "Well fuckin' stop clappin' then!"

---

11 © Sinead O'Connor.

Gordon Brown: Labour Chancellor whose love affair with Prudence came unstuck; subsequently a grumpy Labour Prime Minister:

In his Pre-Budget Report of 9th November 1999 Brown claimed that *"under this Government, Britain will not return to the boom and bust of the past."* Pity about the crash of 2008, which of course had nothing to do with the government hosing the economy with cheap credit...

Brown was often depicted as dour and humourless. Former Cabinet Minister Lord Peter Mandelson knows how unjust that description is: he once asked Gordon for 10 pence to phone a friend from a call-box. *„Have 20 pence and you can phone them all"* volunteered the genial Scot generously.

Brown, claims Jonathan Freedland, *"could be charming in private, but lacked charisma in public. He was untelegenic, a rumpled, sometimes glowering figure prone to firing out machine-gun fusillades of statistics, with 'a face like like a wet winter's morning in Fife'"* according to his colleague and fellow Scotsman, the late Robin Cook.[12]

Warren Buffett: The sage of Omaha and merciless scrutiniser of padded balance sheets, fantasy revenues and freeloading CEOs:

"There is a fool in every market," the sage has said; *"and if you don't know who it is, it is probably you."*

Also: *"The five most dangerous words in business may be 'Everybody else is doing it.'"*

Also: *"Of the billionaires I have known, money just brings out the basic traits in them. If they were jerks before they had money, they are simply jerks with a billion dollars."*

Also: *"We believe that according the name 'investors' to institutions that trade actively is like calling someone who repeatedly engages in one-night stands a 'romantic.'"*

Rejected by Harvard Business School, by 2008 Buffett had become the richest person in the world, with a total net worth estimated at $62 billion. In 1957 he purchased, for $31,500, a five-bedroom stucco house in Omaha, where he still lives.[13] He has given most of his fortune

---

12 Jonathan Freedland: "Who Is Gordon Brown", *The New York Review of Books*, October 25, 2007. Brown was the MP for the Fife constituency of Kirkaldy.

13 However he has also acquired a big spread in Florida and eventually succumbed to the CEO hubris he had previously castigated by purchasing a private jet.

Warren Buffett, ukulele man unimpressed by bullshit from the financial sector.

away (83% to the Melinda Gates Foundation). According to CNN in 2006, Buffett does not carry a mobile phone, does not have a computer at his desk, and drives his own automobile, a Cadillac DTS. In 2013 he had an old Nokia flip phone and had sent one email in his entire life. Buffett reads five newspapers every day, beginning with the *Omaha World Herald*, which his company acquired in 2011.[14]

In a letter to *Fortune Magazine*'s website in 2010 Buffett wrote: "I've worked in an economy that rewards someone who saves the lives of others on a battlefield with a medal, rewards a great teacher with thank-you notes from parents, but rewards those who can detect the mis-pricing of securities with sums reaching into the billions."

Buffett stated that he only paid 19% of his income for 2006 ($48.1 million) in total federal taxes (due to their source as dividends &

14 These details are to be found in Wikipedia's extensive profile of Buffett. Wikipedia does point out that the figure Buffett gives for his very low income tax burden does exclude the taxes paid by his corporations before he is paid the dividends, capital gains etc. on which he is taxed as an individual.

capital gains). His employees were paying on average 33%. *"There's class warfare, all right,"* he added; *"but it's my class, the rich class, that's making war, and we're winning."*

Bunny-boiler: A woman who is miffed at being spurned by a married man and takes action accordingly (e.g. by boiling his family's pet rabbit):

The phrase originated with the film *Fatal Attraction* (1987), in which Glenn Close gives a scary performance as Alex Forrest, who has a one-night stand with a married businessman and turns into a psychopathic stalker after he rejects her. As a matter of fact the original script portrayed Alex as a lonely woman seeking love, but Hollywood demanded a rewrite (no doubt in defence of family values) in which she became a monster. As is well-known, female monsters are apt to boil the pet rabbits of their sexual rivals. So clearly she deserved to get shot by the wronged wife. The audiences loved it.

Bureaucracy: The disease of advanced civilisations (also of unadvanced ones):

The radical anthropologist David Graeber describes (but does not entirely endorse) a widespread view of bureaucracy: "If you create a bureaucratic structure to deal with a problem, that structure will invariably end up creating other problems that seem as if they too can only be solved by bureaucratic means. In universities, this is sometimes informally referred to as the 'creating committees to deal with the problem of too many committees' problem."[15] With the bureaucracy, said the US economist Thomas Sowell, "procedures are everything and outcomes nothing," a sentiment echoed by Javier Pascal de Salcedo, who wrote that "bureaucracy is the art of making the possible impossible." It is indeed an end in itself and one without end.

For example, journalist Victor Mallet reports from New Delhi that there is an exciting local publication bearing the title *Bureaucracy Today* ("Fearless journalism, our habit, our history!"). The issue he is looking at reports agreeably on a "budget-busting 23% pay rise just awarded to more than 10m serving and retired civil servants." The magazine doubt-

15 David Graeber: *The Utopia of Rules: On Technology, Stupidity, and the Secret Joys of Bureaucracy* (Melville House, Brooklyn/London, 2015). This particular quotation is taken from his preview of the book in the *Weekend FT*, 7-8 March, 2105.

less also reported on the grumbles of civil servants obliged by India's new broom Prime Minister, Narendra Modi, *to turn up for work on time* (or indeed at all?) Also to make some effort at clearing their massive backlog of files. However the Indian *babus* have apparently proved even more adept than Sir Humphrey of *Yes Minister* fame at taking revenge on the country's elected leader for such an unparalleled act of *lèse majesté*. One tried and tested technique is to camouflage non-activity with a dense fog of organisational jargon. Mallet gives the example of a not untypical e-mail he received from the Finance Ministry, which evidently likes to keep him informed of its dynamic approach to bureaucratic reform. It begins (and this is just part of the headline): "Chairman, PFRDA calls for increasing the coverage of State Autonomous Bodies (SABs) and to bring the unorganised workers including Anganwadi & Asha workers and SHGs within the ambit of NPS..."[16]

Anyone who has lived in a Latin country that uses the bureaucracy partly as a sponge to mop up potential unemployment, and partly as a means of *clientelismo*, will be familiar with the tactics of bureaucratic inertia. In the Italy of the 1960s, as a book by an Italian journalist[17] pointed out, the bureaucracy was already having such a negative impact that the government, in an unwonted display of energy, set up a Ministry for the Reform of Bureaucracy. Its first task, however, as commentators derisively observed, turned out to be the reform of itself. The only real way to rid oneself of an established bureaucracy, as Max Weber has observed, is simply to kill them all, as Alaric the Goth did in Imperial Rome, or Genghis Khan in certain parts of the Middle East. If you leave any of them alive, they will inevitably end up managing your new kingdom.

Weber also wrote that "every bureaucracy seeks to increase the superiority of the professionally informed by keeping its knowledge and intentions secret ... in so far as it can, it hides its knowledge and action from criticism." This is of course what every one always suspected, what Balzac called "the giant power wielded by pygmies." However, just as people are always clamouring for the government to "do something," whether or not government intervention would be wise or productive, but simultaneously complain about the state having too much power

16 Victor Mallet: *New Delhi Notebook*: "The strangler vine of India's babu bureaucracy," *Financial Times*, 22nd December, 2015.
17 *Gli Italiani* by Luigi Barzini (1965).

(which they have willed it to have), so also many actually want the impersonality and efficiency of the bureaucracy to take the worst of life's burdens off their backs. The schizophrenia of the electorate (where there is one) should never be underestimated in its relations with power and administration.

In the warm water countries it is accepted that you cosy up to and bribe the bureaucrats, because if you don't you will be ignored. So this is a skill people pride themselves on having — and it also helps the bureaucrats, who are usually not all that well paid. In Northern Europe, where manipulating the bureaucracy is altogether a more sophisticated business than handing over grubby brown envelopes stuffed with used notes, the land developer, the powerful businessman, the politician who wants the rules bent, achieves his or her ends by means of a mysterious alchemy of networking and discreet pressure. Often there remains a residual respect — even sympathy — for bureaucrats, particularly in the German-speaking countries, where there is a long tradition of efficient bureaucracy that evidently suits the temperament of the people. Yet that very efficiency may also be seen, for example in the stories of Franz Kafka, as threatening, soulless, grimly absurd and the repository of a terrifyingly hilarious counter-intuitive logic.

"This always confuses liberals," says Grover Norquist, "that conservatives like the military and don't like the bureaucracy. That's because the military has their guns pointed out and the bureaucracy has them pointed in." But where would the military be without its bureaucracies? In many countries these constitute a sort of second military. In the early twentieth century, the Spanish navy had reputedly more admirals than ships; and most European countries have exhibited an exponential rise in defence officials as the numbers of active troops, sailors and airmen decline. A similar bureaucratisation is visible in many other fields, most notoriously in the British National Health Service (q.v.), which reached a point in the early years of the second millennium where there were more managers than beds.

A point well made by Graeber, which often escapes those frustrated by bureaucracy, is that what is nowadays sold as "deregulation" tends to end up as its opposite. What actually happens is a "gradual fusion of public and private power into a single entity, rife with rules and regulations whose ultimate purpose is to extract wealth in the form of profits." In the case of banking, he adds, "'deregulation' has usually meant exactly the opposite: moving away from a situation of managed competition between mid-sized firms to one where a handful of financial conglomerates are allowed to completely dominate the market... Simply by labelling a new regulatory measure 'deregulation', you can frame it in the public mind as a way to reduce bureaucracy and set individual initiative free, even if the result is a fivefold increase in the actual number of forms to be filled in, reports to be filed, rules and regulations for lawyers to interpret, and officious people in office whose entire job seems to be to provide convoluted explanations for why you're not allowed to do things... It fills our days with paperwork. Application forms get longer and more elaborate. Ordinary documents like bills or tickets or membership in sports or book clubs come to be buttressed by pages of legalistic fine print."[18] Those who are sceptical of this view should try setting up an online account to pay the toll for the Dartford Crossing (over the River Thames) by direct debit. The accompanying literature consists of an initial five pages of basic rules and explanations followed by no less than six pages of double-columned small print constituting the *Terms and Conditions*. One whole page is devoted to *"Definitions and Interpretation,"* forty-four in all. This grotesque document is the end result of "outsourcing" a public utility, or "deregulation" by any other name. The *Terms and Conditions* begin with an enchanting statement making it clear that, in the event of the company not fulfilling its obligations, the buck can be passed back to the government before you can say Franz Kafka (*"Sanef enters into this Agreement with you on behalf of and as agent for the Secretary of State for Transport and shall have no liability for any breach of the Agreement by the Secretary of State for Transport."*)

A doctor writing in *The Spectator* relates how he once had a very efficient and knowledgeable secretary of some 45 years' standing. "Three weeks before she retired, she received the order from her 'manager' (she hadn't needed one for more than nine-tenths of her career) that she attend a course to answer the telephone" (*sic*). To no avail she pointed out that she was on the verge of retirement, but the 'manager' was as oblivious both to the insult he was offering to an immensely experienced pro-

---

18 Graeber op cit. P. 17. In a footnote he adds: "About the only policies that can't be referred to as "deregulation" are ones that aim to reverse some other policy that has already been labeled "deregulation," which means it's important , in playing the game, to have your policy labeled "deregulation" first."

fessional who was brilliant at her job as he was to the absurdity of spending money training someone who was retiring in three weeks. Dalrymple explains that the "hospital had contracted a 'consultant', almost certainly personally known to a member of the [NHS] bureaucracy, and possibly a former employee of a nearby hospital, to teach 'telephone skills.' It needed as many staff as possible to attend the course to justify the expense."[19]

Graeber also points out that bureaucracy-breeding "credentialisation" (posing as "professionalisation") has steadily invaded all walks of life, bringing with it the box-ticking culture of "performance reviews, focus groups, time allocation surveys" and so forth. Do tourist guides in Nevada really require *733 days* of "training" before being allowed to ply their trade?[20] The all-conquering advance of "credentialisation" can best be appreciated by the growth of bureaucratic jargon, which he describes as a "peculiar idiom ... full of bright empty terms like vision, quality, stakeholder, leadership, excellence, innovation, strategic goals or best practices. (Much of it traces back to 'self-actualisation' movements like Lifespring, Mind Dynamics, and EST, which were extremely popular in corporate boardrooms in the seventies, but quickly became a language unto itself.)"[21] Although it may be fashionable, chiefly on the incorrigible right, to sneer at this self-serving and often mendacious jargon, it is now well-established, as the job advertisements in *The Guardian* demonstrate. *"Every revolution,"* wrote Kafka, *"evaporates and leaves behind only the slime of a new bureaucracy."* This slime not only dehumanises and pollutes language, it is an effective weapon against change, whether desirable or not, since it talks the language of change in order to conceal the reality of obstruction by vested interests. That's why the old hands say that if "an idea can survive a bureaucratic review and be implemented, it wasn't worth doing."

George W. Bush Jnr., a.k.a. „Shrub" or „Dubya": Former President of the United States and Iraq war hero:

Any Bush presidency has its consolations in the shape of a steady flow of „Bushisms". „The greatness of America" Bush (George.W.) has

---

19 Theodore Dalrymple: "The bureaucrats' boom," *The Spectator* 9 May, 2015.
20 As reported in *The Economist*, December 5th —11th, 2015.
21 Graeber. *The Utopia of Rules*, op cit. P. 21.

said „exists because our country is great. We have people who perform common, common acts of commonplace miracles — commonplace acts of miracle — every day." In an impassioned plea for free trade, he promised to tear down the world's „terriers and bariffs" (Australia notoriously hides behind the Great Bariff Reef); and he has talked lyrically of American families „where wings take dream". As befits a man whose entire career through university and draft-dodging to the presidency was based on privilege, Bush was naturally a great preacher of the self-help gospel. The problem with the French, he is reported as saying, is that they do not have a word for *entrepreneurship* in their language. Quite so. And it is obviously some aberrant quirk of the statistics which indicates that the non-agricultural sector of self-employed in France at 8.6% is higher than in the USA (7.5%)[22]

Still, for all his eloquence, Dubja cannot hold a candle to his father, the great orator George Herbert Walker Bush. Two of his observations have passed into common parlance, as they deserve to: „It's no exaggeration to say the undecideds could go one way or another." And: „I will never apologise for the United States of America, ever. I don't care what the facts are."

The Queen Witch Bratara Buzea: Spokesperson for the Rumanian witches' coven.

This lady has been up in arms since the ignorant and vindictive Rumanian government decided to bring her profession into the tax net (though presumably it will be possible to offset broom-sticks against future earnings.) Worse, it prepared a law making fortune-tellers liable to fines or imprisonment if their predictions turned out to be false.

Reporting on this, the *Financial Times* made an interesting comparison between Romanian witchery and the financial alchemy of New York or London. The latter promised to deliver the "magical disappearance of risk and ever-rising house prices," thus causing the ruination of the alchemists' clients.

Lately the accounting reforms imposed under Basel III require banks to reduce their *risk-weighted assets* (or RWA for short, which also stands for "Really Weird Accounting"). Or at least they must appear to do so. In

22 Ha-Joon Chang: *23 Things They Don't Tell You About Capitalism* (Penguin Books, London, 2011 Pp.158-9).

the course of ingenious "restructuring" to meet the new criteria, the banks have evidently discovered the philosopher's stone that eluded the 16th century alchemists of Rudolf II's court in Prague: they have managed to turn garbage assets into risk-weighted gold. No doubt they will soon turn their attention to the elixir of life.

The Romanian witches' initial tactics in defence of their tax-free status (casting spells on the government and tipping large quantities of mandrake into the Danube) were unfortunately not effective. Subsequently they turned to the PR strategies of Wall Street and the City of London, explaining to a sceptical press that hopelessly wrong predictions were the fault of the *cards*, not the *card reader*. Also, they couldn't help it if clients gave incorrect information about themselves. "This sounds familiar," says the FT. with some asperity. "The models were wrong, not our analysis of them. We are shocked that borrowers overstated their income and that banks marketed products designed to lose value."

The pioneering Rumanian approach to the forecasting problem is nevertheless encouraging and one can see how it could be usefully applied to finance in the West. For example, "estimates" of pension pot growth, currently given mendaciously as 5% or 9%, should be compared with the final pensions actually received and the difference between the real percentage growth and the estimates should be deducted by law from fund managers' salaries. Similarly the accuracy of economic and equity investment forecasts should be assessed annually and the difference between real outcomes and the forecasts should be deducted as a pro rata percentage from the not ungenerous salaries of the economists, analysts and managers concerned.

Of course such measures may well result in an abrupt decline in the number of analysts, fund managers etc., as well as fewer and sometimes better forecasts. But clearly any government that really had the interest of consumers at heart (as opposed to those of powerful financial lobbies) would hasten to implement such a measure, no doubt to general rejoicing.

(See also: *Astrologers* under **A).**

Postscript:

Bankomania: *Singspiel* in three acts rediscovered from the golden age of Viennese operetta. Libretto by Goldman Sachs, music by Gilbert O'Sullivan:

The disunited kingdom of Bankomania is a rich country full of poor people [*Opening chorus of an angry mob waving Equitable Life pension statements* [23]]. Its government doesn't have any policies as such, but it does have a business plan. This is accounted a great success by its protagonists, who indeed have set up their own broadcasting network and newspapers to inform the populace of the great prosperity they are enjoying under the plan. The hospitals, for example, now have more managers than beds, a much more efficient way of running the service because it cuts down on the expense of front-line staff. The new efficiency is also evident from the waiting lists for non-urgent operations (most operations are classified as such) which are constantly decreasing as people on the waiting lists keel over and die. The Bankomania elite of course have private hospitals reserved for those with expensive private health insurance. Unfortunately the latter's policies exclude most of the illnesses that people are likely to get, so the wealthy often go abroad to one of the old-fashioned inefficient countries and have their operations in hospitals that do not seem to be infected with the MRSA bug. [*Trinklied of hospital cleaners.*]

The nominal capital of Bankomania is Apathia, where a unicameral parliament rubber stamps and turns into legislative form the requirements of the real centre of power, known as Bankomat. This is a region to the east of the Parliament known for its triumphalist modern architecture, of which the most impressive examples (mostly skyscrapers) have been given affectionate nicknames, e.g. "heart of glass," "the gouger," "the money launderer" and "Alberich's folly." The enormous cost of constructing these buildings has easily been covered by the profits from finance in Bankomat. This is because Bankomat consists, not of vast stores of wealth, but of tsunami-like flows of money on each ripple of which Bankomat's businesses take a commission. In addition Bankomat is the custodian of huge amounts of money collected from investors in

---

23 The Equitable Life insurance company attracted clients by offering guaranteed annuity rates that were higher than elsewhere, but got caught out when inflation and interest rates declined and tred to renege on its contractual undertakings to 90,000 policy holders. Unfortunately for the company, many of these were lawyers, accountants and other middle class professionals, who were not so easily deprived of their rights as average savers. The company had to be wound up and after years of stalling the government agreed on some compensation for policy holders in 2011 (increased in 2015).

the guise of investment and unit trusts of various kinds, and most notably pension funds. The last named are particularly profitable, because enormous sums can be creamed from them in the form of fees without the putative owners of this money even noticing. Over the life of a pension investment up to half the value is creamed off by Bankomat in this way. The residue is paid out in paltry annuities that are constantly being diminished by means of "market adjustments".

Of course the senior and middle managers in Bankomat have much better guaranteed pensions, actually astronomic ones, arising from the profits their firms make, which in turn arise from the fees and commissions they take from "funds under management" (i.e. other people's money); or from "mergers and acquisitions", whereby they arrange takeovers that turn one ailing firm and one that is apparently solvent into a single, much larger, ailing firm. There is of course a substantial loss of shareholder value in these unnecessary financial manipulations, but that is offset (in the view of Bankomania's government) by the lightly taxed mega- profits that accrue from "advisory" and legal fees. As a matter of fact, Bankomat's managers don't really need their huge pensions, since they receive wonderful "bonuses" each year on top of their salaries, these bonuses reflecting their skills at gambling huge amounts of other people's money and not getting caught out too often.

Bankomania is particularly proud of its education system. This has produced an increased number of higher grades achieved by "Premium Level" GCE candidates each year for the last twenty years. Leading Bankomanians attribute much of this success to the introduction of the scheme known as *"pass one grade, get one free"* which was introduced a few years back, and which has ensured that no pupil is left behind. It is true that young people emerging from school with these grades are only partially literate or numerate, but all of them can use the internet well, an important skill for those later hoping to acquire a Ph.D. on the web. The universities have been modernised and are now mostly business schools with a few other faculties attached. The anachronistic humanities institutes have been abolished or modernised to make them more appropriate to the requirements of Bankomania's business model. For example, history faculties have been transformed into Institutes of Short Term Investment and Risk Concealment, while the time-consuming and irrelevant study of English and foreign literatures has been removed altogether. Moral philosophy has been replaced by an Institute of Compliance and

Tax Avoidance. The science faculties, mostly financed on a charitable basis by Bankomania's two or three remaining industries, attract only a small number of students, many of whom switch to Management Studies or Investment Banking in the second year.

Bankomania has developed a sophisticated system of justice whereby the accused sit together with the judges on the bench and help them to decide what penalties, if any, should be applied. Bankomania did consider abolishing prisons altogether on account of them being rather old-fashioned institutions, sometimes misused for the incarceration of wrongdoers. In the end someone came up with the better idea of placing obstreperous citizens in the cells and appointing recidivist criminals to be the warders (prison governors are usually ex-merchant bankers of considerable repute.)

The police represented a rather tougher problem for Bankomanian constitutionalists. True, they were mostly invisible to the public as they sat in offices all day creatively filling in forms about imaginary arrests they had made or crimes they had solved. Still, there were enough of them driving around with sirens blaring to create a public nuisance at times. After long thought it has been decided to redeploy the police as research assistants to crime syndicates, advising the latter of their rights in regard to unfair tactics by rivals. At first public order ceased to be much of a problem under this imaginative regime as very many people either emigrated or committed suicide. However the process of natural selection has meant that the toughest of the underclass have survived and are liable to cause trouble. A militia has been formed, whose chief task is to guard the banks from the occasional and regrettably hostile demonstrations. This is a volunteer force of youngish investment bankers who are all good shots and for whom service in the militia is a convenient way to keep fit.

Despite the evident success of its business model, all is not well in Bankomania as the operetta opens. Discontent is brewing among an increasing number of people who are too stupid to grasp that, simply because they do not themselves profit from Bankomania's "deregulated economics of globalisation," this certainly doesn't mean it is not the best business model, indeed the only viable one. There has been an attempt on the life of the Chief Cashier as he left the Parliament building and more than one bomb attack on Bankomat itself. The several million Bankomanians who had been paid off over the years with welfare benefits have got bored of daytime television and are increasingly indulging in wanton violence and looting. As Sir Gilbert O'Sullivan's overture swells from the orchestra pit, a chorus of Indignati, all with black face covering, mourns the loss of its Equitable Life pensions and threatens retribution. A banker enters stage right and counterpoints the chorus with contemptuous comment (Aria: *"Making money's what I do / Out of stupid folk like you…"*)

The further development of the operetta *Bankomania* can be imagined according to taste. Perhaps the banker falls in love with a sweet girl living on welfare and abandons licensed looting in Bankomat for a life of illegal looting in shopping malls with her. In the end he emerges as the leader of the Indignati, marries his sweetheart (who turns out to have been the long lost daughter of the Chief Cashier). He himself becomes Chief Cashier and ushers in a period of just rule in which the bankers of Bankomat agree to pay all their taxes and donate an unspecified portion of their bonuses to a pension fund for the needy. The curtain falls on a chorus of bankers singing *"Glücklich ist, wer vergißt / Was doch nicht zu ändern ist,"*[24] while the First Lady draws the numbers in a lottery. Of course one can imagine a darker ending, but then it wouldn't be operetta.

---

24 *"Happy is he who forgets all about what anyway cannot be altered,"* an aria from *Die Fledermaus*, an operetta by Johann Strauss

C

California: From Flower Power to Enron Energy:
„It is a scientific fact," wrote Truman Capote, „that if you stay in California, you lose one point of your I. Q. every year." This can only mean that the long-term workers in Silicon Valley are even cleverer than we thought (or of course that Capote's "fact" isn't one.) Capote seems to be reprising Will Rogers' regrettable observation that "when the Oakies left Oklahoma and moved to California, it raised the I. Q. of both states."

But perhaps parts of California are not so exciting. For example, Gertrude Stein crushingly observed of an otherwise inoffensive place called Oakland that "there is no *there* there." Even California's admirers are not necessarily an asset for the brand: "I love California," said Dan Quayle; "I practically grew up in Phoenix."

One of California's most famous beauty spots is Malibu Beach, which Joan Rivers wittily described as a place where *"You can lie on the sand and gaze at the stars or, if you're lucky, vice versa."* Like all Californian beaches it is supposed to be public; which didn't prevent its richest inhabitant preserving its up-market tone in the 1920's by dynamiting the approach roads…

"California deserves whatever it gets," says a character in Don DeLillo's *White Noise;* "Californians invented the concept of life-style. This alone warrants their doom." People do tend to be rude about California, and especially about Hollywood; but as Orson Welles remarked, *"Hollywood's all right; it's the pictures that are bad."*

Or, as Woody Allen has said: "In California, they don't throw their garbage away - they make it into TV shows."

[*See also* **Enron.**]

Capitalism: A system said by Polish dissidents in the 1980s to be one in which man oppresses man (whereas with Communism it's the other way round):

"Capitalism," said comedian George Carlin, "tries for a delicate balance: it attempts to work things out so that everyone gets just enough stuff to keep them from getting violent and trying to take other people's stuff."

Alex Carey, the leftist Australian commentator, writes that the 20th century has been characterised by three highly significant developments: "the growth of democracy, the growth of corporate power — and the growth of corporate propaganda as a means of protecting corporate power against democracy." Adam Smith (no less) said that the "managers of joint stock companies ... being managers rather of other people's money than their own, it cannot be expected that they would watch over it with the same anxious vigilance with which the partners in a private [partnership with unlimited liability] frequently watch over their own."

To get round this problem, the notion of "shareholder value" was invented in 1981 by Jack Welch, the Chairman of General Electric. The idea was that managers' interests should be "aligned" with those of shareholders, principally by granting stock options to the managers, (though it soon turned out that they tended to get huge salaries, bonuses *and* stock options). Apart from the fact that it is quite easy to manipulate stocks for a while, the rising share prices and profits distribution that this policy seemed to produce was achieved only by cutting jobs and benefits in the real economy, outsourcing (often overseas), lowering wages, squeezing suppliers and threatening governments that wanted to tax the profits with departure to a tax haven.

As the contrarian economist Ha-Joon Chang has it, the reckless distribution of profits that "shareholder value maximisation" involved improved neither the companies concerned, because there was less investment and more distribution, nor society as a whole, because income inequality soared. As he pointed out, *"had General Motors not spent the $20.4 billion that it did in share buybacks between 1986 and 2002... it would have had no problem finding the $35 billion that it needed to* *stave off bankruptcy in 2009."*[1] The founder of "shareholder value" himself cheerfully confessed later that it was probably *"the dumbest idea in the world."* A pity this didn't occur to him while he was in charge…

Jimmy Carter: A successful peanut farmer and (less successful) American President:

Carter was a profoundly decent man who believed that America's mission in the world was to enforce human rights — which is why Washington insiders have generally accounted him a disastrous president. He himself, in a typically self-effacing aside, said "I can't deny I've been a much better ex-President than President," which is true if by "better" one means more effective. Still, the rubbishing of his presidency has been heavily overdone (Mrs Thatcher professed herself "appalled" by him) and the failure to rescue the American hostages in Iran is all the media allow us to remember about him — plus the remark that he had "committed adultery in his heart." The satirists claim that he also once said "I have often wanted to drown my troubles, but I can't get my wife to go swimming."

Carter once visited Wall Street to drum up support for his policies, which had caused a market slump. *"If I weren't President,"* he told the Chairman of the NY Stock Exchange bullishly, *"I'd be buying stocks like crazy right now."* *"Mr President,"* said the Chairman, *"if you weren't President, so would I be."*

Catastrophilia: The drug on which the media are hooked….

In his bestselling book *Thinking Fast and Slow*, Daniel Kahneman explains how irrational concerns among the public are stoked by the "availability cascade," a "self-sustaining chain of events which may start from media reports of a relatively minor event and lead up to public panic and large-scale government action… the cycle is sped along by 'availability entrepreneurs', individuals or organisations who work to ensure a continuous flow of worrying news. The danger is increasingly exaggerated as the media compete for attention-grabbing headlines. Scientists and others who try to dampen the increasing fear and revulsion attract little attention, most of it hostile: anyone

---

1 Ha-Joon Chang: *23 Things They Don't Tell You About Capitalism* (Penguin, London, 2011) P. 20.

who claims that the danger is overstated is suspected of association with a 'heinous cover-up.'"

An example he gives is a scare in 1989 about a chemical sprayed on apples to regulate growth and improve appearance, which, *when consumed in gigantic doses* caused tumours in rats and mice. Of course anything consumed massively in excess is likely to cause harm, but we don't ban alcohol or sugar on that basis and the risk from this substance was so small as to be almost invisible. However the campaign against it attracted attention-seeking celebrities (Meryl Streep testified before Congress!), and a concerned citizen called in to a talk show to ask whether it was *"safe to pour apple juice down the drain or to take it to a toxic waste dump."* Research showed "a very small risk as a possible carcinogen" (just think how many substances we throw down our necks every day which might also constitute such a small risk in massive doses), and the substance was banned. The incident, says Kahneman drily, was not only "an enormous overreaction to a minor problem," but the net effect of it was probably detrimental to public health because fewer apples were consumed."[2]

Chagos Archipelago: Site of ethnic cleansing by the British:
In 1964, in exchange for a $13 million dollar discount on its purchase of Polaris submarines from the US government, Britain agreed to hand over Diego Garcia to the US military and "cleanse" the Chagos Archipelago of its 1,800 inhabitants. It revoked their British citizenship and paid them £325 per head for losing their homes, their livelihoods and their history.

Compulsorily resettled in the Seychelles, unemployed and disease-ridden, the Chagossians eventually (2000) won a High Court action allowing them to go home. Robin Cooke, then the UK's Foreign Secretary, magnanimously said they could have their passports back. Cooke's successor, Jack Straw, reneged on all this with a secret "Order in Council."

Subsequently (2010) the government suddenly declared the islands a marine sanctuary, thus forbidding habitation. The responsible Sir Humphrey at the time let slip that the "marine sanctuary" wheeze was primarily a "greenwash" story to boost Gordon Brown's unpopular gov-

---

2 Daniel Kahneman: *Thinking Fast and Slow* (Penguin Random House UK, 2012), Pp. 142-143.

ernment and leaked communications with the USA showed that the main aim was to make it impossible for the inhabitants to return to their land. Gullible scientists were signed up to support the sanctuary with a promise that the Chagossians would be allowed home (which they weren't, of course).

In 2008 the Law Lords finally voted three to two against the Chagossians right of return, the Government partly basing its appeal on the precedent of the vindictive treatment of entirely loyal Japanese Canadians in World War II (well done, Sir Humphrey!) Described by one FO mandarin as *"Tarzans and Man Fridays"*, and by a Governor of the Seychelles as *"having little aptitude for anything other than growing coconuts,"* the now much reduced Chagossians took their case to the European Court of Human Rights (that's the one that allows rapists and terrorists to avoid deportation from UK, because that would "breach their right to a family life.") The Court does not seem so concerned about the Chagossians right to their home, however, and ruled against them in 2013 on the grounds that they had already received due legal process in the UK (just like the above-mentioned rapists and terrorists.) By 2015, after their petitions to the British and American governments had been met with the usual stonewalling, the Chagossians, spread between Britain, the Seychelles and Mauritius, had been reduced to about half the numbers originally "cleansed." Britain appears to be more concerned about migrants from North Africa and the Middle East than about the people she herself deprived of their homeland.

Robin Chanter: A mildly dissolute Englishman in Florence who kept small reptiles in his bath:

When the youthful Robin Chanter first took up with Ian Greenlees, Director of the British Institute in Florence, he was passionate about art and architecture. The sybaritic and rather lazy Greenlees purported to share this enthusiasm. However whenever they were afoot in Tuscany and Chanter identified a "must see" monument a short walk away, Greenlees, would invariably adopt a mournful mien and explain that, alas, the said building/fresco/ altarpiece had been destroyed in the war. This carried conviction as Greenlees had himself been with the allied invasion and was proud of his heroic contribution to it (he had been driven up to the Fascist radio station at Bari in a jeep, whereat the station's Italian technicians immediately and enthusiastically surrendered to him and opened a bottle of wine.) Years later, Chanter discovered that all the supposedly lost monuments were still there. The portly Greenlees, who hated walking, especially uphill, had developed this ruse to spare himself the unwelcome exertion.

Greenlees had a very fierce and grumpy retainer from Friuli called Else who objected to his constant entertaining (as to most everything else) and would serve the guests at table muttering imprecations under her breath. The non-Italian speaking diners would have no idea that they were being called "nancy boys" or "malformed sons of one-eyed thieves" (if male) or "witches" and "strumpets" (if female). Chanter enjoyed baiting her in his excellent Italian. If Greenlees was away in London, one might hear an exchange like this: Chanter: "So, the master's away in England." Else "Yes, and I hope he doesn't come back!" Chanter: "He's coming on the Tuesday train." Else: "The train might get derailed, mightn't it?" Chanter: "You know what they say about Friulian women: *una donna friuliana è una vera puttana!*"[3] Else: "You know what they say about the English in Italy: *Inglese italianato è un diavolo incarnato!*"[4]

Despite her morose character, Else was in fact fiercely loyal and would have been quite lost if she had been deprived of indulgent employers whom she could happily abuse all day long. On one occasion a robber entered the Greenlees flat, which contained valuable paintings. Else, who was then well into her sixties, emerged suddenly from the kitchen and hurled herself upon the intruder, biting him in the leg. Yelling in pain he fled down the stairs with colourful Friulian epithets ringing in his ears.

3 "Friulian women are total whores"

4 "The Italianised Englishman is a devil incarnate." This saying originally described a brutally effective English mercenary in the Italian wars named Sir John Hawkwood (or "Giovanni Acuto, c.1320–1394), a fresco of whom by Paolo Uccello may be seen in the Duomo of Florence. However the moralistic English scholar Roger Ascham (1515–1568) was the first to apply it to the moral corruption to which young Englishmen on the Grand Tour might be exposed. Ascham says that an Englishman living or travelling in Italy brings home "Papistry or worse," and less learning than he carried forth, not to mention a "factious heart, a discoursing head, a mind to meddle in all men's matters … plenty of new mischieves never known in England before" and of manners "a variety of vanities and change of filthy living." The last charge presumably refers to homosexuality, one of the many "vices" to which Italians were supposedly prone.

69

Chanter's best anecdote about the local expatriates concerned a self-important senior journalist on a leading British broadsheet — let's call him Russell — who married the daughter of a duke and was inordinately proud of her courtesy title. Shortly after Russell's marriage, someone rang to ask him to a function, adding: "And *do* bring Mrs Russell as well." "She is NOT *"Mrs"* Russell," the irate commoner almost bellowed down the phone. "That's quite all right," said his host. "Bring her just the same."

All of which recalls an anecdote of the poet Edith Sitwell concerning the aesthete Lord Berners: "A pompous woman of his acquaintance, complaining that the head-waiter of a restaurant had not shown her and her husband immediately to a table, said, '*We had to tell him who we were.*' Berners, interested, inquired, '*And who were you?*' "

Charity: The red squirrel bonanza:
"*Charity vaunteth not itself, is not puffed up, doth not behave itself unseemly,*" says St Paul in his letter to the Corinthians. He would probably be dismayed if he saw what modern "charities" look like with their highly paid chief executives, their chuggers pursuing old ladies down the High Streets, their subcontracted agencies cold calling donors to bully them into upping their donations and their high profile celeb donors who have incorporated charity into their PR kits.

According to financial journalist Merryn Somerset Webb, the UK government supported charities to the tune of £1.2bn in the 2014-15 tax year through the Gift Aid scheme (you, the humble taxpayer, put in a hundred quid and the government tops that up with a further £25, equivalent to the basic rate tax on the cash.) Which is to say that you also help to give that extra £25 since, after all, the government's money is actually your (and other people's) money. And if the donor is a 40 % taxpayer he claims back the difference between the basic and higher rate tax on his tax return. (That's another £400m or so lost to the Treasury.)

Charities also get 80% relief (often 100% relief) on business rates, which accounts for the ill temper of a struggling rates-paying bookseller located close to Oxfam turning over books on the High Street. The tax loss in this case is estimated at another £1.6 bn. VAT relief for charities comes in at about £250m and stamp duty relief on buying premises at perhaps a further £100m. Other reliefs at the donor end include that on IHT and that for Payroll giving (another £640m), so pretty soon you're talking about serious money, around £4.5bn in fact. Furthermore companies don't pay tax on profits given to charities and charities are themselves exempt from tax on investment income and interest earned (the resultant tax forgiveness costs a mere £3.5bn annually, since you ask.) Of course they are also exempt from Capital Gains Tax. Besides which the state generously hands our money to charities directly — like the £3m given in 2015 to Kids Company in the week it closed down due to financial mismanagement and spiralling debt. So now we're up to circa £6.5 billion of Treasury benevolence. Still, that's only just over half the further £11.1bn government and local government pay to charities for services that have been farmed out to them directly.

Of course all decent people have been nodding along as this narrative unfolds, perhaps enjoying a warm glow at the thought of their (largely involuntary) generosity and heart-warming devotion to good causes. Unfortunately there is an increasingly obnoxious smell emanating from the charitable sector. Firstly many charities are now run like businesses with ridiculously highly paid chief executives, not all of them operating noticeably charitable business practices. Furthermore, says Somerset Webb, there are charities that spend more on their staff's final salary pension scheme than on their charitable activities. She cites also a 24-bed hospice in Cornwall where the remuneration for the top five staff amounts to a total of £500,000.

There are nearly 200,000 charities in the UK inadequately scrutinised or not at all by the Charity Commission. Perhaps this explains why there are *six charities* devoted to *the preservation of the red squirrel* and over eighty dealing with *alcoholism*. And this is before you start asking the hard questions: i.e. should taxpayers be subsidising Oxfam to spend £20m a year on often highly contentious political campaigning? And is it democratic that people should be able to choose to promote their pet causes at taxpayers' expense and be allowed thereby to contribute less than they would otherwise do to the general pot of money that is required for carrying out the mandate of an elected government?

This issue is thrown into stark relief by the decision of Mark Zuckerberg, founder of Facebook, to give away 99% of his wealth. His share of Facebook is worth so many billions that this will still leave him enough to get by on quite comfortably, but every one rightly applauded this unprecedented act of philanthropy. However there is a snag. As Edward Luce pointed out in an article in the *Financial Times*, the many billions that are promised are to be put into a limited liability company, not a charity. The company will not need to spend 5% of its capital every year like a charity but will (like a charity) have a low tax bill. Why does this matter? It matters because the enormous success of Silicon Valley in the USA is built on *federal largesse*: "from the microprocessor to the global positioning system and the computer mouse, to the search engine, Silicon Valley owes its key breakthroughs *to US public research*"[5] [*italics added*]. And why does this matter? Well, Mr Zuckerberg seems un-keen to stress this possibly inconvenient fact — or even mention it in his somewhat mushy 2,234 word letter to his newly born daughter that was coupled with the philanthropic announcement. That may be because "Mr Zuckerberg and his fellow Silicon Valley titans," as Luce points out, "are world leaders at minimising their corporate liabilities. Last year [2014] Facebook paid just over £4,327 — yes £4,327 — in UK corporate taxes. In 2012 it paid none at all." It would therefore be better, says Luce, if Zuckerberg set another kind of example and paid normal taxes at, say, 30%, on his wealth, which would still enable him to put circa $30bn into his charitable investment company. That way the taxpaying public that has helped him get started, and is arguably the foundation of his great wealth, would get a modest return on *their* investment....(*see also Socialism* and Elizabeth Warren).

The word "charity" suggests payment of a voluntary nature for good causes, an image out of which charity organisers extract the maximum mileage. Even when the charity is well run, which is often not the case, if too much of the donated money is going on salaries and pensions schemes, or if it duplicates the work of several other charities, there is no logical justification for taxpayers having to cough up extra for it, especially where they might not be in agreement with its aims or methods. And if the charity has simply become an arm of central or local government, there is no justification for calling it a "charity" anyway — or for treating it as such. Somerset Webb suggests a massive cull, but adds consolingly "anyone who wants to keep financing donkeys, literary festivals, political lobbyists, art projects and the apparently endless UK squirrel crisis can continue to do so. Just out of their post-tax income."[6]

5 Edward Luce: "What Zuckerberg could learn from Buffett," *Weekend FT*, 5th December/6 December 2015.
6 Merryn Somerset Webb: "Vast cost of charity sector is squirrelled away," *Financial Times*, 8 August, 2015.

Chinese democratic credentials: Tips for western states on how to manage protests:

The Chinese *Sonderweg* to democracy was very much on display during the Beijing Olympics, when the regime thoughtfully organised a "Protest Park" to showcase its citizens' right to express their grievances.

Of course you had to get permission to stage your protest, and by the end of the games there had been seventy-seven applications — and... er... no permissions. The Ministry of the Interior explained that most protesters had withdrawn their applications after they had been "interviewed" by officials and some (it omitted to mention) had been sent for re-education through labour. Still, this was enough for the notoriously corrupt members of the International Olympics Committee to hail the "success" of the games and laud their totalitarian organisers.

Meanwhile the ineffable Archbishop of Canterbury became "*concerned*" about the growing "*inequalities*" in China, nostalgically recalling that the dear old Chinese Communist Party of yore had at least "*guaranteed everyone's welfare*" up to the Cultural Revolution. No doubt this is the version taught in the schools of the People's Republic of Lambeth. However, as George Walden disobligingly pointed out, "during the Great Leap Forward of 1958-61, this "*guarantee*" unfortunately ran out for 40 million Chinese, leaving them, it is true, equal, but equally dead. Others survived by eating leaves and bark, or, in remote provinces, babies."

Anjem Choudary: The quiet voice of barbarism:
Choudary, who was given a long and gently ironic interview in *The Observer* in 2014,[7] was a founding member of something called Al-Muhajiroun which was chiefly notable for enthusiastically celebrating the 9/11 attacks. In the interview he says that the Isis atrocities haven't occurred (so why did the perpetrators video them?) and at the end of it breaks off to explain the justification for crucifixions to an acolyte who has wandered in. Some might find it amusing that he is claiming state benefits in Britain, yet hates with an all-consuming hatred the state (and the taxpayers) who provide them. In any case he claims that "*Muslims are imprisoned over here. We can't travel abroad*," although later in the interview

---

7 *The Observer*, 7th September, 2014. "Islamic State is the kind of society I would like to live in with my family." Interview with Anjem Choudary by Andrew Anthony.

he seems to have forgotten this, as he mentions visits to Spain and Denmark. You would think he would try and construct a coherent narrative, however mendacious, but like many of his ilk, he clearly does not see any particular virtue or significance in a true remark as against an untruthful one.

Perhaps we should admire his candour however: he says *"we don't believe in the concepts of freedom or democracy. We believe sovereignty belongs to God."* So when Britain becomes a Muslim country (he thinks by 2050) it would adopt *shari'a*. Asked if the same right of political protest and criticism that he currently enjoys would be available to citizens who opposed such a state, he calmly explains that there would of course be no right of protest, there would be enforced segregation of the sexes, women would be enshrouded, gay people and apostates killed, there would be no alcohol, all music banned (other than Islamic singing — as long as it was not men to women or vice versa), no theatre and the teaching of evolution would be forbidden.

We can hardly wait …

Christians: Victims turned oppressors, turned victims:
Christian intolerance was a by-product of the institutionalisation of Christianity by the Emperors Constantine and Theodosius. During his reign, Julian the Apostate wisely restored the rights and property of pagans ruthlessly persecuted by the Christians, who had been given official status by Constantine. Unfortunately, after Julian's death, Emperor Theodosius again gave Christians a free hand to pillage pagan shrines and temples. The orator Libanius (314-93) pointed out that the pagan temples were the bedrock of country life [like English country churches in the 18th century], where "farming communities rest their hopes for husbands, wives, children, for the oxen and the soil they sow and plant … they believe that their labour will be in vain once they are robbed of the gods who direct their labour to their due end." Further, the country temples were indeed "the soul of the countryside; they mark the beginning of its settlement and have been passed down through many generations to the men of today." Libanius also complains of "hymn-chanting, pious drunkards who eat more than elephants" as they go about their business [like Henry VIII's commissioners] of looting and destruction.

Sixteen centuries later H.L: Mencken appraised religious tolerance in America, where fundamentalist Christianity is ruthlessly promoted by

means of lobbying, well-funded propagandist broadcasting and the infiltration into schools of anti-Darwinist doctrines like "intelligent design":
"I fear," wrote Mencken, that "the meaning of religious freedom is
sometimes greatly misapprehended. It is taken to be a sort of immunity,
not merely from governmental control but also from public opinion.....
Any fool, once he is admitted to holy orders, becomes infallible. Any
half-wit, by the simple device of ascribing his delusions to revelation,
takes on an authority that is denied to all the rest of us. . . . "[8]

The blasphemy laws performed precisely this function, although they
have now fallen into disuse in regard to Christianity. In essence they allowed the views of persons holding to beliefs for which they could provide no evidence other than "revelation" or "scripture" (i.e. propaganda)
to be exempt from the possibly disrespectful scrutiny to which all other
views (and especially those of rival religions) were exposed. The most
pernicious feature of blasphemy laws have now crept back into operation under the guises of "tolerance" and "diversity," by which is meant
not "giving offence" to threatening and intolerant creeds, chiefly Islam,
but also Hinduism. In practice this means appeasement of terrorist fundamentalists and a double standard whereby any insult is permitted if
aimed at Christianity, which is today an almost entirely peaceable religion, but newspapers, broadcasters and indeed governments bow the
knee before groups representing other faiths that claim to be "offended"
by any challenge to their irrational and sometimes malevolent beliefs.

Bruce Bawer in his book *Surrender* has documented the alarming extent to which this appeasement has undermined the basic principle of
democratic freedom, namely that of free speech. The ultimate surrender
of that principle is expressed in the observation of the Dutch Foreign
Minister to the effect that the "freedom of expression doesn't mean the
right to offend."[9] This remark (astonishingly naïve or astonishingly
disingenuous according to taste) neatly dovetails with another by an
imam in Calgary, Canada in 2004, namely that "*Shari'a* cannot be cus-
tomised for specific countries. These universal, divine laws *are for all
people of all countries for all times.*" (Italics added). Much of *shari'a* is
profoundly offensive to western civilisation, sanctioning even practices

8 H. L. Mencken: "Aftermath" in the *Baltimore Evening Sun*, 1925.

9 Quoted in Bruce Bawer: *Surrender: Appeasing Islam, Sacrificing Freedom* (Anchor Books, New York, 2010), P. 236.

that are (with good reason) illegal under western laws. Yet even condemnation of practices approved by *shari'a* now risks accusations of incitement to racial or religious hatred, whereby, as with our former blasphemy laws, religion escapes accountability for its doctrines and perpetrators are turned into victims. In a German case (2007) cited by Bauer the (female!) judge refused to expedite a divorce requested by a Moroccan-German woman from her violent Moroccan husband, arguing that she should have been prepared for such treatment, given that her husband's religion (and *sharia* law) granted him the "right to inflict corporal punishment" on his wife. A Berlin lawyer commented that tolerance for Muslim intolerance was gradually leading to the introduction of a parallel, *sharia*-based legal system.[10] In Britain, the former Archbishop of Canterbury gave a speech in 2008 that seemed to advocate just that.[11]

In the light of all this, the tussle for the right to exclusive victimhood in the ancient world seems almost gentlemanly. Unlike Theodosius, the Apostate Emperor Julian not only had a profound sense of justice, he also had a refined sense of humour: when imposing a heavy fine on the rich Christians of Edessa, he invoked Jesus's praise of the poor and lowly: "since by their most admirable law [the Christians] are bidden to sell all they have and give it to the poor, so that they may attain more easily to the kingdom of heaven ... I have ordered that all their funds pertaining to the church of Edessa... be confiscated; this is in order that poverty may teach them to behave properly and that they may not be deprived of the heavenly kingdom for which they still hope."

---

10 Bruce Bawer, op cit. Pp. 257, 264. The judgement was later reversed, but there have been similar cases. When the website of TV channel ZDF in 2006 dubbed an imam who had referred to Germans as "stinking infidels" a "hate preacher", the imam took the ZDF to court and the judge *condemned ZDF* for using the phrase "hate preacher" and ordered it to cease doing so forthwith (Bawer op cit. P. 264). Laws against, incitement to hatred or racism, it turns out, are often simply a tool to protect violent Islamism from accountability.

11 Speech by Rowan Williams, then Archbishop of Canterbury, at the Royal Courts of Justice, London, February 2008. He proposed *inter alia* expanding the Islamic Sharia Council that was already handing down judgements on marriage and divorce. Bawer describes his speech as a "*six-thousand-word exercise in euphemism and circumlocution*" and indeed it is so convoluted as to be almost unreadable (Bawer op cit. P. 260).

Christmas Wishes: The commodification of Christmas:
Christmas wishes are often little more than marketing gimmicks, as parodied in Tom Lehrer's version of a well-known carol: *"Angels we have heard on high / Tell us to go out and **buy**!"*

In 1948 a Washington radio station contacted ambassadors in the US capital to ask them what they most wished for at Christmas. The French ambassador very properly said he would like to see peace throughout the world. The Russian ambassador wanted freedom for all people enslaved by imperialism (the radio station was too obsequious to inquire whether that included Stalinist imperialism). The British ambassador, Sir Oliver Franks, who was possibly not fully tuned in at that particular moment, said: "Well, it's very kind of you to ask. I'd quite like a box of crystallised fruit."

The American comedienne Chelsea Handler says she considers the ideal gift for her would be a vibrator that also makes tacos.

Churnalism: Contemporary journalism that consists of repackaging news stories from sources such as wire agencies or PR handouts; and generally giving priority to the trivial, manufactured and sensational story over one that may be significant, complex or consensus-challenging:

"Churnalism" is the main topic of Nick Davies' contrarian book entitled *Flat Earth News*.[12] A graduate trainee on a regional tabloid kept a diary of his work schedule for Davies and summarised his week as follows: "Number of stories covered: 48 (9.6 per day). People spoken to: 26. People seen face to face: 4 out of 26. Total hours out of the office: 3 out of 45.5." This, opines Davies, is *churnalism* at work. The number of stories handled by the traineee means that it would be impossible to research any of them properly and the brief periods out of the office mean that contacts could not be built up and cultivated. Furthermore "no reporter who speaks to only twenty-six people in researching forty-eight stories can possibly be checking their truth."[13] According to Davies, "the structure of corporate news has converted journalists from active newsgatherers to passive processors of material — only 12% of which can be shown to be free of the mark of wire agencies and PR consultants."[14]

---

12 Nick Davies: *Flat Earth News: An Award-winning Reporter Exposes Falsehood, Distortion and Propaganda in the Global Media* (Vintage Books, London, 2009).
13 Nick Davies op cit. P. 59.
14 Nick Davies op cit. P. 113.

Although Davies himself worked for the left-leaning *Guardian* newspaper, and his painstaking exposure of double standards, propaganda, bias and untruthfulness in the media was described as "rubbish" by journalistic grandee Simon Jenkins, he does not spare the left or the right in his analysis. For example his account of how the media represented the 1986 Chernobyl disaster is decidedly off-message from the point of view of anti-nuclear campaigners and eco-salvationists, who are generally leftist. He points out that the World Health Organisation, an organisation of some repute, conducted a three-year study of the disaster's health impact and reported its findings in 2005. The report revealed a clear increase in thyroid cancer among children who had drunk milk from cows grazing contaminated grass in the week following the explosion, but most of these children had been successfully treated. There was little hard evidence of other cancers, stillbirths or deformed babies, nor of mutated animals or plants. According to the WHO, the total number of people who had actually died as a result of the accident was not thousands or even hundreds. It was fifty-six.

Not surprisingly, Greenpeace, which is opposed to nuclear energy and needs scary news stories to support its propaganda, responded by producing a counter-report in 2006 for which *The Scotsman*'s headlines, among many similar ones, was "CHERNOBYL'S REAL DEATH TOLL 90,000, SAYS GREENPEACE." "A close reading of the material behind these headlines," writes Davies, "reveals that it was an inaccurate account of a Greenpeace press release, which was itself an inaccurate account of the organisation's own report, which was itself somewhat problematic. The figure of 90,000 deaths came from one single study which was mentioned in the Greenpeace report, among a mass of other studies which put the estimated total deaths from Chernobyl at anywhere between dozens and up to six million. The report itself was honest enough to admit that all this research included 'high levels of speculation and general uncertainty.' In other words they could not really be sure." Furthermore the Greenpeace press release elided the single dramatic figure of 90,000 with other far less dramatic death counts in the weasel-worded formulation "the results of recent studies." "The headlines then removed all remaining uncertainty," pursues Davies "and furthermore failed to reflect that these were deaths [the numbers quoted in the Greenpeace report] which were estimated for the seventy years up to 2056, not deaths which had already occurred."[15]

Elsewhere Pascal Bruckner has written: "The incredible controversy over the number of Chernobyl's victims proves that the radiation also affected the brains of some commentators: 212 dead according to the World Health Organisation, 200,000 according to Greenpeace, nine million according to Corinne Lepage. Nine million, that's genocide, that's serious stuff!"[16]

As Winston Churchill is supposed to have said (must check out that quote some time): "*The only reliable statistic is one which you have yourself falsified...*"

Closet Trackers: Investment funds sold to the unsuspecting as "actively managed" (thus attracting higher fees), but which actually hug an index like a passive fund doing the same thing at ten per cent of the cost:

According to the *Daily Telegraph* a Mr Djanogly has developed an analysis tool that lays bare one of the investment businesses least well kept secrets: namely the existence of funds which pretend that their audaciously brilliant managers are seeking out exciting opportunities in round-the-clock brainstorming on investors' behalf, thus justifying hefty fees — whereas in reality they just buy the relevant index and then go out for coffee.

Mr Djanogly disobligingly points out that investors who dump these closet trackers and go for the real thing could see a net 90% reduction in their costs and would also have "a better idea of what they were getting for their money" (i.e. not much).

Even more disobligingly he identifies no less than 82 closet trackers available to British suckers, I mean savers, in which some £23bn is held.[17] In 2014 the UK's Department for Communities and Local Government became concerned about the sustainability of the Local Government Pension Scheme, one of the world's largest. Based on an independent report by Hymans Robertson, the DCLG discovered what alert

15 Nick Davies op cit. P. 41.

16 Pascal Bruckner: *The Fanaticism of the Apocalypse* (Polity Press, Cambridge, 2013, Translated by Steven Rendall) P. 53. Corinne Lepage was writing in *L'Express*, 20 April 2011.

17 Kyle Caldwell: "Is your ISA fund one of those 'closet trackers'?" *The Telegraph*, September 22nd, 2014.

investors have known for years, namely that "active asset management" is an expensive con.

What out-performance "active" management occasionally produces is usually rendered nugatory by the extra costs charged. "Active fund management," writes Michael Johnson in the *Financial Times*, "has finally been revealed for what it is: a web of meaningless terminology, pseudo-science and sales patter."[18] Fund managers excuse mediocre or poor performance by claiming they invest for the long run; "but," says Johnson, "the long run never arrives. It merely shuffles forward; there is never a day of reckoning. In the meantime, ludicrously expensive talent is deployed in the pointless pursuit of continually trying to outperform one another. Worse, it is a giant negative-sum game in which the savers pay the price, their hard-won capital persistently eroded by recurring charges and fees."

There are some 1,069 investment funds, most of them duds. In the first quarter of 2014 only 46 (4.3 % of them) produced top quartile returns. "Using blind luck," writes Johnson, "one would expect 17 funds to achieve this, which leaves 29 fund managers out of a universe of 1,069, roughly 2.7 %, who could legitimately claim that their success was down to skill. Over the same period… 881 funds did not [produce above-average returns]." Johnson opines that we "do not need" 80% of this industry, particularly since many of them are what are called "closet trackers."

The DCLG has had enough of this sort of thing. It proposes that all the pension assets should be moved to passive fund management with expected savings in charges over the next 20 years of £6.6bn. This would save taxpayers a lot of money, as well as the prospective beneficiaries, who just might get a better pension at the end of it…

The Brits are not alone however. The Swedish government has begun an investigation into closet trackers after a group of indignant investors took legal action against expensive, sleepy funds, while the Danish regulator has discovered that one third of the 188 domestic equity funds in Denmark could be classified as "benchmark-hugging." Furthermore a Brussels-based investor rights group points out that fund fees are in any

18 This and the following quotes and figures are taken from an article by Michael Johnson, a research fellow at the Centre for Policy Studies, in the *Financial Times* of May 12th, 2014.

case too high — in Europe actively managed funds charge 1.70 per cent, in the USA only 0.70 per cent.[19] Some rivals claim that even funds that are genuinely into stock selection (as opposed to following an index), and do outperform from time to time, are no more use to the retail investor than a tracker, because any extra gains they might make are eaten away in "fees, transaction costs and a drag from cash holdings,"[20] which can add up to a princely 2.27%. Many of the victims of these pin-striped scams are of course unaware of how they are being fleeced, especially those whose employers put money into "default funds" for their pensions.

The great Warren Buffett began comparing his own fund's performance against the four largest US mutual funds in 1962; the best of the four (Tri-Continental) had returned 45% over the four years Buffett had been investing, while his Buffett Partnership (forerunner to Berkshire Hathaway) had returned …er… 107%. By 1969 Tri-Continental had managed a 200 per cent return (Terrific! Break open the champagne! But don't mention that Buffett's return by then was 1,403 per cent…). Apart from the fees eating into investor returns, the reason for the underperformance of such mutual funds was that they hugged the Dow Jones Industrial Average — though for most of the 1960s they didn't even manage to keep up with that. "The results of these [Mutual Funds]," observed Buffett, "in some ways resemble the activity of a duck sitting on a pond: when the water (the market) rises, the duck rises; when it falls, back goes the duck. The water level has been of great importance to Buffett Partnership Limited's performance… However, we have occasionally flapped our wings."[21] This sort of thing has been going on for years, the fund managers and "Independent Financial Advisers" getting fat on the fees — and the future pensioners unaware that their nest eggs are quietly haemorrhaging cash…

As a matter of fact the pay of fund managers floats upwards on a rising tide of "funds under management" — the larger the fund, the more

19 Madison Marriage: "Sweden becomes the first in Europe to investigate closet trackers," *Financial Times*, 16th February, 2105.

20 There have been many articles on the topic of fees levied by funds and the effect on investor returns (all negative, of course.) This quotation is taken from an article in the *Financial Times* fund management supplement (*FM*), 18 May, 2015 ("Active fund managers really can pick stocks…[but] outperformance is usually swamped by fees").

21 Quoted in Stephen Foley: "The Buffett duck flaps its wings occasionally," (*Financial Times*, March 2, 2015).

fees it rakes in (and usually the less nimble it can be in the markets, a point your IFA will be less than keen to stress if he or she is getting juicy commission by recommending a particular fund.) As a leader in the *Financial Times* points out with heroic understatement, this means in plain English that firms *"depending on management fees alone tend to focus on size rather than performance."*[22] This is reminiscent of the story about the fund manager naively seeking to impress a client by taking him down to a marina to show him the managers' gin palaces moored there, a visible sign of his firm's success. *"I see that,"* said the client; *"but where are all the investors' yachts?"*

Cold Comfort Farm: An everyday story of country folk:
Stella Gibbons published this engaging tale of pre-BSE country life in 1932.The four cows on the farm (Graceless, Pointless, Aimless and Feckless) compete for the conjugal affections of a hugely well-endowed bull called Big Business. All these erratic ruminants (together with a pony named Viper) are the property of the Starkadder family: Aunt Ada Doom, Seth, Reuben, Urk and Judith. The last-named is married to Amos, the hellfire preacher at the Church of the Quivering Brethren *("Seth, drain the well! There's a neighbour missing.")*

Adam Lambsbreath is an ancient and incompetent shepherd, while Mr Meyerburg, dubbed Mr Mybug by Flora *(see below)*, is an oversexed and presumably Central European intellectual (every village has one). The intelligent but alarmingly unpolished Elfine eventually gets to marry the squire, Richard Hawk-Monitor. This is not without the help of a visiting Starkadder relation, the strong-minded Flora, who administers large doses of "the higher common sense" to the dangerously inbred locals *(" 'That would be delightful,' agreed Flora, thinking how nasty and boring it would be.")*

The book parodies the sub-Lawrentian literary genre agreeably known as *"loam and lovechild"* novels and has supplied us with the ominous and enticing phrase „Something nasty in the woodshed." Like many parodies (e.g. *Don Quixote*), the burlesque version has survived and thrived long after its original target has vanished from cultural memory. The writing has taken on a life of its own, like a successful im-

---

22 "Fund managers face the spotlight of higher pay: Investment has not shared its success with clients" (*Financial Times*, 17th February 2015.)

postor who is more plausible as the identity he has stolen than is the victim of his imposture: surely Mary Webb, or even D.H.Lawrence himself, would have been proud to have penned the following: *"Daisies opened in sly lust to the sun-rays and rain-spears, and eft-flies, locked in a blind embrace, spun radiantly through the glutinous light to their ordained death."*

Commodification of Culture: The contemporary art racket:
"How useless is painting," wrote Pascal, *"which attracts admiration by the resemblance of things, the originals of which we do not admire!"* This is the sort of reaction that might well be engendered in the uninitiated after a visit to the exhibits of the annual Turner Prize in London's Tate Gallery. It may or may not be deemed an adequate response to Piero Manzoni's *Merda d'Artista*, a limited edition of ninety small cans, each containing a thirty gram turd of the artist. (Or possibly not containing the turd, because an obligation enjoined on the purchasers was that the cans should never be opened and so far apparently none of them has been. The last (unopened) can to appear on the market fetched £97,250 at Sothebys in 2008.) Manzoni's inspiration for this line of work was a remark made by his father, namely: *"your art is a load of shit"* (his father happened to own a canning factory). Actually it is not quite true that no Manzoni can has ever been opened: in 1989 Bernard Bazile, a French artist, exhibited a partially opened one as his own work at the Centre Georges Pompidou and labelled it *"Boîte ouverte de Piero Manzoni."* All of which shows that Manzoni was nothing if not inventive in regard to marketing his genius; for example, you could also buy balloons containing the artist's breath (they were labelled *"Fiato d'artista."*)

Pascal's insight could certainly be applied to Jeff Koons, the cult artist of crass consumerism and infantile jokes, whose works include *"Rabbit"* (the cast of an inflatable plastic bunny which allegedly "parodies" Brancusi's bird sculptures), vacuum cleaners framed in Plexiglass or the artist's take on kitsch ornaments like a pig flanked by angels from a series aptly named *"Banality."* Koon's genius is to *"amplify an object's quiddity through a framing device even more puissant than a pedestal,"* as one curator of a Koons show put it in catalogue blurb which is itself beyond parody. This *quiddity* stuff was apparently Koons' big idea; according to the critic Jackie Wullschlager he hasn't had any others. His career, she writes, has been spent in "elaborating that gesture: exaggerating the aura of cheap, ordinary things, aggrandising them into works of art in increasingly expensive materials, and proffering them back to the one per cent as ultimate positional goods."

Of course one should bear in mind that art has always been in some sense a commodity, as well as all the other things that it is. In the Middle Ages the church was the most important commissioner of art — and even those donors pictured kneeling in the corners of Gothic religious paintings would not have been able to sponsor an iconography that was not ecclesiastically sanctioned. From the Renaissance onwards, sponsors would include secular lords and the subjects were often profane, but the *sujets* remained largely at the discretion of the sponsor. Aristocratic and ecclesiastical commissions determined art and architecture from the Counter-Reformation until the 19th century, their various phases (Rococo, Neo-Classical etc.) reflecting broader shifts of taste and artistic demand in societies becoming more secularised as a result of the Enlightenment. Thereafter an ascendant bourgeoisie (earlier in the Netherlands) began to finance artistic production after its own taste, being also prepared to buy what a recognised artist happened to have on offer. The advent of Historicism in the 19th century meant that the institutions of the state provided a huge reservoir of commissions that required their chosen artists to celebrate and interpret a humanistic and primarily heroic national narrative. Romanticism began to salute the free artistic genius, a sloganeering attitude that was later taken up and made the norm by Modernism; but even the Romantics were often responding to perceived interests and wishes of potential buyers, for example in catering to the the new sensibility for landscape and nature.

Such a perception of patronage in the history of western art highlights what is different about art patronage today, at least as it is conducted in the price stratosphere that determines the contemporary canon. The shift to the commodified art world surely begins with the rise of the art dealer as an influential trend-setter and arbiter of taste from the 1870s onwards; it has reached its apotheosis with the dealer-led commodification of contemporary art. Instead of reflecting institutional, social or aesthetic preoccupations as heretofore, much of contemporary art is primarily commodification, a refuge for oligarchs' money and a prestigious type of investment in a world where the global super-rich have more wealth than they can imagine outlets for. This sort of art market, divorced from aesthetic considerations based on any agreed norms or any sponsor-led reflection of a particular social frame-work, is the artistic equivalent of the property market, with the difference that its players have devised a way of keeping it permanently aloft by a system of thinly concealed price-fixing. Institutions as buyers, awards like the Turner Prize in Britain and the much expanded phenomenon of art fairs help to keep the business rolling along.

The immediate consequence is that art is considered to be anything which someone decides to label as such, for example light bulbs going on and off in a gallery room (which won the Turner prize) or a neatly arranged pile of bricks (admittedly architecture is also a neatly arranged pile of bricks). Time was, however, when the success of an artist was measured more in his or her ability to *emulate* (not *copy*, see below) the masterpieces of recognised geniuses; or, by the same token, an ability to push the limits of the status quo to achieve a new angle of vision. Rules had first to be mastered so that genius could break (or reinterpret) them. As there are now no norms to undermine, it is ever harder for artists to produce something that will stimulate the jaded palate of the public that has been led to expect that mere novelty is the essence of genius. "Creativity" today thus tends to be governed by the law of diminishing returns — if there are no rules, there are no rules to break.[23] If everything or anything is art, there is no criterion of artistic quality, other than what the *nouveaux riches* can be persuaded to pay for it. "I don't know what art is," said dissident critic Brian Sewell (now sadly deceased), "but I do know what it isn't. And it isn't someone walking around with a salmon over his shoulder or embroidering the name of everyone they have slept with on the inside of a tent."

Although the Americans and the Brits have expanded the definitions of art most arbirtrarily and enthusiastically, Central Europe has provided key inspiration in the work of Joseph Beuys (1921-1986). The latter's inflated rhetoric about the artist's role in society (unkindly described by a hostile critic as "simple-minded utopian drivel") was complemented by his gift for devising attention-grabbing stunts that launched a thousand imitators in the dreaded field of "Performance Art."[24] One of the

---

23 Writing in *The Spectator* (12th April, 2014) the writer Susan Hill expresses this thought rather more pithily: "Well of course there are no rules, but you have to know the rules there are not, and conform to them, before you are allowed to break them."

24 Beuys is described in the trade as a "Fluxus, Happening and Performance Artist."

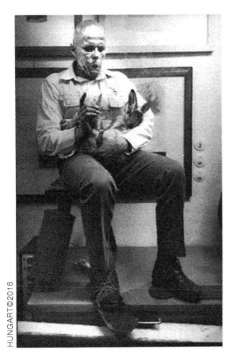

Joseph Beuys: "How to Explain Pictures to a Dead Hare."

most hyped of these performances was *"How to Explain Pictures to a Dead Hare"* (1965).

The *Wikipedia*'s description of the latter runs as follows: "The artist could be viewed through the glass of the gallery's window. His face was covered in honey and gold leaf, an iron slab was attached to his boot. In his arms he cradled a dead hare, into whose ear he mumbled muffled noises as well as explanations of the drawings that lined the walls. Such materials and actions had specific symbolic value for Beuys. For example, honey is the product of bees, and for Beuys (following Rudolf Steiner), bees represented an ideal society of warmth and brotherhood. Gold had its importance within alchemical enquiry, and iron, the metal of Mars, stood for a masculine principle of strength and connection to the earth. A photograph from the performance, in which Beuys is sitting with the hare, has been described „by some critics as a new Mona Lisa of the 20th century," though Beuys disagreed with the description."[25]

This pretty much sums up the problem with Performance Art, as with Conceptual Art, namely it tends to require a lengthy verbal explanation of the arbitrary meanings attached to its component parts, some of which may chime with archetypal symbolism, but most of which appear to have been thought up smoking marijuana in the bathtub. Tom Wolfe first made this point in his coat-trailing book *The Painted Word* (1975), a polemic that made the targeted artists, and especially the pretentious new breed of opinion-forming art critics, satisfyingly apoplectic. By the time we had reached the stage of Conceptual Art, Wolfe implies, the visual had been subordinated to the word, and the word often to ideology. *"Art made its final flight, climbed higher and higher in an ever-decreas-*

25 en.Wikipedia.org/wiki/Joseph_Beuys

ing tighter-turning spiral until... it disappeared up its own fundamental aperture... and came out the other side as Art Theory!" And elsewhere he added: *"In short: frankly, these days, without a theory to go with it, I can't see a painting."*

But this is only part of the problem. The other part is that the frantic search for ideas and actions that scandalise the public (for example with blasphemies and pornography) is highly reductive, just as the reiterated use of formerly taboo words like "fuck" or "fucking" in contemporary drama now has only a deadening and weakening effect rather than a shocking and dramatic one. Since modern culture has insisted on its taboo-breaking role, its duty to shock above all, it has been running out of taboos to break. The last frontier, as Martin Gayford has mischievously suggested, is political correctness. Of Sarah Lucas's sculptures at the 2015 Venice Biennale he writes: "*[There are] a number of life-casts of the lower halves of women with cigarettes protruding from their intimate crevices. This last is outrageously daring, smoking being one of the few truly taboo subjects in the modern world.*"[26]

An exception to the banality of such "shocking" artistic statements might be the "Actionism" of the Austrian artist Hermann Nitsch, whose "*Aktionen*" hark back to pagan sacrifice and symbolic rituals transposed onto a Christian backdrop. His "Orgiastic Mystery Theater" (*Orgien, Mysterien, Theater*) consisted of "actions" that included animal sacrifice and simulated crucifixion with the active participation of helpers (for example to chuck buckets of blood around), as well as music and dancing. This required elaborate staging and quite a lot of participants (indeed audience participation) that raised it somewhat above the level of solo artists, or a small group, simply trying to outdo each other in weirdness. Its mixture of ritual, music and visual effects make it more of a Freudian *Gesamtkunstwerk* travestying certain sacral elements of our civilisation.

However the mingling of ritualistic slaughter with sadomasochistic elements and parody of Eucharistic symbolism still seemed designed to *épater les bourgeois*, an intention shared with the notorious New York happenings that foreshadowed the Orgiastic Mystery Theatre. In particular the crucifixion parodies were evidently intended to outrage, as the following description of the high point of one *Aktion* suggests: "*The*

---

26 Martin Gayford: "More Marx than Dante" [on the 2015 Venice Biennale], *The Spectator*, 16th May, 2015.

naked man lies as if crucified. Viscera (or brains?) are put on his sex organ and doused with buckets of blood by Nitsch. The man is again given blood to drink. He kneads the mess on his own body for a long time with apparent enjoyment. Then he is taken away on the stretcher with a cacophonic noise followed by a charming violin piece."[27] The 130th *Aktion* (in Naples in 2010) involved the "crucifixion" of two "curators" of Personal Structures, an "international contemporary art platform" with which Nitsch's later work is associated. It was considered such a success that its documentation was exhibited at the following year's Biennale, together with Marina Abramović's video installation of her locked in a staring battle with a donkey.

The ritualistic element in Nitsch's work at least gives it a certain coherence compared to the whimsical happenings of much other "performance art." Some early actions led to interventions (on the grounds of blasphemy or obscenity) by the Vienna police, who perhaps were not best equipped to make fine distinctions between artistic authenticity and mere exhibitionism. While Nitsch was brought before the courts several times on grounds that many would now consider anachronistic or reactionary, a fellow Actionist, Otto Mühl spent over six years in prison for sexual interference with minors and drug offences committed as leader of the Friedrichshof Commune in Burgenland. After a while he distanced himself from *Aktion*, calling it "*happening as a bourgeois art form, mere art.*" As an artist with intellectual and political pretensions, Mühl too displayed a remarkable lack of originality in his manifesto for the commune, the aim of which was the Proudhonist destruction of private property, as well as the institution of free love and collective education of children.[28] Since such education evidently included in some cases sexually abusing minors, the courts were not over-impressed by this altruistic mission statement. Normally one should not judge an artistic talent in terms of the artist's biography, but in both cases — Nitsch and Mühl—their artistic output is largely inseparable from their socio-political and philosophical allegiances — and they themselves seem to insist on that.

27 *Bloody Man:The Ritual Art of Hermann Nitsch* by Eugene Gorny (reviewing a retrospective of Nitsch's work in Prague, 1993.) See: www.zhurnal.ru/staff/gorny/englisch/nitsch.htm

28 For the enforced sexual anarchy of the commune and Mühl's exploitation of it, see Jonathan Margolis: "The Price of Freedom," *The Guardian*, 8th October, 1999.

For example Otto Mühl's *obiter dicta* justify the gratuitous hard core pornography of his film-making (including coprophilia, sado-masochism and the consumption of vomit and urine) in the following terms: *"I am for lewdness...I make films to provoke scandals, for audiences that are hidebound, perverted by 'normalcy', mentally stagnating and conformist...The worldwide stupefaction of the masses in the hands of artistic, religious, political swine can be stopped only by the most brutal utilization of all available weapons. Pornography is an appropriate means to cure our society from its genital panic. All kinds of revolt are welcome: only in this manner will this insane society, the product of the fantasies of primeval madmen, finally collapse...I restrict myself to flinging the food to the beasts: let them choke on it."*

Another problematic aspect of the contemporary art scene is the role of the state in promoting culture, which inevitably includes a good deal of junk culture. Much questionable artistic production today is financially underpinned by taxpayer's money and the art of extracting money from the state for art projects is prone to landing up in the hands of well-organised cliques. This is a perennial grievance of the conservative press, whose readers resent having to pay for shows that a small clique of banal anarchists and revolutionary groupies (according to this view) foists on the general public. The left on the other hand believes that it is the mark of a civilised state to encourage dissidence in art as in everything else, sidestepping the fact that state-subsidised art has rather lost its martyr's aura of bold contrarianism. Otto Mühl, for instance, was celebrated with two major shows of his work at Vienna's *Museum für Angewandte Kunst* on exiting gaol in 1997, and thirteen years later he was also exhibited at the *Leopold Museum*. Both of these venues are sustained by taxpayers' money. It is an open question whether the Mühl exhibitions, at least at the MAK whose Director was obsessed with fashionable provocation,[29] were more designed to create a scandal (and thus attract visitors) than to celebrate an important artistic talent. Less open in retrospect is the question as to whether the Province of Burgenland should have supported Mühl's authoritarian and partly criminal commune by offering building subsidies.

---

29 The director since 1986, Peter Noever, was himself *"fristlos entlassen"* in 2011 from his office by the Curatorium of the MAK on account of alleged financial irregularities.

Apart from the tendency of bureaucratic cliques to lavish public money on dubious artistic projects, the growing self-absorption and narcissism of our over-consumerised society has encouraged the notion that "self-expression," however banal, is also "creative." One is tempted to think that Joseph Beuys' most damaging legacy as a Performance Artist was his pronouncement that "everyone is an artist" — to which art critic Andrew Graham-Dixon has drily retorted: "perhaps he should have added that not everyone should necessarily *exhibit* their work." Reviewing the 1993 "BT New Contemporaries" show in Manchester, Graham-Dixon quotes one of its selectors who writes in the catalogue about the difficulty of making a selection, because, of course, doing so means choosing one artwork over another — hard to do if there is really no criterion as to what constitutes an artwork in the first place. "We should have said yes to them all," he wrote, "the man in Brighton who filmed his birthday party; the table with turnips rammed through it; the prolonged video close-up of the artist's vagina; the urinal carved out of soap." The catalogue, writes Graham-Dixon "offers a fascinating insight into the mentality of the right-on art educator, critic and exhibition organiser." This selector believes that the subversive task of the artist is to "explore the territories of mental and emotional strangeness that are closed off to ordinary mortals." He cites the serial murderer Dennis Nilsen as an appropriate hero for the contemporary artist, as Nilsen was himself "an artist who drew the men he murdered: a planner who redesigned his life to suit the dictates of his heart."[30]

The irony of our times is that the more the perceived aesthetic or moral value of art declines or is rendered superfluous, the higher its pecuniary value spirals. *"What's aught but as 'tis valued?"* asks Troilus in *Troilus and Cressida*, a question highly pertinent to modern (and especially post-modern) artworks, many of which acquire extraordinary value because Mr Saatchi or a Russian oligarch has bought them. Stripped of recognised aesthetic value residing in concept, craftsmanship or function, the work of art becomes a mere price tag. Troilus seems to take a similar view of Helen in Shakespeare's play. "In his eyes," writes Terry Eagleton, "Helen is precious because she has been the cause of a glorious war, rather than having caused a war because she is pre-

30 Andrew Graham-Dixon: "That way madness lies…" *The Independent*, 22 June, 1993.

90

cious."[31] An article by the Editor of *Art History News* lifts the lid on how this works in the art market, particularly how it works at auctions. "If you are a dealer representing one of the relatively small number of artists who matter, you can bid (anonymously) on their works yourself, to register new "values." You may have to buy some works back, but in a world where the only thing that matters is the most recent price, paying an auctioneer's commission is merely marketing."

Even more dubious is the so-called 'guarantor purchase,' whereby someone "agrees a certain (undisclosed) price for a work before a sale, *and makes a profit if it sells for more* [italics added]. To liven things up, they are allowed to bid the work up during the sale too. But if they happen to buy it, their pre-sale negotiation (again, undisclosed) means they will not pay anything like the "price" reported by the auction house, and nor will the new "value" of the work be representative."[32] In other words, the auction houses are rigging their sales every bit as much as those despised barrow boys manipulating the Libor and Forex markets in order to enhance the profits of the banks. The latter faced stiff penalties when the well-kept secret of their operations finally leaked out. An analogous practice in the art market provokes, at best, a shrug of the shoulders.[33]

To the fastidious, there is something disgusting about the mismatch between image and reality that obtains in the plush galleries and auction

31 Terry Eagleton: *The Meaning of Life: A Very Short Introduction* (Oxford 2007) P. 72. Commodification as the basis of ever-expanding profits was the direction in which the legendary head of Sotheby's Peter Wilson took the art world. As his obituary in *The Independent* put it: "He was not only able to attract desirable objects (mostly paintings) and sell them at ever-increasing prices at auction, but, himself a hustler, was able to democratise the natural desire to value a widening range of objects in terms of cash rather than mere beauty or sentiment." (*The Independent* 20 June 1993.

32 Bendor Grosvenor: "Contemporary art is judged by its price tag not by aesthetics", *Financial Times*, 19 November, 2014.

33 See also the extraordinary case of dodgy Australian tycoon Alan Bond (1938–2015), who was probably technically bankrupt when he bought Van Gogh's "Irises" at Sotheby's in 1987 for $54m. It turns out that Sotheby's had secretly loaned him much of the money and kept control of the painting. Three years later it sold the picture to the Getty Museum for an "undisclosed" price. It seems that this was all PR, partly to make it appear that Bond's finances were still buoyant, partly to keep art prices buoyant. *The Economist* which reported this in its obituary of Bond (13th June, 2015) added the following: Bond's "father had once predicted he would either become very rich or end up in jail. He achieved both."

houses. Enter one of them in London and you will be approached by an immaculately groomed Sloane ranger, whose simpering manner is belied by her sharp eye calculating whether you are a "serious" (i.e. rich) art lover or a time waster. Her good looks and perfect turn-out parody the homage that aesthetics pays to commerce. If you have something you are contemplating selling, you are passed over to an expert in that kind of object, who discusses its value in a confidential manner and with exceptional delicacy, like a surgeon outlining the prospects of success for an operation on a loved one. The solicitous manner and exquisite tact will probably make you forget altogether that not so long ago the owner of the most famous auction house in the world spent ten months behind bars for colluding with the second most famous auction house in the world in a commission cartel.[34]

Nor will the elegant gentleman or lady expert bring you up to speed on ruses such as "guarantor purchase", still less why auction houses need to take commission on both purchase and sale. (This pernicious practice has been successfully introduced without legal challenge, although it contravenes the basic principle that conflicts of interest arise when an agent is taking commission on both sides of a transaction.)[35] Meanwhile, all these beautiful people you're dealing with create such an aura of discreet grandeur, delicacy and good taste that their business ethics somehow fade into the background. It is only when you look into these that you will realise, if you are a Henry James fan, that this precise mismatch

---

34 Alfred Taubman, Chairman of Sothebys, was convicted in 2002, along with his CEO, Diane Brooks, who was treated less harshly than him for co-operating with the prosecution. The Chairman of Christie's, Sir Anthony Tenant, was also indicted, but refused to go to the USA to stand trial. Despite affecting pleas for leniency from the great and the good (Henry Kissinger and the Queen of Jordan among them) the trial judge was unmoved, pointing out that the conspiracy had swindled customers out of more than $100 million.

35 The double commission scam is now covertly being introduced into the London real estate market which, as once did the auction houses, hitherto has charged commission only to the seller. Businesses do this sort of thing when they can get away with it, or until the law intervenes. The most blatant conflict of interest of this kind was revealed when Goldman Sachs was hauled before the regulators to explain one of its transactions labelled Abacus (q.v.) This involved selling bundled sub-prime mortgages (CDOs) to an unsuspecting buyer while not revealing that the party on the other side of the bargain was a short seller *which had itself selected* some of the assets and was betting against them.

between aesthetic refinement and moral vulgarity has been unforgettably depicted in the character of the emetic Gilbert Osmond in *The Portrait of a Lady*. The more Osmond's faultless good taste is stressed, the more the reader becomes uneasily aware of his avarice and essentially unfeeling nature. His type is to be found everywhere in the contemporary art market.

The artist Bridget Riley takes a sober view of the contemporary art scene in which she is a distinguished protagonist. While what she calls "genuine development" in art will, she thinks, go underground, fashionable art "will come more and more to resemble pop music, with group following group, or movement following movement, supported by a vast promotional structure… the western world will produce an inversion of the effect of totalitarianism, with commercialism replacing party ideology as the dominant factor." [36] Some of the successful artists of the day would probably agree. The most outspoken is the graffiti artist Banksy who has adopted the Greta Garbo or J.D.Salinger policy of hiding from the public in order to become more famous (it doesn't work for everyone of course). Officially he doesn't intend his large works for sale, since the whole point of them is that they are public statements of an ephemeral nature; however his smaller caprices do come in the market. One of his prints offered at Sotheby's in 2014 was evidently prompted by the unexpected success of a previous Sotheby sale of Banksy stuff. It is an illustration of an auction at which the work eagerly bid for bears the rubric: "*I Can't Believe You Morons Actually Buy This Shit*." That may be placed alongside an indiscretion in old age by Peter Wilson, chairman of Sotheby's from 1958 to 1980, who has been described with some generosity as "aristocratic, greedy, aesthetic, unscrupulous and tyrannical": "It has been rubbish all the time," he remarked candidly — by which he meant not so much the art itself but the commodification of it that he had so driven forward. He had spent his life telling potential sellers that it was the perfect moment to secure a huge price, while simultaneously assuring potential buyers that it was the ideal moment to invest.[37]

The problem of authenticity, to which Banksy is perhaps indirectly alluding in his homely way, is one that presents a danger to the money-de-

36 From Robert Kudielka (Ed.): *The Eye's Mind: Bridget Riley Collected Writings 1965–2009* (London, Thames & Hudson Ltd, 2009).
37 See: "Sharp Dealers" in *The Economist*, October 23, 2001.

fined art market, not least since the spirit and often the techniques of much modern art lends itself to fakery. One way of getting round that is to pretend that a copy, at least if blessed by the right galleries and propagandists, is as much a product of creativity as its original. Recently, stunned visitors to MoMA in New York (if visitors to art galleries are still capable of being stunned) found themselves in a retrospective of work by Elaine Sturtevant, "who is known," writes Ariella Budick, "chiefly for not being any of the artists whose works she faithfully reproduced" (e.g. Warhol, Lichtenstein, Stella, Oldenburg among others.) Although some have looked for "the ironic twist of telling difference" (the *ironic* statement is a favourite art publicist's justification for feeble, derivative artworks), it appears that Sturtevant is content just to copy and scrawl her signature on the back of her version. However "slavishness has its perks," writes Budick; "Collectors have bought her works as affordable substitutes for the real thing — and the art market being the lunatic system that it is, her prices have sometimes vaulted beyond the originals'." Such a show as that of MoMA for Sturtevant would not be complete without the added insult of an academic apparatus, where some learned charlatan explains that Sturtevant's copies constitute a fertile dialogue with her sources (the procreators of the sources did not, on the whole, seem to share this view.) Or was Miss Sturtevant making a *statement* (an *ironic* one of course) about the superficiality of easily imitable art ("way down deep, it's shallow," as someone quite memorably said).[38]

Sturtevant and her work are certainly an interesting phenomenon from a sociological and psychological point of view, if not an aesthetic one. Something called the Pictures Generation made a cult out of her in the 1980s, celebrating her as the "elder stateswoman of the so-called image-appropriation movement," which Budick describes as "a school of artists that blended Pop Art's affection for found objects with the conceptualists' hankering for radical ideas." However, you might think to her credit, Sturtevant rejected her crown, saying that the "appropriationists were really about the loss of originality… and I was about the power of thought." "She embraced "replication" rather than the trendier term "appropriation," even though you and I might not be able to tell the difference, and her champions kept telling us that her chosen

---

38 See: Ariella Budick, "Limitations of imitation," *Financial Times* 12 November, 2014.

label didn't actually mean what it seemed to mean. "Replicating might imply "copying", and she was definitely not doing that — nope, not at all." Budick concludes with the observation that it would seem a sign of desperation when a museum pays tribute to those who "find the whole enterprise of artistic creation rather pointless and yet presumably distinguish between their own $700,000 handmade reproductions and $40 posters available in the gift shop downstairs." This is where we end up when originality is defined by its opposite. In 2014 Robert Gober's *Three Urinals* (1988) sold at Christie's for $3.52m. They are indistinguishable, says Grosvenor "from three actual urinals except by virtue of their price and several paragraphs of impenetrable art-speak in a catalogue... expensive, say the experts equals good."[39] The thing is, they are not "original", since Marcel Duchamp touted the same object as art (*Fountain*, 1917). They are, so to speak a rip-off of an "ironic statement" that has already been made. And how soon before we have a rip-off of a rip-off?

Much of the most outré contemporary art is made for galleries and big collectors alone, since collectors of modest means have no space for huge installations and no money to pay inflated prices. Yet they are affected by the scene insofar as they are gallery goers who grapple loyally with enigmatic, outrageous, pretentious, gimmicky or whimsical works of art, always accompanied by catalogues filled with pretentious, impenetrable and possibly meaningless art-speak written by true believers (or, in some cases, utter cynics.) Nobody likes to be thought an intolerant philistine, still less an idiot, so mostly they seem to accept that they don't really understand the more banal objects on show, still less the portentous description of them in the catalogue. This affords a "get-out-of-gaol-free card" for the contemporary artist, who is thus to some extent immunised from public taste, as long as his or her work can be successfully gift-wrapped in words like "edgy," "ironic" or "resonant" by the vested interests promoting him or her.

In the 1990s, Yasmina Reza's highly successful play *Art* deconstructed the psychological confusion and social insecurity that can result when a person who has bought into the prevailing artistic hype (Serge) is confronted by the scepticism of his down-to-earth friend (Marc), who is appalled that Serge has spent 200,000 francs on a monochrome white

39 Bendor Grosvenor, op cit.

canvas with a couple of diagonal scars. In an encounter of some poignance, Marc, having described the picture, asks a mutual friend of his and Serge's (Yvan) to estimate how much Serge had paid for it. Yvan wants to know how fashionable the painter is, to which Marc testily replies "I'm not asking you for a professional valuation. I'm asking you what you, Yvan, would give for a white painting tarted up with a few off-white stripes." The play, as art market researcher Olav Velthuis points out, neatly skewers the clash between those who consider themselves insiders who "get" the point of works of art whose aesthetic appeal they are nevertheless unable to formulate for the benefit of others, or indeed for themselves, and hostile outsiders who think the whole art market is simply a scam. The play is not judgemental, but it does invite the audience to consider the question of aesthetic and pecuniary value, of "sweetness and light" versus commodification, a question that the contemporary art market spends a great deal of time, energy and money attempting to obscure.

Philosopher John Armstrong takes the unfashionable view that the most important role of the arts and the humanities is to guide and educate taste. Unfortunately, at least according to him, "the accumulated wisdom of humanity, concerning what is beautiful, interesting, fine or serious, [has] — to a large extent — [been] left to one side at the precise time when the need for guidance was greatest, and when guidance was hardest to give, and so required maximum effort and confidence." Effort and confidence is not lacking, of course, in the pushing of spurious art, a relentless propaganda drive by modern curators with an attendant band of groupies in the media known to its critics as "the Serota tendency" after the trendy Director of the Tate Gallery. "While the works of [Andy Warhol, Jeff Koons and Damien Hirst] have gained amazing commercial success," pursues Armstrong, "they suggest a loss of purpose in the arts. Loss, that is, of a really central and powerful claim upon the education of taste: upon the sense of what is beautiful, gracious or attractive… We have suffered an astonishing corruption of consciousness practised upon us by a decadent cultural elite… it has been supposed that the point of high culture — of the greatest imaginative and creative effort — is to unseat some fantasized ruling class who had to be provoked and distressed into change. But that is not the task of art or intelligence. Their real task is to shape our longings, to show us what is noble and important. And this is not a task that that requires any kind of cagey , elusive obscurity... Something is good because it is good, not because it was created yesterday or five hundred years ago."[40]

Armstrong's categories of "beautiful, gracious or attractive" are certainly too narrow, if not naïve (where would we be without the ugly brutality of a Bosch, the inspissated melancholy of a Hopper), but his *cri de coeur* is worth quoting at some length precisely because today's art establishment evidently regard such views, which attempt to involve art in notions of beauty, integrity, authenticity and nobility of aspiration, as hopelessly sentimental at best, snobbishly inegalitarian or tiresomely fustian at worst. The fact that a great many potential consumers of art probably share his view is irrelevant. The vast amount of money generated by the Damien Hirst "workshop" is the demonstration of its own worth in a society that can only measure value in terms of cash. Novelty, "provocation," obscurity and whimsy are the aesthetic currency of such an art, which is admiringly discussed in a jargon that is impenetrable to the layman, not least because there is very little of interest to say about it. Its aesthetic and intellectual incoherence is part of its point, though attempts may be made to gloss it as having socio-political significance. The Armstrongs of the world may imply it is fraudulent, but the killer response to that is: "Of course it's fraudulent — like our society itself."

On this analysis, much of "conceptual art" and the like provide the perfect example of the difference between liberty and licence. The artists may sometimes pay lip service to impeccable causes like human rights, feminism or environmental pollution, but this turns out to be mere gesture. The resultant work fails to resonate like Goya's depiction of the French massacring Spanish freedom fighters in Madrid[41] or Picasso's *Guernica*[42] because the artist's self-absorption gets in the way. It's "look at me!" rather than "look at this!" Notwithstanding Ludwig Hevesi's famous motto for the Vienna Secession (*der Zeit ihre Kunst, der Kunst ihre Freiheit* — to the age its art, to art its freedom) it is no longer self-evident that the licence of unconstrained freedom, implying a complete absence of normative standards, is an unmitigated blessing for artists. Of

---

40 John Armstrong: *In Search of Civilization* (Penguin, London, 2010), Pp. 66-67.

41 Francesco de Goya: *Third of May 1808 at Madrid* (Prado, Madrid).

42 Pablo Picasso: *Guernica* (Museo Reina Sofia, Madrid). The picture commemorates in modernistic terms the atrocity of the bombing of this Basque village in 1937 by German and Italian warplanes fighting for General Franco in the Spanish Civil War.

course nobody can say that in public, least of all curators, dealers, art critics, academics and others making good money out of today's gigantic art racket. Leonardo da Vinci could say it though, and did: *"Art breathes from containment and suffocates from freedom."* [43] That, however, is only one side of what Jean Baudrillard calls the "conspiracy" of modern art. *"The other side is that of the spectator who, for want of understanding anything whatever most of the time, consumes his own culture at one remove. He literally consumes the fact that he understands nothing and that there is no necessity in all this except the imperative of culture, of being a part of the integrated circuit of culture. But culture is itself merely an epiphenomenon of global circulation. The idea of art has become rarefied and minimal, leading ultimately to conceptual art, where it ends in the non-exhibition of non-works in non-galleries — the apotheosis of art as a non-event. As a corollary, the consumer circulates in all this in order to experience his non-enjoyment of the works."* [44]

Compensation: American euphemism for excessive managerial remuneration:

In the 1960s and 1970s the ratio of American CEO compensation to that of the average worker was 30-40 to 1 and is now 300-400 to 1, although many of the firms managed by these fabulously remunerated persons are little more productive than they were then. Nor does the argument that "the market" will sort out any anomalies in pay hold water, not least because of what is known as "payment for failure." When Mattel CEO Jill Barad was forced out in 2000 for underperformance, the board forgave her a loan of $4.2 million and added a cash grant of $3.3 million to pay the taxes on forgiveness of another loan. All this was in addition to a contractual termination payment of $26.4 million and retirement benefits exceeding $700,000 a year.[45]

---

43 C.f. the composer Igor Stravinsky's remark: *"The more constraints one imposes* [i.e.the more*"narrowly one limits one's field of action,"*] *the more one frees oneself of the chains that shackle the spirit."*

44 Jean Baudrillard: "Contemporary Art: Art Contemporary with Itself." in: Chris Turner (Translator). *The Intelligence of Evil or the Lucidity Pact (Talking Images).* Berg Publishers, 2005

45 L.A.Bebchuk and J.M.Fried: "Executive Compensation as an Agency Problem" in *Journal of Economic Perspectives*, 2003, vol.17, no.3, P. 81 – quoted in Ha-Joon Chang *op cit.* P. 154.

Then again, during the two years in which the share price of Reuters fell from 800p to 107p, its Chief Executive Tom Glocer received cash bonuses of £1.1 million, salary worth £1.6 million and relocation payments of £1 million. Over the three following years, Reuters lost a further one in five jobs following the 2,250 already axed. Meanwhile the pension pots of some CEOs defied gravity — £15.3 million for GSK's and £12.7 for BP's by 2003. Employee pension schemes of these firms were in huge deficit "not entirely coincidentally," as Ferdinand Mount puts it with gentle understatement.[46]

It is often asked why the big shareholders do not hold companies to account in respect of pay. The answer is quite simple: most of the big shareholders are fund managers who themselves collect outrageous pay packets regardless of performance. As the partner in an executive search firm put it: "If an asset management firm is paying their CEO these kinds of numbers [between $12m and $15m at the top end, when the median CEO pay in the S&P 500 is $8m-$10m] they can't question pay at any other company." A spokeswoman for the High Pay Centre in UK added that asset management executives "benefit from a high pay culture and either don't see anything wrong with excessive executive rewards or don't challenge them. This is why we have argued that shareholders alone are not capable of holding companies to account over pay."[47] In other words investors, savers, pensioners and not infrequently taxpayers are held to ransom by a crony capitalism whose beneficiaries are effectively insulated from the consequences of failure that ordinary people must bear. No wonder commentators speak of the "culture of entitlement" that pervades the financial sector...

Complaint: The solace of the powerless and a way of life for readers of *Which?* magazine:

Many complaints are really part of the struggle between one vested interest and another (for example the recent dispute between traditional taxis and the upstart firm of Uber.) Others seem to assume a supportive constituency which probably does not exist. For example some Edin-

---

46 Ferdinand Mount: *Mind the Gap* (Short books, London, 2004) P. 30. The figures cited for Reuter are from the same.

47 See an article in the *Financial Times*, 19th May, 2014 by Madison Marriage: "Asset management executive pay soars."

burghers complained about a „Festival Erotique" in the city; its perform-ances were competing with those of the renowned Arts Festival, the G-strings of which are traditionally heard rather than seen.

It was pointed out however that sex was always much bigger in Edin-burgh than the arts. Indeed, a survey of 1842 revealed that the city had 200 brothels. Their busiest time of the year was during the annual meet-ing of the General Assembly of the Church of Scotland.

"What is a complaint?" asks Pascal Bruckner, and answers his own question by saying it is "the degraded version of revolt, the essence of democratic talk in a society that allows us to foresee the impossible (for-tune, fulfilment, happiness) and invites us never to be satisfied with our lot… For certain people, complaining is a way of life and true old age, that of the spirit, starts (whether at the age of 20 or 80) when one is no longer able to communicate with others   except by complaints and grumbling — when deploring one's life, defaming it, it lingers on as the best means of doing nothing to change it."

"I could not have any profession in this world unless I was paid for my dissatisfaction" wrote the Austrian journalist and novelist Joseph Roth.[48] This seems also to be the case for City of London traders who are perpet-ually resentful, despite their huge remuneration, because someone else on the trading floor is getting more then they are. Sometimes this boils over into open rebellion, as with the barrow boy who was recklessly em-boldened by string of successful deals to take it out on his supervisor, whom he regarded as an overpaid and under-tasked slob. Accordingly he swaggered over to the said supervisor, jabbed his finger at him and shouted *"Why are you such a fat bastard?"* *"Because,"* said the supervi-sor, *"every time I fuck your wife, she gives me a biscuit."*

Consciousness: "I think, therefore I am. I think."[49]
A Professor Eagleman has written a book demonstrating to his own sat-isfaction (says *The Spectator*) that humans are no more than "bacteria." Evidently we're just a bundle of neurophysiological phenomena that (pre)determine our actions.

---

48 Pascal Bruckner: *The Temptation of Innocence: Living in the Age of Entitlement* (Algora Publishing, New York, 2000 – No translator cited), P. 35.
49 Part of George Carlin's comic routine.

The difficulty with this thesis is that it cannot account for *consciousness* (not even chimpanzees spend time, like philosophers, discussing whether they exist or not.) If humans are really like bacteria, and there is no consciousness, neither can there be free will nor moral choice. Philosopher John Gray says "the human mind serves evolutionary success, not truth. To think otherwise is to resurrect the pre-Darwinian error that humans are different from other animals." Yes, yes. But if we *are* no different, how did we hit upon the *idea* that we are?

The reductionism of the bacteria claim is analogous to the Deconstructionist doctrine of "the death of the author," from which it followed (according to Gallic sage Roland Barthes) that all texts are simply *"multi-dimensional space in which a variety of writings, none of them original, blend and clash."* Of course this would also have to apply to Barthes' own writings: since his theory requires that a text lacks the coherence of a single human agency, a Barthes text must presumably also be arbitrary and/or meaningless. Commenting on Barthes' scintillating exposition of *"The Death of the Author"* (1967), the novelist Malcolm Bradbury made the observation that *"Barthes nevertheless seemed to recognise the role of the author when it was time to collect his royalties."*

Conservative: "A statesman who is enamoured of existing evils, as distinguished from the Liberal, who wishes to replace them with others."[50]

St Joseph of Copertino (1603-1663): Puglian monk known as the "Flying Friar" on account of his prodigious feats of levitation:

Norman Douglas in *Old Calabria*[51] gives us a vivid picture of San Giuseppe, the versatile Conventual Franciscan monk who so impressed visiting celebrities with what may literally be described as his "flights of rapture." Father Rossi, Joseph's indefatigable biographer, relates numerous examples of these, including one that took him to an olive tree, on which he "remained in a kneeling posture for the space of half an hour. It was marvellous to see him swaying slightly on a branch, as though a bird had alighted on it." At an audience with Pope Urban VIII, when kissing

---

50 Ambrose Bierce: *The Devil's Dictionary* (1911).

51 Norman Douglas: *Old Calabria* (1915). The references here are to the Penguin Edition, 1962, Pp. 81-89. See also the *Oxford Dictionary of Saints* compiled by David Farmer (Oxford University Press, Fifth Edition revised, 2011, Pp. 245-246.

the papal feet, "he was raised ecstatically into the air and remained hovering until called down by his Franciscan superior." In the church at Fossombrone he detached himself from the altar "with a cry like thunder and went hither and thither about the chapel like lightning and with such impetus that he made all the cells of the dormitory tremble, so that the monks, issuing thence in consternation, cried 'An earthquake! An earthquake!' " At Grottella he helped workmen raise a Calvary Cross thirty-six feet high by lifting it "as if it were straw" from his hovering position. Ten men had previously failed to shift it.

Sometimes he took passengers, says Douglas, if such a term may properly be applied, once seizing the Confessor of the convent by the hand and raising him into the air and drawing him along, turning him round and round in a *violento ballo*, "the Confessor moved by Joseph, and Joseph by God." On another occasion he induced a flock of sheep to enter the chapel; "while he recited the litany, it was observed with astonishment that the sheep responded at the proper places to his verses, he saying Sancta Maria and they answering '*Bah!*' after their manner."

That was but the half of it. Rossi and other reliable biographers tell us that Saint Joseph multiplied bread and wine, which was an enormous help with the groceries, calmed a tempest, drove out devils (very prevalent in Calabria), caused the lame to walk and the blind to see. Moreover he was everywhere and always accompanied by two guardian angels. However "like all too many saints," writes Douglas, "he duly fell into the clutches of the Inquisition, ever on the look-out for victims, pious or otherwise." It accused him of "drawing crowds around him like a new Messiah through prodigies accomplished on the ignorant who are ready to believe anything" (such as the virgin birth and the resurrection, perhaps?)

Here San Giuseppe deserves every sympathy, especially because he seems to have been illiterate and had to rely on his simple piety to counter the sophisticated witch-hunting of the hierarchy. He later became known as the patron saint of those taking exams, as when he was put to the test, he was miraculously only asked questions that he knew the answer to, something that can happen even today at colleges where the students have paid rather high fees for their courses. Douglas says, not unkindly, that he may have been simple-minded too (he was known as 'the Gaper' in his youth because he went around with his mouth open), but this was not uncommon with Southern Italian saints. Modern physicians, pursues Douglas, would probably describe the more exotic of them as exhibiting symptoms of *gynophobia, glossolalia* or *demono-mania*. Like St Francis himself, he sometimes stripped naked in front of the crucifix, exclaiming *"Here am I, Lord, deprived of everything!"* If anything, this raised the suspicions of the Inquisition even further....

Nor did it like the fact that St Joseph acquired something of a fan club over the years. He was admired and consulted by eight cardinals, Prince Leopold of Tuscany, the Duke of Bouillon, Prince Casimir of Poland, Isabella of Austria, the Infanta Maria of Savoy and the Duke of Brunswick, the last named being converted from Lutheranism after witnessing one of Joseph's flights.

St. Joseph of Copertino (1603–1663), the patron saint of aviators, doing a spot of levitation.

It is touching to learn that Joseph managed a short levitational spin the day before his death on the 18th September 1663 at the convent of Osimo, where he had been confined by the authorities in order that his flying "should not be disturbed by the concourse of the vulgar." What they actually meant, of course, was that he was becoming a bit of an embarrassment to the establishment, as happened with Padre Pio in the twentieth century.[52] Miracles and levitation were all very well in their way, but they should not become a distraction from prayer and obedience to the church, which mostly had less spectacular entertainments to offer.

---

52 "Padre Pio" (Francesco Forgione, 1887–1968) was a Capuchin monk from Benevento who apparently received the stigmata in 1911. He attracted an immense popular following (like St Joseph of Copertino). Exhaustive examination by doctors and Vatican officials confirmed that, like St Francis of Assisi, he did indeed exhibit the wounds of the stigmata on his body. He was canonised as Pius of Pietreicina in 2002 after no less than 104 volumes of evidence had been assembled for his cause. See footnote 37, the *Oxford Dictionary of Saints*, Pp. 364-365.

After 90 years he was canonised in 1753. "Some people," writes Douglas, "will be inclined to detect the hand of Providence in the ordering of the event as a challenge to Voltaire, who was then disquieting Europe with certain doctrines of a pernicious nature."

Corbynism and Corbynomics: Political theories considered to be outside the Washington, BBC, mainstream press and other establishment consensuses, and therefore held up to ridicule at every opportunity:

The media claim to be astonished at the support shown for Jeremy Corbyn, the radical left-winger who won the Labour leadership in 2015.

Here are six good explanations: **1**. Stephen Hester, having collected millions in shares for failing to turn round the Royal Bank of Scotland, collects another £8.5m for failing to turn round Royal Sun Alliance. **2**. After two months in office, Helge Lund qualifies for a £28m pay-off as CEO of British Gas, when Shell launches a takeover. **3**. Léo Apotheker gets $30.4m for 11 months work at Hewlett Packard, during which his masterstroke is the acquisition of software group Autonomy — the said masterstroke leading to a write-down of $8.8bn. **4**. Alan Fishman toils for seventeen days not saving Washington Mutual and gets $11.6m for his pains, plus a $7.5m hiring bonus. **5**. Bill Johnson spends only one day in the office of Duke Energy before being shown the door with severance worth $44.4m. **6**. Elio Leoni Scoti does not even turn up at Coty because the shareholders don't like the cut of his jib; for those of us who are congenitally lazy,, that seems a congenial way of earning $1.8m. Still, the departing AIG boss *did* turn down the $22m pay-off on offer, magnanimously conceding that his restructuring plan had not been the success he had hoped. *"Given the $189bn government bail-out of his company,"* says Matthew Vincent, who supplies the above figures in the *Financial Times*, *"his shareholders had probably guessed as much."*

Corruption: Method of doing business now universal and endemic:
Many smugly imagine corruption to be a Southern European and oriental phenomenon. But Siemens was fined $1.6 billion by the EU for corruption in 2008 and during his term of office Tony Blair stepped in to kill a prosecution for massive alleged bribery involving British Aerospace and Saudi Arabia. In February 2014 a European Commissioner announced that corruption affected all EU states to such an extent that it was collectively costing over $150bn a year.

The OECD Anti-Bribery Convention was signed by 40 countries in 1997, and half of the signatories (according to Transparency International) *have not instituted a single prosecution*. It's like the Catholic Church and paedophilia before bad publicity and a more image-conscious pope compelled action.

Government procurement, "revolving doors" for officials and politicians, planning permission, even "tips" to doctors for preferential treatment: everywhere the Commissioner looked corruption was rampant — refined and insidious in a country like the UK, crude and vulgarly oriental in the former Communist bloc. The mild-mannered and surprisingly candid George Papandreou told the European Commission in his capacity as Prime Minister of Greece that "the trouble with my country is that it is totally corrupt from the top to the bottom." Nobody in Greece turned a hair — to ordinary Greeks that was simply statement of the blindingly obvious. Likewise the Bulgarians have a saying: "Every country has a mafia. In Bulgaria, the mafia has a country."

Curiously the Commissioner's statement made no mention of the corruption *within the administration* of the EU itself. Perhaps, like the Greeks, she felt the point was too obvious to labour.

In 2012 Glaxo Smith Kline was fined $3 billion for allegedly bribing doctors in the USA (mind you, it's in good pharmaceutical company, Abbott Laboratories, Pfizer and others having clocked up $13 billion in bribery penalties over four years.) The allegations were quite colourful, namely of *"cash payments disguised as consulting fees, expensive meals* [for doctors], *weekend boondoggles and lavish entertainment."* By 2016 GSK seemed to have realised that hiring doctors for "seminars" to "educate" their peers in regard to the very wonderful applications of GSK's drugs was not, after all, so good for its image. It discontinued the practice and may prove to be the Judas sheep that leads all the others using this form of propaganda to give it up. The alternative, apparently, is to employ doctors directly to promote new drugs, it apparently being more conducive to public confidence if everybody knows they are in the employ of the drug firm concerned. Or possibly not, of course.

The next year GSK was arraigned in China for spending lavishly on bribes and perks for the Chinese medical profession, although of course the idea that the Chinese should be concerned about corruption was thought to be a splendid joke, until the present Chinese Premier most inopportunely started an ant-corruption drive. This adventure cost GSK another Rmb3bn ($488m).

After each *débâcle*, the CEO of the company concerned says "lessons have been learned" (but why do you need to learn a lesson that you already know?) And of course the damages that have to be paid are borne by firms not individuals; so ultimately the stockholders and consumers pay the penalties, not the perpetrators. No wonder, then, that the "fines" simply become a cost of doing business (GSK made circa $28 billion dollars from the corrupt or illegal business on which the $3 billion fine was levied.) Moreover there is lavish taxpayer support for criminality. Angry voters had no doubt been viewing with quiet satisfaction the penalties levied over the last few years on bankers and international firms for their various and many misdeeds. BP, according to the US Attorney-General, *"received the punishment it deserved"* when forced into a settlement of $20.8bn for the Deepwater Horizon disaster. She forgot to mention that $15.3bn was tax deductible against profits, so really BP would probably only have to cough up $5.5bn or so. Of Bank of America's $17bn settlement in 2014 for mis-selling mortgages, some $12bn was tax deductible as an *"ordinary business expense"* ("ordinary" is nice.) A year earlier J.P. Morgan's Chief Financial Officer was able to boast that $7bn of his bank's $13bn mortgage settlement was tax deductible. In 2015, Volkswagen's Finance Chief was remarkably upbeat about the $6.7bn cost of fixing 11 million vehicles fitted with illegal devices to conceal their noxious (and cumulatively lethal) fumes. He reckoned it would all be, yes, tax deductible!

Matthew Vincent , who has drawn attention to this in the *Financial Times*, says somewhat satirically, that a democracy such as America's or ours would always of course ensure that the same legal generosity applied to individuals as to powerful companies. So it should be possible for a marginal rate taxpayer to deliberately incur a fine for underpaid tax, use the fine to reduce his taxable income to a lower or zero-rate band — and then perhaps successfully appeal the original penalty. Vincent doesn't quite seem to have grasped the principles on which our capitalism operates, namely that every tax saving for criminally behaving companies needs to be subsidised by the rest of us through higher personal tax, spending cuts or increased government debt. The malefactors have perfected the art of "privatising" gains and "socialising" losses, inclusive of those resulting from fines for criminal activities. Don't understand the jargon? Let me put it more simply: *they commit the crimes, we pay the penalties.*

And anyway, despite periodic outcry, the US Foreign Corrupt Practices Act still allows "facilitation payments", which are bribes by any other name. This may serve to remind us that a lot of big business, as we now definitely know about the banks, is little more than a criminal conspiracy with a legitimate front like *Cosa Nostra*'s laundrettes. *Plus ça change*: in the nineteenth century it was allegedly the novelist Honoré de Balzac who remarked that *"behind every great fortune lies a crime."*[53]

Corruption has an *international* as well as a *national* profile. In lavishly funded international sports bodies it is particularly rife. In 2015 the story broke concerning state-organised drug-taking for Russian athletes; but every one had known about this for years, including the people at the international athletics authority who now made great show of "investigating" the miscreants. Even worse, football's world governing body Fifa,(q.v.), has long been simply a stock exchange for kickbacks, its ineffable Chairman Sepp Blatter evidently believing that he and the organisation would remain beyond the reach of the law, and that the football sponsors had too much to lose to kick up a fuss. Indeed the Fifa representative from Guinea-Bissau, which is 130th in the Fifa world rankings for football (but well up at number 13 in Transparency International's world rankings for corruption), said it would be "blasphemy" not to vote in Sepp for a fifth term of office in 2015. This was because (he did not say) Blatter's system assured a constant flow of cash to countries in regions like sub-Saharan Africa, where there wasn't too much good football going on but there are an awful lot of intermediaries with pressing lifestyle expenses to pay. Eventually the corruption became so blatant that even the greedy and hypocritical sponsors, who finance football on a grotesque scale, began to realise that their "image" was suffering from the vulgar spectacle of Fifa delegates feeding at the trough.

53 Actually no one can find this exact quote in Balzac. However in his novel *Le Père Goriot* may be found the rather more subtle observation that *"le secret des grandes fortunes sans cause apparente est un crime oublié, parce qu'il a été proprement fait"* ["The secret of a great fortune made without apparent cause is soon forgotten, if the crime is committed in a respectable way."] Until the financial meltdown of 2007-8, the bankers and financiers of the developed world were able to rely on this to maintain their respectability.

The ultimate in corrupt practice is that which knows no limits at all — not even homicide or murder — indicating that the corrupt person has become completely mentally isolated from the consequences of his (usually it is his) actions. Of course, in Third World countries nurses steal drugs from hospitals and sell them, teachers don't bother to turn up to take their classes and government officials take bribes. People who live in those parts more or less expect it. But what of the real specialists who will do literally anything to extract money from the system? Paul Collier in his book *Exodus* relates an anecdote about the chief official in a Ministry of Health that had been offered aid money to purchase antiretroviral drugs. He secretly set up his own company to import the drugs, then purchased them for the Ministry from the said company. A nice little earner in itself, you might think. *"But onto this abuse of his public office, he added a dramatic twist: in order to cut costs, the drugs he imported were fakes."* As Collier drily puts it *"The chief official in a ministry of health had so failed to internalize the objective of his organisation as to find mass mortality an acceptable price for personal gain."*[54] Now there's a real player!

Council of Europe: Bulwark of democracy:
After many years of cogitation, the Council of Europe finally got around to condemning the *"crimes of totalitarian communist regimes."* Citing Stéphane Courtois' *Black Book of Communism*, the movers of the motion estimated the victims of Communist ideology at around 100 million, of which 65 million perished or were enslaved in China and 20 million in the Soviet Union.

This official condemnation of barbarism produced an amusing outburst from the left, whose strategy of howling louder about Nazism (25 million victims) every time the numerically far greater crimes of their ideological heroes was mentioned, has finally hit the buffers. As one of the Neo-Communist MEPs pathetically complained, the motion "deliberately failed to distinguish between the ideals of communism and its application by totalitarian regimes" — a distinction which doubtless consoled Communism's 100 million victims as they were ushered into torture chambers or lined up for an almost certain death in the Gulags.

54 Paul Collier: *Exodus: Immigration and Multiculturalism in the 21st Century* (Penguin, 2013), P. 205.

Sustained by the media and pinkish academics, the notion that "Germany was the *only* nation to have committed genocide twice within half a century" has, as they say, been in the DNA of the Left for most of the last 75 years. But Stalin deliberately starved thousands of Ukrainian kulaks to death in the 1930s, and also tried to wipe out the Polish elite by massacring its officer corps at Katyn,[55] plus targeting the Soviet Union's ethnic minorities. (This is quite apart from his other butchery on an industrial scale.) Mao Tse Tung did even better, both during the Civil War and the horrific Cultural Revolution of the 1960s. Not to mention the unbridled killing set in train by his protégé, Pol Pot, who wreaked such havoc in the killing fields of Cambodia....

Left wing persons claim to regard it as "tasteless" to compare statistics of mass murder, at least when you introduce non-Nazi ones. But their assumptions about Nazism and Fascism are of course based on just such comparisons, one half of the comparison being seldom mentioned, or, if mentioned, implicitly extenuated. If it is tasteless to compare, perhaps they should stop doing it.

Credit Default Obligations or Collateralised Debt Obligations (CDOs), Synthetic CDOs, (CDO²), Credit Default Swaps **(CDS):** Financial products, many of them swindles, that were heavily sold from the 1990s to the first years of the new millennium, all of them involving what is euphemistically known as "securitisation":

Lest you should be tempted to think otherwise, the phrase "securitisation" in this context turns out to have nothing to do with the usual meaning of "security". Rather the reverse, in fact, since "securitisation" simply meant transforming illiquid bank loans into tradeable "securities." By the time this had been done, nobody (including those selling them) any longer knew which were the good, bad or indifferent loans involved — that indeed was the object of the exercise. Most of the big banks

---

55 The British Foreign Office tried to cover up this appalling Soviet crime for a good thirty years, even when the excuse of not alienating our wartime ally had long since disappeared. The United States was no better (both governments suppressed official reports by their own agents pointing to Soviet guilt beyond a peradventure.) The British attitude may have been influenced by Soviet spies such as Kim Philby in the FO hierarchy. The American agent not only had his report suppressed by Roosevelt, but found his immense Central European expertise was henceforth redirected towards the hugely important sphere of Samoa...

made massive profits — for a while — through deceitfully selling these "products." The rating agencies often aided and abetted them by awarding the "securities" *investment status*. Charitable bodies, small businessmen, gullible investors and even parts of the banks themselves were all victims of this useful scam. Innocent entertainment may be had by leafing through financial articles written while the scam was in full swing, the respectful tone of which show that the journalists couldn't understand them either — but thought they should write as if they did.

Former Greek Finance Minister and "rockstar economist" Yanis Varoufakis points out that most CDOs carried a Triple-A investment rating and returned 1 per cent above US Treasury Bills. A bank could therefore treat the CDOs as *"no riskier than the money with which they had been bought"* and so used their clients' deposits to buy such products, thus enhancing a bank's profitability without limiting its loan-making capacity. *"The CDOs were, in effect, instruments for bending the very rules designed to save the banking system from itself"* writes Varoufakis. Indeed, since the A-rated CDOs were considered so safe that they were not required to be included in the banks' capitalisation computations, the purchases of them were treated as though the money used for such purchases had remained in the bank: or in other words, the bankers' nirvana had been reached whereby there was an apparently risk-free way to print money and turn it almost instantly into paper profits. Of course Warren Buffett spotted this, and lots of those involved probably sensed it, but Hey! Why spoil the party when the money is rolling in and all those underpaid people in the regulatory authorities mostly had one aim in life, namely to cross the lines and join the money moguls with their Porsches and Ferraris…? The Greek gadfly quotes two economists with a good understanding of what was going on: Keynes in the *General Theory*, who wrote that *"when the capital development of a country becomes the by-product of the activities of a casino, the job is likely to be ill-done."* And Marx, who wrote in *Das Kapital* that *"all nations with a capitalist mode of production are.. .seized periodically by a feverish attempt to make money without the intervention of the process of production."*[56]

56 See Yanis Varoufakis: *The Global Minotaur: America, Europe and the Future of the Global Economy* (Zed Books, London, 2015), Pp. 6-9. The quotes from Keynes and Marx are featured on pages 37 and 49.

Cyberchondria: Exciting new affliction characterised by constant internet searches on diseases one has, might have, or possibly could have in the future, together with anxious perusal of medical risks the doctors have now decided to attribute to what you previously thought was harmless — or even beneficial (e.g. reading on the loo, voting Liberal Democrat, not masturbating etc.):

Reserchers at the Karolinska Institute in Stockholm have devised a "death test" (handily available online at *ubble.co.uk*)[57], which allows people to calculate whether they are likely to keel over in the next five years by answering questions about where they have the misfortune to live, the rubbish they eat and alarming aspects of their hideously unhealthy lifestyle.[58] Apparently walking slowly in middle age is a better predictor of early death than smoking; and living near a main road, railway line, or under a flight path "could" make you fat (though one would have thought that stress "could" also make you thin.) (Far more plausibly, Singaporean researchers, according to the *Daily Mail*, have found that living next door to people richer than your self is bad for your blood pressure.)[59] However unnamed "experts" (which usually means "a man I met in the pub" in this sort of newspaper story) have "warned" (as experts are fond of doing) that doing the death test could induce *cyberchondria*. At any rate the Karolinska Institute is taking no risks. There is a magnificent disclaimer on its website which says the following: "YOUR USE OF THE WEBSITE OR ANY CONTENT ON THE WEBSITE IS AT YOUR OWN RISK. WE SPECIFICALLY DISCLAIM ANY LIABILITY, WHETHER BASED IN CONTRACT, TORT, STRICT LIABILITY OR OTHERWISE, FOR ANY DIRECT, INDIRECT, INCIDENTAL, CONSEQUENTIAL, OR SPECIAL DAMAGES ARISING OUT OF OR IN ANY WAY CONNECTED WITH ACCESS TO OR USE OF THE WEBSITE OR THE CONTENT ON THE WEBSITE INCLUDING, BUT NOT LIMITED TO, THE RISK CALCULATOR."[60]

In other words, if you have a heart attack once you've calculated the results of your death test, don't blame us.

57 Actually UbbLE, with ULE standing for UK Longevity Explorer (and the bb standing for...er...something else.)

58 Report in *The Telegraph*, 4th June, 2015.

59 Alexander Chancellor in "Long Life," *The Spectator* 6th June, 2015, quoting *The Daily Mail*.

60 See: httpi//www.ubble.co.uk

Cynic: An idealist's description of a realist:

According to the *Oxford Classical Dictionary*, both Alexander the Great and Jesus Christ have in the past been defined by scholars as Cynics.

Some unduly censorious people condemn attitudes as "cynical" (undesirable in their eyes) which are merely prudent. For example it is surely sensible to follow the maxim "be nice to people on the way up as you will meet the same people on the way down" (good advice for ambitious businessmen or politicians in particular.)

Other definitions of cynicism are perhaps more questionable (e.g. "no man in his heart is quite as cynical as a well bred woman;" or "why be difficult when, with a little more effort, you can be bloody impossible.")

Sometimes unfortunate truths are pejoratively labelled as cynical (e.g. "the world is full of willing people; some willing to work and the rest willing to let them.")

Probably it all depends on your basic outlook on life. As the saying goes "any virtue can be made a vice with practically no effort at all."

D

Darfur: Killing fields in Western Sudan from 2003, where the slaughter was "not genocide," until it could no longer be denied that it was:

Writing in 2006, journalist Mark Steyn pointed out that the good people of Darfur had been spared the "cowboy unilateralism of Bush", only to fall "under the care of the liberal-approved multilateral compassion of the UN. After months of expressing deep concern, grave concern, deep concern over the graves and both deep and grave concern over... etc., Kofi Annan persuaded the UN to *set up a committee* to look into what was going on in Darfur."

Whatever was going on, the committee reported back, *it wasn't genocide*. That was great news for the Darfurians, who doubtless began to feel a lot better about their plight. It was just a statistical quirk that so many of the corpses seemed to come from the same ethnic groups (black Africans). Meanwhile an Editorial in the Egyptian newspaper *Al-Gomhouriya* complained of western propaganda claiming genocide and 400,000 dead in Darfur. Actually, it said, a mere 200,000 had died and not from genocide at all, but simply from common or garden war crimes. *Danke für Ihre wertvolle Ergänzung, Al-Gomhouriya!*[1]

In 2004, Colin Powell, the US Secretary of State did indeed refer to the killings in Dafur as "genocide." The Arab Janjaweed militia targeted ethnic blacks, a specialty being mass rape (even of young children) as a

---

1 *"Thank you for your valuable contribution."* This is a lethal formulation used typically by the Chairman of a German academic committee when a participant has offered a spectacularly dumb and inappropriate comment.

deliberate tactic of total degradation of a non-Arab minority. The Janjaweed (the name means "mounted militia") were about as primitive even as anything thrown up by Arab Africa to date and were supported by the Sudan government in Khartoum, which in turn was liberally supplied with arms by the Chinese. The situation was complicated by the large number of political groupings, ethnicities etc. involved (up to 36 different tribes), so that some twelve of these took part in the early peace talks (which others boycotted.) Political and ethnic struggles were intertwined and peacekeepers (from the African Union or the UN) were often as much at risk from random attacks as anybody else. All this is happening although virtually each group involved is Muslim and there has been intermarriage between the Africans and Arabs here for generations.

In 2005 the Genocide Intervention Fund and the America Progress Action Fund, whoever they are, compared coverage of Darfur with other events featured on US television news. Although casualties in Darfur were by then thought to be pushing the 400,000 mark, Tom Cruise's announcement of his engagement got *twelve times* as much coverage as Darfur and Michael Jackson's trial on charges of child abuse got *fifty times* as much. There were no "western victims" to make a good headline. A year earlier, the killing of eight white tourists by Rwandan guerrillas got about the same coverage as the deaths of *tens of thousands* in Sudan over the whole year. "If television does not cover the genocide in Sudan," concludes the GIF report, "it does not exist in the minds of many Americans." [2]

At least it was reassuring that a Sudanese minister was charged by the International Court at The Hague with 51 war crimes. However Ahmed Haroun felt he had been singled out unfairly and said that he "did not *feel* guilty." He was, after all, the "Minister for Humanitarian Affairs."

Frances Day: Bisexual platinum blonde bombshell with unrivalled sexual skills:

American-born Frankie Schenk, later Frances Day, began performing in speakeasies while in her mid-teens. When she went to England in 1925, she created a sensation in West End nightspots by performing in a G-string with only an ostrich fan for cover. The writer George Bernard

---

2 Information from: Nick Davies: *Flat Earth News* (Vintage Books, London, 2009) Pp. 151-152.

Shaw was said to be enamoured of her (although actually she began to pursue him —he being a sprightly 92 and she 41.) She was also rumoured to have had liaisons with Marlene Dietrich and Tallulah Bankhead.

Frances D

"Little man you've had busy day" was a saccharine 1930s hit sung *inter alia* by Gracie Fields and Paul Robeson, but Frances Day's image was not quite as wholesome as theirs. She had an affair with Anthony Eden (yes, really!), and cut a swathe through the royal family, managing to harpoon the Prince of Wales, his brother and even Lord Mountbatten, who

Frances Day in sultry pose (she pursued George Bernard Shaw when he was 92 and she was 41).

was anyway AC/DC. Eleanor Roosevelt wrote her a love letter. "To put it in army terms," said the actor John Mills, "she sported the largest pair of Bristols it had ever been my pleasure to set eyes on."

Her energy between the sheets was legendary. When she turned up late and dishevelled for a morning rehearsal of one of his revues, Bud Flanagan wagged a finger at her: *"Little Day, you've had a busy man…"*

Death: The elephant in the room: *"Most things may never happen: this one will…."*[3]

Pascal says: *"The last act is tragic, however happy the rest of the play is; at the last a little earth is thrown upon our head, and that is the end for ever."*

And Horace says: *"Omnes eodem cogimur"* ("we are all driven to the same end"), a line inscribed on the Capri tombstone of the writer Norman Douglas, a modern pagan.

Maurice Saatchi in his book about mortality says *"Some lives leave a mark; others leave a stain."*

3 Philip Larkin

I'm in the terminal lounge of life," writes a friend. "Let's hope the planes have been delayed. I'm not tired of life, but life is tired of me."

Arguably the most romantic evocation of death, decline and decay in English was written about Venice by Robert Browning — who died there in the Ca' Rezzonico (then owned by his son) in 1889. By the 19th century, Venice was established in the minds of the romantics as the city that characterised the fall from greatness of a great seaborne empire, an echo chamber of past glories and present decay. Browning captures it in a cameo set a century earlier, where the forms of the past are still preserved but their substance has vanished. Instead the patricians while away their time in elegant amusements, such as listening to Baldassare Galuppi playing his perfect but curiously sterile *Toccatas* in some noble Palazzo that has seen better days... Somehow it was fitting that Richard Wagner had died six years before Browning in just such a Palazzo on the Grand Canal:

A Toccata of Galuppi's

I
Oh Galuppi, Baldassaro, this is very sad to find!
I can hardly misconceive you; it would prove me deaf and blind;
But although I take your meaning, 'tis with such a heavy mind!

II
Here you come with your old music, and here's all the good it brings.
What, they lived once thus at Venice where the merchants were the kings,
Where Saint Mark's is, where the Doges used to wed the sea with rings?

III
Ay, because the sea's the street there; and 'tis arched by . . . what you call
. . . Shylock's bridge with houses on it, where they kept the carnival:
I was never out of England — it's as if I saw it all.

IV
Did young people take their pleasure when the sea was warm in May?
Balls and masks begun at midnight, burning ever to mid-day,
When they made up fresh adventures for the morrow, do you say?

116

V

Was a lady such a lady, cheeks so round and lips so red, —
On her neck the small face buoyant, like a bell-flower on its bed,
O'er the breast's superb abundance where a man might base his head?

VI

Well, and it was graceful of them — they'd break talk off and afford
— She, to bite her mask's black velvet — he, to finger on his sword,
While you sat and played Toccatas, stately at the clavichord?

VII

What? Those lesser thirds so plaintive, sixths diminished, sigh on sigh,
Told them something? Those suspensions, those solutions —
     "Must we die?"
Those commiserating sevenths — "Life might last! We can but try!

VIII

„Were you happy?" — "Yes." — "And are you still as happy?" —
     "Yes. And you?"
— "Then, more kisses!" — "Did *I* stop them, when a million seemed
     so few?"
Hark, the dominant's persistence till it must be answered to!

IX

So, an octave struck the answer. Oh, they praised you, I dare say!
„Brave Galuppi! that was music! good alike at grave and gay!
„I can always leave off talking when I hear a master play!"

X

Then they left you for their pleasure: till in due time, one by one,
Some with lives that came to nothing, some with deeds as well undone,
Death stepped tacitly and took them where they never see the sun.

XI

But when I sit down to reason, think to take my stand nor swerve,
While I triumph o'er a secret wrung from nature's close reserve,
In you come with your cold music till I creep thro' every nerve.

XII

Yes, you, like a ghostly cricket, creaking where a house was burned:
„Dust and ashes, dead and done with, Venice spent what Venice earned.
„The soul, doubtless, is immortal — where a soul can be discerned.

XIII

„Yours for instance: you know physics, something of geology,
„Mathematics are your pastime; souls shall rise in their degree;
„Butterflies may dread extinction, — you'll not die, it cannot be!

XIV

„As for Venice and her people, merely born to bloom and drop,
„Here on earth they bore their fruitage, mirth and folly were the crop:
„What of soul was left, I wonder, when the kissing had to stop?

XV

„Dust and ashes!" So you creak it, and I want the heart to scold.
Dear dead women, with such hair, too — what's become of all the gold
Used to hang and brush their bosoms? I feel chilly and grown old.

Deceit: A business plan:

As the consumer society expands, so too do the opportunities for deceit. Assiduous readers of *Which?* consumer magazine will be wearily familiar with the litany of complaint to be found in its pages regarding sharp practice in almost every sphere, hardy perennials being energy bills, mobile phone tariffs, insurance or banking swindles and food products. The last-named seem to inspire scams of almost comical ingenuity. Manuka honey from Australia and New Zealand costs between ten and twenty times as much as ordinary honey at £45 a jar and as much as 10,000 tonnes of purported Manuka is sold worldwide. Yet New Zealand only produces 1,700 tonnes a year, although the UK alone supposedly consumes 1,800 tonnes of the stuff.

Or how about the common practice of adding lots of water to things like chicken and scallops to bulk up a product sold by weight? Then there is the venerable scam of reducing the content but not the price, which effectively conceals a price *rise*. The simpering ads for Cadbury's Roses portray them as an ideal way of saying thank you. But purchasers are unlikely to say thank you to the ruthless American owners of the brand (the same who promised to keep open the iconic Cadbury's factory in Bristol when negotiating their takeover of the firm — and promptly closed it when the deal was done.) In May 2015 it was reported that tubs of Cadbury's Roses chocolates were being shrunk *for the fourth time in as many years*. Their capacity was reduced from 753g to 729g, while the price was unchanged. In 2010 the Roses were being marketed at 975g a tin.[4] No doubt the accountants are delighted at this simple method of flattering the bottom line.

There is fake cheese on pizzas, basmati rice that isn't, olive oil from Spain passed off as the more prestigious product from Italy, fish that isn't the species it advertises itself to be, horseflesh disguised as other kinds of meat, or clementine and tangerine juices that are merely orange juice. Last but not least there is a gallimaufry of horrible fabrications by food processors (*"meat emulsion"* anybody?), or additives like bromine in juice or antifreeze and methanol in alcohol.[5] What, for example, might be in the final fishy substance whose originals were caught off Norway, decapitated and gutted, shipped to China for filleting, frozen into 7.5kg blocks and shipped on to South Korea (which has the world's largest cold stores), sold on to wholesale traders, who then sell it on to individual companies, or perhaps other traders in other countries, and perhaps arrives back at Scotland, still as 7.5kg blocks of fish confidently labelled as "cod" before ending up in fish fingers or whatever. According to an article in the *Weekend FT,* the financial consulting firm PwC estimates the value of global trade in food fraud at around $40bn a year — and this much travelled and not very transparent fish product is not infrequently a part of it.[6]

It is important to realise that deceit isn't always the same as illegality — which is why the mega-scam of Volkswagen falsifying the emission tests on diesel cars was such a calamitous departure from routine business deceit. That is organised in collaboration with commercial (and tax)

4 Rozina Sabur: "A not-quite-so-big thank you with Cadbury's Roses" — *Sunday Telegraph*, May 24th, 2015.

5 These examples are taken from the May 2014 issue of *Which?*, but experts say they are the tip of the iceberg and there is far more fraudulent food around than ever gets exposed.

6 See Natalie Whittle: "The fight against food fraud: as complex supply chains provide opportunities for crime, is anything we eat actually what we think it is?" (*FT Weekend*, 26/27 March 2016.)

lawyers, who are busier than ever these days and add a significant cost to the state and business, a cost which is ultimately paid by the rest of us. The task of the lawyer is to ensure apparent compliance with laws, rules and regulations through ingenious devices that in fact evade them. Industry and financial lobbies have fought tooth and nail against government attempts to make consumer choice clear and transparent (e.g. the "traffic light code" showing how much saturated fat, or salt or sugar is buried in a food product, or exposure of the hidden costs in pensions sold by the big providers and other financial products like investment funds.) Sometimes the lobbies present their objections as touching concern for the consumer who might be "confused" by too much information, as if they were not confused by too little; at other times they make vaguely threatening noises about the "cost" of meeting regulation, though it can hardly cost more to put accurate and transparent information on a label instead of the thicket of less informative or abstruse stuff, helpfully set in 6 point type, that is currently there.

Some forms of deceit have become such standard practice that consumers seem to expect them as normal (which of course is what their progenitors intend.) The banks indulge in an endless chicanery of interest rate "offers" designed to draw in customers with a favourable headline rate for a limited period before dumping them on a miserable one and hoping they won't notice. Restrictions are applied preventing existing customers from switching out of one agreement to a better one devised to lure in new punters. Financial advisers, besides taking a substantial commission or fee at a product's point of sale, are discovered to be taking a "trail fee" on the sum invested regardless of whether they perform any further services.

It is true that most of these practices have come under attack in the wake of the 2008 financial meltdown, but Christine Lagarde, head of the IMF, was still complaining in 2014 that the industry has fought reform at every turn; and we can be sure that new devices are in incubation to replace the revenue lost from the old ones. A splendid example surfaced in 2015 whereby shops in airport lounges were found to be pocketing VAT rebates due to travellers. To do this they had to identify those who were travelling outside the EU. They therefore demanded that customers show their boarding cards at the till, successfully implying that this was a legal requirement, when in fact it was a ruse enabling them to pocket VAT rebates belonging to non-EU travellers. After this particular deceit was exposed, people were encouraged by the media to refuse to show their boarding cards in future, whereat the ineffable shop assistants' union, USDAW,[7] bossily warned travellers not to be abusive to their members when doing so. The offending firms issued characteristically bland and mendacious statements full of phrases like "normal practice" and "guidelines," but could not conceal the fact they had been well and truly rumbled.

Democracy: A system of governance consisting largely of bribes being paid for by those who are being bribed:

It is remarkable what cachet the word "democracy" has, so that states which have carefully suppressed all aspects of it incorporate the word in their nomenclature. The German Democratic Republic springs to mind, or a criminal hell-hole like the Democratic Republic of the Congo. Usually, if the word "Democratic" is in its name, the state concerned is not. As Lenin said, "industry is indispensable, democracy is not."[8]

According to *The Economist Intelligence Unit,* 15% of all countries were full democracies in 2010 and 31.7% were flawed democracies. So 11.3% of the world's populations enjoyed the benefits of democracy, such as they are, while 37.1% put up with an ersatz version. But of course assessments like this depend not only on the definition of democracy, but who is doing the defining. For example, the Conservative Hungarian government of Viktor Orbán is fiercely attacked by mainstream American and European politicians for its "authoritarian" nature. It is claimed that the Magyar press is not free (although the best-selling daily paper in Hungary fills almost every issue with vitriolic denunciation of the government), that the judiciary has been tampered with, that jobs in the public sector are exclusively reserved for government supporters (although the same practice followed for years in Greece did not provoke outrage), that the constitution is illiberal (although the constitutional jurist and former German cabinet minister Rupert Scholz describes it as "exemplary" and a clear declaration of allegiance to EU values and human rights),[9] that the

7 Union of Shop, Distributive and Allied Workers.

8 Quoted by Neil Harding in *Democracy: The Unfinished Journey* (Oxford University Press, 1992.)

9 At a book presentation and interview held at the Konrad Adenauer Stiftung, 4th June, 2012 on the publication of *"Gespräche über das Grundgesetz Ungarns"* — www.kas.de/wf/ de 33.31225. Scholz is Emeritus Professor at the Ludwig-Maximilians-Universität, München and a former Defence Minister (CDU).

government is abominably corrupt — and much more. Such criticism might be to a greater or lesser extent justified, but there is a problem: Orbán has twice won two thirds of the Hungarian parliamentary seats in OSCE-monitored elections: so either the electors don't care that they are being oppressed, or they are not as oppressed as the Americans and Europeans claim. Either way most people would indeed put Hungary in the category of a "flawed democracy" and Orbán himself characterises his preferred version of democracy as "illiberal."

But now let's look at America, which presumably imagines itself to be a model of democracy, since it takes it upon itself to lecture others, in this case Hungary, on their democratic performance: in the first decade after 2000, the USA *used torture as a judicial mechanism*[10] (you can be sure we would have heard from vigilant American liberals if there was even a single instance of state-authorised torture in Hungary); the revelations of Edward Snowden have shown that the USA *operates massive and generalised surveillance of its citizens*; US prosecutors often *falsify evidence*, especially against black defendants;[11] there are more than *two million people currently in American jails, 40% of them African Americans, who only make up 13% of the population*; new prisons were erected at the rate of *one every ten days between 1990 and 2005*;[12] from time to time cases emerge of *African-Americans being beaten up by the police or shot out of hand* — and these are only the ones caught on video; some American states still administer judicial murder (for which the official euphemism is *"death penalty"*), which every other democracy of the developed world (including Hungary)[13] has abolished; people spend years on death row and it is almost certain that innocent people are periodically executed; in 2015, after a further couple of massacres, it was revealed that there was a "mass shooting" (i.e. a shooting involving more than ten victims) *every single day* in the USA, although all at-

10 Most notoriously the practice known as *"waterboarding"* used against terrorist suspects, which has been juridically defined as torture, but which law officers in the US administration tried to redefine as permissible. It causes the victim to feel he is drowning.

11 See Bryan Stevenson: *Just Mercy: A Story of Justice and Redemption* (Scribe, 2015) for multiple instances of this.

12 Bryan Stevenson, op cit. See also the review by Raymond Banner in the *Weekend FT*, 7th/8th February, 2015.

13 However Orban, no doubt in an attempt to live up to the high standards of American democracy, has floated the idea of reintroducing capital punishment.

tempts to limit gun possession founders on the American constitution, which US politicians evidently think so superior to Hungary's; the members of Congress and the Senate are beholden *to the vested interests that financed their election campaigns* and are monitored by hordes of lobbyists to see that they stick to the script. Instead of addressing this gross infringement of democratic principles, in 2010 the Supreme Court *sanctioned so-called Super-Pacs*. These are vehicles *for raising unlimited amounts of money for a candidate*,[14] with the laughable proviso that their organisers are not supposed to collaborate directly with the beneficiary (is it any wonder that a survey in 2013 found that Congressmen and Congresswomen were less popular than cockroaches and traffic jams?); then again, an American Appeal Court judge recently ruled in the BP oil spill case that the company should pay out compensation *even to claimants who had suffered no loss or damage* (so much for the rule of law and property rights); *electoral boundaries are openly and regularly gerrymandered*, because the boundaries in some states can be set by politicians (as opposed to an independent electoral commission which operates in the UK and elsewhere); and so on, and on, and on...

American academics claim to be outraged by the new Hungarian constitution (which replaces an incompletely amended Stalinist one). However, as Professor Alan Sked has pointed out, the sacred US constitution privileged slave-owners and helped to cause a civil war. Its three different and staggered elections for the Presidency, the Senate and the House were designed as a patriarchal method of obviating popular majorities, with the resulting unedifying gridlock that we see today. Its Supreme Court, of which the American elite is particularly proud, "allows a handful of politically appointed judges to decide the fate of political issues such as abortions, healthcare, gun control, campaign funding and presidential elections."[15] When the conservative Supreme Court judge, An-

14 In most of Europe election expenses are capped by law, precisely to prevent elections being "bought" by well-heeled vested interests – a basic democratic principle.

15 Alan Sked, Professor of International History at the London School of Economics in a letter to the *Financial Times*, July 2015. The politicisation of the Supreme Court came under the spotlight in February 2016 when Judge Antonin Scalia died and it was openly speculated whether the court could be moved politically to the right or the left, depending on whether the outgoing Democratic or an incoming Republican President made the new appointment. When in Hungary soemthing similar happens, there is orchestrated liberal outrage...

tonin Scalia, died suddenly in February 2016, all pretence that the judges were not politically defined was abandoned as Republicans and Democrats manoeuvred over who would get to appoint his successor. (The same American academics who think this is a wonderful system threw all their toys out of their prams when the current Hungarian government merely decided to fix a retirement age for judges...)

So which is the more *democratic* country: America? Or Hungary?

John Stuart Mill, the great Victorian liberal thought that universal suffrage should be open to all those who were literate and numerate, an opinion that a YouGov poll carried out in 2012 found was still shared by 49% of UK voters.[16] (This result might indicate suspicion of the immigrant vote, since literacy and numeracy are now obviously widespread among the host population by comparison with Mill's time.) But another point made by Mill is more obviously still pertinent: he thought that people should not have the vote unless they paid income tax, because "those who pay no taxes, disposing by their votes of other people's money, have every motive to be lavish and none to economise."[17] As soon as a large block of voters is substantially or wholly dependent on the state for its basic income, it is obvious (at least it is obvious to Conservatives) that they will always vote for higher taxes, which they do not pay, and regardless of the adverse effects that this may have on national productivity and wealth creation. The American colonists shouted "*No taxation without representation!*" The conservative today may think (but not say in public) that there should be no representation without taxation....

In reality the situation is more complex: on the one hand voters of all levels of wealth are susceptible to being bribed with their own money (hence the absurd and self-defeating complexity of the tax codes in developed countries with their innumerable "loopholes" and exemptions.) Envy is too simple an explanation of voting habits and defames modestly off voters who are quite without class or wealth hatreds. The practice of democracy is more akin to what the economist and political scientist Joseph Schumpeter foresaw in the 1940s — "a competition for

16 "Democracy on Trial: What Voters Really Think of Parliament and Our Politicians" presented to the Reuters Institute for the Study of Journalism by Peter Kellner, March 2012.

17 John Stuart Mill: *Considerations on Representative Government* (1862).

power between members of the elite who [are] offering the equivalent of bribes to the electorate."[18]

In his illuminating book[19] on the current state of democracy in the developed world, Philip Coggan points to a number of ways in which democracy has effectively been watered down compared to the Athenian model (exclusive and based on slavery though it was). Participation of all citizens in lawmaking being unworkable on the large scale of a modern country, the principle of representation was evolved, so that we elect a body to govern roughly according to a programme we have approved. Now however decisions are often delegated further ("double delegation") to bodies whose transparency and democratic legitimacy are questionable. This is the issue raised by numerous Quangos (q.v.) and NGOs ("technocratic democracy") operating at home or abroad, supposedly on our behalf or with our money. Its most inflammatory example is the EU, which seems, to Europhobes at least, to epitomise the nightmare of an unaccountable apparat, a monster spewing red tape night and day, impervious to the views of those affected by its decisions, wasteful of our money, seriously corrupt and evasive of democratic accountability.

Just as American democracy is almost disabled by the influence of well-financed vested interests, so in Europe it has increasingly been the well financed lobbies that have ultimately dictated the policies. In Britain the Labour Party attacks the vested interests of business influencing Tory policy, but pretends not to notice the strong vested interests by which it is itself influenced. These have been defined by Janan Ganeesh as "teaching unions and other public service lobby groups of the more-money-less-work variety... municipal government fat cats such as the bureaucrats who out-earn the Prime Minister... tax-funded charities and arts bodies... Whitehall is a vested interest of mesmerising guile and tenacity... Even big businesses have a vested interest in the state. Regulation is rarely fatal to them — they have compliance departments brimming with staff — but it can tie down smaller rivals hoping to erode their market share." All this is merely a more sophisticated Northern European version of something we are inclined to sneer at when crudely manifested in Central Europe and

18 Philip Coggan: *The Last Vote: The Threats to Western Democracy* (Penguin, 2014), P. 7 and quoting Joseph Schumpeter: *Capitalism, Socialism and Democracy* (1942).
19 Philip Coggan op cit. *The Last Vote*.

the warm water states of the EU, namely *clientelismo* ("pork barrel" in the USA). It is democracy of a sort, but not as advertised to the voters.[20] "Democracy," wrote the libertarian James Bouvard plaintively, "must be something more than two wolves and a sheep voting on what to have for dinner."[21] "Under democracy," wrote H.L. Mencken, "one party always devotes its chief energies to trying to prove that the other party is unfit to rule — and both commonly succeed, and are right."[22]

But do the voters actually deserve any better? Winston Churchill once said that "the best argument against democracy is a five-minute conversation with the average voter," whereas we might nowadays be inclined to think that it is five minutes conversation with the average politician. Still he did admit on another occasion that "democracy is the worst form of government except all the others that have been tried."[23] This is rather a faint cheer for democracy, to be sure. And "what difference does it make to the dead, the orphans, and the homeless," asked Mahatma Gandhi, "whether the mad destruction is wrought under the name of totalitarianism or the holy name of liberty or democracy?" (It makes a difference to the survivors, that's what.) Robespierre said that "terror is only justice: prompt, severe and inflexible; it is then an emanation of virtue; it is less a distinct principle than a natural consequence of the general principle of democracy, applied to the most pressing wants of the country," a point of view that would give heart to "freedom fighters," totalitarians and others who have causes they believe take precedence over morality or humanity. Robespierre's view was the template for the Communist invention of "people's democracies" that lived in a perpetual state of "pressing wants" and paranoia similar to the terror over which Robespierre presided and of which he himself was in the end a victim. This is what happens to democracy once it is decided that the end will justify the means. After all, Robespierre was a model democrat when he said: "Democracy is a state in which the sovereign people, guided by laws which are its own work, does by itself all it can do well, and delegates all that it could not."[24]

20 Janan Ganeesh: "Miliband's tribal loyalties blind him to vested interests," *Financial Times* 17th February 2015.

21 James Bovard: *Lost Rights: The Destruction of American Liberty*

22 H. L.Mencken: *Minority Report.*

23 Winston S. Churchill: *Churchill Speaks: Collected Speeches in Peace and War, 1897–1963.* (Speech in the House of Commons, 11 November 1947).

24 Quoted in Philip Coggan, op cit. P. 65.

"The whole dream of democracy," wrote Gustave Flaubert, "is to raise the proletarian to the level of stupidity attained by the bourgeois." And H.L. Mencken said "Democracy is a pathetic belief in the collective wisdom of individual ignorance."[25] Elsewhere he remarked that "democracy is the theory that the common people know what they want and deserve to get it good and hard."[26] All such remarks, like Churchill's quoted above, lay stress on the putative unfitness of the people at large to decide their own fate sensibly, but the point of democracy is firstly that no one necessarily knows what is most sensible for all the people, and secondly, even if they did know, that is irrelevant to the right of the people to decide otherwise. The most glaring weakness in democracy is its tendency to obscure the notion of "moral hazard," with the sort of consequences that were seen when the financial sector was absolved from moral hazard by unscrupulous and incompetent governments in the period leading up to the financial crisis of 2008. Just as leaders like to blur distinctions of responsibility for the disasters they have caused, so the voters have forgotten by Friday that they are at least partly responsible for the presently disastrous policy they voted for on Monday. A politician who wants their vote is not about to remind them.

It is widely proclaimed that the basis of democracy, beyond free and genuine elections, is compromise and consensus. Contrary to what many seem to assume, the two are not identical. A compromise is an agreement hammered out between two or more parties and is required even in the cabinet of a government consisting of a single victorious political grouping. Consensus ("general or widespread agreement")[27] may not even be on the table (for example if a majority of voters want the return of the death penalty, but no party is offering that.) Consensus may also be an insidious form of propaganda: for example "metropolitan liberals" who exercise a kind of hegemony over large swathes of the American press and organisations like the BBC or the German broadcasters, often act as if it was self-evident what the "mainstream" or "consensus" view was on any given issue and they were the guardians of it. They are continually surprised when the "mainstream" seems to have flowed elsewhere. Conversely the right-wing media (Fox News, Rush Limbaugh,

25 H. L. Mencken: *Notes on Democracy*.
26 H. L. Mencken: *A Little Book in C Major*
27 The definition in *Collins English Dictionary*, 21st Century Edition.

the Murdoch press in the UK) instinctively feels it represents the "silent" or "moral" majority. It is likewise taken aback when it turns out that many conservatives turn out to be more liberal in their views (on homosexual marriage, say) than expected or assumed.

More importantly "consensus" may not be as inherently desirable as it is presented (and manipulated). Mrs Thatcher put this point with her usual forcefulness: " [Consensus is] the process of abandoning all beliefs, principles, values, and policies in search of something in which no one believes, but to which no one objects; the process of avoiding the very issues that have to be solved, merely because you cannot get agreement on the way ahead. What great cause would have been fought and won under the banner: 'I stand for consensus?'" Consensus as a lazy line of least resistance and a reluctance to face unpleasant realities is widespread in democracies and often encouraged by people who fear that realist attitudes (rather than fudge) are likely to end by making demands on their moral, or even physical, courage. "In order for evil to triumph," said Edmund Burke, "it is sufficient for good men to do nothing."

On the other hand, the success of democracy being dependent on voluntary suspension of absolute freedoms for the sake of political stability and social harmony, it is better to treat it pragmatically. It is, after all, messy, unpredictable and open to abuse. As the American anarchist Edward Abbey has ominously remarked: "Anarchism is democracy taken seriously." *See also*: **M: *H. L. Mencken***

Wendi Deng: Becky Sharp, Chinese version:
The feisty ex-wife of Rupert Murdoch, who famously delivered a karate blow to his cream-pie assailant during a hearing of the Commons Select Committee, finally tired of the old bruiser in 2013. Her career is an impressive example of unstoppable upward mobility.

The sometime waitress in a Los Angeles noodle parlour was born Deng Wen Ge (邓文) (the appellation "*Wen Ge*," given her by her true-believing Communist parents in Eastern China, means „Cultural Revolution," but was perhaps chosen more as a matter of prudence than fashion. (Even London's dreariest metropolitan drones would probably baulk at calling their kids "Diamond" or "Jubilee.")

Wenge hitched a ride out of China with an American couple, bedded, then wedded the husband and eventually made it to Yale Business School; thence to the Murdoch empire, finally lassooing the boss. When the by now fragrant thirties something Wendy married the septuagenarian Murdoch on his yacht it was the stuff of fairytales. Unfortunately it all went belly-up with rumours of temper tantrums and "elder abuse," plus an alleged toe-curling passion for Tony Blair expressed in fragrant Chinglish ("*Because he is so so charming and his clothes are so good. He has such good body and he has really really good legs Butt ... And he is slim tall and good skin. Pierce blue eyes which I love. Love his eyes. Also I love his power on the stage ... and what else and what else and what else…*").[28]

Still, she has travelled a long way from the sort of world where a contestant in a dating-show on Chinese television can be recorded as saying with disarming candour that she'd "*rather cry in the back of a BMW than smile on the back of a bicycle.*"

Lord Denning: Folksy judge with foot-in-mouth problem:
Standing out amidst the barnacled splendour of the British judiciary, Lord Denning was much admired for his avuncular wisdom and fearless pursuit of equal justice for the poor man in his council house as for the rich man in his castle. "I would rather search for justice than for certainty" was one of his more Delphic observations, one which admittedly seemed to take a rather cavalier approach to boring formalities such as evidence and proof.

All agreed that he was an amusing fellow and unusually irreverent for a judge. He once began an address by saying: "The House of Commons starts its proceedings with a prayer. The chaplain looks at the assembled members with their varied intelligence and then prays for the country." Unfortunately Denning's concern for the

Lord Denning: "This is a case of a barmaid badly bitten by a big dog..."

dignity of the legal system eventually overcame his devotion to justice, let alone certainty. He was dead against the first appeal of the wrong-

28 This according to a hatchet job in the American magazine *Vanity Fair*.

fully convicted „Birmingham Six" (accused of IRA terrorism) on the curious grounds that, if it succeeded, it would undermine the reputation of both the judiciary and the police so much that „every sensible person in the land would say 'It cannot be right that these actions should go any further!'" Or at least every member of the Garrick Club would say that.

After the judgement against the Six had not only been overturned, but exposed as a gross miscarriage of justice, he mused nostalgically that it would never have come to this in the good old days, because the Six would have been hanged before the appeal ("If they'd been hanged, they'd have been forgotten and the whole community would have been satisfied.")

"It is better," he once observed, "that some innocent men remain in jail than that the integrity of the English judicial system be impugned."

Well, it's a point of view. As Norman Douglas put it, justice is too good for some people and not good enough for others.[29]

Deprivation: Not getting what you want (or not wanting what you get): "*Deprivation is for me what daffodils were for Wordsworth,*" said the poet Philip Larkin — and indeed there is a good deal more deprivation than there are daffodils in his poetry.

Creative Destruction: Much quoted phrase coined by Austrian economist Joseph Schumpeter which draws attention to the fact that economic progress involves destroying old industries as you create new ones:

Schumpeter stressed that capitalism was dynamic, rather than static. Indeed it is continuously "in turmoil," which is why it works (not for everybody it would seem.) This is a problematic notion for all who believe there is an ideal state of affairs that can be achieved and rested upon once you have the right recipe. As Alan Wolfe has written "Maybe we expect too much from democracy. The economist Joseph Schumpeter, one of the great modern thinkers to address the question, certainly thought so. Eighteenth-century optimists believed that there was such a thing as the common good, that people could determine it for themselves, and that they would then elect representatives to carry out their will. This "classical theory of democracy," as Schumpeter argued in

29 Norman Douglas: *An Almanac* (1945).

1942, was more a quasi-religious expression of hope than an actual description of how democracies worked. There is no such thing as the common good, he delighted in pointing out. And even if there were, ordinary citizens, including the more educated among them, would be too irrational in their desires and too easily fooled to know what it might be. In theory democratic citizens raise and decide issues. In practice, "the issues that shape their fate are normally decided for them."[30]

See also under **S: *Stone Age*.**

The Queen of England's Diamond Jubilee: Opportunities for monarchical gliding:

We learn from *The Economist* (Jan 28, 2012) that the Queen, when celebrating her Diamond Jubilee at garden parties etc., was "careful to choose bright colours and small-brimmed hats" as she glided through crowds "like a liner." And seemingly she never, ever tired. "Oh look! She's keeled over again," she once noted at a stiflingly hot palace reception, spotting her then Prime Minister Margaret Thatcher pale and slumped in a chair." Mrs Thatcher, who once swept out of Downing Street and announced to bemused hacks that "*we* are a grandmother," was reportedly "not amused" to hear of this quip. The genuinely royal "*we*" of course never "keels over," still less "slumps". *We* are either gliding like a liner, or not gliding today.

We also exhibit admirable candour within the rather narrow limits of authenticity that our position allows us. For example, it is said (I cannot confirm it, as *we* never comment on such matters) that *we* once struck the word "*very*" from our speech containing the sentence: "I am very pleased to be back here in Birmingham." *We* were indeed pleased, but not *very* pleased.

Dear Diary: Or in this case, Woodrow Wyatt's misdirected libidinous thoughts:

A lively entry in Wyatt's published diary describes a lustful meeting with Bianca Jagger, as follows: *"She is full of sexual vitality... she grasped my wrist and arm and got her sexuality on me ... she must be like an octopus to go to bed with, wrapping her legs around you."*

---

30 Alan Wolfe: „Democracy Without Accountability" in *Does American democracy still work?* (2006).

The effect of this (a)rousing passage is only slightly diminished by a publisher's note at the bottom of the page, which reads: *"WW refers to a meeting with Bianca Jagger which we now learn did not in fact take place. He mistook someone else for her. We apologise to Ms Jagger for any embarrassment caused."*

Emily Dickinson: The silent minority:
A poem by Emily Dickinson seems apposite to our times (think: "global warming" or "climate change" hysteria.)

> *Much Madness is divinest Sense —*
> *To a discerning Eye —*
> *Much Sense — the starkest Madness —*
> *'Tis the Majority*
> *In this, as All, prevail —*
> *Assent — and you are sane —*
> *Demur — you're straightway dangerous —*
> *And handled with a Chain —*

Dinner: A risky business:
For example a dinner described in Sir Harry Luke's beguiling work *The Tenth Muse* may remind habitual diners of challenging experiences: *"If the soup had been as hot as the claret, the claret as old as the bird, and the bird had had the breast of the parlour-maid, it would have been a damned good dinner…"*

The deficiencies of Luke's dinner remind one of the woebegone comment of General de Gaulle after a particularly punishing English meal in wartime London: *"Les Anglais ont beaucoup de réligions, mais seulement une sauce."*[31]

31 Most anthologies of quotations attribute the original version of this remark to the Sicilian Admiral and Royalist turned Republican Francesco Caracciolo (1752-99) who said or wrote: *"There are in England sixty different religions and only one sauce."* A similar remark is said to have been made more than once by Voltaire. Visitors from countries with refined cuisines have obviously suffered from English "cooking" across the centuries. One must excuse Caracciolo's animus against the English: under their auspices he was condemned in a kangaroo court for his betrayal of the Neapolitan Bourbon King, and hung from a ship's yardarm, his corpse being thrown into the sea at sunset.

Nubar Gulbenkian, the mildly eccentric Armenian millionaire and gourmet, had another take on dinner: "The best number for a dinner party is two," he said. "Myself and a damn good head waiter."

Nubar began his career working without pay for his famously mean father, Calouste Gulbenkian (Mr Five Per Cent — the percentage being on tsunami-like oil revenues). This arrangement came to an abrupt end in 1939. Nubar liked to have his favourite chicken in tarragon jelly with asparagus tips delivered to the office for lunch and charged it to petty cash. Calouste was enraged by such profligacy and gave orders that his son should pay for his lunch out of his own pocket. In retaliation Nubar sued his father for the *$10 million* he said was owed him as a share of a Gulbenkian subsidiary in Canada. The case cost $84,000, which Nubar claimed represented the most expensive tarragon chicken ever supplied.

Cognitive dissonance: Diplomacy for dullards:
It is distressing, but not altogether surprising, that the perfidious inhabitants of Albion are widely regarded as speaking with forked tongues. Foreigners, especially those who imagine they have a good grasp of English, consequently live in a state of perpetually thwarted communication. To rescue them, a frustrated but determined Hungarian lady has made a chart with three columns, namely *"What the British say"*, *"What the British mean"* and *"What others understand"* (**WBS**, WBM and WOU for short.)

Here are some examples:

WBS: "With the greatest respect…". WBM: "I think you are an idiot." WOU: "He is listening to me."

WBS: "You must come for dinner." WBM: "It's not an invitation, I'm just being polite." WOU: "I will get an invitation soon."

WBS: "That is a very brave proposal." WBM: "You are insane." WOU: "He thinks I have courage."

Likewise an interpreter at Strasbourg supplies some engaging examples of **French Eurobabble**, whose exact meaning will only be apparent to experienced Francophobes:

"Il faut la visibilité européenne (translation: "The EU must indulge in some pointless, annoying and, with luck, damaging international grandstanding.")

"Il faut la solidarité européenne" (*"You* must give *me* some money.").

"*Il fait trouver une solution pragmatique*" ("I am about to propose a highly complex, theoretical, legalistic and unworkable way forward.")

And finally: "*Ma réponse est nette et claire*" ("Fuck off!")

Diversity Training: Fashionable policy of promoting victimhood, appeasing Islamism etc.:

In 2010, a meeting of consumer health activists was held under the auspices of Wiltshire County Council to discuss proposed changes to the NHS. At one point, the Chairperson, a courteous lady of a certain age with a distinguished record of community service, stressed the need for an early press release to prevent premature exposure of their proposals and pre-empt "*the jungle drums*" (as in "*bush telegraph,*" or "*grapevine.*") A lady in the public gallery (who turned out to be from the Wiltshire Racial Equality Council) thereupon made "an official complaint" of racism to the (Conservative) Council, which deliberated in secret, upheld the complaint, barred the meeting's participants from council premises and cut off the group's funding.

This however was not enough for the complainant, who insisted on a "full apology" (she had already received one she deemed inadequate); and also that the whole group should have mandatory "diversity training." New Labour's Equality Law (2010) could apparently be interpreted as saying that the *intention* behind a remark is irrelevant if someone claims to feel offended by it.

But what if the Chairperson was herself offended by being (falsely) branded a racist? Will the law protect her? And what is "racist" about "jungle drums," referring to an efficient means of communication formerly used in Africa? It is hardly derogatory like "Dutch courage" or "French leave", which no one objects to (*not yet*, but doubtless a "diversity" hit squad is working on it). Charles Moore traces the leverage of victimhood by means of claimed "racism" to the Macpherson Report (1999) into the appalling murder of Steven Lawrence by racist thugs in South East London in 1993. While the report by a respected High Court judge undoubtedly forced an "institutionally racist" Metropolitan Police to take a good look at itself and reform many of its procedures, all of which was long overdue, it also promulgated the following doctrine: "*A racist incident is any incident which is perceived to be racist by the victim or any other person.*" Moore points out that if a racist incident is so defined anything can be deemed "racist" simply because someone

134

says so. Moreover since the victimhood in respect of racism is (under this doctrine) self-chosen, "the person alleged by them to be guilty is automatically convicted."[32] This is what happened in the Wiltshire County Council case. Such a doctrine is an open invitation to blackmail, character assassination and intrigue. That a senior judge should openly (if unintentionally) issue such an invitation says quite a lot about the bench's decline in intellectual calibre in recent years.

As for "diversity" dogma, that is rapidly becoming the mirror image of the stupidity and intolerance it purports to oppose. Mostly rural Wiltshire scarcely needs a "Racial Equality Council": the latter should be dissolved and the complainant in the above case should be redeployed as something more useful such as a community police officer.

Dull: Outreach in Perthshire:
From *The Spectator*'s "Portrait of the Year 2012": "In April an attempt by the village of Dull in Perthshire to forge ties with Boring in Oregon met with little interest…"

Slim Dusty: Immortal balladeer of the Australian outback (who nevertheless died in 2003).

In 1958 Dusty astonished the world with a ditty written by one Parsons; in the restrained words of his obituarist, this was to become „an erratically sung bar anthem that gave delight to millions" [of drunks].

"Oh it's a' lonesome away from your kindred and all, / By the campfire at night where the wild dingoes call; / But there's nothing so lonesome, morbid or drear / Than to stand in the bar of a pub with no beer."

A late flowering of Dusty's genius gave us the albums: "Beer Drinking Songs of Australia" and "G'Day, G'Day".

One can, of course, think of something even more „morbid and drear" than a pub with no beer; namely, a London pub on a Saturday night with plenty of beer and urinals awash with vomit. But Dusty is essentially right. Even English pubs that used to purvey a tasteless yellow liquid that claimed to be beer, but which was in fact the "own brand" bitter of the big breweries, have now mostly felt constrained to offer their customers a variety of real ales. Sometimes they even offer palatable food as well. The beerage is not what it was (but then neither is the peerage.)

32 Charles Moore: *The Spectator*, 1 March 2014, "*The Spectator*'s Notes."

E

Eulogy:
*Praise of a person who has either the advantages of wealth
and power, or the consideration to be dead.*

Ambrose Bierce: *The Devil's Dictionary*

Economics: "Extremely useful as a form of employment for economists."[1]

Five things they don't tell you about economics (according to a bookmarker stuck inside Ha-Joon Chang's *Economics:The User's Guide*): 1. 95% of economics is common sense. 2. Economics is not a science. 3. Economics is politics. 4. Never trust an economist. 5. Economics is too important to be left to the experts.

If the views of leading economists on economics are hardly encouraging, that does not seem to have deterred armies of students from studying the subject. "Years ago," writes Nassim Nicholas Taleb (one of the handful of experts who saw the 2008 crash coming), "I noticed one thing about economics, and that is that economists didn't get anything right." And further, in his celebrated book *The Black Swan: The Impact of the Highly Improbable*: "If you hear a "prominent" economist using the word 'equilibrium,' or 'normal distribution,' do not argue with him; just ignore him, or try to put a rat down his shirt."

Economists are however quite a reliable guide (albeit unintentionally) to what is *not* going to happen. In 1981 an impressive 364 of them wrote to *The Times* asserting that Mrs Thatcher's policies would lead to rack and ruin. In fact she pulled Britain's economy out of the slough of despond into which, *inter alia*, the advice of economists had plunged it, and it was soon humming along quite merrily.

---

1 John Kenneth Galbraith

136

In a hilarious re-run of economists' fatuousness *The Independent* ran a headline in 2015 saying that "two-thirds of economists" said the coalition government's austerity programme had harmed the economy. This was a magnificent example of the liberal press's regard for the truth, since it turned out on closer inspection that two thirds *out of 33 economists interviewed* claimed this (admittedly this story was run on the 1st of April). Their judgement came not long after the Chief Economist of the IMF had been obliged to apologise publicly for his previous predictions of economic doom when, contrary to his forecast, the economy returned to growth, despite (or because of) the coalition taking painful but necessary measures to cut the deficit. Then again Eurosceptics were greatly encouraged by a *Financial Times* report of January 4th, 2016 that "most of more than 100 economists thought economic prospects following a Brexit would be hit." "For those of us who were unsure about how to vote," wrote a Mr Howe in a letter to the paper on January 8th, "this is decisive. We must vote to leave, because if such a large number of economists believe this will be injurious to the UK, then we know it must be a good thing...."

Comedian Marty Allen has expressed the layman's view of economics and indeed of life in general: "A study of economics" he writes, "usually reveals that the best time to buy anything is last year."

Edgy: Buzz word favoured by trendy TV executives to talk up comedy or drama likely to cause offence:

"*Edgy*," seemingly suggestive of something at the cutting edge of the genre, tends to be wheeled out to counter possibly well-founded critical scepticism and anticipated viewer resistance to the product. If every third line or so contains an obscenity, the show is also said to be "*creative.*"

"*I had a gothic phase, and now I'm more edgy chic,*" the actress Ashley Benson informs us, but presumably she is referring to her clothes. At any rate her blog does not seem especially edgy — more Gwyneth Paltrow ("*When I pass a flowering zucchini plant in a garden, my heart skips a beat*") than Bette Davis ("*In this business, until you're known as a monster you're not a star*") ...[2]

2 Paltrow is celebrated for her health fads and dippy musings on life and love. Davis, on the other hand, is what you might call edgy, as, for example, in her role as the homicidal nanny in the film of that title (1965)...

Ed Stone: Stone monument featuring vague political pledges which was unveiled by Labour Party leader Ed Milliband in the 2015 election. It was described by a Labour shadow minister as a *"12ft granite, marble cock-up"* (it's limestone, actually and only 8ft 6in-tall.)

The "pledges" on this stone ("a strong economic foundation, higher living standards for working families, an NHS with the time to care, controls on immigration, a country where the next generation can do better than the last, homes to buy and action on rent") were vague enough to give few hostages to fortune and Ed was photographed heroically standing in front of it in a marginal Sussex constituency. Then the stone was destined to be placed in the garden of Number 10 Downing Street, into which Ed hoped shortly to be moving.

Alas! The public reaction to this wizard idea by Milliband's policy supremo consisted chiefly of unrestrained mirth. More to the point, anyone who was a bit cynical about politicians' promises would have had their worst suspicions confirmed by Lucy Powell, the Labour campaign's vice-chair, who said in a radio interview: *"I don't think anyone is suggesting that the fact that he's carved them in stone means he's absolutely not going to break them or anything like that"*. Er... precisely.

After the election, in which unhappily the dire performance of Labour meant that the stone became superfluous to requirements, Labour officials refused to disclose its location. *The Daily Telegraph* contacted 50 masonry firms in an attempt to find it, whilst the *Daily Mail* offered a reward of a case of champagne for its location, and *The Sun* set up a hotline for information. Disrespectful comparisons with the Ark of the Covenant as portrayed in *Indiana Jones and the Raiders of the Lost Ark* appeared in the media

The Ed Stone: "I treat opinion polls with a pinch of sugar..."

138

According to Wikipedia, as of 15 May 2015 the Ed Stone is allegedly in storage inside a garage in South London. "The Labour Party reportedly has two plans for its break-up and destruction: throw the rubble away, or sell Berlin Wall-like chunks to party members to raise money."

Education: An optimist's idea of replacing an empty mind with an open one:

"During the holidays from Eton" was for many years the succinct entry under *"Education"* in the *Who's Who* biography of aesthete and writer Sir Francis Osbert Sacheverell Sitwell (5th Baronet). Winston Churchill was no less encouraging about his alma mater, allegedly accusing its teachers of *"casting sham pearls before real swine"* (the second part of that characterization being perhaps more accurate than the first part.) The point that Sitwell and Churchill were making, however, is that self-education is better than any other form. Moreover the quality and content of education may get overlooked in enthusiasm for quantity. Karl Kraus malevolently remarked that *"a great deal of learning can be packed into an empty head,"*[3] while a leftist conspiracy theorist like Noam Chomsky claims to regard education in America, all of it, as a *"system of imposed ignorance."* The writer Flannery O'Connor, a conservative Catholic from the US south, arrives at a similar verdict from the other end of the ideological spectrum: *"Everywhere I go,"* she said, *"I am asked if I think university stifles writers. My opinion is that it doesn't stifle enough of them. There's many a bestseller that could have been prevented by a good teacher."*

Egalitarian ideology allegedly sacrifices excellence in education on the altar of equality, while those who can afford the best education that money can buy stand accused of pulling up the drawbridge on those who can't. Universal state provision of education, say its critics, has fallen prey to the "creeping power of producer vested interest."[4] The latter is defined as the educational establishment (especially the teachers' unions), disrespectfully known in the UK as "the blob." Supposedly the

---

3 Karl Kraus: *Aphorisms and More Aphorisms* (1909).

4 See: Niall Ferguson: *The Great Degeneration: How Institutions Decay and Economies Die* (based on the BBC Radio 4 Reith Lectures 2012), Penguin Books, London, 2014, Pp. 125 ff. for an account of educational decay through "vested producer interest."

blob doesn't believe in the necessary discipline to instil numeracy and literacy, and regards "free schools" that do as a conspiracy of the privileged against the rest. "*In the free society envisioned by the Founders,*" says US Republican Ron Paul, "*schools are held accountable to parents, not to federal bureaucrats.*" His is a view that has not changed much since Mark Twain wrote: "*In the first place God made idiots. That was just practice. Then he made school boards.*" Later he added: "*I have never let schooling interfere with my education.*"

"*The whole purpose of education is to turn mirrors into windows,*" wrote journalist Sydney J. Harris, forlornly echoing idealistic teachers down the ages; and the behaviourist B.F.Skinner wrote that "*education is what survives when what has been learned has been forgotten.*"[5]

Education in this sense is only of real use to people who are inspired by it to educate themselves for the rest of their lives. For that you certainly need an open mind, but also a critical one that interrogates the information passing through it. "*The aim of totalitarian education,*" observed Hannah Arendt, pre-empting Chomsky, "*has never been to instil convictions but to destroy the capacity to form any.*" This is the likely (but fortunately not always inevitable) result of a liberal ideology in educators that has become mandatory rather than indicative. As Daniel Hannan has pointed out, this approach may even engender the very extremism it is seeking to eradicate: "*Children of immigrant parents in Amsterdam or Birmingham or Copenhagen are taught, from the moment they go to primary school, the liberal nostrums that characterize Europe's state sector: no culture is better than any other, patriotism is dangerous, the nation-state is anachronistic, everything is acceptable except sexist language and Euroskepticism. Is it any wonder that some kids cast around for an identity that seems less insipid?*"[6]

"Grade inflation" in the exam results of the secondary schools and degree course dilution at the universities are also blamed for dumbing down education, both by confusing entertainment with learning and mistaking smug conformity to "correct" ways of thinking and speaking for generosity of spirit. Furthermore competition for students among the rapidly expanded places of higher learning in the second half of the

5 B.F.Skinner: *New Scientist*, 21 May, 1964.)
6 Dan Hannan's contribution to washingtonexaminer.com/they'll-like-us-when-we-win-against-isis/article/2560472 , posted 23 February, 2015.

140

twentieth century has brought with it the temptation to offer alluring but not obviously academic courses ("Introduction to Turntablism" for would-be disc jockeys, "Alien Sex," "How to Watch Television" and subjects cashing in on celebrity culture.) Critics in the UK and USA have derided fatuous degree subjects offered by academic charlatans, the notorious example being a course in "Underwater Basket Weaving" (which in fact never existed, except as a lampoon.)

"Only the educated are free," said the Stoic philosopher and former slave Epictetus,[7] a sentiment unquestioned today, but interpreted materialistically. Education is the passport to professional success and upward mobility. Yet the introverted world of fashionable educationalist dogma is obsessed by process and methodology, as if education were an exact science, not an art depending on dedication, good judgement and charisma. Mr Thomas Gradgrind in Dickens' novel *Hard Times* wanted only to inculcate facts in his pupils, but liberal educationalists value instead self-expression which they interpret as creativity. It would be a mistake to think that either of these approaches was sufficient on its own and even if you combine them you can't assume your end-product will actually use his or her education exactly as we might like. This may have been what Theodore Roosevelt had in mind when he said: "*A man who has never gone to school may steal from a freight car; but if he has a university education, he may steal the whole railroad...*"

Efficient Markets Hypothesis (EMH): a dogma masquerading as a hypothesis:

This damaging fantasy, which has held the minds of many economists and city drones in thrall over the last three decades, maintains (*inter alia*) that prices in the stock market are by definition correct ("fair value") because they exactly incorporate and reflect all relevant information about individual stocks. The so-called "strong" version of EMH even claims that markets instantly update to hidden or "insider" information.[8] Were prices really to be accurate in this sense at any given mo-

---

7 Epictetus (c.55-135 AD) studied philosophy as a slave in Rome, was freed and became a revered teacher of Stoicism. His real name at birth is unknown.

8 The masochistic can view the variations on the theme of Efficient Market Hypothesis on en.wikipedia.org/Efficient-market_hypothesis, although it is quite confusing. The clearest concise definition is given at www.investopedia.com/terms/e/efficientmarkethypothesis.asp

ment, it follows that there is no such thing as an overvalued or undervalued asset, so nobody can ever "beat" the market. Stock market bubbles and crashes must simply be the consequence of sudden changes in investor information that transform yesterday's sure fire thing into today's dud, or vice versa. If either yesterday's price of $100 for a particular share, or today's price of only $10, were to be an *anomaly* (rather than "fair value"), the market would not be efficient — whereas according to EMH it is. All this, of course, is hogwash.

Warren Buffett, arguably the world's most successful investor, had no time for EMH, just as he had no time for other self-serving financial wheezes like complex derivatives which he percipiently described as "financial weapons of mass destruction." In 1984, he pointed out that if "the market" was really efficient at reflecting underlying value, it would indeed be impossible to beat it; yet the most successful money managers were, like him, "value" investors, who spotted undervalued stocks and invested in them long term. By contrast, over the 30 years to 1996, more than two-thirds of professional portfolio managers in the USA *under*performed the S&P 500 Index. What, if anything are we to conclude from this (apart from the fact that most fund managers are as incompetent as they are overpaid?) Certainly not that rational decisions based on accurate information govern investment choices in the way that the EMH would require.

EMH is not untypical of contemporary pseudo-science in that its supposed objectivity conceals a *value judgement* identifiable from the word "efficient." Markets that are *efficient* are presumably more desirable than those that are not, so punters are being offered an explanation of markets that is inherently benign. The word "efficient" thus endows the Efficient Market Hypothesis with an air of authority and respectability, although it doesn't actually say anything other than "markets behave like markets because they're markets." Moreover the subtext of EMH suggests that human behaviour can plausibly be analysed almost entirely in terms of microeconomics, an idea that won the Chicago economist Gary Becker a Nobel Prize in 1992. His award sparked a stream of "me too" articles by economists, such as the one in *Journal of Political Economy* which explained that people commit suicide *"when the net present value of their future utility is negative."*[9] The fact that a "scientific" approach to the

9 Quoted in an article by John Kay in the *Financial Times*, 15 January, 2014, "Economists: there is no such thing as the 'economic approach.' "

markets of this kind is full of assumptions about human behaviour that are mostly wrong is the least of deterrents to the dedicated economic behaviourists. Such "models", as John Kay has pointed out, remain in vogue not because they provide practical answers to problems, but because they provide unequivocal ones and "their supporters attach more importance to universality than relevance. If you criticise [a model's] applications, you will be asked what theory you would use instead."

Actually Becker's Nobel Prize citation showed that he was not being honoured for *solving* a problem but for providing what academics nowadays are much more keen on, namely a *methodology* that might or might not be of any practical use, but which can keep them employed for years to come. "To a man with a hammer," observes Kay somewhat caustically, "everything looks like a nail: but the person useful about the house has a toolbox and selects the implement appropriate to the task."[10] Keynes, he reminds us, thought economics would benefit from being conducted like plumbing or dentistry. As it is, "practical men, who believe themselves to be quite exempt from any intellectual influence, are usually the slave of some defunct economist. Madmen in authority, who hear voices in the air, are distilling the frenzy of some academic scribbler of a few years back."[11]

For the amiable traders of the City of London, one of the beauties of EMH is that it neatly sidesteps consideration of morality, social usefulness or any other criterion of *value* that is not purely monetary. It has been well observed that if farming were organised like the stock market, a farmer would sell his farm in the morning when it was raining, only to buy it back again in the afternoon when the sun came out.[12] The market is a mechanism not a morality; it is merely a reflection of what people are prepared to pay for anything at any given moment. It may be an agency created by humans, but its efficacy, if EMH applies, lies in its being outside the control of the investors it serves. EMH thus begins to look like a dogma constructed out of Oscar Wilde's definition of a cynic,

10 John Kay — See Note 2.

11 John Maynard Keynes: *The General Theory of Employment, Interest and Money* (Macmillan, London, 1936), Chapter 24, "Concluding Notes."

12 Economic journalist Will Hutton, misquoting Keynes, who wrote: *"It's as if the farmer, having tapped his barometer after breakfast, would decide to remove his capital from the farming business between 10 and 11 in the morning and reconsider when he should return to it later in the week."*

one who knows the price of everything and the value of nothing. Even here it fails, because it has to assume that investors (and especially professional fund managers and traders) make rational choices of self-interest based on an intelligent assessment of the information they have. The actual behaviour of markets contradicts this at every turn.

The other attraction of EMH, for those who espouse it, is that it replicates the circular logic exploited by Freud and exposed by Karl Popper, whereby the hypothesis is not falsifiable, since its definition of "efficiency" confirms the theory's premise. Just as Freud could explain to his own satisfaction that a person's denial of an analysis was itself a sign that the analysis was right, so the EMH believer can say that any price is correct because by definition all prices in the market are correct. Any person attempting to challenge the definitions of "efficiency" or "value" implicit in the "hypothesis" can be dismissed as being "in denial" (a favourite accusation of dogmatists masquerading as empiricists.) As the Cardinal Archbishop of Vienna once remarked, "we seem to have forgotten that the market is there for mankind, not vice versa."

The slogan of free marketeers is "let the market decide," as if the latter were the collective embodiment of rational decisions by persons presented with an enticing smorgasbord of options. Unfortunately "the market," at any rate the stock market, consists largely of decisions made by professional investors punting with other people's money, participants who are mostly concerned with short term performance and bonuses (for themselves, of course, not their clients). Governments also invoke the wisdom of the market when wanting to raise cash by privatising state assets. The usual result is that the consumer/investor (as taxpaying citizen) is sold something (s)he already owns, and public monopolies or cartels become "privately owned" ones. The experience with British Rail (which the taxpayer has had to sell, then buy back, and now hugely subsidises in its new incarnation as "Railtrack"), and the utilities, not to mention the multiple swindles euphemistically described as "Private Finance Initiatives," should have put an end to this dogmatic faith in the mystical power of the market. It lives on in the context of PFI and the like because it provides convenient cover for governments wishing to cook the books by moving huge amounts of impending liabilities "off balance sheet."

On a deeper level, the market mirrors the ongoing conflict between the individual's craving for instant satisfaction and his dreams of long

144

term security and contentment achieved through restraint and self-discipline. John Armstrong has observed that "the consequences of a free-market economy are dictated in large part by the quality of desire multiplied by affluence… The better the desire, the more we should want affluence. This cannot be captured in a morally neutral account of desire." In the West, material prosperity has increased as spiritual prosperity declined, so "there is a general disproportion between the material wealth of the West and its capacity to use that wealth for self-actualisation."[13] In other words, we would ideally like the market to assist us in realising our noblest aspirations, but unhappily it is equally finely attuned to our craving for the instant gratification provided by expensive crap.

Eheu fugaces labuntur anni *("Alas! The fleeting years glide by…."):*[14] Discouraging recognition that you're past it made bearable by the contemplation of transient reputations:

Hector Berlioz wrote something in a similarly funebrial spirit to that of Horace, namely that *"Time is a great teacher, but unfortunately it kills all its pupils."*

On the whole it's a melancholy prospect for wannabes of immortality: books by formerly fashionable writers gather dust on library shelves; a black hole has swallowed the music of Tomášek, once the composer most admired in Prague, not least by himself; more than 80 operas by Johann Adolph Hasse, who was called *"il padre della musica,"* and in whose shadow Bach and Händel once languished, have sunk into oblivion; the painter Monticelli, avidly collected in the 19th century, is now dismissed as a mere *"dauber."* The Medici Venus, which poor old Ruskin thought *"one of the purest and most elevated incarnations of women conceivable"* sadly turned out not to be the work of Phidias or Praxiteles after all. (A recent art historical tome rates it *"among the most charmless remnants of antiquity."*) Nowadays people have even been known to ask: *"Who was Perry Como?"* As Dr. Johnson observed of erstwhile prodigies and wonders: *"they mount, they shine, evaporate and fall."*

13 John Armstrong: *In Search of Civilization* (Penguin Books, London, 2010, Pp. 83-84).

14 The opening words of Number 14 in Horace's second book of *Odes.*

American Presidential Elections: Quadrennial auction of the highest office in the United States:

In 2000, the campaigns for the presidency cost over a billion dollars (and another two billion or so for the Senate and Congress races). A particularly grotesque element in this election (apart from the fact that the losing candidate, Al Gore, got more votes than the winner) was the posthumous election of Democrat Mel Carnaham to the Missouri Senate seat (this although he was technically disqualified, as he no longer "lived" in the state).

Only a few commentators, for example Nick Cohen in *The Observer* (UK), were prepared to identify the bottom line in this grotesque and insulting parody of democracy: "You cannot be elected President without the approval of the local business mafias. Successful candidates take their bribes — sorry, campaign donations — of about 1.5 billion dollars and promote their interests in office. Half the electorate does not bother to vote. Two million people in prison, most of whom seem to be black, cannot vote. The candidate with the most votes does not win. The dead are elected to the Senate while the living are disenfranchised."

The unfortunate Johnny Chung, who funnelled illicit donations from Red China to Bill Clinton's last campaign, seems to have had a realistic assessment of the "democratic process" in America. Up before the beak for illegal campaign contributions, he explained: "I see the White House like a subway — you have to put in coins to open the gate."

Notwithstanding all this, it is rather amazing how people pop out of nowhere to become President of the United States of America. As comedian George Carlin puts it: "In America anyone can become President. That's the problem."

United States Electoral College: Archaic electoral system originally designed to protect the interests of the slavocracy of the Southern States:

Constitutional expert Akhil Reed Amar has made a study[15] of the bizarre electoral college that decides presidential polls in the USA. The system, he shows, was devised to protect the South, because the latter had so many slaves, who were of course denied the vote. This gave an inbuilt advantage to the North, where most anybody could vote (not

15 Akhil Reed Amar: *America's Constitution: A Biography* (2006).

women of course). So the wise founding fathers, to remedy this, decided to base the electoral college on *populations*, rather than votes actually received. So each southern state could count its slaves as population; but there were an awful lot of slaves, so the wise founding fathers said, after all, they must discount their number by two-fifths, for the purposes of the electoral vote entitlement. Still, the more slaves a southern state bought or bred, the more electoral votes it would receive. As Amar remarks: "Were a state to free any blacks, who then moved North, the state could actually lose electoral votes." For the first thirty-six years of the Republic, this "slavocratic" system ensured that in all but four years slaveholding Virginians held the Presidency. The current electoral system also looks somewhat bizarre and can produce a result (through the "winner takes all" obligation of delegates in individual states), where a candidate can win the "popular vote" (what is the other vote, then?) and still lose the election. Land of the Free!

UK Elections: A system for electing MPs that gives "stable" government (i.e. government by the same old hacks) priority over popular preference:

Foreigners, puzzled by the stupendous fictions of the UK's electoral system, would have needed an extensive glossary to decipher the British press's opaque descriptions of "the world's oldest" (or most decrepit?) democracy in action in 2005:

Press Report: "**New Labour wins by a landslide**". *Gloss:* "One in four of those eligible to vote opted for New Labour".

Press: "**The Conservatives held on to their core vote**". *Gloss*: "The Conservatives assumed that most voters were as greedy, xenophobic, mendacious and mean-spirited as their campaign strategists believed. This turned out not to be the case."

Press: "**The Liberal Democrats are now the party of tax and spend**". *Gloss*: "The Libdems pointed out that if you wanted to stop people being slaughtered on the antiquated railways or dying like flies in the collapsing hospitals, you would have to finance the improvements out of taxes. Everybody knows this to be the case, but it is considered suicidal to say so at election time."

Press: "**The Conservative campaign suffered from confusion over projected tax cuts**". *Gloss* : "There was no confusion. The Tories promised 8 or 20 billion pounds worth of tax cuts (depending on who was speaking), with a simultaneous increase in expenditure on vital services. The voters thought even New Labour were better liars than that."

The above explanations might be received with some dismay, so it would be necessary to further illustrate how amazingly democratic is the UK system compared to the rubbish on the Continent by listing *how many votes* it took to elect an MP of each of the main parties, in order to produce a suitable "first past the post" result. Thus it took just *26,858* votes to elect a Labour MP (the winners, hurrah!), *44,241* to elect a Conservative MP (not surprisingly therefore, the losers, oh dear!) and *98,484* votes to elect a Liberal Democrat (no comment.) (Perhaps this is the place to add that by 2010 the United Kingdom Independence Party had garnered 919,000 votes nationwide, but won not a single seat in Parliament, although parties with half that number of votes, or even one fifth, had six (SNP) and three (Plaid Cymru) seats respectively. This was already a slightly more sane result, however, than that of 1983, when Labour, with **28%** of the vote, got **209** seats, the SDP-Liberal Alliance, with **25%** of the vote got…er…**23** seats.) In the 2010 election David Cameron won a somewhat larger share of the vote than had Tony Blair in 2005, but couldn't form a single party government, whereas Blair, with his smaller vote, had clocked up a substantial parliamentary majority in 2005.

In the 2015 election, the Scottish Nationalists got **4.7 %** of the vote and **56** seats, while the United Kingdom Independence Party got nearly **12.6 %** of the vote and… er… **1** seat.

This is what the British establishment calls "a level playing field."

Elgin Marbles: Sculptural reliefs from the Parthenon in Athens pinched by Lord Elgin between 1801 and 1812:

An American academic called Dr Dorothy King (aka "the female Indiana Jones") is making a career out of insulting the Greeks about the Elgin Marbles. Her characteristic argument for the British retaining the marbles is that "the British Museum cares for them, whereas anyone can see the Greeks haven't taken care of their cultural heritage." (*Note*: Try applying this argument to the Jewish victims of the Holocaust and you have a good chance of being promoted to the board of a Swiss bank.)

Meanwhile the Greeks have built a state of the art museum in Athens to house the marbles. Naturally Dr. King is stridently against this museum, since it contradicts her argument that the Greeks take no care of

148

their heritage. The anger of the Greeks and the solipsism of BM curators (who once described the Elgin Marbles as "part of the [British] family silver,") has the symmetry of pathos: first, the Greeks lost their marbles; and now the British curatorial establishment have completely lost theirs.

Embarrassment, the Dialectics of: What happens if you've not been paying attention:

Barry Miles's book on "alternative" London since 1945 tells of one Emmett Grogan[16] who addressed an exciting *Dialectics of Liberation Congress* at the Roundhouse in 1967. His ten-minute discourse movingly laid out the route-map for "*effecting a real inner transformation*" and was rapturously received by his hippie and vaguely Marxist audience. When the prolonged applause had died down, Grogan thanked them warmly, but confessed that his speech had actually been lifted from elsewhere. It had originally been given by Adolf Hitler to the Reichstag in 1937.

Ralph Waldo Emerson, works of: "German philosophy that crossed the great water and took some on underway."[17]

Emerson was of the splendid Walt Whitman school of thought that considered consistency in one's utterances to be deplorably un-ambitious and certainly not appropriate for poets celebrating themselves. As Whitman put it in an extended literary masturbation known as *Leaves of Grass*: "*Do I contradict myself? Very well, I contradict myself!*"

In *Self-Reliance*, Emerson gave this idea a few embellishments: "A foolish consistency is the hobgoblin of little minds, adored by little statesmen and philosophers and divines. With consistency a great soul has simply nothing to do. He may as well concern himself with his shadow on the wall. Speak what you think now in hard words, and to-morrow speak what to-morrow thinks in hard words again, though it contradict every thing you said to-day. — 'Ah, so you shall be sure to be misunderstood.' — Is it so bad, then, to be misunderstood? Pythago-

---

16 Grogan founded the radical community action group known as The Diggers in San Francisco's Haight-Ashbury district.

17 Karl Kraus: *Dicta and Contradicta* (1923), translated by Jonathan McVity (University of Illinois Press, Urbana & Chicago, 2001, Aphorism 757, P. 110.

ras was misunderstood, and Socrates, and Jesus, and Luther, and Copernicus, and Galileo, and Newton, and every pure and wise spirit that ever took flesh. To be great is to be misunderstood."

Many of us feel very strongly that this is the case.

Empedocles (c.495–c.435 BC): Philosopher who slightly overestimated his powers:

Empedocles is said to have believed he possessed divine powers and was unwise enough to test them by jumping into the crater of Mount Etna. The consequence of this somewhat hubristic act would perhaps have been predictable to less self-important mortals. As Bertrand Russell puts it in his *History of Western Philosophy*, quoting an unnamed poet:

> *"Great Empedocles, that ardent soul,*
> *Leapt into Etna, and was roasted whole."*[18]

Wikipedia tells us the following: "Diogenes Laërtius records the legend that Empedocles died by throwing himself into an active volcano (Mount Etna in Sicily), so that people would believe his body had vanished and he had turned into an immortal god; the volcano, however, threw back one of his bronze sandals, revealing the deceit.... "

Empedocles as portrayed in the Nuremberg Chronicle (before he jumped into Mount Etna).

Below you may view Empedocles' "*cosmic cycle*" based on the conflict between love and strife: "The force that unites the elements to become all things is Love, also called Aphrodite; Love brings together dissimilar elements into a unity, to become a composite thing... Strife, on the other hand, is the force responsible for the dissolution of the one

18 Bertrand Russell, *A History of Western Philosophy*, 1946, p. 60.

Empedocles cosmic cycle

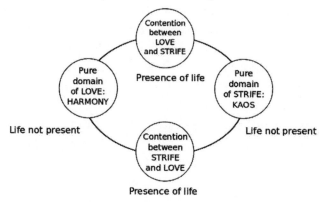

"The nature of God is a circle [whose] centre is everywhere and the circumference is nowhere."

back into [the] many elements of which it was composed." This is what happens in political parties.

Empedocles also said that *"God is a circle whose centre is everywhere, and its circumference nowhere."* The modern configuration of this is a tax-dodging multi-national corporation.

Enronisation: How to corner the market and hold the customers to ransom:

Of the various scams the energy firm Enron perpetrated, the one operated during the California power crisis (itself caused by Neo-Liberal deregulation), had the beauty and simplicity of genius: the firm moved power out of the state via its subsidiaries and then sold it back into California at higher prices, a technique affectionately known as *"ricochet"*. The local inhabitants could sing along with the pop song *"I don't wanna be your ricochet baby"* as much as they liked, but it would be in vain: Enron had correctly identified them as sitting ducks and acted accordingly. As Kenneth Lay, Enron's Chairman and CEO put it: *"We see ourselves as first helping to open up markets to competition."* All the better, of course, if you yourself are the competition…

"If it were not for government regulation of big corporations," wrote P.J. O'Rourke with his customary lack of tact, *"executives at companies like Enron, WorldCom, Tyco, they could have cheated investors out of millions…"*

151

Epicurus (341 BC–270 BC): a philosopher for our times:

Contrary to popular belief and the smears of Christianity, Epicurus did not believe in self-indulgence *per se*; on the contrary he pointed out that happiness, which we should pursue, depends neither on luxury nor power, but on a rational analysis of our desires which could be catered for quite simply: "*Send me a pot of cheese, so that I may have a feast whenever I like!*"

A quotation attributed to Epicurus (albeit doubtfully) fingers what was to become the central weakness of Christian apologetics in regard to theodicy (the attempt to explain the presence of evil in the world if there is an omnipotent and just God.) Epicurus's (?) percipient formulation of the problem was cited (with hostility) by the Christian apologist Lactantius and was later adopted wholesale by the philosopher David Hume (*q.v.*)[19]:

"God," says Epicurus (?), "either wants to eliminate bad things and
     cannot,
or can but does not want to,
or neither wishes to nor can,
or both wants to and can.
If *he wants to and cannot*, then he is *weak* and this does not apply to god.
If *he can but does not want to*, then he is *spiteful* which is equally
     foreign to god's nature.
If *he neither wants to nor can*, he is *both weak and spiteful*, and so not
     a god.
If *he wants to and can*, which is the only thing fitting for a god, *where then do bad things come from? Or why does he not eliminate them?*"

A more streamlined version reads:

---

19 In Book X of David Hume's *Dialogues Concerning Natural Religion* (published posthumously in 1799). Lucius Firmianus Lactantius (c. 240–c. 320 AD) attributes the quotation to Epicurus in *De Ira Dei* [On the Wrath of God – c. 318 AD, 13.19] as one of the philosopher's "famous questions" aka Epicurean aporia. However Lactantius's attack on the Stoics and Epicureans was somewhat hampered by the fact that his learning and rhetoric was rooted in antiquity. The Catholic Encyclopedia indeed complains of another work by him that it displays a "lack of grasp of Christian principles and an almost utter ignorance of the scriptures." Copernicus said of the same work that its mockery of the idea of a round earth was "childish."

Is God willing to prevent evil, but not able? Then he is not omnipotent.
Is he able, but not willing? Then he is malevolent.
Is he both able and willing? Then whence cometh evil?
Is he neither able nor willing? Then why call him God?

There is a counter-argument to this (sort of), namely that we cannot understand the nature of good without the existence of evil, against which the good can be contrasted and in preference to which it can be chosen. In this scenario God is holding the ring and refereeing while allowing humankind the luxury of free choice. Because human beings are ignorant, they choose badly most of the time and are duly punished. How all this squares with events like the Lisbon earthquake and other natural disasters that cause massive casualties among perfectly inoffensive people (*q.v.* **A: *Apocaholics***) is a little obscure — perhaps that is the point.

Epicurus (341–270 BC):
"He who is not satisfied
with a little, is satisfied
with nothing."

About such matters and generally our appetites for wrongdoing and self-indulgence, Epicurus seems to have been a realist. For instance, he believed most businesses stimulate unnecessary desires in people who fail to understand their true needs. This insight has not made much headway in modern societies, whose economies apparently depend on people going out and spending money they have not got on things they do not need, or even really want.

Euphemisms: Misrepresentation designed to spare the feelings of those disadvantaged by a new policy initiative, but especially of those doing the disadvantaging:

The number of euphemisms continues to swell through the agencies of political correctness and bureaucratic self-importance, as well as the customary political and business evasions. As George Orwell remarked of political language, all too often it is designed "to make lies sound truthful and murder respectable, and to give an appearance of solidity to pure wind."

"*Collateral damage*," meaning the annihilation of innumerable civilians by mistake, is now well established. "*Compensation*" (to Chief Executives for getting out of bed) signals a level of remuneration safely insulated from performance. "*Letting people go*," as if it was a kindly act fulfilling what are anyway the victim's wishes, is the requisite euphemism for sacking, which is also concealed under numerous weasel terms like "*redundancy*," "*restructuring*", "*optimisation of assets*," "*reducing payroll*," "*rightsizing*" and even "*ventilating*" underperformers.

Finance is fond of terms like "*market adjustment*" (i.e. adjusting the pay-out on the client's investment *downwards*), while communications warning of an "*improved service*" usually turn out to mean a reduced service costing more.

The London International Group's most successful product was and is the Durex brand of condoms. However for many years it would have been quite difficult to glean this information from the company's literature. By 1994 verbal resourcefulness in avoiding the "C" word had reached new heights of sophistication: LIG's annual report trumpeted its claim to "*global leadership in thin-film barrier technology*".

According to Nigel Rees, who has compiled a *Dictionary of Euphemisms*, *Femhole* is the preferred usage in some quarters for *Manhole* (doubtless the bottle-nosed navvies continually digging up our streets for the utility companies adhere rigorously to the less offensive term.) However, according to the Internet's *Urban Dictionary*, which itself contains a very large number of other alarming "euphemisms" that are not suitable for citation here, *Femhole* doesn't only mean what Rees thinks it means.

Endearing gems from Rees include "*sunshine units*" (to describe lethal radiation escaping from a nuclear power plant) and "*pre-owned vehicles*" for "used cars" (think of the commercial possibilities in "*pre-owned*" husbands or wives!) Lucy Kellaway of the *Financial Times* is continually exposing new attempts at self-aggrandisement through language in the world of business. In her round-up of corporate flannel for 2014 she marked down Tesla for describing its car salesmen as "*Delivery Experience Specialists*" but awarded the annual Golden Flannel prize to PwC in Switzerland, which described its head of Human Resources as "*Territory Human Capital Leader*." "The first three words," says Kellaway, "are intolerably pompous, and the fourth is a lie. HR people don't lead."[20] The next year she spotted an even better example of HR officiousness, whereby managers attending an important meeting were instructed *"to be cognizant of the optics of their personal brand,"* or, as they say on a different planet from that of HR, "dress smartly." While this sort of thing is irritating bordering on offensive, one feels almost affectionate towards some of the attempts to dignify boring or nasty jobs. Who would really want to complain about the verbal reincarnation of supermarket shelf-stackers as *"ambient replenishment assistants"*?

European Union: Dysfunctional body trying to become a federal state by stealth:

Sir Ralf Dahrendorf, a former European Commissioner, once remarked that if the European Community (as it then was) were to apply for membership of itself, it would not be admitted on the grounds of being insufficiently democratic...

The European Parliament, full of persons we have mostly never heard of...

Pieter Brueghel the Elder's Tower of Babel (1563), forerunner of the European Parliament.

In 1992 the people of Denmark voted against the EU's Maastricht Treaty — and were sharply told to come back with a more positive response the following year. Later, Irish voters rejected the Treaty of Nice and were likewise instructed to try again — and this time get it right. French and Dutch voters blew a raspberry at the Constitution

20 Lucy Kellaway: "And the Golden Flannel of the year award goes to..." *Financial Times*, 5 January 2015.

for Europe in 2005, so the EU turned it into the Treaty of Lisbon (2007) which the Constitution's drafter, Valéry Giscard d'Estaing, cheerfully informed anybody who would listen was exactly the same in content as his excellent Constitution. But the cussed Irish rejected this Treaty too (really these voters!), so were again told to come back with a better answer — and did so the following year. As Philip Coggan has mordantly observed, *"What is the point of voting if only one answer is acceptable?"*[21] Of course Joseph Stalin was not worried by such a footling objection, but strangely there are still people around in Europe who are…

Exceptionalism: Phrase coined by American leaders to explain why actions taken by America are morally justified when similar or identical actions taken by other nations are not:

For example, the Monroe Doctrine, which began as a promise not to interfere in South American countries, was transmogrified by means of the "Roosevelt corollary" into a claim that the USA was entitled to interfere with any South American (or Cuban) government whose actions it disapproved of. Naturally the US abhorred any similar behaviour by a European nation (e.g. Britain and France in 1956 in regard to the Suez Canal).

19th century American schoolbooks not only taught "exceptionalism" but also "manifest destiny" (originally used to justify the expansion of the country westwards by force or annexation) and "America as God's country." In common with other expanding imperial powers in history, America adopted "exceptionalism" as a circular argument of uniqueness ("We're more powerful because we're approved by God") while self — interest was sublimated in self-righteousness (c.f. "the white man's burden" borne by the imperialist British). The ideology is as old as the hills, or at least the Old Testament, where we find murderous, racist and chauvinist claims advanced by the Israelites against anyone they regard as rivals — all perfectly OK, because the Jews deemed themselves to be "the chosen race."

It is not immediately clear whether "exceptionalism" was supposed to justify the extermination of native Americans and the institution of

21 Philip Coggan: *The Last Vote: The Threats to Western Democracy* (Penguin Books, 2014), Pp. 180 ff.

156

HUNGART©2016

"Are you eating properly and getting plenty of exercise?"

slavery, or whether God has an opinion on this. Nowadays it is applied to more mundane matters like tax. The US has pursued its own tax evaders ruthlessly through the Foreign Tax Compliance Act (FATCA), which in turn spawned the OECD's Common Reporting Standard (CRS). 96 countries have signed up to that — except… er… the USA. It claims that bilateral data-sharing deals fill the gap, but it turns out they don't in regard to the "beneficial" owners of bank accounts that are part of corporate structures. It turns out further that Delaware does a roaring and lucrative trade in registering foreign firms; likewise money is flowing into states like South Dakota and Nevada with strong secrecy laws and weak oversight, which used to be a speciality of Switzerland — until America took away its business by means of FATCA. The Tax Justice Network says America is the world's third "secrecy jurisdiction" after Switzerland and Hong Kong. As one lawyer puts it: "All this adds up to another example of how the US has elevated exceptionalism to a constitutional principle… Europe has been outfoxed."[22] Once again it's "do as I say, not as I do."

22 See a report in *The Economist*, February 20th, 2016, "The biggest loophole of all: having launched and led the battle against tax evasion, America is now part of the problem."

F

Faith:
*Belief without evidence in what is told by one who speaks
without knowledge of things without parallel.*

Ambrose Bierce: *The Devil's Dictionary*

Facilitating Payments: Bribes:
The rather charming distinction made in US legislation between *"facilitating payments"* (legal, also called *"grease payments"*) and *"bribes"* (illegal) is that the f.p. is merely a backhander given to an official, usually
a minor one, to do for you what you are entitled to have from him or her
anyway, or to do it more quickly. The British are likewise pragmatic,
though the relevant legislation does not really pretend that f.c.s are not
bribes. Until it changed its law some years back, Australia allowed
bribes made in the course of business overseas to be tax deductible.

The problem that arises with anti-bribery laws is that in well over half
the countries of the world, if you don't pay the bribes, you don't get the
business. At least the phrase *"facilitating payment"* provides a pleasant-
sounding verbal fig-leaf for dodgy transactions and is a fitting addition
to the lexicon of financial chicanery that includes items like *"the trickle
down theory"* of *"supply side"* economics, *"securitisation,"* *"leverage,"*
"sell side" analysts and similar euphemisms designed to mislead the layman and supply an aura of respectability to rank exploitation. (See also
C: ***Corruption***.)

Fakelore: The Disneyfication (or dismalisation) of custom, culture and
"heritage."

The phrase describes a lugubrious local canon of costume, ritual and
tradition laid on for tourists, whether it be half-naked African dancers,
the whirling dervishes in Istanbul, or any other fossilised cultural relic.
The scholar Dean MacCannell describes these antics as "staged authen-

ticity"[1] catering to the modern tourist's frustrated yearning for a genuine experience. Such yearning is explained as a sign of deep-rooted disorientation and dissatisfaction in the busy, fretful and restless life of modern man. "Because our life seems complicated to us, at least that of the Greek fisherman should appear simple. Since we are always changing our partners, friends and homes, the Tuscan peasants need to be apprehended as people who live in stable social conditions."[2]

This accounts for the obsession of guidebook cover designers with photographs of grizzled old men at café tables, of peasants riding donkeys, of North Africans riding camels and generally with images of 'pre-industrial' activities. "The technologically dominated present is airbrushed out; the locals who are featured are invariably depicted ... gutting fish or casting nets, harvesting olives, pruning vines, watching over herds of sheep or milking goats."[3] One guidebook series had a standard formula for its front covers featuring a figure in the peasant (or at any rate traditional) costume of the country treated by the guide. On the front of the Austrian guide, however, we are treated to an image of an old man in blue overalls, who might be an old man in blue overalls anywhere, but who is saddled with the caption *"Timeless country character."*[4] In his essay *Simulations*, the French critic and gadfly Jean Baudrillard suggested that, where it existed, the only function of Disneyland itself was to conceal the fact that the entire country had become a vast theme park.

"Most so-called 'sights'" wrote the Austrian Kabarettist Helmut Qualtinger, *"are already completely worn out from being looked at so much...."*

Rev. Jerry Falwell: "Fund-grubbing Bible-basher":
Falwell publicly mused that the horrifying New York terrorist attack of 9/11 might be God's punishment of Americans for the abortionists, pagans, homosexuals etc. in their midst. This could be so, of course, (as

---

1 Dean MacCannell: *The Tourist: A New Theory of the Leisure Class* (New York,1976).

2 Christoph Hennig: *Reiselust: Touristen, Tourismus und Urlaubskultur* (Frankfurt am Main ad Leipzig, 1999), P. 172.

3 *Ibid* P.41. On this topic generally, see Nicholas T. Parsons: *Worth the Detour: A History of the Guidebook* (Sutton Publishing, Stroud, UK, 2007), "The Problem of Authenticity," Pp. 260-263.

4 *Insight Guide Austria*, 3rd edition. (London, 2001.)

Norman Douglas has pointed out: "God, if he exists, must be a monster.") On the other hand, God might simply be "mad at the Americans" (as Falwell puts it) for aiding and abetting the state terrorism of General Pinochet in Chile, whereby rather more people than those who perished in the World Trade Centre were tortured, murdered, or just "disappeared." If so, God is obviously confused, so confused he can't distinguish between "good" terrorism (American-sponsored) and "bad" terrorism. Basically he needs someone like Rev. Falwell to explain it to him.

Being anti-abortion is a signature attitude of conservative Christianity. It is based on the idea of the sanctity of life, which would seem to make the occasional murder by anti-abortion activists of doctors who carry out terminations of pregnancy philosophically incoherent (besides being unpleasant for the doctors). Fanaticism in a cause all too often ends up espousing the very mode of behaviour it purports to oppose. Still one may question whether Karl Kraus hit exactly the right note when he castigated the abortion laws of his day: "Curses on the law! Most of my fellow citizens are the sorry consequences of uncommitted abortions."

The Farm: "Bank robbing is more of a sure thing than farming."[5]
"It is not as if farming brought a great improvement in living standards," writes Bill Bryson; "a typical hunter-gatherer enjoyed a more varied diet and consumed more protein and calories than settled people, and took in five times as much vitamin C as the average person today."[6]

Still, farms do have their uses, as the following *Epigram* from Martial translated by Raymond Oliver demonstrates:

> *You wonder if my farm pays me its share?*
> *It pays me this: I do not see you there.*

Farming: An activity in search of a subsidy:
According to an article by *The Observer*'s economics correspondent, the pre-packaged sandwich industry contributed 0.8% to British GDP in 2001, whereas farming, *if the subsidies were stripped out*, contributed just 0.41 %. **British agriculture (2013) got some £3.1 billion in annual direct and indirect EU subsidies, but overall the UK was a *net con-***

5 Allan Dare Pearce: *Paris in April.*
6 Bill Bryson: *At Home: A Short History of Private Life.*

tributor **to the CAP of £2 billion or £5.5 million a day.**[7] Furthermore it has been calculated by Dr. Lee Rotherham for the Taxpayers' Alliance that the average British household pays an extra £400 a year for its food because of the CAP (more if peripherals are added in, such as extra welfare costs due to higher food prices.)[8] OECD figures have calculated that food prices over recent years were 44% higher in the EU than they would otherwise have been — that is, without the Common Agricultural Policy (CAP); milk costs some 77% more, beef 221% more and sugar 94% more.[9] Despite this (or because of it?) incomes in Britain's farming sector were falling at the beginning of the new millennium and in 2002 alone 52,000 farmers left their land, double as many as in 2001.[10] By contrast, it is claimed, when New Zealand slashed subsidies, its food prices fell to about half of Britain's. Moreover, excluding Greece, about half of all the EU's huge support funds under the CAP go to a small minority of very large farms owned, for example, by UK aristocrats and royals (boo!) or direct to pan-European agribusinesses (double boo!), while 70% of small and middle-sized farmers receive sums of less than €5,000 a year. Welcome to the wonderful world of agricultural and food subsidies.

Nationally France "benefits" most from the CAP, with about 17% of the payments, followed by Spain (13%), then Germany (12%), Italy (10.6%) and the UK (7%).[1] The CAP swallows around 43% of the EU budget and has been described in *The Economist* as "the single most idiotic system of economic mismanagement that the rich Western countries have ever devised."[12] From the importance given to it in the budgeting

7 "European Union Finances 2103", HM Treasury, CM 8740, November 2103, quoted in David Charter: *Europe In Or Out: Everything You need To Know*" (Biteback Publishing, London 2016), P. 194.

8 See a paper for the Taxpayers' Alliance by Dr. Lee Rotherham (2010?) entitled "Food for Thought" – www.taxpayersalliance.com/cap.pdf

9 These specific figures were quoted in an article in the *International Herald Tribune*, 26 June, 2002.

10 This claim, and the figure given to support it, appeared in an article by the environmentalist Zac Goldsmith in an article in the *New Statesman*, 30 June, 2003 ("When common sense is a crime."). Quoted in Jessica Williams: *50 facts that should change the world* (Icon Books, Cambridge, UK, 2004), P. 48.

11 These and other figures following are taken from www.bbc.com/news/world-europe-11216061 . Other sources offer slightly, but not significantly, different figures. The general picture seems clear enough.

12 *International Herald Tribune*, 26 June, 2002, quoting *The Economist*.

and deliberations of the EU, you would hardly guess that agriculture generates just 1.6% of EU GDP and employs only 5% of EU citizens. But then the CAP is entirely a political construct, as it has been since its introduction shortly after the inception of the Common Market, the price that France demanded for agreeing to free trade in industrial goods. In effect, it is the ransom that France exacts for not sabotaging what is now the EU project. Not content with this, France later expanded the reach of its catastrophe economics by forcing on Europe the disastrous EU fisheries policy (*q.v.* below under F: European Fisheries Policy) as part of the price for allowing Britain to join what was then called the European Economic Community in 1973.

Kristian Niemitz of the Institute of Economic Affairs puts it this way: "Imagine there was a Food Tax which had the effect of raising food prices by, say, 17% on average. The tax revenue was collected centrally, and then disbursed to agricultural producers. That tax would be incredibly unpopular, especially in times of rising food prices. The Food Tax would be too obviously recognisable as an instrument of redistributing money from sales assistants and cleaners to wealthy landowners.

The Food Tax is no fiction, of course. Ultimately, the Common Agricultural Policy (CAP) has precisely that effect. It differs from my hypothetical Food Tax only insofar as it is infinitely more complex, consisting of literally hundreds of different support instruments. There is a complex array of tariffs, quotas, and subsidy streams, each of which can, again, be subdivided into lots of different subcategories. Take subsidies, for instance: there are different types of subsidies for different types of agricultural outputs, for different types of agricultural inputs, for different types of agricultural capital goods, and for different types of services related to agriculture. Some subsidies depend on a farm's total farmland area, others depend on the farmland area currently under cultivation, others on the farm's livestock, others on the farm's revenue, and yet others on farmers' income. The OECD's 'PSE Manual' [PSE = Producer Support Estimate], a basic overview of the most important categories of support instruments, has 178 pages."[13]

Is there anything to be said *in favour* of the CAP? Its apologists talk vaguely of "security of food supply" and of the maintenance of con-

13 Kristian Niemitz: see www.iea.org.uk/blog/abolish-the-cap — let-food-prices-tumble (18th January 2013).

sumer choice and quality of produce — but these are features that could be regulated equally well, if not better, by the market. Some supporters even have the gall to suggest the CAP "eases" food shortages in the developing world (would that be by the EU dumping its agricultural products, or by supplying the aid subsequently required because of the dumping?) More plausible is the beneficial role the CAP can play in the preservation of rural lifestyles (e.g. hill farms) and culturally valuable environments. Owen Paterson, formerly Britain's Environment Minister, himself a farmer and a refreshing change from ideologically super-charged[14] predecessors in that office, made clear the distinction between potentially valuable aspects of the CAP and the ocean-going disaster that prevails: "I remain convinced," he told the National Farmers' Union annual conference in 2013, "that farmers' decisions about which crops to grow and which animals to raise should be left to the market. I do believe there is a real role for taxpayer's money in compensating farmers for the work they do in enhancing the environment and providing public goods for which there is no market mechanism." (However the much heralded reforms to the CAP agreed in June 2013 were denounced as "disastrous" and retrograde by environmentalists.)

Writing in 2004, Jessica Williams observed that each of the EU's 21 million cows then attracted a subsidy of $2.50 per day, "although it's unlikely that Europe's cows know how lucky they are — cows are, after all, not known for their intellect." Still, why pick on EU cows in view of the relatively modest support they received to live in the style to which they were accustomed? Japanese cows got *$7.50* a day! Then again, the subsidies racket in the USA (that bastion of free markets and enterprise) makes other regimes look almost sane. There the farming bills are entangled with the system of food stamps which accounts for 80% of their budget. Allegedly these stamps help the poor, some of whom turn out to be millionaires, while others do a secondary trade in them by resale of items back to the stores that supplied them against the stamps. However even contemplating the US government's 126 frequently overlapping

---

14 A good example of how green activists have infiltrated supposedly neutral sources of information is the extremely hostile section on Paterson's views and his role as Environment Secretary inserted into his Wikipedia profile. Clearly designed to portray him as an extremist and unsuitable for the post, the section is currently under dispute with Wikipedia's editors (2014).

anti-poverty programmes is enough to cause brain damage, so it's easier to concentrate on the agricultural part of the farm bill (2014), which, says *The Economist*, is actually worse than the food stamps part (are they sure?).

That has now (2014) been reformed so that farmers will no longer "receive cheques for doing nothing very much" but instead get payments if crops fail or prices fall to an unprofitable level. This sounds like an improvement, but it has the effect of "locking in high prices when farming is profitable." Also, while the farming risk is underwritten by the taxpayer, the requisite insurance policies are provided by insurance companies, "so, in effect, they enjoy a subsidy too." As in the EU, the bulk of the subsidy swag goes to the wealthiest farmers. All this, says *The Economist*, warming to its theme, results in activities that "make no economic sense in the rest of the world, for example making sugar from corn" [making sugar from *corn*?] Furthermore the World Trade Organisation obliges the American government to pay $147 million a year to compensate farmers in Brazil as a penalty for the cotton subsidies it (the USA) keeps in place. The usual reason behind such crazy measures is bribery, which in America is called "political donations." According to Open Secrets, an organisation that tracks such "donations," the ten members of Congress who accepted most from agricultural lobbyists in 2013 took an average of $225,000 in political contributions. Nine of these are Republicans, who are traditionally in favour of free markets until they see an election looming, and the other is a Democrat, whose party habitually uses food stamps as a useful means of bribing its core electorate.[15]

The CAP does not only attract opprobrium from conservative Eurosceptics and free marketeers. It appals many of those who otherwise tend to be the EU's natural supporters, such as eco-warriors and NGOs involved in aid to developing countries. Their frustration is understandable: the CAP is supported by a tariff placed on cheap agricultural produce from poor countries in order to prevent competition with Europe's expensively produced food. In regard to the Common Agricultural Policy, writes Martin Wolf, the Chief Commentator of the pro-Europe *Financial Times,* the EU "seems beyond shame or reason." Probably the most scandalous example of vindictive protectionism has been the sugar

15 See: "A trillion in the trough: Congress passes a bill that gives bipartisanship a bad name", *The Economist*, Feb.8. 2014. Pp. 33-4.

production quotas that heavily disadvantage competing farmers in impoverished countries, while paying huge amounts to giant European agribusinesses. Worse, since one of the erratic effects of the CAP has been to distort markets so that unwanted surpluses emerged (the EU's infamous "butter mountains" and "wine lakes"), surplus European production, as already remarked, was subsequently dumped on world markets, further throttling the economic viability of farmers in poor countries.[16] And as a result of *that* (you guessed it), *aid* has had to be provided by the EU for such countries to deal with their problems of food production, which had largely been caused by the EU in the first place (the aid is another cost to European taxpayers). You could not, as they say, make it up.

Olivier de Schutter, the UN's Special Rapporteur on the Right to Food and specialist on EU Law, is disgusted by the impact of the CAP (and other countries' food subsidies) on developing countries. "They struggle to remain competitive against heavily-subsidised food products being dumped on their markets," he complains. "A number of poor countries have increased their imports of agricultural products, and ... are therefore not investing in their own agricultural sectors. [They] have become addicted to food subsidies from the OECD countries. They have developed a dependency that is not easy to get rid of. Were we to decide tomorrow not to export subsidised foodstuffs to the developing world, the result would be very severe food shortages in the short-term. That is what addiction leads to."

"Let me back-up these statements: first, about one-third of all the food we produce each year is not consumed; about 1.3 billion tons of cereals are being lost or wasted. These are either losses in developing countries, resulting from poor storage facilities or crops rotting before they can be sold and passed onto consumers; or, in developed countries, supermarkets discard food before it is consumed. A quantity of food equivalent to the entire food production of Sub-Saharan Africa is just thrown away each year."[17]

---

16 It is true that CAP subsidies were "decoupled" from production levels in 2003, but distortions remain and the system is essentially just as dysfunctional as before. At least milk quotas were discontinued in 2015; meanwhile the UK's excess production over its milk quota allotted under the CAP (often substantial, as dairy farming is efficient in the UK) is simply poured away. Oh yes, and there is a new "wine lake" of substandard plonk that continues to be produced, although nobody wants to buy it....

17 Quoted in www.debatingeurope.eu/2012/02/20should-europe-scrap-the-cap#comments

Dr. Lee Rotherham concludes the paper he wrote for the Taxpayers' Alliance (*see above*) with the following verdict on the CAP and all its works: "The EU needs to scrap the CAP, and hand back management to national governments. National governments should be made to understand that they can continue to pay their farmers subsidies, but that it must be out of their own tax revenue. Governments of other EU member states might then find their electorates take more of an interest in how their money is being spent. This change should be accompanied by the warning that the consequences for their own protectionism will fall on their own heads in future world trade talks. Alternatively, the money could be saved simply by leaving the EU."

The fact is, we're not at war; the state does not need to ensure an emergency oriented "security of supply," nor to protect farmers in the developed world from market forces. And instead of sending "aid" to Third World countries that disappears into Swiss bank accounts, we should let the poor ones export to us tariff-free the only thing that many of them can currently produce, namely food. In 2004 Jessica Williams cited the Catholic aid agency CAFOD which calculated that the money the EU then spent on protecting its farmers could finance an annual round-the-world trip for each of the EU's 21 million cows, with £400 spending money thrown in. The Japanese cows could fly business class.[18] Not a great deal has changed.

Fart: Audible emission of intestinal gas from the anus:
The Viennese satirist Karl Kraus wrote that *"every man loves the smell of his own farts."* This predilection, which some may find remarkable, must presumably be ascribed to the colourful and pleasing nature of the Viennese diet. Ladies of course never fart, on the principle enshrined in a useful guide to etiquette that runs:

> *Here's a little rhyme you surely ought to know:*
> *Horses sweat and men perspire but ladies only glow.*

Michael O'Mara Books are to be congratulated for their enterprise in publishing a recherché little book on ***The History of Farting*** (1993). With some diligence it classifies for aficionados all known types of fart.

18 Jessica Williams op cit. P. 47.

A typical entry defines the *Junk Fart* (once known as the *Fish and Chip Fart*, the *Pie and Pastie with Sauce Fart* or the *Jellied Eel Fart*, but now as the *Steamed Dimmie Fart*) as "highly processed and brightly packaged."

Horses are great farters, of course (the equestrian art of dressage was once described as "arses showing their horses and horses showing their arses."). On one occasion, when the Queen was riding in the royal landau with a visiting Head of State, the nearside grey let off a tremendous fart. "I do beg your pardon!" exclaimed Her Majesty in some confusion. "That's all right, Ma'am," said the dusky potentate kindly. "I thought it was one of the horses."

John Lanchester remarks that "whereas it is socially unacceptable to talk about money in most contexts in Britain, it is perfectly OK to talk about property prices." People are boasting about money while pretending not to, when they go on about the value of their houses. Such discourse, he says, is *"the conversational equivalent of a perfumed fart."*[19]

Lord St John of Fawsley: A merry fellow sacked from government by Mrs Thatcher for making jokes, *inter alia* about her:

"I cannot recall such a triumph of expediency over principle" complained a Labour drone after an announcement by St John Stevas (as he then was) that touched on some Socialist shibboleth or other. "Has the Right Honourable Gentleman ever considered his own career?" riposted Stevas cheerfully.

When a friend remonstrated with him that he was obsessed with name-dropping," Fawsley replied: "I'm afraid you're right. The Queen said the same to me only yesterday."

Feindbild: Useful (because virtually untranslatable) German word meaning "the hostile image of the other."

Left-liberals in the German-speaking world are always denouncing *"Feindbilder"* as constructs of know-nothing nationalism etc., but closer inspection reveals that they themselves have numerous ideologically based *"Feindbilder."* Communist states, while claiming to be striving

19 John Lanchester: *How To Speak Money: What the money people say – and what they really mean* (Faber & Faber Ltd., London, 2014) P. 241.

for peace in the world, adopted a rhetoric of colourful *Feindbild* abuse full of phrases like "imperialist hyenas," "capitalist running dogs" etc.

Very probably the human psyche requires "*Feindbilder*" to energise it. It is notable that impeccably humane slogans like "*liberté, égalité, fraternité*" provided the chilling cover for bloody massacres during the Jacobin phase of the French Revolution. The "*fraternité*" bit, perhaps significantly, was sometimes dropped altogether, while the addition of "*ou la mort*" to the slogan raised the stakes considerably. Revolutionaries move quickly from an appeal for support to victimisation of doubters. Communists assumed (usually correctly) that any who did not actively support them were actively against them, therefore ripe for torture and liquidation. Hungary's *nomenklatura* got a nasty fright from the 1956 revolution, not least because those who held out longest for freedom were the heavy industry workers on Budapest's Csepel Island, i.e. precisely that level of society with which Communism always claimed a complete alignment of interest. Thereafter János Kádár, the stooge set up by the Russians to "normalise" the country, thought it prudent to reformulate Communism's *Feindbild* by announcing that "*he who is not against us is with us*." This was code for "if you remain apathetic and don't indulge in politics, we'll leave you alone. Or at any rate stop murdering and torturing you."

The Greek historian Thucydides was an early exponent of the ideological *Feindbild*, writing of Athens' opponents that "*your hostility does us less harm than your friendship*." This is more or less the view of militant Islam and renders the liberal stance of appeasement and accommodation irrelevant. What is the point of preaching tolerance to a force that regards tolerance itself as a contemptible vice? On the other hand the jihadists fill a vacuum left by the defeat of Communism, which has not totally been filled by the demonisation of global warming sceptics and so forth. "*The adversary,*" says Pascal Bruckner, "*puts us in the contradictory position of wanting to defeat him and wanting to preserve him in order to retain the energy he instils in us. He is at once detestable and desirable.*"[20] And Balthasar de Gracian has a more refined version of the same insight, namely: "*Enemies are of more use to the wise man than friends are to the fool...*"

---

20 Pascal Bruckner: *The Tyranny of Guilt* (Princeton University Press, Princeton and Oxford, 2010) P. 138 Translated from the French (*La tyrannie de la pénitence: essai sur le masochisme occidental*, 2006) by Steven Rendall.

On the other hand, Michael Corleone makes the wise observation in *The Godfather*: "*Never hate your enemies. It affects your judgement.*" This is not quite identical to Christ's injunction to love one's enemies, but just as difficult...

Fellow traveller: A person who, from the highest motives of course, wishes to betray his country:

The most comprehensive definition of such persons has been offered by David Pryce-Jones: "A fellow traveller is one who commits to a cause, preferably foreign and necessarily hostile to the interests of his own country. He, or as often she, believes that the selected cause is promoting the virtues of Peace, Love and Brotherhood, in contrast to the vices of the home country, its government, its injustices, racism, imperialism or whatever. In most of the world, a dissenting attitude of that kind puts the individual's liberty and life at risk. In the West, the fellow traveller is free to praise what ought to be blamed and blame what ought to be praised, and be rewarded for this with money and a reputation for courage. By means of false moral equivalents, double standards and the assertion that whatever wrongs 'they' are guilty of 'we' have done worse, anyone can become a celebrity fellow traveller."[21]

During the Cold War it was quite fashionable to be a fellow-traveller if you were on the left. The most celebrated was Hewlett Johnson (1874-1966), the so-called "Red Dean" of Canterbury Cathedral from 1931 to 1963. He visited Soviet Russia in 1937 and was shepherded around by officials of VOKS ("The All-Union Society of Cultural Relations with Foreign Countries", a deliberately long-winded name designed to obscure its function as an agent of Soviet control and propaganda.) By the time Johnson went on his trip, the Soviet Union had lost a good deal of its allure except among the silliest or most cynical of Soviet sympathisers, since news of Stalin's show trials, butchery, deportations, torture and deliberately induced famine had trickled out to the West. The Red Dean however had literally sold his soul to the Soviet Union and enthusiastically did the VOKs tour, subsequently rewarding his hosts with a work of stupendous mendacity entitled *The Socialist Sixth of the World*. One sentence from it admirably sums up this enterprise, namely Hewlett Johnson's claim that "*nothing strikes the visitor to the Soviet Union more forcibly than the ab-*

---

21 *The Spectator*, 2013.

sence of fear." This observation, made at a time when virtually nobody in the entire Soviet Union could feel safe, led some reviewers to question whether the Dean had actually written the book himself. In this they were rather near the mark, as it appears that large chunks of it were in fact copied out from material supplied to him by the Society of Cultural relations with the USSR, which in turn had it from VOKS.[22]

Nowadays "fellow travelling" (which always requires an uncompromising and threatening power to identify with) mostly takes the form of timid intellectuals describing Islamic fundamentalism as though it were (a) exaggerated or harmless and (b) ethically on a par with its critics who are smeared as "*secular fundamentalists.*" So someone who, at great personal risk, speaks out against the barbarism of shari'a (which *inter alia* proscribes the death penalty for adultery or homosexual practices) and robustly defends the humane ideas of the Enlightenment, particularly the principle of free speech, finds himself or herself labelled a *(secular) fundamentalist*. It's a tried and tested tactic of the disingenuous liberal, whereby perpetrators are transmogrified into victims and victims into perpetrators. Bruce Bawer calls this the "dialectical scam:"[23] inconvenient criticism, facts or opinions … "[are to be suppressed] if they "offend" the supposed "victims" of "western prejudice," who, however are *themselves* calling for censorship and grisly punishments of dissent under shari'a law (apostasy carries the death penalty).The idea that you can effectively appease the fanaticised apostles of violence ("*accommodation*" is the preferred euphemism) is of course extremely dumb; but as George Orwell remarked "some ideas are so stupid that only an intellectual can believe in them."

FIFA: Fédération Internationale de Football Association: A body that organises international football tournaments and takes bribes:

According to its Financial Report, in 2013 FIFA had revenues of over 1.3 billion U.S. dollars, for a net profit of 72 million, and had cash reserves of over 1.4 billion U.S. dollars. Prince Ali of Jordan, a candidate for the

---

22 See John Butler's admirable book on *The Red Dean of Canterbury: The Public and Private Faces of Hewlett Johnson*, Scala Publishers Ltd., London, 2011, in particular Chapter 7.

23 Bruce Bawer*: Surrender: Appeasing Islam, Sacrificing Freedom* (Anchor Books, NY, 2010) Pp. 22 ff.

FIFA Presidency in 2016, alleges that at least 60 % of FIFA's seemingly unlimited "development funds" have in the past been spent on junketing and flying Fifa grandees around the world rather than on football.[24] The organisation has become synonymous with rapacity, corruption, and bribery. Even the re-election (unopposed) of Sepp Blatter, its aging, mendacious President, was allegedly rigged. FIFA's decision to award the 2018 and 2022 World Cups to Russia and Qatar (the latter with a hopelessly unsuitable climate) appears to have been the result of vote buying. Of the 24 elderly and greedy jobsworths who formerly sat on FIFA's executive committee, at least a third have been accused of corruption and several have been banned from football. An intercepted e-mail sent by the organisation's Secretary General admitted that Qatar had "bought" the world cup (when this came to light, he hastened to say the e-mail had been "misinterpreted," like you can so easily "misinterpret" the word "payment" for "vote" or vice versa.) FIFA's attempted whitewash of the scandal backfired when it buried the report of its own investigator and issued a "summary" which the investigator implied was mostly fiction.[25]

While football associations are now quarrelling with Qatar for its decision to postpone the 2022 tournament to the autumn because of the unbearable summer heat (might someone have thought of that before?), few seem to be concerned about the plight of the migrant workers building the stadium and facilities. These Bangladeshis, Nepalese, Sri Lankans and Indians are slave labour in all but name. As *The Independent* has pointed out, "their deaths, at the rate of two a day last year among the Nepali workers alone, is an inconvenient but persistent reality for Fifa. They are dying in the 50C heat, unable to leave because the Qatari *kafala* system prevents them from going home without their employer's permission."[26] They are also required to pay back huge fees to the intermediary employment agencies if they go home early and their passports are effectively confiscated by their employers while they are there.

24 "On the ball," an interview with Prince Ali of Jordan, *Weekend FT* 9 January, 2016.

25 Lord Triesman, the former chairman of the English Football Association, described FIFA as an organization that "behaves like a mafia family", highlighting the association's "decades-long traditions of bribes, bungs and corruption" (" Fifa 'like a mafia family' says former FA boss Triesman". *BBC News*. 11 June 2014.)

26 Sam Wallace: "Fifa's real crime with Qatar 2022 is ignoring the workers' plight," *The Independent*, 4 March, 2015.

Although the western countries (which founded Fifa in 1904 and ran it until 1974) are outraged at the way the organisation has become football's equivalent of the Camorra, Simon Kuper points out that there is little they can do against the now prevalent non-western countries, which are quite happy with it as it is: "After all, many of these countries are run rather like FIFA."[27] This is also fine by Mr Blatter, who is quite indignant at the idea of having to clean out the Augean stables (you will recall that this labour of Hercules was deemed impossible, since the 1,000 cattle who lived in the stables were divinely healthy and therefore produced an enormous quantity of dung. Moreover the stables had not been cleaned in over 30 years.) For his part, Blatter supposedly believes he should be in line for the Nobel Peace Prize for having united the world through football (and large cheques). [See also C: *Corruption.*]

Financial incentives: Phrase used in the City of London to justify excessive pay:
   A Mr Brett has written to the *Financial Times* to propose a simple and equitable solution to the problem of bankers' bonuses. Henceforth, he suggests, these should be paid solely out of the bank's "toxic assets," for the accumulation of which the bankers have, after all, already been paid gigantic bonuses. True, this might mean that some never got another bonus that actually paid out; but it would at a stroke "align executives' interests with those of shareholders," as company reports are fond of claiming; and also "incentivise" the executives concerned to make more durable profits in future ("*incentives*" are always the justification for huge "compensation.")
   Any bankers who objected could be offered retirement on generous terms, consisting of a huge package of "toxic assets," out of which their pensions should be financed — when and if they ceased to be toxic.
   (See also: **C: *Compensation.***)

EU fisheries policy: An environmental, political and economic catastrophe financed by our taxes:
   Until at least 2012, **up to a million tonnes** of dead fish were being dumped in the sea annually by trawlers, because the species caught did

27 Simon Kuper: "A slow build-up of pressure is the best way to change Fifa" *Weekend FT*, 22 November, 23 November, 2014)

not match the skipper's permit or exceeded his quota or the fish were immature. This had been going on for years with the connivance of the fishing industry, European governments and the EU. The USA, Canada, Norway, the Faroes and Iceland do not allow discarding of fish — after all, existing fish stocks can hardly be monitored if up to a third of the catch has been chucked back in the sea. Greenland actually left the EEC (as it then was) in 1985, on account of the latter's mishandling of fisheries. On the other hand, it is estimated that between a third and a half of the catch made by some EU fisheries is illegally obtained (not surprising when member states like Spain and France are responsible for "policing" their own quotas.) By 2014 the EU had introduced a "reform" of the quota system which stipulated *inter alia* that any excess of fish caught should *not* be thrown back into the sea.[28] Hurray! Instead these fish should be landed and... er... taken to a landfill site.

In an act of calculated betrayal, a Conservative Prime Minister signed away the UK's fishing rights during the negotiations for the UK's entry into the Common Market in 1973. Although there was no mention of a common fisheries policy in the Treaty of Rome (and therefore no legal basis for the decision), the French made it a condition of EEC entry for Britain and Denmark that fishery should henceforth become a "*common resource*" of the Community. The results — near-destruction of the UK fishing industry, boats sitting idly in West Country ports in sight of Spanish trawlers hoovering the mackerel-crowded seas, mountains of red tape, massive corruption, dumping, wastage and "quota-hopping" (similar to the EU's "carbon credits" scam) — are now so awful that even the EU thinks something ought to be done.

The fishermen blame each other and the EU for this fiasco; the EU blames the Council of Ministers for introducing national interests into decision-making, so that deals often involve matters quite unconnected with fishing, or reflect the bullying capacity of countries with powerful fishing lobbies, or lack transparency, or are cavalier in the treatment of expert advice. The Council of Ministers blames its members, the EU bureaucracy and the fishing industry. The environmentalists blame every-

---

28 For a detailed discussion of the fisheries disaster and the EU's efforts to reform it, see David Charter: *Europe In Or Out: Everything you Need To Know* (Biteback Publishing, London, 2016) Pp. 203-210. Statistics from 'CFP reform – Transferable Fishing Concessions', ec.europa.eu/fisheries/reform/docs/tfc_en.pdf

one other than themselves, although their ideological insistence on fish as a *"common resource"* (how soon before oil and gas are declared a *"common resource"* to be apportioned by Brussels bureaucrats?) has produced the chaotic policy, and thus the environmental disaster.

The sensible solution would be for nations to retake control of their territorial waters and enter into bilateral agreements with other countries for fishing in non-sovereign waters. This is the policy followed successfully by countries like Norway, Canada and the USA. It is not ideal, human nature and commercial interest being what they are, but mostly it conserves stocks and ensures a decent livelihood for fishermen. So of course this is what is least likely to happen. Although the UK Conservatives promised to withdraw from the CFP when in opposition, they have quietly reneged on their undertaking when in power. Spain and France have fiercely opposed even the modest "reform" of the policy proposed by the EU in 2013, this despite the fact that the current arrangements have led to the European exclusive zone being perhaps 88% overfished (compared to an average of 25% elsewhere). The leading Green Party negotiator in the EU's deliberations is ideologically against even the halfway house of Individual Tradeable Quotas (effective in Alaska and Norway) because that would mean *"privatising a common resource."* Meanwhile the EU concludes "partnership deals" with Third World countries that allow the EU fishing fleets into African waters, thus often destroying indigenous fish industries — so the locals turn to emigrant smuggling, terrorism and piracy instead.

Flamethrowers: The ultimate gangsters' toy:
"The very existence of flamethrowers proves that sometime, somewhere, someone said to themselves, 'You know, I want to set those people over there on fire, but I'm just not close enough to get the job done.' "[29]

Footnotes: A form of exhibitionism by scholars designed to convey authority and crush rivals:
Anthony Grafton in his classic work *The Footnote* says the following: "In a modern, impersonal society, in which individuals must rely for vital services on others whom they do not know, credentials [such as footnotes provide] perform what used to be the function of guild mem-

29 George Carlin

174

bership or personal recommendations: they give legitimacy. Like the shabby podium, carafe of water, and rambling inaccurate introduction which assert that a particular person deserves to be listened to when giving a public lecture, footnotes confer authority on a writer. Unlike other types of credentials, however, footnotes sometimes afford entertainment — normally in the form of daggers stuck in the backs of the author's colleagues. Some of these are inserted politely... but often the subtle but deadly "c.f." ("compare") is set before [a citation]. This indicates, at least to the expert reader, both that an alternative view appears in the cited work and that it is *wrong*. But not everyone who reads the book will know the code.

Sometimes, accordingly, the stab must be more brutal, more direct. One can, for example, dismiss a work or thesis, briefly and definitively, with a single set-phrase or well-chosen adjective. The English do so with a characteristically sly adverbial construction: "oddly overestimated." Germans use the direct *"ganz abwegig"* ("totally absurd"); the French, a colder, but less blatant, *"discutable."* All these indispensable forms of abuse appear in the same prominent position and carry out the same scholarly version of assassination." He adds that *not* citing a work is as significant a weapon in the scholar's armoury as citing it with an educated sneer. The Italians, for example, have developed a Baroque system of footnotes that combines Machiavellian cunning with prolixity, the whole leaning tower being aimed ultimately at "the coven of the well-informed." "The combined precision and obscurity of the Italian citation code compels admiration — especially in the light of the practical difficulties that confront any Italian scholar who wants to read a given work before not citing it." [30]

Forecasting: The art of incorrectly predicting the future:
Entire industries are devoted to dealing with economic and financial variables, political change, climate change, demographic shifts etc. There is only one reliable aspect of such forecasts: like the pronouncements of the late William Rees-Mogg, they are almost invariably wrong. Jargon-filled forecasts by City "analysts" are aptly described by *The Times* as "no more scientific than alchemy." Digitallook has compared the performance of shares the City said overwhelmingly you should buy

30 Anthony Grafton: *The Footnote: A Curious History* (Faber, London, 1997) Pp. 7-9.

in 2011 with those it overwhelmingly said you should sell. You'd have lost money on all of them, of course; but out of £100 you'd have £64.10 left if you'd bought the "*strong sells*", but only £55.10 if you'd bought the "*strong buys*". A similar analysis can be made for almost any year you care to pick. The Oracle at Delphi actually gave you a better steer than the City's grotesquely over-remunerated seers and can still be consulted at www.askoracle.net

The most spectacularly successful wrong forecast in the twentieth century was that of an obscure lepidopterist named Paul Ehrlich who published a runaway bestseller entitled *The Population Bomb* in 1968. Applying the fallacious Malthusian catastrophe argument[31], he prophesied that hundreds of millions of people would starve to death in the 1970s and 1980s. Ehrlich was not so modern as to suggest that anything could be done about this calamity; however, like other left-wing scientists before him, he was very keen on the enforcement of population control for the future. And those who were so misguided as already to detect an easing in population growth were clearly deluded fools if not arrant knaves (unfortunately the "Green Revolution" in agriculture was even then starting to negate his doom-laden prophecies.)

Despite his predicted meltdown not occurring, Ehrlich made a great career out of doom mongering, sensibly learning in later publications such as the *The Dominant Animal* (2008) not to put a date on the predicted catastrophes. Without a timescale of course, your credibility re-

31 For the record, Ehrlich's thesis rested on two unreliable pillars: firstly, the *ceteris paribus* or "other things being equal" argument, which they never are and are even more unlikely to be in the future; and secondly the extrapolation indefinitely of a linear trend to a presumed conclusion (catastrophe or absurdity, according to taste.) Similar styles of argumentation may be seen in the debates over "climate change" and "global warming."(*q.v.*) Ehrlich was not alone in doom-mongering: about the same time as his book was grabbing attention the Club of Rome's *Limits to Growth* (1973) was prophesying *inter alia* that fossil fuels would run out within thirty years. The critiques of that book, as of Ehrlich's, received little notice. "*Models of Doom*" (also 1973) by Christopher Freeman and Marie Jahoda showed that the modelling on which the Club of Rome's book was based was entirely self-fulfilling in design and failed to allow for any external factors such as exist in the real world. They pointed out that, with minimal alterations to the model's assumptions, the end of the world could be predicted for 1980 — or 2000 — or not at all. Then again, a rise of only 1 per cent in the rate of oil discovery would extend oil reserves by some 200 years. [See: Matthias Horx: *Zukunft wagen* (Deutsche Verlags-Anstalt, München, 2013. P. 95]

mains intact with the true believers — potentially indeed for ever, as with those who regularly troop down to New Mexico to await the end of the world, only to disperse and recalculate the date. The fact that demographers have shown that the world is experiencing what Matt Ridley calls the "second half of a 'demographic transition' from high mortality and high fertility to low mortality and low fertility" is mere statistical observation and therefore of no interest to doom mongers like Ehrlich.

As to Ehrlich's specific predictions, famine on the scale he predicted is "largely history" says Ridley in *The Rational Optimist* (2010), and "where it still occurs — Darfur, Zimbabwe — the fault lies with government policy, not population pressure."[32] Ridley adds that in 1990 the economist Julian Simon won $576.07 in settlement of a wager [with Ehrlich]. Simon had bet him that the prices of five metals (chosen by Ehrlich) would fall during the 1980s and Ehrlich had accepted '*Simon's astonishing offer before other greedy people jump in*' (though later, while calling Simon 'an imbecile,' he claimed he was 'goaded' into it.)"

Ehrlich of course did not take criticism lying down. Failing to admit to the collapse of his thesis in the face of reality, he did say that it was a mistake not to foresee the fate of the rain forests in South America — although since (a) he had not mentioned the rain forests and (b) their destruction anyway reinforced his doom scenario, this can hardly be taken as an admission of error. In any case, despite the colourful language of mass death in the book, he maintained he had not made any "predictions" — again it was "imbeciles" who thought he had. Finally he did get around to making a generous confession of fallibility, admitting that "perhaps the most serious flaw in *The Bomb* was that it was *much too optimistic* about the future" [*sic*]. (Italics added).

Meanwhile it is sad to have to report that the *Astrological Magazine* was obliged to cease publication in 2008 "due to unforeseen circumstances."

Benjamin Franklin: Wit, diplomat, polymath:
Franklin is almost always right about everything, which would be annoying were his remarks not so disarmingly free of cant. "So convenient

---

32 Matt Ridley: *The Rational Optimist* (Fourth estate, London, Fourth Edition, 2011) Pp. 302, 303. "*Ehrlich*" means "honest, sincere or genuine" in German.

a thing it is to be a reasonable creature," he once said, "since it enables one to find or make a reason for everything one has a mind to do."

Or: "Many a long dispute among divines may be thus abridged: It is so. It is not so. It is so. It is not so."

Or: "Time is money".

Or: "Those who can give up essential liberty to obtain a little temporary safety, deserve neither liberty nor safety" (a remark that is as relevant in the second millennium as it was in 1755.) Its pendant is his advice that no one "should ever trust a government that does not trust its own people." This is now considered anachronistic in view of the internet.

Or: "Many people die at twenty-five and aren't buried until they are seventy-five."

Or: "You can bear your own faults, and why not a fault in your wife?"

Or: "He that falls in love with himself will have no rivals."

Or: "I wake up every morning at nine and grab the newspaper. Then I look at the obituary page. If my name is not on it, I get up."

Benjamin Franklin: "We are all born ignorant, but one must work hard to remain stupid."

In 1745 Franklin wrote a now celebrated (or notorious) letter to a young friend, who had evidently complained of uncontrollable sexual urges. Franklin counselled marriage as "the most natural State of Man and therefore the State in which you are most likely to find solid Happiness." This bit of the letter was piously quoted throughout the 19th century in America, which however took care to censor the rest of it. For Franklin went on to advise that, if the young man was set on not marrying for a while but needed to slake his sexual appetite, he should be sure to choose an *older woman* as his mistress.

Was he being serious, cynical or satirical? At any rate his argument of eight points is eminently *reasonable* (e.g. because "the sin is less than debauching a virgin;" because when women "cease to be handsome, they study to be good and supply the Diminution of Beauty by the Augmentation of Utility;" because older women are discreet; because there is no hazard of children; and so forth.) His fifth point seems to have caused most dismay to 19th century prudes (after all, Franklin was one of the Founding Fathers and as such a role-model for young Americans): "Because in every Animal that walks upright the Deficiency of the Fluids that fill the Muscles appears first in the highest Part, the Face first grows lank and wrinkled, then the Neck, then the Breast and Arms, the lower Parts continuing to the last as plump as ever: So that covering all above with a Basket and regarding only what is below the Girdle, it is impossible of two Women to know an old from a young one. And as in the Dark all Cats are grey, the Pleasure of corporal Enjoyment with an old Woman is at least equal, and frequently superior, every Knack being by Practice capable of Improvement." His eighth and final reason for choosing older women was that "they are so *grateful*."

In the light of these sentiments is interesting to look at Franklin's list of 13 virtues compiled when he was 20 years of age in 1726. Number 12 reads: "*Chastity*: Rarely use venery but for health or offspring, never to dullness, weakness or the injury of your own or another's peace or reputation." Note that word "*health*."

Fraudit: Neoliberal version of what used to be called an audit:
The 'Big Four' accountancy firms (Deloitte & Touche, Pricewaterhouse-Coopers, Ernst & Young and KPMG) employ over 700,000 people worldwide and have combined global revenues of some £72 billion, more than half of which is derived from "consultancy services," which in turn

have substantially involved the sale of "tax avoidance" schemes. Since the 'Big Four' between them audit 78% of all companies listed on the main UK market, and since if one firm doesn't sell its client a possibly fraudulent tax avoidance/evasion scheme, another one will, the likelihood of wrongdoing and conflicts of interest is high. In stark contrast to the unctuous tone of their official websites, these firms have in fact been serial offenders in devising tax avoidance that has been ruled illegitimate by Her Majesty's Revenue and Customs (HMRC) or the Inland Revenue Service (IRS) in the United States. Some of their wheezes have a Gilbertian flavour, e.g. helping directors of a company to avoid National Insurance Contributions by paying themselves in gold bars, fine wine and platinum sponge; or developing a trail of tax elimination by shifting a firm's profits to low or no tax jurisdictions through a Byzantine web of corporate structures (for example, the process known as the Double Irish Dutch Sandwich (*q.v.*).) Another feat of prestidigitation involved treating newspaper mastheads as "assets," transferring them to the parent company, then leasing them to the subsidiaries for annual royalties, which effectively deflated taxable profits, while the subsidiaries claimed tax relief on the royalty payments. The company's board minutes exposed in court actually stated that the firm's accountants had advised that this scheme would "*significantly lessen the transparency of reported results,*" but sadly the court was unimpressed and ruled the scheme unlawful.[33]

Apart from their blatant attempts to deceive the tax authorities on a massive scale, the auditors (like the powerful ratings agencies) also conducted a profitable line of business in cooking the books and massaging accounts. It has been pointed out that, just before the greatest financial crash since that of Wall Street in 1929, all the distressed UK banks received a clean bill of health from their auditors. Most spectacularly, Lehman Brothers was given the all clear by Ernst & Young (who collected $31 million in fees in 2007), although it turned out that the bank was borrowing £30 to finance its operations for every £1 provided by shareholders, a leverage rate above 30 to 1.[34] A mere 3.3 per cent drop in the value of its assets was enough to make the bank insolvent. (Ernst &

33 This was the case of Iliffe News and Media Ltd & Ors v Revenue & Customs (2012) UKFTT 696 (TC) (01 November 2012), Paragraph 54.

34 As per the financial satement filed with the SEC for the year to 30 November 2007.

180

Young later settled with the State of New York to the tune of $99 million in order to escape further prosecution for "massive accounting fraud.")

An amusing "fight of the phoenixes" broke out in 2015 over the resurrection of the accounting firm Andersen, which, you will recall, failed to notice that Enron (*q.v.*) had cooked the books and itself imploded when Enron imploded. *Andersen Tax* of the US claims it has the rights to the *"iconic brand name,"* having been founded by twenty-three former Andersen partners who had escaped from the wreckage; but rival *The New Arthur Andersen*, based in France, announced it would launch in 2016. The latter claims that the *"original* [Arthur Andersen] *network has been considerably metamorphosed"*, whatever that means. *"This is an understatement,"* writes Andrew Hill. *"Conflicts at Andersen, which earned more consulting for Enron than from monitoring its cooked books"* resulted in its conviction for *"obstruction of justice, after ordering staff to shred documents relating to Enron,"* although this was overturned in 2005. The CEO of the new Andersen says her firm will be *"inspired by the values behind Andersen,"* the values presumably of that part of the *"iconic brand"* which didn't ignore the cooked books or shred documents. The same mission statement, illustrating that accountants either have a refined sense of humour or alternatively no sense of humour at all, rounds off with a quotation from Mark Twain: *"They didn't know that it was impossible, so they did it."* [35]

Despite some mega-scandals, the "Big Four" have proved too powerful to bring to book, save for a few exceptionally blatant and criminal cases involving individuals or ex-employees. Onetime senior accountancy executives often sit on regulatory bodies or take influential jobs in government, positions that lead to what is picturesquely known as "regulatory capture." In addition the "revolving door" phenomenon means that a number of senior and well-networked former politicians or civil servants become associated with one or other of the "Big Four" (the controversial former head of HMRC, for example, became a consultant with Deloitte.) The door also revolves in the other direction, with accountancy luminaries becoming ministers or civil servants in departments concerned with oversight of their former employers. Although there have been repeated court cases that the firms have lost, it is notable,

35 See Andrew Hill: "Andersen rises from Enron ashes as rivals compete to revive sullied brand," *Financial Times,* 10th September, 2015.

writes accountancy expert Prem Sikka, that "not a single accountancy firm or its partners have ever been disciplined by any UK professional accountancy body for designing, marketing or implementing tax avoidance schemes." [36]

Freedom Fighters: Liberal euphemism for terrorists:
"If crime fighters fight crime and fire fighters fight fires, what do freedom fighters fight?"[37]

French language: A language not spoken by many:
It is greatly to be regretted that the justified pride of the French in their language attracts a rather bilious counter-chauvinism in Anglo-Saxons and others. For example, one Jannes Hartkamp, writing in the now justifiably defunct *Budapest Week*, claimed the following: "France believes French is a world language. Or rather: France wants us to believe French is a world language, because if we believe their make-believe, we may learn French and make it a world language.

"The first problem is that French is not really a world language, the second that it is almost impossible to learn French well, since the French consider you an idiot and break off the conversation immediately the moment you utter *le* where — *naturellement* — it should have been *la*. And it is difficult to find someone else to practise with, because French is not really a world language.

"Why promote a language if you do not accept foreigners speaking it? *Aucune idée.*"

Actually the French are in a perpetual sulk about their language because its decline has reflected the decline of French influence in the world. Some French intellectuals are clear-eyed about this. Jean Cocteau, for example, said that *"les Français sont des Italiens de mauvaise humeur."* Quoting this, Sean Thomas adds: "To me, Frenchness seems like the Islam of nationalities: it still believes in its inherent superiority, and is perpetually irritated by clear evidence that this belief is

---

36 Prem Sikka, "Accounting for Corruption in the ‚Big Four' Accountancy Firms,“ Chapter 14 of David Whyte (Ed.), *How Corrupt Is Britain?* (Pluto Press, London, 2105, Pp. 157-176). The specific examples cited above have all been taken from this chapter, which provides further sources for individual cases in the footnotes.
37 George Carlin

false. The French therefore stand in stark contrast to their neighbours. If you take the short trip from sunny Menton on the Riviera to Ventimiglia on the Ligurian coast, you go from a land of obstinate, proud, rather grumpy Gallic shruggers to a land of bouncy, chirpy, slightly unreliable Latin chancers, in just eight miles."[38]

Frenemy: The enemy of my enemy (therefore my friend — but unfortunately also my enemy):

The unofficial alliance between Israel and Egypt (now even between Israel and Saudi Arabia) against common enemies like Hamas and Iran is a classic *frenemy* situation. However cultivating *frenemies* is a perilous business, *vide* US cultivation of the Mujahideen (heavily supported by one Osama bin Laden) to undermine the Russians, who were then occupying Afghanistan. Part of the Mujahideen eventually morphed into the Taliban, who aren't all that user-friendly. Then again Saddam Hussein was the grateful recipient of US support during his war against Iran, a strategy which sadly turned out not to be the scintillating success that had been expected by the pentagon's policy wonks. The CIA's official term for the implosion of a *frenemy* relationship is *"blowback"* — not a sexual practice as some assume, but a description of the unfortunate boomerang effect of sucking up to murderous governments; for example, the West's cultivation of Saudi Arabia, which pursues the foreign policy the we desire, while simultaneously promoting Salafism in the West, which in turn nurtures Islamic terrorism.

The war in Syria has unfortunately undermined the rule of thumb that the enemy of my enemy is my friend. The enemy of my friend may turn out to be my friend, perhaps also the friend of my other enemy if I'm not paying attention, while the friend of my friend may very well be an enemy. And anyway the whole shooting match hates our guts…. as the Hungarians say, *"just because I'm paranoid, it doesn't mean they're not out to get me."*) [*q.v.* **Feindbild.**]

Fucking: a village in Upper Austria:
The village's population of 104 souls is becoming fed up with the theft of their street furniture by souvenir hunters. It is situated not so very far

38 Sean Thomas: " Borderline personalities: Is national character real? If so, how is it formed?" in *The Spectator*, 13 September, 2014.

from the Bavarian village of **Petting** (three-quarters of the way there, so to speak), but a long way from **Climax** (which is in Colorado). Nor is it twinned with **Wank** (Bavaria) as would seem appropriate. However, in the spirit of collaboration with Asia, **Iron Knob** (Queensland) is said to be thinking of twinning with the Chinese town of **Long Dong**, while it must be only a matter of time before **Muff** (Londonderry) is twinned with **Beaver Head** (Idaho.)

(Incidentally, the population of Fucking was polled in 2004 and over-whelmingly decided not to change the name of its village.)

Fun: First three letters of the word "funeral."

Former Minister for Fun: David Mellor:
Mellor was a member of John Major's ill-fated government and "Minis-ter for Fun" was his (possibly rash) description of his cultural portfolio. A fun-loving character himself, he had to resign after being exposed in the press for alleged toe-sucking sessions with his fiery Spanish mis-tress. The ineffable Sun newspaper headlined its story *"From toe job to no job"* (presumably the equally applicable *"From blow job to no job"* was eschewed on the grounds of taste.)

Mellor was a keen Chelsea fan and it was reported that he liked to wear the club's strip for what the reptiles of the yellow press insisted on calling "sex romps." This prompted his friend and fellow MP Tony Banks to re-mark: *"It's the first time since the great days of Jimmy Greaves that any-one's managed to score five times in a Chelsea shirt...."*

The exposé of the Minister was evidently the revenge of the newspa-pers for his comment that the increasingly unscrupulous gutter press was "drinking in the last chance saloon." The said saloon actually stayed open for another twenty years with its denizens becoming ever more reckless and criminal until finally forced to close (for a while) by the phone-hacking scandals of 2012.

Mellor was agreeably outspoken, even (as a barrister) about his own profession, e.g.: *"Lawyers are like rhinoceroses: thick-skinned, short-sighted, and always ready to charge."* He ended up presenting a music programme on Classic FN, which is not as exciting as toe-sucking, but possibly more useful.

G

Geology: *The geological formations of the globe already noted are catalogued thus: The Primary, or lower one, consists of rocks, bones or mired mules, gas-pipes, miners' tools, antique statues minus the nose, Spanish doubloons and ancestors. The Secondary is largely made up of red worms and moles. The Tertiary comprises railway tracks, patent pavements, grass, snakes, mouldy boots, beer bottles, tomato cans, intoxicated citizens, garbage, anarchists, snap-dogs and fools.*

Ambrose Bierce: *The Devil's Dictionary*

"Gabe ist Aufgabe:" "To have a talent is an obligation to use it": The aphorism (attributed to Käthe Kollwitz) updates the biblical parable of the talents for a secular world. Goethe, on the other hand, seems to have foreseen today's self-absorbed celebrity culture when he wrote: "Everybody wants to *be* somebody: nobody wants to *grow*."

John Kenneth Galbraith: A fount of oracular observations: *"Recessions uncover what the auditors do not"* (*q.v.* **Fraudits**) was a Galbraithian perception, more true today than ever before. Prophetically, he wrote in 1980 that the *"The salary of a chief executive of a large corporation is not a market award for achievement. It is frequently in the nature of a warm personal gesture by the individual to himself."* [*See also* **A:** *Awards*]

Friedmanism, the doctrine of perfect markets and unbridled self-interest, Galbraith dismissed with similar aplomb: *"The modern conservative is engaged in one of man's oldest exercises in moral philosophy: that is, the search for a superior moral justification for selfishness."* Of course the Tea Party would agree, no doubt citing Ayn Rand [*q.v.*], their guardian angel of "Objectivist Philosophy" who published a book in 1964 entitled *"The Virtue of Selfishness: A New Concept of Egoism."* *"Run for your life from any man who tells you that money is evil,"* she wrote. *"That sentence is the leper's bell of an approaching looter."*

185

There was much more in similar vein, all of it guaranteed to give liberals dyspepsia.

Rand was dogmatically opposed to any intervention by government in the free market, however dysfunctional the latter might appear (she got round that by saying that if it was dysfunctional, by definition it wasn't free.) Not that Galbraith was very complimentary about government dogooding either. Of regulators (the sort of people who so spectacularly failed either to foresee or prevent the self-inflicted financial crisis of 2007-8) he remarked: *"Financial regulators are vigorous in youth before rapidly approaching complacent middle age and then either becoming senile or an arm of the industry they were set up to regulate...."* [*See also* **E: Efficient Market Hypothesis**]

"This is what economics now does," wrote Galbraith, "it tells the young and susceptible (and also the old and vulnerable) that economic life has no content of power and politics because the firm is safely subordinate to the market and the state and for this reason it is safely at the command of the consumer and citizen. Such an economics is not neutral. It is the influential and invaluable ally of those whose exercise of power depends on an acquiescent public. If the state is the executive committee of the great corporation and the planning system, it is partly because neoclassical economics is its instrument for neutralizing the suspicion that this is so."[1] Moreover "Few can believe that suffering, especially by others, is in vain. Anything that is disagreeable must surely have beneficial economic effects."[2] As Colin Crouch remarks in *The Strange Non-Death of Neoliberalism* : "The only child pornographer who is unacceptable to the market is one who has no money."[3]

Gaming, Institutionalisation of: Late capitalist society may be summed up simply enough: " 'playing the game' has been replaced by 'gaming the system.' "

Gasputin: Russian statesman who supplies gas to the west and kills people who annoy him with Polonium poisoning.

1 John Kenneth Galbraith: *Power and the Useful Economist* (1973)
2 John Kenneth Galbraith: *The Age of Uncertainty* (1977)
3 Colin Crouch: *The Strange Non-Death of Neoliberalism* (Polity, Cambridge UK, 2011), P. 147.

Gerrymandering: A.k.a. in the UK as "***Shirleymandering***": Method of consolidating the Tory vote in the London Borough of Westminster by putting the homeless in asbestos-riddled tower blocks:

In the late 1980s Dame Shirley Porter DBE, as leader of Westminster Council, sold council houses to potential Tory voters in the Borough, throwing out the homeless families who, inconveniently, were living in them. She called this policy "Building Stable Communities" [that is, of people who would vote Tory]. The courts later surcharged her £37 million for illegal actions, which was small change to the Tesco heiress; however she chose not to pay and fled to Tel Aviv, where she had a nice flat on the seafront. In the first few years only £7,000 was recovered from her, together with a portrait of the lady (value unknown) and her gold-plated lavatory seat. Eventually she was prevailed upon to cough up £12.3 million pounds in recompense for the money illegally spent in this enterprise.

Dame Shirley and the Council also sold off three council cemeteries for *85 pence* to a developer on the grounds that they cost the Council over *£400,000* a year in maintenance and the buyer could develop an adjacent parcel of land, *provided* he maintained the cemeteries. With a financial acumen that only local councils and national government can aspire to, the Council failed to covenant that any *subsequent* buyers of the assets should also be enjoined to maintain the cemeteries. Result: the purchaser at *85 pence* sold the whole package onwards for *£1.25 million* **on *the same day as the purchase***. Once the District Auditor had decided that the transaction was anyway illegal, the Council had to buy the cemeteries back again, the whole boondoggle costing ratepayers *£4.25 million pounds* (instead of saving them *£400,000*). You couldn't make it up (but they did).

Dame Shirley DBE never admitted to having done anything wrong and claimed she was being victimised for being an unrepentant Thatcherite (Mrs Thatcher having once rashly cited Porter as her favourite local government leader.) Her supporters even hinted that anti-Semitism played a role in her prosecution, a tactic briefly tried by the sons of mega-crook Robert Maxwell, but with similar lack of success. The best answer to that sort of ploy was provided by Karl Kraus (himself a Jew) in the notoriously corrupt turn of the century Vienna: "When someone has behaved like an animal, he says: '*I am only human.*' But when he is treated like an animal, he says: '*I, too, am a human being.*'"

W. S. Gilbert: Misogynistic Librettist of "Gilbert and Sullivan" operettas (*"She may very well pass for forty-three / In the dusk with the light behind her"*):

Gilbert's mordant wit was the self-defence mechanism of a somewhat shy person who feared women and sexuality and had a love-hate relationship with the British establishment. On the one hand he was a robust upholder of class distinctions (*"When everyone is somebody, then no one's anybody"*), on the other he despised jobbery and nepotism (*"Stick close to your desks and never go to sea / And you all may be Rulers of the Queen's navee…"* — which was his take in *HMS Pinafore* on the astonishing rise of the bookseller W.H. Smith to First Lord of the Admiralty.) Like most satirists he was a conservative patriot at heart, having little time for *"The idiot who praises with enthusiastic tone / All centuries but this and every country but his own."*

Unlike much wit of earlier ages, Gilbert's humour has worn rather well. A letter he wrote to the Station Manager at Baker Street on the Metropolitan Line could equally well be addressed by one of its victims to Railtrack or a privatised railway company today: " *Sir, Saturday morning, although recurring at regular and well-foreseen intervals, always seems to take this railway by surprise."*

Conservative he may have been, but not prim or prudish: On being told that the title of his operetta *Ruddigore* was indelicate because "*ruddy*" and "*bloody*" meant the same thing, he riposted: *"Not at all, for that would mean that if I said I admired your ruddy countenance, which I do, I would be saying that I liked your bloody cheek, which I don't."*

Mogens Glistrup: Danish politician who won a following by advocating tax evasion:

As a policy proposal, tax evasion proved so appealing that the party Glistrup formed on the back of it got several seats in Parliament. Mogens was probably insane and proud to be a racist, but he did have the clarity of vision that the mentally disturbed frequently display.

For instance, he maintained that, since Denmark was absolutely incapable of defending itself from invasion with its available forces (which was true), the military should be abolished altogether and replaced with a much cheaper recorded message for the border posts simply saying *"We surrender!"* in Russian. (This idea would not catch on in Austria, where hordes of businessmen, "consultants," officials and politicians de-

188

pend on the kickbacks available each time the country's pack of rusty old fighter aircraft needs to be replaced.)

Journalist Gideon Rachman points out that most European armies now exist only on paper, or will do soon. The exception is Switzerland where nearly all males spend many years as part-time members of the armed forces. As the saying goes, Switzerland doesn't have an army; it is an army. On the other hand 75% of Belgian military spending goes on personnel. It has become, in the happy phrase of one military commentator, "an unusually well-armed pension fund."

Globalisation: Process by which international companies achieve parity of power with individual states:

Is globalisation such a menace as the doom-sayers claim? The interconnection of the world through trade, communications and investment is demonised and lauded by opposing political constituencies, and both sides of the argument cannot be entirely right, although neither of them may be totally wrong. In his book *The Rational Optimist*, Matt Ridley has some fun with a "600 page dirge" entitled Agenda 21 that was signed by world leaders at a United Nations conference held in Rio de Janeiro in 1992: "Humanity stands at a defining moment in history," it declared dramatically. "We are confronted with a perpetuation of disparities within and between nations, a worsening of poverty, hunger, ill health and illiteracy, and the continued deterioration of the ecosystems on which we depend for our well-being."

Well, up to a point, Lord Copper. "The following decade," claims Ridley saw the sharpest decrease in poverty, hunger, ill health and illiteracy in human history. In the 1990s numbers in poverty fell in absolute as well as relative terms." Yet the rhetoric of an "unspoken alliance …. [between] reactionaries and radicals, between nostalgic aristocrats, religious conservatives, eco-fundamentalists and angry anarchists [was designed] to persuade people that they should be anxious and alarmed. Their common theme was that individualism, technology and *globalisation* were leading us headlong into hell"[4] (Italics added).

4 Matt Ridley: *The Rational Optimist* (Fourth Estate, London, 2011) P. 290. The unholy alliance between reactionaries and radicals that Ridley refers to was outlined by Charles Leadbetter in *Up the Down Escalator: Why the Global Pessimists Are Wrong* (Viking, NY, 2002).

189

On the other hand Pope Francis, generally thought to be a good egg, is extremely sceptical about the benefits of globalisation, if not of capitalism itself. He complains that the latter is responsible for Catholicism being infiltrated by "hedonistic , consumerist and narcissistic cultures," and remarks that globalisation "is essentially imperialist and instrumentally liberal, but it is not human. In the end it is a way to enslave nations."[5] His view seems to echo that of Harry Magdoff who describes globalisation as "a system by which a small, financial elite expanded its power over the whole globe, inflating commodity and service prices, redistributing wealth from lower-income sectors (usually in the non-Western world) to the higher-income ones."[6]

In any discussion of such a many-faceted (and apparently unstoppable) phenomenon as globalisation, the cacophony of axe-grinding reaches deafening proportions. Identical phenomena may be regarded positively by one side of the argument and negatively by the other — the relevant "facts" (or "factoids") will be adduced accordingly. "Rich nations," asserts Jessica Williams, "have been able to use [globalisation] as a further tool of exploitation, imposing tough barriers on developing countries while lavishly propping up their own economies …. Corporations use cheap labour and materials in poorer countries to further maximise their profits."[7] According to Lori Wallach of Global Trade Watch the latest trade pacts have a more sinister element: they privilege corporations against governments seeking to regulate them, so that "companies can sue countries before an ad hoc panel over the negative impact of laws passed in their parliaments. (Labour groups and non-governmental organisations cannot)." In 2014 the Swedish energy giant Vattenfall

5 This remark comes from a book of exchanges between the future Pope and Rabbi Abraham Skorka published in Spanish in Argentina in 2010 and subsequently published in English in 2014 as *On Heaven and Earth: Pope Francis on Faith, Family and the Church in the Twenty-First Century* by Jorge Mario Bergoglio and Abraham Skorka. Pope Francis had already been strongly critical of the excesses of capitalism in his book *Evangelii Gaudium* (2013).

6 Harry Magdoff: "Globalisation — To What End?" *Socialist Register 1992: New World Order?* Ed. Ralph Milliband and Leo Panitch (New York: *Monthly Review Press*, 1992), Pp 1-32. Quoted in Edward W. Said: *Orientalism: Western Conceptions of the Orient* (Penguin Books, London, 1995), P. 350.

7 Jessica Williams: *50 facts that should change the world* (Icon Books, Cambridge UK, 2004) P. 1.

launched a claim for €3.7bn from the German government over its plans to phase out nuclear power.[8]

It is again Jessica Williams who points out that anti-slavery groups currently estimate that there are 27 million slaves in the world today, many of them working in sweat shops or as bonded labour to produce cheap goods for western consumers (*q.v.* **S: *Slavery***). In India there are 44 million child labourers. The radical Canadian journalist Naomi Klein has been quoted as saying that "*Africa is poor because its investors are incredibly rich*" (whereas it is mostly poor because its governments are incredibly corrupt.) The Brazilian political scientist Roberto Unger has observed that "*one of the striking features of the form of globalisation that has now been established is that it is based on the premise that goods and even capital should be free to roam but labour must remain imprisoned within the nation state*" (hence the desperate attempts of Third World migrants to reach what they believe is the Eldorado of Europe or America.) Or consider the following candid prioritising of business interest before social or political considerations by the CEO of the Swiss engineering firm of Asea Brown Boveri in 1996: "*I would define globalization as the freedom for my group of companies to invest where it wants when it wants, to produce what it wants, to buy and sell where it wants, and support the fewest restrictions possible coming from labour laws and social conventions.*"[9]

Some of the opposition to globalisation comes from those who are ideologically opposed to capitalism *per se* — one suspects they would not be so opposed to a globalisation under the sole aegis of Marxism. Yet such critics are important, since they draw attention to aspects of globalisation that its supporters tend to gloss over. Is outsourcing jobs from Europe and the USA to the Third World really so beneficial for either or both? Can the new jobless poor of the developed world expect any of the benefits that accrue to their more prosperous fellow citizens from the labour of the poorly paid workers overseas whom, we are told, globalisation is benefiting by providing them with an awful job rather than none? Are the estimates that globalisation has closed some 60,000 plants and the North

8 This is Christopher Caldwell's paraphrase of Wallach's view in his column for the *Weekend FT*, 1/2 March 2014, "Popular sentiment is hardening against free trade."

9 Percy Barnevik, President of the ABB Industrial Group, in his address to the annual general meeting of Asea Brown Boveri in 1996.

American Free Trade Agreement eradicated some 5 million manufacturing jobs true, and if so, what were the countervailing advantages?[10] Is the global standardisation of so much urban culture really such a good thing and do we accept the Panglossian implications of Thomas L. Friedman's dubious claim that *"No two countries that both have McDonald's* [hamburger parlours] *have fought a war against each other since each got its McDonald's"*? (Oh no? Moscow got its McDonalds in 1990 and Tbilisi, Georgia in 1999). Are we happy to overlook all the nasty aspects of globalisation and nod approvingly when the distinguished economist Amartya Sen tells us what is undoubtedly true, namely that "[Globalization] *has enriched the world scientifically and culturally and benefited many people economically as well."*[11] And when the President of the European Commission José Manuel Barroso blandly tells us that *"in the age of globalisation, pooled sovereignty means more power, not less,"* are we not inclined to ask "more power *to whom?"*

Still the reality of globalisation is inescapable and perhaps we will come grudgingly to accept it by emphasising and exploiting its benefits. This seems to be the tenor of policy analyst Mark Riebling's robust insertion of realism into the debate: *"Consider the death of Princess Diana. This accident involved an English citizen, with an Egyptian boyfriend, crashed in a French tunnel, driving a German car with a Dutch engine, driven by a Belgian, who was drunk on Scotch whiskey, followed closely by Italian paparazzi, on Japanese motorcycles, and finally treated with Brazilian medicines by an American doctor. In this case, even leaving aside the fame of the victims, a mere neighborhood canvass would hardly have completed the forensic picture, as it might have a generation before."*[12]

Global warming: Oft-repeated claim that the planet is getting exponentially hotter with calamitous consequences for mankind:

10 Figures quoted by Christopher Caldwell *(see Note 4)*. Caldwell adds that NAFTA did not stabilise the US trade balance, or decrease the flood of Mexican migration to the USA, two key advantages touted at its inception. In fact it produced the opposite results.

11 Amartya Sen: *Globalization —The Hopes and the Fears*

12 Mark Riebling: *Hard Won Lessons: The New Paradigm: Merging Law Enforcement and Intelligence Strategies* (The Center for Policing Terrorism at the Manhattan Institute for Policy Research, 2006). P. 2.

Since "global warming" is a form of religious dogma for its adherents, careful note should be taken of any apparent shifts in the "warmist" position. For example, the UK Met Office (which has been in the forefront of GW alarmism, and has struggled to explain its numerous spectacularly wrong longer term forecasts over the past few years) slipped out a statement on Christmas Eve (!) 2012 stating that by 2017 aggregate global temperatures will probably have remained *stable for two decades*. So yes, glaciers are melting in the Andes and the Arctic icecap is receding; but then again the Antarctic ice has thickened, and from Jerusalem to the UK there have been exceptionally cold spells and snow.

An interesting aspect of the global warming debate is the tension between alarmist rhetoric and scientific caution. How to pull off the trick of saying simultaneously (*sotto voce*) that the science about climate risks is confusing — *but* (loudly) that catastrophe is imminent? (*q.v.* under: **Apocaholics**). In the 1980s and 1990s, scientists talked about "the greenhouse effect," then (upping the ante a bit) the "enhanced greenhouse effect." After that came "global warning" — but sceptics disobligingly pointed out that "global warming" seemed to have stalled (warmists say "paused") around 1998. So it was decided in 2005 to adopt the phrase "climate change" (*q.v.* under **C: *Climate Change***). This deplorably anodyne phrase however provoked warmists to angry outbursts — a Mr Read writing in *The Guardian* in 2007 said it was "criminally vague and … dangerous for us to use." He didn't think much of "global warming" either, because he met "lots of people… who say things like, "Yeah, we could use a little global warming round here!" He demanded that we only talk about "climate catastrophe."[13] "Climate chaos" is another popular term, although it has been pointed out that just as "change" is what climate does, so "chaotic" is what climate is. At least it may seem chaotic to mere humans, but doubtless the Almighty has a precise place for it in his "intelligent design." Advocacy groups require both big villains (George W. Bush, Exxon Oil) and apocalyptic scenarios to stand out from the fog of superlatives and distortions that constitute the white noise of everyday press reports. Hence the 1994

13 An excellent chapter on "The Communication of Risk" may be found in Mike Hulme: "*Why We Disagree About Climate Change*" (Cambridge University Press, 2009). Pp. 211 ff. The quote from R. Read in *The Guardian*, 13 Nov. 2007 is to be found in a footnote on P. 234.

Greenpeace report (*Climate Time Bomb*) claimed that the future impact of climate change would be on a par with a nuclear holocaust (*"As bad as a nuclear holocaust, eh? I only get out of bed for exploding super-novas. Pour us another one, Mack!"*)

If, as GW's own protagonists agree, there has been no significant *global* warming since 1998, the whole edifice of *"anthropogenic"* global warming (i.e. that which is man-made due to the carbon emissions our industries and transport produce) begins to look a bit rickety. After all, this has also been a period of unprecedented carbon emissions from developing nations. In fact the race is on to discover the "missing CO2" which should be in the atmosphere but isn't — some say it is "hiding" at the bottom of the oceans, presumably just waiting to leap out and zap us. It appears that the "carbon sinks" that absorb the CO2 have been expanding to meet the increased demand. That's as may be, say the alarmists, but we'll soon reach a "tipping point" where the sinks can't cope. But they still don't know where the "missing" 45% of carbon has actually *gone*. *The Economist*, which is on-message in respect of GW (for example sarcastically linking the idea that GW is "controversial" in the view of Republicans to that of some Republicans that evolution is also "controversial,")[14] quotes a study suggesting that higher air temperatures are strengthening east-west trade winds at equatorial latitudes in the Pacific. This in turn causes more churn in the ocean, and more upwelling of cold water that pushes warm surface water down, sequestering heat that would otherwise have warmed the earth's surface. This elaborate theory might explain the "pause" in GW, and "is clearly good news" says *The Economist*, before adding hastily "but it may not last," because another study says the oceans cannot continue to absorb so much carbon dioxide.[15]

Apart from blandly reassuring viewers in 1987 that there would be no hurricane just before one struck Southern England causing a billion pounds' worth of damage, the UK Met Office used to be quite good at short to middle term forecasts. Unfortunately, however, global warming fanatics have now programmed the Met's computer with an algorithm that only spits out "warmist" longer range forecasts. The predictably hilarious results have been documented with perhaps unwholesome glee by arch-sceptic Christopher Booker and others. For example, in Decem-

14 *The Economist*, Feb.22nd 2014, P. 37 Lexington: "Faith and Reason."
15 *The Economist*, Feb.22nd 2014, P. 49.

194

ber 2012 the Met told us to expect "above average" mean UK temperatures for February-March 2013, but March turned out to be the coldest for fifty years. In March 2012 it told us to expect "drier-than-average April, May and June", but sadly April turned out the wettest "since records began" (as excitable newscasters are fond of saying). Further back, in September 2008, the Met foretold a "milder than average" winter before the coldest winter in a decade and the following year, true to the warmist script, it told us that the trend to milder winters would continue, just before the coldest winter in 30 years. The following autumn it saw an "up to 80 % chance" of a warmer than average winter just before the coldest December "since records began." January and February of 2104 were the wettest in the UK for 250 years, causing extensive flooding, so it was reassuring to have Booker's report that the Met Office had forecast in November 2013 that the three months between December 2013 and February 2014 would be drier than usual.[16]

Of course if you keep predicting the same thing with something as unpredictable as the weather, the law of averages ensures that you occasionally hit the jackpot: as the Magyars say, "even the blind chicken occasionally hits on a grain." Faced with weather that stubbornly refuses to co-operate with their projections (clearly it is "in denial" like global warming sceptics), the Met Office at first tried to suggest that, although its forecasts seemed spectacularly wrong, they weren't *really* wrong to those who understood these things. Regrettably this only produced more hilarity among the benighted public, whereat it deftly changed tack and asserted that actually all these cold and wet "events" were *themselves evidence of global warming*. So it turns out that *any* weather, dry, wet, hot, cold or none of the above, is evidence of global warming. So there![17]

16 Christopher Booker: "How the flooding of Somerset was deliberately engineered", *Sunday Telegraph*, Feb. 23, 2014.

17 The global annual death rate from weather-related natural disasters has declined by 99 per cent since the 1920s. Tropical cyclone intensity hit a thirty-year low in 2008. Global warming will increase the water available through more rainfall caused by greater evaporation from the oceans – as it did in previous warm periods. See Matt Ridley: *The Rational Optimist* (Fourth Estate, London; 2011) pp. 334-5 citing detailed scientific studies by Arnell, Goklany, Pielke and others – full bibliographic details of these are given on P. 421 of Ridley. The IPCC, complained Arnell, misrepresented his paper when it used it by omitting any of its references to the positive outcomes in respect of rainfall from warming.

"Going forward: Corporate yuk-speak for *"in the future:"*
Such pseudo-sophisticated phrases are much favoured by the young men in sharp suits known as "middle managers." The aim is to endow banality with a spurious air of gravitas. Politicians, who hope thereby to appear cool and trendy, have also adopted it, usually in a bid to indicate that the present disastrous policies they are pursuing will, despite all indications to the contrary, have a happy outcome in the end.

In Austria politicians adopt the formulation *"ich gehe davon aus,"* a pompous way of saying "I assume," when the assumption in question, were it not clothed in such verbal pomp, might appear all too implausible. Another much loved cliché is the folksy *"lassen wir mal die Kirche im Dorf"*[18] ("Let's not exaggerate here!") This is delivered with an air of avuncular wisdom by ministers fighting a doomed rearguard action on behalf of some (undeclared) vested interest or other.

Golden Flannel Awards: Annual awards for corporate bullshit published by Lucy Kellaway of the *Financial Times*:
"The bullshit market knows only one phase: the bull phase," remarks Ms Kellaway tartly. The mixture of pretentiousness, mendacious jargon and illiteracy that Orwell once derided in political discourse is now the hallmark of corporate-speak. The head of Cisco tells his colleagues by e-mail *"we'll wake the world up and move the planet a little closer to the future."* Citibank hides its mass redundancy programme inside the notion of *"optimising the customer footprint across geographies."* In 2014 ABN Amro fired 1,000 people in order, it said, to *"further enhance the customer experience,"* while in 2013 an organisation called EY seemed to think that by sacking people it could *"look forward to strengthening* [its] *alumni network.* By that argument, lowering wages should increase employees' loyalty to the firm.

Kellaway has also illustrated the tin ear of CEOs who evidently need some counselling on how to break the news to people that their career is at an end. The head of Microsoft began an e-mail to staff which axed thousands of jobs with a cheery *"Hello there!"* (as in: *"Hello there! You're fired!"*). With similar sensitivity, the CEO of the taxi business Uber began a message to customers, who were getting anxious after the alleged rape of an Indian woman by an Uber driver, with a snappy *"Hey"*

18 Literally: "Let's leave the church in the village."

(as in *"Hey, man! It's only a rape for God's sake."*) Perhaps this was only to be expected from a firm that quadrupled its fares in Sydney for the duration of the siege of a coffee shop by a crazed Islamist in 2014.

Meanwhile our old friend Barclays Bank attempted to revamp its tawdry image by announcing it would henceforth judge staff on *"how they live our Values and bring them to life every day. And we'll judge our 'Go-To' success on a balanced scorecard of impact."* (That makes Barclays, says Kellaway, "the 'Go-To' place for corporate marshmallow and incorrect use of upper case.")

All this pales beside her citation from a project meeting at a major company, as follows: *"You have to appreciate that the milestones we have set in these swim lanes provide a road map for this flow chart. When we get to toll gates, we'll assess where you sit in the waterfall."* In the effluent, surely….

Goldman Sachs: "Great vampire squid wrapped around the face of humanity…":

A 2009 *Rolling Stone* article by Matt Taibbi described investment bank Goldman Sachs as above, adding that it *"relentlessly jammed its blood funnel into anything that smells like money."* Actually this was grossly unfair to vampire squids, since they do not suck blood or have a "blood funnel," and are much nicer than Goldman Sachs; but the Occupy Wall Street movement joyfully used the description anyway in its propaganda.

In a disrespectful tome entitled *"How They Got Away With It"*[19] a Professor Friedrichs lists the amoral, but eye-wateringly profitable, activities of Goldman Sachs. The resultant (rather occasional) fines from the regulators showed up as a barely visible speck of fly shit on the GS balance sheet. In other words, civil penalties (most bank misfeasance seems to be beyond the reach of the criminal law) are customarily treated as "business costs." GS *alumni* go on to be Secretaries of US Treasury or President of the European Bank, which may not be altogether reassuring, since a former GS CEO also ran MFI Global, a firm that collapsed with over $1 billion of clients' funds missing.

In 2001 Goldman Sachs helped Greece conceal the real state of her finances, so as to qualify for the Euro; then it made huge profits selling

---

19 *How They Got Away With It*, Ed. Will, Handelman and Brotherton (N.Y., Columbia University Press, 2013) Pp. 12-15.

instruments that shorted the Greek economy. In the USA, it sold dodgy "*Structured Investment Vehicles*" to municipalities and counties with predictable results for the latter. It "*pumped and dumped*" dud stocks, "*laddered*" (i.e. manipulated) share prices in new offerings, or "*spun*" (discounted) the said shares to crony insiders. It "*gamed*" the oil and commodities markets to the huge detriment of consumers, especially the poor. GS also offered for sale CDOs ("*collateralised debt obligations*") that were designed to fail, in order to make money betting against them.

All this, you may recall, was regarded as "God's work" by the CEO of GS; whereas, says Friedrichs, "*it may more properly be regarded as a form of organised crime.*"

Gold-plating: A tendency of senior British civil servants, known as Sir Humphreys,[20] to smuggle pet schemes that would not survive individual parliamentary scrutiny into EU directives, the latter normally being passed through the House of Commons on the nod:

Exactly how many EU regulations per annum are passed (mostly through statutory instruments) through national parliaments is a matter of dispute. However a former German President claimed that as much as 84% of legislation in the *Bundestag* was EU related. In 2010, the British House of Commons Library came up with the more modest figure of somewhat over 50 % . The measures passed into law ranged from the extremely interventionist Working Time Directive (which is probably why you have difficulty getting medical attention at weekends) to the risible "classification of padded waistcoats in the 'Combined Nomenclature' "[*sic*] [21]

Sir Humphrey is almost invariably a fan of the EU. In many ways it represents that dreamed of utopia where civil servants on high salaries and excellent pensions can pass any laws that take their fancy without the tiresome obligation of democratic accountability.

*Gold-plat**ing*** should not be confused with *gold-plat**ed**,* which refers to Sir Humphrey's pension arrangements.

---

20 Sir Humphrey Appleby was the devious Permanent Secretary in the long-running British TV satire *Yes, Minister*, a programme much enjoyed by Mrs Thatcher.

21 See: an article by Martin Beckford in *The Telegraph* of 28 October, 2010, for details of the House of Commons study.

198

Graffiti: Sticking it to the establishment:

A slogan scrawled on a Viennese tram echoes the feelings of generations of harassed students: *"Knowledge pursues me, but I am faster."* The young person who daubed that will go far, but perhaps only at the speed of a tram (in Vienna an average of 15 km per hour)....

Much graffiti falls under the heading of "the public strikes back." Comedian George Carlin claims to have seen the following scrawled on the loo of a tank station: *"Why do they lock gas station bathrooms? Are they afraid someone will clean them?"*(And while we are on the subject of motorway gas station loos, a *Daily Telegraph* reader reports seeing a hot air hand-dryer in one of them with a series of instructions on the front: *"Press button to start. Place hands under outlet. Rub hands together"* — to which someone had helpfully added: *"Wipe hands on trousers."* This provoked another reader to write: *"I was very pleasantly surprised the first time I used one of these at how rapidly and efficiently they disposed of the water, until I realized that it had simply been blown up my sleeve."*)

Of course graffiti need not only be grumpiness, but rather an idealistic proclamation, like the students' slogan in the Paris of 1968: *"Be realistic: demand the impossible (q.v.* **K: *Nikos Kazantzakis*).** David Graeber, who quotes this, also quotes another 1968 slogan, namely *"All power to the imagination"* — but *"which imagination are we referring to?"* he asks. If this involves the imposition of *"some sort of prefab utopian vision,"* the historical precedents are not encouraging: *"world-class atrocities are likely to be the result."*[22] As was the case, for example, with Soviet communism, of which an American journalist fatuously wrote *"I have seen the future and it works."*[23] On the other hand graffiti is the ultimate defence of the bullied and condescended to, as in this lapidary observation scribbled on a church wall: *"Power corrupts; absolute power corrupts absolutely; God is all-powerful."*

Holy Grail: What is yearned for, but only useful if unobtainable:

In his lecture on *Unbridled Romanticism*, Isaiah Berlin recalled that Dante Gabriel Rossetti, when engaged in his investigation of the Holy

22 David Graeber: *The Utopia of Rules: On Technology, Stupidity, and the Secret Joys of Bureaucracy* (Melville House, Brooklyn.London, 2015) Pp. 88, 92.

23 Lincoln Steffens (1866-1936), the idealistic muckraking journalist. He repeated this phrase many times subsequently, before the news from Soviet Russia compelled a rethink.

Grail, was addressed by a rather malevolent scholar with the words: "But Mr Rossetti, when you have found the Grail, what will you *do* with it?" "This," says Sir Isaiah, "is precisely the type of question the Romantics knew very well how to answer. In their case the Grail was in principle undiscoverable and such that one's whole life could not be prevented from being a perpetual search for it; and that is because of the nature of the universe, such as it is."

Grandeese: Form of language and tone of voice adopted by the Great and the Good to discourage lesser mortals from asking awkward questions:

The thing to look out for in Grandeese pronouncements is any reference to "apples and pears," which is Sir Humphrey's favourite metaphor. Thus, if any of the reptiles disobligingly compares one foreign policy disaster with another, it is explained to him or her that he or she is comparing "apples with pears." So the disaster in Iraq is not to be compared with the meltdown in Libya, defeat in Afghanistan or the failure to have any impact on the mass slaughter in Syria. Some of those situations are "apples," some are "pears." Sir Humphrey's acute antennae are able to distinguish between the two, of course. The rest of us mere mortals are always confusing them and imagining that British policy has been a complete failure; whereas, if they knew their apples and pears, they would realise it had been an enormous success.

Graveyard humour: Hollywood pleasantries exchanged over corpses:
As movie mogul Harry Cohn was being laid to rest, a reporter asked the presiding rabbi : "Can you think of anything good to say about Harry Cohn?" "He's dead," said the rabbi. (The engaging Cohn had once turned down an adaptation of *The Iliad* because there were "too many Greeks in it."). At a fellow-comedian's burial, Charles Coburn was asked his age by one of comedy's thrusting newcomers. "Eighty-nine," said Coburn. "Hardly seems worth while you're going home," said the young man.

Greece: A bottomless pit for EU taxpayers' money:
A *Spectator* cartoon in 2012 showed an advertising slogan in the window of a travel agency: "*This year, go to Greece. Your money is already there.*" Actually this is not a new joke. In the 1990s, the Eastern Euro-

pean mafia was stealing some 60,000 cars a year from Western Europe. A cartoon in a German magazine showed a group of tourists passing a used car lot in Warsaw; over the entrance is written in bold letters *"Willkommen in Polen! Your car is already here."* Nor should we forget South Africa's Kulula airline which is said to have broadcast the following message to the passengers during the aircraft's final descent: *"Welcome to Johannesburg. If you are visiting, we hope you enjoy your stay. If you are returning home, we hope your car is where you left it."*

Greeks will never be able to repay the debts accumulated in their name by sleazy governments, nor adequately service the misnamed "bail-outs" supplied by the EU and others, much of which goes to bondholders, banks etc. On the other hand, perhaps they are not all entirely blameless. It has transpired, for example, that large numbers of them, on paper at least, had suspiciously good genes. For example, remarkably many Greek pensioners continued to draw their pensions into their 110's or above, although they had little use for them, having long retired to the local cemetery. Moreover an island in the Cyclades had apparently been smitten by mass blindness, 90% of its inhabitants drawing benefit for this disability. The heartless authorities began sending oculists here and elsewhere to test the eyesight of these (literally) benighted persons. Such an oppressive action is clearly unacceptable. It probably contravenes Article 14 of the European Convention on Human Rights.

The Greeks are now substantially unemployed, which in some cases is merely a recognition of the fact that previously they were, in far too many cases, overemployed (to put it delicately). On the remote island of Aghios Efstratios, it transpired, there was a school with eighteen students that employed twenty-nine educators, seventeen of which were gym teachers. Then there was the municipally owned radio station of Athens which had an annual revenue of €300,000, but cost €13m to run. A newly appointed reforming manager ran into trouble when he declared: *"We couldn't keep overpaying for* [journalists and others] *who had three or four other jobs, at a time of mass unemployment among journalists..."*[24] (*"Why ever not?!"* protested his critics.) Stories abound of people paid to do nothing in the state sector, a not untypical example

---

24 These examples of abuse of public funds are taken from Vicky Price: *Greekonomics: The Euro crisis and why politicians don't get it* (Biteback Publishing, London, 2013) Pp. 110, 213.

being the employees of the Kopais Lake Agency. This was established in the 1950s to manage the draining of a lake and construction of a stretch of road, all completed by 1957. In 2011 the Agency *still had 30 full-time staff.* As the head of the audit office ruefully observed, *"No one knows what they do — but every year they advertise for new staff."*

It is of course tasteless to slag off the poor Greeks when they're down and out, but someone's got to do it. Someone like Jason Manolopoulos, perhaps, whose book on Greece's "odious debt" finally abandons the customary euphemisms and describes his country as *"a modern day hydra with seven heads: cronyism, statism, nepotism, clientelism, corruption, closed shops and waste."*[25] Attempts to remedy this are not going well. When civil servants were threatened with suspension of their wages unless they logged on to tell the government who they were (*sic*), the computer system crashed. Eventually it was announced that there were 768,009 Greek public sector employees, about six out of every ten employed, and allegedly seven times the ratio of public to private sector employees in the UK. Apparently two-thirds of Greeks aspired to get a state job, preferably a sinecure....

This sort of rebarbative language about the Greeks is of course highly to be condemned by all right-thinking persons. Meanwhile Greece has borrowed from some obscure IMF reserves in order to... er... pay back the IMF; and a concerned EU official has actually suggested that the EU and other creditors should not give Greece more money, but use the money they *were* going to give to Greece to *pay themselves* back the money Greece *can't pay them*. This strategy has the same perfect symmetry as the EU's original brilliant plan: load up a bankrupt country with more debt while simultaneously imposing an austerity programme that prevents the country from recovering enough to repay the debt. Nobel Prizes for Economics all round!

Grievance fundamentalism: Deciding what other people shall be allowed to say or write about a religion, culture or anything else that attracts an emotional allegiance; and threatening (or sometimes killing) people who won't conform:

---

25 Jason Manolopoulos: *Greece's 'Odious' Debt: The Looting of the Hellenic Republic by the Euro, the Political Elite and the Investment Community* (Anthem Press, London and New York, 2011).

Some historical grievances have become a vital part of national identity and are wheeled out to justify any poor performance in the present (for example the Greeks explaining their rotten political culture by reference to 400 years of Turkish occupation); or to rationalise simple ethnic brutality (for example the Serbs, who seem to think atrocities committed against them in the past were atrocities, but atrocities that they committed or commit don't count.) Of course there is a bit of this Serb mentality in all nations, but most of them try to be more discreet about it. The Scots are now successfully marketing their enduring grievance against the English, greatly aided by shrewd populist politicians in Scotland, incompetence at Westminster and mendacious blockbuster films like *Braveheart*. As P.G.Wodehouse once remarked, "*it has never been difficult to distinguish between a Scotsman with a grievance and a ray of sunshine.*"

Islamic grievance fundamentalism is a powerful weapon in preventing people from analysing the illogicality, intolerance and threats dished out by mullahs issuing *fatwas* or the evasiveness of apologists for Islamism. A subtle master of grievance fundamentalism is the Muslim intellectual Tariq Ramadan, the darling of western liberal intellectuals like Ian Buruma, and the subject of various heroising journalistic features, notably Buruma's profile in the *New York Times Magazine* in 2007. According to Ramadan, it is almost entirely the West's embrace of capitalism that is responsible for the evils under which the Muslims feel they live; as he puts it "*the northern model of development* [means] *that a billion and a half human beings live in comfort because almost four billion do not have the means to survive.*" In other words, says Bruce Bawer, who quotes this remarkable statement, "*if Muslims (and others in the so-called developing world) are poor, it's because the West is rich.*" And he adds "*it would seem to me that the last thing the Muslims need is one more "leader" reinforcing an already extremely robust victim mentality by telling them that their relative poverty is the fault not of a lack of individual effort, or ingenuity, or of various cultural deficiencies, but of abuse and exploitation by the evil capitalist West; in such ways are poor people brainwashed into thinking that capitalism, the engine of wealth, is somehow the wellspring of their poverty.*"[26] Brainwashed or not, many poor people are indeed the victims of capitalism at its most ruth-

26 Bruce Bawer: *Surrender: Appeasing Islam, Sacrificing Freedom* (Anchor Books, New York, 2010), P. 128.

less. Ramadan's genius is to link economic grievance to religious ones, in a sleight of hand that manages to obscure the awkward fact that millions of Muslim migrants are trying to reach the wicked capitalist West precisely because it offers a better standard of living and more tolerance than the corrupt, backward and religiously oppressive societies they want to leave.

Ramadan is an extremely supple and fluent communicator and the dogmatism of his remark above is a rare slip (though his critics, like Paul Berman, have unpicked his pronouncements in painstaking detail to expose others.) He himself has said: *"mental ghettos are not mirages; they actually exist in palpable reality: being "open" inside one's mental or intellectual ghetto does not open its door but simply allows one to harbour the illusion that there is no ghetto and no door. The most dangerous prisons are those with invisible bars."* This is a wise remark. It certainly applies to those in the grip of religious intolerance based on the only true faith.

Beppe Grillo: Italian comic who garnered 25% of the vote in the 2012 Italian elections, much to the dismay of the greedy, complacent and corrupt political establishment:

Beppe Grillo, larger than life: "We are all adults. We don't need leaders..."

As befits a stand-up comedian, Grillo has a gift for picturesque abuse and amusing turns of phrase. For example, his coinage *"Rigor Montis"* to describe the Brussels-imposed austerity programme (which of course is quite unsuited to the Italian temperament) proved lethal when pinned on the worthy, but dull, Mario Monti.

The Grillo phenomenon is not new, merely the latest manifestation of what the Italians call *Qualunquismo,* a movement representing the ordinary man (*l'uomo qualunque*). In France this is called *Poujardism* after its founder, Pierre Poujade, who was a bookseller (always dodgy characters.) While Grillo is fond of shouting *"Piss off home!"* [*Tutti a casa!*] at the established politicians, Poujade used to refer to the government as *"rapetout et inhumain,"* and to the parliamentary deputies as "rubbish" and "pederasts."

Many lament the demise of picturesque pre-Grillo parties in Italy, such as the *"partito delle pesci freschi"* and the *"partito della bistecca"*, both of which were doctrinally sound if somewhat narrow in their appeal. But Italians like parties, both political and *bunga bunga* ones; the political system was traditionally organised so that they could have more or less as many of the former as they liked, as long as they confined themselves to demonstrating, collecting subsidies, and other harmless activities.

Economic Growth / GDP: Modern version of the Holy Grail:
David Boyle's **Little Money Book** [27] offers a counter-cultural view of what we are doing to ourselves in the developed economies. For example, the worship of "growth" and "GDP" by economists and politicians is encapsulated in one example that could stand for many: *"The GDP goes up with sales of pesticides that cause cancer and again with sales of drugs to cure it — perhaps made by the same company."*

GDP can't measure anything that isn't done for money, which is about half of all activity (23 million are involved in the voluntary sector in Britain, 22 million are in paid work, many of course in both, but only the paid work counts in GDP.)

GDP growth is a measure, not a value judgement, but economists, politicians and journalists implicitly use it as a measure of "success." *"We destroy the beauty of the countryside,"* wrote John Maynard Keynes in 1933, *"because the unappropriated splendours of nature have no economic value. We are capable of shutting off the sun and stars because they do not pay a dividend."*

27 Published by Alastair Sawday, 2003.

H

Homicide:

The slaying of one human being by another. There are four kinds of homicide: felonious, excusable, justifiable, and praiseworthy, but it makes no great difference to the person slain whether he fell by one kind or another — the classification is for advantage of the lawyers.

Ambrose Bierce: *The Unabridged Devil's Dictionary*

Hair: An intellectual's crowning glory:
"God is dead, but my hair is perfect" is a saying maliciously attributed to the narcissistic left-bank philosopher Bernard-Henri Lévy (or alternatively to Professor A.C.Grayling — he of the exquisite *chevelure*).

Lévy, a "public intellectual" in the French manner, had a bit of bad luck when he published his spectacular refutation of Kant in his 2010 book entitled *De la guerre en philosophie*. The centrepiece of this was the support he felt his position was afforded by the important contemporary philosopher Jean-Baptiste Botul. Alas, Botul was an invention of the journalist (and fellow philosopher) Frédéric Pagès, who made up spoofs for *Le Canard enchâiné*. Botul's most impressive work to date had indeed been his monograph on *La vie sexuelle d'Emmanuel Kant* (that is, if you omit the fascinating but unorthodox *Du Trou au Tout, Correspondance à moi-même*). You might have thought that Bernard-Henri would have smelled a rat when he saw that Jean-Baptiste's philosophic system was described by Pagès as *"Botulism,"* but you have to understand that public intellectuals in France are busy persons with many chat shows to visit and book signings to attend…. They can hardly be expected to actually read all the authors they quote.

Mickey (Miklós) Hargitay: Magyar muscleman and thespian catastrophe zone:
The former "Mr Indianapolis," "Mr Eastern America" and "Mr Universe" was best known for becoming Mr Jayne Mansfield ("Miss Photoflash," "Miss Magnesium Lamp," "Miss Fire Prevention," but

Mickey Hargitay and Jayne Mansfield: "Me Tarzan, you Jane!"

never "Miss Roquefort Cheese", though she was offered it.) In 1955, Hargitay was asked to join the beefcake chorus for Mae West's Las Vegas act, where he danced in a leopardskin G-string. Legend has it that Jayne Mansfield visited the club one night and sat at a table near the front. Asked by her companion what she would like, she said "I'll have a steak and the man on the left."

Hargitay and Mansfield married and appeared in some of the worst movies ever made, in which, as one critic unkindly remarked, his muscles and her tits did most of the acting. The couple were fond of being photographed beside their pink, heart-shaped swimming pool in Beverley Hills, where Jayne shared her profound reflections with respectful hacks, e.g. *"I will do anything for world peace."* And in fact she did take off all her clothes in *Promises, Promises*. Despite propaganda to the contrary from Mansfield fetishists, *Wikipedia* tells us that not Jayne, but "Anita Ekberg, had the largest natural breasts in A-List Hollywood history at 39DD."

Jean Harlow: Author of a novel enigmatically entitled *Today is Tonight*: Although it is now claimed that the best anecdote concerning Margot Asquith (feisty feminist wife of the Liberal Prime Minister) *"non è vero,"* it is certainly *"ben trovato."* The Asquiths were great socialites and one of the many celebrities invited to a party given by them was celluloid sex symbol Jean Harlow. Unfortunately, being very American and unfamiliar with the local usage, Harlow's opening gambit to her hostess was: " *Hey! Aren't you Margot Asquith?*" (pronouncing Margot as if it were "*Mar-got*"). "*Yes Dear,*" replied Margot with a certain lack of warmth, "*but the 't' is silent — as in Harlow.*"

Harlow was indeed by all accounts a bit of a goer. "*Underwear makes me feel uncomfortable,*" she once said, "*and besides my parts have to breathe.*" Also "*I like to wake up each morning feeling a new man.*" Certainly her interests seemed to have been more carnal than intellectual: "*Don't give me a book for Christmas,*" she said; "*I already have a book...*"

Jean Harlow, letting her underparts (and overparts) breathe...

Possibly also *ben trovato* is the sadly ungallant retort of Winston Churchill to Nancy Astor. Irritated by his hostility to feminism, she unwisely snarled at him: "*If I was your wife, I would put poison in your tea!*" "*Madam,*" said Churchill, "*if I was your husband I would drink it.*"

Doris Day was no Jean Harlow, certainly if you believed the studio publicity designed to emphasise her wholesomeness. This provoked Oscar Levant to claim of the fragrant singer and actress from Cincinnati: "*I knew Doris Day before she became a virgin...*" Levant, himself Jewish, finally had his TV show suspended for his comment on Marilyn Monroe's conversion to Judaism, unfortunately unprintable in a family publication like this... Oh, all right then, if you insist: "*Now that Marilyn's kosher, Arthur Miller can eat her.*"

Hatchet reviews: the revenge of talent on genius (sometimes vice versa): Sydney Smith said "*I never read a book before reviewing it; it prejudices a man so.*" Arthur Schopenhauer, ironically addressing the purchaser of his *Die Welt als Wille und Vorstellung¹* in the Foreword to the first edition, remarked that it might have various uses as an artefact, without the proud possessor actually having to read it. For example it could be used to fill an irritating gap on the bookshelf. Or, as a last resort, the non-reader could even write a review of it. On the other hand, *pace* Sydney Smith, actually reading the books often seems to prejudice reviewers even more.

Although many hatchet reviews tend to be wordy and nitpicking, the most effective are succinct. Dorothy Parker was often that and one of her most memorable dismissals ran: "This book should not be tossed aside lightly. It should be hurled with force." The book in question was a youthful effusion by Mussolini entitled "*L'Amante del Cardinale: Grande Romanzo dei Tempi del Cardinale Emanuel Madruzzo.*" "If *The Cardinal's Mistress* is a *Grande Romanzo*," said Parker, "then I am Alexandre Dumas, *père et fils.*"

There are of course hatchet reviews of hatchet reviewers, as when the novelist J. B. Priestley sliced up the notoriously authoritarian and dogmatic critic, F.R. Leavis. Citing a Leavis lecture on *Literature In My Time* given at Nottingham University, Priestley compared the good doctor to Groucho Marx — "whatever it was, he was against it. Virginia Woolf was a 'slender talent'; Lytton Strachey 'irresponsible and unscrupulous'; W. H. Auden 'the career type,' fixed at 'the undergraduate stage;' Spender 'no talent whatsoever;' Day-Lewis 'Book Society author'; the whole age 'dismal' and outlook 'very poor.' By the time Dr Leavis caught his train back to Cambridge, there was hardly anything left to read in Nottingham." Alert readers will notice however that all the authors mentioned are left-wingers and the underlying feud was substantially ideological. Besides Dr Leavis had recently declared that "no time need be wasted on Priestley…"²

Academic spats conducted by means of heavy shelling in the columns of the literary reviews are enjoyable (at least to outsiders), but perhaps not always very edifying. In April 2010 the distinguished historian of Stalin's Russia, Orlando Figes, admitted that he had anonymously been posting on Amazon hatchet reviews of amazing malevolence trashing the

---

1 The earliest translations render this subsequently influential work as "*The World as Will and Idea*," though it is now usually rendered as "*The World as Will and Representation.*"

2 Quoted from: *Thoughts in the Wilderness* by J. B. Priestley (Heinemann).

works of his rivals ("*awful*," "*the sort of book that makes you wonder why it was ever written*" were among the kinder comments).[3] Simultaneously the reviews lauded Figes's works, which gained lustre by comparison with the rubbish turned out by these colleagues ("*Beautifully written… leaves* the *reader awed, humbled and uplifted*" is not uncharacteristic of the rhapsodic, brown-nosing tone.) When the victims began to get suspicious about the authorship of these fusillades (and puffs), Figes at first denied that he was the reviewer, then issued threats of libel action against his accusers, and finally said that actually his wife had written the reviews unbeknown to him. Eventually however he surrendered and apologised for traducing his colleagues, lying to his lawyer and abusing the loyalty of his wife — which is not bad going for a Professor at a respected London university. He then had the gall to imply that he was suffering from depression brought on by researching and writing up the horrific crimes of Stalin: as one of *Figes's* victims, Rachel Polonsky, tartly observed: "Millions of innocent people had their mental health destroyed by Stalin. Take it from me. Whatever his PR man is saying, Orlando Figes is not one of them."

Although senior academics hastened to assure us that the Figes incident was an aberration, "peer reviewing" by scholars of each other's work for journal and book publishers is not always the process of peerless objectivity they would have us believe. Perhaps this is inevitable, given that a manuscript is necessarily sent for assessment to a scholar working in the same field as the aspirant author. It means however that the non-specialist publishing editor is entirely reliant on the honesty of the reviewer, who can either provide an informed and constructive critique — or deliver a disingenuous hatchet job in order to keep out the competition. A few years ago a supposedly distinguished "peer reviewer" of the manuscript of a history of Central Europe rubbished the work as poorly written, badly structured, ahistorical, grossly inaccurate etc., etc., and especially remarked on its unsuitability for teaching. Perhaps he (or she) rather gave the game away by going so far as to say that he (or she) would *actively prevent* it from being used as a textbook

---

3 See, *inter alia*, *The Guardian* of 23 April 2010. Also the tragic-comic account in the *Daily Mail* of 24 April 2010 by Rachel Polonsky of her dogged pursuit of the mountebank. It was her work, *Molotov's Magic Lantern*, that Figes had dismissed as "the sort of book that made you wonder why it was ever written."

if the necessity arose. Despite this attempted ambush, the author did find a publisher and shortly after the book appeared it won an independent award as the *"best history **textbook**"* of its year, besides being an *"Editor's Choice"* for the History Book Club in the USA. It has been in print for nineteen years, and is now a standard work in its third edition.

Of course hatchet reviews need not only be applied to books: drama, music and art (particularly the last-named) all attract brickbats. Nicolas Slonimsky published a *Lexicon of Musical Invective* (1953) which is full of laboured and often *ad hominem* assaults by critics and indeed composers on music they considered an insult to the listening public. The main interest of the book lies in the degree to which posterity has rendered the vituperation redundant, if not absurd. As hatchet reviews, their frequent recourse to zoological, scatological and pathological similes tend to weaken their impact, although occasional gems emerge (e.g. Brahms's characterisation of Bruckner's symphonies as *"symphonic boa-constrictors, the amateurish, confused and illogical abortions of a rustic school-master."* It is not clear that this was necessarily damaging though, since Bruckner's music publisher circulated a poster with both laudatory and vituperative comments on the master's great Seventh Symphony, an early indication of Harold Wilson's perception that all publicity is good publicity.) The saintly and modest Bruckner was a favourite Aunt Sally due to his espousal by the Wagner clique in Vienna and even today remains the butt of jokes (in the Foreword to a new edition of Slonimsky's *Lexicon*, we are told that the "Bruckner Expressway (which traverses the South Bronx in New York City) is so called because it is long and boring and doesn't go anywhere.")

So also in music criticism succinctness (conspicuous by its absence in musical and art reviews) once again proves more effective than long-winded abuse. In 2004 Franz Schreker's opera *Irrelohe*, damned and banned by the Nazis as "degenerate art," was revived at Vienna's *Volksoper*. The then Director of the Vienna opera, himself Jewish and a famously politically incorrect and abrasive gentleman, sat through it with mounting impatience. When the curtain at last fell, he turned to his companion and said: *"There, you see! Not every thing that Hitler banned was good."* Brevity is also a virtue in mounting counter-attacks on critics. The most celebrated example is Max Reger's note to a Munich critic who had savaged his work, which ran as follows: "Sir! I am

211

sitting in the smallest room in my house. I have your review before me. Shortly it will be *behind* me."

Of course the object of a hatchet review must itself be of sufficient stature (or irritation) to warrant the effort expended on demolishing it. This is why reviews of pop music are seldom worth reading. There are exceptions of course, as in this *Guardian* assessment of Marianne Faithfull's CD, *Kissin Time* [*sic*], which runs as follows : "Faithfull's voice could politely be described as characterful: with her received-pronunciation croak labouring roughly in the same vicinity as the tune, she sounds rather like a Woman's Hour presenter with laryngitis… there is something slightly unsettling about hearing Faithfull's ruined voice sing *'If Marianne was born a man she'd show you all a way to piss your life against a wall'*, but it perfectly captures Faithfull's unique candour." (Faithfull is in fact the great-great niece of Leopold Sacher-Masoch, author of a soft porn novel set in Baden bei Wien (*Venus in Furs* — 1870) which put the phrase "masochism" into circulation. Her military father invented a sexual device known as the Sexual Frigidity Machine, while Faithfull herself has lived a colourful life which has even involved an incident when she was busted by police at a country house —- they found her naked but for a fur rug with quite a lot of interesting forbidden substance around. Latterly she became an icon of the drug-fuelled sixties — although, as the saying goes, if you can remember the sixties you weren't really there….)

"*A critic*," wrote the Austrian theatre critic Hans Weigel in a moment of candour, "*is a person who gets very angry when the public likes something he doesn't.*"

Hearse: Vehicle for conveying politicians' reputations:
In the British General Election of 2005, the Conservatives ran a campaign long on the xenophobia but short on policies. This prompted the Tory grandee Chris Patten to describe the Tory leadership as being "*unable to distinguish between a bandwagon and a hearse*".

In 2010, critics of the lugubrious Labour Prime Minister Gordon Brown were even less flattering about their leader. One of them even said: "*if this man was running a funeral parlour, people would stop dying.*"[4]

---

4 Movie buffs will know that this *mot* originated with the ruthless trader Gordon Gecko in the film *Wall Street*.

Hedge Fund: A vehicle constructed to extract huge fees from investors on the false prospectus that it will make money equally in bad markets as in good:

In August 2015 sharp falls in the stock markets illustrated the not very surprising phenomenon that "hedge funds" lose money when everybody else does: for example, the Tiger Global Long-Only opportunities fund lost 7.4% in value, which was 1.4% more than the market itself (beware of funds with words like *"Tiger"* or *"Gold"* in their titles.) The Pershing Square fund dipped 9.2% and many other funds — the majority, it seems — failed to live up to their claims. The *Financial Times* quoted a "professional investor" as saying that the hedge funds aren't really "hedged" anyway, just funds that charge "incentive fees" (i.e. extremely high ones) for pretending to be hedged.[5] You might think the avaricious 20% on profits trousered by fund managers should be offset by rebates on the 2 per cent they take on the tens of billions of investors' money they routinely get their hands on. You might think that, but of course you would be wrong (this "heads I win, tails you lose" practice is known in the trade as "netting.")

In 2012 Simon Lack, himself a toiler at the hedge fund coalface for many years, published an exposé of the industry entitled *The Hedge Fund Mirage* which, needless to say, was not well received by his former colleagues. His central claim, namely that the return for the vast majority of hedge fund investors would have been doubled if their money had instead been in US Treasury Bills, was hotly contested. However even when hedge funds do well, as some do, the investor struggles to see similarly impressive returns because of the relentless gouging of the fee structures. Lack blames the investors for not being more alert, rather than the hedge fund managers who have simply discovered a profitable "business model" (as successful scams are so often called.) Lack is likewise unmoved by protests from the industry: *"The 2% management fee and 20% incentive fee have resulted in an enormous transfer of wealth from clients to the hedge fund industry. My analysis shows that pretty much all the profits earned by hedge funds in excess of the risk free rate have been consumed by fees."* [6]

5 Matthew Vincent: "Hedge funds merit a place on shelf of perfect misnomers," *Financial Times* 5-6 September, 2015.

6 See: *Institutional Investor's Alpha,* June 19, 2012: "Simon Lack responds to AIMA's hedge fund cheerleading."

Heinrich Heine: Poet, journalist and intellectual gadfly who invented the *"feuilleton"* and thereby annoyed Karl Kraus:

In his less than flattering essay *"Heine and the Consequences"*[7] Karl Kraus wrote that Heine's introduction of the French impressionistic essay known as a *feuilleton* had *"so loosened the corsets of the German language that today every sales clerk can fondle her breasts."*

In fact Heine was more than a match for Kraus as a satirist and ran greater risks in view of the tighter censorship that prevailed, especially in Germany, during his lifetime (1797-1856). However the authorities were also quite stupid and the rule that a book of more than 320 pages need not be laid before the censor (who thought thick books must be unreadable and so would not attract impressionable readers) sometimes enabled his publisher to circumvent the censorship by printing shortish books in huge type.

Heine's satires are easier to read than those of Kraus and less parochial: *"Mine is a peaceable disposition,"* he wrote. *"My wishes are a humble cottage with a thatched roof, but a good bed, good food, the freshest milk and butter, flowers before my window; and a few trees before my door; and if God wants to make my happiness complete, he will grant me the joy of seeing some six or seven of my enemies hanging from those trees. Before death I shall be moved in my heart to forgive them all the wrong they did me in their lifetime. One must, it is true, forgive one's enemies — but not before they have been hanged."*

On his deathbed he said: *"Of course God will forgive me: that's his job."*

Hell: Holiday destination in need of better marketing:

Hell is steadily losing adherents, says the *The Economist*.[8] "Accordingly the Infernal Tourist Board, using field-research by Dante Alighieri and John Milton, has produced a promotional flyer containing *inter alia* the following tips for visitors:

"Why Visit? Time stands still here, as the ocean boils and the great abyss yawns before you. Feel the hot sand under your feet, watch the chimeras and gorgons frolic, smell the brimstone on the breeze. You know how you always hope that holidays will never end? This one never will.

---

7 Karl Kraus: *Heine und die Folgen* (1910)
8 *The Economist* (January, 2013)

Getting there: The quickest route is to sin hugely and never show remorse.

Top Sights include: **Satan himself,** frozen in ice at hell's core, gnawing on several sinners at a time, and with his three-horned heads weeping gigantic tears of frustration. Entry staggered at peak times.

What to avoid: Beware belching fire and three-headed dogs.

Dining: **Chez Tantalus**: See your dinner hover over you, but never get to eat it! **Bar Lethe**: A popular, ever crowded, establishment, despite the slow and surly service of barmaid Medusa. You'll soon forget everything, including why you came.

Accommodation: **Holes of the Simoniacs**: Dive head-first into these funnels of fun, and let a devil set the soles of your feet on fire. **The Sacks @Malebolge**: Ten delightful mini-ditches in the trendy 8th circle, specially designed for liars and flatterers.

Book early to avoid disappointment. Pets and suicides extra.

Charon, a people trafficker on the Styx, whose business model inspired Ryanair...

Bertrand Russell wrote: *"The infliction of cruelty with a good conscience is a delight to moralists. That is why they invented Hell."* [9]

9 Bertrand Russell: *Sceptical Essays.*

Hippocampus: The part of the brain that controls our ability to navigate: Apparently taxi drivers have enlarged posterior regions of their hippocampi: doing "the knowledge" (the formidably difficult topographical test you are required to pass before you can be licensed to drive a London black cab), and then applying it, increases the size of the hippocampus over the years. This is the first evidence scientists have discovered that healthy brains can alter depending on how (or perhaps whether) they are used. It was all somewhat bemusing for cabbie Dave Cohen, who said: *"I never noticed part of my brain growing. It makes you wonder what happened to the rest of it."*

Eric Hobsbawm: Hampstead's last Stalinist (as far as we know): Marxist historian and almost the last member standing of the Communist Party of Great Britain, Hobsbawm mourned the fall of the USSR; it was "traumatic," he writes, "not only for Communists but for socialists everywhere" (*"Mir kommen die Tränen ... "*,[10] as the Germans say.)

With characteristic disingenuousness, Hobsbawm avoids referring directly to the Hitler-Stalin pact in his last book, referring blandly to *"temporary episodes such as 1939-41."* Whatever the merits of Hobsbawm *the historian* (and they are many), Hobsbawm *the man* was a master of double standards — ever quick to produce a slur on people who preferred "bourgeois" values to totalitarianism and mass extermination, while stepping daintily over the mega-crimes against humanity committed in the name of the socialist utopia.[11] Asked why he enjoyed a comfortable *haut-bourgeois* lifestyle in Hampstead instead of roughing it with the workers, who (he hoped) would soon establish the Soviet paradise in Britain, Hobsbawm sneered: *"If one is on a sinking ship, one may as well travel first class."*

When he died in 2012, an admiring academe vied with left-wing journalists in paying fulsome tributes. Hobsbawm had once claimed that Stalin's liquidation of millions of Soviet Citizens might well have been justified to establish the Communist utopia, just as the allies had ac-

10 "I already feel the tears coming..."
11 *Plus ça change*: in Iris Murdoch's 1930s Oxford diary we find the youthful moralist complaining that her colleagues do not have the *"right understanding"* [sic] of the recently concluded Hitler-Stalin pact. Likewise her friend Jean-Paul Sartre, being a philosopher like Iris, was disarmingly open about his attitude to truth. *"If you begin by saying 'Thou shalt not lie,'"* he wrote, *"there is no longer any possibility of political action."* Stalin himself could not have put it better.

216

cepted the sacrifice of their soldiers in World War II. This is a much used ploy on the left, suggesting a *moral equivalence* between those fighting for freedom and democracy and those simply butchering people to stay in power. Although the sad collapse of Communist totalitarianism meant that the usefulness of moral equivalence was temporarily diminished, it has subsequently been enjoying a renaissance amongst apologists for Islamism and graduates of the John Pilger school of journalism.

Six months after Hobsbawm's demise, Margaret Thatcher also died. Whatever her faults, it is undeniable that she did not advocate murdering civilians *en masse* as an instrument of Conservative policy. Furthermore she took over a basket case of a country and substantially restored its fortunes and standing in the world, whether or not one agreed with all of her policies. In stark contrast to its wall-to-wall eulogies of Hobsbawm, the broadcast media, with the BBC to the fore, scoured the country collecting soundbites of Thatcher hatred. Channel 4 even fished out an Argentinian who whinged that *"Thatcher invaded the Malvinas [eh?] and ruined my country"* — presumably a reference to Mrs T's robust action having caused the collapse of a murderous regime that was "disappearing" Argentinians at the rate of a thousand a month.

So there you have it: a large section of Britain's academic and media elite clearly *admires* the last Stalinist in Britain *with exactly same fervour* that it *hates* a politician who stood for freedom of the individual and who caused the downfall of a fascist regime. There could be no more eloquent reminder of how the principle of "evil be thou my good" guides many of the most illustrious in our society. Or, as Yeats put it, *"the best lack of all conviction and the worst are full of passionate intensity."*

Homosexuality: A practice now officially countenanced in the armed forces:

It is said that the ancient Spartans took the view that homosexuality had advantages in combat: officers and their favourite companions would often be chained together in battle, so that each fought ferociously to protect the other.

This argument is very compelling and could be used with equal persuasiveness to promote heterosexual relationships in the army, specifically the deployment of women in front-line (or other) positions.

And let us not forget that Lord Nelson's last words were: *"Kiss me, Hardy."*

217

J. Edgar Hoover: Bizarre head of the FBI whom no President dared to sack on account of his card index:

Hoover's sexuality is a matter for debate. One can't really draw any conclusions from his famous statement: "*I regret to say that we of the FBI are powerless to act in the case of oral-genital intimacy, unless it has in some way obstructed interstate commerce.*" There were rumours of cross-dressing and of him being seen painting the toenails of his lifelong friend Clyde Tolson (FBI Vice-Director) on a California beach (but everybody paints toenails on a California beach). Apparently he and Clyde were known as "J. Edna and Mother Tolson", which is rather sweet. Not that J. Edgar was sweet — more of a ruthless blackmailer and smearer of the public figures whom he disapproved of. Richard Nixon called him "one of the greats."

However that may be, he made some quite sensible remarks from time to time, for example: "Banks are an almost irresistible attraction for that element of our society which seeks unearned money." Also: "Justice is incidental to law and order." What people said *about* Hoover was no doubt featured in his famous card index. For instance he surely knew of Lyndon Johnson's (doubtless prudent) observation that "*I guess it's better to have him* [Hoover] *inside the tent pissing out than outside the tent pissing in…*"

Humblebrag: A form of boasting that involves subtly (or not so subtly) drawing attention to your humility:

Plutarch (c.46-127 A.D.) is said to be the originator of this particular ploy, having written an essay entitled "*On Praising Oneself Inoffensively.*" Twitter and tweeting have hugely increased the incidence of humblebrag, as indeed of bragging generally. Actors humblebrag about being recognised ("*It's been 10 years but I still feel so uncomfortable with being recognized. Just a bit shy still I suppose*") and other narcissists rabbit on about important meetings, making it to some public list of celebrities or achievers, or simply being incompetent (but lovable) at some big event. Those who think they can stomach a whole book of such effluent will find lots of it in *Humblebrag: The Art of False Modesty* (2012) by Harris Wittels.

David Hume (1711–1776): Scottish philosopher and master of uncomfortable reasoning:

Hume's take on the age-old problem of theodicy is as follows: "If God is omnipotent, omniscient and wholly good, whence evil? If God wills to

218

prevent evil but cannot, then He is not omnipotent. If He can prevent evil but does not, then he is not good. In either case he is not God." [*See also* **E:** *Epicurus*]. Writing in the *Sunday Telegraph*, someone endearingly described as "Chaplain to the London Stock Exchange" briskly dismisses Hume's argument as "trivial."

Yes, yes, of course! But what is the *counter*argument?

"Generally speaking," wrote Hume, "the errors in religion are dangerous; those in philosophy only ridiculous."[12] Christianity excited his irony, Islam his mistrust: "The admirers and followers of the Al Koran insist on the excellent moral precepts interspersed throughout that wild and absurd performance...Would we know, whether the pretended prophet had really attained a just sentiment of morality, let us attend to his narration, and we shall soon find, that he bestows praise upon such instances of treachery, inhumanity, cruelty, revenge, bigotry, as are utterly incompatible with civilised society. No steady rule of right conduct seems there to be attended to: and every action is blamed or praised, so far only as it is beneficial or harmful to the true believers."

These are sentiments which no one would today dare, or perhaps be allowed, to express on a TV programme, although almost anything can be said about Christianity.... Indeed, in his remarks on miracles, Hume himself said: "Upon the whole, we may conclude, that the *Christian Religion* not only was at first attended with miracles, but even at this day cannot be believed by any reasonable person without one. Mere reason is insufficient to convince us of its veracity: and whoever is moved by *Faith* to assent to it, is conscious of a continued miracle in his own person, which subverts all the principles of his understanding, and gives him a determination to believe what is most contrary to custom and experience." It is notable that he doesn't directly concern himself here with the veracity or otherwise of miracles, only with the psychological process by which the mind accommodates them.

"The Divinity," he wrote, "is a boundless Ocean of Bliss and Glory: Human minds are smaller streams, which, arising at first from the ocean, seek still, amid all wanderings, to return to it, and to lose themselves in that immensity of perfection. When checked in this natural course, by vice or folly, they become furious and enraged, and, swelling

12 Part 4 *Of the sceptical and other systems of philosophy*, Sect. 7 *Conclusion of this book.*

to a torrent, do then spread horror and devastation on the neighboring plains."

"It is an absurdity," he wrote in *Dialogues and Natural History of Religion*, "to believe that the Deity has human passions, and one of the lowest of human passions, a restless appetite for applause."

"*Rousseau* [whom Hume greatly admired] *was mad but influential*," said Bertrand Russell. "*Hume was sane but had no followers*."

Douglas Hurd: "A safe pair of hands" (which is Foreign Office-speak for a politician who is able to present nasty policies as principled and disastrous ones as a success):

In his not very eagerly awaited memoirs, former Foreign Secretary Douglas Hurd claimed the credit for resolutely maintaining the arms embargo on the Bosnians at a time when they were trying to defend themselves against genocidal Serbs armed to the teeth. He asserted that supplying the Bosnians with the wherewithal to defend themselves would only "*create a level killing field*," evidently preferring an un-level one that should soon see the Bosnians eliminated (as Mrs Thatcher tactlessly pointed out.) His bottom still warm from the FO hot seat, Hurd subsequently rushed to do business with the Butcher of Belgrade on behalf of the National Westminster Bank. Milosevich wanted to privatise the Serbian telecom and needed funds to finance his army of thugs and the upcoming ethnic cleansing in Kosovo. Hurd regarded this as a normal business deal and NatWest's fee for its services was allegedly just the $10 million. So that's all right then.

Hurd's attitude may serve as a textbook example of the Foreign Office's interpretation of the word "*neutrality*". The most famous example of this is a plaintive signal sent to the Admiralty by the British Admiral Codrington during the Greek War of Independence, which ran as follows: "*On whose side are we currently neutral?*"

Of course the cynicism of diplomats can be an effective tool of their trade, disarming the opposition by its sheer brazenness. The story goes that Sir Nevile Henderson somewhat redeemed his reputation as an appeaser (he was known as "our Nazi Ambassador in Berlin") when he went to take leave of Hitler in the Chancellery at the outbreak of World War II. The *Führer* was in aggressive mood. "*Remember*," he shouted, banging his fist on the table, "*we have the Italians with us this time!*" "*Well, that's only fair*," replied the Ambassador drily; "*We had them last time*."

Husbands: Slow learners, fast forgetters:
A Word to Husbands from Ogden Nash is probably all the former need to know about keeping their noses clean and staying out of trouble:

> *To keep your marriage brimming,*
> *With love in the loving cup,*
> *Whenever you're wrong, admit it;*
> *Whenever you're right, **shut up**.*

Hypocrites: Persons who claim to believe their own propaganda:
The archetypal hypocrite is *Tartuffe*, the eponymous anti-hero of Molière's play (1664), whose pretended piety is a ruse to advance his schemes of swindling and seduction. Although Louis XIV at first supported the performances of the play, the church rightly perceived it as a threat to its authority (people might get the wrong idea about ostentatious piety). So when the king finally banned it, his justification for doing so (probably supplied by the Archbishop of Paris) was an elegant example of hypocritical censorship:

"…although [the play] was found to be extremely diverting, the king recognized so much conformity between those that a true devotion leads on the path to heaven and those that a vain ostentation of some good works does not prevent from committing some bad ones, that his extreme delicacy to religious matters can not suffer this resemblance of vice to virtue, which could be mistaken for each other; although one does not doubt the good intentions of the author, even so he forbids it in public, and deprived himself of this pleasure, in order not to allow it to be abused by others, less capable of making a just discernment of it."[13]

"…*although one does not doubt the good intentions of the author,*" one "*can not suffer this resemblance of vice to virtue…*" The authorities, especially the ecclesiastical hierarchy, usually advanced arguments like this, namely that they were *protecting* people who might be exposed to the censored product, when in fact they were protecting themselves. In 1978 Judge J. H. Snyman, Chief South African Censor, presented the ultimate refinement of "protective" censorship when he explained the censor's selfless activity as follows: "*Every South African cannot go out*

---

13 Quoted in: François Rey & Jean Lacouture: "*Molière et le roi*" (Éditions du seuil, 2007)

and buy every new book and read it to decide if he will like it. We have a body that can do it for him. We study the book and tell him if he will like it or not."

High-minded hypocrisy is rather a speciality of the Anglophone world. Britain whitewashed its exploitation of its colonies with the doctrine of "the white man's burden." As Jomo Kenyatta once put it with gentle irony: *"When the missionaries arrived, the Africans had the land and the missionaries had the Bible. They taught us to pray with our eyes closed; when we opened them, they had the land and we had the Bible."* The hypocrisy of British imperialism extended of course beyond the oppression of "native" people to the treatment of rivals, most notably in the Boer War, the first war in which concentration camps were used (by the British) and one of the first where propaganda was put on a sophisticated basis. George Orwell describes a debate in the House of Commons in which an opposition member pointed out that, if the government's statistics were to be believed, our British troops had so far killed more Boers than the entire Boer nation contained. Whereat the Tory Prime Minister (A.J.Balfour) rose to his feet, shouted *"Cad!"* and sat down again.

The USA has more or less enshrined hypocrisy as part of the Constitution and the American way of life (c.f. also **Exceptionialism** under "E"). *"Think of how it all started,"* the comedian George Carlin once said: *"America was founded by slave owners who informed us, "All men are created equal." All "men," except Indians, niggers, and women. Remember, the founders were a small group of unelected, white, male, land-holding slave owners who also, by the way, suggested their class be the only one allowed to vote."*

The anarchist writer B. Traven was even more subversive of what he regarded as the hypocrisy ladled into Americans with their mother's milk and reflected in foreign and domestic policy: "In the United States the treatment of Indians is very peculiar. It typifies the remarkable hypocrisy that plagues public life in America. The freedom-loving American found it fully in order to keep negroes in slavery while he fought his revolution for freedom and independence; he found it likewise quite in order to attack weak and unarmed Mexico and to appropriate considerably more than half of that country's territory; he found that he could reconcile with his attachment to freedom the decision to wage a war against Spain, explaining that the oppressed Spanish colonies of Cuba, the Philippines and Puerto Rico would thereby be freed from the

Spanish yoke; and when he had freed them, to place them under his own tutelage. He entered the war in 1917 proclaiming that he had no acquisitive aims, but desired only to bring freedom and democracy into the world — and he emerged from the war with the confiscated wealth of the Germans and Austrians living in America, together with the German colony of Samoa; he allowed neither Mexico nor any of the central American Republics to create and apply laws that these countries considered beneficial for their peoples."[14]

While all this may be true, there is another, arguably more insidious, form of hypocrisy known as *"moral equivalence"* that seeks to elide all *degrees* of misgovernment, so that a totalitarian state can be made to look no worse than a less than perfect democracy, or a less than perfect democracy can be presented as equivalent to a brutal terrorising dictatorship. Defenders of genuine but flawed democracies tend to be at a disadvantage in this case, partly because defending a form of government in which abuses occur can be made to look like defence of the abuses themselves, and partly because the totalitarian state may have been able to silence its most penetrating critics. Also there is always a constituency in the free world for totalitarian ideology. When the "anarcho-syndicalist" philosopher Noam Chomsky claims that *"if the Nuremberg laws were applied, then every post-war [American] president would have been hanged,"* he is suggesting a moral equivalence between democratically elected leaders, who pursued some policies that many opposed, and a bunch of murdering thugs who (*inter alia*) liquidated six million Jews. A more refined version of the same technique is the Marxist historian Herbert Marcuse's characterisation of the freedom enjoyed in the West as *"repressive tolerance."* You may, in your innocence, think repression and tolerance are antithetical, but bulky volumes have been written by

---

14 *"Land of Springtime"* (1928) by B.Traven (aka Ret Marut or Otto Feige). The identity of Traven (1882? or 1890?–1969) is much disputed. He was probably a German revolutionary anarchist who fled to Britain, then the New World, ending up in Mexico. Since he operated under a pseudonym and only submitted manuscripts through intermediaries (some of whom however may have been himself), he was able to maintain an enticing mystery about his person and place of residence. All his novels took the part of the poor and the oppressed against the powerful, wealthy and oppressive. His most successful novel, *The Treasure of the Sierra Madre* (1927) was a hit when filmed by John Huston in 1948. But Traven does not appear to have enjoyed his wealth or to have lived well.

left-wing academics to demonstrate the opposite. George Carlin's says that *"language is a tool for concealing the truth,"* which is true of the Marcusians, who know what they are about. But then again it is consoling to recall that it may equally well be a tool for revealing the truth...

Institutionalised hypocrisy is now rampant in the mature democracies. Bank account holders in the UK not only must constantly prove their identities but may receive letters from the bank demanding to know if they have taxable investments abroad, or be asked *"what the money is for?"* if they wish to transfer funds to a foreign account. Yet these are the very banks that laundered millions round the world simply to avoid tax, as well as falsifying interest and exchange rates, beside sundry other dishonest or illegal activities. The *criminals* have been appointed *to police* the *honest burghers*. You might as well put a benefits cheat in charge of Social Security or Dracula in charge of the blood bank.

Internationally matters are arguably worse. The most spectacular example of hypocrisy used to be a grotesque body called the UN Human Rights Committee, which was reconstituted in 2006 as the Human Rights Council to include *inter alia* Cuba and China, both well-known for their concern about human rights. UN enthusiasts claimed that this was a marked improvement on the previous line-up, that included Colonel Gaddafi's bloodstained Libya (which at one point chaired the Committee), Syria (which displaced the USA on it) and Robert Mugabe's despotic Zimbabwe. [*See also under* **A: *Idi Amin***].

The Council spends a lot of its time censuring Israel (nine resolutions) while ignoring Chinese atrocities in Tibet, genocide in Darfur, murder and torture in Zimbabwe etc. etc. (nil resolutions on those countries). The American diplomat John Bolton was not quite right to say that the UN secretariat in New York could lose 10 of its 39 storeys and no one would notice the difference. Very probably one would notice a marked improvement.

In 2015 the UN Human Rights Council, chaired by an Argentinian who is indignant that the Falkland Islanders have been given the right to decide what national government they wish to live under and universally decided against Argentina, produced a report critical of Britain. The UK, it grandly observed, should *"review its legislation denying all convicted prisoners the right to vote."* The demand was signed off by committee members such as Algeria, Uganda and Egypt, countries where prisoners often shouldn't be in prison at all, and if they are, may be subject to torture. The self-congratulatory bubble of an international institution often produces this sort of double standard: all too often their committees are captured by activists whose concern for human rights extends no further than the extent to which the topic can be exploited in order to distract attention from their own countries' cruel regimes. There is also geopolitical cynicism, as when the United Kingdom in 2015 supported the admission of Saudi Arabia to the Council. *Saudi Arabia,* where women are not allowed to drive a car, domestic and sexual slavery is rife and punishments include beheading with a sword, stoning and lashes, the last named sometimes used for rape victims who cannot name their attacker and are therefore deemed to have committed adultery…

Many who are disgusted by the corrosive influence of institutional hypocrisy are a little more tolerant of individual hypocrisy, since there is after all, a little Tartuffe in every one of us. The press, itself one of the most hypocritical elements in our society, is quick to pounce on conflicts of interest, pharisaism and hypocrisy in public figures. As Humbert Wolfe memorably wrote: *"You cannot hope to bribe or twist / Thank God, the British journalist. / But seeing what the man will do unbribed / There's no occasion to.* Still, the most blatant attempts by public figures to have it both ways usually meet with a justified raspberry, especially where the hypocrites have tried to set themselves up as a moral instance. People expect to have their intelligence insulted by politicians; but to be insulted and morally patronised simultaneously by a shabby careerist is considered to be a bit much

Except, of course, where political correctness is concerned. Here it seems selective indignation is the rule rather than the exception. Stephen Fry, Salman Rushdie and other publicity-addicted intellectuals publicly denounced President Putin's 2013 law that forbad "propaganda of non-traditional relations," which was allegedly designed to prevent proselytism of children by homosexual activists. They demanded that the Winter Olympics at Sochi be boycotted because of this gross discrimination against the gay community which Fry even likened to the Nazis persecution of the Jews (an appeal to the Holocaust will always help to conceal a weak case.) Russia in fact decriminalised homosexuality in 1993. Yet the legal discrimination and even legally sanctioned violence against homosexuals is arguably far worse in countries like Bangla Desh, India, Sri Lanka and Pakistan that regularly play in cricket tournaments with Britain without attracting any foghorn denunciations from the ubiquitous Mr Fry or the conceited Mr Rushdie.

Post-colonial cringe and the instinctive application of double standards often deter the metropolitan liberals of our day from criticising non-white ethnic groups or Muslims. So Bangladesh is allowed to reject United Nations calls to decriminalise homosexuality on the grounds that to do so would "conflict with the socio-cultural values of the country"[15] and the valiant warriors for human dignity and sexual freedom fall silent. Some liberals have even argued that female genital mutilation, one of the most barbaric forms of female abuse in the world today, is "culturally based," implying that we have no right to interfere. Liberal smears against the writer and activist Ayaan Hirsi Ali, herself a victim of genital mutilation, and one who has spoken out fearlessly against the primitive and abusive behaviour of Islamists in regard to women, are clearly rooted in the same cultural cringe and moral cowardice. "I cannot emphasize enough how wrongheaded this is," she writes. "Withholding criticism and ignoring differences are racism in its purest form. Yet these cultural experts fail to notice that, through their anxious avoidance of criticizing non-Western countries, they trap the people who represent these cultures in a state of backwardness. The experts may have the best of intentions, but as we all know, the road to hell is paved with good intentions."[16] And in her autobiographical book *Infidel* she points to the bottom line of liberal equivocation and double standards: "What matters is abuse, and how it is anchored in a religion that denies women their rights as humans. What matters is that atrocities against women and children are carried out in Europe. What matters is that governments and societies must stop hiding behind a hollow pretence of tolerance so that they can recognize and deal with the problem."

If there was a Lifetime Achievement Award for hypocrisy, a strong candidate for it would be German Socialist author Günter Grass. Günter shocked the public (but probably not those who knew the old fraud) with his book "*Peeling the Onion*" [*Beim Häuten der Zwiebel*] in 2006. The Nobel Laureate and author of *The Tin Drum* had spent half a century lecturing Germans about their failure to face up to their Nazi past. Now (after 60 years) he revealed that he himself was recruited to the Waffen-

15 Quoted in "The hypocrisy game" by Leo McKinstry, *The Spectator* 8 March 2014.

16 Ayaan Hirsi Ali: *The Caged Virgin: An Emancipation Proclamation for Women and Islam*.

226

SS *in the dying days of the war*, an admission which, as the leader of the German Jewish Community bitterly and percipiently remarked, was timed to gain maximum publicity (and sales) for his new book.

Like many leftist intellectuals, Grass was a master of the disingenuous formulation. Speaking to Israelis in 1967, he recalled his days in an American prisoner of war camp around 1945, where he met young Jewish survivors from the concentration camps. These people, he claimed airily, had much in common with him — *"the same [Nazi] system had moulded us both."* The sheer effrontery of this, the (as yet unannounced) member of the Waffen-SS suggesting some sort of moral equivalence with its victims, puts Grass in a class of his own for Pharisaism. Joachim Fest, historian and biographer of Adolf Hitler, drily observed in the German weekly *Der Spiegel* of Grass's Waffen SS disclosure:

After 60 years, this confession comes a bit too late. I can't understand how someone who for decades set himself up as a moral authority, a rather smug one, could pull this off.

But pretentious, pipe-smoking Günter, who likened German reunification in 1989 to the *Anschluss* (Hitler's annexation of Austria in 1938), always kept his high horse conveniently tethered nearby. Critics of his more spectacularly self-righteous pronouncements would be trounced with the killer line: *"after Auschwitz you have no right to speak about history."* Apparently this did not apply to him.

Or take Mr George Galloway, an admirer of Saddam Hussein, who is now piously warning (threatening?) us to be "sensitive about people's religion, or deal with the consequences." He means, of course, we shouldn't say anything that might upset the delicate feelings of hair-trigger Islamic crazies, many of whom were his constituents, who equate their psychopathic disorders with true religion. Could this be the same Mr Galloway who still proclaims that the collapse of the Soviet Union was the "biggest catastrophe" of his life? (The Soviet Union, that is, which typically sentenced Baptists to twenty-five years of slave labour for holding prayer meetings…)

The Bog Standard Award for Hypocrisy must go to Gordon Brown, who said: *"I have never believed presentation should be a substitute for policy"* — and then announced a tax cut which, on closer inspection, turned out to be a tax rise. In contention was the inscrutable Roger Scruton, evidently not content with the consolations of philosophy: a right-wing libertarian, Scruton had in the past written touchingly in the *Daily*

Mail of how his Protestant upbringing taught him that *"greed was a vice, so too was sponging. The important thing was to want little and to obtain it by honest means."* These were fine sentiments. Obviously it was just an oversight that the great man forgot to tell the various journals for which he wrote that he was receiving a £54,000 annual retainer from Japan Tobacco International to defend smokers' rights — which he did by writing resounding articles on civil liberties and their incompatibility with restrictions on the sale of tobacco.[17] *The Guardian*, which exposed Scruton's nice little earner, added salaciously that *"Prof. Scruton has denounced single mothers, homosexuals, socialists, feminists, popular culture while defending Enoch Powell and fox hunting* — obviously you can't get more evil than that.[18]

Of course it is a happy coincidence when intellectuals can earn good money writing as their conscience dictates in defence of their beliefs. It certainly beats going to prison for them.

17 Amusingly this matter only came to light in 2002 because of a leaked letter written by Scruton's wife asking for the bung from JTI to be increased to £66,000, in return for which Scruton would place numerous articles in leading journals defending the right to smoke.

18 Kevin Maguire and Julian Borger: "Scruton in media plot to boost the sale of cigarettes" in *The Guardian*, 24th January, 2002

I

Infidel:

In New York, one who does not believe in the Christian religion;
in Constantinople, one who does.

Ambrose Bierce: *The Unabridged Devil's Dictionary*

Iatrogenesis: Diseases and disorders caused by medical intervention:
Iatrogenesis is on the rise as medical science and technical innovation
expands. An article by Werner Bartens in the *Süddeutsche Zeitung Magazin* portrays much well-intentioned intervention by the medical profession today, with its armoury of drugs and scans, as increasingly manic.
For example he cites the case of a seventy-nine year old woman suffering from diabetes, high blood pressure, bronchitis, osteoporosis and
rheumatism ("*not unusual in a person of that age*," as he drily remarks).
She was prescribed twelve different medicines to be taken at five different times of the day in nineteen doses. The likelihood that the old lady
would be able to follow such a regimen was obviously not considered by
the physicians who conscientiously selected the latest dope for each ailment. Some of the medicines even worked against each other, for example that against rheumatism weakens the effect of that against high blood
pressure. In the few moments that were left to her when not swallowing
medicines, the old lady was also urged to pay attention to her diet, attend
to her orthopaedic requirements and take more exercise.

According to Bartens, a further problem of today's medical orthodoxy
(which he does not deny can alleviate many illnesses previously incurable) is the obsession with testing patients that almost invariably reveals
some points of potential or actual illness. He points out that half of those
males who die aged eighty have cancerous prostate cells, but almost all
of them die without developing a tumour. Then again very many people
have back degeneration, at least according to the various x-rays, CT
scans etc. which they are directed to have by their doctors; but these

scans are not necessarily reliable. In a blind test radiologists and orthopaedists in Gemany looked at hundreds of CT scans and in about one third of them diagnosed problems that would require an operation to put right. However, what the experts didn't know, was that all the x-rays and scans had been made of students who were keen sportsmen and complained of no problems. In America the testing culture is not unconnected with commercial profits available to the testing bodies, particularly with potentially dangerous tests like angiograms. In Europe the tendency to constantly raise the bar by lowering the blood pressure or cholesterine level that is considered acceptable produces assessments such that "90% of fifty-year-olds" have a high risk of heart attack or stroke, or 76% of all adults." At some point one has to call a halt. Otherwise one ends making a reality of the current joke doing the rounds among the doctors themselves, namely *"the definition of a healthy person is one who has not been sufficiently examined."*[1]

Iceland: A place where many things are absent (most recently, money): Dr. Johnson was proud of being able to recite an entire chapter of Horrebow's *Natural History of Iceland*, namely Chapter LXXII, which reads: "*Concerning Snakes*: There are no snakes to be met with throughout the island." Even those with age-induced memory problems can probably recite the whole of Chapter XLII, which reads: "There are no owls of any kind in the whole island."

In the 1990s a distinguished banker explained in the gently patronising tones that distinguished bankers assume for telling untruths to lesser mortals, that Iceland (population about the same as the London Borough of Wandsworth) owed its vast and sudden wealth in the early years of the new millennium to … er… the fishing industry and … er … "deregulation."[2] Nice try.

Actually Snorri Sturluson's apparently bottomless pockets owed little or nothing to fish and everything to the cheap money that brought down so many casinos masquerading as banks in the 2007-8 crisis. The com-

---

1 Werner Bartens: "*Machen Sie sich frei: Der Medizin glauben wir alles — dass es vorwärts geht, dass wir immer länger leben. Leider lautet die Diagnose: alles nur Illusionen,*" *Süddeutsche Zeitung Magazin*, Nummer 10, 7 March, 2008.

2 Iceland "deregulated" its banks in 2001, an action which, so far from creating real wealth, in due course bankrupted the country.

bined balance sheets of the three largest Icelandic banks got to be ten times the GNP of Iceland itself, an absurd enough situation made even worse by the crookery and cronyism of these institutions and their main shareholders. As the report[3] into the collapse delicately summarised it: *"When it so happens that the biggest owners of a bank, who appoint members to the board of that same bank and exert for that reason strong influence within the bank, are, at the same time, among the bank's biggest borrowers, questions arise as to whether the lending is done on a commercial basis or whether the borrower possibly benefits from being an owner and has easier access to more advantageous loan facilities than others. This is, in reality, a case of transfer of resources to the parties in question from other shareholders and possibly from creditors. Research has shown that where big owners of banks are, at the same time, borrowers, these owners benefit from their position and get abnormally favourable deals…"* You may feel that this is an all too gentlemanly way of putting it when the single word "theft" would have done.

Here (as reported by *Wikipedia*) is how the system actually worked (in case anyone is tempted to feel *too* sorry for poor little Iceland bullied by the wicked Dutch and Brits, who froze the assets of Icelandic banks operating in the UK, compensated their Dutch and British depositors, and presented Iceland with the bill for doing so:

"Almost half of all the loans made by Icelandic banks were to holding companies, many of which were connected to those same Icelandic banks.

"Money was allegedly lent by the banks to their employees and associates so they could buy shares in those same banks while simply using those same shares as collateral for the loans. Borrowers were then allowed to defer paying interest on the loan until the end of the period, when the whole amount plus interest accrued was due. *These same loans were then allegedly written off days before the banks collapsed* (Italics added).

"Kaupthing [one of the three biggest Icelandic banks] allowed a Qatari investor to purchase 5% of its shares. *It was later revealed that the Qatari investor "bought" the stake using a loan from Kaupthing itself* (Italics added) and a holding company associated with one of its employees (i.e., the bank was, in effect, buying its own shares)."

3 *Causes of the Collapse of the Icelandic Banks — Responsibility, Mistakes and Negligence*, Chapter 21. Posted at www.rna.is/media/skjol/RNAvefurKafli21Enska.pdf

No doubt this sort of thing is what the genial banker quoted above had in mind when he referred to the benign effects of "deregulation."

Iconoclasm: Destruction of images by religious fanatics (also of monuments to leaders considered to be well past their "sell by" date):

Strictly speaking, iconoclasm refers to the destruction wrought on images by *believers* who think members of *their own faith* have strayed from some ur-prohibition, for example the injunction against "graven images" of the Ten Commandments or Islam's prohibition of depictions of Mahomet and other visual taboos spelled out in the *hadith*. In practice, most destruction of artefacts that have a religious or political significance is loosely regarded as iconoclasm, though often also referred to as vandalism. This is bad luck on the Vandals, who were not necessarily any more destructive than other tribes invading an enfeebled Roman Empire in the so-called Dark Ages,[4] although apparently they did make a point of defacing statues when they overran Rome in 455 A.D. Recently there has been some support for vandalism (particularly graffiti), which is seen as legitimate social protest by people who should probably know better — or who just want to advertise their philistinism. For example, in 1974 Norman Mailer [*q.v.*] lauded urban artistic vandalism in an essay entitled *The Faith of Graffiti*,[5] which likened tagging in New York City to the work of Giotto and Rauschenberg [*sic*]. (The New York Authorities responded by coating subway walls with Teflon and jailing taggers.)

The motive for mass cultural destruction in war is presumably to strike at the heart of a cultural identity and humiliate the enemy, so that he is damaged in the very core of his being. This surely lay behind the Persian rampage on the Athenian Acropolis, when they finally took it in 480 BC, smashing all the iconic monuments of the cult of Athena. It was as if they wanted to show how impotent was such a cult, not to mention the people that had embraced it, compared to the mighty Persians. The Athenians, on their return after the Persian defeat at Salamis, reacted with interesting logic by carefully burying the smashed statues, not recycling them,[6] and in due course (under Pericles) re-building the great

4 Some scholars think they actually perpetuated, rather than destroyed, Roman civilisation in late antiquity.

5 *Esquire*, May 1974.

6 Architectural fragments however were incorporated into new northern curtain wall.

symbolic edifices of the Acropolis even more magnificently than before. To this act of pious preservation ("the Persian debris") we owe the fact that the Acropolis museum today features remnants from the Persian devastation still with their pigment intact.

The Acropolis is thus both palimpsest and a place of multiple iconoclasm. In 267 A.D. the East Germanic Heruli smashed it up again; then, under the aegis of Byzantium, the Parthenon became a church, the building's patroness mutating under some duress from Athena to the Virgin Mary. Later, when the crusaders held the city as the Duchy of Athens, the Parthenon became their Latin cathedral. Under Christian ownership "pagan" idols fell victim to Christian zeal or, as the online *Encyclopaedia of Ancient History* chastely puts it, "*in keeping with the church's common practice, all pagan images were destroyed and modifications made to the temples to bring them into alignment with Christian sensibilities.*" Oddly, this is not a phase of iconoclasm much stressed in the relevant tourist literature. The Parthenon's metamorphosis progressed under the Turks, who turned it into a mosque and also stored their gunpowder in it. This ammunition dump blew up after receiving a direct hit from a Venetian mortar in 1687, the first serious reduction of the building in modern times before the depredations of Lord Elgin in 1801. Admittedly Elgin preserved what he looted, but as there is now a state-of-the-art museum *in situ* for the Parthenon frieze to be preserved, this unctuously claimed justification for his action can only be deemed sincere if the marbles are returned to their rightful owners. Meanwhile the archaeologists have also piously performed their own architectural lustration, unceremoniously demolishing Acropolis remnants from Byzantine, Latin and Turkish times in order to restore our sense of pristine awe for the site. For example, in 1874 Heinrich Schliemann[7] took one look at the huge tower (the *Frankopyrgos*) built on the western end of the Acropolis under the Latin Duchy and ordered it to be knocked down...

Théophile Gautier (among others) was strongly critical of this demolition of such an *"integral part of the Athenian horizon,"* while the historian of Frankish Greece William Miller called it *"an act of vandalism unworthy of any people imbued with a sense of the continuity of history."*

---

7 The controversial German excavator of the ancient sites of Troy in Asia Minor and Mycenae in the Peloponnese.

View of the Acropolis (circa 1875) showing the Frankish tower later demolished by Schliemann.

Although the most famous iconoclasm, from which the practice takes its name, is that instituted by the Byzantine Emperor Leo III the Isaurian in 730 A.D. (apparently he thought that the devastating consequences of a volcanic eruption at Thera (Santorini) were a judgement of God on images), the ill-tempered and ill-mannered destruction of religious symbols is as old as religion itself. Early Jewish communities destroyed rival idols, early Christians did the same to pagan idols and Christian colonists from Europe set about the visual religious heritage of the Americas, Africa, Asia and Polynesia. In the Reformation, Protestants set out to eradicate much visual culture associated with Popery, notably in the *Beeldenstorm* ("Statue Storm") that began in the Netherlands in 1566. Of course the opponents of Christianity (or other religions) had always done the same. Hadrian built a Temple of Venus on the supposed tomb of Jesus and around 280 AD a Zoroastrian high priest ordered massive destruction of temples and icons pertaining to all rival beliefs (Jews, Buddhists, Christians and Manichees). The Chinese Emperor Wuzong is said to have razed 4,600 Buddhist monasteries. In modern times gratuitous destruction has been carried out with zest by French revolutionar-

234

ies, Maoist Red Guards, Hindu fanatics and most recently and indiscriminately Islamists wanting to found a new caliphate.

The Vandals may have got a bad press but their actions hardly seem worse than the hypocritical and violent Christians who set out on the fourth Crusade. Ostensibly their aim was to regain the Holy Places of Palestine, but looting their fellow Christians in Constantinople proved to be more fun, not to mention more rewarding financially. In 1204 the Crusaders and Venetians destroyed or carried off most of the treasures of Byzantium in a prolonged orgy of destruction and robbery that stripped the veil for ever from the supposed religious and moral justification for crusades. A modern account by a Greek historian gives some idea of the Christian barbarism involved:

"The Latin soldiery subjected the greatest city in Europe to an indescribable sack. For three days they murdered, raped, looted and destroyed on a scale which even the ancient Vandals and Goths would have found unbelievable. Constantinople had become a veritable museum of ancient and Byzantine art, an emporium of such incredible wealth that the Latins were astounded at the riches they found. Though the Venetians had an appreciation for the art which they discovered (they were themselves semi-Byzantines) and saved much of it, the French and others destroyed indiscriminately, halting to refresh themselves with wine, violation of nuns, and murder of Orthodox clerics. The Crusaders vented their hatred for the Greeks most spectacularly in the desecration of the greatest Church in Christendom. They smashed the silver iconostasis, the icons and the holy books of Hagia Sophia, and seated upon the patriarchal throne a whore who sang coarse songs as they drank wine from the Church's holy vessels. The estrangement of East and West, which had proceeded over the centuries, culminated in the horrible massacre that accompanied the conquest of Constantinople. The Greeks were convinced that even the Turks, had they taken the city, would not have been as cruel as the Latin Christians. The defeat of Byzantium, already in a state of decline, accelerated political degeneration so that the Byzantines eventually became an easy prey to the Turks. The Fourth Crusade and the crusading movement generally thus resulted, ultimately, in the victory of Islam, a result which was of course the exact opposite of its original intention."[8]

8 Speros Vryonis: *Byzantium and Europe* (New York, Harcourt, Brace & World. 1967), P. 152. This quotation is extracted from *Wikipedia*'s extensive account of the 4th Crusade.

Some iconoclasm falls into the category of *damnatio memoriae*, which was the Roman expression for the practice of obliterating the memory of persons whose legacy the new ruling powers wished to remove from public consciousness. This practice lived on into our times, for example in the toppling of the mega-statues of Joseph Stalin in Hungary's 1956 Revolution and the removal of the Prague statue of Stalin in 1962, not to mention the fate of Saddam Hussein's statue in Baghdad after the invasion of Iraq. For the brief period that it existed, the Prague Stalin statue was the biggest in Europe at 15.5 metres high and 22 metres across. It was made of reinforced concrete and faced with 235 granite blocks weighing 17,000 tons. However Stalin's personality cult had already fallen into disfavour by the time it was ready and it was ominous that the principal sculptor, Otokar Svec, killed himself the day before the unveiling. An embarrassed Czech Communist party decided seven years later to get rid of it, but it required 800 kg of explosives to do so. Recently a huge golden statue of Mao Tse Tung erected in China's rural Henan province was "quietly being demolished" according to a report in the *Financial Times*, although of course it is difficult to demolish something 36 meters high "quietly". It

Mao in leaderly pose with seemingly unimpressed locals in the foreground.

is supposed to have cost half a million dollars to erect and Chinese bloggers disobligingly pointed out that it had been erected precisely in an area where millions died from famine in Mao's "Great Leap Forward" during the 1950s.

An Ozymandian fate might have been better as warning to hubristic tyrants, and in fact the Communist statues and monuments of Budapest (some of them made by gifted sculptors) were removed (intact) to a "statue park" outside the city after 1990. The material of the Budapest Stalin statue broken up in 1956 was reused, just as the statue itself had originally been partly constituted by material from monuments to Hungarian patriots broken up by the Communists.

Occasionally it could be risky to back the public mood for *damnatio memoriae* too enthusiastically — witness the fate of the painter Gustave Courbet. In 1871, during the Paris Commune, he proposed disassembling the great statue of Napoleon atop a Corinthian column on the Place Vendôme, which disassembly subsequently occurred after a decision by the Communards. However, when the Commune had collapsed, Adolphe Thiers ordered that the column and statue be re-erected in 1874. Courbet was held to be largely responsible for its removal and ordered to pay the cost of restitution, which was 320,000 Francs. (Perhaps it had been a little rash of the artist also to have advocated the demolition of Thiers' house in Paris and the confiscation of his art collection.) Unable to pay, he went into Swiss exile, so the government seized his paintings and sold them for a meagre sum of cash. Poor old Courbet, "Citizen Courbet," as he had styled himself during the Commune, died penniless in Switzerland in 1877. This is a cautionary tale for those who like knocking down statues, just as iconoclasm is a cautionary tale for those who like putting them up...

Strategic Importance: An importance that is imperceptible without the addition of the word "strategic":

General Colin Powell relates in his autobiography how he served in the Vietnam War with a Vietnamese adviser and went with him to a dangerous outpost near the Laotian border. His Vietnamese counterpart assured him it was a "very important outpost." "But why is it here?" asked Powell. "Outpost is here to protect airfield." "What's the airfield here for?" "Airfield here to resupply outpost."

237

Index: Often the most interesting part of a book, and the only part read with close attention (e.g. by persons wishing to ascertain if their names are featured in it):

The flavour of Francis Wheen's engaging book about the 1970s ("*The Golden Age of Paranoia*") is best conveyed by citing a few items from the index, as follows:

Amin, President Idi: likened to Lady Falkender. Prehistoric monster. Splendid rugger player. Mass-murderer.
Blowing: see cunnnilingus.
Cunnilingus: unknown to Judge Argyle.
Falkender, Baroness: squabbles and screeches. Hates whitebait.
Fellatio: unknown to Judge Argyle.
Geller, Uri: bends cutlery. Meets extra-terrestrials. Turns into a hawk.
Heath, Edward: as Empress of Blandings. Meanness of. Speaks French badly. Grumpiness.
Wash: reluctance to of Lin Biao; of Mao; of author.
Wilson, Harold: as big fat spider. Sees invisible powers. Breaks into Marcia Falkender's garage. As Hercule Poirot.
Yodelling in the canyon: see cunnilingus.

India: A country where more people have access to mobile phones than to toilets:

According to a UN report from a UN Think Tank cited in *The Telegraph* (15th April, 2010), India's mobile subscribers totalled 563.73 million at the last count, enough to serve nearly half of the 1.2 billion population.

But just 366 million people — around a third of the population — had access to proper sanitation in 2008. Apparently, of all India's regions, only Sikkim, the tiny former Kingdom in the Himalayas, has provided indoor lavatories for all its people, and one disgruntled Indian minister has referred to his country as the "world's largest open air toilet" in view of widespread defecation in public.

In another *Telegraph* article of 19th November 2013, reporter Dean Nelson writes: "India has 37 million 'missing lavatories' its government claims to have built in villages throughout the country, but which do not exist, campaigners have said. The claim was made on 'World Toilet Day' on Tuesday by sanitation campaigners who compared figures claimed by the government's rural development ministry and official data from India's census."

But is the infamous Indian bureaucracy really to blame? Nelson goes on to point out that "Advisers had already called on the government to halt its lavatory building programme after it emerged that many of the lavatories were in fact being used as store rooms, guest rooms and kitchens by villagers who preferred to do their ablutions in the open."

T. N. Ninan points out that India is a nuclear power and has sent a satellite to Mars, yet its average per capita income is lower

Baba on the hot line to Shiva...

than those of Laos, Zambia and Sudan. The official (but disputed) figure for formal employment in India is 30 million, just 6 per cent of the total workforce, most of them apparently state employees.[9] Were this to be true, it would suggest that millions are in "informal" employment or the black economy. But how can one know what is true in India? A Harvard Professor has coined the phrase "flailing state" to describe how even the (relatively few) sensible measures enacted by government can seldom be enforced by officials. Repeatedly foreign investors talk of the burgeoning middle class and enormous domestic market as having vast money-spinning potential; after a few years of dealing with local cartels and obstructive officials 99% of them retire hurt.

"India is not, as people keep calling it, an underdeveloped country, but rather, in the context of its history and cultural heritage, a highly developed one in an advanced state of decay." — Shashi Tharoor

9 T. N. Ninan: *The Turn of the Tortoise: the Challenge and Promise of India's Future* (Allen Lane /Penguin India, 2015.)

"No people whose word for 'yesterday' is the same as their word for 'tomorrow' can be said to have a firm grip on the time." — Salman Rushdie, *Midnight's Children*

"The impression [*that India made on me*] was of a plodding indefatigable and distant past that had crashed intact through barriers of time into its own future. I liked it." — Gregory David Roberts, *Shantaram*

"… nothing in India is identifiable, the mere asking of a question causes it to disappear and merge into something else." — E.M. Forster

"The best thing about India is the freedom that one enjoys here, which is also the worst thing about it." — Deepak Rana, *Sky Beyond the Clouds*

"Everything will be alright in the end, so if it is not alright, it is not the end." — The young would-be Indian hotelier in Deborah Moggach's novel *The Best Exotic Marigold Hotel*

Individuals: Persons theoretically lauded by politicians and businesses for their independence of mind, but in practice only approved if they merge into like-minded flocks that can be politically manipulated and more easily sold to:

"*Most people are other people,*" said Oscar Wilde. "*Their thoughts are someone else's opinions, their lives a mimicry, their passions a quotation.*" And Clarence Ayres, a protagonist of the Institutionalist School of Economics, claimed that there "*is no such thing as an individual.*" This would be disputed by many, including intellectuals who pride themselves on independence of mind. But the critic Harold Rosenberg is aware of the sheep-like tendency underlying much of academe's bluster about independent thought and coined the phrase "*the herd of independent minds*" to describe it. Despite claims to the contrary, it is all too often easier to herd intellectuals, or at least academics, than cats…

Intellectuals also tend to be very keen on notions such as "society" and "community," which can be conveniently defined to suit an ideological agenda. Mrs Thatcher, on the other hand, once declared that "*there is no such thing as society. There are individual men and women, and there are families.*" The breast-beating and hysterical denunciation that this latter remark occasioned suggest that it must at least be partly true. Taken out of context it was held up as another example of heartless Tories abandoning the poor and underprivileged to their fate. However William Beveridge who devised the systemic template that underpins the modern welfare state in Britain and is therefore considered to be some sort of secular saint, would have understood what Mrs Thatcher was getting at. In his book *Voluntary Action* (1948), he wrote: "*The making of a good society depends not on the State but on the citizens, acting individually or in free association with one another, acting on motives of various kinds — some selfish, others unselfish, some narrow and material, others inspired by love of man and love of God. The happiness or unhappiness of the society in which we live depends upon ourselves as citizens, not only the instruments of political power which we call the State.*"

William Easterly in his iconoclastic book on global development strategies, points out that all innovation ultimately depends on individuals. Up to the time of the Enlightenment, "innovation," he says, was actually a term of abuse, but thereafter a term of praise. Innovation is produced by those who are able to work outside strictly enforced dogmas policed by hierarchies interested only in conformity. The problem of world improvers today is that they too often believe in top down imposition, for example of the wonders of technology, paying little or no attention as to the culture of individuals on the ground. An example he gives is that of a UN commission on broadband chaired by the Rwandan dictator, Paul Kagame. In a characteristically jargon-filled report Kagame set out targets for broadband expansion, assuming its inherent benefit to all persons in all places. Unfortunately a follow-up study made by a researcher at Berkeley revealed that when this empowering technology was hooked up to a remote village "the dominant use is by young men who are playing games, watching movies or consuming adult content." As Easterly bluntly remarks "wiring the world to end poverty overlooks how many less faddish technologies are still lacking among the poor. The development audience gets excited about farmers in a remote but wired village finding out prices in real time for their crops. It fails to ask whether those farmers have motor vehicles to transport the crops to the market to get that price… top-down leaders and experts in technology do not have enough knowledge or incentives to get it right for the reality of what is happening at the bottom. They promised to end poverty with broadband and they gave us young men watching porn."[10]

10 William Easterly: *The Tyranny of Experts: Economists, Dictators and the Forgotten Rights of the Poor* (Basic Books, New York, 2013) pp. 276, 286-287.

However the institutionalists, behaviourists, and no doubt many other — ists, have a point when they say that socialisation is unavoidable in any context other than Robinson Crusoe's, so people in reality have multiple selves reflecting their upbringing, class, economic circumstances and so forth. Ha-Joon Chang sums up this point of view apodictically: "There *cannot* be such a thing as an individual without society." [11] This idea can be extended — and has been, by the great 19th century Italian poet and recluse Count Giacomo Leopardi, who wrote that: "*Real misanthropes are not found in solitude, but in the world; since it is experience of life, and not philosophy, which produces real hatred of mankind.*"[12]

Inebriation: Something that makes life bearable for the addicted and unbearable for everybody else:

Alcoholics are always, as one's mother used to say, "letting themselves down" — not to mention other people. For example, Michael Steen's *Lives and Times of the Great Composers* contains an anecdote of some pathos about the famous operatic rivalry between Piccini and Gluck. The latter had had a great hit with his mellifluous *Iphigénie en Tauride*. Not to be outdone, Piccini too produced an opera, likewise called *Iphigénie en Tauride*. It was not a success. However, says Steen gallantly in Piccini's defence, its few performances did not really do it justice due to the drinking habits of the leading lady. Indeed its fate was sealed after opera goers began referring to it as "*Iphigénie en Champagne.*"

A Burgenland peasant has claimed that "*reality is a hallucination caused by lack of alcohol,*" which is the sort of thing a Burgenland peasant would say. Unfortunately many writers seem to have subscribed to this view, with mixed results in regard to their creative output and catastrophic ones for their personal relationships [q.v. *Norman Mailer*] .

In his tastefully titled routine "*When Will Jesus Bring the Pork Chops?*" the comedian George Carlin remarked that the "the warning labels on alcoholic beverages were too bland. They should be more vivid. Here is one I would suggest: '*Alcohol will turn you into the same asshole your father was.*'" In similar vein novelist Kingsley Amis once put forward an idea for an advertising campaign for the brewing industry. The campaign, Amis felt, should confine itself to highlighting the product's

11 Ha-Joon Chang: *Economics: The User's Guide* (Pelican, London, 2014), P. 194.
12 Giacomo Leopardi: *Pensieri*, 1834-7.

key selling point; so his posters would simply bear the slogan: "*Beer makes you drunk.*" Adjacent to these words would be an image of someone's mother-in-law falling down stairs. [q.v. **K: *Katja Kabanova.*]** Carlin also had an idiosyncratic input into the debate about responsible drinking among females: "Instead of warning pregnant women not to drink, I think female alcoholics ought to be told not to fuck."

The greatest philosopher of alcohol was W. C. Fields, whose *obiter dicta* on the subject include: "*They say drinking interferes with your sex life, but I figure it's the other way around;*" also: "*My first wife drove me to drink. I always meant to write and thank her.*"

In America they say you're an alcoholic if you drink more than your doctor.

Information: What today is erroneously considered to be synonymous with knowledge:

The accumulation of vast databases has become an end in itself, just as the accumulation of pointless knowledge fuels a thousand television quizzes. Attention spans get shorter and reactions speed up until life itself begins to resemble the mindless jumble of flashing narcissistic images and slogans which fills much of CNN's television programming.

The belief that the endless accumulation of data ("*more research is needed*" is invariably the ominous closing line of an academic study) necessarily brings ultimate wisdom joins the equally entrenched belief that all problems can be solved with more money to make the two unchallengeable orthodoxies of a materialist age.

The phrase "to *problematise*" [an issue], which rises unbidden to the lips of scholars, lifts the veil on academic job creation schemes. By the same token, no project or charity ever admits to having sufficient funding. Yet stock market bubbles are caused (or so the experts tell us) by "over-investment" (*vide* the "dot.com" market collapse) — so shortage of cash is hardly the problem of developed societies; merely misallocation of it.

Anyone who believes, or much worse, demonstrates, that a given problem can be successfully tackled by thinking more carefully, and without an endlessly expanding "database" and a rising tide of "funding," can expect to be pilloried. Such an approach is almost as subversive as suggesting we might all live more satisfactory lives if we consumed less, or that we might have more time for real friends if we spent less time on fake friends who "follow" us on Twitter. As the UK's Chief Rabbi rhetorically inquired recently: "How many of your "friends" on Twitter or Facebook would you go to for support in a real crisis? I fear the answer is none." *"Data is not information,"* wrote the astronomer Clifford Stoll, *"information is not knowledge, knowledge is not understanding, understanding is not wisdom"* (though admittedly he also told us that the internet was going nowhere.) The saintly philosopher Frank Zappa has a more refined take on the problem: *"Information is not knowledge. Knowledge is not wisdom. Wisdom is not truth. Truth is not beauty. Beauty is not love. Love is not music. Music is the best …"*

Financial Innovation: "Something that makes insiders rich, then blows up."[13]

Intellectual clerics: Synonym for left-wing priests:
The previous Archbishop of Canterbury, Rowan Williams, passed among churchmen as an intellectual of great mental subtlety, perhaps because of his beard. It was he who suggested that parts of the corpus of Islamic law known as *shari'a* will soon "unavoidably" be incorporated into British law.

There is a small problem: in *shari'a*, there is no distinction between religious dogma ("revealed truths") and the law; on the other hand British law, especially since the Enlightenment, has evolved from secular concepts like consent, reason, human rights and freedom of the individual. On the whole, *shari'a* is adamantly opposed to precisely these notions, especially in regard to women; it is no wonder that the European Court of Human Rights says it is incompatible with democracy.

None of this seemed greatly to worry the Archbishop, although he was fastidious about the more awesomely barbarous punishments of *shari'a*. However he had a fatherly concern for those with conflicted allegiance: he said he would like to avoid people having to *"choose"* between *"cultural loyalty and state loyalty."*

Unfortunately *state loyalty* and agreement to abide by the laws of the land is for Muslims, as for everybody else in Britain, not a matter of *"choosing"*; it is an obligation. Should Muslims prefer the rule of *shari'a*, which anyway doesn't distinguish between *"cultural loyalty"* and *"state*

---

13 A *Financial Times* columnist – and he should know…

loyalty," and thereby reject "*state loyalty*" when and if it conflicts with *shari'a*, it seems reasonable to ask them to go and live where the environment is more congenial to them.

Intelligence and Security Committee: Satirically named parliamentary body:

Doubtless as part of New Labour's exciting commitment to open government, the Committee once published a review of the work of MI5 and MI6. Journalist Francis Wheen turned the pages, and was unimpressed with sentences like: "We believe that the UK needs to be *** to ensure that the UK remains ***" "There follow," says Wheen, "nine detailed and careful paragraphs, each of which consists of three asterisks and nothing else, after which the Committee concludes: 'We believe the UK cannot afford not to be involved in this work.'"

Intelligent Life: Life like ours, which is capable of obliterating all other forms of life:

According to the cartoon character Calvin Hobbes, the most compelling evidence for the existence of intelligent life on other planets is that it has never tried to make contact with us…

International Investment Bank: A respectable business concealing a criminal enterprise:

In recent decades, most of the largest international banks were involved in falsifying *LIBOR* in London and its equivalents elsewhere in the world, such as *EURIBOR* in Brussels, *FIBOR* in Frankfurt and *TIBOR* in Tokyo. These obscure acronyms stand for interest rates set by a committee of banks, the said rates officially reflecting how much it costs such banks to borrow from each other in various currencies. Scams included "*lowballing*" (pitching a falsely low price to deceive the market into thinking a particular institution's finances were solider than they were) and fiddling the rates to benefit trading positions held by participants. Tiny nudges of *LIBOR* etc. are significant because *$350 trillion's worth* of financial products worldwide is referred to the rates.

Bank divisions operating this racket reported huge profits, which, gentle reader, ultimately stem from a tortuous and well concealed method of parting you from your money. "The business model of modern finance," writes the economist and journalist Will Hutton, "[consists of] banks trading on their own account in rigged derivative markets, skimming investment funds and manipulating interbank lending, all to under-lend to innovative enterprise while over-lending on a stunning scale to private equity and property." Furthermore much of these banks' business was really no more than an alchemy of money creation through complex financial instruments unconnected to productive economic activity.

The size of such business, says Hutton, is mind-boggling. "World GDP is around $70tm. The market in interest rate derivatives is worth $310tm. The idea that this has grown to such a scale because of the demands of the real economy to better manage risk is absurd. And on top it has a curious feature. None of the banks that constitute the market ever loses money. All their divisions that trade interest rate derivatives on their own account report huge profits running into billions. Where does that profit come from?"[14]

It is a good question. Because all this financial wizardry is intertwined with global financial services and the asset-management industry, explains Hutton, global banking is actually a hidden tax on the world economy. The banks didn't lose money on dodgy derivatives, as we see from their results. The final buyers of the derivatives were their customers, the convenient receptacles for any losses that might arise.

Like Fafnir crouched over his hoard, the banks were still sullenly clinging to their rent-seeking and other dubious practices, even as regulators began demanding the separation of retail banking from "investment" banking (a.k.a. gambling with our money and charging losses to the taxpayer.) You doubt it's as bad as that? Wake up and smell the coffee! Before the law caught up with it, sanctimonious mega-bank HSBC had installed *extra-wide cashier windows* in the branches of its Mexican associate to accommodate (as it turned out) the vast piles of drug cartel cash being laundered....

Investment banking in Britain: Activity described by one of its practitioners as "a tax on the saving classes" ("*Tax on*" is banker-speak for "*theft from*"):

As financial journalist Anthony Hilton has pointed out, investment bankers' eye-watering profits, salaries and "bonuses" come from

14 Will Hutton: *"Bank rate-fixing scandals reveal the rotten heart of capitalism," The Observer*, December 23rd 2012.

246

money saved by the public and unwisely handed for safekeeping to the institutions. While ruthless business competition (invariably prescribed by the bankers for others) drives down profits and salaries for mainstream businesses, "competition" among investment banks only causes fees to spiral ever higher. The notion of "performance," ritually proclaimed by "financiers" as requiring astronomic remuneration, is miraculously redefined when their own "performance" is measured. It turns out (according to the *Financial Times* and others) that more than two thirds of the mergers they press on businesses end up *destroying* shareholder value.

The AOL /Time Warner deal has so far managed to dissolve the equivalent of 146 billion Euros of shareholder value, and even the piffling little deal between Quelle and Karstadt in takeover-averse Germany has swallowed 1.4 billion. Huge swathes of this evanescing capital has ended up in the pockets of those who organised the catastrophe in the first place; and who are no doubt laughing … er … all the way to the bank.

However in the wake of the financial crisis the regulators have rather put the kybosh on the easier pickings of investment banking with tiresome restrictions such as caps on bonuses imposed by the EU, attempts to "ring-fence" the investment side from the commercial deposit-taking side to prevent pilfering and conflicts of interest, scrutiny of "proprietary trading" where banks take leveraged bets on their own account — and much more. This has provoked a self-righteous wail from the previously fat, now not noticeably thinner, cats in the investment banking game. All this regulation, not to mention the regrettably misinformed hostility from the press and public, has "inadvertently destroyed the one industry in which the UK was clearly a world leader," they complain.

Leaving aside whether we should actually be proud of being a world leader in overcharging, racketeering and dubious deal-making, Martin Vander Weyer surely has the right response to this disingenuous claim: "No, my friend," he writes, "… we [meaning the government, reacting to public outrage] will merely have encouraged you to operate in a safer, more sustainable way, because you seem to have forgotten that, but for taxpayer and central bank largesse on both sides of the Atlantic, you would already have destroyed yourselves."[15]

15 Martin Vander Weyer: "Are investment bankers being kicked to death? And should we care — or cheer?" *The Spectator*, 17 May, 2014.

Iraq: Happy homeland of *Chemical Ali* and *Comical Ali*:
These two engaging characters held senior posts in Saddam Hussein's Iraq regime. Chemical Ali admittedly contributed little to the gaiety of nations, but a more generous judgement has usually been passed on Comical Ali.

Comical ali and Chemical Ali: Iraq's answer to the Kray brothers, but without the jokes....

"I will kill them all [the Kurdish resistance fighters] *with chemical weapons! Who is going to say anything? The international community? Fuck them!"* A tape of these picturesque sentiments and others of a similar nature was adduced in evidence when Saddam's cousin, Ali Hassan Abd al-Majid al-Tikriti, aka Chemical Ali, was hauled before the courts after the invasion of Iraq in 2003. He was finally given four death sentences, including one for organising the butchery of some 20,000 Shias. Amnesty International's Middle East and North Africa Director Malcolm Smart said Ali's execution was *"only the latest of a mounting number of executions, some of whom* [sic] *did not receive fair trials, in gross violation of human rights..."* For some reason this complaint failed to generate world-wide indignation... Mohammed Saeed al-Sahhaf (Comical Ali), on the other hand, came to prominence in the world's media during the 2003 invasion of Iraq, when he was the Iraqi Information Minister. A sort of Iraqi version of Alastair Campbell, his bombastic and

248

inventive propaganda broadcasts before and during the war extolled the invincibility of the Iraqi Army even as it was surrendering *en masse* — thus providing some much-needed light relief for both combatants and commentators. In Italy he was known as *Alì il Comico*.

Double Irish:[16] A "tax-avoidance" cocktail combining the luck of the Irish with Dutch courage and seasoned with expensive legal chicanery:

This tax "loophole" enables vastly rich multinationals to use Ireland as a foreign operating base, while avoiding its (anyway modest) 12.5% corporation tax. Profits are instead routed to a subsidiary in Bermuda.

The ruse depends, says the *Financial Times*, on "Ireland's permissive view that an Irish-registered business should be taxed where it is managed, even if that is an island where beach shorts are business attire…" The USA has put pressure on Ireland to stop this racket, which it has reluctantly agreed to do by 2020, thus giving time, says the FT unpleasantly, "for tax advisers to dream up replacement schemes." Tax ruses come and go — the Double Irish, for example, was once accompanied by a manoeuvre known as the "Dutch Sandwich" (which unfortunately is not a sexual practice offered in Amsterdam's red light district.)

Investopedia says: "The Double Irish with a Dutch Sandwich technique involves sending profits first through one Irish company, then to a Dutch company and finally to a second Irish company headquartered in a tax haven. This technique has allowed certain corporations to dramatically reduce their overall corporate tax rates." Do not try this on your own (although, if you are an investor or a taxpayer very likely some of your money is involved in it….).

Islam: Monotheism in search of a better image:
We can probably take it that what the founder of modern Turkey, Mustafa Kemal Atatürk, had to say about Islam is not a view shared by the current leader, Recep Tayyip Erdoğan. Turkey's President has, after all, candidly warned any naïve souls who might have thought otherwise that *"democracy is a means, not an end"*[17] — the leader of a Communist cell could not have put it better. In an earlier interview (1994) Erdogan

---

16 *"Lucrative tax loophole exploited by multinationals with Irish operations"* is the definition given in the *Financial Times* (29ᵗʰ December, 2014).

17 In a 1996 interview with the newspaper *Milliyet.*

has made his general position abundantly clear: "For a person who says I am a Muslim, it is not possible to say at the same time I am secularist. You will be either Muslim or secularist. These two cannot exist together." Since gaining power his government has appointed hundreds of judges who are graduates of Koranic schools. Their rulings will make sure that where secular laws and Islamic ones are incompatible, the *shari'a* should prevail.[18]

"For nearly five hundred years," (said Atatürk of Islam) "these rules and theories of an Arab Shaikh and the interpretations of generations of lazy and good-for-nothing priests have decided the civil and criminal law of Turkey. They have decided the form of the Constitution, the details of the lives of each Turk, his food, his hours of rising and sleeping the shape of his clothes, the routine of the midwife who produced his children, what he learned in his schools, his customs, his thoughts — even his most intimate habits. Islam — this theology of an immoral Arab — is a dead thing. Possibly it might have suited tribes in the desert. It is no good for a modern, progressive state. God's revelation! There is no God! These are only the chains by which the priests and bad rulers bound the people down. A ruler who needs religion is a weakling. No weaklings should rule."[19]

Jacques Ellul (1912–1994), a French philosopher and "Christian anarchist" points out that the euphemistic treatment of Islamic aggression (such intellectual appeasement being contemptuously labelled "*dhimmism*" by fundamentalist Muslims) has by now infiltrated even the reference books, either from fear or political correctness: "In a major encyclopedia, one reads phrases such as: "*Islam expanded in the eighth or ninth centuries…*"; "*This or that country passed into Muslim hands…*" But care is taken not to say *how* Islam expanded, *how* countries "passed into [Muslim] hands." Indeed, it would seem as if events happened by themselves, through a miraculous or amicable operation… Regarding this expansion, little is said about *jihad*. And yet it all happened through war! …The *jihad* is an institution and not an event; that is to say it is a part of the normal functioning of the Muslim world… The conquered populations change status (they become *dhimmis*), and the *shari'a* tends

18 Erdogan's strategy is well summarised in an article in *The Washington Times* (March 20, 2006).

19 Quoted in Harold Courtenay Armstrong: *Grey Wolf: Mustafa Kemal – An Intimate Study of a Dictator* (1932) pp. 199-200.

to be put into effect integrally, overthrowing the former law of the country. The conquered territories do not simply change "owners."[20]

This is all very well, but much the same could be said of violent Christianity in its most aggressive phase, together with Judaism. Phenomena like the crusades represent messianic Christian violence, while ancient scripture was formerly invoked to legitimate judicial violence (for example the Boers citing Deuteronomy to justify apartheid.) The Old Testament lists thirty-six misdeeds, including using magic and striking a parent, as meriting death. The Koran lists just two: *hiraba*, which means "spreading mischief," and murder, although admittedly "spreading mischief" could cover anything from poisoning a camel to making bad jokes about the Prophet. But generally execution, lapidation or amputation are reserved for a small number of serious crimes, including theft and adultery, which are gathered under the heading of *hudud*. The argument, however, is really about whether Islam can modernise its judicial practice or indeed tolerate any other religions *today*, and also whether it will ever be possible to free the faith from its army of more or less freelance *mullahs* issuing *fatwahs* right left and centre.

Christianity, though divided doctrinally, agrees fundamentally on how Christians should conduct themselves in the world (peaceably, at least in theory); but Islam is riven between factions, each of which is tempted to gain authority by promulgating the duty of radical and violent action to Islamise the world by force. As the philosopher David Hume (*q.v.*) pointed out, the Qu'ran and *hadith* (alleged sayings of the Prophet) are so impenetrable that texts can be gleaned from them to justify almost anything, however cruel, something mercilessly exploited by *shari'a* judges. The historian Gibbon put his finger on the problem: *"Instead of a perpetual and perfect measure of the divine will, the fragments of the Koran were produced at the discretion of Mahomet; each revelation is suited to the emergencies of his policy or passion; and all contradiction is removed by the saving maxim, that any text of Scripture is abrogated or modified by any subsequent passage."*[21]

20 Jacques Ellul, Foreword to *Les Chrétiens d'Orient entre Jihad et Dhimmitude. VIIe-XXe siècle* (1991); English translation in the preface to Bat Ye'or, *The Decline of Eastern Christianity under Islam* (1996), Pp. 18-19.

21 Edward Gibbon, *Decline and Fall of the Roman Empire* (1788), Vol. 5, Chapter L: **Description of Arabia and its Inhabitants, Part IV.**

Moderate Muslims (the majority) may always find themselves vulnerable to the fanatics' charge that they are not pulling their weight as Muslims if they reject *jihad* and the violent intolerance that goes with it. The widespread reluctance to stand and be counted against *jihadism* may partly be due to intimidation, but also to a feeling that there is an overriding duty to the *ummah* (the community of Islam), which is always depicted as being under attack by the *kaffirs* (infidels). Equally, competitive zeal in punishing supposed crimes amongst the Muslims of backward states that are in thrall to Islamism is a sure recipe for lynchings and barbarous sentences. A Pew survey in 2013 found that many Muslims in South Asia, the Middle East and North Africa favoured cutting off thieves' hands and executing apostates. Moreover, as an article in *The Economist* pointed out, "governments tend to use Islamic law according to their interests"[22] especially in places like Saudi Arabia, where the regime is propped up by hard-line clerics, and Pakistan, where secular politicians are at risk of assassination. Besides which, with the demise of Communism, militant Islam looks to be the only force capable of hindering the Americanisation of the world and the rule of the Great Satan...

It has been claimed that "the Christian religions were bloodthirsty and murderous by deviating from their texts, whereas Islam was the same by following its text more closely — which is why the partisans of a peaceful Islam propose reforming the Qur'an by purging it of the violent verses against infidels."[23] This point may stand up if one similarly purges the Old Testament of bloodthirsty Jewish racism and the vindictive outbursts of a vengeful Jahweh. But even the New Testament can be problematic: in the Gospel according to St. Matthew (10:34-37) Christ says rather alarmingly: *"Think not that I came to send peace on the earth: I came not to send peace, but a sword. For I have come to turn a man against his father, a daughter against her mother, a daughter-in-*

---

22 "Why harsh punishments are more prevalent in the Muslim world," *The Economist*, July 4th, 2015, quoting Ahmed Taleb, a Muslim cleric in Lebanon. This article claims, somewhat implausibly, that in 600 years of Ottoman rule, just one person was stoned to death. The claim is advanced in order to make the point that in recent times punishments by *shari'a* judiciaries have become *more* barbarous than they were in supposedly more barbarous times...

23 Eric Conan: *"N'éteignons pas les lumières,"* L'Express, April 27, 2006.

law against her mother-in-law — a man's enemies will be the members of his own household. Anyone who loves his father or mother more than me is not worthy of me; anyone who loves his son or daughter more than me is not worthy of me; and anyone who does not take up his cross and follow me is not worthy of me. Whoever finds his life will lose it, and whoever loses his life for my sake will find it." Needless to say these sentiments have required some elaborate verbal gymnastics on the part of theologians and apologists trying to put a benign spin on them. "The one key element in this lengthy passage is the word "sword,"" says one James M. Arlandson, "and its meaning is now clear. It indicates that following Jesus in his original Jewish society may not bring peace to a family, but may "split" it up, the precise function of a metaphorical sword…." This is not very convincing. Even if you take refuge in the "metaphorical" sword, which is the approved line, the whole passage bristles with aggression.

In the case of Islam, the real problem is not just dodgy scripture interpreted by dodgy mullahs, but that the non-negotiable premise of the faith holds Islam to be "a revealed religion and hence the only authentic one, with its book directly dictated by God to his Prophet…. not the heir of earlier faiths but rather a successor that invalidates them forever." Since the Qu'ran, not to mention the alleged sayings of the Prophet (*hadith*), require expert exegesis, anything that suits a narrow-minded, psychologically impaired and largely self-appointed priesthood can be incorporated into the obligations and prohibitions of the faith. Hence the persecution and degradation of women, the execution of apostates, the mutilation of sinners and so forth can be represented as the Prophet's unchallengeable commands (which indeed they often are, except for other texts that say they are not). On the one hand the word of the Prophet is inviolable; on the other, the mullahs can apply to it the interpretations they favour. This was exactly how priestly power was maintained in primitive societies, and if there has been such a thing as progress over the last thousand years or so, it has consisted in the dismantling of such a disingenuous and corrupt exercise of power.

Of course the extremist mullahs are acutely aware that the anachronistic features of Islam require special protection if they are not to be overwhelmed by tolerant secularism. To avoid having to justify brutal Islamic acts of the present or the past, extremist Islamists have coined the phrase "*Islamophobia*." "This was a clever invention," writes Pas-

253

cal Bruckner," because it amounts to making Islam a subject that one cannot touch without being accused of racism… In France, a country with an anticlerical tradition, one can make fun of Judeo-Christianity, mock the Pope or the Dalai Lama, and represent Jesus and the prophets in all sorts of postures, including the most obscene, but one must never laugh at Islam, on pain of being accused of discrimination."[24] Moreover the double standards applied by those who have swallowed the Islamist line have actively helped to bring about a situation where some of the most vicious and anti-democratic voices in our western societies are effectively protected from the ridicule they deserve. In the worst case scenario, a *jihadist* creed of violence and oppression may successfully claim victim status for itself, together with the protection afforded by a society it has vowed to destroy…. [*See also under* **P: Peaceful**]

24 This and the previous quotation are from Pascal Bruckner: *The Tyranny of Guilt: An Essay on Western Masochism*, translated by Steven Rendall (Princeton University Press, Princeton and Oxford, 2010), Pp.46, 48.

J

Jargon: Language abuse by mediocre professionals seeking to impress: Every profession has its jargon, but some professions attract a particularly disingenuous form of it: for example, stockbrokers and "analysts", who seek to cloak the banality of their calling in impressive-sounding catch-phrases. Financial journalists have helpfully supplied a gloss on some of the most ubiquitous of these: *Top down investor* (an investment manager who can't read company accounts); *Bottom up investor* (a manager who doesn't understand economics); *Setback* (the market just collapsed); *A long term investment* (a short term speculation gone wrong). *Why's this share going up? More buyers than sellers* (the classic explanation from a stockbroker who has no more idea than you why the share price is rising. Notably less favoured by brokers is: "*Why's this share going down? More sellers than buyers.*") Rather more appealing is the remark of one of the mega-rich Rothschilds, who said he made his money "*by selling too soon*" and "*never buying at the bottom.*"

Lucy Kellaway of the *Financial Times* regularly reports on the most egregious jargon spewing from corporate handouts or executives dressing up disingenuousness and inarticulacy in pompous drivel. For example she quotes a CEO of a multinational electronics company as telling his managers: "*We actually think that the industry is at a place where you can actually see line of sight to the subsidy equation just fundamentally changing in a very short period of time.*" Sell the shares! Unfortunately, says Kellaway, the Church of England now seems to think it has to adopt management-speak to show it's, well, you know, modern and trendy. A paper on training bishops promulgated "*a radical step change in our development of leaders who can shape and articulate a compelling vision and who are skilled and robust enough to create spaces of safe uncertainty in which the Kingdom grows.*" (A "*space of safe uncertainty*" sounds reassuring — could the writer have the Church of England Synod in mind, or perhaps Disneyland?) "*Our Lord,*" writes Kellaway, "*looking down on a sentence in which His Kingdom has been obliterated by a dozen dreary management clichés, must have found his genius for forgiveness sorely tested.*"[1]

Arabic word "Jawn": According to Hava's *Arabic-English Dictionary* (1964), it means: *Black. White. Light red. Day. Intensely black (horse).* **Khàl,** on the other hand, as I suppose everyone knows, means: *Huge mountain. Big camel. Banner of a prince. Shroud. Fancy. Black stallion. Owner of a th. Self-magnified. Caliphate. Lonely place. Opinion. Suspicion. Bachelor. Good manager. Horse's bit. Liberal man. Weak-bodied, weak-hearted man. Free from suspicion. Imaginative man.*

This sort of thing presumably explains why diametrically opposed interpretations of the *Qur'an* appear possible, and shows that the Arabs were Derridians long before the disagreeable French sage thought of proclaiming that texts were susceptible of any meaning that happened to take his (or your) fancy.

"*Jedermaus*": A composite opera ("**Everymouse**") put together from existing stage hits for the benefit of tourists:

Satirist Helmut Qualtinger used to do a sketch about the crass marketing of Austrian culture, in which he impersonated a zealous marketing man anxious to "add value" to the Salzburger Festspiele: "OK now, this *Jedermann* [Everyman] thing really packs 'em in during the Salzburg season and *Die Fledermaus* , Wow! I mean like it's a bi-ig, big hit in Vienna at New Year. So whaddawe do? We offer the punters one product for the price of two, dude! We can call it, like, *Jedermaus* [Everymouse], and it's gonna have everything — sex, death, animals, you name it. This could be really big, I mean bi-ig!!"

"*Jeffrey is Jeffrey*": Explanation (by his wife) of the idiosyncracies of **Jeffery Archer**, "writer", former Tory Vice-President, former peer, and

---

1 Lucy Kellaway: "And the Golden Flannel award goes to …" — *Financial Times*, 5ᵗʰ January, 2015.

ongoing self-publicist, who discovered his vocation for penal reform while doing time for perjury:

There is something about Archer and his wife that seems to bring out the worst in journalists.

Archer's *Prison Diaries*, it was generally agreed, were not exactly on a par with *De Profundis* or *Pilgrim's Progress*; as one critic put it: "Prison has not done for Archer's prose what thirty years of "editing", followed by dinner at the Caprice, never managed to achieve." "*I wrote a million words in the first year, and I could never have done that outside of prison,*" said the great man, thus inadvertently producing quite a good argument against incarceration for wrongdoers. For a start we should definitely take his expert view seriously that "*sixty per cent of people entering prison today are illiterate…*"

What next for Archer in the non-fiction line (though in Jeffrey's work there is always a Post Modernist tension between the concepts of "fiction" and "non-fiction")? How about: "From Shepherd's Pie to the Good Shepherd: How to Lose Everything (Bar a Few Millions) and Find Eternal Lifestyle" ? It would do equally well in the "self-help" and "help yourself" markets.

Jesus: "I mean, like, for example, Jesus is really big right now" (Executive of Creative Talent Agency in LA, 2015.)

Jewish Jokes: The chutzpah of the marginalised:
Jewish jokes are funnier than most, especially those concerned with blackmailing Jewish mothers. This, for example:

A Jew phones his elderly mum to ask how she is. "*Not good,*" she says; "*I've been very weak.*" "*Why are you so weak?*" "*I haven't eaten for thirty-eight days.*" "*That's terrible, Mom! Why ever not?*" "*Because I didn't want my mouth to be full of food if you should call.*"

Woody Allen's jokes revolve around typically Jewish neuroses. When Helena Bonham Carter was filming *Mighty Aphrodite*, Allen insisted on grounds of hygiene that she keep her lips tightly closed when kissing. For bedroom scenes he kept his clothes on under the sheets — and even his shoes. When she asked him why, he said: "*In case there's a fire.*"

A famous self-ironising Jewish joke provides two explanations for the proverbially substantial nose of the Jew. One says that it is because air is gratis, so the Jewish nose is designed to obtain as much of it as possible.

The other explains the Jewish nose with history — for forty years in the wilderness Moses led the Jews by the nose.

Jolly Good Chap: The Establishment's way of looking after itself: A reviewer of Miranda Carter's biography of art historian and Soviet spy Anthony Blunt writes: *"Carter avoids the 'traitor' label, exploring the art historian's complex, divided personality and placing him in the circumstances of his time, painting the portrait of a likeable and in many ways admirable individual, who was stoical and dignified about his fate."*

"*I hear Queen is terribly upset...*"
"*I most certainly am.*"

So that's all right, then. So long as you're part of the British Establishment and belong to the right clubs, and so long as the people whose lives are sacrificed to your vanity are anonymous and distant, calling you a 'traitor' is simply bad form:
    "*Don't you agree, Sir Humphrey?*"
    "*Oh, absolutely! Let me refresh your drink…*"

Journalists: Persons whose profession is despised by those who make the most use of it:

Journalists (who invariably feature in the satirical magazine *Private Eye* as "the reptiles") have now sunk as low in public esteem as the human detritus known as "bankers" or "politicians." This doesn't stop most of the same people who denounce journalists from quoting their work in daily conversation. Indeed just as a politician suddenly becomes popular if he successfully appeals to the electorate's desire to have everything both ways (more services, less taxes), so the journalist will acquire a following if he manipulates the nastier side of human nature (envy, greed, malice, *Schadenfreude* etc.). Janet Malcolm, one of the most gifted journalists, has said that "*every journalist who is not too stu-*

pid or full of himself to notice what is going on knows that what he does is morally indefensible. He is a kind of confidence man, preying on people's vanity, ignorance or loneliness."[2]

In his extremely funny book *Romps, Tots and Boffins*, Robert Hutton gives examples of the language in which journalists write ("journalese") which is both archaic and unused by any normal native speaker of English. As Hutton demonstrates, much of journalese is in fact weasel-worded insinuation, for example the word "*admit*" referring to something not in the least shameful but which the newspaper (usually on ideological grounds) would like to suggest is so. "*There is no suggestion that…*" means that the lawyers have insisted the paper put in this disclaimer to avoid being sued for the insinuations of the previous 500 words. Hutton includes a glossary of code words[3] whose meaning all readers of the daily press will be expected to construe (perhaps not foreigners), although he does not include here the phrase that has passed into the language, again courtesy of *Private Eye*: "*Tired and emotional*" famously got round the problem of how to describe the behaviour George Brown, Britain's drunken Foreign Secretary in the 1960s, without being sued:

Bon viveur: drunk
Concerns for their health: they take drugs
Confirmed bachelor: gay
Didn't suffer fools gladly: nightmare boss
Eccentric: mad
Exotic tastes: we've got the photos in our safe, but they're too
    horrible to print
Flamboyant: gay
Fun-loving: she puts herself about a bit
Gregarious: drunk
He never married: gay.
Ladies' man: they never managed to get the sexual assault charges
    to stick.
Well-turned-out: gay.

---

2 Janet Malcolm: *The Journalist and the Murderer*, quoted in the Introduction by Lee Siegel to *The Freud Archives* by Janet Malcolm (Granta Books, 2012), P. xii.
3 Robert Hutton: *Romps, Tots and Boffins: The Strange Language of News* (Elliott and Thompson Limited, London, 2013), P. 57.

"The Journey": Fashionable journalistic cliché often adduced to lend dignity to brown-nosing articles about uninteresting people:

Nowadays anyone from Nelson Mandela to celebrity airheads wishing to draw attention to themselves may be described as a person on "a journey", which is no longer the ascetic pilgrimage of yore, but more of a must-have humility product and fashion accessory. The expression implies a process of turmoil and transformation at the end of which the "journeyer" emerges smelling distinctly of roses. In the case of a Mandela, the cap fits, but in the case of most semi-reformed addicts, penal-reforming gaolbirds and similar sorts of person soliciting our respect and admiration, it certainly does not. The canny may even manage to piggyback on "the journey" of a more glamorous person, like the artist vicariously cashing in on Barack Obama's "journey" to the White House, whose art documented a personal spiritual "journey" that somehow conveniently got tangled up with that of Saint Barack. "Journeys" may well involve being in a "bad place" for a while, which is traditionally alluded to in the third person as if it was actually someone else who was there, not the journeyer. However the hardened traveller can usually get to a "better place" with the help of some cash and shrewd self-promotion.

Inevitably the "journey" has been adopted as a suitably unctuous expression by management consultants. An FT journalist, Henry Mance, relates how the business doctors descended on the firm where he had his first job and explained to a less than wrapt audience that its members were on a "journey" and had been for some time. Mance was hugely impressed by the consultants' percipience, since the company was located 90 minutes from London "and most people spent almost half the day commuting." Later it turned out that almost everyone, including institutions and businesses, is on a journey — the banks to win back trust from the customers they have cheated, the Labour Party to win back voters and even McDonald's to "*becoming a modern, progressive burger and breakfast restaurant*" (good to get that "*progressive*" claim in there as well.) Rather ungraciously, I thought, Mance thinks the "journey" metaphor is just about the worst possible one for captains of industry to use, as it immediately suggests to employees that a lot of people will soon be on a journey to a new job ("*Every time a chief executive dusts off the metaphor, an underling remembers to update their LinkedIn profile.*") In February of 2014 the CEO of Microsoft told staff that they were starting a "new phase of our journey together," though it turned out that the word "our" did not exactly mean "you" and "you" and "you", who were among the 25,000 he sacked shortly afterwards. Mance says there is no point in asking how long any particular journey will be, since the CEO will merely respond (if not in so many words) that *"like your father, I have a trained ability not to hear you. But at some point I may turn off the engine, pull out the map and seek to blame whoever is sitting beside me. Then, and only then, will you know the journey is over — and that we are simply and irredeemably lost."*[4]

Tony Judt: Jewish Social Democratic historian who specialised in over-turning applecarts:

Judt's massive *Postwar* does not spare the right in politics, but is also the most devastatingly honest account of the continuing *trahison des clercs* of the left in the West since George Orwell first exposed the phe-nomenon. For instance, it is hard to comprehend the full obscenity of Jean-Paul Sartre's apologetics for both Stalinism and Maoism until you realise that the more ruthless Stalin was, *the more he admired him*. In Judt's words: "Western intellectual enthusiasm for [Russian] Commu-nism tended to peak not in times of 'goulash communism' or 'Socialism with a human face', but rather at the moments of the regime's worst cru-elties: 1935-39, 1944-56. Writers, professors, artists, teachers and jour-nalists frequently admired Stalin not in spite of his faults, but *because* of them. It was when he was murdering people on an industrial scale, when the show trials were displaying Soviet Communism at its most theatri-cally macabre, that men and women beyond Stalin's grasp were most se-duced by the man and his cult."

Justice: "You get justice in the next world. In this one you have the law."[5] The notion of justice has arguably attracted more windy rhetoric than any other politico-philosophical idea with the exception of liberty. This is because people have different things in mind when they appeal to it: the rule of law, fairness, social justice, egalitarianism — even animal rights. Some scepticism is in order: after all, even Adolf Hitler claimed

---

4 Henry Mance: "No end in sight to the cliché of the corporate journey," *Financial Times*, 3rd of August, 2015.

5 William Gaddis: *A Frolic of His Own.*

to be valiant for justice (*"as a Christian I have no duty to allow myself to be cheated, but I have the duty to be a fighter for truth and justice."*)[6]

Firstly the rule of law: Cicero said "the more laws, the less justice." Which is one problem. Raymond Chandler's hard-boiled detective Philip Marlow said "the law isn't justice. It's a very imperfect mechanism. If you press exactly the right buttons and are also lucky, justice may show up in the answer. A mechanism is all the law was ever intended to be"[7] — which is another problem. Anatole France was more anarchic on his view: "Justice is the means by which established injustices are sanctioned"[8] — which is a terminal problem.

Lin Yutang has said: "Where there are too many policemen, there is no liberty. Where there are too many soldiers, there is no peace. Where there are too many lawyers, there is no justice."[9] This idea was given a different spin by Jonathan Swift, who distinguished between precedent and natural justice: "It is a maxim among these lawyers, that whatever hath been done before may legally be done again: and therefore they take special care to record all the decisions formerly made against common justice and the general reason of mankind. These, under the name of precedents, they produce as authorities, to justify the most iniquitous opinions; and the judges never fail of decreeing accordingly."[10]

As to "social justice" Friedrich von Hayek observes that "we must face the fact that the preservation of individual freedom is incompatible with a full satisfaction of our views of distributive justice."[11] May be not, but the extent to which "distributive justice" (or any other sort) prevails depends upon the privileged, wealthy and powerful believing that they would rather live in a fairer society than squat anxiously in gated communities fearing the dispossessed mob. They may be motivated by fear or by empathy, but in either case an understanding of the other is a prerequisite for signing up to social justice. "Justice will not come to Athens until those who are not injured are as indignant as those who are injured,"[12] said Thucydides. The same point was allegedly made by Ben-

6 This claim occurs in a speech given by Adolf Hitler in 1922.
7 Raymond Chandler: *The Long Goodbye* (1953).
8 Anatole France: *Crainquebille*
9 Lin Yutang, Chinese writer and philosopher (1895-1976).
10 Jonathan Swift: *Gulliver's Travels*.
11 Friedrich von Hayek: *Individualism: True and False* (1945).
12 Thucydides (c.460–400 BC): *The History of the Peloponnesian War 431-413 BC*.

jamin Franklin: "Justice will not be served until those who are unaffected are as outraged as those who are."[13]

"The simplest way of understanding justice," writes Michael Sandel, "is giving people what they deserve. This idea goes back to Aristotle. The real difficulty begins with figuring out who deserves what and why."[14] So what do people deserve? The answers can be very subjective: "My photographs don't do me justice," complained comedienne Phyllis Diller. "They just look like me."[15]

Isaiah Berlin warned us to beware of people who claimed to have cracked the notion of justice; and not only that, but how to impose it. In his "credo", delivered as a "message to the 21st century," he looked back on the horrors of history and discovered that such people had a lot to answer for: "If you are truly convinced that there is some solution to all human problems, that one can conceive an ideal society which men can reach if only they do what is necessary to attain it, then you and your followers must believe that no price can be too high to pay in order to open the gates of such a paradise. Only the stupid and malevolent will resist once certain simple truths are put to them. Those who resist must be persuaded; if they cannot be persuaded, laws must be passed to restrain them; if that does not work, then coercion, if need be violence, will inevitably have to be used — if necessary, terror, slaughter. Lenin believed this after reading *Das Kapital*, and consistently taught that if a just, peaceful, happy, free, virtuous society could be created by the means he advocated, then the end justified any methods that needed to be used, literally any.

"The root conviction which underlies this is that the central questions of human life, individual or social, have one true answer which can be discovered. It can and must be implemented, and those who have found it are the leaders whose word is law. The idea that to all genuine questions there can be only one true answer is a very old philosophical notion. The great Athenian philosophers, Jews and Christians, the thinkers of the Renaissance and the Paris of Louis XIV, the French radical re-

13 The source of this quotation is doubtful, but it does Franklin no dishonour to attribute it to him.

14 "Michael Sandel on Justice": Interview (by Nigel Warburton) in *Prospect* (January 2011).

15 Phyllis Diller, American comedienne: "*The Joys of Aging and How to Avoid Them*" (1981).

formers of the eighteenth century, the revolutionaries of the nineteenth — however much they differed about what the answer was or how to discover it (and bloody wars were fought over this) — were all convinced that they knew the answer, and that only human vice and stupidity could obstruct its realization.

"This is the idea of which I spoke, and what I wish to tell you is that it is false. Not only because the solutions given by different schools of social thought differ, and none can be demonstrated by rational methods — but for an even deeper reason. The central values by which most men have lived, in a great many lands at a great many times — these values, almost if not entirely universal, are not always harmonious with each other. Some are, some are not. Men have always craved for liberty, security, equality, happiness, justice, knowledge, and so on. But complete liberty is not compatible with complete equality — if men were wholly free, the wolves would be free to eat the sheep. Perfect equality means that human liberties must be restrained so that the ablest and the most gifted are not permitted to advance beyond those who would inevitably lose if there were competition. Security, and indeed freedoms, cannot be preserved if freedom to subvert them is permitted. Indeed, not everyone seeks security or peace, otherwise some would not have sought glory in battle or in dangerous sports.

Karl Marx: "If anything is certain, it is that I myself am not a Marxist."

"Justice has always been a human ideal, but it is not fully compatible with mercy.[16]

16 Isaiah Berlin: "A Message to the 21st Century" (New York Review of Books, 23rd October, 2014). On November 25, 1994 Isaiah Berlin had accepted the honorary degree of Doctor of Laws at the University of Toronto. He prepared a "short credo" for the ceremony (from which this is extracted), which was read on his behalf. © The Isaiah Berlin Literary Trust 2014.

K

Kleptomaniac:
A rich thief.

Ambrose Bierce: *The Devil's Dictionary*

Katja Kabanova: "No matter how bad your mother-in-law is, Katja Kabanova's is worse."[1]

Herbert von Karajan (or ***Heribert, Ritter von Karajan):*** Aromanian born in Salzburg, megalomaniacal conductor and somewhat unrepentant member of the Nazi party:

2008 was the 100th anniversary of the birth of Herbert von Karajan, who was the most successful classical recording artist of all time (200 million records sold according to *Wikipedia*). The apocryphal joke is that he once stepped into a New York cab and the cabbie asked where he should go, to which Karajan replied *"It doesn't matter — I'm known everywhere."*

Karajan's apologists indignantly claim that he only joined the Nazis to advance his career (as if that made it OK). He joined in 1933 and conducted throughout the war (as did many other leading conductors, most notoriously Karl Böhm, whose *obiter dicta* from the period suggest he was a convinced Nazi.) At war's end, they only received short, token performance bans in Vienna, and the Jews were still excluded — as Otto Klemperer bitterly remarked.

There is a nice Austrian joke about Karajan's vanity, viz. *"Mozart came from Salzburg, the birthplace of Herbert von Karajan."*

---

1 Opening line of a review by Shirley Apthorp of the Staatsoper Berlin's production of Janacek's *Katja Kabanova* (*Financial Times* Jan. 29, 2014.)

Genghis Khan: "It is not sufficient that I succeed – all others must fail."

Genghis Khan: Very popular in Mongolia, less so elsewhere:

The hordes of Genghis Khan (actually the 2.5 million Mongolians of today) were forced to give up their surnames by the Communists in the 1920s. However "forenames only" doesn't really work in a modern society with identity cards and phone books etc., so the formerly forbidden surnames are now mandatory. Unfortunately half the population have plumped for **Borjigin**, the clan name of **Genghis Khan**, which doesn't help the bureaucracy a lot. A director of the State Central Library, has come to the rescue with an unlikely bestseller that offers advice to those still in search of a surname. He explains that most available Mongolian names were originally bestowed by villagers on their neighbours. Typical surnames therefore include "**Thief**," "**Numbskull**" and "**Family of Seven Drunks**". "The choice is yours," as the government's advertisements doubtless say…

*Tikhon Khrennikov (***Tikhon Nikolayevich Khrennikov** *(Russian: Ти́хон Никола́евич Хре́нников) 10 June 1913 – 14 August 2007:** Russian person claiming to be a composer:

Not heard of him? Come, come! He won three Stalin Prizes and a Lenin Prize for his "facile, badly orchestrated and comically derivative" compositions (*Guardian* obituary), which also qualified him for the UNESCO Mozart Medal in 2003 (well done UNESCO!) After his runaway success with the *Song of Moscow* for the film *Swineherd and Shepherd*, he was appointed by Stalin to be Secretary of the Union of Soviet Composers. In this position he persecuted real composers, such as Prokofiev and Shostakovich. Ideologically unapproved work was "*noisy mud,*" said Tikhon, adding the unintended compliment that such music "was not representative of Soviet composers." After attacking Russian music with religious tendencies all his life, it was touching to see Khrennikov being blessed by a bishop in 1993. At 80, reported *The*

Guardian, the great man was as creative as ever, "a ballet entitled *Napoleon* causing much mirth."

RIP Tikhon. If there was a Nobel Prize for music, you would surely have been awarded it.

Nikita Sergeyevich Khrushchev (April 15, 1894 – September 11, 1971): Sly Soviet buffoon:

Nikita jokes have acquired a patina of nostalgia in Central Europe. Like this one, for instance: "When Khrushchev died he was asked whether he wanted to go to the capitalist hell, or the Communist one, heaven not being an option. He chose the capitalist one, thinking it would be better. After a few weeks of infernal heat and being chased around twenty-four hours a day by devils with sharp pitchforks, he applied for a transfer to the Communist hell. Lucifer grumbled a bit, but granted his wish. On his arrival there, he was surprised to find it cool and calm, with no devils or pitchforks. He inquired of Lucifer about this remarkable state of affairs, and was told: *"First of all the supplies of heating oil have not been delivered. Then the forks we get from the factory break immediately. And as for the staff, you know how it is: we pretend to pay them and they pretend to work."*

Nikita Krushchev: "If one cannot catch the bird of paradise, better take a wet hen."

"Just kidding": Not all newspaper readers have the same sense of humour as columnists:

Some years ago, according to the late Simon Hoggart, the astrologer on the *Daily Mirror* finally tired of writing *"romance beckons"* or *"be wary of colleagues today."* So instead he wrote under *"**Gemini**"*: *"All the sorrows of yesteryear are as nothing to what will befall you today."* Complaints poured in and he was fired.

And there was once a *Punch* cartoon showing a man listening to a radio broadcast as follows: "*In a major leap forward for astrology, all persons born under the sign of **Scorpio** were yesterday run over by egg lorries.*"

Kim Jong II, a.k.a. "Baby Kim": The world's only hereditary Communist ruler:

"*How's life in North Korea?*" ran a joke current among Kim watchers. "*Well, you can't complain.*"

Kim enjoyed the honorary title of "Dear Leader", thus tactfully avoiding any direct competition with his deceased father, who was of course the "Great Leader" (although this was but one of the many self-awarded titles of the late and not very lamented Kim Il-Sung of North Korea: he was also known as the Ever Victorious Captain and (with becoming modesty) as the Greatest Genius Humankind Has Ever Had.) A journalist suggested the further title of **"Great Lecher"** when the 80-year-old monster fathered a baby girl by a dancer 50 years his junior. Furthermore the Greatest Genius remained President throughout his son's term of office (Baby Kim was a mere "Chairman of the National Defence Commission"), making North Korea the world's only necrocacy.

Pyongyangologists were divided about the intentions of the Dear Leader, who was written off at different times as an alcoholic, a lunatic and a cripple. For a mass murderer, he had a disarming line in self-deprecation: for example, he greeted the film director he had just had abducted from South Korea with the words: "What do you think of my physique? Small as a midget's turd, aren't I?" Just before his birth, according to the official account, a swallow descended from heaven to announce the coming of a general who would rule the world, and a guiding star appeared above the simple hut where he was born. Sounds familiar?

After Baby Kim's death in 2011, he was succeeded by the even babyer, and arguably nastier **Kim Jong-un** (alternatively **Kim Jong-eun**, **Kim Jong Un** or **Kim Jung-eun,** born 8 January 1983) as the Supreme Leader of the Democratic People's Republic of Korea. He is the second son of Kim Jong-il (1941–2011) and the grandson of Kim Il-sung (1912–1994). For a twenty-eight-year-old, he already had a remarkable CV, having held down such demanding posts as First Secretary of the Workers' Party of Korea, Chairman of the Central Military Commission, First Chairman of the National Defence Commission of North Korea, Supreme Commander of the Korean People's Army, and Presidium

Member of the Politburo of the Workers' Party of Korea. He has also attained the highest active military rank (*wonsu*) in the Korean armed forces and was officially declared the Supreme Leader following the state funeral for his father on 28 December 2011. His training for high office apparently consisted of watching basketball videos, playing computer games and listening to Eric Clapton. He is said to live in a cave-like bunker surrounded by stacks of overripe and malodorous Swiss Emmenthal, to which he is addicted.

Kim Jong-un was mentored for his role as Supreme Leader by Ri Yong-ho, Kim Yong-chur, U Tong-chuk and Kim Jong-gak, who sound like characters out of *The Mikado* — and indeed their lives have been just as precarious; all have been demoted or "disappeared" (as *Wikipedia* sinisterly puts it). Five of the seven men who accompanied his father's hearse have been "purged." His uncle, Jang Sung-taek, seems to have got a bit over-confident and made the mistake of being pictured beside Kim with his hands in a posture deemed not to be abjectly respectful enough. He was publicly executed in December 2013 and much of his family was also "disappeared."

Kim proceeds along his father's merry way, even as he tries to obliterate the paternal memory: defectors are killed, public executions keep people on their toes, North Koreans vanish *en masse* into political prison camps. The Deputy Defence Minister, Kim Choi was arrested for "insufficient grieving" for Kim Jong-il's death, which is indeed a hanging offence — except that Choi was taken to a firing range and shelled to death with mortars. Nine female members of the world-renowned Unhasu Orchestra were publicly machine-gunned for annoying Kim's surprisingly glamorous wife, Ri Sol-ju. One of the justifications for his uncle's execution was that he had "the wrong kind of dreams," a crime that must be quite difficult to stand up in court but which is certainly very grave. Even Kim's Chinese sponsors have become rather disheartened because, as one North Korea watcher puts it, "everyone the Chinese used to talk to has been liquidated." Occasionally Kim disappears from view, provoking speculation about his health or a coup, but actually, explained David Letterman, he is just "spending more time executing his family." There was an outbreak of famine in 2013 (a regular feature of the family's rule) and there are rumours of cannibalism. In March 2013 Kim Jong-un threatened the United States with a pre-emptive nuclear strike, a slight over-reaction to some combined military exercises the US was holding with South Korea.

Useful family Tree of North Korea's Ruling Kim Family (courtesy of *Wikipedia*)

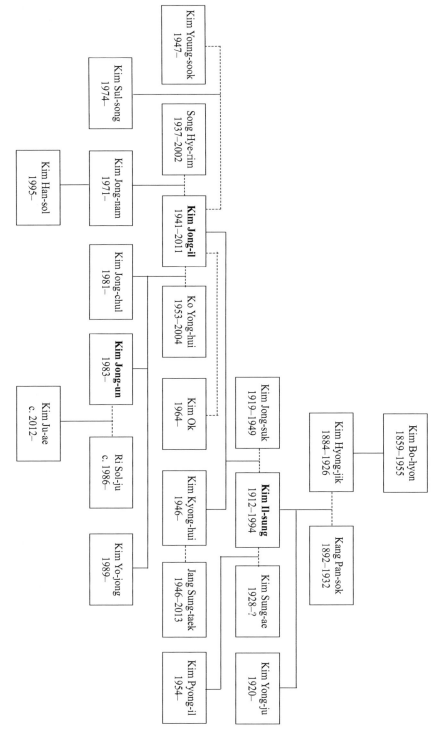

It is not easy for outsiders to enjoy North Korean hospitality, but in February 2015 the North Korean Embassy in Vienna celebrated the 73rd birthday of S.E. Kim Jong II (16th February — "The Day of the Shining Star," which, as everyone knows, illuminated the heavens above Kim's birthplace, like the star at Bethlehem). As mentioned above, Kim Jong II is deceased, according to our way of thinking, but North Korea being a necrocracy, he and his father are still keeping a watchful eye on the socialist paradise now presided over by **Kim Jong Un**. On arrival, guests were ushered into a hall, along the entire south wall of which was a picture of Kims One and Two set against a rugged landscape under a vast expanse of bilious yellow sky. His Excellency Kim Gwang Sop gave a gracious address thanking visitors for their support of the magnificent socialist progress in North Korea, and concluding with a hint that Korea would probably be united today if it were not for the Americans. This is probably true, and is one reason why the South Koreans are so grateful to the latter. There followed a travelogue video of Pyongyang, most of which was devoted to the 70 foot tower erected to Kim II, together with the occasional panoramic shot of a city remarkably devoid of people or cars. At the buffet afterwards a Professor of Korean at Vienna University opined that there was not much to see in North Korea (he had been twice). Moreover it was frustrating not to be able to chat to the locals, whose reticence may possibly be attributed to the fact that they risked being chucked in the gulag if seen talking to foreigners. A lot of the attendees appeared to be of pensionable age and to have come for the excellent buffet, which was enthusiastically consumed while trying not to think of the government-induced famines in North Korea. Few seemed thirsty for North Korean culture, which was perhaps just as well as there does not seem to be a great deal of it. Only one visitor appeared to be a true believer, an elderly gentleman resembling a geriatric Hell's Angel and sporting a Che Guevara beret. Copies of the less than riveting *Pyongyang Times* were on hand, consisting mostly of Kim Jong Un's New Years's Address, which an alert editor could with profit have shortened by about 98% (*Comrades! 2014 was a year in which we clearly demonstrated the spirit and might of the great DPRK that advances by leaps and bounds with confidence in victory…*). On second thoughts, removing even a word of this would probably have cost the said editor his life. As visitors made their way out, they were obliged to run the gauntlet of a number of small North

271

Modest monument to Korean Workers' Party in Pyongyang.

Korean persons in the lobby, all bowing and hissing "*Ub Widelzin!*" (Korean for "*Auf Wiedersehen!*").

Musical Kitsch: If music sales are to be believed, the taste for this is a secret vice shared by the majority and makes pretentious choices made by celebrities for their *Desert Island Discs* look a bit fishy:

Perry Como was perhaps the ultimate kitsch crooner. When he died, Nicholas Foulkes described him in the *Financial Times* as "Como the conformist [who] inhabited a cosy world of golf and fishing, cocktails and knitwear: an agreeably indolent and uncomplicated place in which intellectuals were people who subscribed to the *Readers' Digest* and knew the lyrics of Como's records by heart … Como could make Andy Williams seem like an angry young firebrand railing at the injustices of the world merely by opening his mouth. … [And] his laid-back, almost soporific singing style…lagging behind the beat*"* was no doubt an excellent substitute for Valium.

According to cultural critic Walter Benjamin, kitsch is an artefact that is purely utilitarian and abolishes all critical distance between object and recipient; "*it offers,*" he said, "*instantaneous emotional gratification without intellectual effort, without the requirement of distance, without sublimation"*. Adorno, another poncey intellectual, was very snotty about jazz too. And what's wrong with instant emotional gratification after a hard day at the office, we'd like to know?

A rich source of kitsch is country music, often regarded as hick by boorish urban sophisticates, but full of good tunes and nifty lyrics, like the following: "*She got the goldmine, I got the shaft,*" and "*Honey, I miss you (but my aim is getting better)*". Few girls, surely, could resist a troubadour who serenaded them with: "*If you ever leave me, honey, go out backwards so I think you're coming in*", or "*If I'd killed you when I met you / I'd be out of jail by now.*" Most touching of all is a line from Kinky Friedman that runs: "*Drop kick me Jesus through the goalposts of life.*"

Arthur Koestler: Distinguished writer and journalist who is no longer considered a politically correct figure, but more of a misogynist and a rapist:

Politically, Koestler's Paulite turn came in 1938 when he was one of the first western intellectuals to abandon the avid Communism of his youth. Thereafter he devoted a good deal of his considerable energies to exposing and denouncing atrocities on the right and on the left. In a contribution to *Suicide of a Nation?* (1963) he wrote: "A chimaera, in Greek mythology, was a monster with a lion's head, a goat's trunk, and a serpent's tail; more generally it meant a composite animal. Throughout the ages, painters and writers of fantastic tales have been fond of creating chimaeras. My own favourite brain-child is the *mimophant*. He is a phenomenon most of us have met in life: a hybrid who combines the delicate frailness of the mimosa, crumbling at a touch when his own feelings are hurt, with the thick-skinned robustness of the elephant trampling over the feelings of others. I think the sizeable majority of the Germans of the last generation who supported the *Führer* belonged to the species of *mimophants*. They were capable of shedding genuine tears at the death of their pet canaries; what they did at other times is perhaps better forgotten."

"I think most historians would agree," wrote Koestler, "that the part played by impulses of selfish, individual aggression in the holocausts of history was small; first and foremost, the slaughter was meant as an offering to the gods, to king and country, or the future happiness of mankind. The crimes of a Caligula shrink to insignificance compared to the havoc wrought by Torquemada. The number of victims of robbers, highwaymen, rapists, gangsters and other criminals at any period of history is negligible compared to the massive numbers of those cheerfully slain in the name of the true religion, just policy or correct ideology. Heretics were tortured and burnt not in anger but in sorrow, for the good of their immortal souls. Tribal warfare was waged in the purported interest of the tribe, not of the individual. Wars of religion were fought to decide some fine point in theology or semantics. Wars of succession dynastic wars, national wars, civil wars, were fought to decide issues equally remote from the personal self-interest of the combatants.

"When one contemplates the streak of insanity running through human history, it appears highly probable that *homo sapiens* is a biological freak, the result of some remarkable mistake in the evolutionary process. The ancient doctrine of original sin, variants of which occur independently in the mythologies of diverse cultures, could be a reflection of man's awareness of his own inadequacy, of the intuitive hunch that somewhere along the line of his ascent something has gone wrong."[2]

"Nothing is more sad than the death of an illusion," wrote Koestler in his account of intellectuals' disillusionment with Communism, a disillusionment he himself had experienced so keenly. "I went to Communism as one goes to a spring of fresh water, and I left Communism as one clambers out of a poisoned river strewn with the wreckage of flooded cities and the corpses of the drowned…"

And finally, his encouraging view of the future: "God seems to have left the receiver off the hook, and time is running out."[3]

2 Arthur Koestler: *The Ghost in the Machine* (1967).
3 The Ghost in the Machine (1967).

274

L

Litigation:
*A machine which you go into as a pig and
come out of as a sausage.*

Ambrose Bierce: *The Devil's Dictionary*

Law: An instrument of liberation or repression, depending on who is making or wielding it:

Ralph Waldo Emerson observed that *"people say law, but they mean wealth."* Britain has so constructed its libel laws as to illustrate the truth of this remark.

The rule of thumb is that a repressive state is one where anything that is not specifically allowed is prohibited, while in a free state everything is allowed unless specifically prohibited. The modern supposedly democratic state, with its insatiable appetite for regulation and control, hovers somewhere between these alternative realities. Furthermore governments are constantly debasing the rule of law by delegating disciplinary functions to the private sector (e.g. the handing out of parking tickets to companies that set targets for issuing penalties which their employees must meet), or to Quasi-Autonomous Nongovernmental Organisations (Quangos –*q.v.*). As the latter's evasive, Orwellian nomenclature suggests, these are bodies that evade democratic accountability and covertly accrete power in ever widening fields.

This delegation of legal power is at its most grotesque in regard to the banks, which have been charged with policing the transactions of the private citizen when, as it turns out, the banks themselves laundered money, evaded taxation and generally behaved in a criminal manner. Thus is the criminal given the power to sanction the law-abiding — a situation that occurs otherwise only in totalitarian states and the novels of Franz Kafka.

It is also noticeable that the bankers who made the greatest contribution to the economic crisis beginning in 2007 have been handled very gently by the criminal law, while their shareholders and customers, together with taxpayers and the jobless, are the people who have actually footed the bill for the bankers' misdeeds — and continue to pay for them. By contrast with the aftermath of the 1929 crash, when many financiers ended up in gaol (or committed suicide), the former Fed Chairman Alan Greenspan has observed drily that he doesn't even know any senior bankers who have declared personal bankruptcy or lost their homes in this crisis. Moreover after the 1929 crash, inequality of wealth and income declined in the USA, whereas it has increased after this crash. Lawyers, batteries of whom exist to help banks and companies get round laws they don't like, are a large part of the problem. Apart from ignoring the spirit of laws or regulations and devising financial products of such fiendish complexity that convictions become all but impossible because the courts and juries could not understand them, they have also helped manoeuvre the banks into the position where they are not only "too big to fail," but also "too big to gaol."

This situation is aggravated by contemporary oligarchic capitalism, whereby lawyers and lobbyists with legal training are the source of most legislation in the USA. It is hardly an accident that the most obviously crooked president of modern times was Richard Nixon, a lawyer through and through.

There is also a massive problem with both the origination and drafting of laws, of which there are now anyway far too many to be compatible with healthy democracy. Up to 60% of laws passed on the nod in the parliaments of EU countries originate in Brussels and are weakly legitimated at the ballot box. A speciality of British civil servants is "gold-plating" (*q.v.*) EU legislation in order to smuggle in a pet scheme that they fear would not pass muster if openly debated in the UK. It is no accident that the British (and other) bureaucracies are enthusiastic about the EU and largely indifferent to issues of national sovereignty. Much of the bureaucratic activity in Brussels represents an official's dream of unaccountable power: high salaries and endless opportunities for interfering in the lives of ordinary citizens who are largely powerless to resist.

The United States is a democracy almost smothered by lawyers who dominate the upper echelons of politics and (again like Richard Nixon) often have, to say the least, a somewhat tenuous view of legality. Like

276

most other American lawyers the politicians seem to regard the law as something to be manipulated rather than applied. Because fees are so obscenely high, and because there are far too many laws in the Land of the Free, America is a country drowning in litigation, an open sesame for ambulance chasers, crooked advocates and rent-seeking law firms.

The great Russian dissident Yevgeny Zamyatin had it right about the sort of person cultivated in such a society: "Don't forget that we lawyers, we're a higher breed of intellect, and so it's our privilege to lie. It's as clear as day. Animals can't even imagine lying: if you were to find yourself among some wild islanders, they too would only speak the truth until they learned about European [or American] culture."[1] America seems to have forgotten, if it ever heeded, that wise remark of Richard Lamm: "No nation ever sued its way to greatness."

A relatively new hazard for genuine democrats is the European Court of Human Rights, which has indulged in "mission creep" over the years. It now frequently hands down judgements that support the "rights" of the perpetrators of crimes and ignore those of their law-abiding victims. Illegal immigrants to the UK who have been convicted of terrorist offences or rape, or violent crime, successfully claim the "right to family life" to avoid deportation. As likely as not, their claim will be endorsed by the ECHR, even when (as is frequently the case) they have cynically impregnated a British citizen precisely to in order to claim this right. Furthermore the ECHR, which is not an EU body, has judges presiding on its bench from such model *Rechtsstaaten* as Russia or Montenegro — you may as well put Dracula in charge of the blood-bank. Yet these same judges are able to sit in judgement on the legality of procedures in countries where legal rights were invented and are still generally recognised, however imperfectly. Jurists, of course, living in the sort of professional bubble that insulates them from reality, are perfectly happy to defend all this. No doubt they are keen to expand this splendid example of international co-operation — how about a Communist Chinese judge adjudicating the justice system of Sweden?

Letters to the Papers: Cries of pain and anger from Middle England: J.M.Keynes wrote that there was "one small but extraordinarily silly manifestation of [the] absurd idea of what is 'normal', namely the im-

1 Yevgeny Zamyatin: *Islanders and The Fisher Of Men* (English Translation 1984)

pulse to *protest* — to write a letter to *The Times*, call a meeting in the Guildhall, subscribe to some fund when my presuppositions as to what is is 'normal' are not fulfilled. I behave as if there really existed some authority or standard to which I can successfully appeal if I shout loud enough — perhaps it is some hereditary vestige of a belief in the efficacy of prayer."[2] Many letters to the papers show signs of the assumptions to which Keynes refers and one notices that inveterate letter writers (though some may have been invented by the paper's editor to stir up controversy or flatter his product) seem to have skilfully worked out how to appeal to the paper's usual line in order to have a better chance of getting into print. Letters fall roughly into one of four categories: the pedantic, the pretentious, the petulant and the poopsy. Of course one measures these qualities against one own sense of "normalcy." Still, there are a few which seem refreshingly free of cliché, obsequiousness, hypocrisy and lunacy.

Here is a crisp example from the *Sunday Telegraph* written by one Dr Milton Wainwright:

"Sir: Instead of the futile attempt by the Church of England to curry favour with rationalist opinion by apologising for attacking Charles Darwin, the Church might consider apologising to all those generations of children it has indoctrinated with the nonsense that Jesus was born of a virgin, could turn water into wine, and came back to life after death."

Apologies for things that happened in the past — the Irish famine, the decimation of Aborigines — have become fashionable, which rather highlights the inability of politicians to apologise for anything more recent. They prefer to cite "administrative error", which seems to offer contrition without admitting to anything specific (Tory MP Derek Conway said his son was paid £45,000 out of public funds for doing nothing due to "administrative shortcomings.") "But," asks Leo Hickman in *The Guardian*, "can you imagine the tax man swallowing a line about "administrative errors" leading to discrepancies in your tax return? No, thought not."

As the Greek crisis advanced through 2014 and 2015, it became fashionable among liberals to assert that the plight of Greece was entirely the

2 John Maynard Keynes: "My Early Beliefs," a paper read by the economist at his country house to members of the Bloomsbury group in 1938. Quoted in: *John Maynard Keynes:The Essential Keynes*, Ed. Robert Skidelsky (Penguin/ Random House, UK, 2015) Page 23.

fault of Germany (after all, Germany had put her own house in order by exercising considerable economic self-discipline, had not run up huge unsustainable debts, and had lent or guaranteed huge sums of Euros to Greece to help her out, so in the minds of liberal commentators she was clearly to blame.) In April 2015, the chief commentator of the *Financial Times*, whose disquisitions tend to be sprinkled with appropriate genuflections at the relevant altars of political correctness, wrote that Greece should on no account be allowed to fall out of the Euro by mistake. To prevent this, *more money had to be found*. This suggestion attracted a robust epistolary reaction from a Professor of Economics at Chicago, who pointed out that all the measures recommended in the article boiled down to writing cheques in order to write down Greek debt. "Unfortunately," he continued, "Mr Wolf [author of the article in question] does not say who would happily be parting with that money. Would *he* be so inclined, perhaps? He could, perhaps, follow up his fine article with another one on crowdfunding for Greece, appealing to all who share his view to pitch in, and pointing out that he had done his bit by paying in, say, £10,000. It is the better option than keeping that money to himself, right? "[3]

Leviticus: The third (and unexpectedly entertaining) book of the Pentateuch:

For example Leviticus 20-13 seems to allude to the simultaneous legalisation of marijuana and gay marriage, for which, in a fit of unwonted tolerance, it proposes only one condition: "*If a man lays with another man, he should be stoned.*"

Lexicon of Conservative Cant: Tory-speak catalogued in *The Spectator* by Matthew Parris:

Parris points out that Conservatives have their own version of the much ridiculed Political Correctness (PC), consisting of *Political Soundness* (PS). PS euphemisms are designed to portray the speaker as a broadminded realist, rather than the petty-minded bigot some take him to be. *J* in the Parris Lexicon stands for *Jonathan* [Aitken]: "For the *Politically Sound*, Aitken is a "gallant Etonian" whose only fault was to be a trifle

---

3 Letter to the *Financial Times* from Professor Harold Uhlig, Dept of Economics, University of Chicago on 7th April 2015 in response to an article by the FT's chief commentator, Martin Wolf.

buccaneering in his approach. *'Buccaneer'* is itself a useful PS word to describe any well-connected right-wing crook. Then again Neil Hamilton was a *'maverick'*, while Socialist liars are of course simply *liars.*" [4]

However the new broom in the Tory Party has brought in a number of different phrases, some of which sound more PC than PS. For example "*Compassionate Conservative,*" which, according to liberals, is an oxymoron pioneered by George Bush and test-marketed with limited success by the UK Tories.

The doubtful prospects for "compassionate conservatism" in the UK seemed to be symbolised by a report from the West Midlands, once fertile soil for Thatcherites. In the year 2000 local churches raised £72,000 for a gas-fired "Flame of Hope," donated to the City of Birmingham and intended to burn for the next 1,000 years as a symbol of life-enhancing optimism. It was ceremonially lit by Sir Cliff Richard, whom the press described as the "Peter Pan of Pop." Unfortunately in a couple of years the torch had already gone out because the council couldn't afford the gas bill of £12,000. After new sponsors came forward it flamed until 2004 when the city fathers finally turned it off because *"needlessly burning gas flies in the face of Birmingham's climate change agenda."*

Liberal Implosion: Nemesis of liberal and left-liberal news manipulation: 2015-16 was not a good year for the liberal ideology that has such a firm grip of the media in Germany and Austria and of a large swathe of same in the UK. As a journalist from *Die Zeit* put it: *"when you ask a leftist*

---

4 Jonathan Aitken was convicted in 1999 of perjury and perverting the course of justice after lying about some dubious arms dealing in which he was involved. However he declared himself bankrupt and thereby cost *The Guardian* one and half million pounds in costs for defending itself against a libel action dishonestly brought against it by Aitken. In prison Aitken discovered Christianity and is now President of Christian Solidarity Worldwide, though this remarkable character reform does not seem to have benefited those who lost a lot of money through his antics. Neil Hamilton got into trouble for taking cash in brown envelopes from the owner of Harrods Mohamed Al-Fayed and lost a libel action against the same. A Parliamentary Inquiry decided he had acted improperly and he was forced to abandon his parliamentary career after a former BBC correspondent, Martin Bell, overturned his 16,000 majority in the Tatton constituency at the 1997 election. Tatton was the fourth safest Conservative seat in the country. Hamilton later re-emerged as a Vice-President of the United Kingdom Independence Party, a considerable irony, since the latter draws much of its support from those disgusted by the corruption and arrogance of "politics as usual."

*about a social problem, they will at first deny it, then say that it has al-
ways gone on, and finally that it is good for you."* This has roughly been
the trajectory of the dishonest attempt to manipulate public opinion on
mass migration. *The Economist* tells us week after week that such immigration is a universal good and we should have more of it. People opposed to it are xenophobes, racists and (a new term of abuse being heavily test marketed in the liberal press) "nativist." Initial propaganda
presented all migrants as "refugees" — the News Editor at *Al Jazeera*
actually banned the word migrant as being "racist," which is quite rich
coming from an organization based in the Arab States that don't take any
refugees at all. When this claim failed to fly, it was said that mass migration to Germany could only be a boon, due to the ageing population. Enthusiasm for this line faded after some 500 women were groped and
robbed at New Year's festivities in Cologne.

This was more or less the Waterloo of liberal mendacity, since it
emerged that attempts had been made to suppress the news of this for
four days and only slowly did it emerge that newly arrived asylum seekers were prominent among the mass of offenders, who were all chastely
described as "people of North African or Arab appearance." The lady
Mayor of Cologne delivered schoolmistressy advice to the local girls on
how to behave in public space, a classic example of an old liberal tactic,
whereby responsibility is subtly deflected from perpetrators to victims.
It soon transpired that migrant violence against women had occurred
widely elsewhere too and a Swedish journalist pointed out that the same
had been a regular feature of large gatherings in Sweden for years, news
of it however always being played down or suppressed. True to form,
liberals claimed there was "world wide outrage" when the Danish government applied to migrants the same restrictions on claiming benefits
as applied to Danish citizens, stripping them of assets over the limit that
made them eligible if they wished to have such benefits. (Unhappily for
the left-liberal lobby, this law was also supported by the Social Democrats, so it appeared that the "world-wide outrage" excluded 90 % of Denmark.)

The puzzle of why liberals wish to be the gravediggers of European
culture and society is more a problem for psychiatrists than political scientists. In Germany and Austria it has much to do with assuaging war
guilt; in Britain the lure of self-righteousness seems potent, but also self-
interest. Business welcomes cheap labour that has the happy contingent

effect of suppressing domestic wage militancy. Well remunerated metropolitan liberal journalists are largely immune to the pressure on the health service, education and welfare that sudden mass immigration causes (the same is of course true of the pharisaical journalistic elite of Austria, Germany and Scandinavia.) There are also those useful cleaning ladies and odd job men, many of them happy to be paid in cash. However, apart from betrayal of the poor, liberals have now embarked on the serious business of undermining the main pillar of our democracy, namely free speech. Appeasement of violent militancy is rife, defended by liberals under their various mantras of tolerance, human rights, diversity and multiculturalism. When *Charlie Hebdo* was given the PEN America award in 2015, 145 writers protested. As historian Amanda Foreman observed with some understatement, "*there is something disgusting about writers who defend the assassin's veto.*"

Liberal ideology is based on the pretence that all culturally determined behavior is equally valid. Paul Collier points out in his book *Exodus*[5] that the institutions of European democracies function (when they do) on the basis of mutual regard and trust, but to many migrants these ideas are simply bizarre. Collier quotes a notice in the room of his luxury hotel in Nigeria where logically none of the guests could be poor: "*Honoured guest*," it runs, "*before your departure all the contents of this room will be checked against our inventory*" (the hotel has learned that otherwise the honoured guest will would run off with the contents.) Nigerians, pursues Collier, cannot get life insurance because, "*given the opportunism of the relevant professions, a death certificate can be purchased without the inconvenience of dying.*" Of course, a liberal might claim that this dysfunctionality is precisely what the migrants are fleeing. But then again, in many cases it may be precisely what they bring with them….

Libraries: Once gateways to culture and learning, now considered by local councils to be "*outreach facilities:*"

Matthew Engel, writing in the *Financial Times,*[6] has some poignant words on the decline of the same "According to Manchester Council's

5 Paul Collier: *Exodus: Immigration and Multiculturalism in the 21st Century* (Penguin, 2013), P. 66
6 *Financial Times,* Feb 4th/5th 2012

website: '*In the past libraries were all about books. Now they're about people*' — which is the sort of drivel you expect on council websites."

With the decline of the book as a desirable artefact, it is to be feared that the days of the great eccentric librarians are numbered. The academic librarian, for instance, who obstructed readers from penetrating some little horde of material that he one day hoped to "work up" himself. The lady librarian who left traces of her late breakfast on the pages. Or the legendary Florentine librarian in the 17th century who was famous for his neglect of personal hygiene, which we allow in the great and the good. Antonio Magliabecchi is described as follows in J.G.Keysler's *Travels*: "The books which he frequently consulted bore the marks of snuff… and others which had served him for plates, were daubed with yolks of eggs, which were his principal food. By the length of his nails he resembled a Harpy. He very seldom changed his linen; so that when a shirt was once put on, it remained as long as it would hang on his back. As he lived in this sordid manner and hardly ever washed himself, it is no wonder that the offensive effluvia he emitted could scarce be borne with, but for the pleasure of his conversation."

The librarian Magliabecchi rarely undressed at night, "life being so short and books so plentiful."

Dr Johnson wrote a magnificent prose elegy, not so much for libraries, as for the aspirations of the dear dead authors whose forgotten works repose therein: "No place affords a more striking conviction of the vanity of human hopes than a publick library; for who can see the wall crowded on every side by mighty volumes, the works of laborious meditation, and accurate inquiry, now scarcely known but by the catalogue, and preserved only to increase the pomp of learning, without considering how many hours have been wasted in vain endeavours, how often imagination has anticipated the praises of futurity, how many statues have risen to the eye of vanity, how many ideal converts have elevated zeal, how often wit has exulted in the eternal infamy of his antagonists, and dog-

matism has delighted in the gradual advances of his authority, the im-
mutability of his decrees, and the perpetuity of his power?"

Lies: "Lies have long legs: they are half way round the world, before
truth has got its shoes on…" (French Proverb)

A DEAD STATESMAN

I could not dig: I dared not rob:
Therefore I lied to please the mob.
Now all my lies are proved untrue
And I must face the men I slew.
What tale shall serve me here among
Mine angry and defrauded young?

Rudyard Kipling: *Epitaphs of War, 1914-18*

Lingerie: Desperation dressed for coitus:
There is an old saw of the underwear trade, as follows: "*If love is blind,*
there is no need to spend money on lingerie…."

"Have you read any good books lately?"

Mona Lisa: Picture in the Louvre that serves as a background for "self-ies" taken by Japanese tourists *(q.v.* **S**: *Selfies*):

When the Mona Lisa was stolen from the Louvre in 1911, it was like Christmas and Easter rolled into one for the Parisian satirists. The best spoof to emerge was a five minute film that delighted Franz Kafka and Max Brod when they saw it a month after the theft. The film's hero, evidently a forerunner of Inspector Clouseau, decides that the Director of the Louvre has himself stolen the Mona Lisa. During the uproar that ensues when the unfortunate Director is arrested, the thief quietly returns with *La Gioconda* under his arm, puts it back in its place and removes a Velázquez. No one notices. But then the *La Gioconda* is found with a message pinned to it: *"Sorry, it's my poor eyesight. I wanted the picture next to it."*

Literature, Disappearance of: Now you see it, now you don't:
Despite the tsunami of literary works still rolling off the presses, a group of the most up to date authors known as the *"writers of the No"* have announced that literature is in fact *disappearing* — "like John Cage's mute music" or "the libraries of unpublished or unwritten books and erasure poetry" [*sic*]. According to a reviewer in the *Times Literary Supplement*, the appellation " 'writers of the No' designates authors, who, "taking their cue from [Herman] Melville's agraphic scrivener, 'would prefer not to' " [*sic*]. In 2000 the Spanish writer Enrique Vila-Matas coined the nomenclature for the group in his novel *Bartleby & Co.*, itself inspired by Melville's cult short story, which concerns a legal clerk who stops working, refuses all incentives or encouragement to do anything, and indeed eventually stops living altogether.[7] As our reviewer explains, the "radical negativity" of the 'writers of the No' "is constitutive of artistic modernity, to the point of merging with it."[8] In an article elsewhere we are told by a commentator that Vila-Matas deals with "the endemic disease of contemporary letters, the negative pulsion or attraction towards nothingness."

7 Herman Melville's short story *Bartleby, the Scrivener: A Story of Wall Street* was published in1853.

8 The citations in double quotes are from a review of Aaron Hillyer's *The Disappearance of Literature* (Bloomsbury, 2014) by Andrew Gallix in *The Times Literary Supplement*, 19-26 December, 2014:36. Citations in single quotes are from Gallix's quotations of Hillyer's text.

You might think that nothingness was, well, a bit of a dead end, but on the contrary it has a lot going for it, especially in academe. A right-on young scholar has drilled into this promising new vein of literary theory in his book *The Disappearance of Literature*, which (again according to the TLS reviewer) "asks the crucial question: if language cannot speak the world, 'can the world speak language?' " Apparently words "negate things and beings in their singularity, replacing them with concepts" — which is indeed rather the impression one gains from perusing "literary theory" nowadays, although the author and his enthusiastic reviewer are far too discreet to say so. Still, obviously *something must be done*, even though that something means promotion of nothing; and if not done by readers, who seem to be regarded by literary theorists as a tiresome irrelevance, at least by a hit squad of *No* admirers. Apparently literature must go through a 'zone of decreation' that "deactivates its habitual signifying and informative functions 'in order to communicate communicability itself, openness to the world itself.'" This can be achieved, we are told, by the author "coinciding with his or her work; disappearing momentarily into a thingly, asignifying language that now speaks itself. Only a writer who has vanished into the 'pure event of the word' — where the telling becomes the teller — may express (although not in so many words) 'what absolutely escapes our language.'"

I hope you are with me so far, because there is a good deal more of this. For example we are told that, for "the writers of the No," language becomes a 'procedure' designed 'to indicate what passes beyond it'. Indeed these No fellows sound really exciting, with their novels consisting of "a series of prologues to a novel that never gets going" and "a series of footnotes to an invisible text that exists only in outline" — in other words, the type of script that hitherto was commonly found in the bottom drawers of authors with writer's block, but which now triumphantly emerges as the real mashed potatoes when published by the geniuses of No. According to one Maurice Blanchot, "literature is heading towards itself, towards its essence, which is its disappearance," a notion that has apparently inspired Aaron Hillyer's important work *The Disappearance of Literature*. The TLS reviewer was greatly impressed with it, though he did concede that "combined with the author's subtlety of mind and impressive erudition, it may … leave some readers baffled at times. Hillyer's crucial contention that the 'self-unfolding of the world' is the source of literature and art is taken as given, as is the messianic correlation between the emergence of a new language and a new world. The numerous phrases used to refer to the unindividuated aspect of being — the void, the impersonal, the neuter, the absolute, Genius etc. — may prove confusing, and it is only on Page 91 that the notion of 'forward dawning' is linked to Ernst Bloch (which is rather surprising given that the book derives from a PhD dissertation)." However "these are very minor quibbles," he concludes, asserting that Hillyer's PhD is "a thrilling addition [*sic*] to the growing body of work tracing the emergence of a literature of disappearance." Evidently we can look forward to plenty more nothingness and commentary on it by the Nibelungen of literary academe, until all of them, writers and critics, have literally written themselves out of the script — or, to use a richly *decreating signifiant*, have *disappeared*.

Ken Livingstone, some time Mayor of London: Unsinkable newt fancier who was handbagged by Mrs Thatcher when he was leader of the Greater London Council (which she abolished), but subsequently got his own back by being elected Mayor of London:

Ken's colourful mayoralty (2000-2008) backed by his "Rainbow Coalition" had Conservatives and the right-wing press frothing at the mouth. Perhaps the worst thing he did was to abolish the iconic Routemaster buses (after saying he would never do so), beside which cosying up to the IRA and dubious Islamists, declaring London a nuclear-free zone, and politically correct projects caricatured as Black Lesbian Feminist Workshops or similar, pale into insignificance. However, whisper it not in Gad, he did a good deal for London's infrastructure, particularly the tube and buses. And he was always good for a laugh: his autobiography was entitled "*If Voting Changed Anything, They'd Abolish It.*" Of Parliament he said: "Anyone who enjoys being in the House of Commons probably needs psychiatric help."

Ken ran into trouble over his commendable plan to rid Trafalgar Square of smelly, disease-ridden pigeons (which he called "rats with wings.") His deployment of Harris Hawks (*Parabuteo unicinctus*) to patrol the skies above the square and put the fear of god into the pigeons aroused tearful protests from the ***Pigeon Action Group***. Its spokeswoman modestly described the hawks' occasional meal as "the greatest wildlife cruelty catastrophe that London has ever known." The Group even claimed that, on one occasion, "a hawk swooped *and* *killed a pigeon in front of children.*" According to the Liberal Democrats, for an outlay of £226,000 some 2,500 pigeons have been got rid of, at a cost therefore of circa £90 per bird. This seems poor value and some unregenerate souls have even wondered aloud whether the raptors' remit ought not to have been extended to include children, of whom there are also far too many in the square, many of them a health hazard.

Loneliness: on the "meridian" of which, according to Viennese writer Alfred Polgar, Vienna is located.

The art of being alone and the social arts are equally valued in Vienna. Typically they may be observed in the Viennese coffee house: "*For ten years, every day for hours on end, the two have been sitting quite alone in the coffee house. That is a good marriage, you will say!* **No, that is a good coffee house!**" (Polgar again, who also described the Wiener Kaffeehaus as "*a place where you go when you want to be alone, for which you need other people around.*") And another insight from the same source: *When everyone leaves you it's loneliness you feel; when you leave everyone else it's solitude.*"

"If you're lonely when you're alone, you're in bad company" —
Jean-Paul Sartre.

Sadly, things are not what they were in the loneliness scene. As Stanislaw Jerzy Lec has wistfully observed: "*Einsamkeit, wie bist Du übervölkert...*" ("Oh solitude, how overpopulated you have become...").

Leo Longanesi (1905–1957): Engaging journalist and publisher who pithily summed up his fellow countrymen: "*The Italian is a totalitarian in the kitchen, a democrat in the Parliament, a Catholic in bed and a Communist in the factory.*"[9]

Longanesi was of the opinion: "*Non bisogna appoggiarsi troppo ai principi, perché poi si piegano.*" Rough translation: "It doesn't do to stand too much on principle, because it tends to collapse under your weight." This, we may take it from his oeuvre in general, was intended as a satirical observation. It was apt in a post-war Italy where, as he mournfully remarked: "One third of the voters yearn for the return of the Fascist dictatorship, one third eagerly anticipate the Communist one and the last third hasten to adapt themselves to the Christian Democrat version." This is not really anything new in Italian political attitudes. During the era of anti-clerical so-called Liberal governments following the Risorgimento, there was a popular saying that "*si stava meglio quando si stava peggio*" ("we were better off when we were worse off"). This view is commonly met with in the post-Communist countries of Central Europe (*see* **O: *Ostalgie***).

Luxembourg: Heap of fly-shit on the North European map that supplies dubious heads of the European Commission:

Under the benign rule of Jean-Claude Juncker, the present (2016) devious head of the European Commission, Luxembourg became a centre for "tax avoidance" and profits laundering through "brass plate firms" by multinationals and investors (q.v. ***LuxLeaks***). This proved to be a slight embarrassment to "the Junckernaut" just after he had emerged as Head of the EU Commission following the usual backroom stitch-up. For a while he was obliged to shelter in what the German press delightfully describes as "the deep sea diving station," while the storm raged over questionable tax concessions to powerful companies that took place when he was Luxembourg's Finance Minister. After a while however the

9 *L'italiano: totalitario in cucina, democratico in parlamento, cattolico a letto, comunista in fabbrica.*

caravans had conveniently moved on, and Juncker re-emerged, bland as ever, to continue lecturing the wayward new EU states on "democracy," "the rule of law" and other topics on which Luxembourg is such a notable expert. Indeed, in 2015, a bustling non-person, quaintly described as the "Foreign Minister of Luxembourg," denounced Hungary for building a fence to secure its Serbian border (then being overrun with migrants) as being "*contrary to European values*." Quite different, you see, from the (unmentioned) fence that Bulgaria had long since put in place, or the (unmentioned) one that Austria (another pharisaical little state) was at that very moment in the process of erecting on the Slovenian border, not to mention the 700 mile fence designed to keep illegal Mexican immigrants from the USA, all of which we must therefore assume are fully compatible with "European values" as interpreted by our resident values expert, corrupt little Luxembourg.

Luxembourg's other gift to the EU was Jacques Santer, President of the Commission from 1995 to 1999, when he and the whole commission had to resign because of corruption scandals involving individual members of it. It turned out that it was impossible to sack individual members of the Commission unless their home governments agreed — and France refused to allow the regrettable Edith Cresson (q.v.) to be sacked, despite antics such as appointing her dentist to Euro-jobs. So all in all Luxembourg is a great asset to the EU and an inexhaustible source of jobsworths, busybodies and drones to fill its over-remunerated offices.

LuxLeaks: Revelations in 2014 that up to 340 multinational companies, many of them household names like Ikea or Pepsi, funneled profits through Luxembourg to lower their tax bills, sometimes down to 1 per cent (See also **I: *Double Irish***):

LuxLeaks has had a discombobulating effect on the world elites who quietly make special arrangements to get round inconvenient laws or regulations that are rigorously enforced on the rest of us. The analogy is with *Wikileaks* and other whistleblowing operations which not infrequently resulted in the whistleblower being arrested as well as, or instead of, the crooks. Edward Snowden, like Julian Assange, a somewhat ambiguous figure in all this (somehow the "revelations" they both offer always seem to concern the free western democracies, not totalitarian dictatorships, one of which is giving Snowden asylum) made the key observation: "*It is not the unlawful behaviour of our gov-*

*ernments that should worry us, but the things they are doing that are **entirely lawful**.*"

The same applies to international firms that constantly point out that their tax avoidance schemes are "entirely lawful." Unhappily for this argument, as Pierre Moscovici, the EU Tax Commissioner pointed out in early 2016: "The days are numbered for companies that avoid paying tax at the expense of others." Actually most of these big companies think corporation tax should be abolished anyway…

(PS: Europol reported in 2015 that €500 bills are not accepted by many shops, but still account for one-third of the value of all Euro bank notes in circulation. Basically they are the favoured method of laundering money for crime syndicates and terrorist organizations.

Most undiplomatically, it highlighted the case of **Luxembourg**, which issued **87.5bn's** worth of Euro bills in 2013, "*a significant proportion*" of these in high denominations; all this despite Luxembourg being one of the most "*cash adverse*" countries in the eurozone. €87.5bn is about *twice* the GDP of Luxembourg.[10] "*Curiouser and curiouser*!" as they say in the Luxembourg patois…)

10 See a report by Jim Brunsden and James Shotter in the *Financial Times* of 16th February 2016, "Terrorists, criminals and big-spending Germans, take note — €500 bill to die."

M

Meekness:

Uncommon patience in planning a revenge that is worth while.

Ambrose Bierce: *The Devil's Dictionary*

Madness: "A perfectly rational adjustment to the insane world."[1]

The French utopian philosopher Charles Fourier (1772–1837) has been described as "*mad as a bagful of spanners.*" He believed that work should be compensated according to its value for the common weal (certainly a view that today's bankers would regard as bordering on lunacy.) In the communities which he planned and called *phalanstères* or "grand hotels," the wealthiest would occupy the upper apartments and the poorest be lodged in the lowest. A card index in reception would allow you to select partners from the community for casual sex. (According to Fourier, the Milky Way is the luminous projection of seminal activity by humans and could be multiplied by accelerating the rate of copulation. Thus the problem of providing lighting for large cities at night would be solved if men and women had continuous and varied sex. "This is a project," writes Pas-

Charles Fourier: "...the streets are cluttered with solicitors who swarm without limit or purpose."

1 R.D.Laing.

292

cal Bruckner, "that should immediately be put before the Secretary-General of the United Nations.")[2]

Although you could choose your job, Fourier thought the least agreeable jobs that no one wanted to do should receive the higher pay (another clearly mad idea that George Bernard Shaw later tried to revive, but with similar lack of success.)

Fourier's phalanstère — "Truth and commerce are as incompatible as Jesus and Satan."

Fournier had a number of other ideas that were obviously insane. For example, he proposed that people should be paid high (though not equal) wages and that those without work should be supported by a "decent minimum payment." He thought women should have equal rights and

2 Quoted in Pascal Bruckner: *The Fanaticism of the Apocalypse* (Polity press, Cambridge, 2013) P. 95. Bruckner also mentions that Fourier believed the most recalcitrant species would be tamed in his new dispensation and "anti-whales would draw vessels into calmer waters in the event of a storm, while anti-crocodiles ('river co-operators') and anti-seals (sea-horses) would provide rapid transportation."

homosexuality was a perfectly valid personal choice. So you can see the man was completely off his rocker. An early "climate change" visionary, he believed that the North Pole would become as mild as the Mediterranean and the seas would in due course lose their salinity and turn into lemonade. Who could argue with that?

There are a number of psychiatrists who don't believe that madness exists, or at least not what the rest of us call madness. R.D.Laing (quoted above) said that madness "need not be all *breakdown*. It may also be *breakthrough*. It is potentially liberation and renewal as well as enslavement and existential death."[3] And Thomas Szasz has written that "in the past, men created witches; now they create mental patients."[4] This view is not confined to the psychiatric profession. Antonin Artaud opined that "society has strangled in its asylums all those it wanted to get rid of or protect itself from, because they refused to become its accomplices in certain great nastinesses. For a madman is also a man whom society did not want to hear and whom it wanted to prevent from uttering certain intolerable truths."[5] And Jean Cocteau wants us to believe that "what the public calls madness" is in reality "the extreme limits of wisdom."[6] Obviously all this is tosh — or possibly not. As one of Samuel Beckett's characters puts it: "We are all born mad. Some of us remain so."[7]

Norman Mailer: Wife-batterer with charisma:
Mailer pegged it in 2007 at 84, having clocked up six wives (like Henry VIII) and nine children (one adopted.) He nearly killed his second wife by stabbing her with a penknife when drunk and separated from his fifth the day after the wedding. Remarks like *"you don't know a woman till you've met her in court"* endeared him to feminists, getting parole for murderer Jack Abbott to liberals. (Unfortunately Abbott murdered again six weeks after release, but hey, man! Stuff happens.)

One can't help liking the old fraud, a sort of thinking man's Bruce Willis — and anyone who head-butted Gore Vidal can't be all bad. Mailer's aphorisms, solemnly paraded by fans, leave one gasping for

---

3 R.D. Laing: *The Politics of Experience* (1967)
4 Thomas Szasz: *The Manufacture of Madness* (1973)
5 Antonin Artaud: *Selected Writings* (1976).
6 Jean Cocteau: *Le rappel à l'ordre.* (1926)
7 Samuel Beckett: *Waiting for Godot* (1952).

less (e.g. *"Hip is the wise primitive in a giant jungle."*) His saving grace was self-irony (occasionally): "If a person's not talented enough to be a novelist, nor smart enough to be a lawyer, and his hands are too shaky to perform operations, he becomes a journalist."

And if a journalist drinks and batters his wives, he becomes a Norman Mailer.

Management consultants: The first resort of incompetent managers:
In 2014, management consultant McKinsey celebrated its 50 years of parasitical fee-gouging with a glossy brochure, whose projections for the next fifty years were given in a speed-read summary by Lucy Kellaway in the *Financial Times*.[8] Point 1: The future will not be like the past (in McKinsey-speak: there will be *" more discontinuity and volatility, with long-term charts no longer looking like smooth upward curves, long-held assumptions giving way, and seemingly powerful business models being upended."*). Point 2: There will be new/more technologies, all of them, in Mckinsey-speak, *"turbocharging advances in connectivity."* Point 3: Emerging markets will continue to emerge. Point 4: Everyone will continue to get older. These, as Kellaway points out, are actually present, rather than future, trends. However the brochure is a treasure trove of even deeper insights, e.g. *"It's likely that different regions, countries and individuals will have different fates, depending on the strength and flexibility of their institutions and policies."* Who would believe it? *"Change is hard,"* pursue the authors, "a declaration so crashingly obvious," comments Kellaway rather unkindly, that it is odd that the authors feel the need to back it up with support from *"social scientists and behavioural economists"* who, amazingly, have noticed this too. Apparently the reason why "forecasts" like this are no more than "a sorry exercise in windy platitudes" is because they are not "forecasts" at all but marketing plugs. *"Tomorrow's strategist,"* warn the McKinsey seers will need to be agile enough to *" 'zoom out' in the development of a coherent global approach and to 'zoom in' on extremely granular product or market segments."* Kellaway however has been looking into her own crystal ball and discovers that, notwithstanding all these zoom-ins and -outs on granular segments, the best bet is

8 Lucy Kellaway on Work: "McKinsey's airy platitudes bode ill for its next half-century" (*Financial Times*. 15 September, 2014.)

that in 50 years McKinsey won't exist. A disappointment for the pur-veyors of vacuous business-speak, perhaps, but rather a relief for the rest of us…

The existence of highly paid "management consultants" underlines the extent to which the winners in modern capitalism are those who have mastered the art of providing services at high cost, but are themselves seldom, if ever, being held accountable if the advice they give turns out to be dud. McKinsey have job titles like "Master Experts," "the tautol-ogy," says Kellaway, "no doubt a ploy to soften up the client as a prelude to charging twice the normal rate." A consultant is long gone when and if the results of implementing his or her plans results in chaos or corporate implosion. However their alumni are of course capable of causing plenty of mayhem — Jeff Skilling, for instance who was such a creative Finance Director at Enron (*q.v.*) and landed up in jail; and Michael Pearson, whose "business model" at Valeant involved buying up existing drugs and adding a few hundred per cent to their price. "*Our strategy,*" he said in 2014, "*is basically the education I had through McKinsey,*" which is not such a glowing endorsement in view of the disasters that befell Valeant, half of whose senior executive team were McKinsey men. Both Pearson and Skilling rose to eminence in the glory days of the consul-tancy when it was led by Rajat Gupta, who… er… unfortunately also went to jail…[9]

Similar types of freeloading include the activities of "fiduciary con-sultants," who are now under scrutiny for the way they advise pension funds where to place their assets — there being a conflict of interests if they (Surprise! Surprise!) end up recommending asset managers in which it turns out that they themselves have a stake; and "head-hunters" who act on commission and have a vested interest in whacking up salary packages as high as possible, thus keeping the putatively "international" market in CEO salaries bubbling along in the same way the auction houses and dealers have learned to inflate the market for contemporary art. It appears, however, that if the CEO, lured with a massive welcome package and supposedly picked from an international range of brilliant and expensive candidates, turns out to be a massive flop, the head-hunter is in no way to blame. These things happen….

9 See John Gapper: "McKinsey's fingerprints are all over Valeant," *Financial Times*, 24th March, 2016.

The Man Booker Prize for Fiction: Recognition for novelists that is either premature or overdue:

The Man Booker jury received an unusual entry in 2011, namely the *Timetable for the Number 1 bus service in Bristol.* Simon Holliday, who nominated it, said he could *"personally attest that this is a work of fiction, as it bears absolutely no relation to the times and frequencies of bus journeys."*

Like all such prizes, the Booker generates in-fighting and backbiting amongst the literary cliques and has produced some splendidly eccentric decisions (or not, of course, according to your point of view.) Winners, nominees, judges and commentators have lined up to denounce the recipients or the sponsors of the prize (the Marxist John Berger famously gave half his prize money to the British Black Panthers on the grounds that Booker McConnell had oppressed sugar workers in the Caribbean for 130 years.) *Wikipedia* tells us that nominee John Banville wrote a letter to *The Guardian* requesting that the prize be given to him so that he could use the money to buy every copy of the long-listed books in Ireland and donate them to libraries, *"thus ensuring that the books not only are bought but also read — surely a unique occurrence."*

In 1994, left-wing journalist Richard Gott described the prize as *"a significant and dangerous iceberg in the sea of British culture that serves as a symbol of its current malaise,"* while in 2001, A. L. Kennedy, who had been a judge in 1996, described the prize as *"a pile of crooked nonsense"* with the winner determined by *"who knows who, who's sleeping with who, who's selling drugs to who, who's married to who, whose turn it is"*. [*See also under* **A:** *Awards*, and under **B:** *Thomas Bernhard*]

Mira Markovic: Delightful spouse of Slobodan Milosevic, the charismatic Serb butcher:

Let us eavesdrop on Mira waxing lyrical on husband Slobodan, surely a potential Nobel Peace Prize candidate if Yasser Arafat could get one: *"He is a superior man, as a whole,"* she said. *"He has strong feelings for other people, for their problems and needs ... he has inner stability, strong and natural, genetic inner stability"* ["genetic" is nice].

An article by Blaine Harden in the *New York Times Magazine* (2002) gives us a flavour of the dysfunctional Milosevic family by means of a terrifying interview with Mira, who expresses her pride in her violent and criminal children, as well as her touching affection for her psychopathic husband: "That pride is intense and, in some ways [*sic*], delusional," writes Harden. Indeed, the private life of the Milosevic family has been governed by the same self-deception that has governed their politics.... Marko, their son, became notorious in Serbia for crashing one fancy car after another. Marija, their daughter, once shot her boyfriend's dog. Marko took his guns and bodyguards to nightclubs where he beat up people whose looks he didn't like. [*More recently he had been indicted for threatening to chop up an opposition activist with a rotary saw and throw his body parts in a river. Even in Serbia such sentiments are considered to go a little beyond what good breeding allows.*] Marija took her guns and bodyguards to nightclubs where she looked for cheating boyfriends. During their parents' rule, they cashed in on family connections and made a point of showing off their clothes and cars at times when many Serbs were destitute. Their parents, however, were quite proud of their children. Milosevic told several friends that he admired Marko's business skills. And during our conversation, Markovic told me, "*I have to say that I have a very nice family and well-raised children.*"

Cuddly Mira Markovic with charming husband and well brought up children....

It looks as if the European Court of Human Rights might well have had cause to intervene on Milosevic's behalf during his trial at The Hague in order to protect his "right to private and family life" (Article 8 of the Convention). After all it has intervened on behalf of rapists, murderers and terrorists resisting deportation from the UK on precisely these grounds[10] — and besides, the "family life" of the Milosevices is such a touching and edifying example of togetherness and conscientious upbringing of children.

10 The official figures for 2012-2013 published in the UK show that 324 appeals were allowed for resisting deportation on these grounds. They include a substantial number of violent criminals.

298

Marriage: An attempt to turn a night owl into a homing pigeon (males), or the sexually available into the non-sexually available (women):

According to Albert Einstein, "men marry women with the hope they will never change. Women marry men with the hope they will change. Invariably they are both disappointed."

According to Agatha Christie, "women can accept the fact that a man is a rotter, a swindler, a drug taker, a confirmed liar, and a general swine, without batting an eyelash, and without its impairing their affection for the brute in the least. Women are wonderful realists. "[11] She also said it was great being married to an archaeologist because the older you get the more interested in you he becomes…

Gertrude Stein wrote of her lifelong partner, Alice B. Toklas that she was a "liar of the most sordid, unillumined, undramatic, unimaginative prostitute type, coward, ungenerous, conscienceless, mean, vulgarly triumphant and remorseless, caddish, in short just plain rotten"[12] — so you can see the attraction. Toklas devoted her life to the amazingly unpleasant Stein, doing everything for her from keeping the household to providing fulsome praise for Gertrude's Delphic literary productions. In return Stein gave Toklas orgasms.

Benjamin Franklin, also a realist, tells us: "Keep your eyes wide open before marriage, half shut afterwards."

Beatrice Webb originated the observation that "marriage is the wastepaper basket of the emotions."

"The great thing about marriage," the comedian Rita Rudner has observed, "is finding that one special person you want to annoy for the rest of your life."

"A good marriage," says Montaigne, "would be between a blind wife and a deaf husband." (Which puts one in mind of a lawyer who went to the audiologist because his wife had noticed he was growing hard of hearing. *"How long have you been married?"* was the audiologist's first (and only) question.)

Myfanwy Piper, married to the artist John Piper, was philosophical after 40 years of being exposed to the artistic temperament. As she put it: "I can safely say that I have enjoyed every other minute of it."

11 Agatha Christie: *Murder in Mesopotamia.* (2001).
12 Quoted in Michael Kimmelman: "The Last Act," a review of Janet Malcolm's *"Two Lives: Gertrude and Alice"* (Yale University Press) in *The New York Review of Books*, October 25, 2007.

Jim Slater, the investment guru, married Helen Goodwyn in 1965, describing her as "a long-term hold," (she produced a handsome return until his death in 2015.)

"My husband and I have never considered divorce," says Joyce Brothers. "Murder sometimes, but never divorce."

Anaïs Nin writes: "Someone told me the delightful story of the crusader who put a chastity belt on his wife and gave the key to his best friend for safekeeping, in case of his death. He had ridden only a few miles away when his friend, riding hard, caught up with him, saying *'You gave me the wrong key!'*"

Kahlil Gibran writes in *The Prophet*: "Let the winds of heaven dance between you." As you get older and your digestion gets weaker, there is quite a lot of other wind too.

Socrates says to his pupils (all male): "By all means marry. If you get a good wife, you'll become happy; if you get a bad one, you'll become a philosopher." This of course does not take into account the possibility of changing your spouse regularly, like Zsa Zsa Gabor. However too many changes makes the challenge facing prospective new partners rather formidable. US Senator John McCain showed he was alert to this during his unsuccessful fight for the Republican nomination in 2008. Referring to his difficulty in stirring the conscience of a resigned and flaccid public, he said: *"I feel like Zsa Zsa Gábor's fifth husband. I know what to do, but I don't know how to make it interesting."* Zsa Zsa herself was once asked how many husbands she had had. *"You mean other than my own?"* she asked. Nine times married, Zsa Zsa was something of an expert on the requisite conjugal qualities in a male. *"I want a man,"* she said, *"who is kind, handsome, and understanding. Is that too much to ask of a millionaire?"*

And Oscar Levant said to Harpo Marx: "Harpo, she's a lovely person. She deserves a good husband. Marry her before she finds one."

And Groucho Marx once said to a good-looking widow "Will you marry me? Did he leave you any money? Answer the second question first."

Masturbation: "Don't knock masturbation — it's sex with someone I love":[13]

Mark Twain supposedly had quite a lot to say about this topic, viz: "Homer, in the second book of the Iliad says with fine enthusiasm,

13 Woody Allen.

300

"Give me masturbation or give me death." Caesar, in his Commentaries, says, "To the lonely it is company; to the forsaken it is a friend; to the aged and to the impotent it is a benefactor. They that are penniless are yet rich, in that they still have this majestic diversion." In another place this experienced observer has said, "There are times when I prefer it to sodomy." Robinson Crusoe says, "I cannot describe what I owe to this gentle art." Queen Elizabeth said, "It is the bulwark of virginity." Cetewayo, the Zulu hero, remarked, "A jerk in the hand is worth two in the bush." The immortal Franklin has said, "Masturbation is the best policy." Michelangelo and all of the other old masters-"old masters," I will remark, is an abbreviation, a contraction — have used similar language. Michelangelo said to Pope Julius II, "Self-negation is noble, self-culture beneficent, self-possession is manly, but to the truly great and inspiring soul they are poor and tame compared with self-abuse." Mr. Brown, here, in one of his latest and most graceful poems, refers to it in an eloquent line which is destined to live to the end of time—"None knows it but to love it; none name it but to praise."[14]

An article in *The Spectator* alerted us to the fact that May 2014 was International Masturbation Month, which is sponsored by Marie Stopes International and has been going strong since 1995, if you see what I mean. These days everything must raise money for charity, so readers will be pleased to hear that a feature of Masturbation Months has been *"masturbate-a-thons"* where singletons or groups are encouraged to compete in order to raise money for good causes. Unlike conventional sports competitions, in this one the slowest wins.

According to the article, the NHS has distributed a leaflet in schools advising pupils to masturbate twice a week, remarking helpfully *en passant* that "an orgasm a day" keeps the doctor away, or at any rate is good for cardiovascular health. The BBC's "teen advice" site is apparently even more gung-ho, pointing out that masturbation helps you to sleep well and may "keep your genitals in top working order" [*sic*]. There are

14 This is allegedly from a pamphlet by Mark Twain entitled *Some Thoughts on the Science of Onanism*, the printed version of a speech, subsequently published in a limited edition of 50 copies, and given to The Stomach Club (a society of American expatriates) in 1879 in Paris. The meetings of the Stomach Club (if it existed) were strictly male and strictly private. However the tone and style of the remarks are suggestive of a spoof à la Twain. *Source:* Maria Popova: www.brainpickings.org/2014/12/06/mark-twain-on-masturbation/

"...and these things are not cheap, either...."

signs that the "Health and Safety" people have had an input into this debate, since the Masturbation Month organizers assure their target audience that masturbation is "the safest form of sex a person can have." (Obviously they have forgotten about that Tory MP who choked to death in the course of an elaborate self-love ritual.)

All this goes to show how fickle medical fashion is. Only a generation ago nasty little schoolboys were still being bullied by physicians and clerics who maintained that masturbation sent you mad or made you blind. Now they recommend it unreservedly. It's the same with red wine, which has swung in and out of fashion over the years. The French eat a potentially lethal cholesterol-rich diet, but they have long life expectancy, apparently because all that red meat is washed down with copious drafts of Burgundy and Claret. There is now even an English doctor who *prescribes* red wine to his patients, which makes many of us who have been self-prescribing the Brolio for years feel thoroughly vindicated.

But to return to the subject of masturbation, which you were hoping I had left, it is clear that the NHS leaflets would have more effect if they contained celebrity endorsements rather along the lines of national treas-

302

ure Jimmy Savile's propaganda for the wearing of seat belts in cars. Who does not recall his famous slogan "*Clunk click!*"? It cannot be beyond the powers of the ministerial copy-writers to adapt that to the new campaign and make an arresting splash (as it were) on the public billboards....

Particulate matter: Nasty bits of solid or liquid matter that hang about in the air gradually choking us (and the planet):

A report in *The Economist* (Feb 4/2012) alerts us to the fact that the canals of Holland are "brimming with nitrates and phosphates and the air is clogged with particulate matter." The Dutch Greens, who have dubbed Holland "Europe's drainage hole", came up with 2013's most scary headline, namely the claim that particulate matter in the air diminishes life expectancy in Holland by *155,000 years*. It's enough to make you want to put your head in a dyke! However Pieter Boot of the Dutch planning bureau pointed out that things were not really so bad: the figure quoted amounted to "just *one month* per Dutch person." Clearly he should have been sacked forthwith.

H. L. Mencken: Iconoclastic American journalist and gadfly:
"Civilization," wrote Mencken, "grows more and more maudlin and hysterical; especially under democracy it tends to degenerate into a mere combat of crazes; the whole aim of practical politics is to keep the populace alarmed (and hence clamorous to be led to safety) by menacing it with an endless series of hobgoblins, most of them imaginary. [*See also under* **A: *Apocaholics*** and **C: *Climate Change*.**] Perhaps feeling that the foregoing was too weakly antinomian, he subsequently added: "*the urge to save humanity is almost always a false front for the urge to rule*." Sounds familiar?

According to the usual grumblers in the UK, the function of risk-mongering has now been farmed out to the European Union and its local enforcement arm known (not affectionately) as " *'elf'n'safety*" (a satirical allusion to the Health and Safety Executive). Still, the same sort of people who whinge about *'elf 'n 'safety'* grumbled about the introduction of seat-belts in cars and government sponsored anti-smoking campaigns, which does not greatly enhance their credibility. The trick is to spot when Health and Safety is really advancing something designed to save lives and improve the quality of living, and when it is engaged in mis-

H. L. Mencken: "Conscience is a mother-in-law whose visit never ends."

sion creep, possibly with a concealed ideological agenda. That may have been the case when Britain "opted out" of certain employment laws put forward by the EU, whereupon that sage body simply reintroduced them under Health and Safety provisions, where there is no opt-out. Sir Humphrey greatly admired the elegance of this solution.

If a recent TV programme is to be believed, Britain's Health and Safety Executive is a much maligned body, staffed by mild-mannered men and women working tirelessly for the common good and generally enforcing what is little more than common sense (evidently in astonishingly short supply among the population a whole.) After all, the HSE credits the Health and Safety at Work Act with an 84% reduction in employee fatalities between 1974 and 2010, as well as a 75% fall in non-fatal injuries. We should stop bullying HSE officers in the boulevard press — it is too much like shooting ducks on a pond. In return they should stop bullying us about toothpicks on restaurant tables, or banning dodgems cars from banging into each other, or forbidding school sack races or… er… other things. As to the case where two community policemen could not save a boy from drowning because they lacked the correct swimming qualifications, what do the tabloids actually want? Three drownings instead of one? As Mencken also said: "For every complex problem there is an answer that is clear, simple, and wrong."

I'm sorry to say that Mencken, great man though he was, had regrettably low esteem for democratic government. "The government," he wrote, "consists of a gang of men exactly like you and me. They have, taking one with another, no special talent for the business of government; they have only a talent for getting and holding office. Their principal device to that end is to search out groups who pant and pine for something they can't get and to promise to give it to them. Nine times out of ten that promise is worth nothing. The tenth time it is made good by looting A to satisfy B. In other words, *government is a broker in pillage*, and every election is sort of an advance auction sale of stolen goods.[15]... If a politician found he had cannibals among his constituents, he would promise them missionaries for dinner."

Project Merlin: A strategy deployed by the biggest four British banks in 2011 to divert the government from forcing socially responsible behaviour on them:

The project was evidently so named because merlins (*Falco columbarius*) are birds that are rarely seen — rather like modestly remunerated bankers. The bankers began by demanding that we all *"move on,"* this being a favourite exhortation of politicians, murderers etc., who view the refractory victims of their crimes as the problem, the solution to which is to rebrand the perpetrators (namely themselves) as the real victims. Indeed the smarmy American billionaire in charge of Barclays became quite heated in his castigation of people who demanded to know why bankers needed further huge remuneration to clean up the mess they had caused in the first place. There is a reason for the public's lack of understanding, which Mr Diamond was obviously too intelligent to grasp: the banks had been able to return to profit because of a subsidy of cheap money from the taxpayer, which was estimated by the Bank of England to be worth £100bn a year. So the subsidy led to the profits, and the profits led to the bonuses, and the voters paid for it all through the nose and their taxes.

The Project Merlin agreement was signed in February 2011, the banks having signed up to some vague and unenforceable undertakings to lend more and stop sticking it to their customers. The Chief Executive of the

15 H. L. Mencken: *Prejudices*, First Series (1919).

Bankers Association, a risible lady called Angela Knight whose heart-warming eulogies of bankers had long been a source of innocent merriment among their victims, professed herself well satisfied with the deal. However the Engineering Employers Federation disobligingly pointed out that the agreement did nothing to address the lack of competition amongst banks, which was after all the main reason they were able to get away with behaving so badly for so long. The Liberal Democrat peer Lord Oakeshott resigned as a Treasury spokesman in the House of Lords, remarking that the deal was "pitiful", and adding that officials at the Treasury "couldn't negotiate their way out of a paper bag. [...] If this is robust action on bank bonuses then my name's Bob Diamond [the boss of Barclays Bank] and I'm going to claim my £9m bonus next week" (he said).[16]

Mexico: Country substantially ruled by homicidal drug cartels and populated by persons trying to leave it:
 "Poor Mexico! So far from God, so close to the United States!" (Mexican saying.)

Pippa Middleton: Owner of the most famous bottom in Britain:
"*Das Lesen gefährdet die Dummheit*" ("Reading endangers stupidity") is the motto on a shopping bag supplied by a Viennese bookshop, but the publishers of Pippa Middelton's 2012 book on party planning seemed to believe the opposite. Writing in *The Spectator*, the luscious sister of the Duchess of Cambridge bravely cited a spoof website that supplied ruthlessly accurate parodies of the deathless Pippa prose (e.g. *"Enjoy a glass of water by getting a clean glass and pouring in water from a tap or bottle,"* and *"Avoid early mornings by not getting up too early."*) "All good fun," writes Pippa gamely, "and authors [*sic*] ought to take criticism on the chin." Or on the bottom, perhaps.

Sir Jonathan Miller: Talented narcissist and grump:
Miller, who has a fine sense of his own importance judging from his biography, has said that he hated Mrs Thatcher *"for her odious gentility and sentimental, saccharine patriotism, catering to the worst elements of commuter idiocy."* Like many a comment on Mrs T. this tells us more

16 Quoted by *BBC News*, 9th Feb. 2011 and in *The Independent* 10th Feb, 2011.

about the person making it than it does about her. "Dr Jonathan" descends from 19th century refugees fleeing European anti-Semitism, but it doesn't occur to him that without the "saccharine" patriotism displayed in the past by leaders of the calibre of Mrs Thatcher, his parents, and therefore he, might very well not be here. Why should it? Like the Communist historian Erich Hobsbawm, who found asylum in UK and devoted his life to the destruction of the democratic capitalism that had saved him, Miller seems to believe his socialist ideology absolves him from such vulgarities as loyalty to country or even basic decency.

Like so many metropolitan liberals, Miller is expert at having it both ways. One of his major successes as a producer was his version of *The Mikado*, but according to him Gilbert and Sullivan is "boring self-satisfied drivel…UKIP set to music." Why produce a G&S opera then? He claimed that he was a refugee from the terrible Thatcher regime — so why accept from it the honour of a CBE (*Commander of the Most Excellent Order of the British Empire* — surely an anachronistic honour for persons of Miller's ideological persuasion)? He says he enjoys the "Niagara of praise" that is, after all only his due, but the slightest criticism provokes tantrums and hissy fits. His rival and colleague at the National Theatre, Sir Peter Hall, was rewarded for commissioning Miller productions with the designation "vulgar mediocrity… a safari-suited bureaucrat." Directing Placido Domingo was like "working with King Kong," and even the good doctor's long suffering medical colleagues are rewarded for their super-human tolerance of his boorish egotism with the appellation "uncultured jerks." Although Miller still gets massive applause, it is apparent that it is never quite enough and anyway he despises the applauders ("the foyer at Covent Garden looks like Harrods food hall has offered up its dead" is one of his more robust insults.) Anything less than adulation provokes childish rage — particularly hostile theatre critics, who are "worse than leukaemia" and whose trade is likened to "farting in public." So it's almost comically ironic to read one of Sir Jonathan's own insightful pronouncements, namely: "Errors of taste are very often the outward sign of a deep fault of sensibility." How true! How true!

Millionaires: Nowadays, persons with not much money:
There is an old joke among stockbrokers: "The quickest way to become a millionaire is to start as a billionaire and buy an airline."

307

Shazia Mirza: A devout virgin and teetotal Muslim comedian:

Mirza is the only stand-up comedian in Britain, and possibly the world, who is both female and practising Muslim. This is not a role to be embarked upon lightly, although there is a certain security in the fact that Muslim fundamentalists are not great habitués of the comedy circuit. She begins her act by announcing: "*My name is Shazia Mirza, or at least that is what it says on my pilot's licence.*"

"I could have lived in a big house, had kids and been extremely unhappy."

HUNGART©2016

We are constantly being told that the Prophet used humour in the Koran (like all those rib-ticklers in the Old Testament?) Over the years, says Mirza, this seems to have been forgotten. For example Muslim men have a complete humour failure when she does her joke about having her bum pinched in Mecca — which actually happened — and explains it was "the hand of God." Doubtless our brave feminists will be in the forefront of defending her legacy when she finally gets stoned (and it won't be on ecstasy).

Mission Statement: Statement of how a company would like to behave, other things being equal (which they are not):

"*If your mission statement contains no typos, mentions what your company does, and doesn't go on for a whole page, you're already doing better than these* [see below] *major brands*," says Minda Zetlin, author of *The Geek Gap*.

Are you impressed by a Mission Statement that signs off with the following: "*Our worldwide operations are aligned around a global strategy called the Plan to Win, which center on an exceptional customer experience — People, Products, Place, Price and Promotion.*"? If not, write to McDonalds and tell them to put a sock in it and correct the grammatical error. How about Avery Dennison's determination "*to help make every brand more inspiring, and the world more intelligent*"? Bit over the top for a company whose product is stick-on labels, perhaps?

And here's the fun part of Barnes & Noble's MS: "*To say that our mission exists independent of the product we sell is to demean the importance and the distinction of being booksellers.*" Would they like to repeat that more slowly, please, just so we can work out what is being demeaned, or not, as the case may be. Is it despite the awful content of some of the books that their mission remains intact?

Menu Inc, from which the above is taken, rounds off with a really excellent Statement: "*It is our mission to continue to authoritatively provide access to diverse services to stay relevant in tomorrow's world.*" Then they invite you to guess the company offering it. "*Give up? It was created by the* Mission Statement Generator *which recombines nouns, verbs, and adjectives into prototypical mission statements that are delightfully replete with meaningless corporate-speak.*"[17]

Business schools no doubt spend some time teaching students about mission statements, so it is interesting to know what their own ones look like. In 2009 students at Harvard Business School created an MBA oath that stated *inter alia*: "I will safeguard the interests of my shareholders, co-workers, customers and the society in which we operate." Admirable stuff, I'm sure you'll agree. "A year on," writes Michael Skapinker in the *Financial Times*, "the oath has more than 4,000 signatories from 300 business schools worldwide. But the wording has changed. *The part about co-workers and society has gone.*" Skapinker e-mailed the MBA Oath website to ask why. The language had "***evolved,***" they said. "Perhaps the original wording would come back. They did not seem sure." This is a really difficult one, isn't it? Or may be not: as Upton Sinclair once remarked: "*It is difficult to get a man to understand something when his salary depends on his not understanding it.*"

Inevitably Mission Statements attract a good deal of disrespectful ribaldry, such as the following spoofs from *Humor Times*:

"*To see how far we can get with this sort of business before it becomes illegal.*"

And:

"*To skin alive as many people as it takes to get our second home in the Bahamas.*"[18]

---

17 See www.inc.com /.../9-worst-mission-statements-all-time

18 For these and other examples, see: www.humortimes.com /10067/ corporate-mission-statements-for-our-times

These clearly are the missions of many companies out there, although some such may prefer to dispense with the "Mission Statement" in order not to attract unwelcome attention from the authorities…

Mistakes: Specifically printer's errors, generally a source of innocent mirth, but potentially the cause of wars or worse, if occurring in the printed scriptures:

An article (1997) in the *The Author* listed some book titles that the printers got slightly wrong and proof-readers overlooked: they included *Language, Sausage and Wittgenstein* (for *Language, Saussure and Wittgenstein*), *The Forsyte's Aga*, *A View from the Fridge*, *Deaf in Venice* [a sequel, perhaps to *Venetian Blinds*?], *Gillette* [Charlotte Bronte's advice for the removal of unwanted female hair?], *The Snog of Bernadette* and *Less of the D'Urbervilles*.

Publisher Frederic Warburg's account of the book trade in the 1920's describes the process of book ordering at his firm's warehouse as follows: The publishers' reps ("aged men carrying huge sacks") read out their orders at the trade counter "in a monotonous voice and a system of pronunciation as mysterious as Tibetan". Thus an order for a rather well-known work by Tolstoy was translated to the invoice clerks as *"I'll have twenty Annie Carrie Ninas, and smart about it, please"*.

Although there is a body of educational theory that doesn't seem to think so, literacy and spelling are quite important if we are to avoid tiresome misunderstandings. For example, even those teachers who don't care much about spelling thought it was rather bad luck on that paediatrician whose house was vandalised by ant-paedophile zealots, ever on the look-out for suspicious-sounding professions…

Deborah Moggach: An author unfazed by the casual insults of a book promotion tour:

Here is Moggach writing in *The Author* (a sort of union mag for authors, mostly impoverished, mostly disgruntled) and describing what publishers grandly call a *"Nationwide Publicity Tour"* for her recently published book:

"I travelled down to the Folkestone Literary Festival, a modest affair in the front room of a defunct seafront hotel. On arrival I was offered a small dish of dry-roasted peanuts to be shared between three authors. We had left London in mid-afternoon and wouldn't get back until midnight, but our hostess obviously believed that writers, like Citroën 2CVs, run on very little fuel. Also on very little money, as we were all told, separately, '*Thank you for waiving your usual fee.*'"

At a shopping centre in Maidenhead, every purchaser of her novel was to get a free box of Crabtree & Evelyn freesia soap and a glass of wine — practically bribery. Still no takers. "I can't understand it," said the manageress in a misguided attempt at commiseration. "We had that Rolf Harris last week and the queue was an hour and a half long."

Money: Something which oils the wheels, but probably not yours:
A few years ago the National Consumer Council, theoretically created to protect consumers from abuse by corporate power, launched its "*Friends*" initiative. For a mere ten grand a year, companies could "inform the NCC's thinking on consumer policy". Among the first to sign up were BT (still in deep trouble with the regulator for abusing its sector monopoly) together with the Prudential Insurance, the most unctuous of the companies that persuaded people to purchase dud private pensions in the 1980's. With "*Friends*" like that, the consumer hardly needs enemies...

Meanwhile writer Fay Weldon produced the ultimate in "product placement", a novel commissioned by Bulgari and containing copious references to the sponsor. Clearly the literary classics have so far been scandalously under-exploited in this respect. The celebrated first sentence of *Pride and Prejudice* should obviously be recast to reflect our contemporary preoccupations more accurately, viz. "*It is a truth universally acknowledged that a single man in possession of a large fortune must be in want of a Rolex Oyster Perpetual Cosmograph Daytona in 18 ct white gold with Rolesor and Oysterlock bracelet.*"

Zsa Zsa Gabor said: "There is nothing wrong with a woman welcoming all men's advances as long as they are in cash."

The poet John Dryden said: "All heiresses are beautiful."

Mrs Thatcher said: "No one would remember the Good Samaritan if he'd only had good intentions — he had money, too."

Ambrose Bierce said: "An acquaintance is a person whom we know well enough to borrow from, but not well enough to lend to."

Henny Youngman said: "What's the use of happiness? It can't buy you money."

Dorothy Parker said: "If you want to know what God thinks about money, just look at the people He gives it to."

311

Paris Hilton asked: "What's a soup kitchen?"

An IRS auditor said: "The trick is to stop thinking of it as 'your' money."

Groucho Marx said: "Money frees you from doing things you dislike. Since I dislike doing nearly everything, money is handy."

The Mousetrap: A sclerotic tourist attraction in London's West End:
This gripping whodunnit by Agatha Christie had been running 55 years in the West End by 2007 when the *Financial Times* did a feature on it. The director of *The Mousetrap*, reported the paper, seemed "becalmed" after seventeen years in the job, as perhaps one would be. He regarded himself more as a "custodian" actually, like the Beefeaters at the Tower of London or the ushers at Madame Tussauds. He only came into the theatre (from Worthing) twice a week, presumably to see if the scenery had fallen down or if any of the actors had died. But he had lost none of his enthusiasm for the subtly-drawn characters, like the camp-architect called (would you believe it?) Christopher Wren. Very droll. And of course there's a dimwit martinet called Major Metcalf, whose impersonator once fell asleep in the armchair "*waking up eleven pages ahead of everyone else.*" (It is not recorded whether the audience noticed anything.)

Then there is the token mysterious foreigner, a Mr Paravicini, who just might be of Italian origin. An important company member is the operator of the hand-cranked wind machine that howls every time the window is opened. The director pointed out that Agatha's violence is wholesome ("*a nice little bit of poison and they drop dead quickly.*") He alluded with a shudder to contemporary crime novels, like the one "*where the victims have their throats cut, pubic hair put in their mouths and their lips sewn up. Well, is all that necessary?*"

Most certainly not. Absolutely not!

Eric "The Eel" Moussambani: Olympic swimmer of Equatorial Guinea, who was banned from training in his country's only swimming pool:
Moussambani won the hearts of millions at the Olympics after setting the slowest time ever over 100 m a few months after learning to swim. After the ban on using the swimming pool, he was obliged to train in the sea for the next Olympics, but there were fears for his safety as he was, after all, not such a strong swimmer…

312

Eric the Eel Moussambani, Equatorial Guinea's answer to the UK's Eddie the Eagle...

Murphy's Dicta: The widespread perception that *"things fall apart; the centre cannot hold; / Mere anarchy is loosed upon the world... "*[19]

Murphy's aphorisms are especially annoying to progressive-minded persons who believe that the rational application of sticks and carrots will produce the kind of society they believe is best for us, and which, as it happens, will be ruled by people like them. For example Murphy says:

(1) *"A fine is a tax for doing wrong. A tax is a fine for doing well,"*

and:

(2) *"Give a man a fish and he will eat for a day. Teach a man to fish, and he will sit in a boat all day drinking beer."* (Students of economics will recognize this Murphyism as the inversion of a well-known nostrum of behavioural science which lays down that it is effective to help a man to help himself but counterproductive simply to help him. Tory politicians who urge mobility in search of employment with the slogan "get on your bike" therefore believe people should be given, at least metaphorically speaking, a bike on which to get, rather than ever in-

19 The third and fourth lines of *The Second Coming* by W.B.Yeats (1920).

creasing benefit payments. They describe this policy as "a hand up, not a hand-out." Unfortunately due to another Tory belief that inflating house prices is a good way of stimulating the economy, many people cannot afford to move, with or without a bike.)

Murphy's Dicta are the proliferation of variations on what was originally known as *Murphy's Law*, named after a Captain Edward Murphy,[20] a development engineer at the Wright Airfield Laboratory at Dayton, Ohio. Apparently exasperated by a blundering technician, what he actually said was: "*If there is any way to do it wrong, he will*," a remark subsequently copyrighted on behalf of loyal wives. Later this was turned into the philosophical abstraction, also known as the 4th Law of Thermodynamics, which states that "*if anything can go wrong it will*."

The spin-offs from Murphy's Law have taken us into the world of logic and philosophical abstraction, providing many happy hours of reflection for those with nothing better to do. For example there is *Glasser's Corollary*, which runs as follows:

"*If, of the seven hours you spend at work, six hours and fifty-five minutes are spent working at your desk, and the rest of the time you throw the bull with your cubicle-mate, the time at which your supervisor will walk in and ask what you're doing can be determined to within five minutes.*"[21]

Grave's Law states: "*As soon as you make something idiot-proof, along comes another idiot.*"

Allen's Axiom states: "*When all else fails, read the instructions.*"

Jones's Law states: "*The man who can smile when things go wrong has thought of someone he can blame it on.*"

Judy Sproles' Law states: "*If there is an opinion, facts will be found to support it.*"

Laura's Law states: "*No child ever throws up in the bathroom.*"

There are many eponymous laws featured on Wikipedia, most of them featuring scientific matters beyond the reach of arts graduates who are notorious for being scientifically illiterate. However there are also a few that are not really laws, but which, like those of Murphy or sod, reflect the distressing realities of everyday living:

20 C.f. Nick T. Spark: *A History of Murphy's Law* (Periscope Film Paperback, 2006).
21 *Glasser's Law* and the *Laws* subsequently quoted, together with very many other such laws, may be viewed on the website jcdverha.home.xs-4all.nl/scijokes/9_6.html

Betteridge's Law of Journalism: "*Any headline that ends in a question mark can be answered with the word 'no.'*"

Parkinson's Law (C. Northcote Parkinson): "*Work expands to fit the time available for its completion.*"

The Peter Principle (Dr. Laurence J. Peter): "*In a hierarchy, every employee tends to rise to his level of incompetence.*"

Hutber's Law (Patrick Hutber): "*Improvement means deterioration*" (a reference to disingenuous business habits such as heavily advertising a "new, improved candy bar" which turns out to contain a third less content and cost a third more than the one it replaces.)

Segal's Law: "*A man with a watch knows what time it is. A man with two watches is never sure.*"

Sutton's Law: "*Go where the money is.*" This is taught to medical students with the aim of getting them to use resources in a way that is most likely to pay off. It is said to be derived from Willy Sutton, a famous bank robber. When asked *why* he robbed banks, he said "*Because that's where the money is…*"

N

Inverse Notoriety:
Mark how my fame rings out from zone to zone:
A thousand critics shouting: "He's unknown!"

Ambrose Bierce

Nakations: Vacational therapy for dampening down sexual urges:
Before the fall of the Berlin Wall, it was reported that *OssiUrlaub,* an
East German travel company, was running nudist flights between Erfurt
and the Baltic island of Usedom (or "Not Much in Usedom" as the locals
call it.) No hot drinks were served, doubtless a wise precaution, and each
seat was covered with special cloth to prevent passengers sticking to the
faux-leather upholstery. Herr Garz, the company's founder, was gratified

"I wonder if I left the oven on?"

316

"I wonder if that one's interested in the Good Book...?"

with the success of his marketing wheeze, which he described as a *"new way to get bums on seats."* Indeed, not only bums...

Unfortunately by 2008 the regrettably licentious atmosphere of post-Communist Germany seems to have undermined the admirably disciplined behaviour of the former East Germans. At any rate *OssiUrlaub* felt compelled to cancel their nude flights due to ribaldry on the Internet — and what the firm enigmatically described as *"moral considerations..."*

However a number of firms like *Bare Necessities Tour and Travel* are now offering *"nakations"* — there is even a naked cruise down the River Danube for the hardy nudist traveller, though you do have to put some clothes on for dinner.

An article in *Life* magazine by Paul Thomasch and Jim Loney in 2012 flagged up the increasing popularity of nudist culture, which does seem to flourish in times of austerity. Overt sexual activity, they say, is barred at resorts that fall under the American Association for Nude Recreation's banner, and sexualized clothing or accessories are "not considered appropriate." Visitors are typically advised to sit on towels to avoid sitting naked on furniture.

As for the next nude travel frontier, there is no shortage of ideas. They include nude golf, and a complete nude town, where residents could visit the bank, grocery store or post office in the buff. Imagine a nude bank account! But the bravest new adventure that *Bare Necessities* is considering is a naked cruise to an unlikely destination: Antarctica. "We are looking at ships right now," said a company spokeswoman, adding that *Bare Necessities* had already successfully offered a naked cruise to Alaska.

Napoleon: "I am the successor, not of Louis XVI, but of Charlemagne."

Napoleon: Much admired tyrant who said *"the best way of keeping one's word is not to give it."*

The French (and some Brits with a penchant for authoritarianism) continue to regard Napoleon as a hero whose reputation is not to be sullied by lesser men, especially historians and the like.[1] This is not new. Hazlitt, the English essayist and commentator, wrote a brown-nosing biography of the little Corsican condottiere and the French novelist Stendhal was infatuated with him. When Hegel glimpsed the Emperor riding into Jena after a victory in 1806, the dreadful philosopher rapturously exclaimed that he had seen the "World Spirit on horseback." "World spirits" are definitely a bad idea, especially in the minds, or even worse the hands, of Germans. In our own time, when George Orwell's *Animal Farm* was first published in France,[2] having a leading character as a pig called Napoleon (Orwell's allegory of Joseph Stalin) was considered unpar-

1 In 2015, the 200th anniversary of Waterloo, revisionism was in full swing on the right and the left. Conservative historian Andrew Roberts published his *Napoleon the Great*, while Patrice Gueniffey published the first volume of what promises to be a multi-volume effort entitled simply *Bonaparte.*

2 *Les animaux partout!* (Éditions Odile Pathé, 1947). I am indebted to Piers Burton-Page for this information. He points out that Orwell had previously approved an alternative title of *URSA* for the French edition, an acronym for *Union des Républiques Socialistes Animaux*, which slyly alluded to the French acronym for the Soviet Union (URSS). There was also a hint in "*URSA*" of the Russian bear (*ursa* being Latin for the Great Bear.)

318

donable *lèse-majesté*. The name was diplomatically changed to César, thus appeasing the legendary French *amour propre*.

Some five or six million combatants were killed in the Napoleonic Wars — just one four-day battle at Leipzig (dubbed "the Battle of the Nations") cost the lives of 92,000 men. Goya's horrific prints of *The Disasters of War* record the devastation of the war in Spain. The overall carnage was the greatest since the Thirty Years War. And all this at the instigation of, and to satisfy the ego of, a ruthless little man who could only stay in power through continued military conquest.

Napoleon combined imperial arrogance with a disingenuous advocacy of freedom, which, as is often the case, resulted in those who were "liberated" by him soon being keen to revert to the devil they knew. Despite the Emperor's self-serving claims that Venice was a brutal and reactionary state (a claim reinforced by a propagandist "history" of the Republic written by his own Minister of War), when French troops crushed Venice they were unable to find a single political prisoner to "liberate."

Napoleon also affected an appreciation of culture, by which he meant looting the treasures of others (after all, he argued, they really belonged to him as the Emperor of Europe.) He modestly referred to Charlemagne as his "illustrious predecessor," snatching the crown from the Pope's hands at his coronation and placing it on his own head, thus making it clear that he wouldn't be taking any nonsense from prelates with ideas above their station.

"People of Italy!" he proclaimed in 1796, *"the French army is coming to break your chains… We shall respect your property, your religion and your customs."* This, says David Gilmour in his book *The Pursuit of Italy,* doubtless sounded encouraging to those Italians who had not heard another Bonaparte speech made *only a month earlier* to his army: *"Soldiers! You are hungry and naked; the government* [the Directory in Paris] *owes you much but can give you nothing… I will lead you into the most fertile plains on earth. Rich provinces, opulent towns, all shall be at your disposal; there you will find honour, glory and riches."*[3]

Notwithstanding his own Italian antecedents, Napoleon clearly took a dim view of Italians, though he liked to purloin their art treasures. It is pleasantly ironic that he once complained bitterly to an aristocratic Ital-

3 David Gilmour: *The Pursuit of Italy* (Penguin, London, 2012), Pp.126-127.

ian lady: "*Gli Italiani! Tutti ladroni!*"[4] To which she replied soothingly: "*Non tutti, ma buona parte…*"

Narcissism: The force behind Facebook and Twitter:
A teacher reports that a supposedly backward fourteen-year-old pupil mentioned Narcissus in a classroom project. Intrigued, the teacher asked her what she knew about Narcissus. "*He fell in love with himself,*" replied the pupil. "*Yes; and then what happened?*" asked the teacher. "*The relationship didn't work out,*" she replied. Looking on the bright side, however, it has been said that he who falls in love with himself will have no rivals.

Norman Douglas has concisely summed up narcissism for us in a clerihew that is not entirely suitable for family consumption, but I print it all the same:

> *Narcissus*
> *Doesn't miss us.*
> *He looks in the stream*
> *And has a wet dream.*

(See also under **J**: ***Journey***)

The National Health Service (NHS) of the UK: Money-devouring behemoth with totalitarian features described as the "*nearest thing the British have to a national religion*":[5]
Not content with wasting £12bn on unusable IT and culling the patients with the MRSA superbug, the NHS has discovered a new method of persecuting its victims, who are also its financiers. Many hospitals have *privatised hospital parking*. A builder recently emerged from his local infirmary after visiting a friend and found his vehicle had been clamped. Undaunted, he went to work with the metal cutters he prudently carries for such emergencies and proceeded to get unclamped. Casting around for a suitable place to dispose of the offending article, his eye fell upon a yellow van labelled *Clamping Unit*, whose occupants were evidently taking a well-earned tea-break from harassing frail and

4 "The Italians are all dreadful thieves!" To which she replied: "Not all, but the greater part" (playing on Napoleon's family name.)
5 Ex-Chancellor of the Exchequer Nigel Lawson.

320

anxious hospital visitors. He deftly attached the clamp to their vehicle, adding a heavy duty padlock of his own. It is pleasant to imagine that those who devised this latest form of vindictive rent-seeking may very well end up in hospital themselves one day; which in turn means they may very well catch their death of the MRSA superbug. And their loved ones (if any) may very well not come and visit them on their deathbeds, for fear of being clamped in the hospital car-park...

A letter to the *Sunday Telegraph* points out the flaw in the belief of successive governments that appointing ever more expensive "managers" to the NHS (at one point there were more "managers" than beds) will somehow solve its problems.[6] Actually it makes them worse. The endless paperwork (17% of nurses' time) tells the managers what the staff choose to tell them, and the managers report this information to government (for example, confirming that "targets" for waiting times have been met, while omitting to mention the patients held for hours in ambulances outside the hospital so as to delay the time of formal "admission.") Of course when it turns out, for example, that elderly patients are being killed off through neglect, some of these highly paid "managers" are sacked — 958 of them enjoying golden goodbyes of *more than £100,000* in 2012/13. That may not quite amount to an incentive to kill patients, but hardly looks like one to keep them alive. Meanwhile the astronomical salary of the "interim chairman" of the "troubled" Medway Trust is justified by saying that "the *right person* was needed to make urgent improvements." Which was the justification for the astronomical pay of the Trust's preceding management, consisting so much of the "*right persons*" that they had to be got rid of... Nye Bevan, the Socialist minister who set up the NHS, said of the doctors, who would not join the service unless they were also allowed to continue to practise privately, that he had to "*stuff their mouths with gold*"

---

6 The Conservative-Liberal Democrat coalition in power between 2010-2015 claimed to have taken many managers out of the system through their reforms, but they have a tendency to creep back in each time any new initiative is tried. In 2009, the NHS employed the full-time equivalent of 1,177,056 staff (1,431,996 headcount), of whom 42,509 were managers or senior managers. While the total number of NHS staff increased by around 35 per cent between 1999 and 2009, the number of managers increased by 82 per cent over the same period, from 23,378 to 42,509. Increases in the number of NHS staff and higher pay costs have absorbed more than half the increases in financial resources made available to the NHS since 2002. (*Source*: The King's Fund.)

to get them to co-operate. Now it seems the taxpayer has to stuff every available orifice of the NHS managers with golden goodbyes and golden hullos.

Not to worry, however. The previously unknown Commonwealth Fund reports that the NHS delivers the most cost-effective health care in the world and (according to *The Guardian*) only falls short on one criterion, that of "keeping people alive" (Stop laughing at the back there! This is a reference to "preventive" care.) Then again, the slightly better known OECD ranks the NHS 23rd out of 29 countries' health systems on cost-effectiveness. May be that's because one in six of the managers who leave or are sacked are soon back in work on remarkable salaries in (you've guessed it!) the NHS. The trick is to become a "consultant" and be employed on more than £1000 a day as an "interim" manager. This merry-go-round could possibly help to explain the NHS's declining productivity (at 2.5% per annum between 2001 and 2005) while quite a lot of its "managers" are paid more than the Prime Minister.

On the whole, the British public deserve the dysfunctional NHS that they have, since even the most modest attempt to reform it is met by the same public with the furious accusation that it is being "privatised by the back door." This disingenuous howl is orchestrated by the Labour Party whose 2004 contract awarded to doctors leveraged average GP pay up to £100,000 per annum in return for which the GPs generously ended weekend surgeries and home visits. According to an article in *The Guardian* by Simon Jenkins, the British Medical Association welcomed this contract as "a bit of a laugh," and the King's Fund calculated that it added £30bn to NHS costs with no appreciable benefit. Despite wastage of resources, declining service, difficulty of getting appointments and often lengthy procedures for blood tests and scans that the private sector can supply in 24 hours, nothing dents what Jenkins calls the "carapace of love" enshrouding the NHS. But is all this love not unconnected to a sublimated fear of hospitals, doctors and nurses who, after all, have the power of life and death over patients? At any rate, fear seems to exist in the system itself, since one in four hospital staff tell surveys that they feel "harassed and bullied." Perhaps that is not surprising when, as Jenkins points out, despite a government report in 2015 intending to encourage people to report what is going wrong, one year later "not a single NHS whistleblower had been re-employed or manager reprimanded…"[7] So who would want to risk their career, may be even their chances of re-employment, just so that fewer patients died unnecessarily in hospital? Besides, we have the best health service in the world — and don't you forget it, mate.

Nativism: Originally a political policy of favouring the natives of a country over the immigrants; now, the favoured term of metropolitan liberals to denigrate local patriots, especially those who resist such liberal enthusiasms as the European Union, trans-nationalism, mass immigration etc.

"*Nativism*" is clearly a growth area in sociology faculties. For example, one Dr Ben Pitcher claimed in 2014 that the long-running radio programme *Gardeners' Question Time* was imbued with racist or xenophobic phraseology. Apparently the programme's regular discussions *on soil purity* and *non-native species* reflected (even if unconsciously) *nationalist* and *fascist* beliefs. Dr Ben is a senior lecturer in sociology (like the *History Man* of Malcolm Bradbury's satirical novel about academic opportunism) at the University of Westminster. In 2014 the latter ranked 106 out of 121 universities featured in the *Sunday Times University Guide*; it is rather unlikely to improve its rating any time soon if its teaching corpus is firmly the grip of Pitchers.

But Lola Young, a crossbench peer and "former professor of cultural studies," agreed with Dr Pitcher's remarks. "I remember," she said, "back in the late 80s-early 90s when rhododendrons were seen as this huge problem, and people were talking about going out rhododendron-bashing. That was at a time when Paki-bashing was something that was all too prevalent on our streets." (see also: **A: *Anti-capitalist.*)**

Academics have opened up a promising field with the racist implications of plant names. For example, there's *black man's willy (Rhodochiton volubilis* — a perennial climber), the nomenclature of which clearly betrays the white man's sexual inferiority complex in respect of persons of colour. We should obviously be wary of referring to blackfly, or calling a spade a spade. And what about *Japanese knotweed*, a pest that is nearly impossible to eradicate from your garden?

---

7 Simon Jenkins: "Ailing NHS needs love that's tough: archaic demarcations between GPs, nurses and consultants are costing taxpayers billions. They must go" (*The Guardian Weekly*, 19. 02. 2016).

Happily *The Guardian* newspaper gave Dr Ben a platform to round on his critics, which he did in the time honoured academic's (or politician's) way of denying he had said what was unfortunately on the record by saying it all over again in different words. Of Japanese knotweed he remarked: *"The uprooting of invasive "non-natives" such as the Japanese knotweed is of course not necessarily motivated by racist intent. Yet accounts of alien immigrant invasions, weak native hosts bedevilled by larger, more aggressive, rapidly reproducing foreign species, and stable sustainable environments upset and jeopardised by overpopulation, clearly demonstrate a language that is shared in descriptions of human and nonhuman life."*[8]

Neo-Liberalism: An economic theory promising that wealth will "trickle down" to the poor from the wealthy, but which has resulted in the opposite:

Neo-Liberal protagonists have reason to be well pleased with the total victory of their ideology. Its successes include: imploding infrastructure, prisons bursting at the seams, the routine theft of vast sums from shareholders by company directors, tax-cuts for the mega-rich and rock-bottom wages or unemployment for the poor. Add in the worst financial crisis since the great depression of the 1930s and the fleecing of taxpayers to remedy it, and you begin to see that even the economists paid to push Neo-Liberalism probably don't really believe in it any more.

Have there been any successes of Neo-Liberalism? In the UK, Mrs Thatcher's reduction of the power of the unions, which was destroying the British economy like a flesh-eating virus, may be accounted a success. Also the remorseless logic of her refusal to give public money to build the cross-channel tunnel, thus obviating the customary and unedifying ritual whereby a company obtains a mega-contract from the government by tendering low, but quadruples the price once the government is too far in to extricate itself (c.f. Concorde, Olympic Games etc. etc.).

However the fundamental claim of Neo-Liberalism that the wealth created through the application of its nostrums will trickle down to the less well-off has proved, not very surprisingly, to be a useful myth for rent-seekers. So far from trickling down, wealth has surged upwards,

8 Ben Pitcher: "We talk of native species when in truth nature is as mixed as we are," *The Guardian*, 8th August 2014.

dramatically widening the gap in America and Britain between the mega-rich and the rest. Much of this wealth has been creamed off from those who could least afford to lose it via banks, investment and pension funds and dubious financial alchemy.

All this has come about as a result of theory, unsubstantiated in the real world, concerning *"economic man," "efficient markets"* (*q.v.* under **E: *Efficient market theory***), *"deregulation"* and so forth. "Economic man" (if such actually exists outside the models of behavioural economics) would not be pleasant; you wouldn't want him as a neighbour. The market to which he is allegedly in thrall is by definition amoral. As Colin Crouch puts it in his trenchant book on the subject: *"Any goals or forms of behaviour are acceptable to* [the market]*, provided they can be financed. The only child pornographer who is unacceptable to the market is the one who has no money."*[9]

Neutralisng Logic: Method of disarming tiresome grumblers much used on the Celtic fringe:

An American who took a week's expensive fishing in Scotland expressed his dismay at the paucity of fish. He complained bitterly to the ghillie that the solitary fish he had caught in the whole week had thereby cost him $3,000. *"Ah weel,"* said the ghillie, *"it's a good job you didn'a catch two, then!"*

Neverendums: Referendums either promised but not held; or promised for some future date, thus bedevilling politics for all the years before they occur; or repeated until the "right" answer is achieved (an EU speciality); or held and producing a clear result, thus initiating an immediate campaign on the part of the losers to hold another referendum with a different result (a speciality of Scotland).

Newspaper Gems: How our heroic reporters bring us the dirt:
When boxing hero Frank Bruno was committed to an institution in 2003, *The Sun's* punchy first edition headline read: ***"Bonkers Bruno Locked Up"***. After vitriolic reaction from Bruno fans, the second edition headline was changed to the more diplomatic: ***"Sad Bruno in Mental***

---

9 Colin Crouch: *The Strange Non-Death of Neo-liberalism* (Polity Press, Cambridge, 2011).

Home." In the same year the *Crosby Herald* revealed that many people "*admitted to secret disappointment with their funeral service*"; while in the *Darlington Times* you could read: "*A naked woman seen dangling from a bridge across the A66 could need help, police said.*" Still, it would be wrong to give the impression that journalists are simply cynical, thick-skinned or dumb. As Craig Brown has remarked, "there are moments when we in the British press can show extraordinary sensitivity; these moments usually coincide with the death of a proprietor, or a proprietor's wife."

Crass newspaper reporting is actually one of the incidental pleasures of reading a free press. It is said that Fleet Street's most notorious application of a "house style" that demands pointless amplifications (such as the ritual addition of ages to names, so mercilessly satirised by *Private Eye*) was once printed in the *Daily Telegraph*: Elizabeth Taylor, disembarking from a plane at Heathrow after one of her many marriages, was asked by the *Telegraph* newshound how she felt. The printed version of her reply ran: " '*I feel like a million dollars*' [375,000 pounds]." The *Sun* newspaper is of course always a rich source of crass headlines, such as "HOP OFF YOU FROGS" and other neighbourly sentiments about Britain's oldest European enemy. A wonderful *Sun*-type "special offer" was headlined in *Private Eye* during the Falklands War of 1982: "KILL AN ARGIE AND WIN A METRO".

One of the oddities of journalism is the obscure code in which it is written that makes newspapers such a poor resource for English language learners. A recent book by Robert Hutton[10] listed dozens of words that are constantly found in newspaper headlines but would sound bizarre as staples of every day speech (for example, *don, doff* and *dub*; *rapped, reeling* and *raunchy*; *swoop, slam, secret dossier*; *wannabe, wrangle; bombshell, bigwig* and *boffin* — this last, says a reviewer of the book, certainly not used by a non-journalist since about 1955.)

Strange clichés abound, like for instance *serial entrepreneur*, evidently used approvingly despite the unfortunate acoustic recalling the more usual phrase *serial killer*. On closer inspection, *serial entrepreneur* actually means an eternally optimistic businessman, most of whose ventures went bust. This, suggests Henry Mance, is not ideal as a job de-

10 Robert Hutton: *Romps, Tots and Boffins: The Strange Language of News* (Elliott and Thompson, London, 2013).

scription: "before posting your Linked In status as "serial entrepreneur currently @Wizzteam", try changing your relationship status on Facebook to "Serial monogamist currently with Fiona."[11]

Political and financial journalism is notable for expressions that are opaque, disingenuous or otherwise open to question. *Westminster source* means "the reporter at the desk next to me," while *Westminster sources* means "the barman has heard it too." The important-sounding political art of *triangulation* (a phrase originating with *policy wonks*) was much practised by Bill Clinton and Tony Blair. It turns out to mean a tactic whereby contradictory understandings of a proposed policy are retailed to different interest groups to bring them on board, but the final distillation passed into law seems to have come from somewhere else. There was a brief vogue for George W. Bush's phrase *the reality-based community* which apparently meant 'real people' (i.e. not politicians), and more recently politicians and journalists have been drilling into the rich seam of *the squeezed middle*. This signifies those sections of the middle classes who have been feeling the pinch and whom politicians have identified as winnable voters if they make a suitably affecting show of sympathy for them. On the other hand, few young politicians will want to be designated a *rising star* in the newspapers, as this invariably signifies someone whom the press is looking forward to destroying.

Budget time engenders its own crop of disingenuous jargon, typically with phrases like *expensive giveaways*, which means an electoral bribe consisting of money recycled from that already appropriated from citizens by the Chancellor. Articles concerned with personal finance invariably refer to our *hard-earned cash*, which turns out to mean the income of individuals, whether hard-earned, earned with very little effort or not "earned" at all. *Hard- earned cash* belongs of course to *hard-working families*, i.e. those families whose votes the politicians are trying to court. It is in the nature of modern democracy that all these speculations and commentaries take place in the context of *boom and bust*, or in other words the way in which government policies are co-ordinated (not always successfully) with the electoral cycle.

11 Henry Mance: ft.com/businessblog, 5th February 2015 — "The serial entrepreneur cliché."

New Guinea: Obscure part of the world once insulted by Boris Johnson, the Mayor of London:

At the Versailles Peace Conference in 1919 the victorious allies squabbled over former German territories (each of them, of course, acting from the very highest motives.) Australia had its eye on New Guinea and originally thought of claiming that the grateful natives would welcome Australian rule with open arms. Unfortunately discreet enquiries showed that the reverse was true: New Guineans much preferred the tactful Germans, who never interfered with their genial lifestyle of cannibalism and headhunting. Woodrow Wilson, an extraordinarily prim Protestant, earnestly asked the Australian Prime Minister whether there would be full access for *missionaries* if Australia took over? Absolutely, came the reply; *"There are many days when the poor devils don't get half enough missionaries to eat..."*

Nogress: "Progressive politics" that aren't:

"The reasonable man," said George Bernard Shaw, "adapts himself to the conditions that surround him. The unreasonable man adapts conditions to himself. All progress depends on the unreasonable man."

"A conservative," wrote Ambrose Bierce, "is enamoured of existing evils. A Liberal wishes to replace them with others." (*The Cynic's Word Book* —1906)

"Change is one thing, progress is another," wrote Bertrand Russell. "'Change' is scientific, 'progress' is ethical; change is indubitable, whereas progress is a matter of controversy" (*Unpopular Essays* — 1951)

In politics "change," is a loaded concept — it might be in the direction of desirable reform that improves people's lives, but then again it might not. It may be pertinent to recall here that αλλαγή ("change") was the simplistic electoral slogan in 1981 of Greece's victorious PASOK socialists, whose electoral victory heralded a period of abysmal governance, abject corruption and serious economic mismanagement. PASOK rode to victory on a wave of "progressivism," which in fact threw Greece *back* towards the practices of Third World countries through policies that politicised and multiplied the bureaucracy (Law 1320 of 1983, Law 1505 of 1984 and Law 1586 of 1986,) politicised higher education (Law 1268 of 1982), and misappropriated or misapplied both locally raised state funds and subsequently funds flowing from the EU. *"PASOK effectively justified and modernised rent-seeking,"* writes Stathis N. Kalyvas.

328

"*It justified it via a socialist sounding discourse that stressed concepts such as redistribution and public goods.*" The "people" were anointed the beneficiaries of this redistribution. However, "*since the "people" included almost everyone, this move rendered the idea of redistribution actually moot. Furthermore, the propagation of the idea that "anything is fair game," as long as it represents the legitimate demand of the people, meant that in practice it would be the groups with the highest blackmail potential that would most profit from such redistribution at the expense of weaker ones. Such groups included public-sector workers, particularly those in energy, communications, transport and garbage disposal.*"[12] The Greek experience under the early PASOK governments is extreme, but it has some uncomfortable cross-references to post-Communist democracies, including Hungary. For example, as Kalyvis relates, "*by 1984 it was estimated that 89% of all card-carrying party members of PASOK had some professional connection with the public sector either through a permanent job, a temporary job, or a contract to do business with it.*"[13] Sounds familiar?

The PASOK phenomenon reminds us that resistance to "change," especially of the type unscrupulously masquerading as "progress," may be necessary, principled and democratic. The implication of vulgar political discourse that *any* resistance to "change" is, by definition, "reactionary" is no more than the propaganda of vested interests. This was demonstrated by the anxiousness of the Kadar regime to label the 1956 Hungarian uprising as "*counter*-revolutionary." The historians of 1956 have wiped this accusation from the historical record by repeating the (questionable) mantra that nobody in the uprising, or indeed in the country, wanted a return to any form of conservatism (*nobody*?). The official line written up by the liberals who had got control of the 1956 narrative is that all agreed at that time that socialism, but with a human face, was the

---

12 Stathis N. Kalyvas: *Modern Greece: What Everyone Needs To Know* (Oxford University Press, 2015, pp. 122, and 133-143).

13 Kalyvas op cit. P. 137. It is worth noting that, while the liberal media of Western Europe and America never tire of lambasting Viktor Orbán and the Fidesz government for allegedly trampling on democratic principles, the sustained assault on the same by PASOK under Andreas Papandreou was generally viewed with indulgence by the same media. Trumpeting the magic words "*progressive*" and "*socialist*" was sufficient to give liberal commentators an ample enough fig leaf under which to conceal their double standards....

329

only way forward. A decade of Stalinism, we are led to believe, had turned all those voters who gave the Smallholders Party a 57% majority in 1947 into obedient Socialists. This seems rather unlikely. The successes of Conservative governments in Hungary since 1989, such as they are, implicitly challenge this convenient narrative and are indeed one of the reasons that opposition to these governments sometimes takes on a near-hysterical tone.

The argument about political and societal "progress" is very ancient and much ink has been spilled disputing what is, or is not, to be regarded as "progressive." In the field of pure technology, the dispute is redundant: either something works better than what preceded it, or it does not. This judgement does not however preclude a consideration of collateral damage assessed from the point of view of social value or morality (for example the invention of nuclear weapons may be viewed as a disaster for mankind, while many believe the application of nuclear technology to the production of energy is a boon.) Still, there are grey areas lying between the fields of science and human value, for example in a fundamentally humanitarian activity like medicine, which obviously makes claims founded on scientific discovery. David Wootton, the author of a book called *Bad Medicine*, is in no doubt about post-Hippocratic progress in medicine: until the mid-nineteenth century, he explains, there wasn't any. "*For 2,400 years patients have believed that doctors were doing them good; for 2,300 years they were wrong.*" According to him, until the advent of germ theory and Dr Joseph Lister's demonstration of the principles of antiseptic surgery in 1865, medicine either did virtually nothing to help patients or did more harm than good. Bleeding was the almost universal remedy applied and it either weakened or killed most of its patients (including George Washington and Lord Byron.) As Voltaire once observed of a recovered patient: "Despite the ministrations of the greatest doctors in Europe, he survived."

"*In recent years,*" pursues Wootton somewhat sardonically, "*the medical profession has discovered what it calls 'evidence-based' medicine — that is, medicine that can be shown to work.*"[14] These trenchant views, supported with colourful examples in his text, got him into a lot of trouble — *not* with doctors, but with *fellow medical historians*; they

14 David Wootton: *Bad Medicine: Doctors Doing Harm Since Hippocrates* (Oxford University Press, 2007) pp. 2-3.

preferred to unfold a narrative of continuity and progress — or at least to excuse and explain the complete failure of earlier physicians to achieve remedies by citing the prevailing knowledge and beliefs of the age in which they worked. Of course, even the measurable progress of modern medicine does not mean that every inch of technical progress brings commensurate gain for the patient. As Dr Wootton also points out, iatrogenesis is always possible; that is, when *"medical intervention itself creates conditions that need to be treated."* The alarming spread of hospital infections that have developed resistance to antibiotics is a case in point.

A discussion in historiography has attacked the idea of progress in a different way. In 1931 the English historian Herbert Butterfield wrote a subsequently famous (or notorious) essay entitled ***The Whig Interpretation of History***. *"Butterfield,"* writes his biographer, *"defined "Whig" history as an approach to the past that makes its meaning and its lessons subservient to the demands of the present and to the present's reigning idea of what constitutes "progress." Whig history was history written by and for the winners in historical conflict and change, and as such, it always upheld the present's sense of itself as an unmistakable and inevitable advance on all that preceded it. Such historical writing was likely to be simplistic and one-sided, reducible to white hats and black hats, and thereby offending Butterfield's sense of historical complexity and his insistence on broad sympathies."* There are two criticisms of "history as progress" enunciated here: firstly, that of looking at previous historical events through the lens of today's *bien-pensant* orthodoxy. And secondly, writing history as a narrative of, and from the point of view of, the "winners." The danger is that anachronism crowds out analysis and history becomes a tool of contemporary politics. Truth to tell, it is very difficult to avoid these traps entirely, because a history devoid of interpretation is barely readable. To detach oneself from the *Zeitgeist* is doubtless the duty and the intention of any serious historian, but even contrarians are in a sense held hostage to the shibboleths of the age against which they are reacting. It is more likely that history will simply reflect assumptions, many of them unconsciously held, that are prevalent in the period in which it is written. As E. Hallett Carr observed in a famous lecture, *"the cult of progress reached its climax [in Britain] at the moment when British prosperity, power and self-confidence were at their height; and British* *writers and British historians were among the most ardent votaries of the cult."*[15] The idea of progress, adds Butterfield's biographer needs to be rescued from those who would make of it *"a false religion with a secular and immanent eschatology."*

Ignorant use of history to make present political points is ubiquitous. For example, the French Ambassadress to London recently said that Napoleon, were he alive today, would have struggled passionately to save the EU, because he had dedicated his life to the idea of a united Europe. The historian Simon Schama made short work of this touching sentiment. Firstly, he pointed out that Napoleon's idea of a united Europe meant one under French hegemony, where the subject nations paid for the privilege of being liberated by the French with a hefty annual impost paid to Paris. Secondly, the said nations also had to be content with being ruled in a police state by one of Bonaparte's relations. And thirdly, they enjoyed the further privilege of compulsorily donating their most celebrated and precious works of art to the Louvre. So yes, Napoleon did believe in a "united Europe" (no doubt this is what they are taught in French schools); but no, the aspirations of the European Union today are not those of Napoleon. That is to say, we hope they are not; but the Ambassadress's devotion to the cause is undoubtedly in line with "progressive" advocacy of "ever closer union" in Europe. She may inadvertently have alerted us to the sort of post-democracy that a European super-state might involve — a new version of "democratic centralism"[16] no less. The attempted imposition of refugee quotas on the EU's eastern states through the device of majority voting at Brussels, heavily influenced by a Germany whose irresponsible policy has vastly exacerbated the migrant problem in the first place, seems to take us further in that direction.

All this reflects an ongoing schizophrenia about European "values." If the EU *does* represent the gold standard of values, then it seems not unreasonable to expect immigrants to integrate themselves fully with the host societies of Europe. However the protagonists of "multicultural-

---

15 Edward Hallett Carr: *What Is History? The George Macaulay Trevelyan Lectures* delivered in the University of Cambridge January-March 1961 (Macmillan & Co Ltd., London, 1962), P. 105.

16 This was the euphemism employed by Communist states in an attempt to portray totalitarian rule as democratic.

ism" seem to believe the opposite. A universalist conception of values, as Isaiah Berlin has stressed, was fundamental to the mind-set of the Enlightenment. He remarks that ..."progressive French thinkers" of the Enlightenment believed that "human nature was fundamentally the same in all times and places."[17] This being so, it was entirely achievable that "a logically connected structure of laws... could be constructed [to] replace the chaotic amalgam of ignorance, mental laziness, guesswork, superstition, prejudice, dogma, fantasy, and, above all, the 'interested error' maintained by rulers of mankind and largely responsible for the blunders, vices and misfortunes of humanity." Opposed to this fundamentally optimistic and confident outlook were not only the expected forces of reaction such as the church, but more damagingly what Berlin calls "the relativist and sceptical tradition that went back to the ancient world." In mature democracies, the forces of reaction have been weakened to the point of inefficacy (even the Pope is worried about 'inequality' and 'climate change'), so the political debate is now largely between the optimists and the sceptics. To put it another way, the optimists believe that legislation can probably change human nature, while the sceptics believe that it probably can't — and is moreover always vulnerable to perverse outcomes.

It would be wrong however to place the sceptics automatically in the politically conservative camp. For example, the fashionable philosopher John Gray has moved from right to left in his political stance over the years, but insists that "advances in science and technology do not run in parallel with improvement in civilisation." In his *The Silence of Animals: On Progress and Other Modern Myths* (2013) he is sharply at odds with the teleology of liberal progressivism in his Darwinian insistence that humans are just animals among other animals, "not the exalted species apart that Christianity or its liberal humanist descendants would have us to be." This implies an uncompromising pessimism about mankind which is summed up in the book's citation of Curzio Malaparte: "There are not two kinds of human being, savage and civilised. There is only the human animal, forever at war with itself." While Gray accepts the desirability of practical assistance for the underprivileged and oppressed to make the

17 Isaiah Berlin: "The Counter-Enlightenment," republished in *Isaiah Berlin: Against the Current: Essays in the History of Ideas*, Edited by Henry Hardy (The Hogarth Press, London, 1979) Pp. 1-24.

world a better place, he seems convinced that the expansion of human power in the world is always ethically ambiguous.[18] Yet there is an empirical weakness in Gray's relentlessly histrionic and one-dimensional dismissal of the elevated power of reason, which the Enlightenment felt set man above the animals: as the Marxist Terry Eagleton put it in his blistering *Guardian* review of Gray's *Straw Dogs: Thoughts on Humans and Other Animals* (2002): "A creature like Gray can fulminate against genocide but we have yet to meet the giraffe that can do so.*"[19]

J.B.Bury in his great work on *The Idea of Progress* points out that the notion of the *inevitability* of progress is really only as old as the Enlightenment, in the writings of which it gets mixed up with optimistic assumptions about the perfectibility of mankind. This was the view of Condorcet, who observed that the *"perfectibility of the human race must be seen as susceptible to indefinite progress."*[20] The medieval mind, for instance, was chiefly concerned with what might happen on judgement day, apprehension of coming before his maker with only a poor life record to show being the chief incentive for the good behaviour of sinful man. *"The idea of a life beyond the grave was in control,"* writes Bury, *"and the great things of this life were conducted with reference to the next."*[21] One may contrast this with the Enlightenment's quasi-teleological confidence that mankind was on a trajectory of improvement in this life, a life that counted just as much as, or even more than, the unknowable fate of individuals in the hereafter. Even Gibbon, the ironic chronicler of Rome's decline, had few doubts about the apparently inexorable advance of comfort, reason and civilized governance. He had come, he wrote, to *"the pleasing conclusion that every age of the world has increased, and still increases, the real wealth, the happiness, the knowledge, and perhaps the virtue, of the human race."*[22] *Pace* Gibbon, it is unfortunately also possible that civilisational *regress* may occur, often retaining and exploiting the great technological

18 See an interview with John Gray in *Oxford Today*, Michaelmas Term 2015 — Volume 28 No 1, pp. 35-37 from which these quotes are taken.

19 *The Guardian*, 7th September, 2002.

20 Quoted in Sudhir Hazareesingh: *How the French Think* (Allen Lane, 2015, P. 87) from Nicolas de Condorcet: *Esquisse d'un tableau historique des progrès de l'esprit humain* (Paris, 1970, P. 236.)

21 J. B. Bury: *The Idea of Progress: An Inquiry into its Origin and Growth* (1920), *Preface.*

22 Edward Gibbon: *The Decline and Fall of the Roman Empire*, Ch. xxxviii.

334

progress that has accrued. Many people would cite today's Islamic State or the Third Reich in the twentieth century as cases in point; on the other hand, progressive persons are usually desperate to rescue the notion of "progress" from the mass-murdering regimes of Stalin and Mao Tse Tung. Writing shortly after the Bolshevik revolution, Bury had thought about this problem too: *"This idea* [of Progress] *means that civilisation has moved, is moving, and will move in a desirable direction. But in order to judge that we are moving in a desirable direction we should have to know precisely what the destination is."* Furthermore: *"the Progress of humanity belongs to the same order of ideas as Providence or personal immortality. It is true or it is false, and like them it cannot be proved either true or false. Belief in it is an act of faith."*[23]

This sort of scepticism about progress as a concept is characteristically, if not peculiarly, English. It is out of tune with much continental (especially French) assumption about its ineluctable force and also with American eudaemonism. As far as politics are concerned, such scepticism has tended to be allied to a political conservatism stemming from Locke's theory of government. As Bury puts it, *"English thinkers were generally inclined to hold, with Locke, that the proper function of government is principally negative, to preserve order and defend life and property, not to aim directly at the improvement of society, but to secure the conditions in which men may pursue their own legitimate aims."*[24] Although such an attitude is a good bulwark against tyranny for the articulate and the well-educated, it is obviously not one that is conducive to what we may call progressive legislation aiming to emancipate the oppressed. For that we have had to look, in Britain at least, to non-conformists or evangelicals like William Wilberforce (the abolition of slavery), liberals like Lloyd George (the introduction of pensions) and William Beveridge (the blueprint for a welfare state) — or, more recently, moderate Socialists like Roy Jenkins (the abolition of the death penalty and the repeal of cruel laws against homosexuality.) Although Conservative governments have been in power in Britain for more years than their opponents since the introduction of universal suffrage, the idea of "progress" has nevertheless carried all before it among most of the intelligentsia and in the liberal media. It has also been tacitly accepted as in-

23 Bury op cit., *Introduction*.
24 Bury op cit., Ch. xii.

evitable, if not always positive, in society at large (as they say, "*You can't hold up progress…*"). However, if we hold to the idea of "universal values," it is perfectly possible to distinguish between "progress" that is positive and that which is not. Conservatives are concerned to do just that, and in order to do so, they recognise the need to be proactive, if necessary, against evils that have crept in under the banner of "progress." Their attitude could be summed up in the aphorism of Prince Tancredi Falconieri in Giuseppe di Lampedusa's *The Leopard*: "*If we want things to stay as they are, things will have to change.*"

So what has gone wrong with the notion of progress today and why have mainstream conservatives, and those further to the right of them, staged such a remarkable comeback in the UK and other European countries? One reason is that the word progress itself has become associated with trimmers and opportunists, rather than persons of clear principles fighting clearly defined causes. As Janan Ganesh explains in an article in the *Financial Times*, British Conservatives have often retained clarity of purpose and an instinct for the concerns of ordinary people where clever left-leaning intellectuals have not. Moreover, as has also been mischievously pointed out, it is now more than forty years since the Conservatives selected a woman leader and only in 2015 did the Labour Party contemplate doing so (but did not). Then again it took the supposed progressive parties (Liberals then Labour) 142 years to catch up with the Tories by selecting a Jewish leader. "*John Stuart Mill, the great liberal,*" writes Ganeesh, "*described the Tories as stupid. The Liberals closed down in 1988. The Tories are still running the country … In the post mortem of electoral defeat, 'progressives' grope for a 'critique' of their electoral loss. They 'work towards' an 'analysis' of modern Britain and an 'agenda' for 'renewal,' which must be 'radical' or at least 'empowering.' The candidates* [for the Labour Party leadership], *themselves reared in this junk language of abstract nouns and undergraduate sociology, go along with the joyless charade, always primed with an allusion to the 'changing workforce' and something about the internet. This is not sophistication, it is sophistry.*" [25] That this became apparent to Labour Party members was a contributory factor in the victory in the party's leadership contest of radical Socialist diehard Jeremy Corbin (although

---

25 Janan Ganesh: "Analysis paralysis blights a party of clever fools", *Financial Times*, 19 May, 2015.

336

letting anyone join the party and gain a vote in the leadership contest on payment of £3 was probably the proximate cause of his success.)

There are many examples of how putting sloganeering and "virtue-signalling" ahead of analysis and thought have landed progressives in their current cul-de-sac. One has been well described by the philosopher Slavoj Žižek: he points out that, by choosing identity politics over economic analysis, progressives have become entangled in contradictions of their own making. This includes "an uncritical acceptance of anti-American and anti-Western Muslim groups as representing "progressive" forms of struggle… groups like Hamas and Hezbollah all of a sudden appear as revolutionary agents, even though their ideology is explicitly anti-modern, rejecting the entire egalitarian legacy of the French Revolution. (Things have gone so far that some on the contemporary Left consider even an emphasis on atheism as a Western colonialist plot.)" Against this temptation, writes Žižek, "we should insist on the unconditional right to conduct a public, critical analysis of all religions, Islam included… While many a Leftist would concede this point, he or she would be quick to add that any such critique should be carried out in a respectful way to avoid a patronising cultural imperialism — which *de facto* means that every real critique is to be abandoned, since a genuine critique of religion will by definition be "disrespectful" of the latter's sacred character and truth claims." The double standards in regard to "respect" for religion he underlines by citing the row over the Swiss referendum that disallowed the building of minarets in Switzerland, a ban which Turkey, among others, loudly condemned. But Turkey, a candidate for EU membership, forbids all religious buildings other than mosques (and how about applying to construct a Catholic church or a synagogue in Riyadh?)[26]

All too often the label "progressive" tries to sprinkle holy water on policies that can be damaging, anti-democratic or actually regressive. Slogans like "social justice" and "equality" mean little without the policies they engender being specifically spelled out — they merely recall the grocer in Communist Prague who placed a placard with the words *"Workers of the world unite!"* in his shop window beside the tomatoes and the cucumbers. Indeed "Progressive politics" often seems to have got little more specific than its formulation by Condorcet in 1795: *"Our hopes regarding the future state of humanity can be reduced to these*

26 Slavoj Žižek: *Living In The End Times* (Verso, 2011, Pp. 137-138).

three important points: the destruction of inequality between nations; the progress of equality within one and the same nation; and finally, the real perfecting of mankind." This could almost be the rhetoric of today's progressives, but unfortunately Condorcet had not heard of political correctness, and added the question: "*Shall all nations some day approach the state of civilisation attained by the most enlightened, the freest, the most emancipated from prejudices of present-day peoples, such as the French, for example, and the Anglo-Americans?*"[27]

Nomenclature: *Nomen est omen:*
According to an article in *The Arts Club Journal* the name for Canada was derived from Spanish "*acanada*" ("Here is nothing."). The Spaniards, having found that this was more or less true, as the land was barren and without gold, soon left it. The Indians repeated this phrase to the French in the hope of getting rid of them too; but the French, not understanding, thought it was the name of the country and stayed."

Actually the French have form when it comes to names: in January 2015 a French court prevented a couple from Valenciennes from naming their daughter "Nutella" after a well-known hazelnut spread, because she might be subjected to "mockery or disobliging remarks." And in 2013, a boy named "Jihad" caught the notice of school authorities when the three-year-old was seen wearing a T-shirt emblazoned with the words "*I am a bomb*" on the front, and his name and date of birth, 11 September, on the back. His mother was acquitted of supporting terrorism by a court in Avignon.

Most of us make do with a surname and at most two Christian names, but Arabs seem to have a LEGO-like approach to personal nomenclature full of apostrophes, "*al*"s, "*Abd*"s etc. and indications of a the person's heritage by the word *ibn* (ابن "son", colloquially *bin*) or *ibnat* (ابنت "daughter", also *bint*, abbreviated *bte.*). *Wikipedia* gives a not untypical Arab name for a person of distinction as follows:

محمد بن سعيد بن عبد العزيز الفلسطيني (would this go on the postbox?) Muhammad ibn Saeed ibn Abd al-Aziz Ahl-Filasteeni *muhammad ibn saīdi ibn abdi l-azīzi l-filastīnī*

---

27 Condorcet op cit., quoted in Harry Elmer Barnes: *An Intellectual and Cultural History of the Western World*, Vol.2., P. 834 (Dover Publications, reprint 1965 of a work published in 1937 and revised in 1941.)

Ism — (proper name) Muhammad (lit. "praised")

Nasab — (father's name) Saeed (lit. "happy")

Nasab — (grandfather's name) Abd al-Aziz ("servant of the Almighty or the Honourable")

Nisbah — (origin) Ahl-Filasteeni ("the Palestinian", from *Filasteen* "Palestine").

So: "Muhammad, son of Saeed, son of Abdul-Aziz, the Palestinian"

"This person would simply be referred to as "Muhammad" or by relating him to his first-born son, e.g. *Abu Kareem* ("father of Kareem")… To signify respect or to specify which Muhammad one is speaking about, the name could be lengthened to the extent necessary or desired." This is presumably why conversations with distinguished Arabs take a long time and require many cups of tea… Also it seems you have to remember the name of his male first-born, as well as the name of his father and grandfather, apart from all the other stuff…

On the other hand, scions of European aristocratic or royal houses are obliged to include any number of forebears who brought money or some other advantage into the family, plus names of symbolic or religious significance designed to underpin legitimacy of title and rank. Currently the person with surely the most complicated passport page in Europe is the Habsburg who is Hungary's Ambassador to the Holy See and to the Sovereign Order of the Knights of Malta in Rome. The full name of this talented theologian, author and film-maker, the great-great-grandson of Emperor Franz Joseph and Empress Elisabeth, is as follows:

Eduard Karl Joseph Michael Marcus Antonius Koloman Volkhold Maria Habsburg-Lothringen — or "Ed" to his friends…

Nomenclaturik:[28] A tactic devised by the English to catch out Smart Alec foreigners who think they have mastered English sufficiently to pronounce impossible names correctly:

> There was a young fellow named Cholmondeley
> Whose bride was so mellow and colmondeley
> That the best man, Colquhoun,
> An inane young bolqufoun,
> Could only stand still and stare dolmondeley.

28 This witty doggerel is by Harry Hearson.

The bridegroom's first cousin, young Belvoir,
Whose dad was a Lancashire welvoir,
Arrived with George Bohun
At just about nohun
When excitement was mounting to felvoir.

The vicar — his surname was Beauchamp —
Of marriage endeavoured to teauchamp,
While the bridesmaid, Miss Marjoribanks[29],
Played one or two harjoripranks;
But the shoe that she threw failed to reauchamp.

Other English or Scottish names designed to discombobulate the unwary include Mainwaring [*Mannering*], St John [*Sinjun*], Woolfhardisworthy [*Woolsey*], Menzies [*Mingis*], Dalziel [*Die-ell*] and *Fotheringay* (Fungee).

Non-Statements, the Art of: How to say nothing profoundly:
This is a skill that some public figures have mastered very elegantly. Paul Volcker, perhaps the most impressive post-war head of the US Federal Reserve Bank, once produced a gem that combines the elliptical profundity of Gertrude Stein with the low level bombast of Barack Obama: *"We did what we did, we didn't do what we didn't do, and the result was what happened."*

Donald Rumsfeld is famous (or notorious) for his witty observations on Iraq in which he identified the *"known knowns,"* the *"known unknowns,"* and the *"unknown unknowns."* Following the war, Errol Morris made a film about Rumsfeld that bore the title the *"Unknown Known."* Journalists were unjustly dismissive of the Rumsfeld philosophical riff on language and knowledge which bears the clear stamp of Wittgensteinian genius.

The unchallenged British protagonist of the profound non-statement in recent years was Deputy Prime Minister Willie Whitelaw (of whom Mrs Thatcher famously said *"everybody needs a Willie."*) Faced with a hatchet-faced woman at the hustings who was pressing him on the capital punishment, Whitelaw wiggled his famous eyebrows, drew himself up and intoned *"I thank you Madam! So there it is, that's it and there you are!"* Then he swept out.

29 Pronounced *"Marshbanks."*

O

Ocean:
*A body of water occupying about two-thirds of a world
made for man — who has no gills.*

Ambrose Bierce: *The Unabridged Devil's Dictionary*

Obstinacy in error: *"Even then I'm right!"* (as the Magyars say):
Newspaper commentators, while competing in belligerence in support
of the war in Afghanistan, were vociferous in their condemnation of the
bombing of Yugoslavia, which they assured readers could only benefit
Milosevic: *"Milosevic is now politically impregnable"* (Simon Jenkins,
The Times), *"... more popular with his people than ever"* (Paul Rout-
ledge, *Daily Mirror*); *"All observers agree,* "declared Lord Healey, *"that
the bombing has strengthened Milosevic's political position in Yugoslavia."* Nor should we forget the former Foreign Secretary, Lord
Hurd, who rushed out to Belgrade to help the Natwest Bank tap into fees
for "privatising" the Serbian telephone monopoly. (Slobo needed cash
for his genocidal campaign in Kosovo, and 12.4m Deutschmarks are
said to have found their way into his Natwest account — *"a legitimate
commercial transaction"* was Hurd's description of the proposed telephone deal).

For all these people, the arrest and trial of Slobo must indeed have
been galling. Eventually he wound up at the International Court in The
Hague charged with crimes against humanity. When he died during the
trial, Austria's most self-righteous avant-garde writer, Peter Handke, delivered a fulsome necrology in Serbian at his graveside. Previously, during the NATO bombing which was designed to stop genocide by the
Serbs in Kosovo, Handke had rushed to Belgrade, nobly declaring *"my
place is with the Serbs"* — obviously, as a distinguished writer and caring intellectual, "his place" was not with the victims of Serbian ethnic
cleansing. *"My way of thinking is often so wrong,"* writes an alter ego of

Handke in one of the latter's much praised literary effusions, "*so untenable, because I think as if I were talking to someone else.*"

In 1999, Salman Rushdie pointed out that Handke had received the Order of the Serbian Knight from Milosevic for his propaganda services during a visit to Belgrade, and that his "*previous idiocies include the suggestion that Sarajevo's Muslims regularly massacred themselves and then blamed the Serbs;*" furthermore, according to Handke, the massacre of 8,000 Bosniak Muslims carried out by his Serb heroes at Srebrenica had never occurred. None of this seemed to worry the jurors of the Heinrich Heine Prize in 2006, which was awarded to Handke. Unfortunately the 50,000 Euros pay-out had to be approved by the city council of Düsseldorf and the Councillors decided that artistic freedom was all very well, but preferred not to have their names associated with apologetics for genocide. So Handke missed out on the cash. Literary prizes are an incestuous world however; after the furore had died down, in 2014 the jurors of the International Ibsen Award thought Handke should have that one too (the insults to the memory of both Heine and Ibsen are not the least bizarre aspects of these decisions.) The decision was condemned by PEN Norway and a historian remarked that "*awarding Handke the Ibsen Prize is comparable to awarding the Immanuel Kant Prize to Goebbels.*" On the other hand, a former Ibsen Award winner opined that not only should Handke get the Ibsen, he should get the Nobel Prize for literature as well. After all, an author is bound to tell the truth as he sees it…

Michael O'Leary: Genial Irish boss of Ryanair who made a fortune by offering a "no frills" airline and insulting passengers ("*In economy no frills. In business class, it'll all be free including the blow job.*"):

The world according to O'Leary is not for the faint-hearted — as his *obiter dicta* constantly remind nervous customers:

"Anyone who thinks Ryanair flights are some sort of bastion of sanctity where you can contemplate your navel is wrong. Anyone who looks like sleeping, we wake them up and sell them things."

This was the sort of remark that endeared O'Leary to his fan-club among the reptiles, together with his shameless admission of money-grubbing (he once contemplated fitting coin slots to the loos on planes.) He has also considered offering porn films which passengers could access, appropriately enough, on a "hand-held device."

Other endearing gems include the following:

"Do we carry rich people on our flights? Yes, I flew on one this morning and I am very rich."

"Germans will crawl bollock-naked over glass to get to low fares."

"One of the weaknesses of the company now is it is a bit cheap and cheerful and overly nasty — and that reflects my personality."

"Ryanair brings a lot of different cultures to the beaches of Spain, Greece and Italy where they copulate in the interests of pan-European peace."

Michael O'Leary: "All flights are fuelled with Leprechaun wee and my bullshit."

O'Leary does not hold with "environmentalists", whom he calls "fuckers" (he is fond of pointing out that less than 2% of CO2 emissions are anthropogenic), still less with "consultants," who he believes should be hired to run the company if they were any good at managing change. But they never are and they are not. "Every idiot who gets fired in the industry shows up as a consultant somewhere." And he doesn't like whingeing passengers who complain about arbitrary treatment: "You're not getting a refund so fuck off. We don't want to hear your sob stories. What part of 'no refund' don't you understand?" As to his fellow toilers in the airline business, he likes to point out that "the industry is full of bullshitters, liars and drunks. We excel at all three in Ireland." Rival airlines get short shrift too: the partnership between BA and Iberia was likened to two drunks propping each other up. Altalia he said he would not want to have even if it were offered to him for free (most of us who have flown Alitalia could agree with that.) And when his bride had not arrived some 35 minutes past the hour for their wedding he reassured the assembled guests (who were getting a bit restive) by telling them that "she's coming here with Aer Lingus."

Oligarchy: The end-game of Neo-Liberalism:
In 2011 (a difficult year for business) pay packages of directors of FTSE 100 companies rose *on average* by 49%, average workers' pay rose by just 2.7%, and that of those at the bottom of the heap by 0.1%, both the last two rises being less than inflation.

Neo-Liberal propagandists like to claim that wages in the west are forced down by the imports of goods produced by cheap labour in China and elsewhere. But if that is the case, how come that the salaries of executives are immune to the undercutting process which devastates the wages of everybody else? A century ago, the financier J.P.Morgan said that the head of a company should never earn more than twenty times the pay of those at the bottom end of its pay scale. Nowadays we have some CEOs earning as much as *900 times* the average salary of his employees, and the usual ratio for those in the USA is now around 300 to 400 times. According to Ferdinand Mount (a Tory, by the way,) the explanation for this strange state of affairs is obvious, though denied daily by the oligarchs' handmaidens in the media: *"the market for "top talent" in business has been rigged by professional cartels, boardroom stitch-ups and the "ancient arts of carve-up, scam and outright looting."*

In her book on *Plutocrats*, Chrystia Freeland documents the trajectory of Neo-Liberal ideas from the so-called "Treaty of Detroit" in 1950 (that guaranteed American auto workers *inter alia* generous health care and pensions) to the so-called "Washington Consensus" that arose in the Reagan / Thatcher years. Strong unions, high taxes and a high minimum wage gave way to tax cuts for the wealthy, union attrition, diminished spending on welfare and deregulation. The greatest triumph of the latter policy was its export: the collapse of the Soviet Union and the adoption of market economics in Communist China. The red peril and its ideological appeal was in fact the reason that the plutocrats of the 1950s had

344

accepted the need for the Detroit Treaty. Now that the red peril had been removed, the new plutocrats, who were anyway much richer and more powerful than their predecessors, saw no need to pander to the low paid. The "plutonomy" that has resulted enables the wealthiest to capture the political narrative and influence policy-making in their favour. *"It is one thing,"* writes Freeland, *"for Steve Jobs* [of Apple] *or Bill Gates* [of Microsoft] *to accumulate billions"* through their visionary business skills; *"it is quite another for multi-million dollar compensation to be paid to bankers whose institutions were bailed out by taxpayer trillions, or for private equity fund managers to pay 15 per cent tax on most of their earnings, or for the CEOs of multinational companies to take home higher paychecks than their billion-dollar firms pay in tax in the United States."*[1]

The dissident economist Ha-Joon Chang is the most candid of his tribe to have broken ranks and exposed the self-serving rhetoric of the modern careerist CEO and Neo-Liberals. He says bluntly that US managers are "over-priced" both in respect of their predecessors who ran companies in the 1960's that were more successful in relative terms than today's, but were paid ten times less as a proportion of average worker compensation; and also in respect of their counterparts in other rich countries (though these are now trying to ramp up their pay using the US as a benchmark), who are paid twenty times less on a comparable basis; and finally they are overpriced because they do not get punished for poor performance. Nor is this ("unlike what many people argue") dictated by market forces. On the contrary, *"the managerial class in the US has gained such economic, political and ideological power that it has been able to manipulate the forces that determine its pay."*[2]

Ha-Joon Chang also points out the unhealthy nexus between business and government, whereby senior employees of Goldman Sachs (for example) end up in political office where they reinforce Neo-Liberal ideology (he might have added that there is also a drift in the opposite direction, where senior politicians move from government and are rewarded for their support of business shibboleths with plum, if not very demand-

1 Chrystia Freeland: *Plutocrats: The Rise of the Super-Rich* (Penguin, London, 2013) Pp. 190-191.

2 Ha-Joon Chang: *23 Things They Don't Tell You About Capitalism* (Penguin, London, 2011), Pp. 148-149.

ing, positions on company boards.) When the US Congress, which still contains some Congressmen concerned about their tax-paying constituents, tried to put a cap on pay of the managers of financial firms receiving a massive taxpayer bail-out, there was effective resistance from the business lobby and their cronies in government. The British government also declined to do anything about the £15-20 million pension payout (generating an annual income of some £700,000) to the disgraced former boss of the Royal bank of Scotland, "although the negative publicity forced him subsequently to return £4 million." Chang concludes that "markets weed out inefficient practices, but only when no one has sufficient power to manipulate them."[3]

On the other hand the protagonists of the plutonomy argue that the existence of "ultra-high net worth" individuals merely reflects the successes of the third industrial (technological) revolution which has also brought inestimable benefits through globalisation. Jim O'Neill of Goldman Sachs claims that *"two billion people are going to be brought into the global middle class between now (2012) and 2030 as the BRIC (Brazil, Russia, India and China) and N-11 (Next 11) economies develop"* and that *"tens of millions of people from the BRICs and beyond are being taken out of poverty by the growth of their economies."*[4] What the evangelists of the plutonomy and globalisation are less keen to dwell on is the fact that the developed countries must pay a price for these happy outcomes — and so do the poor in the dangerous Third World sweatshops supplying cheap garments to the middle class of that same developed world. According to the leftist American economist Joe Stiglitz, full globalisation logically means a depression of average living standards of the richer countries: *"... what happens when you bring together two countries which are very different, like the United States and China — what happens is that the wages in the high-wage country get depressed down [sic]. ... Full globalisation would in fact mean that the wages in the United States would be the same as the wages in China. That's what you mean by a perfect market. We don't like that."*[5]

Elsewhere Stiglitz has pointed out that *"over the past 40 years average worker productivity in the US has roughly doubled, while real wages*

3 Ha-Joon Chang, op cit. Pp. 155-156.
4 Quoted in Freeland, op cit. Pp. 29-30.
5 Quoted in Freeland op cit. P. 27

have stagnated." This sort of statistic is widely accepted but few can agree on a remedy since the implosion of the Communist "command economies" discredited the idea of totalitarian coercive egalitarianism. "*It doesn't matter, ethically speaking if the heiress to the L'Oréal fortune has six yachts or none,*" writes Professor Deirdre N. McCloskey of the libertarian Chicago School. "*True, she ought to be ashamed that she spends her wealth on baubles and not on good works. **But her wealth is not what made people poor** [emphasis added]. Taking it will not much improve their condition.*" Her Neo-Liberal solution is to make a bonfire of regulations and job protection for the "precariat" (q.v.) (i.e. people experiencing declining and volatile real wages and labour insecurities): "*Give up the minimum wage, the "protection" of jobs, the over-regulation of banking [sic!] and the support for monopolies from taxis to surgeons… Yes, I know: hopeless politically. But so people said under all the ancient regimes.*"

Presumably at the opposite end of the political spectrum, Guy Standing of the University of London says the rich countries should start by giving everyone a guaranteed basic income paid for by the state (i.e. the taxpayer). A major advantage of this is that it would do away with the "***ludicrous array of subsidies that go predominantly to upper-income groups and corporations***" [*Emphasis added*]. Moreover "*we should recognise that our individual wealth is due far more to the collective efforts of our forebears than to anything we do. A basic income should be seen as a social dividend on their efforts.*"[6] Standing's ideas seem quite rational and logical, so we can be fairly sure no political party will embrace them… (*See also under **P: Plutonomy**.*)

London Olympics: Triumph of British sportsmanship and financial management (only three times over original budget) that helped to revitalise East London:

Not everyone was quite so enthused about the Olympics (for example those who had failed to get tickets and subsequently noticed acres of unused "corporate sponsor" seats when watching the games on TV.)

Amazingly, given the hype, some people were against the whole thing — disruption of traffic in London, waste of money, ostentatious VIP and

---

6 Comments from Stiglitz, McCloskey and Standing come from a one page symposium on "Pay Pressure" in the *Financial Times*, 19 September, 2014.

corporate privilege and much more. The most curmudgeonly comment came from professional gadfly Rod Liddle, who opined: *"If I want to see drugged foreign persons running very fast, I can do that any evening in Tower Hamlets"*

The Onion: a satirical American magazine with excellent articles in questionable taste:

An anthology of pieces from the magazine (entitled *Our Dumb Century*) contains one of its best spoof headlines, namely:

"APOLLO 13 ASTRONAUTS DROWN AS TED KENNEDY FLEES SPLASHDOWN SITE".

Another spoof under the headline "Homosexual-Recruitment Drive Nearing Goal" (July 29, 1998) upset some Baptist preachers (not, one would have thought, typical readers of *The Onion*) who responded angrily to this "homosexual recruitment drive":

"Spokespersons for the National Gay & Lesbian Recruitment Task Force announced Monday that more than 288,000 straights have been converted to homosexuality since Jan. 1, 1998, putting the group well on pace to reach its goal of 350,000 conversions by the end of the year.

"Thanks to the tireless efforts of our missionaries nationwide, in the first seven months of 1998, nearly 300,000 heterosexuals were ensnared in the Pink Triangle," said NGLRTF co-director Patricia Emmonds. "Clearly, the activist homosexual lobby is winning."

Emmonds credited much of the recruiting success to the gay lobby's infiltration of America's public schools, where programs promoting the homosexual lifestyle are regularly presented to children as young as 5."

Orientals: Stereotypes of endearing rapacity created by western travellers:

Baedeker's advice (1906) for travellers to the Middle East deals with what it delicately describes as "Intercourse with Orientals":

"Most Orientals regard the European traveller as a Croesus, and sometimes as a madman, so unintelligible to them are the objects and pleasures of travelling. They therefore demand Bakhshîsh almost as a right from those who seem so much better supplied with this world's goods. He who gives is a good man....The custom of scattering small coins for the sake of the amusement furnished by the consequent scramble is an insult to poverty that no right-minded traveller will offer.

348

*Beneath the interminable protestations of friendship with which the trav-
eller is overwhelmed lurks in most cases the demon of cupidity."*

No doubt it was against such stereotyping that Edward Said was reacting when he wrote in his influential *Orientalism*: "The Orient and Islam
have a kind of extra-real, phenomenologically reduced status that puts
them out of reach of everyone except the Western expert. From the beginning of Western speculation about the Orient, the one thing the orient
could not do was to represent itself. Evidence of the Orient was credible
only after it had passed through and been made firm by the refining fire
of the Orientalist's work."

And elsewhere in the same work: "The Orient is watched, since its almost (but never quite) offensive behaviour issues out of a reservoir of infinite peculiarity; the European, whose sensibility tours the Orient, is a
watcher, never involved, always detached, always ready for new examples of what the *Description de l'Egypte* called *"bizarre jouissance."*
The Orient becomes a living tableau of queerness."[7]

The problem, which used to be one of the European's superiority
complex, became in the twentieth century (according to Pascal Bruckner) its reverse. But the new idealisation of whole nations or peoples
that concerned anti-colonialists promoted in place of the patronising
contempt implied by Said reproduces the same flaw, namely a lack of
authenticity. Orientals (or Asians, or Africans or South Americans according to ideological context) *"are seen in pathological perspective
because we can only talk about them in numbers. They are the masses;
we are the individuals."*[8]

Osama bin Laden: Spoiled rich boy gone slightly off the rails:
Overheard in a New York theatre: *"Osama bin Laden? Typical middle
child. He's twenty-sixth out of 51."*

Ostalgie: Nostalgia of East Germans for their lovable Stalinist state:
The Czech writer and former dissident Milan Kundera has pointed out
that "the Greek word for "return" is *nostos*, while *algos* means "suffer-

---

7 Edward Said: *Orientalism* (Vintage Books, 1978). Said is an interesting commentator due to the fact that, as a Palestinian Christian, he straddles the cultures he describes.
8 Pascal Bruckner: *The Tears of the White Man: Compassion as Contempt* (The Free
Press, New York and London, 1986), Translated and with an Introduction by William
R. Beer. P. 79.

ing."[9] So nostalgia is the suffering caused by an unappeased yearning to return." The twist in *Ostalgie* is that East Germans are arguably suffering from being deprived of their former suffering. Nostalgia, says the critic Stephen Bayley "was originally identified as a psychosis, a mental aberration describing a state of mind that could find delight only in the past."[10]

Ostalgie (derived from German "*Nostalgie*") is of course a phenomenon not confined to "*Ossies*" (East Germans), who resented the arrival in the East of frequently self-righteous and arrogant "*Wessies*." The latter often treated them as if they were backward children who should be grateful for the sagacious supervision of *Wessies*, rather as Britain treated the inhabitants of its empire. Most of the countries of the former Soviet empire had a large demographic, usually but not always older people, who understandably regarded the loss of womb to tomb state provision of all life's necessities as more threatening than enticing. The painful transition of the economies of these countries (job losses, instability, rapacity of western businesses, rampant corruption, political uncertainty) meant that many yearned for the (relatively) quiet life of the past. Added to which, in some countries the old Communists appeared before our wondering eyes as the new Neo-Liberals, managing to hold onto the levers of political power, the economy and the media for a remarkably long time. In Hungary, at the turn of the millennium, the former Communist leader János Kádár was still coming top in polls that recorded the nation's votes for the greatest Hungarians in history.

It is a little easier to understand Hungarians nostalgia for mild Kádárism than East German enthusiasm for a state that had very nearly achieved the ideal of Plato's Republic, in which there was no privacy at all. Perhaps East Germans intuitively knew that the Federal Republic was not absolutely desperate to join up with them, despite the retrospective rhetoric… *See also* **L: *Leo Longanesi***.

Outer space: Area filled with detritus of old satellites etc. left there by earthlings, besides a few planets, stars and so forth:

"Humans have left almost 400,000 pounds of junk on the Moon," writes Jennifer Welsh, adding "…OK, it's more like 200 tons."

---

9 Milan Kundera: *Ignorance* (Faber, London, 2002), translated by Linda Asher. The novel deals with false or falsified memories of the past, voluntary and involuntary.
10 *The Spectator*, 23 May 2015.

"At the Apollo 11 landing site, called Tranquility Base [items] include: two pairs of space boots (Neil Armstrong's and Buzz Aldrin's); empty food bags and storage containers; multiple cameras and leftover film; multiple tools; and even "defecation collection devices" and "urine collection assemblies" (aka astronaut toilets, which still contain deposits made by Neil Armstrong).

"A group called the *Lunar Legacy Project* are working to preserve the site. As we learn from a recent *Boing Boing* article:

"While bags of frozen astronaut poop may sound unimportant, even a little gross, some "extreme heritage" conservationists are very concerned about their protection — as well as the other detritus left behind by humanity's first moon walkers. For now, Tranquility Base is still tranquil (there is no wind or rain up there to damage things), but preservationists worry that private space enterprises will one day endanger the Apollo landing site, as well as other important landmarks on the moon."[11]

Meanwhile, a survey by the Roper (or ropey?) organisation estimates that 2% of the American population have been abducted by aliens at some time in their lives — around five million a year, or 22 million, if you extend it globally. This means that *4000 abductions are taking place every night*.

It is a sign of how well aliens are embedded in positions of influence in our societies that nobody seems to have noticed this...

Oversight: Things the newspapers unaccountably missed:
Take the Kentucky Lexington Herald-Leader, for example. On the 40th anniversary of the passing of the Civil Rights Act in the USA, its editorial contained the following apology: *"It has come to the Editor's attention that the Herald-Leader neglected to cover the Civil Rights Movement. We regret the omission."*

OK, OK, so they got it a bit wrong. But journalists are awfully busy people and you can't expect them to catch everything that's going on...

Anyway, as A. J. Liebling once wrote in *The New Yorker: "People everywhere confuse what they read in the newspapers with news."*

11 *Business Insider* (July 30, 2012).

P

Platitude: *The fundamental element and special glory of popular literature. A thought that snores in words that smoke. The wisdom of a million fools in the diction of a dullard. A fossil sentiment in artificial rock... All that is mortal of departed truth. A demitasse of milk- and — morality. The pope's nose of a featherless peacock. A jelly-fish withering on the shore of the sea of thought. The cackle surviving the egg.*

Ambrose Bierce: *The Devil's Dictionary*

Panomphaean: Insights that may seem less resonant when sobriety returns:

The word appears in older editions Chambers, but seems to have been overlooked by the slipshod new breed of lexicographers. The Chambers definition is: "all-oracular, an epithet of Zeus: applied (after Rabelais) to the word "drink" which is celebrated by all nations. [Gr. *omphé*, a divine voice].

Papuan cannibals: Much maligned persons with a consuming interest in their neighbours:

"I believe in compulsory cannibalism," said the American revolutionary Abbie Hoffman. *"If people were forced to eat what they killed, there would be no more wars."* Papuans would consider this remark amazingly wrong-headed, even tasteless. In any case it wrongly assumes that human flesh is unpalatable, whereas all who have tried it say it is excellent — a little like veal, only better.

Some valuable research on cannibalism surfaced from Manchester Metropolitan University a few years back, the summary of which ran as follows: "This paper uses the work of Jacques Derrida to 'read' the case of consensual cannibalism in Germany [in 2001]... [It] aims to create a dialogue between Derrida's notion of symbolic cannibalism and the actual case of consensual cannibalism, in order to potentially offer critical insights into humanist ethical responses and discourse that surround and contribute to a dominant thinking on consensual cannibalism, but also to shed light on ways in which ethical dimensions are not only made on a day to day basis, but how they are constructed, embodied and 'voiced' in Western Society."

If you are not up to speed on the "dominant thinking on consensual cannibalism," you can always ask a man in the pub if he would be so kind as to 'voice' his view of it (also his opinion of Derrida). They would likely be no more intelligible than the "discourse" of Manchester Metropolitan University, but very probably a great deal more colourful.

It is of course an indication of the progressive nature of the western democracies that its cannibalism is "consensual." According to *Wikipedia*, the Korowai tribe of south-eastern Papua may be one of the last surviving tribes in the world engaging in cannibalism, possibly not the consensual kind. (On the other hand, there have been reports suggesting that the Papuans have been coaxed into encouraging tourism by perpetuating the myth that it is still an active practice; if true, this is a lively and interesting variation on *fakelore* (q.v.) on which the tourist authorities should obviously be congratulated.)

Parentectomy: Alarming physician-speak that makes the removal of children from their parents sound objectively necessary:

Parentectomy, a term which becomes more sinister than scientific when you think of medical terms like "appendectomy," appears to have been coined by our old friend Bruno Bettelheim (*q.v.*). He launched the idea that autistic children were in many cases reacting against mistreatment by their parents (although the view now most widespread is that it is genetically determined.) Autistic children (a fertile field for medical conjecture) are also sometimes said to suffer from "refrigerator" mothers, that is, maternal icebergs who unfroze just sufficiently to achieve coitus but have little or no maternal feelings.

Another angle on parentectomy is provided by the custody quarrel in divorce cases. An influential novel by Kimber Adams (Xlibris, 2009) describes in dismaying detail a not uncommon situation where one parent (in this case the father) uses the children as pawns in a divorce battle. This sort of thing has, of course, always happened; but now it has been medicalised (Parent Alienation, Parentectomy etc.) with the usual paraphernalia of support groups, therapists and so forth. But as Adams mentions right at the beginning of her book, there is in principle a simple test that could be applied right at the beginning of negotiations, which is that of King Solomon. He, you will recall, decided in a dispute between two claimant mothers to cut the disputed child in half and award one half to each "mother." The real mother immediately gave up her claim. Perhaps it would be difficult to do it this way nowadays; all the same counsellors could probably devise some simple psychological tests that would flush out which parent had the child's interest at heart rather than their own. Of course, if neither had, there is a problem…

Patter: In England, a form of speech peculiar to salesmen for Everest Double Glazing:

Michael Munro's the *The Complete Patter* (Birlinn, 2001) is an indispensable and now world-famous guide to the picturesque *Glaswegian* speech that also goes under the name of patter. In contrast to the salesman's patter down south, Glasgow's is more attuned to colourful insult of the mean, the bad, the ugly and other persons who are annoying or don't drink enough whisky on a Saturday night

Much out of the way information can be gleaned from books of this kind. For instance, how many people know that the standard greeting be-

Flyting : "I will not insult idiots by calling you one…"

tween young Glaswegian males is: *"How's yer arse for love-bites?"*? The dictionary lists some 19 expressions, none of them complimentary, to describe the sort of visage that may be arresting for the wrong reasons. These include: *"a face like a melted welly,"* and *"a face like it went on fire and somebody put the flames out with a shovel."* Irresistible is the locals' name for Glasgow's somewhat forbidding St Mungo Museum of Religion, which is known as *"Fort Weetabix."*

Ian Crofton's *Dictionary of Scottish Phrase and Fable* (Birlinn, 2013) offers some profitable browsing for lovers of arcane abuse. He quotes, for instance, the 16th century *Flyting of Dunbar and Kennedie,* a *tour de force* of mutual vituperation by the two makars at the court of James IV.

Kennedy calls Dunbar an *ignorant elf, aip owl irregular,*

> *Skaldit skaitbird, and common skamelar;*
> *Wanfukkit, funling, that natour made ane yrie*

[*skaldit*, scabby, *skaitbird*, skua (which is thought to feed on the excrement (*scat*) of other birds), *skamelar*, scrounger and sycophant, *wannfukit funling*, misbegotten foundling, *yrie*, dwarf.]

Dunbar fights back with

> *Cuntbitten, crawdoun Kennedie coward of kind*
> [*cuntbitten*, pox-ridden,?hen-pecked, *crawdoun*, dwarf]

One is reminded of the fact that Donald Trump is partly of Scottish origin...

Peaceful: A claim made by aggressive faiths or ideologies that they intend no one any harm:

As, for example, in the manifestly false, but currently expedient, claim that Islam is a "peaceful" religion. The message of peace does not seem to have percolated to the aggressive activists in the rival Sunni and Shia sects of Islam, even if millions of Muslims are entirely peaceful to the extent that they are quite secularised and therefore not very interested in such kindly shari'a precepts as murdering apostates or beheading homosexuals. Even so, surveys of Muslim opinion on 9/11 and other atrocities seem to show that some 15% of the faithful are to a greater or lesser extent radicalised[1] and the overwhelming majority believe that

---

1 See, for example, Douglas Murray: *"The Dangerous Lie"* in The Spectator, 17th January, 2015.

blasphemers (defined by whom?) should be punished. Infidels (*"kuf-fars"* — often Christians, but also Buddhists, Hindus, Shintoists etc.) are subject to violence and village-burning in several African states like Nigeria, Sudan, Mauritania, Mali, Niger, Algeria and Senegal, as well as Indonesia and the Philippines. Nor can it be truthfully stated that all the leaders of orthodox branches of Islam are men of peace — Iran's Ayatollah Khomeini, for example, was one of the most revered Islamic scholars of his age, not to mention one of the most cruel and vindictive. A flavour of his method of governance is given in a message to the Iranian people in 1980 and many similar outbursts: *"These criminals that have been arrested are not accused, but their crimes have been proven. We only have to prove their identity and then kill them all. There is absolutely no need for a trial. No compassion for them will be allowed. We believe that the guilty party does not need a trial and must be killed."*[2] Most notoriously he issued the following *fatwa* against Salman Rushdie, the author of *The Satanic Verses*: *"The author of the Satanic Verses book, which is against Islam, the Prophet and the Koran, and all those involved in its publication who were aware of its content, are sentenced to death. I ask all Moslems to execute them wherever they find them."*

On the other hand, nor did the message of peace supposedly embedded in their Christian faith deter President Bush and Tony Blair (both ardent believers) from conducting wars in Iraq and Afghanistan, even if the professed aim of these campaigns was to establish peace and democracy, which could hardly be said to be the aim of jihadists. St Augustine of Hippo (354-430 AD) conveniently provided a pretext, which he called *"a just war"*, to explain why wars waged by Christians were legitimate when he said that *"the purpose of all wars is peace."* Was this the purpose of the crusades? It certainly didn't seem to be the purpose of the religious wars of the 16th and 17th centuries. The Thirty Years War (1618-1648), to take the worst example, was a toxic mixture of religious pretext and territorial aggression. The population of Germany was reduced by at least a third and the Protestant Swedish armies alone destroyed up to 2,000 castles, 18,000 villages and 1,500 towns in that country, about a third of the total. The French religious wars between

2 Ayatollah Khomeini (in a message to the Iranian people, June 30, 1980). Taken from *Quotes from Ayatollah I Khomeini* collected by Dr. Jalal Matini and translated by Farhad Mafie, July 25, 2003 (Mafie@att.net)

1562 and 1598, which included such edifying demonstrations of religious zeal as the St Bartholomew's Day Massacre in 1572, are estimated to have cost something between two and four million lives. As late as the First World War, priests on both the German and Allied fronts were blessing the weapons about to be used for slaughtering the fellow Christians. *"God is not great!"* as the late Christopher Hitchens observed, with considerable understatement, in his book of the same title.

Adherents of the two most widespread monotheistic religions (Christianity and Islam) traditionally advanced against their rivals, enemies or prospective subjects with a weapon in one hand and scripture in the other. Of course the Devil can quote scripture, but this does not quite explain away the differences between the New Testament and the Qu'ran. For example, *sūrah* 8:12 of the Qu'ran describes God's support for believers as follows: *"I shall cast terror into the hearts of the infidels. Strike off their heads, strike off the very tips of their fingers!"*[3] This sort of thing (and there is quite a lot of it) is in stark contrast to the mainstream teaching of Jesus as recorded in the Gospels (*"Love your enemies and pray for those who persecute you"* — Matthew 5:44; *"Let he who is without sin cast the first stone"* — John 8:7; *"If someone strikes you on the right cheek, turn to him the other also* — Matthew 5:39 — and so on.) The effect of all that is admittedly slightly marred by Christ's statement, as recorded in St Matthew's Gospel (Matthew 10, Verses 34-35), that he had come *"not to bring peace, but the sword,"* (for discussion of this passage which is somewhat embarrassing for Christians, see under **I: *Islam***).[4]

Even more striking, however, is the difference between the biographical profiles of the two prophets: Muhammad was a polygamous warrior with slaves, the details of whose personal life, even when presented in as sanitised a form as possible, suggest a ruthless and violent streak. Although the Qu'ran often recommends mercy for those that repent and convert to Islam it also prescribes that those who *"make war against God and his Apostle... shall be ... slain or crucified or have*

3 *The Koran* with a parallel Arabic text, translated by N. J. Dawood (Penguin Books, London, 50th Anniversary Edition, revised, 2014), P. 177. This translation was first published in 1956 and has been through nine revisions. It uses extremely circumspect language, but even so the Prophet (or Allah's) outbursts of violent ill temper and ruthlessness are evident.

4 A 1730 edition of The Bible offers copious commentary and annotation throughout, but is silent on Verse 34 of St Matthew's gospel...

their hands and feet cut off on alternate sides, or be banished from the land."[5] This suggests a very different sort of God and a different sort of intermediary with the Divinity to the one who was himself crucified. Christ, as a celibate pacifist and teacher of forgiveness, could hardly be more different. "*The world would be an infinitely safer place,*" writes Douglas Murray, "*if the historical Mohammed had behaved more like Buddha or Jesus. But he did not and an increasing number of people — Muslim and non-Muslim — have been able to learn this for themselves in recent years.*"[6]

A particularly horrifying aspect of the Prophet's violence, at least from our contemporary perspective, is the slaughter of Jews at his command, the most notorious such taking place at Khaybar. As a result of this unprovoked attack led by the Prophet, over 600 male Jewish captives were beheaded and their women and children sold into slavery. Mohammed himself took as wife an attractive, "freshly widowed" Jewish girl. This incident is well attested in the biographical sources for Mohammed and even *sūrahs* 33:26 and 33:27 of the Qu'ran mention it in the customary form of conversation between Allah and his Prophet.[7] The biographical account suggests an early example of the pogroms that became so notorious a weapon of medieval Christians against the Jews, with considerable emphasis being placed on the torture of leading Jews to persuade them to reveal where their treasures were hidden. Later slaughters of Jews and adherents of other faiths by Muslims offer a grisly correlative of Christian brutality: 4,000 Jews massacred at Granada in 1066, 100,000 thousand Hindu slaves slaughtered, allegedly on a single day, at Delhi in 1399, while between 1894 and 1896 over 100,000 inhabitants of (Christian) Armenian villages were liquidated during pogroms conducted by the Sultan's special regiments. Intra-Islam slaughters also mirror the sectarian wars of Christianity, for example when the Shia version of Islam was forced on Sunni Persians in the early 16th century, a bloody conflict that was reversed in the mid-18th century when attempts were made to impose Sunni hegemony.

5 *The Koran* op cit., *sūrah* 5.33 (P. 112).

6 Douglas Murray op cit.

7 *The Koran* op cit. *sūrahs* 33:26 -27, P. 420 and a footnote on the extent of the slaughter. See also, for an account of the planning and execution of the attack, *The Biography of Mahomet and Rise of Islam*, Vol. IV, Chapter 21, by William Muir (Smith, Elder & Co., London, 1861) which may be viewed on the internet.

The shari'a law (q.v.) of Islam perpetuates the note of violence, revenge and savagery that we find in the Old Testament and in some passages of the Qu'ran. In Pakistan this has become totally out of control and threatens to replace a weak civil society with arbitrary and homicidal theocracy. The main weapon against religious minorities, or even liberal Muslims, is the blasphemy laws administered by cowed or complicit judges. When the Governor of Punjab was assassinated for calling for mercy for a Christian woman unjustly arraigned under these laws, *lawyers* greeted his assassin at court with a shower of rose petals.

The advantage for prospective murderers of exploiting "blasphemy" is that the latter is always in the eye of the beholder and the mere accusation of it is often sufficient to condemn the victim. It is an instrument of arbitrary censorship seldom given up willingly — Britain only repealed its "blasphemy" law in 2008, although it had been virtually a dead letter since the last successful prosecution against *Gay News* in 1979.[8] "Blasphemy" in Pakistan and other nations subject to the vicious rule of religious vigilantes can include spelling errors by children or throwing away a visiting card bearing the name "Muhammad." Vendettas in the slums can be settled by playing the blasphemy card, something which is reminiscent of Arthur Miller's play *The Crucible* (1953). Yet, while liberals were enthusiastic about *The Crucible*, which they saw as targeting the totalitarian mindset of the right following the excesses of McCarthyism, many remain silent and afraid to denounce the same tendency in Islam. Instead they shoot the messenger, accusing those who raise such problems of "Islamophobia." "Almost two years after mobs burned down 100 Christian homes in Lahore," writes *The Economist*, "the only person behind bars is the man whose alleged blasphemy triggered the riots."[9]

It should be obvious to anyone concerned to uphold democracy and freedom of speech that the acid test of the latter is the right to "offend"

8 This was a private prosecution initiated by a Christian campaigner who sought to purge the media, especially the BBC, of unwholesome material. *Gay News* had published a poem by James Kirkup which *inter alia* described the thoughts of a Roman centurion at the Crucifixion as he dreamed of having sex with Christ. The conviction was upheld on appeal to the House of Lords, but one of the law lords did point out the anomaly that only Christianity was protected by the blasphemy law in the UK. Theoretically you could say or write what you liked about Judaism, Islam, Hinduism etc.

9 *The Economist*, November 29, 2014. The preceding information about Pakistan's blasphemy laws is taken from this article.

— governments, religions, ideologies, beliefs etc. If representatives of any of these are allowed to decide what is "offensive", and there is a law banning articles or statements that give "offence" to back them up, freedom of speech has been abolished. It is not obvious to the EU however, whose European Commissioner for the grandly named External Relations and European Neighborhood Policy told journalists in 2006 to "regulate [them]selves" in the cause of "mutual respect and understanding" between cultures, and explained that "freedom of expression is not the freedom to insult or offend."[10] Although the author of these sentiments was a dimwitted political retread promoted to an EU post wildly beyond her capabilities, her views are mainstream among the *bien pensant*. The blindness is of course diplomatic, which is to say intentional — appease the growling monster of what Flemming Rose calls "*grievance fundamentalism*"[11] and it will go away. The events in Paris on the 7th of January 2015,[12] in November 2015 (and other similarly gruesome terrorist acts) indicate what is likely to happen once the right to decide what gives offence is exercised by a group that hates democracy and fears freedom of speech.

Notwithstanding that Islam (like Christianity) has a violent past and (unlike Christianity) has not really come to terms with its violent tendencies today, in a broad historical perspective it is probably no more violent than its monotheist rival. According to David Landes, the author of *The Wealth and Poverty of Nations*,[13] the laurels for cumulative religion-inspired butchery across the course of history should probably be awarded to the Christians. Perhaps that is why the American comedian George Carlin has observed: "*I would never want to be a member of a group whose symbol was a man nailed to two pieces of wood.*" If your faith is defined by a divinely sanctioned victimhood, what happens when you become top dog? All too often the psychology of self-sacrifice and

---

10 Quoted in: Bruce Bawer: *Surrender: Appeasing Islam, Sacrificing Freedom* (Anchor Books, New York, 2010), P. 243.

11 In an interview with the *Weekend FT* 10-11 January, 2015. Rose was editor of the Danish newspaper *Jyllands-Posten* which published riot-provoking cartoons depicting the Prophet Mohammed in 2005.

12 The killing of journalists and cartoonists at the satirical magazine Charlie Hebdo by Islamist extremists.

13 David Landes: *The Wealth and Poverty of Nations: Why Some Are So Rich and Some Are So Poor* (W.W.Norton, New York, 1998).

victimhood is revealed as the obverse of a coin whose reverse is violence and the infliction of suffering. Today's empowered victim is tomorrow's tyrant. An example of this is the manipulation of victimhood by Serb nationalism during the 1990s war that broke up Yugoslavia. In his paschal address in 1991 Patriarch Paul of Belgrade quoted one of his predecessors who had said that "if the Serbs were to avenge themselves in proportion to all the crimes that have been inflicted on them during this century... they would have to bury men alive, roast the living on an open fire, skin them alive, cut the children into pieces under the eyes of their parents. The Serbs have never done this, not even to wild beasts, much less to humans." As Pascal Bruckner drily observes, the most remarkable aspect of this list of atrocities is that it "exactly describes those that the Serb troops would perpetrate from June 1991 onward, as soon as the war began."[14]

The very words "peace" and "peaceful" have been systematically misused by propagandists promoting appeasement of ideologies or powers that are by no means "peaceful." During the cold war, western sympathisers with the Soviet Union and its "allies," who included the word "peace" in their self-descriptions, engaged in elaborate semantic manoeuvres to avoid mentioning the far from peaceful nature of doctrines espoused by the Communist powers, while of course condemning the measures taken by the West to defend itself as "aggression." Many sincere and idealistic people in Britain joined the Campaign for Nuclear Disarmament, which turned out to be a campaign for *unilateral* nuclear disarmament. The idea was that the Soviets would be so impressed by such an unequivocal demonstration of peaceful intent that they would immediately follow suit when the West destroyed its nuclear weapons. The question of what would happen if, owing to some petty bureaucratic difficulties, they did *not* follow suit was not one to which the "peace movement" had an answer. Indeed, even to pose it was likely to arouse even greater indignation aimed at the "warmongering" West.

All this was music to the ears of Communist apologists and fellow-travellers, not to mention Soviet or Chinese propagandists. The latter were of course apologists for atheistic violence that rather puts the reli-

14 Quotation from Patriarch Paul and comments thereon in Pascal Bruckner: *The Temptation of Innocence: Living in the Age of Entitlement* (Algora Publishing, New York, 2000), P. 237.

gious version in the shade: Hitler's aggression led to the deaths of some 55 million people worldwide, including 11 million non-combatants and six million Jews herded into camps and murdered;[15] Stalin's slaughter of his own people included the deliberate use of starvation and the latest tally is between two and three million dead;[16] Mao Tse Tung easily wins the prize for the greatest murderer in history with between 40 and 70 million estimated to have been executed, murdered or starved to death under his rule.[17] In the Introduction to the *Black Book of Communism* may be found an estimate of the number of deaths round the world *directly attributable* to that creed, as follows:

- 65 million in the People's Republic of China
- 20 million in the Soviet Union
- 2 million in Cambodia
- 2 million in North Korea
- 1.7 million in Ethiopia
- 1.5 million in Afghanistan
- 1 million in the Communist states of Eastern Europe
- 1 million in Vietnam
- 150,000 in Latin America mainly Cuba
- 10,000 deaths "resulting from actions of the international Communist movement and Communist parties not in power."

According to the book's editor, Stéphane Courtois, this total of 94 millions killed by Communist regimes is greater than for any other political ideal or movement, including Nazism. The statistics of victims includes executions, famine, deaths resulting from deportations, physical confinement, or through forced labor.

15 See, for example a recent estimate in Jürgen Weber: *Germany 1945-1990: A parallel history*, Translated by Nicholas T. Parsons (CEU Press, Budapest and New York, 2004), P. 1 "The Audit of Horror."

16 See Timothy Snyder: "Hitler versus Stalin: Who Killed More?" in *The New York Review of Books*, March 10th, 2011. Also the same author's *Bloodlands: Europe between Hitler and Stalin* (Basic Books, 2010) and *The Black Book of Communism: Crime, Terror, Repression*, Edited by Stéphane Courtois (Harvard University Press, 1999).

17 Latest research into this ideologically motivated slaughter comes from Dutch historian Frank Dikötter, whose book *Mao's Great Famine* (Bloomsbury Publishing, London 2010) documents in horrific detail the suffering of ordinary people under Mao's rule. He was able to conduct research in the (partially) opened Chinese archives.

Nevertheless "Peace" was a very popular word in the Communist lexicon — even the Hungarian church hierarchy which indeed made its own peace with the regime after the fiercely anti-Communist Primate of Hungary was holed up in the American Embassy following Hungary's 1956 revolution, imposed the nomenclature "peace priests" (*béke papak*) on its clergy. This gave a touchy-feely flavour to a body of prelates who had now agreed to be complicit with violent totalitarianism.

Philologists at McDonald's (the hamburger people): How to make philology a branch of PR:

Corporate gurus at Oak Brook, Illinois have decided that the definition of "*McJob*," as it appears in most lexicons, is misleading. They are offering (free with every order over six dollars?) a much better one. So it's out with "*low-paid or menial job with few prospects and little job satisfaction*" and in with "*opportunities for career progression and skills that last a lifetime*." Quite so. If you last a lifetime, which you probably won't if you eat hamburgers, you'll still only be good for shovelling French fries and picking Big Macs off the belt when you're eighty.

According to know-all journalist Thomas Friedman, no country with a McDonald's has ever gone to war with another one that also boasts a McDonald's (forget Panama, Serbia, Lebanon etc.). This is known as "The Golden Arches Theory of Conflict Prevention." Really. It says so in *Wikipedia*.

Pablo Picasso: Rebarbative Spanish painter with superiority complex: That Picasso did not exactly live like an earnest clean-living Christian may perhaps have been a reaction against his pious parents, who tried to fix him on the straight and narrow by burdening him with half a hagiographer's index of Christian names, viz., *Pablo Diego José Francisco de Paula Juan Nepomuceno María de los Remedios Cipriano de la Santísima Trinidad Clito Rula y Picasso.* Stuck with such a moniker, is it any wonder he made remarks like "*Art is a finger up the arse of the bourgeoisie*"? His response to his critics, especially his bourgeois critics, was always splendidly disdainful, e.g. "*The world doesn't make sense today, so why should I paint pictures that do?*"

Picasso sometimes sounded like a cynic, even a charlatan, but so do many geniuses to mere mortals. His *obiter dicta* reveal that he was good at overturning applecarts by adopting a quasi-surrealist view of things, a bit like his fellow Spanish genius, Luis Buñuel:

"When art critics get together they talk about Form and Structure and Meaning. When artists get together they talk about where you can buy cheap turpentine."

"The genius of Einstein leads to Hiroshima."

"Computers are useless. They can only give you answers."

"God is really only another artist. He invented the giraffe, the elephant and the cat. He has no real style, He just goes on trying other things."

Picasso's views on women, though doubtless shared by many men (especially creative geniuses) would perhaps meet with some resistance today:

"There are only two types of women - goddesses and doormats."

"Every time I change wives I should burn the last one. That way I'd be rid of them. They wouldn't be around to complicate my existence. Maybe that would bring back my youth too. You kill the woman and you wipe out the past she represents."

On the other hand, like many over-achievers who have a ruthless way with women, Picasso had an uncritically supportive mum who was convinced he was destined for greatness:

"When I was a child my mother said to me, 'If you become a soldier, you'll be a general. If you become a monk, you'll be the pope.' Instead I became a painter and wound up as Picasso."

Salvador Dali, considerably more of a cynic than Picasso, is supposed to have said of his fellow genius: *"Picasso is a painter, so am I; Picasso is Spanish, so am I; Picasso is a communist, neither am I."*

It is said that a German officer visited Picasso in his Paris studio during the Second World War. There he saw the artist's *Guernica* and was shocked at the modernist 'chaos' of the painting. He asked Picasso: *"Did you do this?"* Picasso calmly replied: *"No, you did this!"* "[18]

Plagiarism: A backhanded compliment from indifferent writers to good ones, or sometimes vice versa.

18 Quoted by the philosopher Slavoj Žižek in an essay on "Violence."

Plagiarism has only really been regarded as sinful since the establishment of Copyright. Shakespeare stole almost all his plots from Holinshed, but nobody minds. However people got quite shirty when one of the British royals, aka Princess Pushy, lifted chunks from genuine historians for her book on *Royal Brides*. While "passing off" is rightly seen as earning money you're not entitled to from someone else's text, much of perfectly respectable literature and academic writing consists of recycling earlier material and putting your own spin on it. Come to that, the same applies to much of unrespectable writing, like the *Devil's Dictionary*. Voltaire has justly observed somewhere that *"originality is no more than a plagiarism that has not yet been found out."*

Charges of plagiarism are best faced down with shameless chutzpah. After Graham Swift, a Booker Prize winner, was accused of copying a novel by William Faulkner, Julian Barnes remarked: *"When Brahms wrote his First Symphony, he was accused of having used a big theme from Beethoven's Ninth. His reply was that any fool could see that."* [I got all this out of an article in *The Guardian*].

No Platform(ing): Censorship exercised by student activists, *bien pensant* communicators and others who believe that freedom of expression should be limited to *their* opinions:

Students Union rulebooks invented the concept of *"No Platform"* to prevent racists, fascists and neo-Nazis from standing for office in the union or speaking at its meetings. Predictably the procedure soon escalated into disallowing anyone with whom (almost always left-wing) activists disagreed from taking part in public debates. Although the Cambridge Union opposes the principle of *No Platform* in both its actions and laws, its enlightened policy has resulted in aggressive student protests against the hosting of a whole range of speakers, simply because activists disliked their point of view. Targets included Tories like Universities Minister David Willetts and the Local Government Minister Eric Pickles (at which time the Union building was broken into), as well as former IMF chief Dominique Strauss-Kahn, Marine Le Pen and (somewhat puzzlingly) Julian Assange. In February 2010, the NUS was heavily criticised after two of its officers forced the cancellation of a proposed debate on *multiculturalism* at the University of Durham, a significant escalation of *no platforming* beyond banning individuals into censoring whole topics.

Leftists were once big supporters of Israel, but contemporary left-wing agitprop decrees there should be bans and boycotts for anyone (invariably labeled "Zionist') putting the case for Israel, while an uncritical attitude to the Palestinian cause, and even Palestinian terrorism, is now *de rigueur* in such circles. Amusingly some of the most fierce and effective rights activists of a previous generation (e. g. feminist Germaine Greer and gay rights campaigner Peter Tatchell) have fallen foul of today's *No Platform* zealots, whose remit is remorselessly being extended to cover whole areas like transsexuality, immigration and alleged "Islamophobia." (See also **Z: *Zeal and Climate Change Zealotry***)

Plutonomy: An economy that is driven by, or that disproportionately benefits, wealthy people:

"Plutocracy is not an American word," the liberal American TV presenter Bill Moyers has written, *"but it's become an American phenomenon. Back in the fall of 2005, the Wall Street giant Citigroup even coined a variation on it, plutonomy, an economic system where the privileged few make sure the rich get richer with government on their side. By the* next *spring, Citigroup decided the time had come to publicly "bang the drum on plutonomy." ... over the past 30 years the plutocrats, or plutonomists, choose your poison, have used their vastly increased wealth to capture the flag and assure the government does their bidding. ... This marriage of money and politics has produced an America of gross inequality at the top and low social mobility at the bottom, with little but anxiety and dread in between, as middle class Americans feel the ground falling out from under their feet."*

Citigroup later regretted its candour in boasting about the triumph of the "plutonomy" and had the relevant memoranda removed from the web. However Matthew Yglesias, speaking at the *International Herald Tribune*'s Luxury Business Conference in 2011 resurrected the piece, much to Citigroup's dismay (Ajay Kapur's "*Plutonomy: Buying Luxury, Explaining Imbalances*"). "The analysis itself is a mixed bag," says Yglesias, "but the bullet point summary is a brilliant instance of summarization so I'll just quote it:

— The World is dividing into two blocs - the *plutonomy* and the rest. The US, UK, and Canada are the key *plutonomies* - economies powered by the wealthy. Continental Europe (ex-Italy) and Japan are in the egalitarian bloc.

— Equity risk premium embedded in "global imbalances" are unwarranted. In *plutonomies* the rich absorb a disproportionate chunk of the economy and have a massive impact on reported aggregate numbers like savings rates, current account deficits, consumption levels, etc. This imbalance in inequality expresses itself in the standard scary "global imbalances." We worry less.

— There is no "average consumer" in a *plutonomy*. Consensus analyses focusing on the "average" consumer are flawed from the start. The *Plutonomy* Stock Basket outperformed MSCI AC World by 6.8% per year since 1985. Does even better if equities beat housing."

According to the Global Wealth Report, which Boston Consulting Group published in June 2014 in Washington D.C., the liquid wealth of what are called "Ultra-High-Net-Worth Households" in the jargon (those with more than $100 million liquid financial assets), increased by 20% in 2013. BCG claims that 15,000 households globally belong in this group of the super-rich and control 5.5% of global financial wealth. 5,000 of them live in the US, followed by China, Britain and Germany.

However the outlook is not entirely rosy since, as Citigroup regretfully points out, "political enfranchisement remains as was — one person, one vote, [and] at some point it is likely that labor will fight back against the rising profit share of the rich and there will be a political backlash against their rising wealth." Very disagreeable.

The most candid definition of plutonomy may be found in the Urban Dictionary, as follows: *"Plutonomy: (ECONOMICS) economies in which consumption by the very rich is what drives most growth: Bulgari watches, Maybach limousines, Gulfstream V business jets, vacations in the Maldives, Dolce & Gabbana suits, private security services, money laundering, and income tax evasion."*

According to the heretical economist Ha-Joon Chang, the standard justification for a plutonomy is as follows: "It may sound harsh, but in the long run poor people can become richer only by making the rich even richer. When you give the rich a bigger slice of the pie, the slices of the others may become smaller in the short run, but the poor will enjoy bigger slices in absolute terms in the long run, because the pie will get bigger." But, says Chang inconveniently for this soothing argument, "pro-rich policies have failed to accelerate growth in the last three decades" [i.e. up to 2010]. The idea of "trickle-down economics" is a

367

great get-out-of-gaol-free card for those who have a slight conscience about the "money breeds money" syndrome, but it doesn't stack up in practice. Actually, says Chang, *"we need the electric pump of the welfare state to make the water at the top trickle down in any significant quantity... The economy-boosting effect of the extra billion dollars given to the lower-income households through increased welfare spending will be bigger than the same amount given to the rich through tax cuts."*[19] *In short, instead of income "trickle-down" in our economy we currently have a formidable amount of "trickle-up," since those at the bottom are having their wages screwed down and those at the top are enjoying an ever greater bonus from the productivity of the poorly paid...*

Not that Chang is sentimental about the behaviour of the rich in *poor* countries. He points out that, although a Swedish bus driver is paid fifty times more than one in New Delhi, he is obviously not fifty times more skilled or fifty times more productive. But he does share his labour market with people (top scientists, managers and engineers) who are perhaps a hundred times more productive than their Indian counterparts. This drags up the average national productivity of Sweden. The bus driver gets to keep his advantage chiefly by protectionism (keeping out too many people who might do the job for much less.) It is the *low productivity of the rich* in poor countries that keeps those countries poor (plus massive corruption, of course). *"Instead of blaming their own poor people for dragging the country down, the rich of the poor countries should ask themselves why they cannot pull the rest of their countries up as much as the rich countries do."*[20]

Of course, not everyone thinks indignation about inequality is healthy either for democracy or the economy. Ben Shapiro, the conservative American talk show host, is a robust protagonist of the contrarian view: *"The story of Detroit's bankruptcy was simple enough: Allow capitalism to grow the city, campaign against income inequality, tax the job creators until they flee, increase government spending in order to boost employment, promise generous pension plans to keep people voting for failure. Rinse, wash and repeat."*

See also under **O: Oligarchy**.

---

19 Ha-Joon Chang: *23 Things They Don't Tell You About Capitalism* (Penguin, London, 2011) Pp. 137, 146.

20 Ha-Joon Chang: *op cit.* P. 29.

Political Correctness: Originally a well-meaning campaign to shame people into avoiding expressions that are offensive to ethnic minorities, non-heterosexuals, women and other constituencies deemed to be vulnerable to discriminative thought or behaviour. Now a blackmailing methodology for suppressing the views of people you happen to disagree with:

According to the *Cynic's Dictionary*, a Liberal is *"one who tolerates all beliefs and opinions except those with which he disagrees; a benevolent soul who advocates progressive measures for the sake of people with whom he would never associate."*[21] This is a view that is no longer confined to cynics and the techniques of opinion enforcement have become more powerful and ruthless through the agency of Facebook and Twitter. One such technique is to keep changing the acceptable terminology for "minorities", in the hope of catching someone out using the no longer acceptable term. Certain words are reserved for use by particular interest groups, but unacceptable if used by anyone outside the group. So "bitch" is of course politically incorrect, but right-on sassy women can use the term amongst themselves, just as Pakistanis can use the word "Paki," otherwise deemed a term of abuse. While most could understand the distinctions being made in these cases, the rules for a word like "queer" are too complex for many of us to unravel. "Faggot" can apparently be used among gay men referring to themselves, but anyone else gets into serious trouble for using it. In a surreal PC incident during the Afghanistan war, American Navymen were solemnly rebuked for writing *"Hijack this, you faggots"* on a bomb destined for the Taleban. They were told to *"more closely edit their spontaneous acts of penmanship,"*[22] which is nice considering the Taleban would be blown up by the bomb before being able to read it and anyway consider that homosexuals should be beheaded. But perhaps the idea was to assuage the delicate sensibilities of gay colleagues who might surmise that the word had been written on the bomb by someone who was not himself gay?

The actor Benedict Cumberbatch (amusingly himself politically correct to the nth degree) was pilloried in America in 2015 for using the

21 Rick Bayan: *The Cynic's Dictionary* (Quill / William Morrow, New York, 1994) P. 103.

22 Quoted in Brendan O'Neill: "The new PC from A to Z" in *The Spectator*, 7th of February 2015.

phrase "coloured people" when evidently only "people of colour" is now acceptable (but for how long?) The attacks on such a pure-minded individual as Cumberbatch illustrate that political correctness now has little relevance to perceived offence and is more concerned with a totalitarian approach to speech and a lust to demonstrate power. Just as whole categories of persons are deemed to be off limits (which in effect means that persons in these categories should not be criticised, even if the criticism is justified or indeed urgently required), so others are deemed to be in a category that is not permitted to air a view: the simple phrase "*check your privilege*" is flung at them to discredit unanalysed what they have to say on this or that issue. This is a convenient way of slamming the door on free speech for those the PC police disagree with. As Robert Wargas has written, "*PC is like a church whose only sacrament is excommunication.*"[23]

In 2015, a freshman's fair at the University of East Anglia was enlivened by the sight of sombreros being worn by students who had been handed them by an enterprising Mexican restaurant in Norwich to promote Pedro's Tex-Mex Cantina. The Student Union decided that wearing these hats was offensive and potentially racist on the grounds of something called "*cultural appropriation*" and stereotyping. A gentleman described as the union's "democracy officer" issued a statement that helpfully illustrates the required mind-set for those contemplating a career in political correctness enforcement, as follows: "*At the student union we want all members to feel safe and accepted, so at all events we try to ensure that there is no behaviour, language or imagery which could be considered racist, homophobic, transphobic, sexist or ableist. We know that when it comes to cultural appropriation the issues can sometimes be difficult to understand and many don't realise that they may be about to cause offence or break a policy. So we're discussing internally how we can improve our briefing to both external organisations and our own members so that people aren't caught out at the last minute.*"[24] The patronising language of this astonishing policy statement — note that "breaking a policy" is as important as "causing offence" —

23 Quoted in Damian Thompson: "Rise of the new young puritans," *The Spectator*, 7th February, 2015.

24 Quoted in a report of the incident in *The Sunday Telegraph*, 27th September, 2015.

suggests that its authors are sublimely unaware of the way it echoes the paternalistic censorship of the past.

By 2015 censorship under the guise of "political correctness" was swiftly gaining ground in universities, particularly in America. Students at Princeton occupied the President's office demanding that all references to Woodrow Wilson (former head of the university and 28th President of the USA) be removed from campus and the prestigious (and very liberal) Woodrow Wilson School of Public Policy and International Affairs be renamed. Wilson's offence is that he reintroduced segregation into the federal workforce. His efforts at the Peace of Versailles and in founding the League of Nations apparently count for nothing. Logically, as Edward Luce pointed out in the *Financial Times*, monuments to, or institutions named after, George Washington, Thomas Jefferson (a liberal hero) and James Madison should also be purged, since all of them kept slaves; and Winston Churchill's generally well-received stand against Nazism should count for nothing because he was an avowed imperialist. Then again Franklin D. Roosevelt, hitherto an icon on the left, should presumably be erased from our consciousness because he didn't do anything for civil rights and interned 120,000 Japanese-Americans during World War II. Like the Students Union at the University of East Anglia, the Princeton activists issued patronising demands to their elders, whom they do not regard as their betters, no matter how experienced they may be as scholars and teachers. Not untypical was the risible demand that faculty members should undergo *"cultural competence training."*[25] "Cultural competence" training today, the cultural revolution tomorrow...

Partly the new Puritanism is a job creation scheme for victimhood opportunists (*q.v.* **A: *Apologism***); indeed the American universities are taking on multicultural guidance counsellors and diversity officers by the bucket-load. All of these of course need to justify their positions, sniffing out heresies and imposing what George Orwell called the "smelly little orthodoxies" contending for our souls. Although you might think the point of universities was that people should learn to debate points of view with which they disagree, PC power has devoted itself to the opposite, a policy which is called *"no-platforming."* This simply means imposing a ban on speakers you don't like (recent victims of this totalitar-

25 See Edward Luce: "The rise of liberal intolerance," *Financial Times* 30th November, 2015.

ian practice masquerading as liberalism have included Christine Lagarde of the IMF for allegedly victimising poor countries, Condoleeza Rice for being Secretary of State at the time of the Iraq War and Ayaan Hirsi Ali. Ostracisation of the last-named is particularly revealing, since Hirsi Ali supports the emancipation of women who suffer from the widespread subjection of women in conservative Islam, and is thereby branded "*Islamophobic.*")

The wheel has come full circle: politically correct liberals now openly defend oppression, but only that which chimes with their multicultural dogmas. None of this censorship, or exploitation of real or imagined "*microaggression*" (unconsciously giving verbal offence to marginalised groups), or abuse of those who don't subscribe to the ordained group-think, does anything to help the people of colour being gunned down by trigger-happy American cops, of course. But that is not the point of it. The point of it is power and the activists hope to become the bullying, self-righteous, freedom-denying politicians of tomorrow.

Pope Benedict XVI was certainly not "politically correct" as that notion is currently perceived and exploited — it is unlikely that a Catholic dogmatist ever could be. For example, he caused an uproar by quoting an opinion based on experience voiced by the Byzantine Emperor, Manuel II Palaeologos, namely that the only new idea thought up by Mohammed was to spread his religion by the sword. (Christians found this such a good idea they soon decided to do the same with the Crusades.)

Curiously enough, the following far more explosive paragraph of the Pope's lecture was ignored. There he said that it is repellent to the God of the Christians when men behave against the tenets of reason. For the Mohammedans however (according to the Pope) such a notion as God *preferring reason* is impossible, indeed blasphemous, because their God is a transcendent entity and his will is neither defined nor bound by any human categories such as "reason". In other words, if one were to try and describe the God of the mullahs in *human* terms, he would look very much like a transcendent psychopath.

This sort of argument (that God is all-powerful *and* all-merciful but doesn't act like or on it) has often proved a cul-de sac for the faithful (of whatever faith) because of the insurmountable problem of *theodicy* (*q.v.*). Fortunately it is improbable that the more subtle aspects of this discussion can be presented in terms that smelly mobs of Islamists on the streets of the Middle East are likely to grasp ("smelly mobs" is a po-

372

litically incorrect phrase that I use here *only by way of example* of the non-PC way to describe intensely peaceful and fragrant groups of concerned Islamists or Jihadists respectfully demonstrating in favour of their faith and the beheading of homosexuals, apostates etc.)

Populism: Dismissive description applied by the liberal establishment and media to opposition politics with popular support:

"The people," said Edmund Burke, *"should not be trusted as advisers on policy or even necessarily as true reckoners of their interests in the short run, but they are always the best judges of their own oppression — so much so that we ought to fear any power on earth that sets itself above them."*[26]

Chambers Dictionary defines a populist as *"someone who believes in the right and ability of the common people to play a major part in governing themselves."* "It is understandable that advocates of Brussels centralist government should regard this as a term of abuse but why do you all continue to portray populism as some sort of extremist and undesirable activity?" complains the writer of a letter to the *Financial Times.*[27] Eric Foner of Columbia University says that the word 'populist' has simply become "a term of disdain employed by purveyors of a presupposed consensus seeking to disparage popular passions… [the opposite of populist thus becomes the voter who is] "responsible or middle of the road or rational" — or in other words, agrees with me.

This complaint more or less sums up the cognitive dissonance between those who believe that democratic government should be *representative* and those who think it should be *delegatory*. The MEP Daniel Hannan pours scorn on the anxiety spread by EU President Herman Van Rompuy, who fears that the whole European structure will be blown away by the 'winds of populism.' "Populism," writes Hannan, "is a favourite Eurocrat word, meaning 'when politicians do what their constituents want'— or, as we call it in English, 'democracy.'" He also points out that, until the 2014 elections to the EU Parliament made this particular fiction unsustainable, EU apologists presented anti-EU parties as interchangeably "extremist,"

26 David Bromwich: *The Intellectual Life of Edmund Burke: From the Sublime and Beautiful to American Independence* (Harvard, 2014).

27 Stephen Hazell-Smith of Penshurst, Kent, UK (*Financial Times* letters, May 29, 2014).

while the liberal media contrived to give the impression that they were all "far right". "It is amazing," pursues Hannan "how common this narcissism is: I disagree with person A, and I also disagree with person B, therefore A and B are identical."

America is rather less hypocritical about populism than the EU federalists. Merriam Webster defines a populist as *"a member of a political party claiming to represent the common people"* or *"a believer in the rights, wisdom or virtues of the common people."* Populists in the USA were those who supported the People's Party which won five states in the 1893 presidential election representing the agrarian interest; it was also an advocate of a more flexible currency and agitator for government restraint of monopolies. The Populists were, says Gary Silverman "serious people who believed … in the central promise of American life: the democratisation of intelligence."[28] Other causes they espoused (the secret ballot, the eight-hour workday, the graduated income tax) eventually came about. Their insistence on curtailing the power of giant corporations was prescient to say the least. The increasing pressure they brought to bear on mainstream parties finally bore fruit in the Sherman Antitrust Act of 1890 which became the cornerstone of democratic control over appallingly unscrupulous robber barons like John Pierpoint Morgan and John D. Rockefeller. Although the Populists declined after throwing in their lot with the Democrats, they were the precursors of the Progressives who converted Theodore Roosevelt to his vigorous action against vested interests, just such as is again needed today against a greedy, narcissistic financial sector that makes "the people" pay the bill for its negligence, corruption and incompetence. In 1913 Woodrow Wilson, again under Progressive influence, wrote that "if monopoly persists, monopoly will always sit at the helm of government. I do not expect to see monopoly restrain itself. If there are men in this country big enough to own the government of the United States, they are going to own it."[29]

This observation is disagreeably relevant today where there are reportedly at least three highly-paid lobbyists for the drugs and health insurance industry assigned to every congressman and senator in the

28 Gary Silverman: "An all-American cheer for populism" (*Financial Times*, May 30th, 2014).

29 Woodrow Wilson: *The New Freedom, A Call for the Emancipation of the Generous Energies of a People* (1913), P. 286.

374

United States. Yet contemporary American populists are far more Jekyll and Hyde-like than those of the twentieth century, exhibiting a rage against the establishment that is as undiscriminating as it is often effective. The lack of a clear focus makes the populist movement vulnerable to manipulation. For example, the violence of the opposition to Obamacare, where the principle aim was to bring the forty-five million Americans without health insurance into a comprehensive plan, bears all the hallmarks of the forces stirring Dr Stockmann's opponents in Ibsen's play *An Enemy of the People*. The Tea Party campaign against Obamacare, together with massively funded negative propaganda from an evangelically hypocritical healthcare industry, was able to focus on the coercive element in the plan and present it as a "socialist" measure of wealth redistribution. It is revealing that 61% of Hispanics approve the plan and so do 91% of African Americans — but only 21% of whites.[30] This would seem to indicate pretty conclusively that the plan did indeed benefit the least privileged in American society and that white Americans, from the lower middle class upwards, had no intention of voluntarily paying for it. The dog whistle "socialist" slogan in American political parlance is enough to damn any proposal, good, bad or indifferent, just as the charge of "anti-Semitic" in Central European political discourse is effectively used to smear opponents or close down debates that may not have anything to do with anti-Semitism. Tea Party supporters merely responded to the dog whistle.

Writing in *The Spectator*, Peter Oborne describes Nigel Farage (leader of the United Kingdom Independence Party, who has a French-sounding name, and is married to a German wife, but has built up his support by opposing immigration) as a *"subversive who has reintroduced the vanished concept of political opposition into British politics."*[31] In the British case there is characteristically a good deal of snobbery involved in the attacks on him since he deliberately cultivates an image of the man in the pub (for which read "pub bore") who likes a pint, or possibly three, and unrepentantly smokes like a chimney. Raising the issue of im-

30 Poll conducted by the Pew Research Centre, September 2013.

31 Since that article was written by Oborne, Jeremy Corbyn has been elected to the leadership pf the Labour Party. Arguably this makes UKIP even more the real opposition, as the official opposition seemed unable to fight its way out of a paper bag, but UKIP threatened to upend the Conservatives over Europe.

Poujadists, tax-averse populists, take to the streets of Paris in 1955 ...

migration, in this analysis, typically attracts a liberal reaction combining snobbery with hypocrisy: "For affluent political correspondents, it [immigration] made domestic help cheaper, enabling them to pay for nannies, au pairs, cleaning ladies, gardeners and tradesmen who make middle class life comfortable. These journalists were often provided with private health schemes and were therefore immune from the pressure on NHS hospitals from immigration. They tended to send their children to private schools. This meant they rarely faced the problems of poorer parents whose children find themselves in schools where scores of different languages were spoken in the playground. Meanwhile the corporate bosses who funded all the main political parties (and owned the big media groups) tended to love immigration because it meant cheaper labour and higher profits." Oborne concludes that the most powerful and influential figures in British public life "entered into a conspiracy to ignore and to denigrate millions of British voters. ... for them politics is neither more nor less than a cynical game, the possession of the elite."

Similarly journalist Janan Ganesh explains the rise of populism as an indication of the mood of "anti-politics" sweeping through the disillusioned electorates of Europe. Part of the problem, he thinks, is the narrowness of the political class: *"Parliament has become a job guarantee for apparatchiks and activists who relax by watching television dramas set in other political capitals. In Britain politics is not just showbiz for ugly people, but for weirdly obsessive people too."*

These analyses sum up the *perceptions* of many in the UK who feel that they have been powerless to resist or guide the two massive social and political experiments stealthily inflicted on them over recent decades

376

through immigration and the extension of EU powers. The public frustration is palpable, but not entirely rational (not only the affluent classes have benefited from hard-working immigrants, the NHS would hardly function at all without the massive input of immigrants from what used to be called the Third World, and immigrants have been a net plus to GDP, in Britain as elsewhere); but Oborne is surely right that the main parties can no longer stay largely silent on the greatest social and political issues of the day, while a largely like-minded press contributes to this conspiracy by abusively picturing political dissidents as the barbarians at the gates of democracy. The success that Marine le Pen has had in nearly making her Front National what the Germans call "*salonfähig*" (i.e. not only appealing enough to attract votes from both disillusioned Socialists and Conservatives, but consequently "respectable" enough to be treated slightly more respectfully by the media) is even more alarming for "mainstream" politicians.

There are of course other definitions of "populist" from those quoted above from Chambers and Merriam Webster. Not untypical is the definition in Collins English Dictionary: "*populism: a political strategy based on a calculated appeal to the interests or prejudices of ordinary people.*" The words that stand out here are "calculated" and "prejudices," which not only imply something pretty disreputable, but also seem to hint at the existence of an alternative political strategy (to populism) that is not "calculated" and never stoops to appeal to the "prejudices" of ordinary people. This is presumably the sense preferred by the metropolitan liberal elite, most academics and the "mainstream" political parties. Unfortunately it is also deceitful. If Mr Miliband, the Labour leader in the UK until the 2015 election, suddenly announced a plan to force the energy companies to "freeze" energy prices for a couple of years, or if he ran around the country expressing sympathy for a newly discovered disadvantaged demographic known as "the squeezed middle [class]," was this the height of disinterested statesmanship or a "calculated" strategy? When the Conservative Home Secretary sent a placarded lorry around immigrant districts of London bearing the message in huge letters that illegal immigrants should go home, was this coherent policy or simply an appeal to people's prejudices? When Prime Minister David Cameron rode to the House of Commons on his bicycle to show how environmentally conscious he was, but omitted to tell us that all his necessary papers were being carried by a car travelling behind him, is that a populist gimmick or principled leadership? The idea that "mainstream" political parties do not adopt the same tactics as their "populist" opponents is, of course, moonshine. Mr Obama assured the electorate before his first election to the Presidency that he would immediately close the notorious Guantanamo Bay camp but the promise was not kept and it stretches credulity to pretend that he could not have known of the difficulties this would involve. Sometimes the attempts of mainstream politicians to emulate the wicked populists end in farce: a Labour Minister called Michael Meacher used to speechify affectingly on the theme of his poor agrarian upbringing, implying a boyhood of struggle and rural poverty. The political journalist Alan Watkins enjoyed pointing out that the Minister's supposedly horny-handed father actually trained as an accountant (and the Minister himself went to a prestigious Oxford college). Watkins was (recklessly) sued by the indignant would-be proletarian, who of course lost the case — an interesting example of the tendency of politicians to believe their own propaganda and the dangers of doing so.

A more insidious form of populism by the parties that claim to eschew it is the use of abstractions such as *"fairness"*, *"equality"*, *"society"* and so forth in political propaganda designed to create a touchy-feely image that has little or nothing to do with the tough decisions and difficult mediation required of effective and ethical governance. In 2014 the British Labour Party polled its members under the slogan *"What does Labour mean for you?"* Interviewees were invited to choose from a rather limited range of qualities: "compassion, equality, fairness, opportunity, progress and solidarity." They were also asked to complete a sentence that began: *"Above all, I believe Britain should be…"* — here the choice was "compassionate, diverse, fair, pioneering and respectful."

All this is an egregious example of populism dreamed up by spin doctors, since it is evidently designed to promote the party's caring image without putting forward anything so vulgar as a policy with which the party members might or might not agree. You may as well ask people whether, as party members, they are in favour of paedophilia or homicide. Moreover *"solidarity"* is a particularly weaselly abstraction: in a democracy people show solidarity on *opposing sides* of important issues. Mediating between them is what democracy is for. *"Progress"* is even worse, another dog whistle slogan, this time on the left of the ideological spectrum. A dark side of the otherwise mainly altruistic Progressives in the USA referred to above was that they enthusiastically espoused the idea of eugenics. It was indeed an enthusiasm of most progressive persons at that time, carried away as they were by the scientific potential of manipulating the gene pool. However the horrors of Nazi crimes have resulted in most people today considering such ideas dangerous and unacceptable in a civilised and humane society. The Labour Party's poll is therefore not much to do with "progressive" ideas as its devisers no doubt hoped to imply, but essentially a marketing exercise which, like any other sales campaign, tries to associate feeling good about the product with feeling good about yourself.

A problem for those taking the higher ground against populism is the difficulty of distinguishing between their own self-interest and the democratic principles they seek to uphold. According to Max Weber, the state is defined as having "the monopoly of legitimate violence," but this definition does not tell us whether the state in question is democratic or not. Without such a monopoly, the state cannot carry out its function of enforcing law and order, as we can observe in places like Somalia or for that matter the Ukraine. Populism is often seen as stoking the forces that would challenge the state's monopoly on coercion, a movement with democratic roots that would however sooner or later bring down democracy itself. Such an objection to populism cannot simply be waved away, but on the other hand constantly evoking the potential horrors of anarchy or worse ("Hitler came to power democratically" is a favourite cry) may equally be a tactic to distract attention from the behaviour of the entrenched elite that has provoked the mass discontent in the first place. In mature democracies with inclusive institutions, it is not very likely, though it is always possible, that a Robespierre will succeed in establishing a reign of terror.

The most common excoriation of populism, but also the most ambiguous, may be found in the disdainful rant of Shakespeare's Coriolanus. Deprived by intrigue of the consulship that he felt was his due on account of his patriotic military feats, Coriolanus rages at the impressionable crowds who are easily led by the nose, the "*common fools*" and "*mutable, rank-scented many*" as he calls them. Allowing the plebs to have power over patricians, he decides, would be like allowing "*crows to peck eagles.*" Yet Coriolanus's pose of disinterested patriotism seems a bit hollow when he later joins the Volscian enemy, in the wars against whom his military reputation had originally been earned. It is an uncomfortable play (George Bernard Shaw mischievously called it Shakespeare's greatest comedy),

379

its moral compass difficult to read, its main protagonist by turns noble and petty, his final murder hovering between good riddance and tragedy. And that's the problem with populism too: it is a great force for beneficial change and social justice, except when it's a great force for their opposite. The career of the archetypal populist, a tribune of medieval Rome, illustrates this very well. Rienzi came to power with the support of the church and started well by passing sweeping laws that checked the noble factions then bleeding Rome dry, as well as clearing streets and roads infested with robbers. Yet power corrupted him, the church became alarmed and the people turned against him. After a few years in internal exile, the whole process was repeated — a triumphant return to power, misuse of same, finally assassination on the Capitol where he had taken refuge.

It is not surprising that the career of Rienzi fascinated Wagner, who made him the protagonist of his first successful opera premiered in Dresden in 1842. Wagner fancied himself as a Socialist revolutionary and the story's ingredients of popular liberation vitiated by hubris and corruption enabled him to project the corruption of power in a dramatic setting. It is even less surprising that the semi-educated and impressionable Adolf Hitler was bowled over by the opera when he first saw it as a young man in 1906 or 1907. The manuscript was given to him as a fiftieth birthday present in 1939 and was reportedly with him in the Berlin bunker when, like the Rienzi of Wagner's opera, he was himself immolated. The Wagner scholar Thomas Grey has written that "in every step of Rienzi's career — from acclamation as leader of the *Volk* through military struggle, violent suppression of mutinous factions, betrayal and final immolation — Hitler would doubtless have found sustenance for his fantasies."[32] Rienzi's charisma, his famed eloquence, were sufficient initially to bring order and temporary stability or to restrain others, but not sufficient to restrain himself.

While all politicians tell the people what they want to hear and then invoke the small print or unforeseen circumstances in order to avoid delivering what they should never have promised, the populist tends to become a prisoner of his own rhetoric. He invites the assumption that he is *delegated* by certain sections of the electorate to deliver what they demand, rather than acting as *representative* of the public interest as a

32 Thomas S. Grey (Ed): *The Cambridge Companion to Wagner* (Cambridge University Press, 2008), P. 36.

whole, one who has to make judgements between competing interests. Trapped in a sort of political Ponzi scheme, he has to keep making new promises that are paid for by people to whom he has made previous promises. While he tells the people what they want to hear, the braver leader, like Dr Stockmann in Ibsen's *An Enemy of the People*, tells the people precisely what they do not want to hear (and by doing so, may end up paying the same price as the spurned populist.) The perspective of a play like *An Enemy of the People* is somewhat Coriolanian, the "common fools" of the town being easily manipulated by financial interests to believe that the man who intends only good actually intends them harm. Just as Shaw claimed to see Coriolanus as a comedy, Ibsen himself said he couldn't quite decide whether *An Enemy of the People* was "a comedy or a straight drama" (most audiences are in little doubt.) The stupidity of people may be a matter for humour, but lynch mobs are usually not. Mark Twain, a master of comedy and an acute, if benevolent, observer of human frailty summed up the danger of the herd mentality thus: *"Whenever you find yourself on the side of the majority, it is time to pause and reflect."*[33]

It is possible, but extremely rare, to become a figure as widely admired as the charismatic populist by telling people truths about their behaviour that do not flatter their self-images, but yet flatter them enough to suggest that they are capable of attitudes that are infinitely more dignified than those they currently aspire to. Mahatma Gandhi is perhaps the most celebrated example of this and the secret of his success seems surprisingly simple: he practised what he preached, which is a great deal more than can be said of most populists. Since he did not seek power for himself, but rather sought to influence people by moral axioms and personal example, it was impossible to accuse him either of opportunism or hypocrisy. When he said that *"in matters of conscience the law of the majority has no place,"* he was enunciating one of the fundamental principles of a civilised democratic society. As a moral force, Gandhi's courage and persistence are almost unequalled; importantly, we can verify the facts of his life, and know that he spoke the words that he did,

---

33 This is generally attributed to Twain, who used the same ideas in variant forms from time to time in public speaking. In *Mark Twain's Notebook*, edited by Albert Bigelow Paine (1935), P. 393, the quotation appears as *"whenever you find that you are on the side of the majority, it is time to reform"*

which we cannot in the case of Jesus Christ whose words and deeds we only have at second-hand from propagandists. However as a political strategy, his influence depended on his opponents actually having a conscience and a code of morals, as well as being at least partly accountable to the population of the mother nation at home. Gandhi would not have lasted long, for instance, under Stalinist or Nazi rule — indeed we might very well never have heard of many Gandhi-like figures that were liquidated under such regimes. This is not to diminish Gandhi's stature, any more than the fact that white South Africans changed course partly through sanctions and outside pressure in any way diminishes the achievement of Nelson Mandela. It is merely to say that the political environment ultimately determines whether such figures prevail, whereas in another context they would simply be murdered and forgotten like so many others. The moral force of a Gandhian commitment to non-violence (as opposed to St Augustine's legitimisation of the "just war") is something that appeals unequivocally to the best in human nature. The danger of the populist's rhetoric is that it may achieve its effect through appealing to the worst.

Precariat: Replaces the stable Marxist concept of the proletariat with a wobbly one:

One of the many triumphs of Neo-Liberalism is the creation of the *Precariat*, a demographic defined by the least privileged class in society who indeed live precariously, not to say on the edge of a precipice. That means they are likely to be constantly in debt and will always be fearing for their jobs. The *Precariat* being on PAYE, the sort of tax loopholes that government has traditionally, if surreptitiously, offered the wealthy are not available to it. Indeed, until the idea of a "living wage" caught on among politicians, much of the *Precariat* struggled to earn even enough to bring their net incomes after tax above those living on benefits — a situation which is another consequence of Neo-Liberalism. The *Precariat*, like the rest of us, have all sorts of hobbies and pastimes they'd like to indulge in, but cannot because they have no money, lead highly insecure lives, and are usually trapped in decaying post-industrial parts of the country.

Professor Guy Standing of London University points out that the *Precariat* experiences a *loss of control over time* and is offered only "*commodified schooling that de-emphasises culture, history, art and subversive knowledge.*" All that is really expected of it is that it "*labours*

382

flexibly, shops, consumes and plays."[34] When it becomes apparent that it can't even afford to do those things, no doubt governments will be obliged to think of remedies….

As a consequence of unbridled Neo-Liberalism euphemistically known as the "Washington Consensus," much of the world seems to have relapsed into the class conditions of the industrial revolution. Standing's analysis uncannily echoes a complaint made in an earlier age by Paul Lafargue[35] in his celebrated essay *The Right To Be Lazy*: "*Confronted with this double madness of the labourers killing themselves with over-production and vegetating in abstinence, the great problem of capitalist production is no longer to find producers and to multiply their powers but to discover consumers, to excite their appetites and create in them fictitious needs.*"

Prescottisms: Aphorisms from the Deputy Leader of the Labour Party: Politics would have been even duller than they already were without the strangled syntax and colourfully inappropriate similes of John Prescott, renowned for his two Jaguar motor cars and his wife's remarkable hairdos.

The late Simon Hoggart was an indefatigable chronicler of Prescottisms ("Prescott triumphs on the slippery slopes of syntax") and has recorded the following: (*When Prescott was unveiling his transport white paper*): "When you do a gas, the gas comes out of the car and if the car's not moving you get less gas." (*As he came off a plane*): "I am glad to be back on terra cotta". (*In Parliament*): "Liberal Demoprats" and "coming to a collusion". Also: "The Government intend to reduce — and probably eliminate — the homeless by 2008." "I notice from the papers and on television today that the Tories have now brought in a new person to get people to vote Tory, and I could not help noticing that the person is named, as I saw on the website, "Mr. Tosser". I do not know which person on the Front Bench this man is modelled on, but let me tell the right hon. Gentleman that I always thought that his party was full of them, and that is why they have lost three elections."

---

34 Quoted in a review of Standing's book on the *Precariat* and an essay he wrote for the Open Democracy Forum. See: *http://righttobelazy.com/blog/2012/02/the-precariat-and-control-of-time/*

35 Lafargue was Karl Marx's son-in-law and a revolutionary theorist and activist. *The Right to be Lazy* was published in 1883.

John Prescott canvassing vigorously....

Prescott had as much sense of humour as his detractors. During a general election campaign he was struck by a tomato thrown by a heckler and reacted with a fancy right hook that felled the assailant. Tony Blair rang him up to ask if he was all right: "I said 'Yes', and he said 'Well, what happened?' and I said 'I was just carrying out your orders. You told us to connect with the electorate, so I did."

Other masterly quips include his claim that "most Tories seem to think that 'ethics' is a county near Middlesex," and "Enjoy your holiday — make it a long one." The Prescott masterpiece, however, is surely his championing of the Green Belt: "It's a Labour achievement, and we mean to build on it."

***Private Eye*'s opera review:** A superbly crafted critique by one of the world's most respected musicologists:

"*BBC Radio 3 Opera Highlights*: ***The Damnation of Silvio* by Hector Berliozsconi:** As the curtain rises, we see the Robber Baron Silvio hosting a lavish banquet at the Palazzo Copulazione. He is surrounded by a chorus of beautiful young women, many of whom are members of the European Parliament. They are singing the famous Rumpipumpi Chorus from the popular operetta *Orgy and Bess*. As the festivities proceed, there is a peal of thunder and we see his Holiness the Pope arriving in his Popemobile flanked by a chorus of Cardinals on motorbikes wearing red helmets and dark glasses. Despite the papal curse condemning Silvio to hell, another chorus of Italian voters suddenly appears and carries the robber baron shoulder-high to his favourite brothel. The Pope sadly withdraws as they sing triumphantly '*Papa gono*' ("His Holiness has left the building."). (*Curtain*). "

Privacy: A concept considered anachronistic by those who are determined to intrude on it for commercial gain or political control — and now have the means to do so:

Pascal says: "*If all men knew what each said of the other, there would not be four friends in the world.*"

The classic response of ideologues to pleas for the right to a private life is to say that those who have nothing to hide have nothing to fear. This was the totalitarian argument of Plato (who argued that the houses of Athens should have no covered windows, so it could be seen by anyone what a citizen was up to in the privacy of his own home.) This view begs the question of why we should interest ourselves in matters that do not concern us other than to exert control and power over such persons — the control and power of the mob. In practice, however, such control becomes that of a narrow *nomenklatura*, a form of oppression that reached a kind of apotheosis with the activities of the Stasi in the misnamed German Democratic Republic.

The demise of privacy amongst consumers nowadays is an evil that is largely self-inflicted. Lately Samsung's SmartTVs have been marketed with an incorporated microphone for those too lazy to choose their channels by using the remote control. It turns out the microphone can also pick up some of what is being said elsewhere in the room: the "telescreen" of George Orwell's dystopian novel *1984* is apparently being given its first test drive. There are already all sorts of inquisitive "smart" gadgets ranging from mobile phones to energy meters. The beauty of all these (from the providers' point of view) is that they can endlessly gather information about their users — their habits, preferences, tastes and spending patterns. The "internet of things" connects up gizmos and home appliances, theoretically to make life easier for the consumer; but his or her life will not be so enhanced if they are used to flood the homeowner with sales offers, or indeed when the hackers get hold of them. Helen Lewis of the *New Statesman* has pointed to the imminent danger of internet trolls tampering with smoke alarms — or for that matter getting the dishwasher to order things on eBay. Trolls have already hacked a popular internet-connected doll to make it swear, which is quite funny; but doubtless soon it will be able to do more sinister things,[36] like maliciously accusing parents of paedophilia and reporting them to social workers...

However there is a difference between the advance of privacy-destroying consumer phenomena and the totalitarian oppression practised through the telescreens in Orwell's novel, namely that people are willingly submitting to the invasion of their privacy out of material greed and a solipsistic desire to put themselves on display. If the Orwellian telescreen becomes a reality, it will be because people are too lazy to stop it, preferring convenience over freedom and self-absorption over self-discipline. Facebook and Twitter are already awash with the detritus of our imploding civilisation — ingratiating politicians posting would-be blokeish comments, attention-seeking celebrities spouting cringe-inducing banalities, trolls spewing poison. Why should we feel sorry for a future population that ends up being locked inside shopping malls, sent to gulags or simply thrown in the sea just because it can't be bothered to protect its privacy any more?

Private pensions: A system devised by the financial services industry for skimming the savings of the unwary:

Among the achievements of Neo-Liberalism in Britain (*see* **Precariat** *above*) — selling the national assets to tax-payers who already own them, turning state monopolies into private cartels etc. — smashing the private pension system must take pride of place. During the Thatcher government companies began appropriating (i.e. stealing) surpluses that existed in many company pension schemes. The Inland Revenue gave cover for this by decreeing that any scheme holding more than 105% of its liabilities was a tax dodge. Next came "payment holidays," when annual payments to a scheme would be suspended (forget about the actuarial principle that surpluses built up in good times should smooth out the

36 Helen Lewis: "Why couch potatoes choose to relinquish their private lives," *Financial Times*, 11th February 2015.

losses accrued in bad times.) Not very surprisingly, surpluses on pension schemes soon became burgeoning deficits.

On the principle that once you have robbed your victims you shouldn't forget to knee them in the groin as well, Chancellor Gordon Brown then weighed in with his removal of tax credits on pension funds. Final salary pension schemes, the only reliable ones, were now deemed "unaffordable" and withdrawn — except, of course, for the Neo-Liberal big hitters in management who had stolen the money from employees' schemes in the first place. (Meanwhile directors made off from the ruins of the firms they had devastated loaded to the gunwales with pay-offs, cashed-in options and, yes, *pensions*. A not unusual pre-departure pay rise of £100,000 for a CEO implied a further 1 million needed to fund his £66,000 pension hike, money which was quietly stolen from the shareholders.)

Savers of more modest means were pushed into the arms of the seriously misnamed "pension providers," where greedy jobsworths mismanaged their pension pots and stole up to 25% of the latter in opaque "fees and charges." This sorry tale all too perfectly characterises the banana republic Britain had become, where the poor help the rich and the rich help themselves.

Privilege: Anything that annoys egalitarians:
A modish way of silencing your opponent nowadays is simply to hiss at him or her "*Check your privilege!*" A favourite with trolls (*q.v.*) on social media, the accusatory phrase is seemingly animated by the assumption that a white person has no right to give an opinion on racism, or a male on feminism, or a straight person on homosexuality, or a rich person on poverty and so on and so forth. That is to say, it is permissible to endorse what the people in these categories themselves have to say about their preferences or situation, but any attempt to challenge their statements is an unacceptable exercise of "privilege" over "disadvantaged" or "vulnerable" groups.

This is certainly one of the more effective forms of the censorship increasingly favoured by today's liberals, many of whom seem to have abandoned the difficult task of coherent argument in favour of shutting down opinions they don't wish to hear. Entire classes of people with their tiresomely unorthodox opinions can thereby be removed ("no platformed") from forums of public discussion merely on the basis of who or what they are.

The "social privilege" checklist was the brainchild of one Peggy McIntosh in a 1998 article titled "*White Privilege: Unpacking the Invisible Knapsack*." She came up with a list of 26 (later extended to 50) "white and male" advantages which white people possess due to their skin color. These include:

• I can if I wish arrange to be in the company of people of my race most of the time.
• I can turn on the television or open to the front page of the paper and see people of my race widely represented.
• I can swear, or dress in second hand clothes, or not answer letters, without having people attribute these choices to the bad morals, the poverty, or the illiteracy of my race.
• I can do well in a challenging situation without being called a credit to my race.
• If a traffic cop pulls me over or if the IRS audits my tax return, I can be sure I haven't been singled out because of my race.

The article rather cleverly juxtaposes the self-confidence of whites with (not unjustified) black feelings of victimhood in the USA. Unfortunately it triggered a boom in grievance mongering and offence-taking. By September 2006, the "social justice" blog *Alas!* had compiled (alas!) a list of fifteen types of privilege, including that pertaining to able-bodied people, black males, members of the upper class, Americans [*sic*!] and heterosexuals. It is only a matter of time before law-abiding citizens will be obliged to "check their privilege" before commenting on criminals (the European Court of Human Rights has taken a bold step in this direction by demanding that prisoners be given the right to vote). And may be persons who live in reasonably stable democracies will soon have to "check their privilege" before making nasty remarks about terrorists. This is what happens when a reasonable appeal for good manners, which basically involves consideration for others, is turned into a slogan of "identity politics."

But hope is on the horizon: even the left are getting apprehensive about such a two-edged weapon as the concept of "privilege", not least because some of them are doing OK and have fallen into the privilege category themselves, whereas the idea was that all those nasty right-wing, sexist and reactionary persons who fail the "progressive" test are supposed to be the culprits. Dan Hodges, a renegade from the Left and former trades union official who now writes a blog for the conservative

Daily Telegraph, points out the flaw in assuming a definition of privilege that accords only with left-liberal orthodoxy: *"For a start, how do we actually define privilege? Let's go back to the example* [of] *welfare. Who really holds the privilege in this debate? Is it someone like me, who has never taken a penny of welfare, except to make regular withdrawals from the bank of mum and dad? Or is it those who are actually subsisting on, and benefiting from, welfare themselves? Who, in this case, actually enters the debate from a position of self-interest? Shouldn't it be those Shameless types who we all know are merely idling and scrounging and swinging the lead, who should be giving their own privilege the run down?"*[37] It is seriously "off-message" to describe people living off the welfare as enjoying a privilege, but quite a lot of the people who actually pay the taxes that enable them to do so seem to think that they do.

However there is a deeper philosophical objection to this way of thinking, well-expressed by Blair Spowart in the magazine *Spiked* put out by students at Edinburgh University: *"Beyond the usual Student Union muppetry, there's a darker side to all this. Student radicals have started to take as given the idea that we simply cannot understand anything outside of our own experience. In essence, this worldview insists that we must consider society as ultimately divided along the lines of race, gender, sexuality and so on. This allegedly radical idea insists that society has little common experience and no recourse for inter-group understanding or empathy. This is a middle-finger to universalism and is, in the end, the opposite of true equality: the phenomenological equivalent of the pernicious doctrine of 'separate but equal'"*[38] That, you will recall, used to be the mantra of apartheid…

Profits: The surplus from successful enterprises or the fruits of exploitation, depending upon your view and salary:

Many profits are of course a combination of both the above, besides much else. The Financial Officers of banks and businesses have perfected techniques for reconstituting losses as profits, booking as presently occurring profits those which might or might not materialise in the future, or creating other plausible but mostly fictive profits that

---

37 Dan Hodges, *Telegraph* blog, May 30th, 2013.

38 Blair Spowart: "'Check your privilege' – a dark and divisive politics." *Spiked*, 8th May 2015.

only turn out not to be such when the faecal matter hits the oscillating device much further down the line. John Lanchester in his book *How To $peak Mone¥* remarks that "one of the most brilliant things the financial services industry ever did was to take the word 'debt,' which people thought was a bad thing that you wanted to avoid, and to re-name it as 'credit,' which sounds like a good thing you want more of." He calls this process "*reversification*," whereby the meaning of words used in the realm of finance gradually rotate until they end up meaning their opposites…[39]

According to the FT, the US banks "have booked unrealised profits from marking to market the value of their own debt to their creditors." Bank bonds having plunged in value due to solvency fears, accounting alchemy enables their issuers to record profits from their own weakness. Were Greece to use the same accountancy trick, adds the writer satiri-cally, "Athens would be flaunting a public sector surplus bigger than Norway's."

But that's nothing compared to the Franco-Belgian bank Dexia (the one that went belly up a few weeks after passing the EBA's stress test with flying colours.) It created a "special purpose vehicle" and leant it one heap of money. The vehicle's "special purpose"? To buy wodges of Dexia shares (come back Robert Maxwell, all is forgiven!) None of this diminished the revenue flow in the form of salaries to the bankers them-selves of course.

The resentment against banks, pursues the article, lies in the fact that one segment of society has insured itself against the pain it has helped to inflict on everyone else. In the bankers' world, you see, only the pi-lots have parachutes, and the lifeboats are exclusively reserved for the ship's crew.

Psychiatrists: The priests of a secular society:
According to some Anglican bishops, the services of psychiatrists are re-quired in order to "cure" homosexuals. A letter to *The Guardian* points out that it is the bishops who need a psychiatrist. These are men who have delusions that an all-powerful benevolent being is watching over them, and who cling to this fantasy in the face of overwhelming evi-

39 John Lanchester: *How To $peak Mone¥: What the money people say — and what they really mean* (Faber and Faber, London, 2014), P. 107.

dence to the contrary. They also seem to think this being is male and make frequent statements about him that suggest a repressed and unrequited homosexual love.

That's just typical of the sort of superior attitude that psychiatrists like to adopt! What do they know that the rest of us don't? It is clear that a regrettable scepticism has crept into the evaluation of psychiatrists from people who should know better. For instance, it has been said that "a neurotic is a man who builds a castle in the air. A psychotic is a man who lives in it. A psychiatrist is the man who collects the rent and psychopaths smash the windows."[40]

All this echoes a recurrent suspicion that psychoanalysis is an indulgence available to people with money and the American psychiatrist, like the specialist in Alan Bennetts's comedy *Habeas Corpus*, is one who specialises in "diseases of the rich." A French psychiatrist, Pierre Janet (1859-1947) had a similar take on the nexus between treatment and money: "If a patient is poor he is committed to a public hospital as a 'psychotic.' If he can afford a sanatorium, the diagnosis is 'neurasthenia'. If he is wealthy enough to be in his own home under the constant supervision of nurses and physicians, he is simply 'an indisposed eccentric.'"[41]

However a spoof that allegedly appeared in *Reader's Digest* indicated a way of making psychiatry more widely and rapidly available to those short of time and cash by using a telephone menu of the type so irritatingly used by utilities, local councils etc. : "*Hullo, welcome to the psychiatric hotline! If you are obsessive-compulsive, please press 1 repeatedly. If you are co-dependent, please ask someone to press 2. If you have multiple personalities, please press 3,4,5 and 6. If you are paranoid-delusional, we know who you are and what you want. Just stay on the line until we can trace the call. If you are schizophrenic, listen carefully and the little voices will tell you what number to press. If you are manic-depressive, it doesn't matter which number you press, no one will answer.*"[42]

---

40 Alan Hull: Rock musician.

41 Pierre Janet, quoted in *The Wit of Medicine* ed. L. and M. Cowan (1972).

42 Attributed to *Reader's Digest* and quoted in Salamon Gábor and Zalotay Melinda: *Melyik a nemdohányzó mentőcsónak?/ Which is the Non-Smoking Lifeboat?* (Pécsi Direkt Kft., Alexandra Kiadója, 2007).

The first deeply unkind verdict on psychoanalysis was made by Karl Kraus, who strongly objected to people being "psychoanalysed" in their absence at meetings of the Vienna Psychoanalytic Society. "Psycho-analysis," he said, "is that mental illness for which it regards itself as therapy."[43] However this broadside did nothing to deter its extremely profitable onward march, especially in America. In 1972 the Nobel prize-winning scientist Sir Peter Medawar had another go: "Considered in its entirety, psychoanalysis won't do. It is an end product, moreover, like a dinosaur or a zeppelin; no better theory can be erected on its ruins, which will remain for ever one of the saddest and strangest of all land-marks in the history of 20th century thought."[44]

He obviously needed help....

43 Karl Kraus, quoted in *No Compromise: Selected Writings of Karl Kraus*, Edited and with an Introduction by Frederick Ungar (Frederick Ungar Publishing Co., New York, 1977), P. 227.

44 Sir Peter Medawar: *The Hope of Progress* (1972).

Q

Quotation:
The act of repeating erroneously the words of another.

Ambrose Bierce: *The Unabridged Devil's Dictionary*

Quangos: Quasi-Autonomous-Non-Governmental-Organisations (largely unaccountable bodies chaired by political retreads or collectors of salaries and offices):

Modern governments come to power promising to reform and reduce these highly undemocratic bodies, but usually the promise is not kept. Quangos are simply too useful for shifting political responsibilities from the politicians to some more or less obscure bureaucratic body. Characteristically Tony Blair gave one of his soapy undertakings to consign Quangos to "the dustbin of history" when in opposition — and of course doubled them over his time in office. Deliberately vague mission statements made it difficult for the public to know what, for example the "Museums, Libraries and Archives Council" (abolished 2012) actually did all day. It claimed to be "building knowledge, supporting learning, inspiring creativity and celebrating identity" (love that last one). Apparently it also "made regulations", not accepted by the Tate Gallery, for example, because the latter had a de-accessioning policy which would have been in conflict with said regulations. For this *lèse majesté* the MLAC threatened the Tate that it would no longer receive donations in lieu of Inheritance Tax. In other words, the MLAC did very little that was useful, may be very little, period; but its jobsworths could bully people who were doing a proper job for public benefit. The MLAC has now been "merged" with the Arts Council, itself a body embroiled in constant bickering and disputes such as the celebrated "poetry wars" of the 1970s.

The Tories also promised to hack back the number of Quangos, but to relatively little effect (of the 262 slated for abolition from the amazing

393

1,200 that Labour had by then arrived at, only 56 had gone by 2014).[1] At least the Hearing Aid Council and the Teenage Pregnancy Advisory Board were no longer spending our money….

Lib Dems share with Labour a preference for getting ideologically like-minded people on to Quangos, since they afford an opportunity of sabotaging those policies of the elected governments which they happen to disapprove of. Tories would doubtless do the same, but there aren't so many of them on Quangos, probably because they tend to be ideologically opposed to them.

Journalist Philip Coggan points out the democratic deficit in Quangos, observing that voters can do nothing to influence their activities, let alone their existence: *"Nor are these organisations subject to the discipline of the market: if they are bad at their job, they will not necessarily lose their revenues and go out of business."*[2] It may of course be difficult to know if they are good or bad at their jobs when it is not very clear what the job is… In 2014 Quangos were still estimated to be spending £80 billion of public money, and some of their chiefs earned more than the Prime Minister himself.

Quantitive Easing: the euphemism preferred by our leaders for "printing money":

This quaint exercise, formerly frowned upon as being associated with despotic Third World regimes whose tyrants were careful to keep their own wealth in dollars or Swiss francs, is now apparently designed to keep the economies of the developed world afloat. First it was employed as part of the strategy to save the banks from implosion, which turned out to mean rescuing risk takers from the consequences of their actions; then, like a mutating virus, it emerged as the indispensable device to boost demand in flagging economies. Since the banks kept swallowing

---

1 Philip Coggan, in his book *The Last Vote: The Threats to Western Democracy* (Penguin Books, London, 2014) Pp. 228 ff., ascribes somewhat more success to the coalition government of 2010-2014, saying it had examined 901 Quangos and marked 120 for closure. But the claim to have closed *or merged* one hundred of them by 2012 gives the game away: "merging" is not "closing." Surviving Quangos merely get bigger and therefore demand more public money for their operations. The difference in assessments of the problem is probably accounted for by slightly different definitions of a Quango (e.g. some of them are partially disguised as registered charities.)

2 Phlip Coggan *op cit*. Pp. 228-9.

the excess cash to repair their balance sheets, this proved to be a self-per-petuating and ever expanding expedient, desperately aimed at getting consumers fired up about consuming. At one point it was quite seriously suggested you could do the job more efficiently by dropping money on the populace by helicopter.

In 2015 the European Central Bank finally followed the US Federal Bank and the Bank of England down the path of QE, despite the resist-ance of Germany, which is allergic to any suggestion of money printing since its experience in the Weimar Republic. Actually the ECB was for-bidden by the Rome Treaty from creating new money to finance govern-ment deficits or to bail out feckless administrations. No matter! In 2007 the ECB invented a stratagem called the *Securities Market Programme* (SMP) to get round the prohibitions of the Rome Treaty. The idea was to buy Spanish and Italian government bonds and claim that this wasn't a "bail-out," as the purchases were "sterilised" by withdrawing the same amount of money from the markets (I hope you are following all this.)

After spending about €200 billion on this manoeuvre without any ob-vious impact on the problem, the ECB had another go in 2011 with a new wheeze called *Long-Term Refinancing Operation* (LTRO), which provided cheap cash (at 1%) for the Spanish and Italian banks for three years. The banks took the money (about €1 trillion in loans this time) and invested it in their own government's bonds, making a turn on the transaction. (Some naïve persons had hoped the banks would actually lend some of this cash to businesses and consumers, but they obviously hadn't been paying attention.) Again the letter of the Rome Treaty was not broken as the ECB was bailing out banks, which in turn were…er… bailing out governments. The ECB's collateral was government bonds, which was not exactly reassuring given the condition of the respective governments' economies.[3] If the banks don't or can't pay the money back, the ECB is stuck with the government bonds. And if the govern-ments concerned default, other governments with healthier economies in Northern Europe will no doubt have to cough up to repair the ECB's bal-ance sheet…

3 In February 2015 the ECB stopped accepting Greece's bonds as collateral, which was quite sensible, as they were probably worthless. The decision however was not un-connected with the recently elected Greek government's attempt to blackmail the EU into writing off much of its debt. Blackmail of course invites retaliatory blackmail.

However even this largesse from the ECB seemed not to be working, so in 2012 *another* mechanism was wheeled out called *Outright Monetary Transactions* (OMT), whereby the ECB would buy unlimited amounts of — you've guessed it — short-term Spanish and Italian government bonds. And all this very wonderful SMP, LTRO and OMT, which sound rather like obscure sexual practices, occurred *before* the Germans could be persuaded to accept (which in fact they didn't) outright *Quantitive Easing* (QE) in 2015. The ECB, described as the "soup kitchen" for Europe's banks, *"was starting to resemble one of those problem drinkers, who started off life teetotal. One day they try a small sherry, then before you know it they are on the scotch, and they end up sleeping on a park bench with a bottle of lighter fluid."*[4] The scale of QE is indeed a little worrying to those of a nervous disposition. It took the US Federal Reserve 94 years to grow its balance sheet to $900bn. Within *six weeks* of the Lehman collapse in September 2008 it had *doubled its balance sheet* and by the end of the year the latter had ballooned it *to over $4 trillion*. It is interesting to learn that by October 1981 the US national debt had reached $1 trillion — a sum that had taken *more than 205 years to accumulate*. The second trillion dollars was accomplished *in less than five years*. Does that make you a bit queasy? Similar policies elsewhere have brought Central Bank balance sheets worldwide up to three times pre-crisis level at $16 trillion. Getting scared? The effect has been massive inflation of asset prices — but meanwhile the world's aggregate debt burden has continued to grow from 175 per cent of world GDP to almost 220 per cent, despite all the talk of austerity. Feeling suicidal yet? The Central Bankers seem to be.[5]

The Director of Asian Capital Partners writing to the *Financial Times* says that all this has to stop, since we know from the example of Japan (twenty years and climbing of stagnation) what happens when you pour money into banks that does not magically flow out again into investment and consumption. All you do is rescue — or in fact reward – fecklessness, drive up asset prices and ruin people on fixed incomes. His solution?

---

4 Philip Coggan: *The Last Vote: The Threats to Western Democracy* (Penguin Books, London, 2014) Pp. 186-189.

5 Figures quoted by Helena Morrissey in "QE addiction has made us too complacent", *Sunday Telegraph* 21 December 2014.

Stop policies of extend and pretend: *"Bite the bullet. Reprice the assets. Write off the unpayable debt. Smite the unwary. Start again with a new confidence that there is an upside."*[6] The Greeks want something similar — without them having to pay for it, of course.

Realistically it will be impossible to determine whether QE has actually worked until the fall-out from withdrawing it is over. However another Asia-based strategist quoted in the *Financial Times*[7] observes that it has effectively been a device for channelling money to the "Mayfair economy" of the rich and "boosting the price of Warhols". For pensioners on fixed incomes or ordinary citizens with bank deposits, on the other hand, it has resulted in negative real returns over several years. As they get poorer, they are also underpinning (according to the McKinsey Global Institute) a cumulative interest rate windfall for US companies of $310bn since 2007, which increased profits by 20%. Since savers of modest means were effectively paying for this, economists at the University of Berkeley have calculated that the top 1% of the American workforce captured 95% of income gains in the first three years of the recovery. As the bankers say, that's capitalism for you.

Dan Quayle: Vice-President of the USA, the thinking American's John Prescott:

"I'm Dan Quayle. Who are you? (extending his hand during a campaign stop): Woman: *"I'm your Secret Service agent."*

Dan Quayle was Vice-President to George Bush Senior (1988-1993), causing some alarm to those (they were many) who thought he was an idiot and not fit to be a heartbeat away from the Presidency. His *obiter dicta* did indeed range from the oxymoronic or fatuous to the mildly unhinged, e.g. "I believe we are on an irreversible trend toward more freedom and democracy — but that could change"[8] or: "A low voter turnout is an indication of fewer people going to the polls." Or: "Who would

6 Letter to the *Financial Times*, by Paul Serfaty of Asian Capital Partners, 22nd of January 2015.

7 Quoted in an article by John Plender in the *Financial Times*, 11/12-01-2014, *"Recession has revived labour's struggle against capital."*

8 Compare and contrast Dwight D. Eisenhower's profound observation: *"Things have never been more like the way they are today in history."*

Dan Quayle: "I deserve respect for the things I did not do."

have predicted that Dubcek, who brought the tanks into Czechoslovakia in 1968 is now being proclaimed a hero in Czechoslovakia. Unbelievable!" Or: "When I have been asked during these last weeks who caused the riots and the killing in L.A., my answer has been direct and simple: Who is to blame for the riots? The rioters are to blame. Who is to blame for the killings? The killers are to blame".

A school of thought claims that Quayle was in fact a first-rate comedian who was simply misunderstood by the joyless critics of the liberal press. Seen in that light, some of his gags are excellent, for example "Republicans have been accused of abandoning the poor. It's the other way around. They never vote for us." Or: "Bank failures are caused by depositors who don't deposit enough money to cover losses due to mismanagement." Or: "I am not part of the problem. I am a Republican." Or: "This President is going to lead us out of this recovery." Or: "Our party has been accused of fooling the public by calling tax increases 'revenue enhancement'. Not so. No one was fooled ."

Nor did the reptiles seem to appreciate his subtle satirical cameo on the relations between education and power when he wrongly corrected a 12-year-old's spelling of the plural of the word "potato" on a visit to a school. As Quayle himself has perceptively observed, "people that are

398

really very weird can get into sensitive positions and have a tremendous impact on history." And surely no one could quarrel with his remark "What a waste it is to lose one's mind. Or not to have a mind is being very wasteful. How true that is."

To the end Quayle remained insouciantly cheerful and unrepentant against the onslaught of the press, saying defiantly that he "stood by all his misstatements" and adding "I deserve respect for the things I did not do" — which was certainly true. He then made a dignified exit with a splendid parting shot: "This isn't a man who is leaving with his head between his legs."

Queen Mother: National treasure with a fondness for gin:
The Queen Mother's 100th birthday was celebrated by the British press with a fulsomeness which would surely have made Stalin green with envy. There was a 12 page supplement in the *Sunday Times*, a "definitive" 16 page pull out in the *Sunday Telegraph* and a *Mail on Sunday* part-work running to more than 50 pages. 50 pages! This was a stupendous feat by the reptiles, considering there wasn't much to say about the Queen Mum, but besotted royalist Paul Johnson said it anyway, listing her achievements as: "opening things and saying a few well-chosen words, fishing, remembering faces, singing in church ..." Lord Bell of Belgravia (*sic*) let us in on her secret weapon in the ratings war: "Not giving interviews — it's a brilliant ploy. Absolutely nobody knows what she thinks about anything." Assuming, of course, that she actually did think anything about anything...

Awkward questions: For example those posed by Euro-MP Daniel Hannan, a thorn in the flesh for EU-zealots:
According to the OECD, writes Hannan, per capita GDP in the EFTA countries (Norway, Switzerland, Liechtenstein and Iceland before the crash) was *double* that in the EU. "But Iceland has fish!" (So would we have, but for the ocean-going disaster of the Common Fisheries Policy.) "Norway has oil!" (Britain is the only net exporter of oil in the EU.) "Switzerland has banks!" (London is the world's premier financial centre, though the EU is trying to change that.) It is true that Britain does not export false teeth, like Liechtenstein, but our huge ***trade deficit*** with the **EU** is not only down to false teeth. EFTA nations export *more per head to the EU from outside than Britain does from inside.*

I mention in passing that in 2013 the EU's auditors refused to sign off the accounts for the 19th year running, with six billion pounds spent in error in that year…

The West Lothian Question: A question concerning the right of Scottish MPs to vote in the British House of Commons on matters purely affecting England, when and if English MPs cannot vote on matters devolved to Scotland:

This question was first raised in 1977 by the political gadfly Tam Dalyell, Labour MP for West Lothian, and has been annoying constitutionalists and pedants ever since. It is doubtful whether people outside the Westminster village understand what the question actually is, still less what the answer to it might be. There has been talk of "Grand Committees," "Double Majorities" and "Fourth Readings" as possible solutions, but no one has the foggiest idea what all that means.

On the other hand, people could well understand that Labour, with its 40 Scottish seats controlled by hitherto "genetically programmed" Labour voters, could and did bring in legislation whereby university fees were charged to students in England and Wales but not to Scottish students (because legislation on education is devolved there). This produced the Gilbertian situation whereby students from the EU could attend the Scottish universities without paying fees (since discrimination between EU countries is not allowed), but English students were charged the full whack of nine thousand pounds a year.

After the referendum of September 2014 which rejected Scottish independence, the role of the 40 Scottish labour seats became even more topical, especially when it appeared that the labour-programmed genes of their electors had mutated to Scottish Nationalist. Apparently they were no longer content to be represented by drunks and incompetents who were chiefly there to serve as cannon fodder for a Labour government in the House of Commons.

The simple answer to the West Lothian question is of course equal devolution for all the constituent parts of the United Kingdom including England, which is recommended by dissident Tory MPs like Daniel Hannan. However this looks menacingly like the break-up of the UK. Besides which there could be disputes about whether an issue really only affects one part of the United Kingdom rather than another. As Andy McSmith puts it: "Even if the political party that controls the Commons also holds a majority of English seats, there could be arguments about what constitutes "English" legislation. For instance, suppose the government decided to abolish the London Assembly - is that an "English" or a "UK" matter? By what logic does it concern the MP for Berwick, in the far north of England, but not his parliamentary neighbour in Berwickshire, on the other side of the border?

But the real difficulties would begin if there was one party or coalition in control of the UK Parliament, while a different party or coalition controlled a majority of English seats. You would then have a Prime Minister who could not introduce legislation affecting the public services for 85 per cent of the population, and an opposition leader who controls these public services but has no formal position in the government. Would the English MPs be allowed to make decisions that cost money, and how would they raise the necessary taxes?"[9]

At this point in the discussion most people heave a sigh and go off to the pub: as a political wiseacre has put it, *"The best answer to the West Lothian question is to stop asking it."*

Questionable aphrodisiacs: What to use when Viagra fails:
According to Aristotle, "erection is chiefly caused by parsnips, artichokes, turnips, asparagus, candied ginger, acorns bruised to powder and drunk in muscadet, scallion and shellfish." Pliny's recommended Viagra was a gum known as dragon's blood, but it is expensive to obtain and is therefore unlikely to become available on the NHS. It can only be extracted from a dragon crushed by a dying elephant.

The Qianlong Emperor [Chien-lung Emperor; born Hongli (**Hung-li**; *Chinese*: 弘曆)]: Genocidal Chinese ruler who appears to have suffered from *cacoethes scribendi*:[10]

The genocide visited upon the Zunghars (a Mongolian people) and the Qing extermination of the Jinchuan Tibetans in 1776 are a slight

9 Andy McSmith: "What is the West Lothian Question and can it be resolved satisfactorily?" *The Independent*, 4th July, 2006.

10 Wikipedia translates this famous Latin tag as *"the insatiable desire to write:"* Cacoëthes ("bad habit", or medically, "malignant disease") is a borrowing from Greek *kakóēthes*. The phrase is derived from a line in the *Satires* of Juvenal: *Tenet insanabile multos scribendi cacoethes*, or "the incurable desire (or itch) for writing affects many". See also *hypergraphia* (which, however, is a medical condition associated with epilepsy.)

The Quianlong emperor posing for a publicity shot...

embarrassment by comparison with the cultural and other military achievements of Qianlong's very successful rule (1736-1795). The Emperor was *inter alia* a great patron, a collector and prolix author. Unnervingly for those who had to read and praise them, he produced over 40,000 poems and 1,300 prose texts. On the other hand, he was equally assiduous in destroying texts he disapproved of, namely those that betrayed even a hint of criticism of the Manchus. The censor would "judge any single character or any single sentence's neutrality; if the authority had decided these words, or that sentence were derogatory or cynical towards the rulers, then persecution would begin."[11] In Qianlong's time, says Wikipedia, there were 53 cases of *literary inquisition*, resulting in the victims being beheaded, or corpses being mutilated, or victims being slowly sliced into pieces until death occurred. In addition about 3,100 works and 150,000 copies of books were either burned or banned. At least it can be said that Qianlong preferred incinerating the books to executing their authors, except in the most recidivist cases.

In 1792 George III sent an emissary to the Emperor in a bid to open up Chinese trade, then limited to Canton. One reason for this initiative was that the British were running a large deficit with China due to the fashionable obsession with tea-drinking in the United Kingdom. Sadly Qianlong sent the emissary packing with a note to the king pointing out that the Celestial Empire *"possesses all things in prolific abundance and lacks no product within its borders. There was therefore no need to*

11 R. Kent Guy: *The Emperor's Four Treasures* (Harvard University Press, 1987). P. 167.

402

import the manufactures of outside barbarians in exchange for our own produce."[12] Like the Americans today, the British could not understand how something so beneficial to themselves should be resisted on such piffling grounds. They stepped up their Indian opium supplies to China and in 1840 started the first Opium War, in which the Chinese were brutally crushed and forced into the arrangements that the victors were absolutely sure were for the Chinese's own good. Ha-Joon Chang has pointed out that Qianlong's economic theory was "*in line with the mainstream view among European economists, including Adam Smith, at the time.*" The British government's view, however, backed up by violent and criminal action, was a portent of things to come, whereby an economically powerful country forces weaker nations to open up their markets under the slogan of "free trade" (themselves always being ready, of course, to slap on import tariffs at home should domestic politics require them.)

Quintin Hogg (Lord Hailsham): A Conservative loose canon:
Hailsham invented the phrase "*elective dictatorship*" to characterise the way in which British parliamentary majorities increasingly failed to reflect the views of the voters under the "first past the post" electoral system. This was a surprising admission from a Tory (and certainly not well-received by his colleagues, who preferred to keep quiet about such things), but it was prescient. It applied to varying degrees both to eighteen years of Tory hegemony and to New Labour. Towards the end of the latter's long period in government (1997 to 2010) Tony Blair was being elected with handsome parliamentary majorities by around a quarter of those eligible to vote.

In June 1963, when his fellow Minister John Profumo had to resign after admitting having lied to Parliament about having slept with Christine Keeler, Hailsham extravagantly and self-righteously attacked his errant colleague in a television interview. Fox-hunting Labour MP Sir Reginald Paget dubbed this "a virtuoso performance of the art of kicking a friend in the guts," adding magnificently:"*When self-indulgence has reduced a man to the shape of Lord Hailsham, sexual continence involves no more than a sense of the ridiculous*"

12 Ha-Joon Chang: *Economics: The User's Guide* (Pelican, London, 2014), Pp. 407-8.

Quintin Hogg, Lord Hailsham, anticipating Vladimir Putin's naked self-promotion...

"*The best way I know of to win an argument is to start by being in the right*" was one of his more engaging insights, but nothing provoked such disrespectful hilarity as his casual reference to "*the total integrity that marks all leaders of the legal profession.*" Lord Denning (q.v.) could not have put it better…

Family quotations: An English-Hungarian book of 1,000 Family Quotations (*1,000 családias idézet*) bears the engaging title: "*If You Leave Me, Can I Come Too?*"[13]

A subsequent volume in this popular series is entitled "*Which is the Non-Smoking Lifeboat?*"

The two nations, Britain and Hungary, share a penchant for black humour, e.g. "I can't think of anything worse after a night of drinking than

13 Compiled by Salamon Gábor and Zalotay Melinda and published by Pécsi Direkt Kft. and Alexandra Kiadója, Pécs, Hungary.

waking up next to someone and not being able to remember their name, or how we met, or why they're dead."

And what about: "Sacred cows make the best hamburger"?

Or: "The only evidence against evolution is its opponents."

Or this from American comedienne Elayne Boosler: "Have you ever noticed that the same people who are against abortion are for capital punishment? Typical fisherman's attitude: throw them back when they're small and kill them when they're bigger."

And here's one for Central Europeans, attributed to Bette Midler: "I married a German. Every night I dress up as Poland and he invades me."

R

Road:

A strip of land along which one may pass from where it is too tiresome to be to where it is futile to go.

Ambrose Bierce: *The Devil's Dictionary*

Rabbi: Counsellor on religious rectitude with remarkable rules-bending skills:

Rabbis are essentially teachers (not simply priests, as gentiles commonly suppose.) Tales of their pawky humour and sly wisdom are legion, the following being not untypical:

"Rabbi Bloom was having trouble getting together a *minyan* (quorum of ten for prayers). Several families with strong anti-war views had recently left his synagogue and taken up the Quaker faith. "It can't be helped," he lamented. "It seems some of my best Jews are Friends.""[1]

There are of course many jokes *about* rabbis, some of them unintentional. *The Guardian*, for instance, has a reputation for entertaining misprints, followed by equally entertaining corrections to their gaffes, e.g.: "*In our panel of Glastonbury highlights this summer we listed a band as 'Frightened Rabbi.' Several readers have pointed out that this should read 'Frightened Rabbit.' *" Rabbis, of course, are never frightened; on the contrary they exhibit the Jewish quality of *chutzpah* to an advanced degree. "Rabbi Bloom," said an admirer, "you really know everything!" "That too," said Bloom…

It has been said that "*calling a taxi in Texas is like calling a rabbi in Iraq*":[2] And if you travel in an exorbitantly expensive black cab in Lon-

---

1 David Minkoff: *The Ultimate Book of Jewish Jokes* (Portico Books, London, 2010), P. 206.
2 Fran Lebowitz.

don, you are quite likely to be lectured by a rabbinical simulacrum whose wisdom alone is worth the price of the ride.

Unfortunately, however, not all rabbis are such pussycats. One Rabbi Yaacov Perrin, speaking at the funeral of a Jewish extremist who had massacred 29 Palestinians, is quoted in *The New York Times* (1994)[3] as saying that "one million Arabs are not worth a Jewish fingernail"

Railtrack: A business model pioneered in the UK for selling, buying and reselling the same entity, always at the cost of the taxpayers:

In November 2000 Railtrack's stockmarket value was 5 billion pounds, or exactly the amount that had been paid to it in subsidies by the Labour government since 1997. At this time, it was aptly described as *"a bankrupt private monopoly subsidised by taxpayers,"* the latter having been expropriated without compensation, or, (if they were shareholders) having been sold something they already owned. Not so much "property is theft" as "theft is property"…[4]

Rant: Expression used by conservative-minded commentators to describe a well-argued leftist polemic to which, for the moment, they do not have the answers. Conversely a term used by liberal or left-liberal commentators to avoid engaging with a well-calibrated critique of their shibboleths that has somehow avoided their policing and got into the mainstream media.

In his book on *The Tyranny of Experts* William Easterly demonstrates how this left-right syndrome works in the field of development, though it could be applied equally well elsewhere: "If you deviate from what the political Center deems to be Centrist, you slide down a perceptional slippery slope toward "ideologue." Audiences sometimes look for code words that imply the writer is too extreme. Mention *markets* and you are presumed to favour a world with zero government. Mention *liberty* too often and you are presumed to be in favour of some extreme right-wing ideology. Mention Friedrich Hayek's book *The Road to Serfdom* and you are presumed to be to the right of ranting talk-show hosts.

---

3 Quoted in *The New York Times* of February 28th, 1994, the remark having been made the day before at the funeral of Baruch Goldstein, an extremist who had run amok.

4 Pierre-Joseph Proudhon: *"Qu'est- ce que la propriété? C'est le vol."* (1840).

Less commonly recognized is a perceptional slippery slope on the left. If you mention *colonialism, racism,* or *imperialism* too often, as concepts still relevant to understanding development past and present, you risk being seen as a leftist ideologue." In fact, he says, "rebels against the technocratic consensus come from both left and right, and they often hold incompatible views on almost everything else."[5] It would be helpful if someone told the BBC Current Affairs editors this; they could bear it in mind as they prepare another non-productive discussion whereby a dreary propagandist perceived to be "on the left" tries to score points off an equally dreary propagandist "on the right" [*See also* **B: Bias**].

So "*rant,*" like "*bias,*" is a slippery concept in the hands of our media princes and their myrmidons. The tendency is to believe one's own propaganda. This was not the mistake made by Adlai Stevenson, the wet dream of a presidential candidate for American liberals in the 1950s. On being told that he would have the support of "*every thinking man in America,*" he replied: "*Yes, but I need a majority.*"

The London Library's Readership Survey: Lost books and lost causes: The survey threw up, *inter alia,* this response: "I would caution against discarding any book solely on the grounds that it has not been taken out for a long time. I relish the fact that we have a *two-volume history of the wheelbarrow* and a *folio volume on the history of the telephone in Brazil before 1908.* We must not lose such as these."

As Thomas Fuller (1608-1661) sagely observed, "*Learning hath gained most by those books by which the printers have lost.*"

And as Frank Zappa, with equal sagacity, pointed out: "*If you want to get laid, go to college. If you want an education, go to the library.*"

***Readers' letters in* The Guardian:** A useful barometer of political correctness:

One rather charming feature of letters to *The Guardian* used to be the effort devoted by left-leaning intellectuals to correcting misunderstandings that had regrettably arisen over Communism. After the reunification of Germany, one writer informed us that 73% of his former compatriots in East Germany still hankered after "socialism," and "a significant per-

---

5 William Easterly: *The Tyranny of Experts: Economists, Dictators, and the Forgotten Rights of the Poor* (Basic Books, New York, 2013) Pp.12-13.

centage" wanted the wall back. "The image of the GDR as a totally repressive regime, as portrayed in the film *The Lives of Others*," he continues, "is as much a travesty as the image of it as a socialist paradise." So true! Now let's see if this one will fly: "*The image of Stalin's Russia as a place where some twenty million people were judicially murdered and/or sent to labour camps is as much a travesty as the image of it as 'the future that works.'*" Not bad, eh? The *Guardian* letter writer himself (an asylum-seeker from the Federal Republic of Germany?) actually lives in Aberystwyth, presumably intending to return home only when the wall is rebuilt.

Readers' Letters in **The Daily Telegraph:** A useful barometer of political incorrectness:

Letters to the *The Telegraph* not infrequently begin with the phrase "*Am I alone in thinking…?*" — to which usually the correct response is: "*Yes, you are, you reactionary old fart…*"

Religion: A justification for good behaviour — or bad behaviour:

> *The inhabitants of the earth are of two sorts:*
> *Those with brains but no religion,*
> *And those with religion, but no brains.*

> Abu'l-Alā' al-Ma'arri (died 1057)

The following anecdote once appeared in the annual newsletter for the alumni of an English preparatory school: "An ancient Dean of Christ Church is said to have given three reasons for the study of Greek: the first was that it enabled you to read the words of our Saviour in the original tongue; the second, that it gave you a proper contempt for those who were ignorant of it; and the third that it led to situations of emolument." Commenting on this, A.C. Benson observed: "The first reason is probably erroneous, the second is un-Christian, and the third is a gross motive which would equally apply to any professional training whatsoever."

Reparations: Useful tactic by means of which poor, misgoverned, countries extract money from richer and better governed ones. Following a war, reparations are a method of putting together the ingredients for the next one:

A Mr Kaur, writing to the *Financial Times* from the Punjab, points out that "the reparation movement" (such as the demands of Jamaica for large sums of money from the UK for having sponsored the slave trade) is not so much about justice as about blackmailing the descendants of European colonizers, since the latter, unlike their non-European counterparts, tend to feel overly guilty about their ancestor's deeds. "Take, for example the case of India. The country was colonized, wholly or partly, not just by the British but also by the Turks, Persians, Afghans, Portuguese, Uzbeks and Mongols. Why are Indians singling out the British for reparations, while letting other colonizers get away with it, although their rule did far more damage to India's cultural heritage? Maybe Indians know only too well that not only will they receive no reparations from the Turks, Arabs, Persians etc.; they will also politely be told where to get off" (or possibly not so politely.) And while we're on the subject, how's that Nigerian court case going, by means of which the descendants of those sold into slavery by tribal chiefs are suing descendants of the said chiefs for repayment to them of the monies they earned by betraying their own people into slavery? Not too well, I fear.

Ronald Reagan: "Government's first duty is to protect the people, not run their lives."

Ronald "Sunrise in America" Reagan: American politician after whom the Ronald Reagan Roundabout in Wroclaw (Poland) is named:

Leftist historians have spilled much ink in a desperate effort to demonstrate that Reagan contributed *nothing*, but **nothing**, to the demise of the Soviet Union, but it is hard to make the resentments of academe stick to the Teflon president. Likewise he got away with a splendidly cavalier attitude to the enormous deficits that now worry us all so much. "*I don't worry about the deficit*," he once said cheerily, "*it's big enough to take care of itself.*"

410

Reagan's Republican successors and would-be successors just don't have the right touch to woo the reptiles. Not untypical is Florence King's thumbnail sketch in *The Spectator* of Mitt Romney, he of the mortician's smile and implausible jeans. According to King, "*Romney gives the distinct impression that somebody started to embalm him and then stopped.*"

Which reminds one of Disraeli's crack about Robert Peel, namely that he had "*a smile like the silver fittings on a coffin.*"

Regietheater: Terrifying German word for "director-dominated" opera, in which left-leaning egomaniacs turn some inoffensive masterpiece into a vehicle for clichéd agitprop:

For example, *New Yorker* music critic Alex Ross tells of a "*Ballo in maschera*," that "featured the ruins of the World Trade Centre, a cast of Elvis impersonators, naked elderly persons in Mickey Mouse masks and a woman dressed as Hitler." "I have seen," he says wearily, " a *Tristan* which took place entirely inside a pulsating pink cube, a *Ring* whose Wotan expressed his desperation by feeding papers into a shredder, and a *Parsifal* where the climactic transfiguration of the Grail Temple was accompanied by footage of decomposing rabbits."

Regietheater also involved ideological programme notes, often written by East Germans, whose sense of humour is of course legendary. Beside the half-baked Marxist guff about "issues" and "alienation", Sigmund Fraud was an obligatory "name-check" (e.g. in a note on *Elektra*: "Hugo von Hofmannsthal knew Freud, whereas the Greeks did not" — who would have believed it?) The great Viennese critic, Marcel Prawy, finally could stand it no longer: "*Regietheater*," he thundered, "is the AIDS of the opera world."

Remuneration: "*Too much for what I do, too little for what I can do*" (Mozart commenting on his salary for a minor musical post at the Habsburg court.)

In these troubled times jokes tend to surface about remuneration, or lack of it. For instance, the website RollOnFriday jests that "*lawyers, hookers and plumbers are the only people who still charge by the hour,*" though it seems to have overlooked accountants preparing "frandits." (q.v.)

Authors mostly do not charge by the hour, or if they do, no one takes any notice. They are lucky if they get paid at all since publishing is no longer producer-led and publishers are obliged to give ruinous discounts to Amazon etc. Authors are paid a percentage of the discounted "recommended retail price" and since the discounts demanded by the retailers are not uncommonly 50–60 per cent, the average author will get an occasional paltry cheque — that is, when the publishers remember to send it. Still, since there is probably a two or three hundred per cent oversupply of would-be authors, the publishers have rightly spotted that the latter don't really need to be paid at all according to the principles of demand and supply, save in the unlikely event an author hits bestsellerdom and becomes a valuable property.

Small wonder therefore that an embitterd scribbler has claimed *"nowadays, if your book is not on Richard and Judy's list* [of titles recommended by these popular TV presenters], *the only profitable form of writing is ransom notes."* Bankers, on the other hand, have devised a bullet-proof form of remuneration to be paid regardless of performance (if the bank has done well you deserve a bonus, and if it has imploded, the staff must be "incentivised" to put it right.) There are remuneration committees to enforce this system for the CEOs of large companies, which traditionally include two or three "compensation consultants" identified by the saintly Warren Buffet as the ever-pliable "Messrs. Ratchet, Ratchet and Bingo." Speaking at a Berkshire Hathaway annual shareholders meeting, Buffett rather bluntly referred to these compensation consultants as prostitutes; whereat his vice chairman Charles Munger objected that *"prostitution would be a step up for them."* (See also **B: *Warren Buffett.***)

Ernest Renan: Liberal scholar who managed the remarkable feat of enraging *both* Jews *and* Christians:

Renan regarded Judaism as pretty much hocus pocus, while Jesus Christ he believed should be researched like any other historical figure, two approaches that did not go down well with pious Jews and the Christian hierarchy... "Never has any one been less a priest than Jesus," he wrote in his *Life of Christ* (1863), "never a greater enemy of forms, which stifle religion under the pretext of protecting it. By this we are all his disciples and his successors; by this he has laid the eternal foundation-stone of true religion..."

Renan also annoyed patriots. According to Renan, *"a nation ... is a group of people united by a mistaken view of the past and a hatred of their neighbours*"[6] (but then he was, of course, a Frenchman.) For good measure he added that "*Forgetfulness and historical error are essential in the creation of a nation.*"

The great Viennese playwright and comedian Johann Nestroy had a more oblique view of nationhood, perhaps stemming from the Austrian experience of running a fractious multi-national empire: "*Of all nations,*" he wrote, "*the noblest nation is resignation…*"

Ernest Renan: "*God, if there is a God, take my soul, if I have a soul…*"

Rent-seeking: "Using market position to make money without adding value:"[7]

Rent-seeking, a close relative of monopoly, is somewhat more subjectively defined than the latter. However its core notion is the process whereby businesses are able to screw money out of customers or clients without providing anything of commensurate value in return, neither in terms of goods nor services.

For example, in the 1970s there was a patch of tarmac adjacent to London's Battersea tennis courts where those who had booked and paid for an hour's play could park their cars. One day the would-be Federers drove up to find a shabby and faintly inebriated individual in a yellow flare jacket standing beside a small portable sign at the entrance to this area and demanding money on behalf a car-parking firm that had just been awarded the concession by the local council. Most people just drove straight at him, causing him to jump for his life.

Then again firms in the business of parking control abuse their concessions from the borough councils by setting quotas for their operatives

6 In a lecture entitled *Qu'est-ce qu'une nation* given in 1882.

7 As defined by former Labour Party activist Matthew Taylor, Chief Executive of the charity RSA.

to rake in a specified minimum of money, which of course leads to falsely issued penalties and arbitrary interpretation of the regulations. Something sold as being for the advantage of the local tax payers has been turned into rent-seeking persecution of the same, with the added refinement that the victims are paying the salaries of the persecutors.

Rent-seeking thrives where customers can be faced with a Hobson's choice — accept the blackmail of the rent-seeker, or let yourself in for endless hassle that costs as much in time and money as the amount you would save by achieving a reasonable charge. Hire car franchises are particularly adept at working this one — quietly adding the cost of a full tank of petrol to a car that was returned filled up, accidentally charging twice for "cleaning," and other "clerical errors" such as transferring some damage from another car to the one you hired. Since they have an open-ended charge on your credit card, it is extremely difficult to challenge all these items which are down to the company's word against yours — something that is of course built into the "business model." By the same token, venerable institutions such as the postal service exploit the captive customer by keeping rent-seeking below the radar until the victim unexpectedly finds himself confronted with it. Take, for example, cross-border parcel deliveries in the EU. The *Financial Times* reported in 2015 that a finely calibrated racket had opened up on the postage front to exploit trans-national deliveries of internet purchases. The European Commission discovered that a 2kg parcel delivery in Austria with the national post operator would cost 4.44 Euros; but to have the same parcel sent to neighbouring Italy would cost *14 Euros*. Bit steep? Try then sending the same parcel back to Austria from Italy and the cost rose to *25 Euros*. To send the same parcel weight from the Netherlands to Spain cost 13 Euros, which is quite a lot, given that we supposedly live in something claiming to be a single market; but *to send it back again* from Spain to the Netherlands *cost a staggering 32.74 Euros*.[8] So obviously the amount charged has not the faintest relation to the cost of providing the service and the system is no more ethical than a protection racket.

Philip Coggan has described the rent-seeking of the financial sector leading up to the crisis of 2008. The enormous rise in incomes for those working in the sector could be explained neither by the superior skills of

8 Jim Brunsden: "Brussels vows to crack down on cross-border postal prices" (*Financial Times*, 22nd December, 2015.)

those working there, nor by new technology (for example, the pay rates of engineers did not boom in the same way.) The real reason was that someone else was taking the business risk for their activities (e.g. via implicit or explicit government guarantees), while insured deposits meant that banks enjoyed cheap funding.

Another factor is that fund managers' fees are based on a percentage of the value of funds under management, so they profited inordinately in the long bull market from 1982 to 2000 — and again as a result of Quantitive Easing following the financial crisis. Such matters of chance were allied to chicanery and information asymmetry — the clients could not inform themselves as well as the insiders and were frequently sold dud investments as a result, while the financial adviser took his cut whether investments did well or badly. Clients of fund managers also didn't realise that the latter were charging them to look after their money and then dipping into customers' funds to buy the services to do the job, a gravy train that *inter alia* generated reams of unread research. Practitioners claim the research business will be hugely affected if fund managers have to finance it themselves, which *"speaks volumes about the perceived value of the product"* in what the *Financial Times* describes as a *"producer racket."*

Lastly, with so much money at its disposal the finance sector could lobby its way out of regulation. When the US Commodity Futures Trading Commission wanted to regulate financial derivatives in 1997, its Chairman was telephoned by the Deputy Treasury Secretary (Larry Summers), who said: *"I have thirteen bankers in my office and they say if you go forward with this you will cause the worst financial crisis since the World War II."*[9] (It was of course the bankers themselves who caused the worst financial crisis since World War II.)

Devastating Replies: The Hungarian for this is *"Lépcsőházi szelle-messég,"* or *"the brilliantly witty retort that I failed to think of at the dinner party, but which occurred to me as I was departing down the stairs"* (Hungarian is a very condensed language). The French call it *"l'esprit de l'escalier."*

Politicians of course need to be well equipped mentally for the knock-down reply, since they are almost daily subjected to impertinence and

---

9 Philip Coggan: *The Last Vote: The Threats to Western Democracy* (Penguin Books, London, 2014) Pp. 208-9.

abuse which is best dealt with by replying in kind but with more wit. Disraeli and Churchill were masters of this art. For example, the former was once told by an irate member of Parliament that he (Disraeli) would *"either die on the gallows or of some unspeakable disease."* *"That depends,"* said Disraeli, *"on whether I embrace your policies or your mistress."* But the crushing reply may not occur to the person concerned soon enough. G.K. Chesterton described a rising young politician who had got his public speaking act admirably together: "When he thought of a joke, he made it, and was called brilliant. When he could not think of a joke, he said that this was no time for trifling, and was called able…"

Harold Macmillan excelled at excellently honed punchlines. When Lord Carrington reported to him that Senator Muskie, campaigning for the US presidency, had broken down in tears on the hustings because a newspaper had accused his wife of being a drunkard, Macmillan expressed astonishment. *"Well,"* said Lord Carrington, *"what would you have done if Lady Dorothy*[10] *was similarly accused?"* Macmillan thought for a moment and replied: *"I would have said: '***You should have seen her mother***!'* "

A lot of liberals underestimated Ronald Reagan's capacity for good humoured but highly effective mockery of po-faced opponents. In the 1984 TV debate with Walter Mondale, the presidential candidate for the Democrats, Mondale evidently thought that stressing Reagan's age (he was 73) was a promising tactic to unsettle the old boy in front of the cameras. Reagan landed the perfect riposte: *"I will not make age an issue of this campaign,"* he said. *"I am not going to exploit, for political purposes, my opponent's youth and inexperience."*

A mistress of the devastating reply was the feisty Liverpudlian actress, Thora Hird. On an evening during World War II, she was making her way across London's Piccadilly in the black-out after performing in a show. A drunken G.I. mistook her for a prostitute and demanded to know how much she charged. She thought this over carefully for a minute, but no figure came to mind. *"Well, luv,"* she said at last, *"I really don't know. How much do your mother and sisters charge?"*

Restructuring: Business euphemism for panic-stricken measures following a company's near-death experience:

10 Macmillan's wife.

416

Restructuring businesses: Sacking people, cutting the dividend, paying off the megalomaniacal CEO with a huge cheque, selling off the dud businesses very expensively acquired by said megalomaniac (which is described as "*concentrating on the core business*"), sacking people, stopping the dividend, selling off the executive jet(s) and yachts, abolishing "defined benefit" pensions (except of course for senior managers), sacking people, buying cheaper coffee and fewer toilet rolls for the offices, sacking people....

Restructuring banks: Revealing the true state of the bank's liabilities previously concealed by fraudits, sacking people, removing the dividend, paying off the CEO with an enormous cheque, sacking people, placing advertisements on the London underground featuring a wholesome young lady saying she wants the bank to be your friend, paying out compensation for all the products the bank had previously mis-sold, paying enormous fines to the financial regulators for same, sacking people...

Economists and the financial pages of the newspapers are also fond of referring to "*structural reforms*" required by the EU in those member states that are technically or actually insolvent. In the case of Greece these requirements included undertakings to sack about a third of the country's civil servants, reduce spending on pensions, welfare and Greece's practically non-existent health service, stop corruption, sell (or pretend to sell) state assets at knockdown prices, embrace the novel idea of collecting taxes due, politely explain to oligarchs that it is customary in a democracy for rich people also to pay taxes, stop corruption, stop complaining so much, pay down debt, stop complaining so much, stop corruption, stop referring to Chancellor Merkel as a "Nazi" in public, stop mentioning the gold reserves stolen by Germany from Greece during World War II, sell the port of Piraeus to a Chinese gangster syndicate, sell the Akropolis to Disneyland, stop corruption, stop complaining so much...

Dr Roídi of Zante: An unfortunate poet (most poets are unfortunate): Students of the Heptanese (they are not many) have long debated whether Dr Roídi's incompetence as a medical practitioner was greater than his ineptness as a poet. After Roídi had rashly depreciated the verses of the powerful Zantean Count Comuto, the latter retaliated by destroying his medical practice. "This step," writes Romilly Jenkins, "no doubt saved many lives, but unfortunately meant he had more time for poetry."

Roídi considered his own poem on *The Passion* to be his masterpiece and was inveigled into reciting it from the cathedral pulpit before an audience "gasping and shaking with laughter," although "by turning their heads aside and cramming their handkerchiefs into their mouths they were able to convey the impression that their heavings were due to emotion." The performance ended abruptly however when Roídi himself, "moved at his own eloquence, broke down into sobs and was unable to continue."

Jean-Jacques Rousseau: Secular saint who wrote sentimentally about childhood and packed off his four (?) children to the foundling hospital:

Diderot said of Rousseau that he was "false, vain as Satan, ungrateful, cruel, hypocritical, and wicked … He sucked ideas from me, used them himself, and then affected to despise me".

However a good deal of the *philosophes'* abuse of Rousseau was down to the fact that he was unforgivably successful, each of his publications being received rapturously by the public. No author can abide another one who is praised more and sells better than himself or herself. Since his death however Rousseau has been accused of almost everything undesirable, not excluding laying the basis for nationalism and Nazism. Even the promulgation of the idea of the "noble savage" has been wrongly foisted on him by a Scots racial supremacist, who of course believed the Scots were the most racially impressive of all nations (the same line was taken by an Englishman, who of course believed that the Anglo-Saxons were the best race.)

That distinguished intellectual Mandy Rice Davies got Rousseau bang to rights with an observation she made when roughing it on a camping weekend: "*I have this innate instinct not to be unhappy. Back to nature, huh! Did you know that Rousseau used to send his laundry home to his mum?*" — which would have been quite a feat, since Rousseau's mother died of puerperal fever nine days after his birth. (Characteristically he described this as "the first of my misfortunes—" i.e. seeing the prospect of a free laundry service evaporate.) Rice Davies had obviously overlooked her antihero's assertion that "*Hatred, as well as love, renders its votaries credulous.*"

Regardless of all this, David A. Bell has given Rousseau a handy get-out-of-gaol-free card, observing that "as with any truly great writer, it is foolish to judge Rousseau by the instances where people tried to follow his advice literally, still less by the harmful things done in his name (by

418

which standard Jesus Christ does not exactly come off unblemished.)"[11] This would seem to imply that, as long as the writings can plausibly be given differing or even diametrically opposed interpretations, no author can be blamed for anything that he wrote. This is certainly a very just opinion. Could one apply it perhaps to *Mein Kampf?* It certainly is applied to the *Qur'an*…

Rousseau's genius was to achieve among his contemporaries and posterity an image that was a major improvement on the reality of his nasty selfish nature. The trick was to appeal to "authenticity." "In the name of [his] good inner nature," writes Pascal Bruckner, Rousseau "decided for himself for which faults he owes repentance and for which he can be exonerated: a lie that he told a girl in his youth bothers him more than the fact that he abandoned his offspring, a fault for which the world and society castigate him. For he knows only one idol: 'the holy truth which my heart adores,' far more real than the 'abstract concepts of the true and the false'… This is the "consummate sophistry, the entire modern movement of relativism. If only authenticity counts, then everyone is entitled, in the name of himself, to hold himself apart from the common laws that would deprive him of his fidelity to himself. Don't judge me: you would have to be me to understand me!"[12] In the same way the protagonists of modern celebrity culture have learned, often with the help of a compliant press, to project an image deeply at odds with the sordid narcissism, greed and hypocrisy of their actual lives; indeed they have perfected what Rousseau invented.

Rubbish: It's either that or art (or both).
For example, we read in the newspapers of some rubbish cleared and burned by Frankfurt's dustmen (abandoned plastic sheets of an unpleasant yellow colour.) Unfortunately this was actually a sculpture by one Michael Beutler. "*I thought construction workers had dumped their stuff on the street*," said the dustman, not unreasonably. "*There was no sign or anything to show it was a work of art.*"

11 David A. Bell, "Happy Birthday to Jean-Jacques Rousseau: Why the World's First Celebrity Intellectual Still Matters", *New Republic*, June 22nd, 2012.
12 Pascal Bruckner: *The Temptation of Innocence: Living in the Age of Entitlement* (Algora Publishing, New York, 2000) Pp. 135-136. Bruckner is quoting from Rousseau's *Les rêveries du promeneur solitaire.*

This is an artwork entitled "Where shall we go dancing tonight?" that represents the hedonism and political corruption of the 1980s. It is not the detritus from the vernissage…

In 2015 the same thing happened in a Bolzano museum. An installation supposed to represent 1980s hedonism, political corruption and … er… that sort of thing, was created by Sara Goldschmied and Eleonora Chiari, two artists from Milan. It consisted of cigarette butts, empty bottles, paper streamers, confetti, discarded shoes and clothing. Unfortunately, when cleaning staff turned up for work the next morning, they assumed that the mess was left over from the previous night's party. They promptly started throwing the objects into bin bags, after conscientiously dividing them into recycling sacks for glass, plastic and paper.

According to *The Telegraph*'s somewhat gleeful report on this,[13] work by the British artist Damien Hirst fell victim to something similar at a London gallery in 2001. A cleaner assumed that a work featuring piles of overflowing ashtrays, beer bottles and coffee cups were the

---

13 *The Telegraph*, 26th October, 2015. Nick Squires: "Art installation ends up in the bin because the cleaners thought it was rubbish."

remnants of a wild party and threw them away. *"As soon as I clapped eyes on it I sighed because there was so much mess,"* said Emmanuel Asare, the cleaner. *"I didn't think for a second that it was a work of art — it didn't look much like art to me. So I cleared it all into bin bags and dumped it."*

Willie Rushton: Humourist who didn't suffer fools gladly:
Rushton did a profitable sideline speaking at dull Rotarian dinners for not inconsiderable fees. On one occasion, as he tucked into the prawn cocktail, the businessman next to him said: "You'd better be funny tonight, considering we are paying you all this money." "I'm getting that," replied Willie, "for having to sit next to you."

Post-Soviet Russia: Dysfunctional state experiencing glorious resurgence under Gasputin (q.v.):
Writing in *The Observer,* James Meek gave us a flavour of the place: "Post-Soviet Russia is like an old prison. Everyone has been liberated. The prisoners and their jailers are free to come and go. But the prisoners have nowhere else to live, so they do up their cells and make themselves comfortable, while the jailers, with no other job to do, continue wearing their uniforms, drawing their salary and making occasional assaults on the inmates."

S

Sabbath:
*A weekly festival having its origin in the fact that
God made the world in six days and was arrested on the seventh.*

Ambrose Bierce: *The Devil's Dictionary*

Satire: What, according to Tom Lehrer, became obsolete when Henry Kissinger was awarded the Nobel Peace Prize:

Likewise the Czech-German- Austrian satirist Alexander Roda Roda observed that *"in many countries satirists are superfluous; the government makes itself ridiculous...."*

Saudi Arabia: Vicious shari'a state much courted by the British Establishment:

Not since the Foreign Office organised honorary degrees from British universities for the murderous Nicolai and Eleanor Ceauşescu of Romania had an official welcome been so oleaginous as that for King Abdullah of Saudi Arabia when he paid a visit to Britain in 2007. In a welcoming speech from which lesser men would have recoiled, the then Foreign Office Minister went out of his way to extol the *"values that we* [and the Saudis] *have in common"* [sic].

Doubtless these would be the values in the observance of which Saudi religious police once prevented teenage inmates from escaping a blazing school, because the girls weren't wearing Islamic dress. Or those in the Wahhabi literature identified by Freedom House in American mosques, which included statements that Muslims should not only "always oppose" infidels "in every way", but "hate them for their religion ... for Allah's sake", that democracy "is responsible for all the horrible wars... the number of wars it started in the 20th century alone is more than 130 wars," and that Shia and certain Sunni Muslims were infidel. Or those set out in pamphlets distributed by Saudi agencies in Britain urging the

422

beheading of apostate Muslims and the persecution of homosexuals. Not forgetting genital mutilation of women, lopping off the hands of thieves and flogging a rape *victim* for meeting a man unaccompanied by a family member. Or the death penalty for adultery, sodomy, witchcraft and sorcery. (There's a lot more of this).

Still, it was obviously reassuring to hear that the Saudis are bursting with enthusiasm for *our* values in Western Europe. For example: religious tolerance, free elections and the ability of women to live their own lives without being held hostage, battered or murdered by members of their own family. For a full list of our shared values, apply to Sir Humphrey Appleby at the FO.[1]

Selfare: The inverse of *welfare* — and very probably just as ruinous to the taxpayer and *Normalverbraucher:*[2]

The phrase describes a tendency in powerful organisations whereby the wealth created by others is appropriated by the powerful for their own consumption. Under Communism the state appropriated the fruits of individual endeavour so that, for instance, the creator of the famously frustrating Rubik Cube was denied access to most of the revenue arising from his patent. Inventions or improvements made by Communist workers in factories were appropriated by the management in the name of the factory as a whole and the rewards arising (if any) were shared out, together with a few backhanders to the factory leaders. This effectively dampened any enthusiasm there might have been for making such improvements.

Under capitalism a grisly inversion of the Communist practice now appears to be common. Unsuspecting inventors try to interest big companies in their inventions. The said companies demand to see blueprints, keep them for a month or two before turning the invention down on some more or less plausible grounds; after a few more months however

---

1 There are some who seem to think that Sir Humphrey is losing his grip these days due to the cuts and so forth. But obviously he is still at his desk navigating the tricky rapids of international diplomacy with his customary aplomb. For example, in January 2015 it was reported that Susan Kramer, the amazingly earnest Lib Dem who was then Minister for Transport in the coalition government, was provided with a valuable watch to give to Mayor of Taipei on her visit to that city. Sir Humphrey forgot to inform her that a watch is an omen of death for the Chinese...

2 "*Humorous*" [Langenscheidt] — German nomenclature for the average consumer.

they are found to be producing something amazingly similar or using an identical technical process.

In academe, selfare has long been established, though officially it is frowned upon. At its most ruthless, busy and image-conscious professors get students to do massive research which they then write up and publish to great acclaim under their own names. In many university faculties the pedagogues are far more interested in pursuing their own research than in teaching, with the consequences that may be expected. This is not entirely their fault: as the economist John Kay has pointed out, modern universities tend to prize research over teaching.[3] The triennial review of the academic production of faculty members also militates against quality teaching time, besides producing a brain-dulling flood of indifferent and jargon-ridden publications.

Another form of selfare is what J. K. Galbraith called *"corporate welfare."* This distortion of the tax system runs right across party ideologies in the USA, where candidates for office, Republican or Democrat, are dependent on huge bungs from industry and millionaires. Hence the $1.3tn of exemptions in the US tax code, *"most of which are, in effect, a welfare state for the rich."*[4]

Selfie: Advertisements for oneself in the form of photographs taken with a smart phone, often against some much less interesting or beautiful background (e.g. the *Mona Lisa*):[5]

"*Selfie*" was the "Austrian youth word of the year" in 2014, which tells you quite a lot about young Austrians. The practice of making *selfies* and the technology to do it has overtaken the old-fashioned custom whereby ladies placed their vulvas on the flash plate of the office photocopying machine and circulated the resultant images to interested parties. There are variations on the art of the *selfie*, e.g. "*belfie*" (a portrait of one's backside), "*shelfie*" (a portrait of one's bookcase full of unread but impressive-looking volumes), and "*nelfie*" (a naked "*selfie*", usually communicated through "*sexting*.")

3 In the *Financial Times*, May 21st, 2014.

4 John Micklethwait and Adrian Wooldridge, "What happened to the idea of the Great Society?" — *Financial Times*, May 23, 2014.

5 The guides at the Louvre say that the average time spent by a tourist in front of the Mona Lisa is 15 seconds.

It is said that Australians invented the term *selfie*, which would not be so surprising in that verbally inventive nation. They also gave us *"shiny bum"* for a bureaucrat and *"sticker licker"* for a traffic warden. Brevity is the soul of Australian wit and their humour wastes no time in getting to the point. As, for example, in the joke about the Bondai Beach bum, a dazzling apparition of rippling muscles with impressive equipment held together by a minuscule budgies comforter. As he strides up to a curvaceous blonde dozing on the sand, he shifts his gum to the side of his mouth and inquires with admirable conciseness: *"Say, Sheila, you wanna fuck?"* Whereat the blonde very slowly opens one eye, looks at him appraisingly, and replies: *"You sweet-talking bastard, you talked me into it."*

Sentencing consultants: American persons whose skills lie in devising arguments that persuade judges to give lenient sentences to crooked businessmen:

The consultants have had a number of successes, sparing such charmers as Michael Milken, Ivan Boesky and mega-meanie Leona Helmsley the worst rigours of punishments destined for lesser mortals.

Meanwhile one hears that the authorities have "tightened up" on the "white-collar" prison engagingly known as "Club Fed", the inmates of which have progressively "been stripped of … tennis courts, swimming pools and even golf courses."

This is really dreadful: soon they'll be putting them in cells…

Sentimentality: What was often taken to be evidence of a kind heart until we heard about lachrymose Gestapo officers swooning over the music of Schubert:

"Sentimental people," writes philosopher Roger Scruton, "respond more warmly to strangers than to those who are close to them, and are more heatedly concerned by abstract issues which demand no personal sacrifice, than by concrete obligations that cost time and energy to fulfil. Sentimental emotions are *artefacts*: they are designed to reflect credit on the one who claims them… The sentimentalist is not your friend. He enters human relationships by seduction, and leaves them by betrayal."[6]

6 Roger Scruton: *The Aesthetics of Music* (Oxford University Press, 1997), P. 486.

Sex: *"The only reason for putting a woman on a pedestal is to get a better view of her legs"*:[7]

"Sex is not the answer. Sex is the question. "Yes" is the answer" according to the American humorist Swami X. But not everyone is so enthusiastic: A.R.Ammons, acerbic poet and author of the award-winning *Garbage*, has summed matters up in a plaintive couplet entitled *Their Sex Lives*:

> *One failure on*
> *Top of another.*

"There is," wrote Karl Kraus, "no unhappier creature on earth than a fetishist who yearns for a woman's shoe and has to embrace the whole woman."

Kraus's fastidiousness puts one in mind of the disgusted complaint of *"No muffin in here!"* overheard in a London bar from a young lady on the prowl with her girlfriend. Apparently groups of girls going to night-clubs in England always make sure that at least one of them is extremely unattractive to enhance the effect of their own supposed charms. In Newcastle this anti-decoy is known as *"the grilled tomato."* The analogy is with the full English breakfast where the role of the boringly anaemic tomato is merely to highlight the devilish cholesterolic attractions of the sausage, bacon and eggs.

Brendan Francis has said that the "big difference between sex for money and sex for free is that sex for money usually costs a lot less." Money and opportunity are the perennial bugbears in the quest for sex, but Woody Allen has helpfully pointed out that "bisexuality immediately doubles your chances for a date on Saturday night."

But let's hear it from the ladies' point of view: "Sex appeal is 50% what you've got and 50% what people think you've got" (Sophia Loren). "Nature abhors a virgin — a frozen asset" (Clare Booth Luce). "Sex is a bad thing because it rumples ones clothes" (Jackie Onassis). "I thought *coq au vin* was love in a lorry" (Victoria Wood).

And let's hear it also from officialdom: "The proliferation of massage establishments in London in the last few years appears to indicate a dramatic increase in muscular disorders amongst the male population." (Environmental Health Officer quoted in the *New Statesman* in 1980).

---

7 Attributed to Vladimir Nabokov

"If this is really so, I'm glad I do not have long to live..." (Liverpool Stipendiary Magistrate in 1978, on being told that oral sex is widely practised in Britain.)

People tend not to be very candid about their sexual performance, but Richard Pryor was the exception in *Richard Pryor in Concert* (1980): "I like making love myself and I can make love for about *three minutes*. Three minutes of serious fucking and I need eight hours sleep, and a bowl of Wheaties."

Shari'a: Corpus of barbaric and vindictive laws presented by its apologists as a model of justice and mercy:

Shari'a, meaning "the way" or "the path," regulates the personal behaviour of Muslims in excruciating detail and seems to be applied either parallel to, or in place of, the secular laws of the land, depending on the prevailing degree of conservatism in the country concerned. Its best side is the mediation it may offer in civil or marital disputes, but unfortunately its bad side is enforced by zealots and vigilantes of uncertain legitimacy and has become a licence for violent persecution, especially of women. Though you would hardly think it from the presentation of *shari'a* by Islamic apologists, and the down-playing of its obnoxious oppression by anxious western liberals, *shari'a* has been declared "*incompatible with the fundamental principles of democracy*" by the European Court of Human Rights (2003). This did not prevent the Law Society in the UK effectively trying to smuggle *shari'a* into Britain's legal system as parallel law when it issued guidelines to England's 125,000 solicitors on how to draw up "*shari'a* compliant" wills. Nicholas Fluck, the then President of The Law Society, had the gall to say the guidance would promote "good practice" in applying Islamic principles in the British legal system.

Although this was initially done very discreetly, when the news got out it provoked outrage, especially among those concerned to protect Muslim women from discrimination. After sullenly defending the move for a while, the Law Society eventually caved in and apologised. As *The Telegraph* wrote at the time: "*The Society had issued a practice note to solicitors effectively enshrining aspects of Islamic law in the British legal system. The guidelines advised High Street solicitors on how to write Islamic wills in a way that would be recognised by courts in England and Wales. They set out principles which meant that women could*

In Paradise the 72 'gazelle-eyed' houris with 'swelling breasts' await the Jihadist heroes...

be denied an equal share of inheritances while unbelievers could be excluded altogether." [8]

One of the more amusing aspects of this was the behaviour of the lady at the Law Society leading its "equality and diversity committee," who had recently been on a "speed networking" day in the City of London to highlight the fact that women lawyers were being discriminated against by the male-dominated legal establishment. However when the Law Society decided to reinforce the male chauvinism of Islam and the *shari'a*, the same lady turned on a sixpence and supported female discrimination in the interests of multiculturalism. [9] Obviously if you are a Muslim battered wife and feel strongly you should be represented by a women lawyer, it would probably be best not to choose this one...

8 John Bingham: "Sharia law guidelines abandoned as Law Society apologises," *The Telegraph* 24th November 2014.
9 See a report in *Private Eye*, 12th–19th December, 2014, P. 34.

All this followed an extraordinary speech by the Archbishop of Canterbury a year or two earlier suggesting that parts of *shari'a* would sooner or later be incorporated into British law, which he evidently thought desirable. It transpired that there were already numerous quasi-judicial *shari'a* bodies already operating in Britain, although it is claimed that these are for "mediation" — a distinction that Muslim women obliged to engage with them might not appreciate.

ISIS, the newly founded "caliphate" causing such mayhem in Iraq and Syria, has obligingly laid out the list of penalties people can expect to receive for doing things it disapproves of, a list it claims is legitimised by *shari'a* law:

Complete List of "Offences and Punishments" Laid out by ISIS under Shari'a Law

Crime	*Punishment*
Insulting Allah	To be killed by beheading or any other form found suitable
Insulting Messenger of Allah	Beheading, even if the offender repents for his crime
Insulting the religion	To be killed
Zinah (a woman sleeping with someone)	If married, stoned to death. If not married, 100 lashes and banning from the land for the period of 1 year.
Homosexuality	Killing the one who does such an act, and the one who it's done to
Stealing	Cutting off the hand
Drinking alcohol	80 lashes
Slander	80 lashes
Spying for *kūfar* (any enemy of ISIS) interests	To be killed by any form found fit
Turning one's back on Islam (apostasy)	To be killed by any form found fit
A bandit who kills and takes money	Should be killed and crucified
A goon who threatens people	Should be banished from the land

As of September 2010, stoning as a punishment for *Zinah* ("adultery by married persons") was still included in the laws of several Muslim countries including Saudi Arabia, Sudan, Somalia, Yemen and some predominantly Muslim states in northern Nigeria. Brunei actually *added* stoning to its laws in 2013 "in accordance with *Shari'a*." In early 2013, a spokesman for the judicial committee of Iran's parliament stated that stoning is no longer mentioned in Iran's legislation, but that the punishment will remain the same as it is Islamic law. In some countries like Somalia, stoning is a spectator sport. For example, in October 2008, a girl called Aisha Ibrahim Duhulow was buried up to her neck at a Somalian football stadium, then stoned to death in front of more than 1,000 people. You should also avoid being raped, especially gang-raped, in a *Shari'a* state, as there are several chilling instances of girls who have been raped and are then being stoned for having had illicit sex.[10]

Connoisseurs of black comedy will relish a letter sent to the *Financial Times* in February 2015 in which Iran's Ayatollah Seyyed Safavi condemned the atrocities of ISIS as undemocratic and non-Islamic and asserts that its "ugly behaviour towards women, and indeed towards minorities, particularly Christians, is utterly contrary to Islamic values." This attracted a response from an Iranian exile welcoming the Ayatollah's unexpected support for democracy, human rights and women's rights and adding: "*I dream of the day that these pronouncements* [of the Ayatollah], *as well as respect for freedom of speech and respect for all minorities become a reality in Iran.*"[11]

It may, or may not, be reassuring to hear from Islamic apologists that stoning is an aberration resulting from a misinterpretation or misapplication (it's not quite clear which) of *shari'a.* For instance, one Dr Ask Joommal, Member of the Islamic Research Foundation International Inc., located at 7102 W. Shefford Lane Louisville, KY, says quite indignantly on his website: "*Stoning to death has been emphasized time and again as the "Shariah" law. It most certainly is NOT! The punishment prescribed by the Shariah of the Quran is* **ONE HUNDRED LASHES** *each to the adulterer and the adulteress, in public.*" Truly, Allah is merciful!

---

10 For the preceding details and other information about lapidation see *en.wikipedia.org/wiki/stoning*.

11 Letter to the *Financial Times*, 10th February, 2015, from Zia Ebrahimzadeh, Washington DC, US.

The Taliban religious police politely explain to a woman that she shouldn't remove her burqa.

"Hudud" is an Islamic concept that defines "crimes against God" as described in the *Qur'an* and the *Hadiths* (the sayings and practices of the Prophet and the record of Islamic tradition). *Sūrah* 5:38 of the *Qur'an* says *"As for the man or woman who is guilty of theft, cut off their hands to punish them for what they did. That is the punishment enjoined by God"*[12] (though it does allow the possibility of repentance and pardon.) But are we sure that such brutality is "enjoined by God"? Has anybody asked him?

Slavery: Man's inhumanity to man — and still going strong:
"The fact is," wrote Oscar Wilde in *The Soul of Man under Socialism* (1895), "that civilisation requires slaves. The Greeks were quite right there. Unless there are slaves to do the ugly, horrible, uninteresting work, culture and contemplation become almost impossible." But he did have the decency to add: "Human slavery is wrong, insecure, and de-

---

12 *The Koran: With Parallel Arabic Text*, translated by N.J.Dawood (Penguin Books, 2014), P. 113.

moralising. On mechanical slavery, on the slavery of the machine, the future of the world depends." As so often, Wilde's antinomian flippancy sums up the layered paradox of civilisation. Slavery was regarded as an economic necessity that underpinned to varying degrees virtually all tribal and national cultures until modern times (that is, until 1808 when the slave trade in the British Empire was outlawed, followed in 1833 by the abolition of slavery itself—at least officially.)

The oldest known legal code, that of Sumeria dating to circa 2050 BC, includes provisions dealing with slavery, which was an institution of all ancient civilisations, whether Hittite, Persian, Egyptian or later Minoan, Greek and Roman. Slavery was established in China under the Shang dynasty (circa 1600-1046 BC), when some 5% of the population were slaves, and not abolished there until the mid-nineteenth century. Its incidence fluctuated according to reforms made by successive Emperors, usually followed by a reversion to the old systems. In the main however it seems to have been criminals who were enslaved (e.g. eunuchs who had been castrated for committing rape), together with their families, as well as foreigners (mostly prisoners taken in wars). It is estimated that the majority of citizens in Athens at the height of its civilisation owned at least one slave. Most ancient writers considered slavery not only a natural phenomenon but also a necessary one, although doubts begin to surface in the Socratic dialogues and the first recorded condemnation of slavery appears in the writings of the Stoics. Seneca exhorted his correspondent Lucilius: "Kindly remember that he whom you call your slave sprang from the same stock, is smiled upon by the same skies, and on equal terms with yourself breathes, lives, and dies."[13] The Stoic Epictetus (circa AD 55–135) was actually born a slave (his Greek name simply means "acquired.")

Aristotle provided the philosophical justification of slavery. In book I of the *Politics*, he addresses the questions of whether slavery can be natural or whether it is contrary to nature, and whether it is better for certain types of people to be slaves. He concludes that *those who are as different [from other men] as the soul from the body or man from beast — and they are in this state if their work is the use of the body, and if this is the best that can come from them — are slaves by nature. For them it is better to be ruled in accordance with this sort of rule, if such is the case for the*

---

13 Seneca: *Moral Letters to Lucilius*. Letter 47: *On Master and Slave* (circa AD 65.)

432

other things mentioned. However he contends that it is not advantageous for someone to be held in slavery who is not a "natural slave," because such a condition is sustained solely by force and results in enmity (how those factors differ from those governing a "natural slave" is not entirely clear). Anyway he is quite definite "that some men are by nature free, and others slaves, and that for these latter slavery is both expedient and right," just as he is clear that women are "naturally" subservient to men and "barbarians" to Greeks. Today Aristotle would presumably be labelled a male chauvinist racist.

It is noticeable however that Aristotle's notion of the slave *per se* is not racist in a way that depends on specific ethnicities: this refinement was added by Western Europeans and transplanted to America. When the Confederacy was founded in the American South, its Vice-President declared that its cornerstone was "the great truth that the Negro is not equal to the white man, that slavery — subordination to the superior race — is his natural and normal condition."[14] "[Slavery]," proclaimed Jefferson Davis, the President of the Confederate States of America, "was established by decree of Almighty God…it is sanctioned in the Bible, in both Testaments, from Genesis to Revelation…it has existed in all ages, has been found among the people of the highest civilization, and in nations of the highest proficiency in the arts."

The Israelites had precise rules about their slaves, rules which were also racially based: if the slaves were themselves Israelites, they should be manumitted after six years or at the next Jubilee, whichever was the sooner. However non-Israelites were treated as their masters' permanent property. Both the Old Testament and the New Testament sanction slavery. There is no statement by Jesus that could be taken as explicitly condemning it. St Paul was of the view that slaves should serve their masters "*as to the Lord, and not to men.*" In the *Epistle of Paul to Titus*, he writes: "Tell slaves to be submissive to their masters and to give satisfaction in every respect; they are not to talk back, not to pilfer, but to show complete and perfect fidelity, so that in everything they may be an ornament to the doctrine of God our Saviour." It is hard to read this any other way than as the sanction of slavery by God. This was evidently the view of the Protestant Society for the Propagation of the Gospel in Foreign

14 Quoted in James W. Loewen: *Lies My Teacher Told Me* (Simon & Schuster, New York, 2007) P. 193.

Parts owned by the British Codrington Plantation, in Barbados, where several hundred slaves were put to work. All of them were branded on their chests, a red hot iron imprinting the word *Society* to signify their ownership by the Christian organisation. (The Church of England has apologised for the "sinfulness of our predecessors").

While Christians now condemn slavery as contrary to God's will, this is a comparatively modern view, and chiefly the result of Low Church agitators against slavery, especially Quakers and Methodists (although the Southern Baptist Conference in America was founded in 1845 to *defend* slavery, and later segregation.) Nor should one forget the centuries during which the papal galleys were filled not only with Muslim slaves, but periodically with dissident Christians from cities like Florence or Venice when the latter were in conflict with the Papal States. Roman Catholic teaching began to condemn "unjust" [*sic*] forms of slavery from 1435, when it was decided that the enslavement of the recently baptised was somewhat counterproductive.

According to a book by Murray Gordon, the Arab slave trade predates the Christian European one by a millennium and continued a hundred years after the latter's abolition. He states that "no moral opprobrium has clung to slavery since it is sanctioned by the Koran and enjoyed an undisputed place in Arab society."[15] Bernard Lewis explains that "Islamic law, in contrast to the ancient and colonial systems, accords the slave a certain legal status and assigns obligations as well as rights to the slave owner. The manumission of slaves, though recommended as a meritorious act, is not required, and the institution of slavery not only is recognized but is elaborately regulated by *shari'a* law. Perhaps for this very reason the position of the domestic slave in Muslim society was in most respects better than in either classical antiquity or the nineteenth-century Americas. While, however, the life of the slave in Muslim society was no worse, and in some ways was better, than that of the free poor, the processes of acquisition and transportation often imposed appalling hardships. It was these which drew the main attention of European opponents of slavery, and it was to the elimination of this traffic, particularly in Africa, that their main efforts were directed."

Although some care might be taken of the slave-goods (particularly of girls destined to be sex slaves), since they were after all a valuable

15 See: Murray Gordon: *Slavery in the Arab World* (New York, 1989).

commodity, other culturally based practices had the reverse effect. For example, boys might be mutilated to make them eunuchs (much in demand for oversight of the harem and other sensitive positions). It has been estimated that only about one in ten of the boys castrated under conditions that lacked any hygienic precautions actually survived the mutilation. Saudi Arabia officially abolished slavery only in 1962, but it is known still to exist there and in some other Arab states, albeit not officially so described. Mauritania declared slavery illegal in 1980(!), Yemen in 1962, while the first Muslim state to officially abolish the trade was Tunisia in 1846, although the law wasn't enforced until the French arrived in 1881. There seems to be a degree of selectivity in the denunciation of Arab slavery. George Schöpflin, writing in the *Hungarian Review*, puts it this way: "… historians have turned towards the marginal, the dispossessed, the oppressed as a means of legitimating their position in society and/or delegitimating the claims of the majority. The fashion for, the current focus on (take your pick) the history of the Atlantic slave trade is a good illustration. The Arab slaving past in East Africa does not have this attention."[16] Pascal Bruckner remarks on the irony that demands for reparations and apologies are directed at the western countries that repented of the slave trade and abolished it. He reminds us that there were three slave trades: "the Eastern one, which began in the seventeenth century (an estimated seventeen million captives); the African, which provided slaves for use both in Africa and abroad (fourteen million persons); and the Atlantic, which, in a shorter period, led to the deportation of almost eleven million men, women, and children. Amy historian who dares to discuss this is running the risk of being accused of revisionism."[17]

"The abolition of slavery itself," continues Lewis, "would hardly have been possible [in the Islamic world of the 19th century]. From a Muslim point of view, to forbid what God permits is almost as great an offence as to permit what God forbids — and slavery was authorized and regulated by the holy law. More specifically, it formed part of the

16 George Schöpflin: "*History and Historians: Parts of a Memoir*" in Hungarian Review, Volume V., No. 3, May 2014, P. 63.
17 Pascal Bruckner: *The Tyranny of Guilt: An Essay on Western Masochism* (Translated by Steven Rendall. Princeton University Press, Princeton and Oxford, 2010) Pp. 155-156.

law of personal status, the central core of social usage, which remained intact and effective even when other sections of the holy law, dealing with civil, criminal, and similar matters, were tactically or even openly modified and replaced by modern codes. It was from conservative religious quarters and notably from the holy cities of Mecca and Medina that the strongest resistance to the proposed reform came. The emergence of the holy men and the holy places as the last ditch defenders of slavery against reform is only an apparent paradox. They were upholding an institution sanctified by scripture, law, and tradition and one which in their eyes was necessary to the maintenance of the social structure of Muslim life."[18] (This attitude scarcely differs from that of the Anglican bishops in Britain, who voted against the Abolition of Slavery Act in 1833 — as they had done on almost all reform bills. The Act provided for compensation of *slave owners* (there was no compensation for the slaves, of course) and £20 million was to be paid to the proprietors of West Indian plantation slaves in compensation for the loss of their 'property'. The Anglican Church as such received a paltry £8,823 8s 9d, which was for the loss of slave labour on its Codrington plantation in Barbados (*see above*), but individual Churchmen were compensated separately. For example, Henry Phillpotts, Bishop of Exeter, and three business associates received nearly £13,000.)[19]

The Barbary pirates based on the North African coast enslaved large numbers of white Christians whom they took captive on their plundering raids which stretched from Europe as far as America and Iceland. By 1620 it is estimated there were 20,000 white Christian slaves in Algiers and by the 1630s some 30,000 men and 2,000 women. One of the most famous of this type of slave was Miguel de Cervantes, the author of *Don Quixote*, who was captured by Algerian corsairs in 1575 and only ransomed by his parents and the Trinitarians after five years of servitude. Since the conditions in which these slaves lived were so miserable, free Europeans living along the North African shore provided them with es-

18 Bernard Lewis: *Race and Slavery in the Middle East: An Historical Enquiry* (Oxford University Press, 1990).

19 Compensation recorded in the British Parliamentary Papers 1836 (597) Vol. 49. For a fact-filled and extremely hostile account of Christianity and slavery (accompanied by many horrifying illustrations) see:
www.badnewsaboutchristianity.com/gaa_slavery.htm

sential food and clothing. Spanish Catholic priests in Algeria even built a hospital to care for the white Christian slaves.[20]

The Atlantic slave trade on a systematic capitalist basis lasted for some 245 years. The first to practise it in the 15th century seem to have been the Portuguese but by the mid-eighteenth century it was dominated by the British, who were then shipping half of the 80,000 odd slaves annually transported. One reason why so many African slaves were needed was that the diseases brought by European "settlers" in the New World had had a devastating impact on the local populations, which were decimated by smallpox, influenza, plague and other illnesses against which they had no resistance. As Charles Darwin wrote in 1839, *"Wherever the European had trod, death seems to pursue the aboriginal."*[21] The supply of cheap labour made plantation owners rich, many of them English and Scottish aristocratic families who ultimately owe their present wealth to the exploitation of slaves in the past. Some historians believe the impetus for the industrial revolution, and hence Britain's rise to prosperity and empire, rests on the sweated labour of slaves and the raw materials they produced at minimal cost. Certainly the economy of the Southern States of America depended almost entirely on slavery until the Civil War.

While both the USA and Britain have apologised for their involvement in the slave trade and the iniquity of the human misery it caused, the abolition of the trade by the British (who deployed thirty ships against traders and lost 2,000 men in enforcing the ban) highlighted an awkward aspect of slavery. Namely that the African tribal chiefs were complicit in it, just as much as the Arab traders who escorted the caravans of "black ivory" to the coast. Even the American Indians sold their people into slavery on occasion. James Loewen tells us that northern Indian tribes specialised in fur but "certain southern tribes specialised in people," a trade that of course multiplied exponentially once there were was steady demand from the European settlers.[22] The British and American apologies have thus generated demands for a similar apology from the descendants of the African chiefs and others who sold their own people into slavery.

---

20 See: Paul Baepler (Ed.): *White Slaves, African Masters* (University of Chicago Press, 1999).
21 Charles Darwin: *Voyage of the Beagle*, quoted in Loewen, op cit. P. 78.
22 Loewen op cit. P. 104.

Slavery: in 2009 it was estimated that 29 millon slaves still existed worldwide...

According to a report in *The Guardian* in 2009,[23] the Civil Rights Congress of Nigeria had written to tribal chiefs saying: "We cannot continue to blame the white men, as Africans, particularly the traditional rulers, are not blameless." The congress argued that the ancestors of the chiefs had helped to raid and kidnap defenceless communities and traded them to Europeans. "In view of the fact that the Americans and Europe have accepted the cruelty of their roles and have forcefully apologised, it would be logical, reasonable and humbling if African traditional rulers ... [can] accept blame and formally apologise to the descendants of the victims of their collaborative and exploitative slave trade."

Because the corrupt governments of Africa prefer to cover their crimes with anti-colonialist rhetoric and blame the misgovernment of the present on imperial exploitation in the past, there are rather few takers for the idea of an apology. However there was an exception in 1998 when Yoweri Museveni, the President of Uganda, told an audience that included Bill Clinton: "African chiefs were the ones waging war on each

23 *The Guardian*, 18 November 2009.

other and capturing their own people and selling them. If anyone should apologise it should be the African chiefs. We still have those traitors here even today." (Unfortunately Museveni also passed a law in 2014 that prescribed life imprisonment for practising homosexuals, but one can't have everything.[24])

Tunde Obadina of Africa Business Information Services points out that "when Britain abolished the slave trade in 1807 it not only had to contend with opposition from white slavers but also from African rulers who had become accustomed to wealth gained from selling slaves or from taxes collected on slaves passing through their domains. African slave-trading classes were greatly distressed by the news that legislators sitting in parliament in London had decided to end their source of livelihood. But for as long as there was demand from the Americas for slaves, the lucrative business continued." Furthermore "British efforts to suppress the trade made it even more profitable because the price of slaves rose in the Americas. The numerous wars that plagued Yorubaland for half a century following the fall of the Oyo Empire was largely driven by demand for slaves." In addition "a consequence of the ending of the slave trade was the *expansion of domestic slavery* [italics added] as African businessmen replaced trade in human chattel with increased export of primary commodities. Labour was needed to cultivate the new source of wealth for the African elite."

Now that there are laws against slavery in every country in the world, can we assume that it is no longer a problem? The answer to that question is a chilling negative: there are *more* slaves in the world *than there have ever been*, writes Jessica Williams; the upper estimate of anti-slavery groups is 27 to 29 million. The definitions may have changed slightly, but the victims of debt bondage, serfdom, sale of women into marriage or prostitution and child servitude are slaves by any other name. Of these, perhaps 20 million are bonded labour, a particularly grotesque feature of India and some other Asian countries. Such people have been forced or tricked into taking out a loan, for which their labour is the collateral. The

---

24 The Uganda Anti-Homosexuality Act was originally introduced as a Bill prescribing the death penalty for homosexual activity — the so-called *"Kill The Gays Bill."* Some visiting American Christian fundamentalists have been active in support of brutal anti-gay legislation in Uganda, where attitudes to homosexuality are not significantly different from those in several sub-Saharan states.

terms of the loan prove to be such that they never succeed in paying it off. The debt can be passed on to future generations condemning them to the same fate. Slaves in the narrower sense of persons who are trafficked were estimated to be 2.7 million by the Anti-Slavery Society in 1995, while the Global Slavery Index claims there are still 4,500 slaves in Britain (2103).[25]

Then there are the thousands of labourers whose wages are barely at subsistence level working in garment factories that are in danger of collapse or burning down. The real slave masters of these thousands are ourselves, the comparatively prosperous consumers of the developed world who enjoy the fruits of sweated labour — the stylish but cheap garments and trainers, the daily fix of coffee and perhaps other products and commodities whose mode of production we are not even aware of. "The new slavery," writes Williams, "is even more dehumanising than the slavery of old…" In the past there was an incentive to look after your slave properly, as you could expect to get "little valuable work out of a slave who was hungry or ill… [but] in the modern era, the slave is perceived to be a disposable asset, bought and sold cheaply, eminently replaceable. The average slave in the American South cost \$40,000 in today's money. Today, a slave costs an average of just \$90."[26] It's the cost of a less than gourmet meal for two in a trendy New York eatery…

Socialism: A method of distributing wealth:
"The problem with Socialism," Mrs Thatcher once said, *"is that eventually you run out of other people's money."*

Although Proudhon maintained that *"property is theft,"* a good case can be made for the proposition that Socialism is also mostly theft, albeit of the Robin Hood type. By the same token, the American salon revolutionary Abbie Hoffman extolled stealing as a justified attack on bourgeois capitalist oppression. He wrote a work with the title *Steal*

25 Figures quoted are from the Walk Free Foundation (2013), the International Labour Organisation (2012), the Anti-Slavery Society (1995) and the Global Slavery Index (2013).

26 Jessica Williams: *50 facts that should change the world* (Icon Books, Cambridge UK, 2004) Pp. 262-267, *"There are 27 million slaves in the world today."* The main facts from this paragraph (other than the specific figures which are sourced in Note 11) are taken from Williams. She in turn sources Amnesty International and a website www.freetheslaves.net.

This Book for a publisher who was presumably either extremely masochistic or extremely radical. However, writes Michael Skapinker in the FT, he "felt the need to refine his philosophy when his apartment was burgled." "In advocating stealing as a revolutionary act, "Hoffman declared, "I guess I didn't make clear the difference between stealing from General Motors and stealing from me."

Winston Churchill said that "the inherent vice of capitalism is the unequal sharing of blessings; the inherent virtue of socialism is the equal sharing of miseries."

Norman Mailer said that "the function of socialism is to raise suffering to a higher level."

George Orwell said that "as with the Christian religion, the worst advertisement for Socialism is its adherents."

R.H.Tawney wrote in *The Acquisitive Society* (1920) that "wealth in modern societies is distributed according to opportunity; and while opportunity depends partly upon talent and energy, it depends still more upon birth, social position, access to education and inherited wealth; in a word, upon property."

In *Essays on Political Economy* (c. 1850s), Frederic Bastiat (*q.v.*) wrote that: "It is the law which socialism invokes. It aspires to legal, not extra-legal plunder.... It is absolutely necessary that this question of legal plunder should be determined, and there are only three solutions of it:

1. When the few plunder the many.
2. When everybody plunders everybody else.
3. When nobody plunders anybody.

Partial plunder, universal plunder, absence of plunder, amongst these we have to make our choice. The law can only produce one of these results. Partial plunder: This is the system which prevailed so long as the elective privilege was partial; a system which is resorted to, to avoid the invasion of socialism.

Universal plunder: We have been threatened by this system when the elective privilege has become universal; the masses having conceived the idea of making law, on the principle of legislators who had preceded them.

Absence of plunder: This is the principle of justice, peace, order, stability, conciliation, and of good sense."

Adam Smith wrote: "Civil government, so far as it is instituted for the security of property, is in reality instituted for the defence of the rich against the poor, or of those who have some property against those who have none at all."

Karl Popper wrote in *Unended Quest*: "I remained a socialist for several years, even after my rejection of Marxism; and if there could be such a thing as socialism combined with individual liberty, I would be a socialist still. For nothing could be better than living a modest, simple, and free life in an egalitarian society. It took some time before I recognized this as no more than a beautiful dream; that freedom is more important than equality; that the attempt to realize equality endangers freedom; and that, if freedom is lost, there will not even be equality among the unfree."

Senator Elizabeth Warren has said: "There is nobody in this country [the USA] who got rich on their own. Nobody. You built a factory out there - good for you. But I want to be clear. You moved your goods to market on roads the rest of us paid for. You hired workers the rest of us paid to educate. You were safe in your factory because of police forces and fire forces that the rest of us paid for. You didn't have to worry that marauding bands would come and seize everything at your factory... Now look. You built a factory and it turned into something terrific or a great idea - God bless! Keep a hunk of it. But part of the underlying social contract is you take a hunk of that and pay forward for the next kid who comes along."

Oscar Wilde wrote in *The Soul of Man under Socialism:* "The recognition of private property has really harmed Individualism, and obscured it, by confusing a man with what he possesses."

Tony Benn said, "If we can find the money to kill people, we can find the money to help people."

Karl Hess said: "It is curious to note that when for reasons of conscience, people refuse to kill, they are often exempted from active military duty. But there are no exemptions for people who, for reasons of conscience, refuse to financially support the bureaucracy that actually does the killing. Apparently, the state takes money more seriously than life."

Chief Justice Earl Warren wrote: "Many people consider the things government does for them to be social progress but they regard the things government does for others as socialism."

442

Jonah Goldberg wrote in his book *Liberal Fascism: The Secret History of the American Left from Mussolini to the Politics of Meaning*: "If there is ever a fascist takeover in America, it will come not in the form of storm troopers kicking down doors but with lawyers and social workers saying. 'I'm from the government and I'm here to help.'"

In the *Communist Manifesto*, Karl Marx wrote: "The bourgeoisie, by the rapid improvement of all instruments of production, by the immensely facilitated means of communication, draws all, even the most barbarian, nations into civilization. The cheap prices of its commodities are the heavy artillery with which it batters down all Chinese walls, with which it forces the barbarians' intensely obstinate hatred of foreigners to capitulate. It compels all nations, on pain of extinction, to adopt the bourgeois mode of production; it compels them to introduce what it calls civilization into their midst, i.e., to become bourgeois themselves. In one word, it creates a world after its own image."

In *Political Philosophy: Arguments for Conservatism* (2006) Roger Scruton wrote that "it is not the truth of Marxism that explains the willingness of intellectuals to believe it, but the power that it confers on intellectuals, in their attempts to control the world. And since, as Swift says, it is futile to reason someone out of a thing that he was not reasoned into, we can conclude that Marxism owes its remarkable power to survive every criticism to the fact that it is not a truth-directed but a power-directed system of thought."

Slavoj Žižek wrote in his book *Revolution at the Gates*: "There is an old joke about socialism as the synthesis of the highest achievements of the whole human history to date: from prehistoric societies it took primitivism; from the ancient world it took slavery; from medieval society brutal domination; from capitalism exploitation; and from socialism the name."

Mikhail Gorbachev said, "Jesus was the first socialist, the first to seek a better life for mankind."

Mao Zedong said: "Socialism…must have a dictatorship, it will not work without it."

Alexis de Tocqueville wrote: "Democracy and socialism have nothing in common but one word, equality. But notice the difference: while democracy seeks equality in liberty, socialism seeks equality in restraint and servitude."

Czech President Vaclav Klaus said: "To pursue a so-called Third Way is foolish. We had our experience with this in the 1960s when we looked

443

for a socialism with a human face. It did not work, and we must be explicit that we are not aiming for a more efficient version of a system that has failed."

Nassim Nicholas Taleb said: "What we do today has nothing to do with capitalism or socialism. It is a crony type of system that transfers money to the coffers of bureaucrats."

Solipsism: A consequence of excessive use of Facebook and Twitter:
In his book *Human Knowledge*,[27] Bertrand Russell recounts how he received a letter from a logician who said she was a solipsist and that she was surprised that there were no others.

Sothebys: Ruthless and vulgar capitalists pretending to be persons of refinement and taste:
What with Christies turning federal evidence on price-fixing between the two biggest auction houses and various other dubious practices, the elaborately honed air of respectability which Sothebys and Christies traditionally tried to present took a bit of a knock in the 1990s. This followed decades of faking auctions (Christies), fleecing buyers and sellers with enormous commissions and sometimes auctioning stolen works. Vienna's Dorotheum, which also tries to present itself as a venerable institution, did a roaring trade in the Nazi era in works confiscated from about-to-be liquidated Jews. It later appeared that many of the sales documents relating to the Nazi era had "been destroyed." Most unfortunate.

Spelling checkers: Bossy software that knows better than you what you want to write:
A contribution to *The Author* (a sort of trades union magazine for British writers) begins as follows:

> *Eye halve a spelling chequer;*
> *It came with my pea sea*
> *It plane lee marques four my revue*
> *miss steaks eye cannot sea.*

---

27 Bertrand Russell: *Human Knowledge: Its Scope and Limits* (George Allen & Unwin, 1948).

And continues:

> *Eye stryke a quay and tipe a wurd,*
> *And weight four it to sey*
> *Weather eye am write oar rong:*
> *It shoughs me strait a weigh*

And ends:

> *Four eye have run this pome threw it:*
> *And I'm shore you're pleased two no —*
> *It's letter perfick awl the weigh;*
> *My chequer tolled me sew.*

Starchitects: Architects as celebrities with egos to match:
Take Rem Koolhaas, "starchitect" and an almost perfectly formed example of the wealthy western left-liberal. Koolhaas declined to participate in the competition to design a replacement for the Twin Towers in New York, describing the project as a *"monument to self-pity on a Stalinist scale."* However he was not so fastidious about working for the murderously oppressive Chinese regime, for whose propaganda organ, Central China TV, he has proudly created a new building.

A clue to Koolhaas's ideological-aesthetic agenda is provided by Graham Owen writing in *Architecture, Ethics and Globalization,* where we learn that allegiance to what is euphemistically called "the generic" frees the architect from such vulgar notions as "nostalgia or provincial habit." *"While for critics of*

Rem Koolhaas's Chinese CTV building. As the great man opined, "People can inhabit anything..."

445

sprawl the generic signifies a loss of local identity and connection to place, for Koolhaas it represents an opportunity for reinvention and fantasy.... He admires the generic's accessibility, impermanence, economy of imagination, and malleable lack of authenticity or moralizing agenda."

Good to know that a "moralising agenda" has been kept out of it, an approach that would doubtless have appealed to his Chinese patrons. Koolhaas has also said that *"People can inhabit anything. And they can be miserable in anything and ecstatic in anything. More and more I think that architecture has nothing to do with it. Of course, that's both liberating and alarming"* — but perhaps more alarming than liberating for those destined to live in buildings designed by someone who thinks thy can live in anything. Nevertheless *"The good is not a category that interests me,"* says the starchitect firmly.

Not all starchitects are on the left of course: Le Corbusier (*"a house is a machine for living"*) expended a lot of time and energy brownnosing fascist governments. Mussolini gave him a lectureship in Rome in 1928 and he hung out in Vichy during the French regime's residence there. But he didn't get much in the way of commissions for all his fawning. Jonathan Meades, who absolves Le Corbusier from the allegation (if it is one) that his architecture was influenced by his political beliefs (if he really had any), observes crisply that *"He was an architect, thus a promiscuous tart,"* an idea rather supported by the fact that Le Corbusier's first building, the Centrosoyuz in Moscow, was done for the Soviets. This caused the influential fellow Swiss architect Alexander von Senger to denounce him as a Communist. (Senger, a servile Nazi, wrote a learned tome entitled *Race and Architecture* after being expelled from Switzerland as a Nazi agent and was appointed to a chair at the Munich school of architecture.)

Senger wasn't really a starchitect, of course, but Albert Speer most certainly was. Indeed he has been rehabilitated to such an extent that today, says Meades, he is *"the acceptable face of war criminals, doted on by bloated classicism's clownish admirers, his complicity in enormities forgotten."*[28] *"We shape our buildings; thereafter they shape us,"* said Winston Churchill, no doubt thinking of monumental public build-

28 Jonathan Meades: "Dedicated follower of fashion?" in *The Spectator*, 23 May, 2015.

ings, perhaps even of the aptly named "brutalism" in public architecture that took hold in London at the end of Churchill's life. Residents squatting in an ugly sub-Corbusierian block of flats with low ceilings might also experience the truth of Churchill's remark differently from what he had in mind…

Statistics: Compilations of figures designed to bamboozle your ideological opponents and persuade the public of a meretricious argument:

In 1954 one Darrell Huff published a book called *How To Lie With Statistics* which, says *The Economist*, was "a guide to getting the figures to say whatever you want them to." Nowadays there are numerous competing "performance indices" which measure all sorts of things round the world, some all too tangible like corruption, some intangible like happiness. Sociologists make up theories and politicians construct policies based on these statistical surveys, the politicians choosing those which seem to support their ideological predilections. (This is why different "think tanks" produce statistics on much the same the topic which yet come up with different, or at least differently interpreted, figures.)

A Nobel Prize Winner in Economics writes in the *Financial Times* that "Statistics are far from politics-free; indeed, politics is encoded in their genes. This is ultimately a good thing." He likens politics to the springs, cogs and wheels that lie behind a clock-face and adds that "down in the works, even where the decisions are delegated to bureaucrats and statisticians, there is room for politics to masquerade as science."[29] But occasionally the mask slips, as is the case with consumer price indexes, which have been manipulated ever since their inception in 1904. A political scientist is quoted as saying that "statistics are how the state sees. The state decides what it needs to see and how to see it." But Deaton does not see this as such a bad thing, since it also implies a source for monitoring and accountability. Or, as Ben Goldacre, the scourge of big pharma and bad science puts it, "it is impossible for someone to lie unless he thinks he knows the truth. Producing bullshit requires no such conviction…"

29 Angus Deaton: "Statistical objectivity is a cloak spun from political yarn," *Financial Times*, 3rd November, 2015.

In the spirit of Huff, *The Economist* offered its own guide to "concocting a spurious index," which may be summarised as follows: First use only the figures you can easily get hold of, whether old or new, or from wildly differing sources, or from very small or biased samples. If the figures for a particular country are lacking, substitute those from some other country ("one index of slavery, short of numbers for Ireland and Iceland, uses British figures for both (aren't all island nations alike?))" If the numbers don't seem to be producing the conclusions you want, call in academics or businessmen of your persuasion to supply "expert opinion" on the basis of which the numbers can be made more compiler friendly. You can also "tweak the weighting of the elements to suit."

Then there is presentation and marketing to think of. Hide the dodgy methodology in an obscure corner of your website, get celebrity endorsements of the conclusions and exaggerate small movements in the figures ("minor year-on-year moves in the rankings may be statistical noise, but they make great copy.") The point is, you can choose what to put in your index (it's like the government's wonderfully plausible index of the cost of living). You having decided what the problem is (or indeed invented the problem), your figures can be made to deliver your preferred solution. In this way, those you approve of may get an easy ride and those you disapprove of may be made to look pretty bad. Rankings of business-friendly countries may ignore the fact that their admirable laws are never enforced, those of women's status may overlook the fact that, "in Saudi Arabia, women outnumber men in universities because they are allowed to do little else but study." No matter —"criticism," concludes *The Economist*, "can always be dismissed as sour grapes and special pleading. The numbers, after all, are on your side. You've made sure of that."[30]

Perhaps reacting to this piece, an emeritus professor from the University of Michigan wrote to *The Economist* a few weeks later reminding readers of the dangers of policy decisions based on averages. He cited in support of his view a sign posted on the door of a visiting African scholar at his university which read: "*A statistician is a fellow who says that if you ate a chicken and I ate nothing, we each ate, on average, half a chicken.*"[31]

---

30 *The Economist*, November 8th, 2014. "Performance indicators: How to lie with indices."

31 *The Economist*, November 29th, 2014. Letters.

Racial Stereotypes: Prejudices based on everyday experience, e.g. that German holidaymakers go to the hotel pool at 7 a.m. and book all the loungers by placing their towels on them:

An Englishman, Scotsman and Irishman meet in the pub and each orders a pint of Guinness. Just as they are about to drink, a fly lands in each pint and gets trapped in the froth. The Englishman makes a face and pushes away the beer. The Scotsman fishes out the fly and drinks the beer with evident satisfaction. The Irishman too fishes out the fly, holds it over his glass, and yells at it furiously: *"Spit it out, spit it out, you bastard!"*

In one of his essays George Orwell offers a classic of the genre: a Jew and a Scotsman go to a public talk in aid of some good cause. Towards the end it becomes appallingly clear that there will be a public collection by passing round the tin. At this point the Jew faints and the Scotsman carries him out.

Anyone, if interviewed on the *Today* programme, will say they abhor racial stereotyping. It is after all, nothing to do with being German that you place your towel on the pool loungers at 7 a.m. and everything to do with being sharper and more disciplined than the British wallies in the hotel who are still sleeping off their hangovers — which in turn is nothing to do with being British. Is it?

Stock Options: Stock given to CEOs and senior managers so they can manipulate the share price in order to cash in at a high price in due course:

This is the latest wheeze devised by the captains of industry for stealing money from shareholders. Here's how it works: stock is granted free to employees (normally ones who are already extremely well paid) at the price ruling when the grant is made, with an option to sell in the future when the stock (hopefully) has gone up. If it doesn't go up much or at all, probably because the beneficiaries of the scam are running the business badly, you simply backdate the price to a level where profits can be booked anyway. This is known in the trade as *"incentivising"* managers, though exactly what incentive exists when you get the money whether performance is good or bad is a question considered to be in bad taste.

Actually, as the *Financial Times* points out, fraudulently manipulating stock options probably has the reverse effect, encouraging the hubris and recklessness of managers who get rich if a mega-risk pays off but lose nothing if it results in melt-down. As the late and great J.K.Galbraith observed, *"the remuneration of the chief executive of the large corporation is not a market award for achievement. It is frequently in the nature of a warm personal gesture by the individual to himself."*

Stone Age: The Stone Age did not end because they ran out of stones…
See also **D: *Creative Destruction***

Tom Stoppard: Rare example of playwright who is not interested in pandering to fashionable shibboleths:

Refusing support for the self-important Harold Pinter, who was lobbying to have the "Comedy Theatre" renamed the "Pinter Theatre", Stoppard wrote back to the egomaniacal playwright: *"Have you thought instead of changing your name to Harold Comedy?"*

The London *Evening Standard* once mischievously sent a questionnaire round the capital's leading theatre producers asking if they would ever consider putting on a *right-wing* play? Almost all of them replied that they *"wouldn't know what a right-wing play was."* In other words, the answer was *"No."*

Strategy: A claim by politicians that they have a plan, or at least a clue:
For example Ronald Reagan once delivered the following statement to alarmed liberal journalists: *"Here is my strategy for the Cold War. We win, they lose."*

Hannen Swaffer: The Pope of Fleet Street:
"Freedom of the press in Britain," wrote Swaffer, "means freedom to print such of the proprietor's prejudices as the advertisers don't object to."

Gloria Swanson: Collector of husbands (six in all):
Swanson was originally a silent screen star who made a late comeback in *Sunset Boulevard*. "I am big," she once said, "it's only the pictures that got small." Also: "I've given my memoirs far more thought than any of my marriages. You can't divorce a book."

Latterly she had had so many facelifts that only her eyes could move: *"Sic transit Gloria Swanson,"* as they say in Hollywood.

Gloria Swanson with friend.

Leó Szilárd: Nuclear physicist who pointed out that if America had lost the war after dropping the atomic bomb, it would have been prosecuted for war crimes...

"I have been asked," said Szilárd, "whether I would agree that the tragedy of the scientist is that he is able to bring about great advances in our knowledge, which mankind may then proceed to use for purposes of destruction. My answer is that this is not the tragedy of the scientist; it is the tragedy of mankind."

Szilárd once told a friend he was keeping a diary, not for publication but "to record the facts for the information of God." "Don't you think God already knows the facts?" asked his friend. "Yes," said Szilárd; "He knows the facts, but he doesn't know *this version of the facts.*"

451

T

Truth:

*An ingenious compound of desirability and appearance.
Discovery of truth is the sole purpose of philosophy, which is the
most ancient occupation of the human mind and has a fair
prospect of existing with increasing activity to the end of time.*

Ambrose Bierce: *The Devil's Dictionary*

Takeovers: "Displacement activity by strategically challenged chief executives."[1]

As the *Financial Times* and others have repeatedly pointed out, 70% of company takeovers leave shareholders worse off in the medium to long term, often far worse off. Not untypical are two examples that Matthew Vincent recently cited in the *Financial Times*: The consequences of the "merger" between Lafarge and Holcim in July of 2015 were that "*earnings, margins, cash flow and share price [were] all down — the latter by 45 per cent in 12 months. At Alcatel-Lucent, the telecoms equals that merged in 2006, the shares fell 80 per cent in the next eight profitless years.*"[2] "Takeover-itis" can even destroy a company altogether, as happened in short order with Arnold Weinstein's beloved GEC. Within in a year or two of his retirement, the new managers had destroyed the fruits of a lifetime's good stewardship through their manic takeover activity. The responsible directors danced from the wreckage of this once great company with handsome pensions and pay-offs, an *ex gratia* salute, one supposes, to the record speed with which they had turned a silk purse into a diseased sow's ear; in two years the share price sank from £11 to 4 pence. The uncharitable remarked that they also left with their knighthoods intact (honours that were of course

---

1 John Plender: "Politicians have the treatment for Pfizer syndrome" *Financial Times*, May 13, 2014.

2 Matthew Vincent: "Beware of buying into the 'merger' euphemism," *FT Weekend*, 27/28 February, 2016.

452

unconnected to the generous contributions to Tory party finances made during their tenure.)

To reverse Joseph Schumpeter's much quoted justification for capitalism, takeovers have come to represent "*uncreative* destruction." Sometimes they are sold to us as "mergers" in order to save the faces of the executives whose companies are being taken over. There will be much accompanying propaganda from stockbrokers and the like touting the "added value" thereby arising; but the end result is all too often the same: asset stripping, dismissal of employees, the enormous enrichment of the participating executives on both sides of the deal — and the erosion of shareholder value. Apart from rent-seeking managers, the only people who benefit from the majority of takeovers are flashy lawyers in the City of London or on Wall Street and fee-gouging merchant bankers.

Even when the takeover is achieved illegally, as was the case when Guinness bought the Distillers Company in the 1985 (it employed the simple expedient of "incentivising" cronies of Guinness's CEO to ramp the Guinness shares), the law showed itself impotent to reverse it. Everyone soon reverted to business as usual with analysts and share pushers warbling enthusiastically about the money-making potential ("*synergy*") of the new entity. Who would want to spoil a good (remunerative) story by gurning on about legal niceties? True, some of those involved in the takeover scam did do a spell in gaol — a feeble gesture of contrition by the establishment; but then again, Ernest Saunders (the Guinness CEO) won early release from prison by pleading that he suffered from Alzheimers disease. Poor man, he'd already forgotten what he'd done: clearly only exceedingly heartless and excessively censorious persons would fail to do the same. After his release Saunders made a remarkably swift recovery from his illness, indeed one that made medical history, since hitherto no remission of Alzheimers had been recorded. He was soon involved in new business projects, doubtless with the support of indulgent former colleagues in the city whose own memories were perhaps a little impaired...

In regard to pharmaceutical companies the takeover culture is even more insulting to those who end up paying the bill for it. In 2014 Pfizer was prepared to pay a multiple of 21 times' current earnings to take over the Swedish/British firm Astra Zeneca, chiefly so it (Pfizer) could move its business to a lower tax zone. Such a huge multiple would inevitably be paid for *inter alia* in job losses and cuts to expenditure, the easiest way to achieve substantial savings being to slash risky and expensive R&D (especially "R"). This put AZ's longstanding and successful UK research base in the firing line. But it gets worse: as with other drug companies, most of Pfizers's money-spinning patented drugs had benefited from *publicly funded* research (in Pfizer's case the US National Institutes of Health, which disbursed a cool 32 billion dollars of taxpayer funds for research in 2012 alone.)[3] Drug companies of course do develop drugs that look promising, but the risky and commercially unappealing business of primary research is increasingly provided by "small biotech and large public labs" — a beneficial process for big pharma that it disguises with the corporate euphemism of "open innovation." Naturally this does not stop the said pharma from constantly seeking further hand-outs from the Revenue in the form of R&D tax credits; or through the UK's Patent Box tax scheme which offers a 10% tax for income earned on patented drugs (although patents are already monopolies with 17 years' protection.) Drug companies have become true votaries of what the economist John Kenneth Galbraith used to call "corporate welfare."

If you're with me so far, you can see where all this is heading: effectively the taxpayer is coughing up twice to keep big pharma in the style to which it is accustomed: "once for research, then for the high prices justified by the supposedly high risk that big pharma is taking on" (but actually shedding as much as it can). As Mariana Mazzucato points out,[4] there is an uncanny resemblance in such a business model to that of the banks: risk is socialized (i.e. borne by the taxpayer) and rewards are privatised. To add insult to injury, in order to justify rip-off pricing, big pharma's lobby in the USA (PhRMA) grossly exaggerates the amount needed to create a "research-driven powerhouse," quoting a figure of $2.6 billion. But the charity Médecins Sans Frontières says it is possible to develop new drugs for as little as $50m and no more than $190m, even taking into account drugs that fail during trials.[5] Meanwhile big pharma buys smaller

3 The figures in this paragraph are taken from an article in *The Observer* of 11th May, 2014 by Mariana Mazzucato: "Big pharma relies on public money but shirks its obligations to society." She is also the author of a book questioning Neo-Liberal shibboleths: "*The Entrepreneurial State: Debunking Private vs Public Sector Myths.*"

4 See Note 2.

5 See "Billion-dollar babies: the high cost of R&D is used to explain why drug giants merge, and why they must charge high prices. The reality is somewhat different" in *The Economist*, November 28th, 2015.

drug firms with one or two successful products in order to seize control of same and ramp up the price to a largely captive market. For example, in 2015 Valeant increased its prices for two heart medications — Isuprel and Nitropress — by about 525% and 212% immediately after buying the drugs from Marathon Pharmaceuticals in February. Valeant is the only company that sells these two life-saving medications.

John Plender[6] reinforces the point that there is little evidence that takeover activity "adds value" to companies, as the city claims. Pfizer, for example, had spent $240bn on three acquisitions in the 15 years prior to 2014, but its market value in that year was a mere $185bn. "A big acquisition," he says, conveniently muddies the waters and makes financial performance harder to judge for a while" — something which those of you with suspicious minds may feel is part of the point of them. To add insult to injury, assurances given to bodies such as the parliamentary committees are seldom worth the paper they are generally not written on. This is confirmed by the fall-out from hubristic takeovers in the past (ICI, Marconi, Royal Bank of Scotland and Lloyds TSB have all ended up costing the taxpayer and/or shareholders a great deal of money for no visible benefit, except to the bank accounts of participating executives and swarms of parasitic middlemen in the City of London.)

Some sort of nadir was reached with the arrogant performance of Irene Rosenfeld, Chief Executive of Mondelez and Kraft Foods, who decided to take over Cadbury, the iconic British chocolate maker in 2010. Naturally her assurances in regard to jobs at Cadbury's Bristol factory were reneged on as soon as the takeover was in the bag. She then refused to appear before the British parliamentary committee investigating the matter — why should she care about a few job losses on her salary package, which was probably more than that of all the committee members added together? In 2015 it was reported that insult had been added to injury, since no corporation tax was being paid on the company's British subsidiary. According to an online report in *The Guardian* dated 6th December, 2015: "*Mondelez was able to pay no UK corporation tax as a result of a Channel Islands-based bond, despite Cadbury making £96.5m profit in 2014.*" It added: "*An investigation by the* Sunday Times *found the company was wiping out Cadbury's bills using interest payments on an unsecured debt, which is listed as a bond on the Channel*

6 See Note 1.

Islands' stock exchange. The interest paid on the loan can be offset as a loss against gains made elsewhere in the company."

According to the *Financial Times*, Rosenfeld's 2013 pay package increased by over 30% (despite falling revenues at Mondelez) bringing it to £18.9 million (masterminding the split between Kraft and Mondelez had already brought her a bonus of over £6 million.) According to a BBC report in February 2011, after taking into account integration costs, the Cadbury acquisition knocked about 33% off Kraft's earnings per share. Kraft is famous for its nasty processed cheese, while Mondelez markets an assortment of unhealthy snacks, so perhaps there is a certain appropriateness in a board of shits presiding over a heap of crap. However the former employees of Cadbury may not find that particularly comforting...

Is there anything to be said *in favour* of takeovers? Certainly some have delivered those famous synergies and Astra Zeneca was itself the product of a successful merger in the past, likewise its rival drugs company GlaxoSmith Kline. Still, it is worth recalling that the Monopolies Commission blocked a takeover of Glaxo (as it then was) by Beecham in 1972 on the grounds that it would reduce the number of independent centres for drug research in the UK. Sure enough, within a few years Glaxo's research team had produced a series of blockbuster drugs, which they probably wouldn't have done if Beecham, with its focus on over-the-counter remedies, had had its way).[7] The above-mentioned Guinness was itself later folded into a rather anonymous but profitable drinks conglomerate named Diageo (the trend towards abstruse names or boring acronyms for big companies is perhaps an indication of how they are perceived as characterless chips in the modern investment casino). Reckitt Benckiser is the product of a merger many years ago and is one of the most successful British companies, resisting the takeover megalomania and contenting itself with smaller strategic "bolt-ons."

On the other hand Hanson, a company that lived from takeovers and asset stripping in the 1980s and 90s, has all but sunk below the radar.

---

7 Beecham soon languished and was taken over by SmithKline Beckman, which in turn was eventually subsumed into Glaxo. However it looks as if the latter — and its research department — had a lucky escape from Beecham's original takeover attempt. Just possibly the strategically challenged CEO of Beecham had launched it as a displacement manoeuvre?

Typically takeover splurges financed with a wall of funny money are rife when funds are cheap, but are replaced by retrenchment and a "return to core functions" (for which read "dumping unwise acquisitions") when the economic cycle turns. Whether all these bouts of frenetic financial activity, followed by hangover-induced policy reversal, are beneficial for society or capitalism itself is, to say the least, doubtful. Usually, there being honour among thieves, the fiction is maintained that they promote market liquidity and further the "creative destruction" (*see Schumpeter above*) which makes capitalism work effectively for the common good. Lord Adair Turner was the first establishment figure (in 2011) to break with this *omertà* — prescribed dogma, much to the consternation of the city, when he mused aloud that not everything the latter cooked up could be described as socially useful.

The greatest takeover scandal of recent years was that of the infamous Phoenix Four businessmen who paid BMW a princely ten pounds in 2000 to take the basket case known Rover Group off its hands. BMW threw in a "dowry" consisting of an interest-free loan of £427 million plus stock, so they must have been pretty keen to get shot of the business. The enterprise collapsed in 2005 with 6,300 out of work and debts of £1.3 billion. Of course such things happen, but the workforce and the public were first amazed, then enraged, to discover that the Phoenix Four had extracted some £42 million in pay and pensions over the five years of their mismanagement. When queried about this, they explained that it was compensation for the great risks they were taking with their investment, though £10 doesn't seem such an awfully big risk. At any rate the authorities didn't think it was and persuaded them to disbar themselves from being directors for a combined 19 years.

Although the Director of Public Prosecutions decided there was not enough evidence to convict the Phoenix Four of fraud, a public inquiry into the firm's collapse took the lid off an incredible can of worms. A Chinese assistant who had "a relationship" with one of the directors was paid over a million pounds in fees, ostensibly for translations; accountants and a leading bank assisted with a dubious tax avoidance scheme aptly code-named Project Slag. The directors had actually been planning to extract some £75 million over the five years; when the inquiry was announced, one of them hastily installed software on his computer which significantly bore the name of "Evidence Eliminator" and used it to delete files that could have been relevant to the investigation.

The Phoenix Four were of course self-righteously indignant at the contents of the report and described it as "a whitewash [of the government] and a witch-hunt [against them]." After all they had not actually been prosecuted for anything — a fact that tells us as much about the state of business law in Britain as it does about their guilt or otherwise. In one of the masterly understatements that are often a feature of such reports, the authors of the inquiry remarked *en passant* that there was no evidence from the business skills displayed by the Phoenix Four in their previous careers that would seem to justify their sudden leap into bulge bracket salaries... A takeover, it seems, can do wonders for your market value, at least between the day it is completed and the day on which the enterprise goes belly up.

Tariq Aziz: Saddam Hussein's former Deputy and a devout Chaldean Catholic:[8]

Tariq has lost a loved one and no doubt his plight will have many westerners weeping into their beer: *"Saddam was a friend,"* he told a reporter mournfully, *"a colleague, a boss and I loved him as a person. I loved [him] and his imagination and view of Iraq. ... After the death of Saddam Husssein, nothing in life is a joy."* It must indeed be depressing to have been banged up in a foetid cell at Baghdad Airport for so long without even being able to look forward to the weekend turkey shoot of a few thousand Shias and Kurds.

Tariq Aziz, the Chaldean fixer for Saddam Hussein, asked the Pope if he had a spare room...

After a while, Saddam's Deputy Prime Minister wrote to Pope Benedict asking him, as a co-religionist, to fix him up with more comfortable quarters in Italy while he awaited trial. The Holy Father, said Tariq's spokesman, was considering the request, understanding that this was a "humanitarian issue." I'm sure we all hoped Mr Aziz would soon be resuming the style of living to

8 The Chaldean Church "of Babylon" is in communion with Rome.

458

which he was accustomed. And it would be charming to think of these two old gentlemen, the erstwhile member of the Nazi youth movement and the genocidal Chaldean, sharing their thoughts on "humanitarian issues" in the papal apartments over a glass of *Vin Santo*.

Taxation: Politicians bribing people with their own money:

Benjamin Franklin observed that nothing in this world is certain but death and taxes. He might have added that it is even more certain that politicians will lie about the second. George Bush Senior famously said *"Read my lips: no more taxes!"* before raising them once he became President. In the 1980s taxes remained overall remarkably high despite the Thatcher government's rhetoric about lowering them. The incoming New Labour government of 1997 claimed that John Major's unpopular administration had made "the biggest tax hike in peacetime history." It was all going to be different under them — so, for example, in the decade between 1997 and 2007, taxes outpaced by some 2.5 times the rise in earnings.[9]

The Adam Smith Institute usefully calculates the Tax Freedom Day based on the date in the year when all the tax demanded by the government has been earned in the economy. After that date we finally start working for ourselves. In 1965 Tax Freedom Day was 27th April, but by the end of the Blair years it was around the end of May. Blair's tax-obsessed Chancellor was Gordon Brown, the most disingenuous occupant of that office in living memory. Apart from producing budgets full of charlatanism, misleading figures and insulting spin such as "re-announcing" previously assigned funds as if they were new money, he was the master of "stealth taxes." These began as soon as he took office — £5 billion on pensions, taxes on health insurance and foreign investments. Then came higher National Insurance and tax on workplace training, plus a freeze on tax thresholds so that inflation caused people to pay more tax through a process known as "fiscal drag." After that came higher Council Tax on second homes, a levy on people using the courts, taxes on nursery schools and school buses, a doubling of passport fees, a "lighthouse tax" on boats, rises in air passenger duty (known as 'skyway robbery'), higher fees for fishing licences, higher NHS dentistry charges, hospital car park charges, new taxes on Premium Bonds, a twenty-fold rise in the cost of pub and restaurant licences, litter tax on

9 Figures from David Craig: *Squandered* (Constable, London, 2008) Pp. 115 ff.

takeaways, further Council Tax rises for houses considered to be well situated, higher vehicle registration fees, new charges for wheelie-bins, new duties on longer vehicles. There was also a huge increase in speed cameras and in draconian parking rules, considered by many people to be extortion practiced on captive motorists by local authorities.[10]

According to libertarian Conservatives, Neo-Liberals and some economists the purpose of taxation is to provide services that are understood to be in the interests of the people as a whole. So the money raised should finance goods and services, such as infrastructure, the health system, education and so forth, which are regarded as collective goods in a civilized society. It is also thought desirable by some that the budget should be balanced, or in other words that expenditure is kept roughly within the limits of income. One of the paramount dishonesties of a modern democracy is that lip service is still paid to these fundamental principles, whereas politicians of all shades actually administer something quite different, namely an ideologically based regime known as the "tax-and-benefits" system. The object of this system is not simply to finance useful services and infrastructure, not even to provide a net for the indigent, the sick, the unemployed and an old age pension; rather it is to transfer wealth from the rich, or the richer, to the poor or the poorer with an eye to electoral advantage.

Such a system exacts retribution in the form of confiscation from those who are thought to be too rich, the proceeds (theoretically) being handed to those who are thought to be too poor. Lurking in the background is the notion that really all wealth belongs to the state, as once all land belonged to the king. Hence the amazingly brazen way in which financial journalists speak of the Chancellor "giving away" money (that does not belong to him anyway) by generously lowering, abolishing, or simply not raising a tax. Mrs Thatcher expressed (for egalitarian ideologues) an outrageously subversive view when she remarked that the trouble with socialism is that "eventually you run out of other people's money" (*see also* **S: *Socialism***). This is no more than the truth, since

---

10 This list, which may very well not be complete, is compiled by Eamonn Butler in *The Alternative Manifesto* (Gibson Square, n.d.) pp. 218-219. True, Brown introduced a 10p. tax rate in 1999 — and then in 2007 abolished it with a sleight of hand which, unfortunately for him, did not fool a media by then fully cognizant of his not so cunning ruses.

460

excessive taxation eventually kills the goose laying the golden egg, but for a public figure to state it is guaranteed to draw opprobrium from the massed ranks of those who believe their activities should be compulsorily financed by the taxpayer. Curiously enough, the loudest voices among these are usually not "the poor" themselves, who may well aspire to greater wealth lightly taxed, but those posing as their advocates, or trades unionists on handsome salaries and perks, or well-remunerated people in the public sector or charity bigwigs and so forth. This is before you even start on left-wing comedians like Jimmie Carr, who turn out to have been keeping their money in tax havens…

So taxation has evolved from the financing of public goods and services to a form of "social engineering," and beyond that to a form of punishment for the rich, regardless of whether their wealth is inherited, obtained by dubious means or achieved by immensely hard work and personal sacrifice. It is not at all clear from opinion polls that the majority of the electorate actually wants a punitive tax system. Equality of opportunity, primarily through taxpayer- supported education and health, is one thing, equality of income quite another. In reality, when the latter has been imposed under Communism by force (as it had to be), the quality of life slowly sank for most people, not only through lack of income but more especially through the oppressive governance required to snuff out personal initiative, innovation, business development and much else, simply to keep the system going. But the worst element was that this supposedly egalitarian society was no such thing: it was simply the rule of a ruthless and greedy Communist *Nomenklatura* that kept the economic plums for itself and doled out the rest to a subservient populace. Once a government is taking 50% or more out of the economy in taxes, or, to put it another way, once the average salaried employee is working "for the government" beyond June in any one year, we are well on the way to the Communist dystopia. The system soon goes into an accelerating spiral: low productivity due to excessive taxes begins to reduce the actual tax take, so new imposts have to be invented to fill the widening gaps. The public sector grows and with it waste. Talented people flee to more friendly tax jurisdictions. Government grows more oppressive as the taxpayer, whose standard of living may be dropping, grows more recalcitrant. Populist parties arise, attracting increasing support with their hostile rhetoric focused on the "plunder and squander" of government. And so it goes on.

On the other hand, the electorate has been steadily conditioned to want ever more things from government, most of them expensive. Elections become a hideous bidding war between the parties in which costly commitments are trumpeted and the acres of small print attached to them are concealed. Taxpayers are not only wooed with their own money, they are often insulted with it. Large sums are squandered on corrupt governments through bilateral overseas aid and the EU pays lobbyists *to lobby itself*, using our money. Local authorities blithely shell out taxpayers' money on "charities", which are therefore no such thing but outsourced taxpayer-financed service providers. NGOs, unelected, largely unaccountable and lavishly remunerated, are awash with taxpayer's money. Sometimes it seems as if the taxpayer is no longer simply paying his share of the necessary expenses to support a civilized society, but also financing the lifestyles of all sorts of busybodies, empire-builders, pressure groups — even illegal immigrants or non-deportable criminals living on benefits. Meanwhile the state is at pains to conceal from him where a lot of his money is going by an accounting device known as "*off balance sheet,*" which turns out to mean ruinously expensive "Public Private Partnerships" or the like. He is helpless, bound like Gulliver, his vitals gnawed like Prometheus, his finances and enthusiasm drained by a voracious, plundering state that cannot look at anything without wondering whether it too can be taxed.

Meanwhile the vested interests determined to protect a hideously complex and dysfunctional tax system have proved to be massive and vocal. When Hungary's Conservatives opted for a "flat tax" at 16% on coming to power in 2010, members and supporters of the amazingly corrupt former government set up a caterwauling of pretended concern for those on lower incomes who had not noticeably benefited from the kleptocracy run by them, which had bankrupted the country and necessitated rescue by the IMF. A flat tax simply means that the same percentage of income is paid in tax by everyone, though there is an income threshold before tax starts to be paid. According to Gordon Brown, Britain's arrogant and incompetent former Chancellor, this is an outrage because the millionaire "pays the same tax rate as the young nurse, the home help, the worker on the minimum wage." Exactly why this should be so dreadful, since 20%, say, of an income of a million is a great deal more than 20% of an income of £25,000 a year, is never explained. The hullabaloo got up in Hungary by a press still boasting a strong contingent of former

Communists was also designed to give the false impression that the government's measure was uniquely wicked, something no civilized government would even contemplate. As it happens, more than 40 countries have introduced flat taxes of one form or another, including all the Baltic States, as well as Russia, Ukraine, Macedonia, Bulgaria and (for local taxes) seven American states. Slovakia and the Czech Republic also had successful flat taxes for a while until governments of different ideological persuasions reversed them. All these countries introduced the tax in environments where collecting tax was difficult because of Communism's legacy and because it was thought that a flat tax boosts economic growth — and in many cases it has.

Why then are western liberals so opposed? After all the flat tax has been proposed by serious economists for such model welfare states as Germany and the Netherlands — and even the British Conservatives have been pondering it. The fact is that liberals like a complex tax system in which many of them can hide their own wealth while they posture about equality and social justice. Governments, especially ones with dodgy finance ministers, like the complexity because it helps them impose "stealth taxes." And business likes it because they can bully governments into all sorts of tax breaks and "corporate welfare" which would be hideously exposed to public view in a much simpler system. All these dishonest motives for maintaining, for example, a US tax code that is 9 million words long and riddled with loopholes, deductions and exemptions, and which distorts economic incentives and encourages a vast and parasitic industry devoted to "tax avoidance," are concealed in the slogan "progressive taxation." Tax revenues actually rose in Russia when it first introduced its flat tax and the Baltic countries boomed until their economies were trashed by the 2008 meltdown and EU folly.

Comedian Dave Barry has admirably summed up the humbug surrounding the flat tax: **Question:** *"I understand that Congress is considering a so-called 'flat' tax system. How would this work?"* **Answer:** *"If Congress were to pass a 'flat' tax, you'd simply pay a fixed percentage of your income, and you wouldn't have to fill out any complicated forms, and there would be no loopholes for politically connected groups, and normal people would actually understand the tax laws, and giant talking broccoli stalks would come around and mow your lawn for free, because Congress is NOT going to pass a flat tax, you pathetic fool."*

Likewise Ronald Reagan has summed up the economic imperatives of modern western governments with an accuracy that is as distressing as it is accurate: *"The government's view of the economy may be summed up in a few short phrases. If it moves, tax it. If it keeps moving, regulate it. And if it stops moving, subsidise it."*

But contempt for disingenuous tax regimes is not necessarily the exclusive preserve of the rich and greedy, as liberals would have you believe. That great radical Thomas Paine was just as outspoken on the subject.: *"If, from the more wretched parts of the old world, we look at those which are in an advanced stage of improvement, we still find the greedy hand of government thrusting itself into every corner and crevice of industry, and grasping the spoil of the multitudes. Invention is continually exercised to furnish new pretenses for revenues and taxation. It watches prosperity as its prey and permits none to escape without tribute."* Those words could have been written about Britain's former Chancellor of the Exchequer, Gordon Brown, who once admitted that in Britain *"we spend more on cows than the poor."* (Well, whose fault was that then?)

Technocracy: A society ruled by technocrats, for which read "experts," who do not really see the point of democracy, especially if it results in people choosing what they want rather than what they should want (according to technocrats):

William Easterly in his book *The Tyranny of Experts* describes how the agency worlds of "development" and "aid" have become inherently, if unconsciously, authoritarian. As he puts it: "Any approach to development will either respect the rights of the poor or it will violate them. One cannot avoid this moral choice by appealing to 'non-ideological evidence-based policies' (a popular phrase in development today.)"

Easterly gives a startling example of the autocratic rule of "experts" as manifest in a Ugandan project sponsored by the World Bank to promote forestry in order to raise local incomes. Unfortunately it had overlooked the property rights of the local farmers, who were in the way. They were driven from their farms at gunpoint by the authorities and had to watch their grain stores being burned and their cattle being slaughtered. The promised "investigation" by the World Bank somehow got stuck in the works.

The bank's jargon-ridden and evasive report on "governance" (2007) is also quoted by Easterly and provides a "horrible example" of a large, bureaucratic organisation trying to pretend it is proposing reform when it is not: *"Implementing the strengthened approach to governance... will require... careful development of a ... detailed results framework, consideration of budget and staffing implications... and further consultations with stakeholders... The specific initiatives needed to fully operationalize this strategy will be outlined in an Implementation Plan."*[11] Despite all this "considering", "consulting," "implementing" and "operationalizing," four years on, the Ugandan farmers of the Mubende District were still chased off their land in some nifty "operationalizing" ultimately (if unintentionally) sponsored by the Bank. "The technocratic illusion," says Easterly, "is that poverty results from a shortage of expertise, whereas poverty is really about a shortage of rights... the technical problems of the poor (and the absence of technical solutions for those problems) are a *symptom* of poverty, not a *cause* of poverty."[12]

See also **A: *Aid to Third World Governments.***

6th Grade History Tests: In Canada, a test of original thinking and imagination:

At a school, which shall be nameless, answers to some of the trickier biographical questions in one of the 6th Grade tests included the following: *"Socrates was a famous Greek teacher who went around giving people advice. They killed him. Socrates died from an overdose of wedlock. After his death, his career suffered a dramatic decline"*. And: *"Johann Bach wrote a great many musical compositions and had a large number of children. In between he practised on an old spinster which he kept in his attic"*.

And a few more interesting insights into historical movers and shakers:

Writing at the same time as Shakespeare was Miguel Cervantes. He wrote Donkey Hote. The next great author was John Milton. Milton wrote Paradise Lost. Then his wife died and he wrote Paradise Regained.

Sir Francis Drake circumcised the world with a 100-foot clipper.

Joan of Arc was burnt to a steak and was cannonized by Bernard Shaw.

11 World Bank, "Strengthening World Bank Engagement on Governance and Anticorruption," March 21, 2007, P. 33. Quoted in Easterly op cit. (*see note 11*).

12 William Easterly: *The Tyranny of Experts: Economists, Dictators, and the Forgotten Rights of the Poor*, Basic Books, New York, 2013, Pp. 3-7. The Ugandan scandal was exposed in an Oxfam report of 22 September 2011 and was also reported a day earlier in the *New York Times*.

The Greeks were a highly sculptured people, and without them we wouldn't have history. The Greeks also had myths. A myth is a female moth.

Moses led the Hebrew slaves to the Red Sea, where they made unleavened bread, which is bread made without any ingredients. Moses went up on Mount Cyanide to get the ten commandments. He died before he ever reached Canada.

Ancient Egypt was inhabited by mummies and they all wrote in hydraulics. They lived in the Sarah Dessert. The climate of the Sarah is such that the inhabitants have to live elsewhere.[13]

Paul Theroux: Famously dyspeptic American author who reckoned Britain was on the way out:

Theroux spent 18 years in England from 1972 and his unflattering view of Britain and the British is an uncomfortable reminder of how far that nation has fallen in international esteem.

For example, he cites the elevation of crooks to the House of Lords as symptomatic. That began with Prime Minister Harold Wilson's dubious friends (e.g. Lord Kagan, the inventor of hideous crinkly raincoats that were even given the establishment's seal of approval when worn by the royal corgis), and continued later with the so-called "Baron Archer of Weston-Super-Mare," a former Vice(*sic*)-Chairman of the Conservative Party who was banged up for perjury.

In the early years of the new millennium we had lords and commoners on the take, some building duck-ponds at taxpayers' expense, or "flipping" subsidised residences free of Capital Gains Tax, or lying on mortgage applications, or putting family members on the public payroll.

The House of Lords is supposed to have been reformed, but that did not prevent the ennoblement of a former Speaker of the House of Commons who had disgraced his office. As a member of his own Labour party put it, "*he has been a Speaker who had actually tried to prevent some of this information* [about the abuse of MPs' expenses] *coming out, spent money trying to get us exempted from the Freedom of Information Act — part of what seemed to be a very, very small coterie of the establishment who wanted things not to change.*" The Establishment however

---

13 These are allegedly real answers to 6th Grade History Tests in Canada collected at www.superkids.com/aweb/pages/humor/052899.sht

is forgiving of its own, so in due course this deeply undistinguished person was kicked upstairs as Baron Martin of Springburn, of Port Dundas in the City of Glasgow…

Still Theroux is not always much kinder about other countries, writing for instance that "the *Australian Book of Etiquette* is a very slim volume."

Or: "The Japanese have perfected good manners and made them indistinguishable from rudeness."

Or: "You must not judge people by their country. In South America, it is always wise to judge people by their altitude."

Or: "Less frightening, but no less disgusting, is the Iranian taste for jam made out of carrots."

Paul Theroux at home in Hawaii with the dii familiares

All the same his account of Britain's "*Sleazy aristocrats, crooked politicians, spies and trimmers…*" is sobering. Nowadays many of the worst elements in the UK seem to have risen from the depths to the surface of a putrefying society; and there they rest, like the graveolent imbrication of human sewage.

Celebrity-owned tigers: More sensitive than other tigers:
Following the demise of pop-idol Michael Jackson, *London Lite* reported that *"Two tigers kept by Jackson were told of his death by their guardian, the former actress Tippi Hedren."*

Time Out's New York Theatre Guide: How the theatre tries to keep up with our tastes:

The following shows were advertised in the New York summer theatre guide in 1996: "Nuns against Filth," "One of our Monsters is Mything," "Sexual Perversity in Chicago," "Tit Tales," "Unzipped," "The Vagina Monologues" and "Vampire Lesbians of Sodom."

Nothing much there to upset your grandmother, you might think — but why no *"Clitoridectomy for Beginners," "Gay Cannibalism Cookbook"* or *"Lapidation's Greatest Hits"*?

Free trade: Slogan under which powerful nations impose their goods on weak ones, while protecting their own producers with subsidies and (when necessary) tariffs:

George W. Bush was an outspoken devotee of free trade. *Schadenfreude* all round, therefore, when Dubya's *steel tariffs*, designed to win votes in steel-producing states, resulted in raised steel prices to Michigan carmakers, who duly shed 30,000 jobs. Meanwhile, of 900 million people in the world trying to survive on $1 a day, three-quarters are farmers competing with Europe (where every cow is subsidised to the tune of $600 a year) or Japan ($1,372 per cow per year). French farmers are pocketing $17, 283 a year in subsidies and each British farmer (according to Policy Exchange) costs the taxpayer an average of $27,707 a year.

As the (now defunct) newspaper *The Business* has mordantly observed: "This obscene system, which makes it profitable to grow sugarbeet in snowy Finland, while bankrupting Caribbean sugar-cane producers, also impoverishes consumers in rich countries …who pay 42% more than the market price for their food."

Not everybody is so keen on free trade however. An American labour leader called Lane Kirkland has complained that *"To hear the Japanese plead for free trade is like hearing the word love on the lips a harlot."*

Translations: "Like women, if they are beautiful, they are not true; if they are true, they are certainly not beautiful."[14]

This of course is not true, but it makes a good *mot* (*see also under* **A:** *Aphorisms.*)

14 Attributed to Yevgeny Yevtushenko, but possibly originating with Michel de Montaigne.

In *"What Have We Lost, & Where Did it Go?"* Michael Bywater writes: *"In England it's the Lost Property Office. In France, it's the Bureau des Objets Trouvés. Make of it what you will."* A better example, perhaps, is the fact that we talk of *"love-hatred"* in English, while the Germans talk of *"Hassliebe"* (may as well get it the right way round).

Mistranslations are another matter altogether. The story goes that a novice Budapest translator once came on a passage in German dealing with *Jacob's Ladder*. Clearly this was a reference to some fellow Hungarian Jew called "Leiter Jakab," and he rendered it accordingly, to the unrestrained joy of the coffee house wits. Ever since, solecisms in Hungarian translation are referred to as *"Leiter Jakabs"*.

Translations, to be readable, may not be all that accurate. Harold Bloom has observed that "the Greek New Testament is the strongest and most successful misreading of a great prior text in the entire history of influence," a statement which reminds us that the mere recording, let alone translation, of religious texts is fraught with danger. How many massacres in the history of religious conflict depend on a mistranslation (or for that matter, an accurate one)? And what about a misreading of the Greek itself? Saint Augustine's depressing doctrine of original sin, the idea that all mankind has inherited sin and mortality from Adam, is said to be derived from the fact that the great man's Greek was not too hot and he mistranslated a line from St Paul's *Letter to the Romans*.[15] In this case a mistranslation has been the cause of endless psychological misery for generations of innocent people, not to mention providing fire and brimstone ammunition for power-hungry preachers…

"Poetry is what gets lost in translation," said Robert Frost (the maximalist view). "The original is unfaithful to the translation," said Jorge Luis Borges (the minimalist view).

Truth: That which traditionally is in short supply:
Emily Dickinson wrote a characteristically acute poem about telling the truth:

15 See: Robin Lane Fox: *Augustine: Conversions and Confessions* (Basic Books / Allen Lane, 2015).

Tell all the truth, but tell it slant,

Success in circuit lies.
Too bright for our infirm delight

As lightning to the children
eased
With explanation kind,
The truth should dazzle
gradually.

Town twinning: Bumbledom's expression of civic fraternalism that cynics suspect is mostly a device to enable local councillors to go on junkets abroad:

Comedian Linda Smith has memorably remarked: "*I come from Erith. It isn't twinned with anywhere, but it does have a suicide pact with Dagenham.*"

Kenneth Tynan: Spanker and theatre critic:

It being reported to him that an irascible Rex Harrison (star of *My Fair Lady* etc.) had punched a harmless autograph hunter, Tynan remarked that this was "*the only known real life example of the shit hitting the fan.*"

Trinitarianism: The Christian Church's version of "triangulation", later much favoured by Bill Clinton and Tony Blair, whereby two propositions that people passionately support are melded into a third that nobody does:

Trinitarianism posits "one God in three Divine Persons" and should not be confused with *Binitarianism* (one deity, two persons), *Unitarianism* (one deity, one person) or *Modalism* (one deity with three separate aspects.) Some have found all this rather tedious, not to say ridiculous:

Il y avait un jeune homme de Dijon
Qui n'avait que peu de religion.
Il dit, "Quant à moi
Je déteste tous les trois:
Le père, le fils et le pigeon!"

U

Un-American:
Wicked, intolerable, heathenish.

Ambrose Bierce: *The Devil's Dictionary*

Unloved allies: The English for the French (also *vice versa*):
A recent book reveals what the radical French Socialist Prime Minister, Édouard Daladier (1884–1970), really thought of the British who pressed him into appeasement of Hitler at the Munich summit of 1938. He regarded Chamberlain as a *"desiccated stick"*, George VI as a *"moron"* and Eden as an *"idiot"*. He also said he had never met *"a single Englishman for whose intellectual equipment and character he had respect."* This is what happens, evidently, if you only meet with royalty or Tories… (*See also* **F**: *Frenemies* and *Feindbild*).

Not that he had a much higher opinion of his fellow-countrymen: returning from the disaster of Munich he was greeted by wildly cheering crowds. *"Idiots!"* he muttered under his breath.

The remark made under your breath, but loud enough for some to hear, is rather a French speciality. The corrupt French President Jacques Chirac liked to employ it as noises off, for example muttering *"couillons"* when Mrs Thatcher was in full flood at an EU summit. This was not an effective way of stopping her, of course; rather the reverse.

Madame Cresson, Prime Minister of France until she annoyed people so much that her "sponsor" Francois Mitterand had to remove her and give her a job as European Commissioner for Education, Research and Sciences, was arguably even less enamoured of the English than Daladier. In an interview with Naim Attallah published in *The Observer*, she claimed that 25% of Englishmen were gay (evidently her irresistible female charms had not been sufficiently appreciated in London; but to be fair she asserted that the same was true of American

471

and German men.) In Brussels she appointed her own dental surgeon, René Berthelot, as her personal adviser on HTV/AIDS, about which he knew next to nothing. "After two years," writes Attallah "though eighty-five thousand pounds the richer, Berthelot had produced a total of twenty-four pages of notes later deemed to be unqualified and grossly deficient."

"Another project she generated, known as the Leonardo da Vinci Vocational Training Scheme, which she claimed was the best-administered programme in Brussels, became implicated in massive fraud, and the company she had chosen to run it was stripped of its five-hundred-million-pound contract. Investigations uncovered a whole nest of falsified contracts, forged handwriting and embezzled funds, leading to the resignation of the entire Santer Commission in 1999. Though the Advocate General of the European Court of Justice recommended that she be stripped of half her forty-seven-thousand-euro pension, she was allowed to escape the imposition of any financial penalty. '*Maybe I was a little careless,*' was the extent of her public admission."[1]

Probably straight "Anglo-Saxons" and "Germans" should not have been too miffed at Madame's remarks about them, since she was quite generous with her aspersions. The Japanese, she said, wanted to conquer the world, and were too busy plotting against the American and European economies to be able to sleep at night. They were 'ants … little yellow men who sit up all night thinking how to screw us'. Almost as bad as the perfidious and gay inhabitants of Albion in fact. Unfortunately this sort of thing brings out the worst in the tabloids, and as everyone knows, the worst tabloids are the British ones. The *Sun*, for example, offered this as a return match: "*Édith Cresson, France's first woman PM, claims one in four Englishmen is homosexual. That's a bit rich coming from the leader of a nation where most men carry handbags and kiss each other in public. They don't call Paris Gay Paree for nothing, you know.*" Then Mr David Jones of Bolton, Greater Manchester, suggested in a letter to *The Observer* that for Mme Cresson's next state visit to Britain he could envisage a 'guard of honour of scaffolders at Heathrow, ready to receive the premier by ceremoniously intoning, "*Cor, I bet she does the business.*"

1 See: Naim Attallah Online: "Edith Cresson: The Other Femme Fatale," posted 16/10/2012.

The unreasonable man: A familiar type of humankind, as characterised by Theophrastus (c.370–285 B.C.):

"[He] is the kind who comes up to you when you have no time to spare and asks your advice. He sings a serenade to his sweetheart when she has influenza … He is certain to bring along a buyer who offers more, when you have just sold your house. When people have heard a matter and know it by heart, he stands up and explains the whole thing from the beginning."

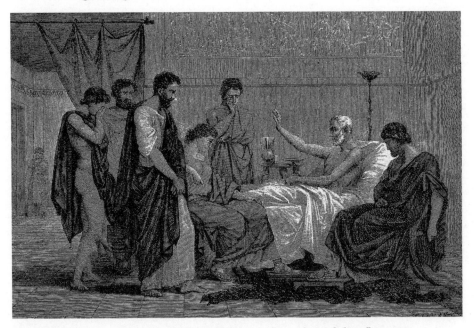

Theophrastus on his deathbed offering a few cheerful reflections...

Theophrastus 'Five Characters are fun: "The ***abominable man***… is one who, on meeting respectable women, will lift his clothing and display his private parts. In the theatre he claps when the rest have stopped; and hisses players whom everyone else is enjoying; and when there is a silence, he will lift his head and belch, to make the audience turn round. The ***presumptuous man***… will go to his father and tell him that his mother is still fast asleep in their bedroom. When a woman relative has died, he inscribes on her tombstone her husband's name and her father's and mother's, as well as her own name and her place of birth and adds that "they were all estimable people." And when about to take an oath he remarks to those standing round: "I've done this scores of times." The *late learner*, when wrestling at the baths, wiggles his bottom rapidly, so that people may think he has been properly trained … he rides out to the country on a borrowed horse, practises horsemanship on the way, falls off and breaks his neck."'

The Characters of Theoprastus
Theoprastus (319 BCE)

- The Dissembler
- The Flatterer
- The Garrulous Man
- The Boor
- The Self-Seeking Affable Man
- The Willfully Disreputable Man
- The Loquacious Man
- The Newsmaker
- The Unconscionable Man
- The Penurious Man
- The Buffoon
- The Tactless Man
- The Officious Man
- The Stupid Man
- The Surly Man
- The Superstitious Man
- The Querulous or Grumbling Man
- The Distrustful Man
- The Nasty Man
- The Ill-Bred Man
- The Man of Petty Pride
- The Parsimonious Man
- The Pretentious Man
- The Arrogant Man
- The Coward
- The Oligarch
- The Opsimath or Late-Learner
- The Backbiter
- The Friend of Rascals
- The Mean Man

"Unhelpful": Sir Humphrey's word for any intervention that interferes with his world view:

In diplomatic jargon it is "unhelpful" when Vladimir Putin annexes the Crimea and even more so when and if he does the same to East Ukraine. The Syriza party in Greece is "unhelpful," firstly by getting elected and secondly by pointing out what everybody knows (including Sir Humphrey who has been pretending otherwise), namely that Greece can never repay its debts and a large part of them will have to be written off. Hitler and Stalin were "unhelpful" persons, of course, but there are a surprising number of persons closer to home of whom the same could be said — bossy academics who produce reports advocating cuts to the diplomatic service, for instance; or journalists who view Sir Humphrey's heroic efforts on behalf of us all with totally unjustified cynicism. Really obstructive persons who have rumbled one or other of Sir Humphrey's clever ruses to outwit his political masters are known as *"difficile"* — even worse than unhelpful.

United Nations' Expenditure: How the money of the world's taxpayers goes to a good cause:

A book many of you may have missed in 2006 is a catchily titled tome that cost the UN a mere $567,379 to produce. It's called *The United Nations Development Programme: A Better Way* (hurry, while stocks last). The author was paid a fee of $252,000, of course with a travel budget of $37,299. No wonder the introduction offers profuse thanks to Mark Malloch Brown for authorising this blizzard of greenbacks (Malloch Brown, you will recall, was Kofi Annan's anti-corruption investigator, so obviously the right chap for the job.)

But there is more: a "project co-ordinator" got $87,639, while research and editing cost $91,559; $26,752 was spent on office space (or "waste of space," as UN offices and their occupants are called.) Cambridge University Press received $55,000, to relieve them of copies that would otherwise have been more difficult to shift than refrigerators to Eskimos. The American activist who unearthed all this complained pathetically that the money would have been better spent carrying out the organisation's mandate of helping the world's poor. What a disgraceful slur on the conscientious and dedicated folk at the UN!

Universities: "A man is not necessarily intelligent because he has plenty of ideas, any more than he is a good general because he has plenty of soldiers."[2]

In his *Counsels and Maxims* Arthur Schopenhauer muses that "extensive reflection and knowledge without much experience resemble one of those editions with two lines of text on a page and forty lines of commentary." On the other hand, "extensive experience without much reflection and knowledge is like an edition without notes which is often unintelligible."[3] This is one way of summing up the conundrum of university life, its trade-off between the ivory tower and the rat race. In point of fact the rat race has now entered the hallowed precincts of the university itself, whereby triennial audits of publications and other activities increase the measurable output of struggling academics, but not necessarily the quality (*q.v.* **B: Bureaucracy**).

2 Nicolas Chamfort: *Maximes et pensées*, 1805.
3 Arthur Schopenhauer: *Parerga and Paralipomena*, 1851.

Politicians must be seen to espouse the aim of having an ever increasing number of university students, both to produce more qualified people and to give the underprivileged more access to social and economic power. Like apple pie and mother love nobody who isn't a monster could possibly object to such worthy aims. So it is not done to talk about the problems that result from such a policy. Such as (1) the devaluation of Honours Degrees and even PhDs in the job market due to there being too many of them; (2) the escalation of student debt, ever greater proportions of which may not be paid back due to (3) the escalation of tuition and other fees (around $26,000 on average in the USA in 2014); (4) the creation of what a leftist Swedish academic called "an academic proletariat" — people with all sorts of higher qualifications in disciplines such as the social sciences, who join an overcrowded field and help to churn out more members of the same proletariat. Paul Collier, the distinguished Professor of Economics at Oxford, is candid enough to write in his book *Exodus* that "anyone familiar with universities will recognize that some of their students, and indeed some of their staff, are virtually unemployable despite being highly educated."[4]

Of course a university education still assists its beneficiaries to social and economic advantages if they can get jobs. However, while it helps those individuals, the writer Christopher Caldwell has wondered aloud whether it benefits the broader community, as is tacitly assumed: "It is leading the US closer to a social structure," he writes, "that resembles the Spanish army of a century ago, with its shortage of foot soldiers and its bloated high command."[5]

These are of course reactionary thoughts and anyone who has themselves enjoyed a university education would be ill-advised to voice them in public. It was typically the *enfant terrible* of post-war letters, the writer Kingsley Amis, who made the point most brutally. As the huge expansion of higher education got under way in the 1960s creating what were snobbishly dubbed "red brick" universities out of former polytechnics, Amis (himself a former university lecturer) contemplated the scene with dismay. "*More means worse*", he said, instantly provoking a chorus

4 Paul Collier: *Exodus: Immigration and Multiculturalism in the 21st Century* (Penguin Books, 2014) P. 261.

5 Christopher Caldwell: *Weekend FT*, February 22/23, 2014. It was once claimed that the Spanish navy had more Admirals than ships…

of abuse. There were other renegades, notably the novelist Malcolm Bradbury whose hilarious exposé of academic opportunism and charlatanism in *The History Man* did nothing for the prestige of the higher learning. Not that misapplied learning had gone uncriticized in the past: *"A learned fool,"* said Molière, *"is more a fool than an ignorant fool…"*

Getting up: "What can you expect of a day that begins with getting up in the morning?"

"I know an Englishman," said Goethe, *"who hanged himself rather than having to get dressed every morning."*

Peter Ustinov: Corpulent multilingual sage and mimic:
Two Ustinovisms: "We used to have lots of questions to which there were no answers. Now, with the computer, there are lots of answers to which we haven't thought up the questions."

And this rather topical one: "American democracy is the inalienable right to sit on your own front porch, in your pyjamas, drinking a can of beer and shouting out: 'Where else is this possible?' Which doesn't seem to me to be freedom, really."

Peter Ustinov as a decidedly dodgey Nero in Quo Vadis .

T. E. Utley: High Tory journalist who turned down a job as TV critic:
Utley, who was blind from birth, is said to have been the Editor's first choice for TV reviewer on the newly founded *Sunday Telegraph* (1961). The Editor (Donald McLachlan) argued that he was best for the job as he wouldn't be distracted by the pictures …

The writer Clive James almost single-handedly raised television criticism to the level of an art form, because he captured very well its unashamed reflection of the most banal and narcissistic elements of our grossly materialist society. As he put it: *"Anyone afraid of what he thinks television is doing to the world is probably just afraid of the world."* Dreadful TV programmes are used by James as the inspiration not just for gags, but for gags that may well upset your sanguine view of life as well as your appetite for your TV dinner. Like this, for instance, his take on a celebrity sport programme: *"In the Bob Hope Golf Classic, the participation of President Gerald Ford was more than enough to remind you that the nuclear button was at one stage at the disposal of a man who might have either pressed it by mistake or else pressed it deliberately in order to obtain room service."*

Skewering the crass and the grotesque tends to be the staple of TV criticism, if only because the medium constantly goes out of its way to try and convince the viewers that everybody who appears on the box is a genius, or at least fascinating in some indeterminate way. James gave that sort of thing short shrift, viz. *"A traditional fixture at Wimbledon is the way the BBC TV commentary box fills up with British players eliminated in the early rounds."* Feeble left-wing orthodoxy in the culture department was also unceremoniously dispatched: *"Among artists without talent Marxism will always be popular, since it enables them to blame society for the fact that nobody wants to hear what they have to say."*

Clive James perfected the kind of abuse that Dorothy Parker pioneered, but tailored it perfectly to its targets in a casual *ad hominem* manner that somehow avoids letting you feel sorry for the victims in all their awfulness. *"Hi! I'm Liza"* was his ominous headline for a review that might have been sufficient to encourage some TV licence fee payers to withhold payment of the same:

"Bad Sight and Bad Sound of the Week were twin titles both won by 'Love from A to Z' (BBC1), a river of drivel featuring Liza Minnelli and Charles Aznavour. To begin with (and to go on with and end with, since the phenomenon was continuous), there was the matter of how Charles had contrived to get himself billed above the normally omni-dominant Liza. Not only was his name foremost in the opening titles, but the between-song lectures, instead of being delivered by Charles on the subject of Liza's talent, were mainly delivered by Liza on the subject of Charles's genius. "Hi!" Liza would yell intimately, her features suffused by that racking spasm of narcissistic coyness which she fondly imagines looks like a blush, "I'm Liza." (Such a coup is supposed to stun you with its humility, but in the event it is difficult to choke back the urge to belch.) She would then impart a couple of hundred words of material … on the topic of Charles Aznavour, with particular reference to his creativity, magnanimity and vision.

"This would be followed by a lengthy and devastating assault on '*My Funny Valentine*' by Charles himself, in which the song's subtlety would be translated into the standard emotional intensity of the French cabaret ballad, leaving the viewer plenty of opportunity to note how the tortured singer's eyebrows had been wrinkled by hard times, lost loves and the decline of the franc…

"Liza, who can't even walk up a flight of stairs sincerely (a flight of stairs was wheeled on for the specific purpose of allowing her to prove this), is more touching than she knows. She began her career with a preposterous amount of talent, the shreds of which she still retains, but like her mother she doesn't know how to do anything small, and, like almost every other young success, she has embraced the standards of excellence proposed by Showbiz, which will agree to love you only if your heart is in the right place — where your brain should be."[6]

Another TV critic who has elevated the genre is Nancy Banks Smith of *The Guardian*. Her approach is less *ad hominem* than James and her rather more informative pieces are laced with witticisms and gentle humour, e.g. "*Anthropology is the science which tells us that people are the same the whole world over — except when they are different.*" Or: "*Agatha Christie has given more pleasure in bed than any other woman.*" Reporting on a Royal Jubilee programme she captured in a few words the portentous manner of a royal correspondent, in this case Tom Fleming: "He knows the State Coach weighs four and a half tons, and was delivered at five in the morning, and the names of all the horses: Budapest, Beaufort, Rio, Santiago, and so forth. So forth not being a horse, of course. They are greys because it shows the red and gold harness so well and that must be one reason why London, grey in style and stone, lends itself to such pageantry. When most truly moved, Fleming is barely rational: 'One wonders what the conversation will be in the stables tonight when the horses get home.'

"However, let joy be unconfined and criticism minimal. The walkabout was a genuinely gay and pretty business with the Queen being handed a painting here, a posy there. I watched with close attention and

6 Clive James: *Visions Before Midnight* (Jonathan Cape Ltd.).

fed my findings into a computer. The conclusion is that the Queen is likeliest to stop and talk to you if you are a young, male foreigner in a funny hat sitting in a wheel-chair near a Boy Scout; the Duke if you are a nun with a periscope."[7]

Utopianism: "Utopianism is the populism of the elite."[8]

A lot of (possibly) well-meaning and otherwise intelligent people are rather too keen to believe in utopias, especially the one supposedly ushered in by Lenin and his gang in Russia. Apart from Lincoln Steffens quoted elsewhere ("*I have seen the future and it works*"), a string of leftist intellectuals including George Bernard Shaw, Beatrice and Sydney Webb and Hewlett Johnson (the 'Red Dean' of Canterbury) professed themselves delighted with the "progressive" nature of the Soviet state at a time when slaughter on an industrial scale was well under way. For connoisseurs of fatuousness the most egregious eulogy of Stalin was provided by a Labour Chancellor of the Exchequer, Sir Stafford Cripps, who said of the great butcher that he was "*direct, honest-minded, no pretentiousness, no sign of wishing to be a personage, in short a businessman, completely absorbed in scientific humanism and in bringing health and happiness to all people.*" This is quoted by Richard Ingrams in his commonplace book. He also quotes how this paragon of "scientific humanism" prepared to wreak vengeance on his enemies, real or imagined: "*To choose the victim, carefully prepare the blow, satisfy an implacable vengeance, then go to bed. There is nothing sweeter in the world.*"[9]

---

7 Nancy Banks Smith, TV critique in *The Guardian*.
8 John O'Sullivan.
9 Richard Ingrams: *Quips and Quotes: A Journalist's Commonplace Book* (Oldie Publications, London, 2012), Pp. 67 and 97.

V

Vote:

*The instrument and symbol of a freeman's power to make
a fool of himself and a wreck of his country*

— Ambrose Bierce

Günther Verheugen: European Commissioner who rashly applied the notion of accountability to the Brussels apparat:

Verheugen's skilfully selective vision in respect of human rights abuse amongst new member states of the European Union had won him justified plaudits from colleagues. But just as they were admiring and applauding Günther's slippery passage between *Dichtung und Wahrheit,* he overturned the applecart by denouncing the Brussels bureaucracy as power-hungry, grossly inflated and costing European companies up to 600 billion Euros annually. Alas, poor Günther! Revenge for such *lèse-majesté* was not slow in coming from the 24,000 gourmet *apparatchiks.* They immediately prepared a new law in Günther's area of competence (competition) to be nodded through behind his back, the draft of which ignored all the policies the great man had advocated on the issue. They also let it be known why his immediate resignation would be desirable, so as to demonstrate unequivocally what happens to whistleblowers… er… that is, to protect an altruistic public servant who had evidently suffered some kind of breakdown and was in need of prolonged rest (*apparatchiks* have "tenure" of course).

If anyone was still inclined to doubt the totalitarian tendencies of the Brussels *apparat,* President of the Commission Barroso (a former Maoist) did his best to clarify the situation: he allied himself immediately with the unelected bureaucracy against the commissioner (admittedly also unelected, but nominally accountable.) It seems that the view of Brussels insiders is sadly reminiscent of an attitude we had rather hoped that Europe had outgrown. In 1979 it was neatly summed up by the Czech Communist organ, *Rude Pravo* : *"Those who lie on the rails of history must expect to have their legs chopped off."*

"There are twenty-seven commissioners," Verheugen had said, *"which means twenty-seven directorate-generals. And twenty-seven directorate-generals means that everyone needs to prove that they are needed by constantly producing new directives, strategies or projects. In any case the rule is: More and more, more and more, all the time."*[1] Clearly such a man is not fitted to hold a high post in the EU…

Paul Verlaine (1844–1896): "Take eloquence and wring its neck": Whether or not Verlaine definitively succeeded in wringing the neck of eloquence, it is clear that he was actually a forerunner of Buddy Holly. Compare, for example *"Il pleure dans mon cœur / Comme il pleut sur la ville"* with the rock'n'roll master's lyric "The sun is out, the sky is blue / There's not a cloud to spoil the view; / But it's raining, raining in my heart." This is a classic example of what the critic Harold Bloom calls the "anxiety of influence" and no doubt many Eng. Lit. majors are contemplating a Ph.D. on it.

Actually Verlaine's poem may well have been inspired by a spell teaching French in rain-swept Lincolnshire, an experience which is almost bound to contribute to a generally gloomy outlook and alcohol addiction…

In World War II, another Verlaine poem *"Chanson d'automne"* was used to broadcast the start of D-Day operations to the French Resistance in 1944. The first three rather unencouraging lines of the poem, *"Les sanglots longs / Des violons / De l'automne"* ("Long sobs of autumn violins"), meant that the invasion was to start within two weeks. The next set of lines, not a lot more encouraging (*"Blessent mon coeur / D'une langueur / Monotone"* — "wound my heart with a monotonous languor"), signalled that it would start within 48 hours and that the Resistance should begin sabotage operations, especially on the French railroad system.

---

1 Quoted in: David Charter: *Europe In Or Out: Everything You Need To Know* (Biteback Publishing, London, 2016) P. 258.

What have you done, you standing there
In floods of tears?
Tell me what you have done
With your young life?[2]

Verlaine was the archetypal *poète maudit,* a pitiful figure but also a genius. As a very young man he was convicted of shooting (but in fact only grazing) his lover and fellow poet Arthur Rimbaud. Of Rimbaud, the police report said: *"In morality and talent, this Raimbaud (sic), aged between 15 and 16, was and is a monster. He can construct poems like nobody else, but his works are completely incomprehensible and repulsive."* The shooting incident was the combination of a lovers' tiff and alcoholic excess, and Rimbaud did not lodge a complaint against his friend. The law banged up Verlaine anyway because the shooting provided a good excuse to punish homosexuality (although it was not illegal in France); also Verlaine had been a Communard (supporter of the 1871 Paris Commune.)

Removed from the temptations of the Parisian cafes (especially the absinthe) Verlaine converted to Roman Catholicism and spent his 555 days behind bars writing masterpieces that later earned him the title of "prince of poets." Unfortunately, once released from the reliable discomforts of prison back into the world of unreliable comforts such as alcohol and drugs, the poet went steadily downhill. By the end of his life he was an alcoholic and destitute, moving between his haunts of slums, hospitals and cafes. Diabetes, ulcers, syphilis and absinthe finally did for him and he died of pneumonia in January 1896 at the age of 51.[3]

Bernard Bousmanne, curator in 2015 of a comprehensive Verlaine exhibition in Mons (where Verlaine was incarcerated), spent years collecting material on the unfortunate genius. Nevertheless his final assessment is well this side of idolatry: while he concedes that Verlaine has emerged as one of France's four greatest poets — along with Baudelaire, Mallarmé and Rimbaud — he points out that his violence towards his wife and mother suggest he was not a pleasant character, but a man who appeared

2 Translation by Martin Sorrell: *Selected Poems: Paul Verlaine* (Oxford University Press World Classics, 2009).

3 See: Kim Willsher: "How 555 nights in jail helped to make Paul Verlaine a 'prince of poets,' *The Observer,* 18 October, 2015.

Paul Verlaine, a martyr to absinthe...

to seek out misery and melodrama. *"He is often moaning in his letters, but it was always someone else's fault, never his. He often writes that he is going to kill himself or end it all, but doesn't."*

Or, as Verlaine himself put it:

Ton cœur bat-il toujours à mon seul nom ?
— Toujours vois-tu mon âme en rêve ? — Non."

Victimhood: Fiercely competed ground in the identity wars:

It started with feminist Suzanne Moore complaining in print that women were being pressured to acquire the ideal body shape, which was apparently *"that of a Brazilian transsexual."* Moore was immediately engulfed via the Internet in a tsunami of terrifying abuse from the transsexual lobby. Forced to retreat from Twitter altogether, her graceful parting shot was: *"People can just fuck off really. Cut off their dicks and be more feminist than me."*

Enter from the left (or possibly from the right) journalist Julie Burchill, well-known Rottweiler and friend of Moore, who wrote a characteristically tasteful piece in *The Observer* accusing transsexuals *inter alia* of being *"bed wetters in bad wigs."* As one commentator wrote,

"Julie Burchill poured oil on troubled waters. Then she put some seabirds in the oil. Then she set fire to it."

Whereat *another set* of outraged liberals (keep up at the back there!) denounced Burchill, demanding that both she and the Editor of *The Observer* be sacked (pity the poor editors of left-wing journals trying to keep abreast of ever more categories of person who may not be spoken ill of.)

Some of you may be a little bewildered by all this, but the explanation is simple: the most valuable commodity in identity politics is *victimhood*, of which sadly there is not quite enough to go round for all the groups laying claim to it. This gives rise to violent turf wars between gangs of liberals seeking to establish new victimhoods and hate crimes, naturally also with slogans to go with them (*"cissexist," "cultural appropriation"* and so forth (but see also under **A: *Apologism*** and **N: *Nativism***, plus **W: *Trigger Warnings***.)

But surely it is outrageous that no one has denounced the use of the word *"Brazilian"* in this case? Ever since an unfortunate Brazilian was mistakenly liquidated by the anti-terrorist squad on the London underground, it is clear that Brazilians have an unimpeachable claim to victimhood. Being "transsexual" *and* "a Brazilian" is therefore a sort of victimhood jackpot. Yet there isn't even a Transsexual Support Group exclusively for persons of Brazilian nationality! How uncaring can you get?

Inverted victimhood is another interesting modern development in the field, being the art of turning perpetrators into victims. Writing in the *Guardian*, a minor academic laments that he can't complain in public (so what's he doing here?) about the practice of white artistes blacking their skins for performance, because the "threat of being labelled *politically correct* creates an environment where we are scared to voice our objections." Substitute the word *incorrect* for *correct* in this sentence and you will see how this gentleman has elegantly inverted the reality on the ground. Nevertheless this handily reversible form of the "politically correct" ploy has great potential. Up and down the country there are obviously thousands of people for whom the mere accusation of "political correctness" is a new form of fascistic intimidation *by the very people who should have been intimidated by now, but have not been!* The authorities should act immediately.

Fake accounts of victimhood have become very popular in recent years, often receiving fulsome praise from papers like the *New York Times* and in a few cases even wining prizes. The most common are fabricated accounts of surviving the worst horrors of World War II; or of growing up in hideously deprived circumstances, e.g. oppressed by a violent alcoholic father and/or an abusive drug-taking mother, plus a further colourful cast of dysfunctional ogres. An amusingly brazen attempt to cash in simultaneously on both victim culture and politically correct "diversity" was Margaret Jones's "memoir" of her life as a half-American Indian girl adopted into a black family in Los Angeles (*"raw, tender and tough-minded"* according to the *New York Times*.) It turned out that the author was actually the white middle-class product of a creative writing programme. As journalist Christopher Caldwell has drily remarked "For a writer, gaining access to moral authority is an imperative. How does one do that in a system that confers moral authority based on someone's race or birth?"

Then again, in an increasingly competitive market for victimhood, to be sure of success you must locate yourself in the comparatively narrow zone approved by liberal intellectuals. They can hardly be expected to flagellate themselves if you are simply white, desperate and non-newsworthy.

Gore Vidal (1925–2012): Collector of enemies who said *"Whenever a friend succeeds, a little something in me dies."*

Vidal has also observed with disarming candour: *"It is not enough to succeed. Others must fail."*

And: *"The four most beautiful words in our common language: I told you so."*

And: *"I'm all for bringing back the birch, but only between consenting adults."*

And: *"There's a lot to be said for being nouveau riche, and the Reagans mean to say it all."*

On monotheism he had rather decided views which were not calculated to endear him to the mainstream in America, or indeed anywhere else where Judaism, Christianity or Islam are in vogue: *"The great unmentionable evil at the center of our culture is monotheism. From a barbaric Bronze Age text known as the Old Testament, three anti-human religions have evolved — Judaism, Christianity, Islam. These are sky-god religions. They are, literally, patriarchal — God is the Omnipotent Father — hence the loathing of women for 2,000 years in those countries afflicted by the sky-god and his earthly male delegates. The sky-god is a jealous god, of course. He requires total obedience from everyone on earth, as he*

486

is in place not for just one tribe but for all creation. Those who would reject him must be converted or killed for their own good. Ultimately, totalitarianism is the only sort of politics that can truly serve the sky-god's purpose."[4]

Of Vidal's insouciant sexual provocations Martin Amis wrote: *Vidal gives the impression of believing that the entire heterosexual edifice — registry offices,* Romeo and Juliet, *the disposable diaper — is just a sorry story of self-hypnosis and mass hysteria: a hoax, a racket, or sheer propaganda.*[5] This is perhaps an example of how the fate of aging gadflies is to be treated with amused indulgence rather than outrage…

Gore Vidal: "A narcissist is someone better looking than you are…."

On the other hand, his abrasive take on sensitive issues often still resonates, for example in his full-frontal demolition of liberal naivete in regard to mass migration (Vidal was generally accounted a Democrat and a Liberal). In a 1999 lecture entitled "*The Folly of Mass Immigration*" he said: "*A characteristic of our present chaos is the dramatic migration of tribes. They are on the move from east to west, from south to north. Liberal tradition requires that borders must always be open to those in search of safety, or even the pursuit of happiness. But now, with so many millions of people on the move, even the great-hearted are becoming edgy. Norway is large enough and empty enough to take in 40 to 50 million homeless Bengalis. If the Norwegians say that, all in all, they would rather not take them in, is this to be considered racism? I think not. It is simply self-preservation, the first law of species.*"[6]

4 "America First? America Last? America at Last?", Lowell Lecture, Harvard University (1992)

5 Martin Amis: Review of *Palimpsest*, in *The Sunday Times*, October 1995, reprinted in *The War Against Cliché* (2001)

6 Quoted by Anthony Browne (April 30, 2003), "*The Folly of Mass Immigration*" (See: *Opendemocracy.net*, November 7, 2011) from a lecture of the same name given by Gore Vidal in Dublin in 1999.

Viennese jokes: Almost as funny as Jewish jokes:

Take this one, an everyday story of Viennese guile: A man nursing a beer in a restaurant is suddenly caught short. But he hasn't finished his beer, and you can't leave unfinished beer unattended, certainly not in Vienna. His ingenious solution to the problem is to affix a scrap of paper to the beer glass on which he has scribbled in large letters *"I've spat in this beer!"* When he comes back from the relieving himself, the beer level has dropped by several centimetres and there's another scrap of paper on the glass, on which has been scribbled: *"So have I!"* (OK, OK! But it's the way they tell them …)

Actually there are quite a lot of beer jokes, many of them agreeably sexist, ageist, non-politically correct etc. For example: at the *Opernball* (Vienna's annual ball held in the opera house) a handsome young man approaches a wallflower and asks if she is free for the next dance. *"Yes, rather…"* says the wallflower eagerly. *"Oh that's wonderful,"* says the man; *"then could you mind my beer for me till I get back…?"*

Many other jokes envisage farcically erotic scenarios, which indeed still occur in the city that has not quite slipped its reputation, bestowed by Schiller, of being inhabited by the lubricious tribe of Phaeacians mentioned in the *Odyssey*. For example: two men meet at a party for the first time. By way of breaking the ice with bracing small talk, one of them says to the other: *"Do you see those two ladies chatting away in that corner? The pretty blonde is my mistress and the curvy brunette is my wife."* *"That's funny,"* says his interlocutor; *"I was just about to say the same thing — only the other way round…"*

A perennial figure of Viennese humour is a dumb minor aristocrat named Graf Bobby, who emerged as a popular butt of ridicule around 1900. As Republican Austria, following each World War, looked back ironically on the days when birth implied privilege, the character enjoyed a further lease of life. Indeed the affection in which the naïve Graf Bobby was held demonstrated an admirable lack of rancour on the part of the Austrians, while his unerring eye for missing the point became emblematic of the Viennese type who was simultaneously stupid and unwittingly sly. The French Republicans after the Revolution of 1789 decapitated their aristocrats; after 1918 the Austrians made fun of them:

Graf Bobby is called up for the army and is asked how he wishes to perform his military service. *"As a General of course!"* *"Are you mad?"* *"Why do you ask? Is that a condition?"*

Graf Bobby comes back from a shooting party earlier than expected and finds his wife in bed with another man. *"Johann!"* he shouts to his butler, *"Bring me my gun; I will shoot them both here and now."* *"You can't do that, Sir,"* says the butler; *"As a passionate stalker you must know that during the rutting season they are protected."*

Graf Bobby meets his friend Baron Mucki in the coffeehouse. He has just heard a rumour: *"Tell me, is it true what they say that you have separated from Mitzi simply because she has to wear glasses now?"* *"Absolute nonsense!"* says the Baron. *"To tell the truth, as soon as she got her glasses I was dismissed!"*

Graf Bobby arrives at the Austrian border. A bored customs official routinely asks him: *"Alcohol, cigarettes, chocolate?"* *"No, thank you,"* says Bobby. *"Just a cup of tea for me."*

Many Viennese jokes depend on sophisticated wordplay, making them hard to translate, but others revolve around the deadpan application of logic, rather as Tristram Shandy in Laurence Sterne's novel of the same name remarks somewhat inappropriately to his father *"You, Sir, slept with my mother, so why should not I sleep with yours?"* The great Viennese actor/producer Johann Nestroy filled his comedies with this kind of thing and even drew a smile from the po-faced bureaucrats looking to censor anything they thought was subversive. *"What has posterity done for us?"* was a typical Nestroy sally. *"I will tell you: it has done nothing. So I will do nothing for posterity."* (This is an argument that could be used to annoy "climate change" zealots.)

There is a sense in which Vienna is the incarnation of a witticism, or at least a shaggy dog story, the "theatre city" shaped by Habsburg mythology described by Egon Friedell: *"The world was supposed to pattern itself on [the Habsburgs], not they on the world. Therefore they could make use of creatures who had no will of their own, and so arose the 'Nation of Privy Councillors.' Then came the Baroque with its double reversal of the idea of worldliness. It first rejected the world as mere dream. But since at the same time it affirmed dream as the only reality, it again returned to the world by a roundabout way. Thus it became the philosophy of the most worldly worldliness, since it rejected every accountability on the grounds that the world is just a dream. So arose that odd mixture of withdrawal from life and love of life, of submissiveness and pride, of incense and musk."*

Virgin Birth: Parturition of mothers who have signed a chastity pledge: An article in the British Medical Journal reports that a study carried out between 1995 and 2009 shows that one in 200 US women claimed to have given birth while still a virgin. 31 per cent of these ladies had also signed a *chastity pledge.* Clearly this represents a triumphant vindication of one of the central tenets of Christian doctrine. It is greatly to be re-gretted that the nitpicking psilanthropist researchers who carried out the survey seemed to cast doubt on what is obviously a widespread phenom-enon. Their spokesman even said that "fallible memory [it is all too easy to forget *how* you got pregnant], beliefs [for example, in the *virgin birth*] and wishes [many wish they had not got so *drunk*] can cause people to err in what they tell scientists" — or indeed apostles.

Virtue Signalling: Coded references in newspaper commentaries, speeches, interviews with celebrities etc., designed to show that the communicator is safely on message in respect of the age's fashionable shibboleths, and is therefore a very wonderful and deeply concerned individual (as opposed to those sceptical of said shibboleths, who are obviously nasty, selfish and generally worthless persons):

Virtue signalling was originally invented by the Pharisees, who were accused by Jesus of ostentatiously praying in public and going around saying things like *"Lord, I thank thee I am not as other men are."* Nowa-days Facebook, Twitter and blogging have provided new and fertile ground for virtue signalling. Sometimes punishments for sinners are also suggested (for example Nuremberg-style trials to deal with anyone who doubts either the extent of the danger posed by climate change or is crit-ical of the methods proposed to deal with it.)

The migrant crisis in 2015 provided excellent opportunities for virtue signalling, which were eagerly embraced, for instance, by the Austrian establishment. At first, when huge numbers of migrants flooded into the country from Hungary, the authorities simply sluiced the new arrivals directly through to Germany, while loudly denouncing the Magyars for their alleged inhumane treatment of same. From the Austrian point of view, this operation combined the twin attractions of *seamless buck passing* with *unlimited opportunities for self-righteousness.* Alas! The policy hit the buffers when Germany abruptly clamped down on its bor-der with Austria, sparking near panic in the Chancellery. Thereafter Austria (which had vilified Hungary for using troops) began sending troops to its own borders (cuddly *Austrian* troops, you understand, quite unlike the *thuggish Magyar soldiery*, which, the ORF (Austrian Broadcasting) did its best to persuade us, were only sent to the frontier to beat up defenceless refugees.) By December, Austria was itself *building a fence* on its border with Slovenia (not a nasty Magyar *of*-fence, of course, but a cheerful *Austrian* fence designed to make the migrants feel more at home. No doubt loudspeakers playing Strauss waltzes and dirndl-clad maidens handing out *Sachertorte* would soon be part of the welcoming package.) In November the Austrian Foreign Minister had gone off-message altogether and said that the current EU migrant policy could best be described as a *"subsidy for people traffickers."* By then even the Austrian Chancellor Werner Faymann was thinking better of his rhetoric implying that the Hungarians were the new Nazis ("playing the Nazi card" in Austria has a habit of blowing up in its user's face.) The ORF (a sort of left-liberal version of Fox News) also began recalibrating its mendacious anti-Hungarian propaganda as the strain of misrepresenting the government's pursuit of policies it had just condemned became all too apparent. By February 2016 the EU was accusing Austria of violating the European Charter of Fundamental Rights, the European Convention of Human Rights and the Geneva Convention for capping the daily quota of asylum seekers it would take, shipping most of the rest to Germany and saying it would cap the yearly intake of migrants. All the prior bum-sucking to the EU and Germany was to no avail: it had merely turned them into the playground bullies — and there was no longer even the consolation of being able to bully Hungary, safe behind its fence.

Meanwhile propaganda pictures were shown on TV of migrants in Athens on the ramp of a plane bound for Luxembourg. This was to celebrate the EU's brilliant redistribution policy for migrants (147 redistributed by November out of 116,000 earmarked, so clearly a triumph!) What the liberal media were less keen to report was that this group of beaming migrants was a *second attempt* to ship such to Europe's money-laundering and tax evasion centre formerly ruled by the Junckernaut. The first group chosen by the authorities *had flatly refused to go*. Oh dear! A similar affront to *amour propre* had earlier been offered to the French who had sent buses to Munich to bring back migrants longing for the joys of France. Alas! There were not very many of these of these (no doubt they'd seen the TV pictures of the *banlieux* and read up on the generosity of French welfare compared to Germany and Sweden, and decided that the joys of France were, after all, not for them.) The buses had to trundle home less than one third full.

Finally a non-person, quaintly described as the "Foreign Minister" of Luxembourg, weighed in with his own virtue signalling. He denounced Hungary's border fence as *"contrary to Europe's humanitarian and democratic values."* That's as opposed, presumably, to the Croatian, Bulgarian, Greek (on the land border with Turkey) and Austrian ones (not to mention the 700 mile fence protecting the US border with Mexico), which are obviously shining examples of said humanitarian values…Still, it's always safe to bash a small country like Hungary, especially when its Prime Minister is tactless enough to point out home truths before the smug elite in the EU has thought of a plausible way of obscuring them…

Vodaphone: Model of corporate governance and greed:
Vodaphone's CEO was "rewarded" with a "bonus" of ten million pounds for engineering the takeover of Mannesmann in Germany in 1999. Subsequently some of the Mannesmann board were brought before the German courts on suspicion of having been bribed for their support, one of them having received a "bonus" of 15 million Euros. "We are not talking here about a cashier putting his hand in the till," said his defence lawyer sniffily, and indeed the average crooked cashier would be satisfied with much less…

Meanwhile the great man at Vodaphone seemed to feel that 10 million pounds was barely adequate recognition of his services to the firm (and himself). So a grandly titled "global market remuneration programme" was proposed, which should have added 13 million pounds of options to his heist — but the scrooge-like remuneration committee opted for a measly 8 million instead. (Meanwhile Vodaphone shares fell from a peak in 2000 by 205 billion pounds, which is more than the national output of Belgium…)

According to the Neo Liberals, this sort of thing is just "the market" at work, by which they mean, in the words of J. K. Galbraith (*q.v.*), that *"the rich should be made richer to make them work harder, and the poor should be made poorer, to achieve the same result."* Certainly Sir Christopher Gent, Vodaphone's deal-maker, could not be accused of lack of generosity to his fellow rich. For example he sat on the Compensation

Committee of Lehmann Brothers as a Non Executive Director. That committee approved truly remarkable pay-outs to Dick Fuld, the less than delightful and spectacularly failed CEO of Lehman Brothers. His haul was $40.5m in 2006 and $34m in 2007.

Vodaphone has often spectacularly been in conflict with tax authorities (notably in UK and India) due to its creative accounting. In March 2016 its 2015 Luxembourg accounts showed profits of €1bn from lending €42.4bn to companies worldwide, on which it paid tax of €5m or 0.5 percent. It doesn't actually sell any telephones in Luxembourg of course, but income diverted to Luxembourg is not taxed because Luxembourg (former fiefdom of the Junckernaut, friend of the multinational tax dodgers and now President of the EU Commission) allows paper losses from writing down investments to be set against income. Vodaphone had £70bn of such losses, which it expected to exploit over the next 55 to 65 years.[7] Nice work if you can get it!

7 See a detailed report in *Private Eye* (19th February – 3rd March 2016).

W

War:

War is God's way of teaching Americans geography.

Ambrose Bierce:

Pascal's Wager: A risk-free bet that could save you a lot of trouble:
"Belief," wrote Pascal, "is a wise wager. Granted that faith cannot be proved, what harm will come upon you if you gamble on its truth and it proves false? If you gain, you gain all. If you lose, you lose nothing. Wager then, without hesitation that He [i.e. God] exists."

This advice may solve the dilemma of faith in general terms, but not in specific. The latter is probably insoluble, something which the "*Mathematical Description of Religions*" purports to illustrate as follows: "Since there are hundreds of religions in existence, some having thousands of sects with competing interpretations, the probability that a given person's religion should happen to be the one that is true (to the exclusion of others) is diminishingly small. Additionally, it must be considered that the set from which a person must choose is not simply the set of existing faiths, but the set of all possible faiths. It is, for example, possible that the "true" faith is one which was revealed long ago, but has since been forgotten, or one which has never yet been revealed. This problem is further complicated by those religions which posit the existence of evil spirits capable of misleading humans, since any claimed revelation could have been a false production of such spirits, and any initially true revelation could have afterwards been corrupted and made false by such spirits. And so, if such evil spirits existed, the truth value of any proposed religion must become zero."[1]

1 en.wikipedia.org/wiki/Argument_from_inconsistent_revelations

494

Wages of sin: Not what they used to be, possibly due to the recession… In his *Diaries*, the novelist Evelyn Waugh mentions the story of a somewhat inexperienced judge trying a sodomy case in the 1950s. Being uncertain about the sentencing guidelines that applied to this sort of thing, he decided to consult the Lord Chancellor, Lord Birkenhead, who was getting on a bit and prone to absentmindedness. Accordingly he rang up the latter and asked him *"What should you give a man who allows himself to be buggered?"* *"Oh, thirty shillings or two pounds,"* said Birkenhead; *"whatever you happen to have about you."*

"Waiting for Godot": *"A play in which nothing happens, twice."*[2]

War: A demonstration of the law of diminishing returns:
Bertrand Russell, the pacifist British philosopher, claimed that *"war does not determine who is right — only who is left."* Karl Kraus, an Austrian scarred by the horrors and hypocrisies of the First World War which sealed the fate of his country, wrote the following: "War is at first the hope that things will get better for oneself; after that the expectation that things will get worse for the other; then satisfaction that things are no better for the other; and after that astonishment that things are going badly for both."[3]

Trigger warnings: A new technique of censorship currently being piloted in American academe:
For example, Ovid's *Metamorphoses*, according to the student-led Multicultural Affairs Advisory Board (*sic*) of Columbia University, could "trigger" harmful effects in sensitive students. This is because "like so many texts in the western canon, it contains triggering and offensive material that marginalises student identities in the classroom." But why is it "offensive" to the students, or rather why should we care? Any literature worth the name is probably offensive to someone or to some set of beliefs — that is the point of it. And why should a student feel "marginalised" if he or she reads something with which they disagree?

---

2 Martin Esslin, literary critic.
3 Karl Kraus: *No Compromise: Selected Writings of Karl Kraus*, edited with an Introduction by Frederick Ungar (Frederick Ungar Publishing Co. New York, 1977) P. 232.

Is the aim of learning simply to reaffirm 'student identities in the class-room,' prejudices and all? Does that include students who believe deeply in god as well as those who think the whole notion of god is a con? Those who are pro legal abortion and those who are fiercely opposed? Or would all such opposed factions be expected to recuse themselves from any course where discussion of such issues might occur? May be it would be worthwhile for them to reach beyond their 'identities' and learn how to analyse, discuss and argue their position? In the "trigger warning" world, there wouldn't be much of that if all the course material has been sanitised in advance for fear of "marginalising identities" and "triggering post traumatic stress disorder."

Meanwhile professors are being advised to flag up works that depict rape, misogyny, racism, homophobia and violence, rather like those warnings on the TV news that the upcoming item contains flash photography. Presumably sensitive students would have to absent themselves from the relevant parts of a literature course that included, for example, *To Kill A Mockingbird*, Harper Lee's classic novel about racism as it influenced a rape trial in the American south. The idea seems to be that students should be spared contact with anything that reminds them of the terrible things that happen in the world, or indeed anything that might unsettle their preconceived opinions. Instead of education there is to be reduction, instead of candour, euphemism, instead of debate, dogma — all in all the exact opposite of what education has hitherto been about.

According to historian Amanda Foreman, one of the journalists who survived the Charlie Hebdo massacre in Paris in 2014 later gave a talk to students at Chicago University, necessarily under armed guard. Her defence of free speech was attacked by members of the audience who denounced her for using her "privileged position" to oppress others [*sic*] and the organisers were ticked off for giving her a "free pass to make condescending attacks" on the students who disagreed with her. As all good liberals know, victims are really perpetrators who haven't "checked their privilege" (*q.v.*)

Meanwhile a feminist professor at Northwestern University is being sued for "mental harassment" by two female graduate students because she wrote an article in *The Chronicle of Higher Education* criticising the trigger movement's unhealthy "obsession with helpless victims," (she might have added, but didn't, that this is a condition to which ever larger numbers of students and others lay claim in order to keep out of

496

the teaching or public domain any sentiments, or arguments, or even facts, of which they disapprove.) As Foreman puts it, *"the trigger movement has enabled legions of self-proclaimed victims to become the victimisers."*[4]

Wash trades: Dirty financial washing:

"Wash trades" is one of the latest pieces of jargon to emerge from the criminal world of neo-liberal finance. It means matching buy and sell trades placed with the same counterparty for the same amount on the same day. Its sole function is to steer massive commission to crooked brokers who assist traders in their dodgy activities.

Years ago the City's motto was *"my word is my bond,"* which at least confirms that there *is* honour among thieves. However, after some spectacular examples of (illegal) "bond washing," this was changed to *"my word is my bond wash."* How innocuous all that seems today…

Wegelin & Co.: Founded in 1741, Wegelin was Switzerland's oldest (and arguably most corrupt) bank until its abrupt closure in 2013:

"Also the one," writes Martin Vander Weyer in *The Spectator*, "with the simplest strategy for growth — which was to offer secret accounts to American tax-evaders who could no longer obtain that valuable service from the bigger Swiss banks like UBS." US citizens evaded $1.2 billion in taxes thanks to Wegelin.

One might think that explosive growth of the bank's funds under management — despite Wegelin being headquartered "in a house reminiscent of a giant cuckoo-clock in the modest town of St Gallen — must have looked suspicious, even to the complacent Swiss authorities." Inquisitive reporters were told by the bank's spokesperson that it was better "to avoid the emotions of greed and fear" of a big financial centre, and that the bank "combined 'client servicing with modern financial theory' " — presumably a reference to the late Leona Helmsley's very modern theory that 'only the little people pay taxes.'

The US Department of Justice's ruthless tactics have been most unsettling to the unctuous Swiss burghers, who no doubt look back fondly to

---

4 All the examples here are taken from an article by Amanda Foreman ("Here's a trigger warning for all campus censors: I shall fight you,") in the *Sunday Times*, 31st May, 2015.

the good old days when the Nazis deposited in Swiss vaults the gold reserves they had plundered from occupied countries. "Nowadays," says Vander Weyer somewhat uncharitably, "it's easier for a camel to pass through the eye of a needle than for an American to open a new bank account in the Alps."

Arnold Weinstock: Businessman of blessed memory whose successors destroyed his entire life's work almost overnight:

Some readers will recall that Weinstock built one of the greatest British businesses ever; admittedly this was not without ruthless cost-cutting — one of the Communist union leaders was moved to describe him as "Britain's greatest unemployer."

Because he refused to indulge in acquisitions that destroy shareholder value, but *do* line the pockets of parasitical "investment" bankers, he was endlessly criticised by the City for accumulating a pile of cash and paying a good dividend. Weinstock, in turn, expressed his contempt for the sort of entrepreneurs who were then all the rage, creating spectacular, but phoney, results through highly-geared takeovers. *"We don't deal in companies,"* he said, *"I don't approve of raising money to plunder other companies."*

It took his successors under five years to get into bed with the bankers and destroy Weinstock's brilliant legacy. In the process they reduced the value of his holding in GEC from £480 million to £2 million. *"Dreams have their place in managerial activity,"* the old boy had once said prophetically, *"but they need to be kept severely under control."*

"On the day Lord Weinstock died," wrote *The Economist* in a melancholy obituary, "the rump of the company he created slid closer to bankruptcy, with sales falling further as debts rose. Its shares were down to 4 pence from £12.50 at their peak. He would have cried… His friend Lord (James) Hanson said he probably died of a broken heart."

The men responsible then disappeared into the blue, after trousering several million pounds in severance pay and pension contributions. This is known in the trade as "reward for failure."

Mae West: American actress and *provocatrice:*
The first play that Mae West wrote was called *Sex*, was staged by the Morals Production Company [sic], and cost her ten days in the workhouse.

498

Mae West: "A hard man is good to find…"

The opening dialogue in her first Hollywood film (1932) ran as follows: [Hat Check Girl]: *"Goodness, what beautiful diamonds!* [Mae West]: *"Goodness had nothing to do with it, dearie!"*

Although she lied about her age, her biographer says West was **eighty-three** when she uttered the famous line in her last film, *Sextette*: *"Is that a gun in your pocket, or are you just glad to see me?"*

Everyone has their favourite Mae West quote: *"I used to be Snow White, but I drifted;" "Between two evils, I always pick the one I never tried before;" "Ten men waiting for me at the door? Send one of them home, I'm tired." "I've been in more laps than a napkin."*

One of her most prescient pieces of advice is nowadays enthusiastically followed by almost anyone in a position to dish a bit of dirt for monetary reward after his or her career has hit the buffers: *"Keep a diary,"* she said, *"and one day it'll keep you…"*

Jessica Williams: author of provocative *50 Facts That Should Change The World*[5] (but probably won't):

This well-documented and not quite despairing cry for action deserves a wider circulation than it is likely to get. Here are some of the fifty facts (as recorded in 2004) that are polemically formulated in the book:

"Brazil has more Avon ladies than members of its armed services."

"Every cow in the European Union is subsidised by $2.50 a day. That's more than what 75 per cent of Africans have to live on." [2004 figures]

"There are 44 million child labourers in India and 44 million missing women in China."

"There are 27 million slaves in the world today."

"There are 300,000 child soldiers fighting in conflicts around the world."

"Two million girls and women are subjected to female genital mutilation each year."

"The world's trade in illegal drugs is worth about the same as the legal pharmaceutical industry ($400 billion in 2004)."

"There are 67,000 people in the lobbying industry in Washington DC — 125 for each elected member of Congress."

"In 2004, golfer Tiger Woods was earning $148 every second."

Wind Farms: Government-instigated environmental vandalism:
The indefatigable Christopher Booker unpicked the propaganda for the huge Thanet wind farm that opened in September 2010. Its boasted "capacity" is 300 MW of electricity, but the website for the then Environment Minister (before he was put in gaol) had admitted that the previous year's average output of the UK's offshore turbines was 25% of capacity (the problem is that the wind does not always blow, astonishing though it may seem.) So the hideous turbines will actually produce circa 75 MW, powering less than half the 240,000 homes claimed.

Wind power not being commercially viable, taxpayers subsidise each kilowatt hour of wind electricity by £100, or 200 per cent, or £1.2 billion guaranteed over the 20-year estimated working life of the turbines. That would buy *1,000MW* of carbon-free nuclear generating capacity avail-

5 Icon Books, London, 2004.

500

able 24 hours whether the wind blows or not, which is 13 times the average wind farm output. The Minister however was jubilant about the "green jobs" created (subsidy cost: £3 million per job.) It seems rather a lot to pay for so much hot air…

Booker keeps an alert eye on other wind turbines despoiling the countryside, such as the one built in Somerset in 2014: "A giant new 2 megawatt turbine… now spins at 330 feet above [the Mendips]," he writes, "a Canadian-made Endeavour E3120. Despite being 120 feet high, its "capacity" is … a mere 50 kilowatts, just a 40th of that of its nearby big brother. Allowing for the intermittency of the wind, this means that its actual output averages some 13 kilowatts, *enough to power just 13 kettles*." It will however generate some £24,000 a year for its owner, of which "£17,500 is what we all pay in "feed-in-tariff" subsidies." He calculates that the "pitiful" amount of electricity produced by this monster is being subsidized to the tune of 260 per cent — even more than the 200 per cent subsidy for offshore wind farms. (The following week he apologized for getting his figures wrong: modern kettles are apparently 3 kilowatt plus, so actually the Endeavour produces enough on average to power just over 4 kettles.)

Winter Wonderland: Christmas consumption of religion confused with the religion of consumption:

Located in the exciting environment of Milton Keynes, Winter Wonderland closed less than 24 hours into its projected nine-day run in December 2013 following complaints about fag-sucking elves, Father Christmas being played by skinny teenagers with squeaky voices and an "enchanted woodland," which consisted of two antlerless reindeer.

Not only does Christmas marketing start in early November nowadays, but Christmas itself stretches over an ever extending holiday during which the families that have gathered for a love fest grow increasingly fractious. This has made the opening lines of a Christmas ditty by the great Tom Lehrer look curiously anachronistic: *"On Christmas Day you can't get sore / Your fellow man you must adore / There's time to rob him all the more / The other three hundred and sixty four…"*

Jay Leno has drawn attention to the fact that the US Supreme Court has ruled that there cannot be a nativity scene in Washington, D.C. over the festive season. This wasn't for any religious reasons. They couldn't find three wise men and a virgin.

Shirley Temple stopped believing in Santa Claus when she was six. Her mother took her to see him in a department store and he asked for her autograph.

Phyllis Diller has said that what she doesn't like about office Christmas parties is looking for a job the next day.

Ludwig Wittgenstein: Brilliant philosopher unsuited to schoolmastering: Wittgenstein cheered us all up by observing that "*it doesn't necessarily mean you are stupid, if you don't understand something.*" Sadly the Austrian sage also went on to say: "*...but not everything is stupid that you don't understand.*" Pascal's view, on the other hand, was that "*you always admire what you don't really understand*"— quantitive easing for example, or Collateralised Debt Obligations.

Bertrand Russell tells us that he once wrote a recommendation for the philosopher to the Cambridge Syndics as follows: "*I recommend Wittgenstein for the Faculty of Philosophy*. Russell." The Syndics wrote back asking whether perhaps he could enlarge on this somewhat cryptic recommendation, which was, after all, several pages shorter than was customary. Whereupon Russell wrote a full page, adding at the bottom: "*This says exactly the same as my previous recommendation, but in prolix, convoluted and obscure language that the Syndics may find easier to understand. Russell.*"

Possibly Wittgenstein's most commonly cited observation runs "*whereof one cannot speak, thereof must one be silent.*" The world would undoubtedly be a happier place, or at least a less irritating one, if more people followed this advice, but Wittgenstein was actually pointing to the limitations of language rather than castigating airheads. For the latter there is a more appropriate traditional saw, namely "*one should not confuse the wisdom of the silent with the silence of the wise...*"

In 1920, Wittengenstein took a job as a primary school teacher in a small village in Lower Austria. His views on the villagers were unflattering and he wrote to Russell that he was "*surrounded, as ever, by odiousness and baseness. I know that human beings on the average are not worth much anywhere, but here they are much more good-for-nothing and irresponsible than elsewhere.*" On the whole the villagers had a no less unflattering view of the philosopher in their midst; he became a byword for eccentricity, shouting "*Krautsalat!*" ("cabbage!") when the headmaster played the piano, and "*Nonsense!*" when a priest was answering children's

502

questions. On the other hand he was a passionate teacher, to those with any intelligence that is, and some of them loved him; his sister Hermine came to watch him teach and claimed that the students *"literally crawled over each other in their desire to be chosen for answers or demonstrations"*.

Unfortunately Wittgenstein was unable to feign similar enthusiasm for the less intelligent, who were not enthralled by endless maths lessons. The great man resorted to decidedly un-philosophical methods, caning recalcitrant boys or boxing their ears, and allegedly also pulling the girls' hair, those who failed to show the faintest glimmering of application or intelligence. His attitude to life was anyway not terribly encouraging for young persons just starting out on it and one wonders if his pupils were happy to be told: *"I don't know why we are here, but I'm pretty sure that it is not in order to enjoy ourselves."* Especially as he was probably right...[6]

Writing: a practice often equated with sex by professional writers:
Chekhov said *"Medicine is my lawful wedded wife and literature my mistress. When one gets on my nerves, I spend the night with the other."* And the Hungarian playwright Ferenc Molnár, when asked how he got started in writing, replied: *"The same way a woman becomes a prostitute. First I did it to please myself; then I did it to please my friends; then I did it for money."*

World Endings: A deeply satisfying prospect for many, but difficult to predict:
According to the Mayan calendar, the world was supposed to end on the 24th of December 2012 (although, when it didn't end, the would-be Mayans interviewed on TV hastened to explain that what they actually meant was, there would be a *"new beginning"*, which is not quite the same thing.)

According to Karl Kraus, writing at the turn of the 19th century, Vienna was *"an experimental laboratory for world endings"*, which looks quite prescient with hindsight, since two World Wars were in the offing. However Gustav Mahler said that if he was informed that the end of the

---

6 An amusing account of Wittgenstein's life, including his teaching career, is to be found in Ray Monk: *Ludwig Wittgenstein: The Duty of Genius* (Free Press, 1990). Hermine's remark is quoted there.

world was imminent, he would immediately go to Vienna. *"Why so?"* he was asked. *"Because everything happens fifty years late in Vienna."*

Work: Described by Philip Larkin as a *toad* in a poem expressing sentiments incompatible with the pursuit of excellence, economic growth and other shibboleths of modern society:

> Why should I let the toad work
> Squat on my life?
> Can't I use my wit as a pitchfork
> And drive the brute off?
> Six days of the week it soils
> With its sickening poison —
> Just for paying a few bills!
> That's out of proportion.
>
> Lots of folk live on their wits:
> Lecturers, lispers,
> Losers, loblolly-men, louts —
> They don't end as paupers;
>
> Lots of folk live up lanes
> With fires in a bucket,
> Eat windfalls and tinned sardines —
> They seem to like it.
>
> Their nippers have got bare feet,
> Their unspeakable wives
> Are skinny as whippets — and yet
> No one actually starves.
>
> Ah, were I courageous enough
> To shout, Stuff your pension!
> But I know, all too well, that's the stuff
> That dreams are made on:
>
> ...

Some other views on work:

504

"The world is full of willing people; some willing to work and the rest willing to let them."[7]

"When a man tells you that he got rich through hard work, ask him: 'Whose?' "[8]

"Choose a job you love, and you will never have to work a day in your life."[9]

"One of the symptoms of an approaching nervous breakdown is the belief that one's work is terribly important."[10]

Worse Things: Fleur Adcock, poetess of sleepless nights in which the past rises up to torment us, tells us what they are:

> There are worse things than having behaved foolishly in public.
> There are worse things than these miniature betrayals,
> committed or endured or suspected; there are worse things
> Than not being able to sleep for thinking about them.
> It is 5 a.m. All the worse things come stalking in
> And stand icily about the bed looking worse and worse and worse.

"Everything you have forgotten," writes Elias Canetti, *"cries out for help in your dreams."*

7 Robert Frost.
8 Don Marquis
9 Confucius
10 Bertrand Russell: *The Conquest of Happiness.*

X

Chico Xavier: a Brazilian medium, always busy:
Xavier published more than 400 books, all of them dictated by the spirits of the dead, and including new poems by 56 deceased Brazilian poets. The widow of one of these tried to sue Xavier for royalties, but the court ruled that "*the* [poet] *is dead, and the dead have no rights.*"

This seems a perverse judgement. Unless they have waived their moral rights, the "*mighty poets in their misery dead*" should surely have copyright protection for their latest efforts, while Chico's excellent contacts on "the other side" should easily have enabled him to find out where the royalties should be sent.

"Though nobody can go back and make a new beginning," said Chico delphically. "Anyone can start over and make a new ending."

Chico Xavier getting it all from the horse's mouth...

HUNGART©2016

506

Xenophanes of Colophon (c. 570 – c. 475 BC): Pre-Socratic Greek philosopher, lampooner and vagrant rhapsodist, one of the first to realise that the anthropomorphic visualisation of god or gods often turned out like a boomerang with a hand-grenade attached:

Xenophanes earned the approval of Clement of Alexandria and other Christian apologists battling the smorgasbord of deities available to their contemporaries. Clement quoted approvingly the philosopher's witty summary of the pagan concept of religion, namely: *"Ethiopians have gods with snub noses and black hair; Thracians have gods with gray eyes and red hair."* A modern version of this irreverent attitude is encapsulated in an observation by the actor Robert Morley, who wrote that *"up to the time of going to press, there is no definite indication as to which religion the Almighty himself prefers."*

"If cattle and horses, or lions, had hands, or were able to draw with their feet and produce the works which men do," said Xenophanes, *"horses would draw the forms of gods like horses, and cattle like cattle, and they would make the gods' bodies the same shape as their own... If an ox could paint a picture, his god would look like an ox."*

Actually Xenophanes may have been the first western monotheist, another reason for earning brownie points with Christians: *"There is one God - supreme among gods and men — who is like mortals in neither body nor mind"* was quite radical stuff at the time. His scepticism has also found favour with modern thinkers; Karl Popper in particular was appealed by such observations as: *"No man knows distinctly anything, and no man ever will."* Moreover *"no human being will ever know the Truth, for even if they happen to say it by chance, they would not even have known they had done so."* Of course this is a bit discouraging for the founders of religions.

Xenophanes may well have had in mind institutions like the Open University, when he said: *"education is the best viaticum of old age."* And he could be sardonic in his commentaries on other sages: "Plato having defined man to be a two-legged animal without feathers, Diogenes plucked a cock and brought it into the Academy, and said, *'This is Plato's man.'* On which account this addition was made to the definition, *'With broad flat nails.'"*

Xenophobia: The American way:

Saint Barack Obama has compared the oil spill in the Gulf of Mexico[1] to 9/11 (which, you may recall, was a terrorist attack) and lambasted sneaky *British* Petroleum (40% American owned) for its negligence. Following the disastrous Macondo blow-out, the oil major BP rightly shouldered responsibility and by 2014 had paid *$43bn* in penalties and clean-up costs (although the poor oversight of the Swiss-domiciled rig owner, Transocean, and the American contractor Halliburton, was the proximate cause of the explosion.) Of course it was just accidental that American officials continually referred to *British* Petroleum (although its official name is BP) during their subsequent briefings. Moreover the US treatment of a penitent BP makes the Mafia look like a *Rechtsstaat*. The wily windbag in the White House summoned the CEO for what a Republican Senator incautiously described as *"the biggest shakedown in history"* (he was immediately threatened into silence by voices in the Senate and Congress, two bodies whose members are not known for being backward in coming forward when sweeteners and kickbacks are in the offing.)

Meanwhile BP had unwisely signed up to decisions on compensation claims being adjudicated by an American legal person. The result was what you would expect: virtually anyone who put in a claim, including law firms (!), and in one case a business that had already closed down before the spill, plus many others that were many miles away from being affected by it — all got loads of dosh. When BP tried to appeal against this blatant chicanery, the American appeal courts simply said that they (BP) had signed the contract giving the adjudicator discretion, so *it didn't matter if the claims themselves were spurious* (two judges vigorously dissenting however.) Besides, they said, BP's agreement with the Adjudicator *did not expressly exclude paying money to those who had suffered no damage.* This is a novel concept of justice: it is as if I agreed to replace your car, because I had damaged it, whereupon anybody else who felt they would rather like a new car would be entitled to claim one off me.

---

1 There was an explosion at BP's Deepwater drilling platform off the coast of Louisiana in April 2010 that killed 11 workers and injured 16 more, besides causing massive pollution in the area.

Of course anyone putting themselves at the mercy of the American legal system should not really be surprised at this outcome. Perry Mason it is not. So BP faces billions more in payments, many of them fraudulently obtained, besides the $12 billion it has already coughed up in compensation and $14 billion in clean-up response. And let us not forget that BP has itself engaged expensively incompetent American lawyers, who have got it into this mess and are no doubt earning eye-watering hourly fees in their pathetically unsuccessful attempts to get it out again. But what do they care whether BP actually wins or loses a case? The more litigation, the better for them.

It is interesting to compare all this with what happens when an American firm is culpable. In the 1984 Bhopal chemical leak disaster, the Indian subsidiary of Union Carbide killed 2,000 people (Macondo killed 11) and poisoned half a million, besides causing massive environmental damage. After five years a settlement (approved by the Indian High Court) was reached, whereby UCC paid a derisory $470m in compensation (after all, they were only Indians.) The victims and various activist groups supporting them fight on for better compensation, but Dow Chemical (which took over UCC) says it's nothing to do with them.

It was not much reported in the press, but Saint Barack's environment adviser announced after a remarkably short period that most of the oil pollution in the Gulf of Mexico had miraculously disappeared (well, an election was in the offing.) This is good news, though furiously disputed by those with a vested interest in prolonging the catastrophe scenario. In one respect it is a pity: we will definitely miss those jolly local politicians from Louisiana, Michelin-man look-alikes in their ten-gallon hats with wobbly jowls and drifting paunches, who were fond of drawling to television interviewers: *"If you hear someone talking with a British accent, he's lying."* Bless!

Xenophon: (Born circa 430 BC in Athens, died circa 354 BC in Thrace): Greek historian with a dry wit:

In his account of the campaigns of Alexander the Great, Xenophon gives us an amusing cameo of Alexander's vanity (it also shows the tendency of the Celts, then as now, to be unimpressed by outsiders wishing to throw their weight around):

"At this point Alexander was visited by envoys from Syrmus, the King of the Triballians, and from the various other independent tribes along the Danube. The Celts from the Adriatic Sea also sent representatives — men of haughty demeanour and tall in proportion. All professed a desire for Alexander's friendship, and mutual pledges were given and received. Alexander asked the Celtic envoys what they were most afraid of in this world, hoping that the power of his own name had got as far as their country, or even further, and that they would answer, '*You, my lord!*' However, he was disappointed; for the Celts, who lived a long way off in country not easy to penetrate, and could see that Alexander's expedition was directed elsewhere, replied that their worst fear was that *the sky might fall on their heads*. None the less, he concluded an alliance of friendship with them and sent them home, merely remarking under his breath that the Celts thought too much of themselves."[2]

Xenophon provides many vivid, if not exactly PC, descriptions of peoples who the Greeks encountered on their expeditions, all of whom are naturally on a lower level of civilisation than themselves, e.g.: "When, in the course of their march, they came upon a friendly population, these would entertain them with exhibitions of fatted children belonging to the wealthy classes, fed up on boiled chestnuts until they were as white as white can be, of skin plump and delicate, and very nearly as broad as they were long, with their backs variegated and their breasts tattooed with patterns of all sorts of flowers. They sought after the women in the Hellenic army, and would fain have laid with them openly in broad daylight, for that was their custom. The whole community, male and female alike, were fair-complexioned and white-skinned. It was agreed that this was the most barbaric and outlandish people that they had passed through on the whole expedition, and the furthest removed from the Hellenic customs, doing in a crowd precisely what other people would prefer to do in solitude, and when alone behaving exactly as others would behave in company, talking to themselves and laughing at their own expense, standing still and then again capering about, wherever they might chance to be, without rhyme or reason, as if their sole business were to show off to the rest of the world."[3]

In the Persian expedition, in which Xenophon took part and describes in his *Anabasis*, he relates the dramatic moment that produced a tremen-

2 Xenophon: *The Campaigns of Alexander*
3 Xenophon: *Anabasis*

Xenophon (430–354 BC): "Thalassa! Thalassa!"

dous shout among the desperate Greek mercenaries making their way home after betrayal and defeat, a shout that has echoed down the ages:

"When the men in front reached the summit and caught sight of the sea [the Black Sea near Trebizond] there was great shouting. Xenophon and the rearguard heard it and thought that there were enemies attacking in the front. However, the shouting got louder and drew nearer. Those who were constantly going forward started running towards the men in front, who kept on shouting. And the more there were of them, the more shouting there was. It looked then as though this was something of considerable importance. So Xenophon mounted his horse, and taking Lycus and the cavalry with him, rode forward to give support.

"And quite soon they heard the soldiers shouting out ***thalassa, thalassa***, 'The sea!, the sea!' and passing the word down the column. Then certainly they all began to run, the rearguard and all, and drove on the baggage animals and the horses at full speed; and when they had all got to the top, the soldiers, with tears in their eyes, embraced each other and their generals and captains."[4]

4 *The Persian Expedition*, translated by Rex Warner (Penguin 1949, 1972), Page 211.

It had been a costly adventure however, and many Greeks who embarked on it never returned to their homeland. Xenophon's lapidary comment was: *"Excess of grief for the dead is madness; for it is an injury to the living, and the dead know it not."*

Xeroderma: an abnormal dryness of the skin as the result of diminished secretions from the sebaceous glands:

Of little interest, as it has not yet been featured on the *Millionaire Show*. It is also known as ***ichthyosis*** or ***fishskin disease.***

Ximénès Doudan (1800–1872): Discouraging philosopher-journalist and author of *Pensées et Fragments Suivis des Révolutions du Goût* (1881), with which you are doubtless familiar:

One of Doudan's better *pensées* may serve to convey his general outlook on life: "Providence gives us the same reply as the soldier who was begged by a prisoner to spare his life: *'Impossible'*, he said, *'but you can ask me for anything else.'*"

Xoanon: an image of God supposedly fallen from Heaven — like Warren Beatty:

Someone once remarked to Katharine Hepburn that Warren and his wife, Anette Bening, seemed very much in love. *"Sure,"* agreed that feisty old trooper; *"And with the same man."*

Y

A period of three hundred and sixty-five disappointments.

Ambrose Bierce: *The Devil's Dictionary*

The annual yawn known as the Turner Prize: "Irritart" encouraged by "the Serota tendency":[1]

"Mock inflatable sex dolls cast in bronze, real rotting apples and a transvestite potter's ceramics inscribed with the line "*Fuck off you middle-class tourist*" can only mean one thing," wrote *The Guardian* a few years back: "The Turner prize shortlist exhibition has opened in London." Or as the *Times* put it: "If Duchamp's urinal were exhibited today, people would probably just use it." The previous year's winner was a fried chicken styled in lead.

The prediction about Duchamp's urinal has, in a sense, been anticipated by an exhibit titled "*Piss Christ*" in a retrospective of work by Andres Serrano in New York, which depicted a crucifix drenched in urine. According to the *New York Times* reviewer,[2] Mr Serrano's use of bodily fluids was seen by the artist as "*a form of purification,*" "*the fluids make us look at* the *images harder and consider basic religious doctrine about matter and spirit.*" The trouble with this explanation, says philosopher Slavoj Žižek, is that it covers anything you care to name. For example, if he (Žižek) published a video clip showing him in the act of defecation ("*how the anal hole gets wider until the excremental sausage falls out, while also showing the stupidly satisfied expression on my face when the business is over,*") much the same argument from "purification" could

---

1 After Sir Nicholas Serota, Director of London's Tate Gallery.

2 Michael Benson" "Andres Serrano: Provocation and Spirituality," *New York Times*, December 8, 1989.

Is it a genuine Emin (£10,000) or a worthless fake?

HUNGART©2016

Charles Thomson , Stuckist and scourge of "the Serota tendency."

be adduced in support of it (the body gets purified by ejecting excrement.)[3] Žižek might well attract state support for such a significant work — after all Serrano did. We should probably be grateful that the emollient reception of *Piss Christ* didn't tempt the artist to create further works in similar vein (*Piss Off Christ, Christ Taking The /A Piss*, etc.)

A group known as The Stuckists[4] have long campaigned without obvious success against "conceptual art" in general and the Turner Prize selections in particular. In a satirical reference to the notorious unmade bed, a copulatory *lieu de mémoire* that made artist Tracy Emin famous, they exhibited a painting of her knickers with Sir Nicholas Serota as their purchaser in the background:

Stuckists say they exist to defend figurative art and are anti-anti-art (anti-art being Conceptual Art and much of Post-Modernism.) This of course makes them highly suspect for right-on trendy artists. A group of these calling itself the London Surrealists has denounced Stuckists (and the similarly suspect Young British Painters) in terms reminiscent of *Private Eye*'s resident revolutionary Dave Spart: according to them, Stuckism *"is a childish kicking against modernity that fails, pathetically, to challenge the underlying realities of capitalism, of the capitalist art market, of material, psychological, psychic and spiritual repression."* Quite so.

Rather surprisingly Stuckism has gained a good deal of traction in a world otherwise dominated by sponsorship (and media coverage) of the

---

3 Slavoj Žižek: *Living in the End Times* (Verso, London and New York, 2011), P. 325.

4 The name arose because a leading light of the movement, unfortunately called Billy Childish, was told by his then girlfriend, one Tracey Emin, that he was "Stuck! Stuck! Stuck!" with his painting, poetry and music.

514

latest art gimmicks and associated Stuckist groups have formed around the world. In Colombia, for example, they are known as *Los Stuckistas* and there are even Stuckists in the Ivory Coast, where no doubt hardly a day passes without the proponents of Conceptual Art clashing dramatically with local adherents of figurative painting. The movement is also very busy issuing manifestoes, sending round robins, inviting Nicholas Serota to resign etc. etc. Charles Thomson remains one of its most eloquent protagonists, a thorn in the flesh of the Tate and an unrepentantly abusive opponent of Turner Prizery. "The result of walking round Tate Modern," he has written, "is not an experience of the marvel of creative profundity which gives meaning to life, but more akin to the detritus of a dryly analytical bureaucrat reverting to an infantile stage during an extended breakdown."[5] The critics of Stuckism have returned fire in similar vein, many of them being heavily committed to the pretentious buzz of Conceptual Art and the market-determining nexus of Serota and multimillionaire Charles Saatchi. According to Rachel Campbell-Johnson of *The Times*, Stuckist painting is formulaic: "Each picks on a painter — Egon Schiele or Toulouse Lautrec, for instance — and restyles his aesthetic in a brash cartoon format. The Stuckists are indeed stuck — even worse, they are stuck being Stuckists."[6]

A yawning prospect: Competition prizes announced in an Ohio paper: "First Prize*: One week in Cleveland.* Second Prize*: Two weeks in Cleveland.*"

Yearning: A satisfying mixture of implausible aspiration and abject self-pity:
   "*The unobtainable is whatever we have not sufficiently desired...*"[7] wrote Nikos Kazantzakis in his fulminating autobiography.[8] The latter work is full of similarly questionable, but appealingly Zorba-ish, statements, as indeed are his other works:
   "*Where are we going? Do not ask! Ascend, descend. There is no beginning and no end.*"

5 *Artistica 29. 1. 06.*
6 Rachel Campbell-Johnston, *The Times 3. 10. 06*
7 Nikos Kazantzakis*: Report to Greco.*
8 *Report to Greco* (English translation by Bruno Cassirer, 1965.)

"What a strange machine man is! You fill him with bread, wine, fish, and radishes, and out come sighs, laughter, and dreams" [also quite a lot of wind.]

"A woman's body is a dark and monstrous mystery; between her supple thighs a heavy whirlpool swirls, two rivers crash, and woe to him who slips and falls!"

In Wagner's *Tristan und Isolde,* Tristan signs off with the line *"... still yearning as death approaches, but not to die from yearning."* Actually the whole opera turns on Isolde being given the wrong elixir by her maid Brangäne, which turns her yearning for death into a yearning for Tristan's love — which in turn is resolved by them both yearning to die together in an erotic embrace, a practice known in Germany as *Liebestod.* It's extraordinary what complications can follow from a simple mix-up at the pharmacy.

"Wagner's music is better than it sounds," as Mark Twain[9] sagely remarked, possibly having the celebrated "Tristan chord" in mind. In *The Shrine of St Wagner* he writes: "... there isn't often anything in Wagner opera that one would call by such a violent name as acting; as a rule all you would see would be a couple of people, one of them standing, the other catching flies. Of course I do not really mean that he would be catching flies; I only mean that the usual operatic gestures which consist in reaching first one hand out into the air then the other might suggest the sport I speak of if the operator attended strictly to business..." There is quite a lot of this sort of thing in Tristan and it is probably connected to yearning, *Liebestod* etc. The music also well reflects yearning, insofar as, to the average listener, it does not appear likely to stop: "The principle of [Wagner's] endless melody," said Stravinsky, "is the perpetual becoming of a music that never had any reason for starting, any more than it has any reason for ending." "The prelude to *Tristan und Isolde,*" wrote the critic Eduard Hanslick, "reminds us of one of the old Italian paintings of a martyr whose intestines are slowly unwound from his body on to a reel." "After a couple of hours," said Mark Twain, "I looked at my watch and found that the opera had already been going for fifteen minutes..."

9 Generally attributed to Mark Twain, but now thought to have originated with an American humorist called Bill Nye.

Boris Yeltsin: Russian drunk stumbling around in the Kremlin between 1991 and 1999:

British Prime Minister John Major once asked Yeltsin to sum up "in a word" how things were in Russia. "In a word," said Yeltsin, "*good.*" Thinking this a little inadequate, Major asked him if he could perhaps enlarge on the situation in *two* words. "In two words," said Yeltsin, "*not good.*"

Boris Yeltsin: "That's the wrong speech, Mikhail! Wake up and smell the coffee..."

General Alexander Lebed, a contender in the 1996 Russian presidential election, said this of his opponent Boris Yeltsin: "*He's been on the verge of death so many times. ... His doctors themselves are in shock that he's still alive. Half the blood vessels in his brain are about to burst after his strokes, his intestines are spotted all over with holes, he has giant ulcers in his stomach, his heart is in absolutely disgusting condition, he is literally rotting ... He could die from any one of dozens of physical problems that he has, but contrary to all laws of nature — he lives.*" (Lebed died — admittedly in a helicopter accident — in 2002; Yeltsin lived until 2007.)

Yobs in the classroom: Education recalibrated as entertainment:
In 2004 the Germans, tiring of the prevailing attitude in English schools
that the only things that ever happened in Germany were the Nazis and
the holocaust, invited English history teachers to visit them and discuss
the issue. They needn't have bothered. Asked why he mostly taught
about the Nazis and little or nothing about 2,000 years of German history, one of these veterans of the classroom explained: *"Kids find the
Nazi period interesting. A lot of things happen. There is plenty of violence."* Post-war German history was, he thought, *"a bit dry"* by comparison…

Yogi Berra (1925–2015): Baseball star and homespun philosopher:
The *obiter dicta* of Yogi Berra are rightly admired by the cognoscenti:
"When you come to a fork in the road, take it,' is authentic Berra, although he did also say *"I didn't say most of the things I said."* Another
valuable insight is his advice that *"you should always go to other people's funerals, otherwise they won't come to yours."* This is all too true,
as, sadly, is his observation that *"the future ain't what it used to be."* He
once berated a colleague for not spelling his name properly after he gave
him a cheque inscribed as *"Pay to bearer."*
   Other Yogiisms:

   "Even Napoleon had his Watergate."
   "It's tough to make predictions, especially about the future."
   "Nobody goes to that restaurant anymore because it's too crowded."
   "Never answer an anonymous letter."

Brigham Young: The Moses of the Mormons:
In his book *It All Started with Columbus* Richard Armour describes the
apocalyptic moment for the Mormons: "Their leader in the early days in
Utah was Bigamy Young. When he arrived in Salt Lake City he said to
his followers, *'This is the place!'* — although he had never been there
before. It was uncanny." (Armour's remark is in the same reliable history book in which he says: *"Explorers returned with Chinaware from
China, Indiaware from India, and Underware from Down Under."*)
   Brigham Young, who famously practised polygamy, claimed that
*"any young man who is unmarried at the age of twenty one is a menace
to the community."* A realistic observer of human nature, he also pointed

518

out that *"in the adversity of our best friends we often find something that does not displease us."* Also: *"Remember, a chip on the shoulder is a sure sign of wood higher up."*

Here is Young's interesting take on the Creation [italics added]: "Now hear it, O inhabitants of the earth, Jew and Gentile, Saint and sinner! When our father Adam came into the Garden of Eden, he came into it with a celestial body, and brought Eve, *one of his wives*, with him. He helped to make and organize this world... They came here, organized the raw material, and arranged in their order the herbs of the field, the trees, the apple, the peach, the plum, the pear, and every other fruit that is desirable and good for man; the seed was brought from another sphere, and planted in this earth. *The thistle, the thorn, the brier, and the obnoxious weed did not appear until after the earth was cursed.* When Adam and Eve had eaten of the forbidden fruit, their bodies became mortal from its effects, and therefore their offspring were mortal... *It is true that the earth was organized by three distinct characters, namely, Eloheim, Yahovah, and Michael*, these three forming a quorum, as in all heavenly bodies, and in organizing element, perfectly represented in the Deity, as Father, Son, and Holy Ghost."[10]

That seems clear enough, then. "Those who would assail *The Book of Mormon*," writes Jon Krakauer sensibly, "should bear in mind that its veracity is no more dubious than the veracity of the Bible, say, or the Qur'an, or the sacred texts of most other religions. The latter texts simply enjoy the considerable advantage of having made their public debut in the shadowy recesses of the ancient past, and are thus much harder to refute."[11] And San Francisco journalist Mark Morford says: "It is, after all, far too easy to pinch and kick the bizarre Mormon Church; to say it's ripe for satire and parody is to say a Catholic schoolgirl is ripe for debauchery. It's like shooting polygamist fish in a barrel of coffee."

Mark Twain wrote of Mormonism and Christian Science in his *Autobiography*: "*The Book of Mormon*," engraved upon metal plates, was dug up out of the ground in some out-of-the-way corner of Canada by Joseph Smith, a man of no repute and of no authority, and upon this extravagantly doubtful document the Mormon Church was built, and upon it stands to-day and flourishes. "*Science and Health*" was sent down

10 *Journal of Discourses* 1:50-51 (April 9, 1852).
11 Jon Krakauer, *Under the Banner of Heaven: A Story of Violent Faith.*

from heaven to Mother Eddy, after having been sent up there by Brother Quimby, and upon *"Science and Health"* stands the great and growing and prosperous Christian Science Church to-day. Evidently one of the least difficult things in the world, to-day, is to humbug the human race.[12]

Yuppy or Yuppie: Annoyingly affluent young person whose golden future is however behind him or her — or so everybody secretly hopes:

Yuppies attract an astonishing lack of sympathy for the special diseases to which they are prone, and which indeed are known as "yuppie diseases" (*"informal, sometimes considered offensive"* says *Collins English Dictionary* guardedly.) These tend to be "viral disorders" associated with "stress", which in turn is associated with wondering whether your colleague got a better bonus than you this year. But hey, that's not fair to yuppies! We all get "chronic fatigue syndrome," even if we're poor — so we should empathise.

According to *Wikipedia*, yuppie is short for "young urban professional" or "young upwardly-mobile professional" and defined by one source as being "a young college-educated adult who has a job that pays a lot of money and who lives and works in or near a large city". The acronym became current in the early 1980s. We learn further that *yuppie food stamp"* is a slang term in the United States for a $20 bill, because ATMs there typically dispense only $20 bills. This illustrates the importance of distinguishing yuppies from *puppies* (poor urban professionals, a.k.a. *welfies* and *cheapies*.)

The vitriol yuppies have attracted, they would say, is pure envy. And so it is. It is also directed at smugness, greed, arrogance and the sort of philistinism that manifests itself as fashion-conscious cultural consumption. "Yuppies never gamble, they calculate," claims writer Douglas Coupland. "They have no aura: ever been to a yuppie party? It's like being in an empty room: empty hologram people walking around peeking at themselves in mirrors and surreptitiously misting their tonsils with Bianca spray, just in case they have to kiss another ghost like themselves. There's just nothing there." And Jean Baudrillard's objections to them is typically and ideologically French: "The Yuppies are not defec-

---

12 *Autobiography of Mark Twain,* Edited by Benjamin Griffin, Harriet Elinor Smith and other editors of the Mark Twain Project, Vol. 2 (University of California Press, 2013) P. 247.

tors from revolt, they are a new race, assured, amnestied, exculpated, moving with ease in the world of performance, mentally indifferent to any objective other than that of change and advertising."

May be the yuppies have had their day, however, what with the never-ending financial crisis and the deplorable lack of indulgence shown to wealthy professionals these days: "The media have just buried the last yuppie," writes Barbara Ehrenreich, "a pathetic creature who had not heard the news that the great pendulum of public consciousness has just swung from Greed to Compassion and from Tex-Mex to meatballs."

Related terms to *yuppy* include the following:

Buppie (a black urban professional.)
Huppie (a Hispanic/Latino urban professional.)
Guppie (a gay urban professional.)
Scuppie (a Socially Conscious Upwardly-Mobile Person)

Dink or *Dinky*, meaning *Dual Income, No Kids [Yet]*, is often considered to be synonymous with *Yuppy*.

These terms are very important to Estate Agents.

A "*Yuppy*" should not ordinarily be confused with a "*Yippie*", who was a member of radical Jerry Rubin's so-called Youth International Party ("Don't trust anyone over thirty.") However, like many persons who in their drug-fuelled youth despised wealth and stuff, Rubin began to feel the pinch a bit and also realised that marketing sixties radicalism was more fun and more profitable than actually living the anti-capitalist dream. In 1982 he founded a "business networking group", prompting some of the reptiles to point out that he had gone from being a *yippie* to being a *yuppie*. This was the fate of most sixty-eighters, that is those who didn't become President and do good works. As Rubin himself justly pointed out: "I didn't get my ideas from Mao, Lenin, or Ho. I got my ideas from the Lone Ranger." And as he also pointed out: "the individual who signs the check has the ultimate power."

Z

Zeal:
*"A certain nervous disorder afflicting
the young and inexperienced."*

Ambrose Bierce: *The Devil's Dictionary*

Frank Zappa: One of the great thinkers of our time:
Not all of Zappa's philosophising is printable in a family publication like
this one, but here is an observation by him that gives us something

Zappa: *"A reason for bad mental
health in USA is that people have
been raised on 'love lyrics'."*

to ponder in the new millennium:
*"In the fight between you and the
world, back the world."* The only
thing is, this remark was originally
made by Franz Kafka (no relation).[1] Still it *might* have been
made by Frank Z. Here are some
zappy Zappaisms that are undoubtedly 24 carat Frank:

*"Some scientists claim that hy-
drogen, because it is so plentiful,
is the basic building block of the
universe. I dispute that. I say there
is more stupidity than hydrogen,
and that is the basic building
block of the universe."*

*"Most rock journalism is people
who can't write, interviewing people who can't talk, for people who
can't read."*

1 Franz Kafka: Aphorism 52 in *Unpublished Works 1916–1918*

"Take the Kama Sutra. *How many people died from the* Kama Sutra, *as opposed to the Bible? Who wins?"*

"Government is the Entertainment division of the military-industrial complex."

"The essence of Christianity is told us in the Garden of Eden history. The fruit that was forbidden was on the tree of knowledge. The subtext is: all the suffering you have is because you wanted to find out what was going on. You could be in the Garden of Eden if you had just kept your fucking mouth shut and hadn't asked any questions."

"Love lyrics have contributed to the general aura of bad mental health in America."

Zealot: A person with no sense of the ridiculous:
Rowan Williams, the former Archbishop of Canterbury, has expressed himself *"genuinely puzzled by political parties, governments or churches that appear to find a greater moral problem in abortion than in the manufacture, marketing and use of indiscriminate weaponry, from cluster bombs and poison gas to nuclear warheads."* American anti-abortionist zealots, some of whom murder doctors who do abortions, will doubtless be able to clear up any confusion Archbishop Williams may have regarding the philosophical underpinnings of their "right to life" campaign. For those who do not share their view, they have an incontrovertible argument: *"Hey, man! You're undermining the sanctity of life;* **so we're gonna kill you!***"* Only a nitpicking liberal could fail to be impressed by the logic of that.

The anonymous author of the 18th century *Letters of Junius* described the mindset of zealots with considerable acumen when he wrote: *"There is a holy mistaken zeal in politics as well as in religion. By persuading others, we convince ourselves."* This sounds right, but then again some of the most evil despots have been cynics rather than zealots. Mátyás Rákosi, the Stalinist dictator of Hungary in the 1950s, once delivered the following admonition to his Politburo colleagues: *"Comrades! Have we sunk so low that we have begun to believe our own propaganda?"*

Louis D. Brandeis, the American Supreme Court judge, was also sceptical of the value of zealots: *"The greatest dangers to liberty,"* he remarked, *"lurk in the insidious encroachment by men of zeal, well meaning but without understanding."* And the English Catholic convert Frederick William Faber went further, claiming that *"kindness has con-*

verted more sinners than zeal, eloquence, or learning" (unfortunately this is not the view of the Islamic State of Iraq and al-Sham, which has found the threat of decapitation an extremely effective method of conversion.)

The enduring psychological appeal of zealotry has been rather charmingly analysed by the Christian apologist C. S. Lewis, as follows: "The 'average sensual man' who is sometimes unfaithful to his wife, sometimes tipsy, always a little selfish, now and then (within the law) a trifle sharp in his deals, is certainly, by ordinary standards, a 'lower' type than the man whose soul is filled with some great Cause, to which he will subordinate his appetites, his fortune, and even his safety. But it is out of the second man that something really fiendish can be made; an Inquisitor, a Member of the Committee of Public Safety. It is great men, potential saints, not little men, who become merciless fanatics. Those who are readiest to die for a cause may easily become those who are readiest to kill for it."[2] As Anatole France said: "*It is the certainty that they possess the truth that makes men cruel.*"

According to the historian Josephus, the original zealots around 70 AD had an "*inviolable attachment to liberty and said that God is their only ruler and lord*", a view the Romans found thoroughly unhelpful. They were also identified with the Sicarii who practised assassination of their political opponents and ended up being massacred at Masada.[3] In short, they were a nuisance.

Carl Sagan said: "*The fact is that far more crime and child abuse has been committed by zealots in the name of God, Jesus and Mohammed than has ever been committed in the name of Satan. Many people don't like that statement, but few can argue with it.*"[4]

Isaac Asimov said: "*When a religionist denounced me in unmeasured terms, I sent him a card saying, 'I am sure you believe that I will go to hell when I die, and that once there I will suffer all the pains and tortures the sadistic ingenuity of your deity can devise and that this torture will continue forever. Isn't that enough for you? Must you call me bad names in addition?'*"

2 C. S. Lewis: *Reflections on the Psalms*

3 See *The Oxford Dictionary of the Christian Church*, edited by F.L.Cross and E.A.Livingstone (Oxford University Press, Third Edition, 1997) Pp. 1778-1779.

4 — Carl Sagan: *The Demon-Haunted World: Science as a Candle in the Dark*

The Austrian writer Karl Heinz Waggerl wrote: *"What a tragic error to die for something rather than to live for it!"*

Climate Change Zealotry: "Climate is what you expect; weather is what you get"[5]:

"Climate change" (CC) is not exactly a new phenomenon: the climate has been "changing" for four and a half billion years, "change" being what climate does. However it was officially discovered as an imminent threat to the planet and humanity on 3 February 2005 at a conference in Exeter (UK) co-ordinated by the Meterological Office's Hadley Centre. "The Exeter meeting had two main aims," writes the palaeoclimatologist Professor Robert Carter: "First, replacing the term global warming (which was no longer happening) with climate change (which always would be); and, second, adopting, for entirely political reasons, a fanciful 2°C target as the 'dangerous' amount of warming that politicians should be advised that they were to prevent." Actually "climate change" had already crept into the United Nations' Framework Convention on Climate Change (1994) where it was defined as the purely man-made (*anthropogenic*) part of it, thus skilfully leaving out the majority of climate change that has natural causes.[6]

Nevertheless many climate change protagonists are convinced that *man-made* climate change is the villain of the piece because it will lead to a *tipping point* ("tipping points" are very fashionable amongst futurologists, even if they can only really be worked out in retrospect). The culprits must not only be fingered, but also made to pay for their crimes against the planet. Possibly we have been here before: "The most active period of the witchcraft trials," wrote Dr. Emily Oster in *The Journal of Economic Perspectives* in 2004, "coincides with a period of lower than average temperature known to climatologists as the "little ice age"…In a time period when the reasons for changes in weather were largely a mystery, people would have searched for a scapegoat in the face of deadly changes in weather patterns. 'Witches'

---

5 Mark Twain.

6 See: Robert M. Carter: *Climate: The Counter Consensus* (Stacey International, London, 2010), Pp. 34-5. Also Pp. 72-75, where he documents that "man's carbon dioxide contribution is small in the context of the planetary carbon system" (CO_2 emissions are accused of causing "global warming", alias "climate change" etc. etc.)

became targets for blame because there was an existing cultural framework that both allowed their persecution and suggested that they could control the weather."

CC alarmists are extremely hostile to the idea that man might *adapt* to climate change, rather than trying to predict what cannot be accurately predicted and prevent what, to a large degree, cannot be prevented. Adaptation is, after all, what mankind has practised since it first appeared on earth and is the reason for its survival. As Nigel Lawson[7] has observed, two of the most successful economies in the world, Finland and Singapore, have annual average temperatures that differ by more than 22 degrees centigrade. As to *"global warming,"* (*q.v.* under **G: *Global Warming***) alarmists are notably unkeen to mention any of the *benefits* it might engender, preferring the disaster scenarios that bring them fame and research funding. However, as Björn Lomborg pointed out in 2009, "winter regularly takes many more lives than any heat wave: 25,000 to 50,000 each year die in Britain from excess cold. Across Europe, there are six times more cold-related deaths than heat-related deaths… By 2050… warmer temperatures will save 1.4 million lives each year."[8] Observations of this kind got him into a lot of hot water.

You certainly wouldn't think that the alarming *projections* of climate change models were not *predictions* from the way the press reports them; nor would you be aware that, if you tweak a model just a little, a future catastrophe becomes a benign scenario — or vice versa. As has frequently been pointed out, the modellers themselves do not say they "predict" the future climate: they make models of possible socio-economic scenarios from their outputs, which of course are substantially dependent on the assumptions behind their inputs. In any case, for many parts of the climate system (for example the processes that occur within

---

7 However Ex-Chancellor, ex-Energy Secretary Lawson is the bogeyman of "climate change" and "global warming" fundamentalists since he founded an institute to examine their claims and to question current energy policies. *The Observer*'s Environment Correspondent dismissed his views on the highly scientific grounds that he (Lawson) is "fat and elderly."

8 Unless otherwise indicated, the quotations in this section have been taken from a list of 450 compiled by the author Steve Goreham. Although Goreham is sceptical about the claims of climate change protagonists, this extensive list includes statements from all sides of the debate and is helpfully structured under different topics. It may be located at www.climatism.net/quotes-on-climate-change-environment-and-energy/.

clouds), the scientists' incomplete knowledge of the relevant physics requires *"parameterisation"* in the models — for which, says Robert Carter, read *"educated guesses."*[9]

Like all religions, climate change also has its own eschatology, a sort of inverted millenarianism in which an ecological "tipping point" will shortly be reached, or has been reached, beyond which our planet is doomed. Anyone who questions this assertion, or the "science" adduced to support it, is clearly aligned with the devil. Hence the character assassination, abuse and accusations of bad faith that characterise the debate between true believers (who claim to have all "serious" scientists on their side) and sceptics who refuse to conform, unmoved by threats and ridicule. As C.S.Lewis remarked, "of all tyrannies, a tyranny sincerely exercised for the good of its victims may be the most oppressive...those who torment us for our own good will torment us without end for they do so with the approval of their own conscience." Isaiah Berlin put the same idea in a historical context when he wrote: "Disregard for the preferences and interests of individuals alive today in order to pursue some distant social goal that their rulers have claimed is their duty to promote has been a common cause of misery for people throughout the ages."[10]

Like all true believers, the warmists and alarmists *know* that they are in possession of *"the truth"*, which means of course that they are *morally superior* to the sceptics. The latter, they say, are simply stooges financed by the fossil fuel industry. The fact that virtually all research grants and state sponsorship go to those who are clearly working with the underlying assumptions of climate change orthodoxy, and that such people are therefore much better financed than their opponents, obviously doesn't count. Currently, writes Professor Carter in 2010, "global warming alarmism is fuelled by an estimated worldwide expenditure on related research and greenhouse bureaucracy of more than US$10 billion annually." Diplomatically he adds that the "power of such sums of money to corrupt, not only the politics of greenhouse but even the scientific process itself, should not be underestimated."[11] As Matthew Sin-

9 Robert M.Carter, op cit. Introduction, P. 31.

10 Quoted in I.Byatt: *Climate Change Policy: Challenging the Activists* (Institute of Economic Affairs, 2008).

11 Carter op cit. Pp. 188-9.

clair[12] has pointed out, the cumulative funding of environmental lobbies hugely exceeds the funds raised by those questioning aspects of their work. Characteristically the EU even *funds* environmental bodies (with our money) *to lobby itself* on this issue!

AGW (*anthropogenic global warming*) and CC propaganda justifies runaway expenditure and counterproductive policies (e.g. biofuel subsidy that *inter alia* reduces world food supplies for the poorest and in America seems to be destroying the bee population) in order to forestall an *unproven* future scenario by applying the so-called *"precautionary principle."* This is predicated on the idea that something *might* happen, and would be so *disastrous* if it did that we must spend *trillions of dollars* on prophylactic measures, regardless of potentially devastating effects on our economies. Just as the possible benign effects of GW are seldom mentioned, so also is it taboo to point out that the costs of the measures currently proposed (and to some extent already being implemented) may far exceed the relative costs of dealing with anticipated damage when and *if* it occurs. To the true green fundamentalist cost — benefit analysis is just another part of capitalism's "false consciousness." The huge sums to be spent on the putative prevention of warming through emission reduction schemes, subsidies to uneconomic green energy such as wind turbines, job losses, green taxes and all the rest of it will not dismay someone who is engaged on the important business of saving the planet. The respected climatologist John Christy, testifying before the US Congress Ways and Means Committee on this topic in 2009, said that he had used the *International Panel on Climate Change* (IPCC)[13] climate models in his calculations. He found that if the mooted (and costly) carbon dioxide cap-and-trade system were to be adopted by the USA, the net global impact would

---

12 Matthew Sinclair: *Let Them Eat Carbon: The price of failing climate change policies, and how governments and big business profit from them* (Biteback Publishing, London, 2011) Pp. 217 ff. Sinclair adds that "activists who claim that they would prevail if it wasn't for corporations and well-funded lobby groups are deluded. The world's largest companies are generally lobbying for more climate change regulation not less." (P. 210). This is not least because of the subsidies available to them for toeing the line on climate change or investing in renewables. With some big industries, such "corporate welfare" has effectively become part of the business model.

13 The International Panel on Climate Change is the world body leading CC alarmism, but increasingly discredited through revelations of doctored inputs, misrepresentation of scientists' views and much else.

at most be [a warming reduction] of one hundredth of a degree by 2100; and if the whole world adopted the same measure, the effect would be less than four hundredths of a degree by 2100, both amounts too small to be instrumentally measured anyway.[14]

Since the IPCC itself assumes that people alive in 2100 will, on average, be between four and eighteen times as wealthy as people are today due to economic growth, it seems odd to recommend throttling our own generation's prosperity on their behalf. As Matt Ridley puts it in *The Rational Optimist*, such a view implies "that your impoverished great great great grandfather, whose standard of living was roughly that of a modern Zambian, should have put aside most of his income to pay your bills today."[15] Conversely the 4 °C, let alone the implausible 6 °C, of future warming conjured by the *Stern Report* (*see below*) can only actually occur (assuming we accept the AGW argument) if it is accompanied by exponential increases in human prosperity brought about by the very growth which (it is claimed) will have caused the climate change in the first place. So *either* countries in the future will easily be rich enough to cope with the *possible* fall-out from *possible* global warming (the IPCC's own assessments suggest that they should be), *or* they will fail to grow economically, in which case their carbon dioxide emissions will be insufficient to cause the rapid global warming that the IPCC asserts is man-made. The sages of the IPCC can hardly have it both ways. Besides which, Stern only gets to his dramatic spending requirements by using a very low *discount rate*, which is "the cost of doing something now versus the benefit accrued in the future." Economists typically use a discount rate of 6% in analogous calculations, but Stern arbitrarily uses 2.1% for the twenty-first century, 1.9% for the twenty-second and 1.4% for subsequent centuries in order to get projections that even "warmists" like the economist William Nordhaus say are nonsense.[16]

And all this is before one even gets into the question of wind-farms that frequently operate at around 30% of capacity and require fossil fuel power stations to back them up when the wind doesn't blow, not to mention dozens of other costly "green energy" commitments. Consumers

---

14 Carter op cit. P. 215.
http://waysandmeans.house.gov/hearings.asp?formmode=view&id=7847
15 Matt Ridley: *The Rational Optimist* (Fourth Estate, London, 2011) P. 331.
16 Ridley op cit P. 331.

and taxpayers have begun to realise what "green energy" solutions actually mean for them — much higher energy prices for a start, as well as subsidies to rich landowners, corporate welfare for big companies and sundry other dysfunctional consequences. Even the warmist *Financial Times* points out that Germany's energy policy is "an unholy mess," partly as a consequence of the panicked and ill considered decision to decommission all the country's nuclear power plants, and partly because of a "renewables" policy designed to appease Green fundamentalists. The consequence was that by 2014 German electricity was 40% more costly for consumers and 20% more expensive for industrial users than the European Union average. German companies must pay almost three times as much as their US competitors for electricity. Meanwhile her carbon emissions are rising because the US shale gas boom means more cheap coal is being exported from the USA to Germany (and Europe) — mostly to keep going all those coal-fired stations that are required to step in when the wind doesn't turn the wind turbines.[17] It's a story out of *Angela im Wunderland*.

But surely if all these distinguished and saintly experts from Barack Obama to Cate Blanchett have embraced the cause of "Climate Change", there must be something in it? Surely, if Dame Vivienne Westwood tells us that our "rotten economic system" (of which her multimillion dollar fashion business is not, of course, a part) is "destroying the planet,"[18] or George Monbiot is applauded by *Guardian* readers for his

---

17 See: Tony Barber: "Subsidy distortion has generated German energy chaos," *Financial Times* Sept. 27, 2013. Despite such a lucid demonstration of the incoherence in energy policy resulting from "global warming" alarmism, the FT editorial line to date continues faithfully to adhere to "Climate Change" orthodoxy. A lead article by its senior commentator Martin Wolf even complained pathetically that the opponents of this orthodoxy had done their job "too well" and people were beginning to doubt if it was well-founded. Not the FT however. In a separate and unrelated article Wolf draws attention to the dangerous disillusion with democracy consequent on the recent failures of the governing and opinion-forming elites in the western democracies — two disastrous and ill-considered wars, financial meltdown, Euro crisis and (what he doesn't say) climate change zealotry leading to damaging economic policies…

18 In 2015 it was revealed that Dame Vivienne's business was paying £2 million per annum to an offshore company located in Luxembourg, a tax avoidance scheme costing the UK treasury about £500,000 a year. This is a similar model to the one used by Starbucks that had earlier caused such outrage. Dame Vivienne had just donated £300,000 to Britain's Green Party — which was calling for a Tax Dodgers Bill to outlaw

demand that "every time someone dies as a result of floods in Bangladesh, an airline executive should be dragged out of his office and drowned,"[19] we should drop what we're doing and rush to the nearest Climate Change protest venue? Mike Hulme, a Professor of Climate Change at the University of East Anglia, has written a candid book in which he is quite open about the ideological (as opposed to purely scientific) basis of the movement he supports: "I came to view global climate change caused by greenhouse gas emissions as a manifestation of a free-market, consumption driven, capitalist economy — an ideology to which I was opposed... I began to see climate change increasingly as an issue of public policy and strategic decision making and less as an object of *detached quantitive scientific analysis*" (italics added).[20]

Once the belief that the matter is too urgent to be left to scientific analysis has been embraced, any means used to persuade people of the purported problem and to advance the proposed solution become legitimate [*See also under* "A" —Advocacy Science]. For example, a secret meeting in 2006 between a group of green activists and the BBC hierarchy resulted in the latter agreeing to refuse airtime for the views of those who (however well qualified) were sceptical of the approved line on climate change and global warming. The BBC spent years in legal manoeuvres trying to conceal the names of the participants at this meeting, not surprisingly since the agreement that was reached directly contradicts the mission to inform embodied in the Corporation's Charter.[21]

such payments to offshore companies, when used as a manoeuvre to avoid tax in the country where the profits arose. See: Robert Mendick: "Westwood accused of hypocrisy over offshore tax base," *The Sunday Telegraph*, 8 March, 2015. According to *Private Eye* (20 March–2 April, 2015) Vivienne Westwood Ltd. paid another £4m to Vivienne Westwood Srl in Italy for "commission" on designer, PR and advertising agreements "which would also seem to fall foul of the Greens proposed bill, which would stop UK firms channelling large fees through subsidiaries to "related companies in tax havens for the use of intellectual property such as brands and software."

19 *The Guardian*, Dec 5th, 2006. Carbon emissions from airlines are said by CC scientists to account for some 2% of total anthropogenic (man-made) emissions.

20 Mike Hulme*: Why We Disagree About Climate Change* (Cambridge University Press, 2009), Pp. xxx, xxxi, xxxii).

21 The meeting was co-hosted by the Director of Television and the Director of News. "*The (untrue) message delivered was that the science supporting global warming was so certain that it was the BBC's public duty to cease providing airtime to alternative viewpoints.*" — Robert Carter op cit. P. 232.

The battle for hearts and minds, as with all religions, has taken on a more sinister aspect with attempts to pre-empt the climate change discussion in schools, including the use of *"An Inconvenient Truth,"* Al Gore's apocalyptic cod science film. After protests, the High Court intervened and ordered that it should not be shown without "corrective" guidance from teachers, since it contained nine fundamental scientific errors. Given the hysteria on climate change generated in the media and by government or academe, one has reasonable grounds for scepticism in regard to the zeal with which teachers supply such guidance…. Later, an "infotainment" video,[22] filmed at Camden School for Girls in 2010 and intended for use as global warming propaganda in cinemas and on TV, proved to be a spectacular own goal. *Inter alia* it featured a chirpy teacher asking her class if they were going to support the 10.10 campaign to reduce their carbon footprints. When two pupils seem insufficiently enthusiastic, the teacher presses a detonator to blow up the refuseniks, whose blood and guts explode all over their fellow pupils. This was too much for the mainstream tree-hugging fraternity, which was evidently unimpressed by the film's Monty Python-style insouciance in regard to violence (the ensuing row was known as "splattergate") and the film was withdrawn. Its co-producer Fran Armstrong said: "Clearly we didn't really think [people] should be blown up. That's just a joke for the mini-movie; but may be a little amputation would be a good place to start."

Although climate change fanatics are usually among the keenest to protect children in every possible way, evidently subjecting them to propaganda on this subject at an early age is considered acceptable and the Curtis film was not alone. The website of Australia's public broadcaster (ABC) was a case in point. It provided a "greenhouse gas calculator," by means of which "primary school children were encouraged to work out the amount of carbon dioxide that their activities produce, and thereby 'find out what age you should die at, so you don't use more than your fair share of the earth's resources.' "[23] Professor Richard Dawkins

---

22 *"No Pressure"* produced by the Global Warming Mitigation Campaign 10.10 and made by the well-known film director Richard Curtis. If satire (on either side of the argument) has become taboo in dealing with a topic, you know you're into fundamentalist territory, where threats have replaced arguments. For example an AGW blogger suggests that sceptics should be brought before courts modelled on the Nuremberg trials of the Nazis.

23 Carter op cit. P. 182.

has suggested that bringing up children to believe in God constitutes "child abuse." This website seems to demonstrate an analogous misuse of pedagogic authority.

1988 was the year when "climate change" took off and so did the language used to describe it. A study in 2006/7 explained how "the alarmist repertoire adopts an inflated language with terms such as 'catastrophe,' 'chaos' and 'havoc...' It employs a quasi-religious register of doom, death, judgement, heaven and hell. It also uses the language of acceleration, increase, intractability, irreversibility and momentum."[24] This makes good press headlines, good publicity for opportunist politicians — and good money for research scientists in the field. It also assists the hijacking of the issue by apocalyptic ideologists. A former Environment Minister in Canada let the cat out of the bag when she said: "No matter if the science of global warming is all phoney... climate change [provides] the greatest opportunity to bring about justice and equality in the world."[25] A similar desire to scare people into behaving as authority desires (one of the oldest psychological tactics of religion) has been evident in a string of apocalyptic narratives from Rachel Carson's *Silent Spring* (1962) through Paul Ehrlich's *The Population Bomb* (1968) and the Club of Rome's *Limits to Growth* (1972). It matters not that Ehrlich's apocalyptic population scenario wholly failed to tally with subsequent developments in the real world, or that the Club of Rome's assertion that "fossil fuel" would have run out (not "might" or "could have" run out) by the turn of the millennium was simply false. In 2011(!), the renowned energy expert Dr. Dieter Helm wrote in *The Guardian* that "the real problem is that there may be too much fossil fuel, not too little." The accuracy or otherwise of previous predictions are, it seems, not the point.

What then *is* the point? Reading the propaganda carefully and looking between the lines, you will discover that "the point" is that capitalism is the evil mechanism destroying the planet through exploitative growth. Growth is the great Satan that has to be checked by "transnational" solutions customarily supplied by universalist utopian ideologies, which in turn segue into totalitarian forms of government. Eric Hobsbawm, the Marxist historian and a long-standing Communist, helpfully let another

24 Quoted in Hulme op cit. P. 67.
25 Christine Stewart, Environment Minister for Canada, 1998. Quoted in Mike Hulme op cit. P. 354.

cat out of the bag when he blandly observed that "democracy, however desirable, is not an effective device for solving global or transnational problems"[26] ("*however desirable*" is nice).

The propaganda battle between believers and sceptics was long an uneven one, since people had little way of knowing the extent to which they were being manipulated. Recently, to the dismay of zealots, it has seemed that the sceptics are making headway. Nevertheless claims are constantly made that the "science is settled", although if that were true, it would not be science, and anyway this was the view espoused by Galileo's persecutors in the Inquisition. "I would remind you to notice where the claim of consensus is invoked," said the late Michael Crichton, the author of *Jurassic Park*: "Consensus is invoked only in situations where the science is not solid enough. Nobody says the consensus of scientists agrees that E=mc2. Nobody says the consensus is that the sun is 93 million miles away. It would never occur to anyone to speak that way." Speaking in 2003 he said: "Historically the claim of consensus has been the first refuge of scoundrels; it is a way to avoid debate by claiming that the matter is already settled… consensus is the business of politics. Science, on the contrary, requires only one investigator who happens to be right, which means he or she has results that are verifiable by reference to the real world … The greatest scientists in history are great precisely because they broke with the consensus… If it's consensus it isn't science. If it's science, it isn't consensus. Period."[27]

Actually, even the oft claimed "consensus" is misrepresented in its own terms. In 2013, headlines in the press trumpeted that 97% of scientists who had looked into the matter believed global warming was man-made. As so often with press misrepresentation, it was probably assumed no one would look more closely at the source of this information. Anyone who did would find that the relevant report actually said the following: "We analyze the evolution of the scientific consensus on anthro-

---

26 Eric Hobsbawm in *Globalisation, Democracy and Terrorism* (Ed.Hobsbawm), Little Brown, London, 2007. Evidently he didn't think democracy all that desirable anyway, since he once suggested that Stalin's mass murdering might have been justifiable if the Communist utopia had actually resulted therefrom. P. 118. Quoted in Hulme op cit. P. 308.

27 Michael Crichton: Aliens cause global warming. Speech at the California Institute of Technology, 17 Jan 2003 and available at
http://www.michaelcrichton.net/speech-alienscauseglobalwarming.html.

pogenic global warming (AGW) in the peer-reviewed scientific literature, examining 11,944 climate abstracts from 1991–2011 matching the topics 'global climate change' or 'global warming'. We find that *66.4% of abstracts expressed no position on AGW, 32.6% endorsed AGW, 0.7% rejected AGW and 0.3% were uncertain about the cause of global warming. Among abstracts expressing a position on AGW, 97.1% endorsed the consensus position that humans are causing global warming.*"[28] (Italics added). Even those with weak mathematical skills can probably work out that 66% expressing no opinion is rather more than 32% expressing a specific one, even if that 32% almost all blamed humans for GW.

Then again rhetorical attempts are constantly made to imply that sceptics of current claims by APW and CC protagonists may be likened to those who *deny the holocaust*. Clearly such persons must not only be refuted but also punished (as are holocaust deniers under German and Austrian law). A writer in the Christian Science Monitor in 2009 "*wonders what sentences judges might hand down at future international criminal tribunals on those who will be partially but directly responsible for millions of deaths from starvation, famine, and disease in the decades ahead.*" Politicians and activists constantly invoke comparisons of climate change catastrophe with terrorism, war, even in one case with the asteroid that is said to have wiped out the dinosaurs. "*Climate change is a result of the greatest market failure the world has seen...We risk damages on a scale larger than the two world wars of the last century*" writes Sir Nicholas Stern in *The Guardian* (2007). Stern is the British Al Gore; his headline-grabbing report [*see above*] made for the British government was comprehensively rubbished by Richard Tol, the Dutch Professor of the Economics of Climate Change, who opined that it was alarmist, incompetent and preposterous,[29] and that "its academic value was zero." As previously stated, Stern's most dramatic scenarios depended on his manipulation of the "*discount rate*" [*see above*] customarily applied in economic project planning. Sol said the Stern report contained "errors that were systematic and suggestive of ideological bias." Needless to say that has not stopped it being constantly cited as authoritative.

Bias of another kind surfaced in the amusing "*climategate*" scandal, where e-mails intercepted between AGW/CC protagonists at the Univer-

---

28 See: iopscience.iop.org/1748-9326/8/2/02402/article
29 Matt Ridley op cit. P. 331.

535

sity of East Anglia and colleagues elsewhere seemed to show attempts to manipulate scientific evidence in order to arrive at a pre-determined outcome. "*I received an astonishing email from a major researcher in the area of climate change*," testified Dr David Deming[30] before a Senate Committee in 2006. "*He said, 'We have to get rid of the **Medieval Warm Period**!... In 1999, Michael Mann and his colleagues published a reconstruction of past temperatures in which the MWP simply vanished*" [The MWP is sensitive because there were infinitesimal carbon emissions caused by human activity in the Middle Ages compared to the period since the industrial revolution, yet the planet warmed.]

All this is irrelevant to fundamentalists of course: "The Earth has cancer and the cancer is man," proclaimed the second report of the Club of Rome, 1974. "The existence of the Little Ice Age and the Medieval Warm Period were an embarrassment to the global-warming establishment, because they showed that the current warming is almost indistinguishable from previous warming and coolings that had nothing to do with burning fossil fuel," wrote the physicist Dr.William Happer in 2011. "The organization charged with producing scientific support for the climate change crusade, the Intergovernmental Panel on Climate Change (IPCC), finally found a solution. They rewrote the climate history of the past 1000 years with the celebrated 'hockey stick' temperature record (for "*hockey stick*" see below)."

The IPCC and Dr Michael Mann are indeed the pantomime villains of the piece. The dubious practices of the IPCC (exclusion of papers that don't follow the required line, abuse of the peer review process, cherry-picking data) have been repeatedly highlighted by opponents whom the "warmists" try to depict as a tiny handful of disgruntled pseudo-scientists in the pay of "fossil fuel." "In my more than 60 years as a member of the American scientific community, including service as president of both the National Academy of Sciences and the American Physical Society, I have never witnessed a more disturbing corruption of the peer-review process than the events that led to this IPCC report" wrote the

---

30 Deming, a geologist and geophysicist, has right-wing views that don't accord with liberal orthodoxy in American academe and has been targeted by his university in a way that, were he a liberal, would result in a nationwide outcry. However most liberals seemed to think it is right to marginalise him, if necessary by unconstitutional means.

536

physicist Dr. Fredrick Seitz in *The Wall Street Journal* in 1996, commenting on the IPCC Second Assessment Report; similar views have been voiced by others who found their papers had been included but tampered with. Dr Seitz is a controversial figure on the sceptics' side, but his controversiality pales beside that of the Dr Michael Mann on the other side who invented the "*hockey- stick graph*" purporting to show a sudden and dramatic upward surge in global warming in the twentieth century. This remarkable discovery conveniently underpinned the main ideological thrust of the IPCC, which gave it prominence in its third report in 2001. After some devastating analyses of its methodology (it took time, because Dr Mann long refused to divulge his raw material) the hockey stick's blade began to show distinct signs of brewer's droop and the IPCC thought it prudent to drop it in the next report.

It is somewhat refreshing to read by contrast the following contribution from a scientifically-minded lady blogger, which is perhaps just as likely to be right as the alarmists' prophecies of doom — especially in view of the fact that there was a global warming "pause" between 1998 and 2015: "The true situation," she wrote, "is probably just what most informed people thought before the IPCC and Mann invented the hockey-stick. To whit: the Earth has been typically warm (and pleasant) for more than a half billion years. There have been four relatively short ice ages for reasons not perfectly understood. We have been in an ice age for about two million years. For at least the last million years there has been a cycle of about ninety thousand years of cold (very cold indeed) alternating with about ten thousand warm years. Within our present interglacial there seem to be smaller cycles of warmth and cold of about five hundred years. There was the Roman Warm Period followed by the cold Dark Ages, followed by the Medieval Warm Period, followed by the Little Ice Age. We seem to be about a century into the Modern Warm Period which should last for a couple more centuries if the pattern holds. This is very good news."

Perhaps the last word on the subject should go to comedian Jay Leno, who said: "According to a new UN report, the global warming outlook is *much worse* than originally predicted. Which is pretty bad, when they originally predicted it would destroy the planet."

Then again, an alarm was raised in the respected ecology magazine *Nature* on March 6th *1975:* "A recent flurry of papers has provided further evidence for the belief that *the Earth is cooling*. There now seems *little doubt* that changes over the past few years are more than a minor statistical fluctuation." (Italics added).

"Al Gore," writes climatologist Dr Roy Spencer, "likes to say that mankind puts 70 million tons of carbon dioxide into the atmosphere every day. What he probably doesn't know is that mother nature puts 24,000 times that amount of our main greenhouse gas — water vapour — into the atmosphere every day and removes about the same amount every day. While this does not 'prove' that global warming is not man-made, it shows that weather systems have by far the greatest control over the Earth's greenhouse effect, which is dominated by water vapour and clouds."[31] [Admittedly Dr Spencer believes in "intelligent design", rather than evolution, but one can't have everything.]

Zen: "Zen is to religion what a Japanese 'rock garden' is to a garden:"
"Zen knows no god, no afterlife, no good and no evil, as the rock-garden knows no flowers, herbs or shrubs. It has no doctrine or holy writ: its teaching is transmitted mainly in the form of parables as ambiguous as the pebbles in the rock-garden which symbolise now a mountain, now a fleeting tiger. When a disciple asks *"What is Zen?"* the master's traditional answer is *"Three pounds of flax"* or *"A decaying noodle"* or *"A toilet stick"* or a whack on the pupil's head."[32]

The best reaction to this sort of thing would be a kick in the master's balls.

Zeugma: Subversive figure of speech likely to bring its targets into disrepute:

The following is not actually a true zeugma (aka *semantic syllepsis*, if you're a pedant), but it's difficult to find items for the letter "**Z**". At any rate it's a Schopenhauerian insight into the rigours of life in Greenwich Village, viz., *"Not only is there no God, but try getting a plumber at weekends."*[33]

A true zeugma is more like: *"You are free to execute your laws and your citizens as you see fit."* [34]

---

31 This is from Dr. Spencer's website, *"Global Warming and Nature's Thermostat,"* January 28, 2008.
32 Arthur Koestler: "A Taste of Zen" in *Bricks to Babel* (1980).
33 Woody Allen.
34 William Riker: *Star Trek: The Next Generation.*

Sam Leith, in his exhaustive discussion of figures of speech, quotes a classic zeugma from the Flanders and Swann song about a dirty old man who is planning seduction of a fair-cheeked maiden:

> *"He had slyly inveigled her up to his flat*
> *To view his collection of stamps*
> *And he said as he hastened to put out the cat*
> *The wine, his cigar and the lamps...*
> *Have some Madeira, M'Dear..."*

There is also a thing called a *diazeugma*, roughly a zeugma backwards with knobs on, of which Leith gives the following example: "*The man standing in the dock, Your Honour, killed my wife, abused my children, twisted the head off my cat, painted the walls with the blood of my pet tortoise and afterwards wiped his hands on my budgerigar.*"[35]

Grammarians say the zeugma should be used with caution — beware the dangling modifier! You have been warned...

Zimbabwe: Potentially very prosperous African state long ruled by a now nonagenarian psychopath:

Zimbabwe's President, the much-loved world statesman Robert Mugabe, once remarked *en passant:* "*Tony Blair was a troublesome and difficult little boy. He is still that.*" This is possibly the only truthful remark Mugabe is recorded as making.

According to *The Economist*, in 2008 Zimbabwe's inflation was climbing towards 80 billion, the dead were buried without coffins and there was 80% unemployment. The hyper-inflation was stopped overnight by switching to dollars and since then Zimbabwe is kept afloat by $500m a year from the Zimbabwean diaspora, foreign aid and the Americans who discreetly pay a quarter of the country's health-care costs.[36] Welcome to Mugabe's world, where the chief kleptocrat and murderer lives in the largest palace in Africa built for him by the ever-obliging Chinese — and all of the rest of us are helping to keep his regime going through our taxes...

The country's Minister for Environment and Tourism (Francis Nhema) "owns" a once thriving farm "liberated" by ZANU thugs in 2002. Formerly 220 acres of maize, 200 acres of tobacco, and productive

35 Sam Leith: *You Talkin' To Me?* (Profile Books, London, 2012) Pp. 268, 277.
36 *The Economist*, February 14th, 2015: "Zimbabwe's economy: Nothing for money."

Robert Mugabe: "The only white man you can trust is a dead white man"

of quality beef cattle, pigs and sheep, the farm is now a wasteland. And Mr Nhema? He was elected head of the United Nations Commission on Sustainable Development.

Zimbabwe was a net exporter of food until 2000, when the white farms were seized. The Famine Early Warning Systems Network has warned that the country now produces less than half the maize it needs to feed its population. So Mr Nhema sounds just the man for the job. As he remarked to his critics: "*I think it's not time to point fingers. There is never a perfect method.*" Evidently not.

Slavoj Žižek: Non-PC Slovenian Marxist philosopher who has attracted a following with remarks like: "*Humanity is OK, but 99% of people are boring idiots.*"

"*There is an old story,*" writes Žižek, "*about a worker suspected of stealing: every evening, as he leaves the factory, the wheelbarrow he rolls in front of him is carefully inspected. The guards can find nothing. It is always empty. Finally, the penny drops: what the worker is stealing are the wheelbarrows themselves...*"[37]

540

Slavoj on toilets: "In a traditional German toilet, the hole into which shit disappears after we flush is right at the front, so that shit is first laid out for us to sniff and inspect for traces of illness. In the typical French toilet, on the contrary, the hole is at the back, i.e. shit is supposed to disappear as quickly as possible. Finally, the American (Anglo-Saxon) toilet presents a synthesis, a mediation between these opposites: the toilet basin is full of water, so that the shit floats in it, visible, but not to be inspected. [...] It is clear that none of these versions can be accounted for in purely utilitarian terms: each involves a certain ideological perception of how the subject should relate to excrement. Hegel was among the first to see in the geographical triad of Germany, France and England an expression of three different existential attitudes: reflective thoroughness (German), revolutionary hastiness (French), utilitarian pragmatism (English). In political terms, this triad can be read as German conservatism, French revolutionary radicalism and English liberalism."[38]

Slavoj on liberal guilt: "Postcolonialism is the invention of rich Indian guys who wanted to make a good career in the west by playing on the guilt of white liberals."

Slavoj on sex: "Love is what makes sex more than masturbation."[39]

Žižek, it has to be said, is not taken very seriously by most of his co-toilers in academe. For example philosopher Adrian Johnston writes, with rather unnecessary venom: "Maybe, many years ago, Zizek made a bet with some of his Slovenian colleagues about how much post-modern sounding gibberish he could get contemporary academics to swallow —[40] keep in mind that, recently, he's been trying to persuade people to embrace as unproblematic the juxtaposition of Stalinist dialectical materialism and Christian theology."

It could be that Žižek's less than reverent attitude to his colleagues is also a factor in their sniffiness (not to mention his media success). For example, in his book 2010 *Living in the End Times*,[41] he describes an academic dinner in America where the presiding professor asked each par-

---

37 In an essay on "Violence."

38 In *"The Plague of Fantasies."*

39 A remark made on BBC World's "Hardtalk," 12th January, 2010.

40 Adrian Johnston, "Review of *"The Fright of Real Tears: Krzysztof Kieslowski Between Theory and Post-Theory"* by Slavoj Žižek, *Metapsychology* (2001)

ticipant to introduce himself by stating his or her *"professional position, field of research and sexual orientation."* American academics are now such an unutterably pathetic species that they all meekly complied with the last request. Žižek however was strongly tempted to say that *his* sexual preference was *"for penetrating boys under five years old and then drinking their blood."* Given that the average PC academic neither understands nor approves of jokes, he wisely decided against this. The incident reminded him of a TV interview with Gore Vidal in which the latter was asked *"Was your first sexual experience with a man or with a woman?"* To which he replied: *"I was too polite to ask."*

The human zoo: "Man is the cruellest animal."[42]
Dostoevsky wrote: *"People speak sometimes about the "bestial" cruelty of man, but that is terribly unjust and offensive to beasts, no animal could ever be so cruel as a man, so artfully, so artistically cruel."*

Or as one commentator has put it: *"There are too many people in our society who fall into the category of children who murder their parents and then claim sympathy and support on the grounds that they are now orphans..."*

Zuck's Books: Young billionaire learns to read:
Mark Zuckerberg announced that 2015 would be a "year of books", during which his faithful Facebook followers (180,000 of them) would read what he told them to every two weeks and then discuss their reflections with their benevolent mentor. This burst of altruism is evidently designed to present him as a cyber democrat rather than the CEO of a dodgy data-collecting and privacy-stealing technological behemoth.

"I've found reading books very intellectually fulfilling," the young genius wrote solemnly. *"Books allow you to fully explore a topic and immerse yourself in a deeper way than most media today."* Who would have thought it? *"Next up,"* tweeted a journalist in response, *"Mark Zuckerberg discovers cutlery. 'A knife and fork allow you to eat more kinds of food than using your fingers.'"*[43]

41 Slavoj Žižek: *Living in the End Times*, Verso, London, 2010
42 Friedrich Nietzsche.

Among today's breed of ruthless, tax-avoiding entrepreneurs Zuckerberg is arguably the most unctuous, although in the case of China he has difficulty concealing from his Facebook clientele (known as "*netizens*") the extent to which his lust for revenues trumps his concern for civil liberties. In 2016 he publicised his Beijing trip (which the netizens mocked as the great "Zuck-up") with stunts like running in Tiananmen Square and posting on his Facebook page a picture of himself smiling smugly as he jogged past the Forbidden City. This was not considered tactful by netizens who remember the Tiananmen massacre. Indeed reaction to this, and clips of his obsequious demeanour while listening to the Communist head of "propaganda and ideological purity," which the state television made much of, attracted such venom from Chinese netizens that the authorities ordered that malicious Facebook commentary should be "controlled" and the media should "stop hyping" Zuckerberg's visit. Oh dear!

Zuck seems however to be undeterred in his pursuit of profit through Facebook access to China, even though, as Jamil Anderlini pointed out in the *Financial Times*, he knows that access would be granted only if he agreed to base Facebook servers in China, hand over users' private information and communications to the security apparatus and employ an army of censors to delete 'sensitive' content." The Chinese phrase for sycophancy, pursues Mr Anderlini unpleasantly, is *pai ma pi*, meaning "to stroke the horse's posterior" (perhaps this is a sanitised translation?). "But there is an associated saying that warns if you stroke the horse's posterior too hard and run your hand down its leg, then you are likely to be kicked in the head."[44] Since Zuck's head is nothing if not swollen he might find it particularly hard to avoid this fate.

43 Andrew Hill: "No sneering at Zuck's books," *Financial Times*, 8 January, 2105.

44 See Jamil Anderlini: "Beijing's price for liking Facebook," *Financial Times*, 24th March, 2016.

Some Other Books by
Nicholas T. Parsons

Guidebooks

Hungary: A Traveller's Guide
Blue Guide to Austria
Blue Guide to Vienna

Anthologies and Humour

Dipped in Vitriol
A Letter Does Not Blush
The Book of Literary Lists
The Joy of Bad Verse
The Xenophobe's Guide to the Austrians
(writing as Louis James)

Cultural Topics

Worth the Detour: A History of the Guidebook
Vienna: A Cultural and Literary History

Printed in Great Britain
by Amazon